Real Time Computing

NATO ASI Series
Advanced Science Institutes Series

A series presenting the results of activities sponsored by the NATO Science Committee, which aims at the dissemination of advanced scientific and technological knowledge, with a view to strengthening links between scientific communities.

The Series is published by an international board of publishers in conjunction with the NATO Scientific Affairs Division

A Life Sciences	Plenum Publishing Corporation
B Physics	London and New York
C Mathematical and Physical Sciences	Kluwer Academic Publishers Dordrecht, Boston and London
D Behavioural and Social Sciences	
E Applied Sciences	
F Computer and Systems Sciences	Springer-Verlag Berlin Heidelberg New York
G Ecological Sciences	London Paris Tokyo Hong Kong
H Cell Biology	Barcelona Budapest
I Global Environmental Change	

NATO-PCO DATABASE

The electronic index to the NATO ASI Series provides full bibliographical references (with keywords and/or abstracts) to more than 30 000 contributions from international scientists published in all sections of the NATO ASI Series. Access to the NATO-PCO DATABASE compiled by the NATO Publication Coordination Office is possible in two ways:

- via online FILE 128 (NATO-PCO DATABASE) hosted by ESRIN, Via Galileo Galilei, I-00044 Frascati, Italy.

- via CD-ROM "NATO Science & Technology Disk" with user-friendly retrieval software in English, French and German (© WTV GmbH and DATAWARE Technologies Inc. 1992).

The CD-ROM can be ordered through any member of the Board of Publishers or through NATO-PCO, Overijse, Belgium.

Series F: Computer and Systems Sciences Vol. 127

Real Time Computing

Edited by

Wolfgang A. Halang

Vakgroep Informatica, Rijksuniversiteit Groningen
Postbus 800, 9700 AV Groningen, The Netherlands

New address:

Fachbereich Elektrotechnik und Informationstechnik
FernUniversität Hagen, D-58084 Hagen, Germany

Alexander D. Stoyenko

Department of Computer and Information Science
New Jersey Institute of Technology
Newark, NJ 07102, USA

Springer-Verlag Berlin Heidelberg GmbH

Proceedings of the NATO Advanced Study Institute on Real Time Computing, held in Sint Maarten, Dutch Antilles, October 5–17, 1992

CR Subject Classification (1991): C.3, J.7

ISBN 978-3-642-88051-3   ISBN 978-3-642-88049-0 (eBook)
DOI 10.1007/978-3-642-88049-0

Library of Congress Cataloging-in-Publication Data. Real time computing / edited by Wolfgang A. Halang and Alexander D. Stoyenko. p. cm. – (NATO ASI series. Series F, Computer and systems sciences; v. 127) Proceedings of the NATO Advanced Study Institute on Real Time Computing, held in Sint Maarten, Dutch Antilles, Oct. 5-17, 1992.

1. Real-time data processing–Congresses. I. Halang, Wolfgang A., 1951- . II. Stoyenko, Alexander D., 1962- . III. NATO Advanced Study Institute on Real Time Computing (1992: Aint Maarten, Netherlands Antilles) IV. Series. QA76.54.R4216   1994   004'.33–dc20   93-46646

© Springer-Verlag Berlin Heidelberg 1994
Originally published by Springer-Verlag Berlin Heidelberg New York in 1994

Typesetting: Camera ready by authors
45/3140 - 5 4 3 2 1 0 - Printed on acid-free paper

Foreword

NATO's Division of Scientific and Environmental Affairs sponsored this Advanced Study Institute because it was felt to be timely to cover this important and challenging subject for the first time in the framework of NATO's ASI programme. The significance of real-time systems in everyones' life is rapidly growing. The vast spectrum of these systems can be characterised by just a few examples of increasing complexity: controllers in washing machines, air traffic control systems, control and safety systems of nuclear power plants and, finally, future military systems like the Strategic Defense Initiative (SDI). The importance of such systems for the well-being of people requires considerable efforts in research and development of highly reliable real-time systems. Furthermore, the competitiveness and prosperity of entire nations now depend on the early application and efficient utilisation of computer integrated manufacturing systems (CIM), of which real-time systems are an essential and decisive part. Owing to its key significance in computerised defence systems, real-time computing has also a special importance for the Alliance.

The early research and development activities in this field in the 1960s and 1970s aimed towards improving the then unsatisfactory software situation. Thus, the first high-level real-time languages were defined and developed: RTL/2, Coral 66, Procol, LTR, and PEARL. In close connection with these language developments and with the utilisation of special purpose process control peripherals, the research on real-time operating systems advanced considerably. Comprehensive software tools for supporting the entire development process of real-time systems from hardware configuration and software requirements specification to code generation and documentation were developed and are now in widespread use.

Currently, real-time systems work is undergoing a revival. Many new and challenging applications are being developed in the areas of command and control systems, process control systems, automated manufacturing, flight control systems, avionics and aerospace, automated defence systems, shipboard systems, submarine systems, visions, and robotics. Hence, there is a wealth of new results being produced in industry and in academia, and the community of real-time experts is growing at a fast pace. The main topics of the present interest in real-time systems include requirements engineering methods and design tools, reliability engineering and software quality assurance in hard real-time environments, high-level real-time programming languages and their implementation of tasking, concurrency, synchronisation, and timing concepts, real-time operating systems and task scheduling algorithms, distributed and fault-tolerant novel real-time systems architectures, hardware and software support for process interfacing, communications, distributed databases, and, finally, artificial intelligence aspects with special emphasis on real-time expert systems.

Existing international research activities in real-time systems are characterised by a number of parallel developments and repetitions, which can, to a large extent, be referred to the lack of communication between the different national research groups. The primary reasons for this are language barriers and the inaccessibility of the literature, which is scattered over many journals and conference proceedings due to its interdisciplinary nature, and often only available in the form of internal reports. In this situation, the Advanced Study Institute on Real-Time Computing served as an appropriate medium to foster international communication and to present the state of available knowledge in a comprehensive form. An additional, practical advantage of the ASI was that it enabled a large number of European and North American top researchers to meet personally for the first time. Owing to the ASI's breadth, this volume will constitute, for a number of years, the urgently needed English-language compendium on the state of the art in real-time computing.

As the list of main lectures shows, the majority of leading specialists with an international reputation in the field were present at the ASI, covering the entire span of the present interest in real-time computing. The discussions revealed that consensus has been reached on many points. In particular, it has been almost unanimously concluded that there is a large gap between academic research, user needs, and industry practice, that enough work has taken place on such theoretical fundamentals as scheduling and formal specification, and that more "system" work is needed, as well as that technology-minded approaches would now be of use, especially where safety-critical, real-time operation is concerned. There is a need for new approaches to deal with the synchrony spectrum, especially when developing complex large-scale systems. Determinism and behavioural predictability were identified as indispensable prerequisites for trusting mission-critical and safety-critical systems. As a consequence of the still rapidly decreasing hardware costs, the general design philosophy must shift from resource limitation to resource adequacy, rendering more understandable solutions possible. With respect to formal methods it was concluded that while formal descriptions are valuable, the state of the art has not evolved to a point, yet, where they can be widely applied. In particular, the number of people who could be trusted to make formal descriptions of non-trivial systems is extremely limited. In order to make formal descriptions useful, they must be animated and augmented with appropriate means of decomposition. The obvious appeal of exploiting a well-developed tool set and existing knowledge was pointed to as a strong motivation for employing the operating system UNIX also in real-time applications. On the other hand, there are severe reservations to this approach due to the non-real-time nature of UNIX. An essential activity to be vigorously pursued is that of education in multiple directions. The parties involved in real-time computing must become aware of each others' problems and points of view. One needs to work closer with various groups of application engineers in the future and to take account of the real needs of applications in developing appropriate solutions. Consequently, many case studies must be documented and examined in this regard.

Wolfgang A. Halang   Alexander D. Stoyenko

October 1993

Acknowledgements

First and foremost, we should like to express our deep appreciation to the NATO Science Committee and to NATO's Division of Scientific and Environmental Affairs for their interest in the field of real time computing, for their confidence extended to the two co-directors, and for making this Advanced Study Institute possible by a generous grant. Our thanks go also to Dr. L. Veiga da Cunha, the ASI Programme Director, for the smooth co-operation in preparing this ASI and for his patience and understanding in resolving whatever problems arose.

We are very grateful to industrial corporations and government agencies for their generous and altruistic scientific and financial contributions to the success of the ASI. Listed in alphabetical order, these institutions are:

Bailey Controls Company

Digital Equipment Corporation

Philips Corporate Research

TÜBITAK

U.S. National Science Foundation

U.S. Office of Naval Research

We should like to thankfully acknowledge the large amount of work invested by the following persons into the administrative and co-ordinating efforts associate with the ASI and into the preparation of its proceedings: Mr. Bo-Chao Cheng for mailing and co-ordinating assistance, Ms. M. Craddock for financial reimbursement, Dr. J. Wichmann for carefully reading all contributions and removing language, consistency, and other flaws, Mrs. G. Kock for formatting the submitted documents according to the style prescribed by Springer-Verlag, and Ms. J. Halbeisen, M.A., for proof-reading, implementing corrections, and layouting this book.

The final ASI programme featured 10 working days with 26 lectures, 30 industrial and government experience sessions, 12 panels, some 50 student posters, and 10 spontaneous "birds-of-a-feather" sessions. We thank all ASI participants for their immense collective and individual contributions to the success of our meeting. While the contributions of those who participated in lectures, panels, and experience presentations have also been reflected in these printed proceedings, we should like to offer special thanks to everyone else and, especially, to the volunteers of the "birds-of-a-feather" sessions, that met after hours and on weekends (organisers in parentheses):

1. Deterministic Scheduling for Distributed Real-Time Systems (Hammer, Verhoosel)
2. Scheduling in Communication Networks (Ecker)
3. Safety-Critical Systems (addressing 4 different subtopics) (Cullyer)
4. Hierarchical Object Oriented Design (Tempelmeier)
5. Real-Time Services and Protocols in Communication Transport Systems/Networks (Rebensburg)
6. Worst-Case Execution Time Analysis of Programs (Chapman)
7. Formal Specifications with special regard to Petri Net Related Methods (Ghezzi)
8. Education in Real-Time Computing (Zalewski)
9. CAN (Frederiksson)
10. Formal Methods — How to make them understandable and usable for engineers? (Bareiß)

The enthusiasm, determination, and dedication of all participants was exemplary, and the attendance at daily sessions was extremely high; hence, the ASI has clearly achieved its objectives.

Contents

1 Lectures

2 Experiences

3 Panels

3.1 Contributions to Panel I: What is the State-of-the-Art in Real-Time Computing Research, Development and Technology?

3.2 Contributions to Panel II: The Role of Academia, Industry and Government in Real-Time Computing

3.3 Contributions to Panel III: The Next Generation of Real-Time Operating Systems and Languages

3.4 Contributions to Panel IV: Hard, Soft, Hybrid Real-Time Systems and Their Uses

3.5 Contributions to Panel V: What is the Right Specification/Design/Implementation Paradigm for Real-Time Applications?

3.9 Contributions to Panel IX: The Role of Standards in Real-Time Computing

3.10 Contributions to Panel X: Life Cycle of Real-Time Software Development

3.11 Contributions to Panel XI: What Should We Focus on in the Next Five Years?

4 Posters

5 Birds-of-a-Feather Sessions

Fundamentals of Real-Time Scheduling (Extended Abstract)

C. L. Liu

Department of Computer Science
University of Illinois at Urbana-Champaign
Urbana, IL 61801
U.S.A.

1 Introduction

For a given set of jobs the general scheduling problem asks for an order according to which the jobs are to be executed such that various constraints are satisfied. Typically, a job is characterized by its execution time, ready time, deadline, and recourse requirements. The execution of a job might or might not be interrupted (pre-emptive) or (non-preemptive scheduling). Over the set of jobs, there is a precedence relation which constrains the order of execution. Specifically, the execution of a job cannot begin until the execution of all its predecessors (according to the precedence relation) is completed. The system on which the jobs are to be executed is characterized by the amounts of resources available.

Scheduling problems arise in various applications including PERT (Programming Evaluation and Review Technique), transportation scheduling, process control, robotics, avionics, parallel computation, synthesis of VLSI circuits, and so on.

A key parameter (if not *the* key parameter) in any scheduling problem is *time*. A job should be completed before its deadline or a set of jobs should be completed before a pre-specified time of completion. By a real-time scheduling problem, we refer specifically to the case in which each job has its individual ready time and deadline.

There is extensive literature on the subject of scheduling theory, in this chapter, we shall give a brief survey on a number of topics in order to illustrate the many dimensions of a fascinating and important area of research.

2 Scheduling to Meet an Overall Deadline

One of the simplest models of the scheduling problem which has been studied extensively can be described as follows:

(1) The execution time of each job is given.
(2) All jobs have the same ready time and the same deadline (which is referred to as the overall deadline).

(3) Execution of a job cannot be interrupted (non-preemptive execution).
(4) There is a precedence relation over the jobs.
(5) There is a given number of identical processors. A job can be executed on any one of the processors.

The problem is to determine a schedule for the execution of the jobs so that they are all completed before the overall deadline.

Although this problem appears to be exceedingly simple, very little is known about algorithms that produce an optimal schedule, namely, a schedule that will complete the execution of all the jobs in minimum time. In fact, efficient algorithms[1] that produce optimal schedules are known only for the following cases:

(1) Jobs with unit execution time and with the precedence relation over them being a forest are to be scheduled on a set of identical processors [1].
(2) Jobs with unit execution time are to be scheduled on two identical processors [2].

3 Jobs with Un-uniform Ready-Times and Deadlines

3.1 Earliest Deadline First

Consider the following model:

(1) The execution time, ready time, and deadline of each job are given.
(2) The jobs are independent (i.e. the precedence relation over the jobs is empty).
(3) Exection of a job can be interrupted (preemptive execution).
(4) There is only one processor.

As it turns out, for this model, the *earliest deadline first* scheduling algorithm will produce an optimal schedule in the sense that if a set of jobs can be scheduled to meet all the deadlines, the earliest deadline first scheduling algorithm will produce one such schedule. On the other hand, if according to the earliest deadline first scheduling algorithm, one or more jobs will miss their deadlines, then there is no schedule in which all jobs will meet their deadlines. By *earliest deadline first* we mean that at any time instant among the jobs that are ready for execution the one which has the earliest deadline will be executed [3, 4, 5].

The result stated above can be extended to the case when there is a precedence relation over the job. In this case, we introduce the notion of the "modified deadline" of a job. Let d_R denote the given deadline of a job J_R. The modified deadline of J_R, denoted d_R^*, is computed according to the formula

$$d_R^* = min(d_R, min(d_i^* | J_i \text{ is a successor of } J_R))$$

In fact, for the extended case, the *earliest modified deadline first* scheduling algorithm also produces an optimal schedule.

---

[1] We emphasize the word "efficient". Otherwise, we can always construct exhaustively all possible schedules and pick an optimal one.

3.2 Earliest Critical Time First

At any time instant, the critical time of a job is defined to be

critical time = deadline - remaining computation time of job

Note that the critical time of a job is a dynamical quantity which changes as the job is being executed. For the case of a single processor, the *earliest critical time first* scheduling algorithm is also optimal. For the multi-processor case we have, however, the following result:

Theorem 1 [6]: For the multi-processor case the earliest critical time first scheduling algorithm is optimal if (1) The ready times of all jobs are the same, or (2) The deadlines of all jobs are the same.

4 Periodic Jobs

A periodic job consists of an infinite sequence of requests with periodic ready times, where the deadline of a request is the ready time of the succeeding request. Furthermore, the execution times of all the requests of a job are the same. A periodic job is characterized by two parameters T, the period of the request, and C, the execution time. The utilization factor of a set of n periodic jobs is defined to be the sum $\sum_{i=1}^{n} \frac{C_i}{T_i}$ where $T_1, \ldots, T_i, \ldots, T_n$ are the periods and $C_1, \ldots, C_i, \ldots, C_n$ are the execution times of the n jobs.

According to the result stated above, the earliest deadline first algorithm is optimal for any given set of periodic jobs. The following theorem states the fact in a quantative way:

Theorem 2 [4]: A set of periodic jobs can be scheduled by the earliest deadline first scheduling algorithm if and only if its utilization factor, $\sum_{i=1}^{n} \frac{C_i}{T_i}$, is less than or equal to 1.

The earliest deadline first scheduling algorithm is a priority driven algorithm in which priorities are assigned to requests with highest priority being assigned to the request that has the earlier deadline, and a higher priority request always pre-empts a lower priority one. Another priority driven scheduling algorithm, known as the *rate monotonic* scheduling algorithm, assigns higher priorities to the requests of jobs with shorter periods. The earliest deadline first scheduling algorithm is an example of priority driven algorithms with dynamic priority assignment in the sense that the priority of a request is assigned as the request arrives. On the other hand, the rate monotonic scheduling algorithm is an example of priority driven algorithms with static priority assignment in the sense that the priorities of all requests are known even before their arrival. The priorities of all requests of each job are the same. (They are determined only by the period of the job.)

The rate monotonic scheduling algorithm is not optimal. As as example, one can easily check that it fails to schedule the two jobs $C_1 = 1, T_1 = 2, C_2 = 2.5, T_2 = 5$ which, as was indicated above, can be scheduled by the earliest deadline first algorithm. We note, however, that the rate monotonic scheduling algorithm is optimal among all static priority scheduling algorithms in the sense that if a set of periodic jobs can be scheduled by any static priority scheduling algorithm then it is also schedulable by the rate monotonic scheduling algorithm.

The following theorem provides an effective way to determine whether a set of period jobs can be scheduled by the rate monotonic scheduling algorithm.

Theorem 3 [4, 5]: A set of n period jobs can be scheduled by the rate monotonic algorithm if the utilization factor of the set is less than or equal to $n(2^{\frac{1}{n}} - 1)$.

Note than for $n = 2$

$$n(2^{\frac{1}{n}} - 1) = 2(\sqrt{2} - 1) = 0.828$$

for $n \to \infty$

$$n(2^{\frac{1}{n}} - 1) \to 0.693$$

We note the Theorem 3 provides a useful utilization bound in the sense that if the utilization factor of a set of jobs is below the utilization bound then the set is guaranteed to be schedulable. On the other hand, for a set of jobs the utilization factor of which exceeds the utilization bound then there is no such guarantee. Furthermore, it can be shown that for each n there exists a set of n jobs which are unschedulable with the utilization factor of which being only slightly above the utilization bound.

5 Variations of the Periodic Job Model

In Sec. 4, we specify that there is an infinite periodic sequence of requests in a periodic job with the deadline of a request being the arrival time of the subsequent request. In this section, we present results related to variations of the model of periodic jobs in which the deadline of a request is not necessarily the arrival time of the next request. Consequently, a periodic job is specified by three parameters T, C, and D, where T is the period of the request, C is the execution time, and D is the deadline of each request meaning that the deadline of a request which arrives at t is $t + D$.

5.1 The Case $D \le T$

We examine first the case $D \le T$. The *deadline monotonic* scheduling algorithm is a static priority scheduling algorithm in which priorities are assigned to periodic jobs inversely with respect to the deadlines $D_1, D_2, \ldots, D_n$, of the jobs. We note that

Theorem 4 [7]: For a set of n periodic jobs specified by the parameters $(C_1, T_1, D_1), \ldots (C_i, T_i, D_i) \ldots (C_n, T_n, D_n)$, if $D_i \le T_i$, for $i = 1, \ldots, n$, the deadline monotonic scheduling algorithm is optimal among all static priority scheduling algorithms.

For the special case $D_i = \Delta T_i$, $1 \le i \le n$, the rate monotonic and deadline monotonic scheduling algorithms are the same. We have the following result on the utilization bound:

Theorem 5 [8, 9, 10]: A set of n periodic jobs with $D_i = \Delta T_i$, $1 \le i \le n$, is schedulable by the rate-monotonic scheduling algorithm if

$$\sum_{i=1}^{n} \frac{C_i}{T_i} \le \begin{cases} n[(2\Delta)^{1/n} - 1] + (1 - \Delta) & \frac{1}{2} \le \Delta \le 1 \\ \Delta & 0 \le \Delta \le \frac{1}{2} \end{cases}$$

5.2 The Case $D \ge T$

The case $D \ge T$, which shall be referred to as the case of *scheduling with extended deadlines*, was studied extensively in recent years. For the case $D_i = \Delta T_i$, $i \le 1 \le n$, we have

Theorem 6 [8]: A set of n periodic jobs with $D_i = \Delta T_i$, $1 \le i \le n$, is schedulable by the rate-monotomic algorithm if

$$\sum_{i=1}^{n} \frac{C_i}{T_i} \le \begin{cases} n[(\Delta + 1)^{1/n} - 1] = n(2^{1/n} - 1) & \Delta = 1 \\ \Delta \left[(n-1) \left((\frac{\Delta+1}{\Delta})^{1/n-1} - 1 \right) \right] & \Delta = 2, 3, \ldots \end{cases}$$

As $n \to \infty$, both expressions on the right hand side become

$$\Delta \, ln \left(\frac{\Delta + 1}{\Delta} \right) \qquad \Delta = 1, 2, 3, \ldots$$

For the case $D \ge T$, a new scheduling algorithm known as the *modified rate-monotonic* scheduling algorithm was introduced [11].

The modified rate-monotonic scheduling algorithm, like the rate-monotonic scheduling algorithm, is preemptive and priority-driven. It divides all the requests into two groups, current requests and old requests, and assigns two sets of priorities to them according to the following rules:

(1) All current requests have priorities lower than that of all old requests.
(2) The priorities of the requests in each group are assigned on a rate-monotonic basis. In other words, the current request of a job with a shorter period has a higher priority over the current request of a job with a longer period. Similarly, an old request of a job with a shorter period has a higher priority over an old request of a job with a longer period.
(3) All old requests of the same job are scheduled and executed on the first-in-first-out basis.

Hence, two priorities are assigned to each job J_i : i and $i + n$.

We have the following results concerning the modified rate-monotonic scheduling algorithm:

Theorem 7 [11]: Let δ be a constant larger than or equal to 2. The modified rate-monotonic algorithm is optimal for a set of n periodic jobs if

(1) $D_i \geq (\delta - 1)T_i, i = 1, 2, \ldots n$

(2) The ratio between the longest and the shortest period is less than or equal to δ.

Theorem 8 [11]: A set of n periodic jobs with $D_i \geq 2T_i, 1 \leq i \leq n$, is schedulable by the modified rate-monotonic algorithm if

$$\sum_{i=1}^{n} \frac{C_i}{T_i} \leq \begin{cases} 1 & n = 2, 3 \\ \frac{1}{2}[1 + n(2^{1/n} - 1)] & n > 3 \end{cases}$$

It should be noted that for the case of scheduling of extended deadlines, the rate-monotonic algorithm and the modified rate-montonic algorithm are incomparable in the sense that there are examples in which a set of periodic jobs with extended deadlines are schedulable by the rate monotonic scheduling algorithm but not by the modified rate monotonic scheduling algorithm, and there are also examples in which a set of periodic jobs with extended deadlines are schedulable by the modified rate monotonic algorithm but not by the rate monotonic scheduling algorithm.

6 Variations and Extensions

There are several variations and extensions to the problem of periodic job scheduling described in Sec. 4 and 5. Some of these are Pinwheel scheduling [12], periodic maintenance [13], and scheduling for multiprocessor systems [14].

References

1. Hu, T. C., *Parallel scheduling and assembly line problems*, Oper. Res., Vol. 9, 1961, 841-848.

2. Coffman, E. G., Jr. and R. L. Graham, *Optimal scheduling for two processor systems*, Acta Informatica, Vol. 1, 1972, 200-213.

3. Labetoulle, J., *Some theorems on real time scheduling*, Computer Architectures and Networks, E. Gelenbe and R. Mehl (eds.), North-Holland Publ. Co., 1974, 285-298.

4. Liu, C. L., and J. W. Layland, *Scheduling algorithms for multiprogramming in a Hard-real-time environment*, J. ACM, Vol. 20, 1973, 46-61.

5. Serlin, O., *Scheduling of time critical processes* Proc. of the Spring Joint Computers Conference, 1972, 925-932.

6. Mok, A. K., *Fundamental Design Problems of Distributed Systems for Hard Real-Time Environment*, Ph.D. Thesis, MIT, 1983.

7. Leung, J. and Whitehead, J., *On the complexity of fixed-priority scheduling of periodic, real-time tasks*, Performance Evaluation, Vol. 2, 1982, 237-250.

8. Lehoczky, J. P., *Fixed priority scheduling of periodic task sets with arbitrary deadlines*, Proceedings of the 11th IEEE Real-Time Systems Symposium, December 1990, 201-209.

9. Lehoczky, J. P., and Sha, L., *Performance of real-time bus scheduling algorithms*, ACM Performance Evaluation Review, Vol. 14, 1986.

10. Peng, D-T. and Shin, K. G., *A new performance measure for scheduling independent real-time tasks*, Technical Report, Real-Time Computing Laboratory, University of Michigan, 1989.
11. Shih, Wei Kuan, J. W. S. Liu, and C. L. Liu, *Modified Rate-Monotonic Algorithm for Scheduling Periodic Jobs with Deferred Deadlines*, submitted.
12. Chan, M. Y. and F. Y. L. Chin, *General Schedulers for the Pinwheel Problem Based on Double-Integer Reduction*, IEEE Trans. on Computers, Vol. 41, No. 6, 1992, 755-768.
13. Wei, W. D. and C. L. Liu, *On a Periodic Maintenance Problem*, Operations Research Letters, Vol. 2, No. 2, 1983, 90-93.
14. Dhall, S. K. and C. L. Liu, *On a real-time scheduling problem*, Operations Research, Vol. 26, 1978, 127-140.

Algorithmic Methods for Real-Time Scheduling

K. Ecker

Technische Universität Clausthal
Erzstraße 1
38678 Clausthal
Germany

Abstract

Task scheduling is a wide research area whose results gained increasing interest during the last decades. A great variety of different algorithmic methods has been developed. Though these methods are very often adjusted to the specifics of the various scheduling problems, there are few principles along which scheduling algorithms work. The purpose of this contribution is to give an overview on the main algorithmic approaches applied in real-time scheduling. Different methods for solving selected problem classes are discussed.

1 Motivation

In general, scheduling problems can be understood as the problems of the allocation of resources over time to perform a set of tasks. By resources we understand arbitrary means tasks compete for. They can be of very different nature, such as man power, money, processors or machines, energy, and tools. Tasks, too, can have a variety of interpretations starting from machining parts in manufacturing systems up to processing information in computer systems. In case of real-time scheduling, besides other criteria the usefulness of a production part or a computational result depends on the time it is produced. In many application areas today highly sophisticated, complex and distributed systems are required which include coordination and control of time critical activities.

One concern in the analysis and in the development of strategies for task scheduling is the question of predictability of the systems behavior. In deterministic scheduling, assumptions about the model parameters are postulated which allow to predict the behavior of the real-time system. Especially in manufacturing environments this kind of scheduling is often called *predictive*. If there is no sufficient knowledge to predict the system's behavior, *reactive* scheduling using a shorter planning horizon leads often to acceptable results. But in many situations, especially if deadlines have to be met, reactive scheduling cannot be applied. When for instance task processing times are unknown, the only way to solve the problem is to assume upper bounds on the processing times. If all deadlines are met with respect to these upper bounds, no deadline will be exceeded for the real task processing times. This approach is often used in a broad class of computer control systems working in hard real-time environments, where a certain set of control programs must be processed before taking the next sample from the same sensing device. Another possibility would be to enter mean values of system parameters in cases where exact values are not available.

2 Scheduling Models and Problem Complexity

2.1 Notation

The scheduling problems considered here are characterized by a set of *tasks* $T = \{T_1, T_2, \ldots, T_n\}$ and a set of *processors (machines)* $P = \{P_1, P_2, \ldots, P_m\}$ the tasks are to be processed on. Besides processors, tasks may require certain additional *resources* $R = \{R_1, R_2, \ldots, R_s\}$ during their execution. Scheduling, generally speaking, means the assignment of processors from P and resources from R to tasks from T in order to complete all tasks under certain imposed constraints. In classical scheduling theory it is also assumed that each task is to be processed by at most one processor at a time and each processor is capable of processing at most one task at a time.

We begin with an analysis of processors, $P = \{P_1, P_2, \ldots, P_m\}$. There are three different types of processors: *Parallel processors* may be interpreted as central processors which are able to process every task (i.e. every program). *Uniform processors* differ from each other by their speeds, but they do not prefer any type of tasks. *Unrelated processors*, on the contrary, are specialized in the sense that they prefer certain types of tasks, for example numerical computations, logical programs, or simulation procedures. The processors may have different instruction sets, but they are still of comparable processing capacity so they can process tasks of any type, only processing times may be different.

By an *additional resource* we understand a "facility" besides processors the tasks compete for. The competition aspect in this definition should be stressed, since "facilities" dedicated to only one task will not be treated as resources in this paper. In computer systems, for example, messages sent from one task to another specified task will not be considered as resources. In manufacturing environments tools, material, transport facilities, etc. can be treated as additional resources. Let us now consider the assumptions associated with the task set T. In general, a task $T_j \in T$ is characterized by the following data.

- *Vector of processing times* $p_j = [p_{1j}, p_{2j}, \ldots, p_{mj}]^T$, where p_{ij} is the time needed by processor P_i to process T_j. In case of identical processors we have $p_{ij} = p_j, i = 1, 2, \ldots, m$. If the processors in P are uniform then $p_{ij} = p_j/b_i, i = 1, 2, \ldots, m$, where p_j is the *standard processing time* (usually measured on the slowest processor) and b_i is the *processing speed factor* of processor P_i.
- *Precedence constraints* among tasks. $T_i \prec T_j$ means that processing of T_i must be completed before T_j can be started. In other words, set T is partially

ordered by a precedence relation $\prec$. The tasks in set T are called *dependent* if the order of execution of at least two tasks in T is restricted by this relation. Otherwise, the tasks are called *independent*.

- *Release time* (or *ready time*) r_j is the time at which task T_j is ready for processing. If the ready times are the same for all tasks from T, then $r_j = 0$ is assumed for all j.
- *Due date* d_j specifies a time limit by which T_j should be completed; usually, penalty functions are defined in accordance with due dates.
- *Deadline* $\tilde{d}_j$ is a "hard" real-time limit by which T_j must be completed.
- *Periodicy* of tasks: In some applications a task T_j may need repeated service with some given period c_j. This is especially the case in control systems where a computer has to run a set of tasks in an infinite loop. Values of task periods then depend on the dynamic of the physical process associated with them. Because of limited space we will not consider periodical tasks.
- Weight (or priority) w expresses the relative urgency of T_j.

In deterministic scheduling theory a priori knowledge of ready times and processing times of tasks is usually assumed. As opposed to other applications, the question of a priori knowledge of these parameters in computer systems needs a thorough comment. As far as processing times are concerned, they are usually not known a priori in computer systems. Despite this fact the solution of a deterministic scheduling problem may have an important interpretation in these systems. One approach would be to solve the problem with assumed upper bounds on the processing times. In hard real-time environments with given task deadlines, this approach is often used; if all deadlines are met with respect to their upper bounds, no deadline will be exceeded for the real task processing times. Another possibility would be to take mean task processing times instead of exact values and calculate an optimistic estimate of the mean value of the schedule length.

Next, some definitions concerning *schedules* and *optimality criteria* are discussed. A schedule is an assignment of processors from set P (and possibly resources from set R) to tasks from set T in time such that the following conditions are satisfied:

- At every moment each processor is assigned to at most one task and each task is processed by at most one processor.
- Task T_j is processed in the time interval $[r_j, \infty)$, or, if deadlines are specified, in the time interval $[r_j, \tilde{d}_j)$.
- All tasks are completed.
- If tasks T_i, T_j are in relation $T_i \prec T_j$, the processing of T_j is not started before T_i has been completed.
- A schedule is called *preemptive* if each task may be preempted at any time and restarted later at no cost, perhaps on another processor. If preemption is not allowed we will call the schedule *nonpreemptive*.
- Resource constraints are satisfied.

The following parameters can be calculated for each task $T_j, j = 1, 2, \ldots, n$, processed in a given schedule:

Completion time C_j;
Flow time $F_j = C_j - r_j$ being the sum of waiting and processing times;
Lateness $L_j = C_j - d_j$;
Tardiness $D_j = \max \{C_j - d_j, 0\}$.

Depending on the type of application we are confronted with, different *performance measures or optimality criteria* are used to evaluate schedules. Among the most common measures in scheduling theory are *schedule length (makespan)* $C_{\max} = \max \{C_j\}$, and *mean flow time* $F = \frac{1}{n} \sum_{j=1}^{n} F_j$ or *mean weighted flow time* $F_w = \sum_{j=1}^{n} w_j F_j / \sum_{j=1}^{n} w_j$. Minimizing schedule length is important from the viewpoint of the owner of a set of processors or machines, since it leads to both, the maximization of the processor utilization within makespan $C_{\max}$, and the minimization of the maximum in-process time of the scheduled set of tasks. The *mean flow time* criterion is important from the user's viewpoint since its minimization yields a minimization of the mean response time and the mean in-process time of the scheduled task set.

In real-time applications, performance measures are used that take lateness or tardiness of tasks into account. Examples are the *maximum lateness* $L_{\max} = \max \{L_j\}$, the mean tardiness $\overline{D} = \frac{1}{n} \sum_{j=1}^{n} D_j$ or *mean weighted tardiness* $\overline{D}_w = (\sum_{j=1}^{n} w_j D_j) / \sum_{j=1}^{n} w_j$, the number of *tardy tasks* $U = \sum_{j=1}^{n} U_j$ where $U_j = 1$, if $C_j > d_j$, and 0 otherwise, or *weighted number of tardy tasks* $U_w = \sum_{j=1}^{n} w_j U_j$. *These due date involving criteria* are of great importance in many applications, as for example in control or manufacturing systems. These criteria are also of significance in computer control systems working in a hard real-time environment since their minimization leads to the construction of schedules with no task late whenever such schedules exist. There is another optimality criterion based on task due dates or deadlines: If a task is not finished on time, the yet unprocessed part of it contributes to the schedule value that has to be minimized.

A schedule for which the value of a particular performance measure γ is at its minimum will be called *optimal*, and the corresponding value of γ will be denoted by γ^*.

We now define a *scheduling problem* Π as a set of parameters as described above, together with an optimality criterion.

The criteria mentioned above are basic in the sense that they require specific approaches to the construction of schedules. A *scheduling algorithm* is an algorithm which constructs a schedule for a given problem Π. In general, we are interested in optimization algorithms, but because of the inherent complexity of many problems of that type, also approximation or heuristic algorithms are applied. It is rather obvious that very often the time available for solving particular scheduling problems is seriously limited so that only low order polynomial-time algorithms can be applied. Thus, the examination of the complexity of these problems should be the basis of any further analysis.

Scheduling problems belong to the broad class of *combinatorial search problems*. It has been known for some time [19], [41] that there exists a large class of combinatorial optimization problems for which most probably *no efficient optimization* algorithms exist. These optimization problems are called *NP-hard*.

We refer to [30] for a comprehensive treatment of the NP-completeness theory. The complexity analysis answers the question whether or not a given scheduling problem can be solved optimally in time bounded from above by a polynomial in the input length of the problem.

2.2 Classification of Deterministic Scheduling Problems

The great variety of scheduling problems motivates the introduction of a systematic notation that could serve as a basis for a classification scheme. Such a notation of problem types would greatly facilate the presentation and discussion of scheduling problems. A notation proposed by Graham et al. [33] and Błażewicz et al. [9] is composed of three fields $\alpha \mid \beta \mid \gamma$ that have the following meaning. α describes the processor environment, i.e. type and number of processors. β describes task and resource characteristics such as processing times, precedence constraints, ready times, deadlines, resource requirements. γ denotes the optimality criterion, as for example maximum lateness ($min L_{max}$), or weighted number of tardy tasks ($min \sum w_j U_j$).

3 Algorithmic Approaches

As already mentioned, scheduling problems such as real-time problems belong to the broad class of combinatorial optimization problems. To solve these problems one tends to use algorithms which for sure always find optimal solutions. General methods for solving such problems are *dynamic programming and branch and bound*. Both methods use *implicit enumeration* because they consider certain solutions only indirectly without actually evaluating them explicitly. The computation time of these methods usually increases exponentially with the number of tasks. For special optimization problems, however, polynomial-time optimization algorithms can be constructed. In other cases *heuristic (suboptimal) algorithms* can be applied which tend toward but do not guarantee optimal solutions.

3.1 Dynamic Programming

In *dynamic programming* the given problem is divided into a number of *stages*, and at each stage a decision is required which impacts on the decisions to be made in later stages. Bellman's principle [3] of optimality is applied to draw up a recursive equation which describes the optimal criterion value at a given stage in terms of the previously obtained value. In order to calculate the optimal criterion value for any subset of size k, we have to know the optimal value for the subsets of size $k - 1$. Thus, if the problem is characterized by a set of n elements, the number of subsets to be considered is 2^n. This means that dynamic programming algorithms are of exponential computational complexity. However, for problems which are NP-hard (but not in the strong sense) it is often possible to construct *pseudopolynomial* dynamic programming algorithms which are of practical value for reasonable instance sizes.

3.2 Branch and Bound

Suppose that for a given finite set S of feasible solutions and an optimality criterion $\gamma\colon \mathsf{S} \to \mathbf{R}$, we want to find $S^* \in \mathsf{S}$ such that $\gamma(S^*) = min\{S \in \mathsf{S}\}$. *Branch and bound finds S^** by implicit enumeration of all $S \in \mathsf{S}$ through examination of sets of solutions belonging to subproblems of the original problem.

The method of branch and bound consists of two fundamental procedures, branching and bounding. In *branching*, the problem is divided into two or more subproblems. For each subproblem generated in the branching process, *bounding* calculates a *lower bound* on the value of an optimal solution. The branching procedure can be conveniently represented as a *search* (or *branching*) *tree*. This tree consists at level O of a single node representing the original problem, and at further levels of nodes representing particular subproblems of the problem at the previous level. Edges are introduced from each problem node to each of its subproblem nodes. A list of unprocessed nodes (also called *active nodes*) is maintained where each node corresponds to a subproblem that is not eliminated and whose own subproblems have not yet been investigated.

Suppose that at some stage of the branch and bound process a solution S of value $\gamma(S)$ has been obtained. Suppose also that a node encountered in the process has an associated lower bound $LB > \gamma(S)$. Then the node needs not be considered any further in the search for S^*, since the resulting solution can never have a value less than $\gamma(S)$. When such a node is found, it is eliminated, and we do not continue the branching process from it. The solutions used for checking elimination of nodes are sometimes called *trial solutions*. At the beginning a trial solution may be found e.g. by using a special heuristic procedure, and at any later stage the best solution found so far can be chosen. In many cases a node can be eliminated not only on the basis of lower bounds but also by means of so-called elimination criteria provided by dominance properties or feasibility conditions developed for a given problem.

The choice of a node from the set of generated nodes which have so far neither been eliminated nor led to branching is due to the chosen *search strategy*. Two search strategies are used most frequently: jumptracking and backtracking. *Jumptracking* implements a *frontier search* where a node with a minimal lower bound is selected for examination, while *backtracking* implements a *depth first search* where the descendant nodes of a parent node are examined either in an arbitrary order or in order of nondecreasing lower bounds. Thus, in the jumptracking strategy the branching process jumps from one branch of the tree to another, whereas in the backtracking strategy it first proceeds directly to the bottom along some path to find a trial solution and then backtracks up to the first level with active nodes, and so on. It is easy to realize that jumptracking tends to construct a fairly large list of active nodes, while backtracking maintains relatively few nodes on the list at any time. However, an advantage of jumptracking is the quality of its trial solutions which are usually much closer to optimum than the trial solutions generated by backtracking, especially at early stages.

The actual computational behavior of branch and bound algorithms remains unpredictable and large computational experiments are necessary to recognize their quality. It is obvious that the computational complexity function of a branch and bound algorithm is exponential in problem size. However, the approach is often used for finding approximation solutions by stopping the branching process at a certain stage or after a certain time period elapsed.

3.3 Relaxation

One may try to relax some constraints imposed on the original scheduling problem and then solve the simplified problem. Solution algorithms for the latter might give rise for interesting approximation algorithms for the original problem. Such a relaxation could consist of

- allowing preemptions, even if the original problem dealt with non-preemptive schedules,
- assuming unit-length tasks, when arbitrary-length tasks were considered in the original problem,
- assuming certain types of precedence graphs, e.g. trees or chains, when arbitrary graphs were considered in the original problem, etc.

3.4 Heuristic and Approximation Algorithms

When solving NP-hard scheduling problems one often applies approximation algorithms which try to find optimal schedules but do not always succeed. One of the most often used approximation approaches is the so-called *list scheduling*. Such an algorithm starts with a given sequence of tasks where tasks are arranged according to some reasonable priority, and at each step the first available processor is selected to process the first available task on the list. The accuracy of a particular list scheduling algorithm depends on the given optimality criterion and the way the list has been constructed.

To mention an example, a very often used heuristics is the earliest due date (EDD) rule, where tasks are processed in order of nonincreasing due dates. Another way to create a task list is the application of so-called interchange relations. Here, due to certain properties inherent in the given problem, decisions about the processing order, e.g. of pairs of tasks, are made.

Of course, a necessary condition for list algorithms to be applicable in practice is that their worst-case time complexity function is limited from above by a low-order polynomial in the input length. A sufficient condition follows from an evaluation of the distance between the solution value they produce and the value of an optimal solution. This evaluation may concern the *worst case* or a *mean behavior*. Heuristic algorithms with analytically evaluated accuracy are often called *approximation algorithms*. To be more precise, if A is an approximation algorithm for a minimization scheduling problem Π, and I is any instance of it, we may define the ratio $R_A(I)$ as

$$R_A(I) = \frac{A(I)}{OPT(I)}$$

where $A(I)$ is the value of the solution constructed by algorithm A for instance I, and $OPT(I)$ is the value of an optimal solution for I. The *absolute performance ratio* R_A for an approximation algorithm A for problem Π is then given as

$$R_A = \inf\{r \geq 1 \mid R_A(I) \leq r \text{ for all instances of } \Pi\},$$

and the *asymptotic performance ratio* R_A^∞ for A is

$$R_A^\infty = \inf \{r \geq 1 \mid \text{ for some positive integer } K, R_A(I) \leq r \text{ for}$$
$$\text{all instances of } \Pi \text{ satisfying } OPT(I) \geq K\}.$$

The above formulas define a measure of "goodness" of an approximation algorithm. The closer R_A^∞ is to 1, the better performs algorithm A. However, for some combinatorial problems it can be proved that there is no hope of finding an approximation algorithm of a specified accuracy, i.e. this question is as hard as finding a polynomial-time algorithm for any NP-complete problem.

Besides the worst-case behavior of an approximation algorithm, also its mean behavior may be analyzed. One way of doing this is assuming that the parameters of instances of the considered problem Π are drawn from a certain distribution, and then the *mean performance* of algorithm A is analyzed. The second way of evaluating the mean behavior of approximation algorithms consists in experimental studies. In the latter approach solutions constructed by a given approximation algorithm are compared to optimal solutions.

3.5 Other Approaches

There are few attempts to apply neural nets for the process of schedule generation. Also, in some applications as for example in production planning systems within computer integrated manufacturing, methods of artificial intelligence are used to support decision processes especially for the so-called short term production scheduling. In this contribution we will not consider these types of scheduling approaches.

4 Real-Time Problems and Their Solutions

In the following we give a short overview on a selection of available results in soft and hard real-time scheduling under different optimality criteria.

4.1 Minimizing Schedule Length

First we will analyze the schedule length criterion. The first problem considered is $P \mid \mid C_{\max}$ where a set of independent tasks is to be scheduled on some given set of identical processors in order to minimize schedule length. Complexity analysis of this problem leads to the conclusion that the problem is not easy to solve since even the simple case $P2 \mid \mid C_{\max}$ of scheduling on two processors is NP-hard [41]. Hence there is no hope of finding an optimization polynomial time algorithm for $P \mid\mid C_{\max}$, and one may try to solve the problem along the lines explained in Section 3. If we relax the problem $P \mid\mid C_{\max}$ by allowing task preemption, it turns out that the problem can be solved very efficiently. It can easily be seen that the length of a preemptive schedule cannot be smaller than the maximum of the two values: maximum processing time of a task, and mean processing requirement on a processor, i.e.

$$C^*_{\max} \geq \max \{\max_j\{p_j\}, \tfrac{1}{m} \sum_{j=l}^{n} p_j\}. \tag{4.1}$$

An algorithm given by McNaughton [57] ("McNaughton's wrap around rule") constructs an optimal schedule of length equal to $C^*_{\max}$. Its time complexity is $O(n)$. We see that allowing preemptions made the problem easy to solve. However, there remains the question of practical applicability of the solution obtained this way. It appears that in particular in multiprocessor systems with a common primary memory the assumption of task preemptions can be justified. In cases where task preemption is not allowed, as for instance in most manufacturing systems, one may try to find an approximation algorithm for the original problem and evaluate its worst case as well as its mean behavior.

One of the most often used general approximation strategies for solving scheduling problems is list scheduling, where a priority list of the tasks is given, and at each step the first available processor is selected to process the first available task on the list [34]. The accuracy of a given list scheduling algorithm depends on the order in which tasks appear on the list. Unfortunately, this strategy may result in an unexpected behavior of constructed schedules, since the schedule length for problem $P \mid prec \mid C_{\max}$ (with arbitrary precedence constraints) may increase even if the number of processors increases, task processing times decrease, or precedence constraints are weakened.

These scheduling anomalies have been discovered by Graham [34], who has also evaluated the maximum change in schedule length that may be induced by varying one or more problem parameters. Suppose L and L' are task lists for a problem of type $P \mid prec \mid C_{\max}$, and the number m of processors is changed to m'. For the lengths C and C' of schedules created by the lists L and L', resp. we have

$$\frac{C'}{C} \leq l + \frac{m-l}{m'}.$$

From this we can follow that an arbitrary list scheduling algorithm can produce schedules almost twice as long as optimal ones. An improvement could be gained if tasks are ordered properly in the list. One of the simplest algorithms is the *LPT algorithm* in which the tasks are arranged in order of nonincreasing p_j.

LPT Algorithm for $P \parallel C_{\max}$.
`begin`
Order tasks on a list in nonincreasing order of their processing times;
$--$ i.e. $p_1 \geq \ldots \geq p_n$
`for` $i = 1$ `step` 1 `until` m `do` $s_i := 0$;
    $--$ processors P_i are assumed to be idle from time $s_i = 0$ on, $i = l, \ldots, m$
$j := 1$;
`repeat`
    $s_k := \min \{s_i\}$;
    Assign task T_j to processor P_k at time s_k;
        $--$ the first nonassigned task from the list is scheduled on the first processor
        $--$ that becomes free
    $s_k := s_k + p_j$; $j := j + 1$;
`until` $j = n$;   all tasks have been scheduled
`end`;

The worst case behavior of the *LPT* rule is known to be [34]

$$R_{LPT} = \frac{4}{3} - \frac{1}{3m}.$$

We see that in the worst case an *LPT* schedule can be up to 33% longer than an optimal schedule. However, one is led to expect better performance from the *LPT* algorithm, especially when the number of tasks becomes large. In [20] another absolute performance ratio for the *LPT* rule was proved, taking into account the number k of tasks assigned to a processor whose last task terminates the schedule. Then the performance ratio reduces to

$$R_{LPT}(k) = 1 + \frac{1}{k} - \frac{1}{km}.$$

To conclude the above analysis we may say that the *LPT* algorithm behaves quite well and may be useful in practice. However, if one wants to have better performance guarantees, other approximation algorithms should be used, as for example MULTIFIT introduced by Coffman et al. [16] or the algorithm proposed by Hochbaum and Shmoys [37]. A comprehensive treatment of approximation algorithms for this and related problems is given by Coffman et al. [17].
Under the assumption that tasks have unit processing times, Hu [38] proved that for tree-like precedence constraints and an arbitrary number of processors the problem can be solved by a simple algorithm called level algorithm or critical path algorithm. The algorithm is based on the notion of a task level in an in-tree which is defined as the number of tasks on the path to the root of the graph. It is interesting to note that the problem of scheduling opposing forests (that is, combinations of in-trees and out-trees) on an arbitrary number of processors is NP-hard [32]. However, if the number of processors is limited to 2, the problem is easily solvable even for arbitrary precedence graphs [14], [27], [28].
The algorithm given by Coffman and Graham [14] uses labels assigned to tasks,

which take into account the levels of the tasks and the numbers of their immediate successors. It should be stressed that the question concerning the complexity of problem $Pm \mid prec, p_j = 1 \mid C_{\max}$ with a *fixed* number m of processors
is still open despite the fact that many papers have been devoted to solving
various subcases of precedence constraints. Some results are also available for
the subcases in which task processing times may take only two values. Problems
$P2 \mid prec, p_j = 1$ or $2 \mid C_{\max}$ and $P \mid prec, p_j = 1or k \mid C_{\max}$ are NP-hard [23],
while problems $P2 \mid tree, p_j = 1$ or $2 \mid C_{\max}$ and $P2 \mid tree, p_j = 1$ or $3 \mid C_{\max}$ are
solvable in time $O(n\log n)$ [63] and $O(n^2\log n)$ [24], respectively. Furthermore, several papers deal with approximation algorithms for $P \mid prec, p_j = 1 \mid C_{\max}$
and more general problems. The application of the level algorithm to solve
$P \mid prec, p_j = 1 \mid C_{\max}$ has been analyzed by Chen and Liu [18] and Kunde
[44].
Preemptions can be profitable, as was recently shown by Coffman and Garey
[15] who proved that for problem $P2 \mid prec \mid C_{\max}$ the least schedule length
achievable by a nonpreemptive schedule is no more than 4/3 the least schedule
length achievable when preemptions are allowed.

4.2 Minimizing Flow Time

This section deals with scheduling problems subject to minimizing $\sum w_j C_j$. The
problem $1 \mid\mid \sum w_j C_j$, i.e. scheduling a set of n tasks in such a way that the
weighted sum of completion times is minimal, can be optimally solved by scheduling the tasks in order of nondecreasing ratios of processing times and weights,
p_j/w_j. This is known as *Smith's weighted shortest processing time (WSPT)* rule
[70]. In the special case that all tasks have equal weights, any schedule is optimal which places the tasks according to *SPT* rule, i.e. in nondecreasing order of
processing times.
Optimality of the WSPT rule for $1 \mid\mid \sum w_j C_j$ can be shown by proving a far
more general result due to Lawler [50] that includes $1 \mid\mid \sum w_j C_j$ as a special
case: Given a set T of n tasks and a real-valued function γ which assigns value
$\gamma(\pi)$ to each permutation π of tasks, find permutation π^* such that $\gamma(\pi^*) = \min$
$\{\gamma(\pi) \mid \pi$ is a permutation of task set T}. If we know nothing about the structure
of function γ, there is clearly nothing to be done except evaluating $\gamma(\pi)$ for each
of the n ! possible different permutations of the task set. But for a given function
γ we can sometimes find a transitive and complete relation $<$ on the set of tasks
with the property that for any two tasks T_i, T_k, and for any permutation of the
form $\alpha T_i T_k \delta$ we have

$$T_i \stackrel{.}{<} T_k \Rightarrow \gamma(\alpha T_i T_k \delta) \leq \gamma(\alpha T_k T_i \delta) \tag{4.2}$$

If such a relation exists for a given function γ, we say: "γ *admits the relation* $<$".
This means that whenever T_i and T_k occur as adjacent tasks with T_k before T_i
in a schedule, we are at least as well off to interchange their order. This relation
is also referred to as the *adjacent pairwise interchange property*. Hence we have

the following theorem:

Theorem 4.1 *If γ admits a task interchange relation $<$, then an optimal permutation π^* can be found by ordering the tasks according to $<$.* ∎

Consider, for example, *Smith's WSPT rule,*

$$T_i \overset{\cdot}{<} T_k \Leftrightarrow p_i/w_i \leq p_k/w_k. \tag{4.3}$$

If the last task in the subsequence α in (4.2) finishes at time t, the cost $\sum w_j C_j$ of $\alpha T_i T_k \delta$ will be $w_i(t + p_i) + w_k(t + p_i + p_k) + C$ where C considers all the costs of tasks in the subsequences α and δ. If T_i and T_k are interchanged, the cost of $\alpha T_k T_i \delta$ will be $w_k(t + p_k) + w_i(t + p_k + p_i) + C$. Clearly, because of (4.3), the first sequence is of smaller cost than the second. As a consequence, the function $\sum w_j C_j$ admits Smith's *WSPT* rule, hence, by Theorem 4.1, this rule solves $1 \,||\, \sum w_j C_j$ optimally.

The problem of minimizing the sum of *weighted* completion times subject to release dates is strongly NP-hard, even if all weights are 1 [55]. We just mention two heuristic algorithms for scheduling the tasks, where each rule specifies priority criteria for adding a task to an existing partial schedule S_U of already scheduled tasks $U \subseteq T$, starting with $U = \emptyset$.

Suppose that the schedule is constructed by adding one task at a time, starting from the empty schedule. At any point, we have a partial schedule S_U of task set $U \subseteq T$, $S_U = (T_{a_1}, \ldots, T_{a_{|U|}})$. The earliest start time of task $T_j \in U, s_j$ and its completion time, C_j, are given by

$$s_1 = \begin{cases} r_i & \text{if } i = \alpha_1 \\ \max\{r_i, C_{\alpha_{j-1}}\} & \text{if } i = \alpha_j, i \neq 1, \\ \max\{r_i, C_{\alpha_{|U|}}\} & \text{if } T_i \in T - U; \end{cases} \tag{4.4}$$

$$C_i = s_i + p_i. \tag{4.5}$$

The two heuristics are as follows.

- *Earliest completion time (ECT)* rule: Select task T_i with min $\{C_i \mid T_i \in T - U\}$. Break ties by choosing T_i with $\max_i\{s_i\}$, and further ties by choosing T_i with minimum index i. Update s_i and C_i using (4.4) and (4.5).
- *Earliest start time (EST)* rule: Select task T_i with min $\{s_i \mid T_i \in T - U\}$. Break ties by choosing T_i with min $\{C_i\}$, and further ties by choosing T_i with min $\{i\}$. Update s_i and C_i using (4.4) and (4.5).

For these two heuristics, no accuracy bounds are known. The main difficulty arises from the fact that, since $r_j \geq 0$, idle times may be inserted in the optimal schedule.

For the case of *equal weights*, a branch and bound algorithm for solving the problem optimally was presented by Dessouky and Deogun [22]. An extension of this branch and bound algorithm to the case of unequal weights is presented in [11]. The case in which the tasks have unit processing times can be solved in polynomial time [54].

If the order of task execution is restricted by arbitrary precedence constraints, the problem $1 \mid prec \mid \sum w_j C_j$ becomes NP-hard [53]. Among others, Potts [65] presented an especially interesting branch and bound algorithm where lower bounds are derived using a Lagrangian relaxation technique in which the multipliers are determined by the cost reduction method. Optimization scheduling algorithms running in polynomial time have been presented for tree-like precedences [35], [1], for series-parallel precedences [69], [39], and for more general precedence relations [10], [62]. For series-parallel precedence graphs, Lawler [48] presented an $O(n\log n)$ time algorithm where an interchange relation similar to that presented in (4.2) is applied.

There is another class of promising scheduling algorithms. These algorithms obtain optimal schedules by finding optimal subschedules for progressively larger *modules* of tasks until all tasks are scheduled. This idea can be, for example, applied to series-parallel graphs which are built up recursively from smaller modules. Möhring and Radermacher [60] considered the class of all precedence graphs built up by substitution from *prime* (indecomposable) *modules* of size $\leq k$, k arbitrary, and proved that there is an optimization algorithm of complexity $O(n^{(k^2)})$ to minimize $\sum w_j C_j$.

Sidney and Steiner [71] improved this algorithm to run in $O(n^{w+1})$ time, where w denotes the maximum width of a prime module.

The idea of decomposing posets into prime modules can also be applied to optimization criteria other than $\sum w_j C_j$, as for example for the exponential cost function criterion. Monma and Sidney[61] proved that if the objective function obeys certain interchange properties then the so-called *job module property* is satisfied. The job module property says that any optimal solution to a subproblem defined by a task module is consistent with at least one optimal schedule for the entire problem.

4.3 Minimizing Due Date Involving Criteria

In the following we will concentrate on minimization of the $L_{\max}$ criterion. It seems to be quite natural that in this case the general rule should be to schedule tasks according to their earliest due dates. However, this simple rule of Jackson [45] produces optimal schedules only under very restricted assumptions. In other cases more sophisticated algorithms are necessary, or the problems are NP-hard. Let us start with nonpreemptive scheduling of independent tasks, $P \parallel L_{\max}$. Taking into account simple transformations between scheduling problems and the relationship between the $C_{\max}$ and $L_{\max}$ criteria, we see that all the problems that are NP-hard under the $C_{\max}$ criterion remain NP-hard under the $L_{\max}$ criterion. Hence, for example, $P2 \parallel L_{\max}$ is NP-hard. On the other hand, unit processing times of tasks make the problem easy, and $P \mid p_j = 1, r_j \mid L_{\max}$

can be solved by an obvious application of the *EDD* rule [7]. Moreover, problem
$P \mid p_j = p, r_j \mid L_{\max}$ can be solved in polynomial time. Unfortunately very
little is known about the worst-case behavior of approximation algorithms for
the NP-hard problems in question.

The *preemptive* mode of processing makes the solution of the scheduling problem
much easier. The fundamental approach in that area is testing feasibility of
problem $P \mid pmtn, r_j, \tilde{d_j} \mid -$ via the network flow approach of Horn [36]. Using
this approach repetitively, one can then solve the original problem $P \mid pmtn \mid$
$L_{\max}$ by changing due dates (deadlines) according to a binary search procedure.
A general approach for the case $P \mid prec, p_j = 1 \mid L_{\max}$ consists in assigning
modified due dates to tasks, depending on the number and due dates of their
successors. An optimal polynomial time algorithm for problem $P \mid in-tree, p_j =$
$1 \mid L_{\max}$ using modified due dates was presented by Brucker [12]. Surprisingly
out-tree precedence constraints result in the NP-hardness of the problem [6].
However, when limiting to two processors, a different way of computing modified
due dates allows to solve the problem in $O(n^2)$ time [29].

4.4 Minimizing the Number of Tardy Tasks

The next sections deal with single processor scheduling where due dates are involved. The first optimization criterion considered is the minimization of the
weighted number of tasks exceeding their due dates. The problem of finding
a schedule that minimizes the weighted number $\sum w_j U_j$ of tardy tasks is NP-
hard [41]. Villarreal et al. [72] presented a branch and bound algorithm for
$1 \parallel \sum w_j U_j$.

For the (simpler) case of minimizing the unweighted number of tardy tasks Moore
[59] published an optimization algorithm that solves the problem in $O(n \log n)$
time. This algorithm first sorts the tasks according to *EDD* rule. Next the subset
$T^\leq$ of tasks of T that can be processed on time is determined; finally a schedule
is constructed from the subsets $T^\leq$ and $T - T^\leq$. This algorithm generates a schedule with minimum number of tardy tasks. A generalization of this algorithm
to the case that only certain specified tasks have to be finished within their due
dates was discussed by Sidney [68].

The weighted problem $1 \parallel \sum w_j U_j$, however, remains NP-hard, even if all the due
dates d_j are equal. In fact, this problem is equivalent to the knapsack problem.
As in the unweighted case, an optimal solution for $1 \parallel \sum w_j U_j$ can be specified
by a partition of the task set T into two subsets, say $T^\leq$ and $T^>$. The set $T^\leq$,
also called feasible on-time set, represents those tasks that are completed before
their due dates, while the set $T^>$ represents the tasks that are tardy. A schedule
is found by placing the tasks in $T^\leq$ in *EDD* order, followed by the tasks in $T^>$
in arbitrary order. Thus it suffices to find an optimal partition of the task set T.
Sahni [67] developed an exact pseudopolynomial time algorithm for $1 \parallel \sum w_j U_j$
which is based on dynamic programming and requires $O(n \sum w_j)$ time.

When all processing times are equal, the problem $1 \mid p_j = 1 \mid \sum w_j U_j$ can easily
be solved. For the more general case of $1 \parallel \sum w_j U_j$ with agreeable processing

times and weights, i.e. $p_i < p_j$ implies $w_i \geq w_j$, an exact $O(n\log n)$ time algorithm can be obtained by a simple modification of the *EDD* algorithm [46].

If in addition to the above specifications tasks are released for execution at different times, the problem is known from Lenstra et al. [55] to be NP-hard in the strong sense. If, however, all weights are 1 and if release times and due dates are *consistent*, i.e. $r_i < r_j$ implies $d_i \leq d_j$ for all tasks T_i, T_j, then optimal schedules can be constructed in $O(n^2)$ time [42], [49].

If task preemptions are allowed, dynamic programming algorithms can be applied to solve $1 \mid pmtn, r_j \mid \sum U_j$ in $O(n^5)$ time, and $1 \mid pmtn, r_j \mid \sum w_j U_j$ in $O(n^3(\sum w_j)^2)$ time.

Finally we turn to scheduling problems where task precedences are given. Lenstra and Rinnooy Kan [54] proved that the 3-PARTITION problem (see [30]) is reducible to the problem $1 \mid chains, p_j = 1 \mid \sum U_j$. Hence, scheduling unit time tasks on a single processor subject to chain-like precedence constraints so as to minimize the unweighted number of late tasks is NP-hard in the strong sense. For $1 \mid forest \mid \sum w_j U_j$, Ibarra and Kim [40] discussed an algorithm that finds for any positive integer k an approximate schedule S^k such that

$$U_w^k/U_w^* < 1 + \frac{1}{k+1}.$$

The approximate solution is found in $O(kn^{k+2})$ time. They give also examples showing that the algorithm is not applicable to arbitrary precedence graphs.

4.5 Tardiness Problems

Another possibility of evaluating schedules where due dates are involved is mean tardiness. For the mean weighted tardiness problem $1 \mid\mid \sum w_j D_j$, we know from Lawler [47] and from Lenstra et al. [55] that the problem is NP-hard in the strong sense. McNaughton [57] has shown that preemption cannot reduce mean weighted tardiness for any given set of tasks. If all weights are equal, the problem is still NP-hard in the ordinary sense [25]. If unit processing times are assumed, the problem of scheduling independent tasks can be formulated as a linear assignment problem, and hence it can be solved in $O(n^3)$ time [33]. If in addition all tasks have unit weights, simply sequencing tasks in nondecreasing order of their due dates minimizes the total tardiness, and hence this special problem can be solved in $O(n\log n)$ time.

For another special problem of type $1 \mid\mid \sum w_j D_j$ where processing times and weights of tasks are *agreeable*, Lawler [47] presented a pseudopolynomial dynamic programming algorithm of the worst-case running time $O(n^4 p)$ or $O(n^5 p_{\max})$, if $p = \sum_{j=1}^n p_j$, and $p_{\max} = \max \{p_j\}$, respectively. The algorithm is pseudopolynomial because its time complexity is polynomial only with respect to an encoding in which p_j values are expressed in unary notation.

Lenstra and Rinooy Kan [53] studied the complexity of the mean tardiness problem $1 \mid prec \mid \sum w_j D_j$ when precedence constraints are introduced. They showed that $1 \mid prec, p_j = 1 \mid \sum D_j$ is NP-hard in the strong sense. For chain-like precedence constraints, they proved the problem $1 \mid chains, p_j = 1 \mid \sum w_j D_j$ to be NP-hard, and Leung and Young [56] were able to prove that the problem remains NP-hard even in the case of equal weights.

4.6 Scheduling with Deadlines

In case of problem $1 \mid r_j, \tilde{d_j} \mid C_{\max}$, i.e. if the tasks are allowed to have arbitrary processing times, a transformation from the 3-PARTITION problem shows that the problem is NP-hard in the strong sense, even for integer release times and deadlines [55]. Only if all tasks have unit processing times, an optimization algorithm of polynomial time complexity is available. The general problem can be solved by applying a branch and bound algorithm, e.g. as proposed by Bratley et al. [73].

If task preemption is allowed, the problem $1 \mid pmtn, r_j, \tilde{d_j} \mid C_{\max}$ can be formulated as a maximum flow problem and can thus be solved in polynomial time [5].

Problem $1 \mid prec, r_j, \tilde{d_j} \mid C_{\max}$ is NP-hard in the strong sense because problem $1 \mid r_j, \tilde{d_j} \mid C_{\max}$ already is. However, if all tasks have unit processing times, i.e. for the problem $1 \mid prec, r_j, p_j = 1, \tilde{d_j} \mid C_{\max}$ and if all release times and deadlines are integer multiples of a given unit of time, a modification of the earliest deadline scheduling rule solves the problem optimally in polynomial time [31].

We now turn to scheduling problems $1 \mid \tilde{d_j} \mid \sum w_j C_j$ where the sum $\sum w_j C_j$ of weighted completion times is to be minimized, subject to meeting deadlines. The tasks are to be processed without preemption. This problem was first studied by Smith, who found a simple solution procedure both for situations with no deadlines, and for situations with deadlines, but with equal weights. Emmons [26] showed that Smith's procedure does not extend to the case of unequal weights, and from Lenstra [51] we know that this problem is NP-hard. Burns [13] constructed a pairwise interchange heuristic for the problem that was improved by Miyazaki [58]. Bansal [4] developed an optimization algorithm based on a branch and bound approach and dominance criteria, and used Smith's *WSPT* rule to calculate lower bounds. Potts and van Wassenhove [66] presented a branch and bound algorithm based on a Lagrangian relaxation of the problem and found additional dominance criteria. Similar improvements have been presented by Kalra and Khurana [43], Posner [64] and Bagchi and Ahmadi [2]. The latter used a task-splitting procedure to compute lower bounds for the weighted sum of completion times.

In the following we will assume that at least one feasible schedule exists for the given problem; this is easily checked by ordering the tasks in nondecreasing order of deadlines. If a task in this sequence is completed after its deadline, then no feasible schedule exists. It can be shown that if tasks have especially agreeable deadlines, i.e. $p_j/w_j \leq p_k/w_k$ implies $\tilde{d_j} \leq \tilde{d_k}$ for all tasks T_j and T_k, then an optimal solution is obtained by ordering the tasks in nondecreasing order of their deadlines.

Another interesting heuristic algorithm for $1 \mid \tilde{d_j} \mid \sum w_j C_j$ is *Smith's backward scheduling rule* [70]. Provided there exists a schedule in which all tasks meet their deadlines, the algorithm chooses one task of largest processing time among all tasks T_j with $\tilde{d_j} \geq p_1 + \ldots + p_n$, and schedules the selected task last. It then continues by choosing an element of largest processing time among the remaining $n - 1$ tasks and placing it in front of the already scheduled tasks, etc. This algorithm can be implemented to run in $O(n \log n)$ time. We also know that the algorithm is exact in the following cases (cf. [66]):

(i) unit processing times, i.e. for the problem $1 \mid p_j = 1, \tilde{d_j} \mid \sum w_j C_j$,

(ii) unit weights, i.e. for problem $1 \mid \tilde{d_j} \mid \sum C_j$,

(iii) agreeable processing times and weights of tasks.

However, in case of arbitrary weights, simple examples show that this algorithm is not exact.

Finally, if precedence constraints among the tasks are specified, Lenstra and Rinnoy Kan [54] proved that the special problem $1 \mid chains, \tilde{d_j}, p_j = 1 \mid \sum w_j C_j$ of scheduling is NP-hard.

An interesting modification of the deadline problem is to allow tasks to be tardy up to a given *maximum allowable tardiness* $D \geq 0$, i.e. the objective is to minimize $\sum w_j C_j$ subject to $C_j - \tilde{d_j} \leq D$ for $j = 1, \ldots, n$. This problem is called *constrained weighted completion time (CWCT) problem* [21]. It has been shown to be NP-hard by Lenstra et al. [55]. From Chand and Schneeberger [21] we know that the CWCT problem can be solved optimally in some special cases, e.g. when processing times and weights of tasks are agreeable. Furthermore they discussed a worst-case analysis of the *WSPT* heusistic and showed that the accuracy performance ratio can become arbitrarily large in the worst case.

4.7 Imprecise Computations

Usually scheduling algorithms developed for soft real-time scheduling problems are of no value in a hard real-time environment. On the other hand, there are situations where tardy tasks are acceptable. As an example consider computations which improve the quality of their results step by step. If such a computation is abandoned before completion, the result obtained so far might already be acceptable. Note that in a real-time production environment the process of task or job scheduling itself is of that type. If e.g. the schedule is produced by a branch and bound approach, it usually improves over time. So, before a solution known to be optimal is found, an approximate solution is already available.

Instead taking the number of tardy tasks one should rather choose a measure that considers the uncompleted portions of tasks. A proposal made by Blazewicz [8] is to schedule tasks as to minimize the (weighted) sum of values $R_j := \max \{0, \min \{p_j, C_j - \tilde{d_j}\}\}, j = 1, \ldots, n$.

A variation of this model considers each task as consisting of two subtasks, a mandatory part and an optional part. The mandatory subtask is the portion that must be done in order to produce a result of an acceptable quality. This subtask must be completed before the deadline of the task. The optional subtask, or a portion of it, is left unfinished if the deadline is reached. To guarantee all timing constraints, only the mandatory subtasks must be allocated sufficient processor time to complete by their deadlines. The leftover processing time can be used to complete as many subtasks as possible. For an overview we refer to [52].

5 Conclusion

We know that there is a huge area of a variety of different kinds of scheduling problems, each of which needs an individual algorithmic approach. On the other hand, only few fundamental scheduling techniques are available. The aim of this contribution is to shed light on the question of what techniques are applied in some of the more important scheduling areas.

References

1. D. Adolphson, and T.C. Hu, *Optimal linear ordering*, SIAM J. Appl. Math., Vol. 25, 1973, 403–423.
2. U. Bagchi, and R. H. Ahmadi, *An improved lower bound for minimizing weighted completion times with deadlines*, Oper. Res., Vol. 35, 1987, 311–313.
3. R. Bellman, S. E. Dreyfus, *Applied Dynamic Programming*, Princeton University Press, Princeton, New Jersey, 1962.
4. S. P. Bansal, *Single machine scheduling to minimize weighted sum of completion times with secondary criterion — a branch-and-bound approach*, European J. Oper. Res., Vol. 5, 1980, 177–181.
5. P. Bratley, M. Florian, P. Robillard, *Scheduling with earliest start and due date constraints*, Naval Res. Logist. Quart., Vol. 18, 1971, 511–517.
6. P. Brucker, M.R. Garey, and D.S. Johnson, *Scheduling equal-length tasks under treelike precedence constraints to minimize maximum lateness*, Math. Oper. Res., Vol. 2, 1977, 275–284.
7. J. Blażewicz, *Simple algorithms for multiprocessor scheduling to meet deadlines*, Inform. Process. Lett., Vol. 6, 1977, 162–164.
8. J. Blażewicz, *Scheduling preemptible tasks on parallel processors with information loss*, Tech. Sci. Inform., Vol. 3, 1984, 415–420.
9. J. Blażewicz, J. K. Lenstra, A. H. G. Rinnooy Kan, Scheduling subject to resource constraints: *classification and complexity*, Discrete Appl. Math., Vol. 5, 1983, 11–24.
10. H. Buer, R. H. Möhring, *A fast algorithm for the decomposition of graphs and posets*, Math. Oper. Res., Vol. 8, 1983, 170–184.

11. L. Bianco, and S. Ricciardelli, *Scheduling of a single machine to minimize total weighted completion time subject to release dates*, Naval Res. Logist. Quart., Vol. 29, 1982, 151–167.

12. P. J. Brucker, *Sequencing unit-time jobs with treelike precedence on m machines to minimize maximum lateness*, Proceedings IX International Symposium on Mathematical Programming, Budapest, 1976.

13. R. N. Burns, *Scheduling to minimize the weighted sum of completion times with secondary criteria*, Naval Res. Logist. Quart., Vol. 23, 1976, 25–129.

14. E. G. Coffman, Jr., R. L. Graham, *Optimal scheduling for two-processor systems*, Acta Inform., Vol. 1, 1972, 200–213.

15. E. G. Coffman, Jr., M. R. Garey, *Proof of the 4/3 conjecture for preemptive versus nonpreemptive two-processor scheduling*, Report Bell Laboratories, Murray Hill, 1991.

16. E. G. Coffman, Jr., M. R. Garey, D. S. Johnson, *An application of bin-packing to multiprocessor scheduling*, SIAM J.Comput., Vol. 7, 1978, 1–17.

17. E. G. Coffman, Jr., M. R. Garey, D. S. Johnson, Appoximation algorithms for bin packing — an updated survey, in: G. Ausiello, M. Lucertini, P. Serafini (eds.), *Algorithm Design for Computer System Design*, Springer Verlag, Vienna, 1984, 49–106.

18. N.-F. Chen, C. L. Liu, *On a class of scheduling algorithms for multiprocessors computing systems*, in: T.-Y. Feng (ed.), Parallel Processing, Lecture Notes in Computer Science 24, Springer Verlag, Berlin, 1975, 1–16.

19. S. A. Cook, *The complexity of theorem proving procedures*, Proc. 3rd ACM Symposium on Theory of Computing, 1971, 151–158.

20. E. G. Coffman, Jr., and R. Sethi, *A generalized bound on lpt sequencing*, RAIRO-Informatique 10, 1976, 17–25.

21. S. Chand, H. Schneeberger, *A note on the single-machine scheduling problem with minimum weighted completion time and maximum allowable tardiness*, Naval Res. Logist. Quart., Vol. 33, 1986, 551–557.

22. M. I. Dessouky, and J. S. Deogun, *Sequencing jobs with unequal ready times to minimize mean flow time*, SIAM J. Comput., Vol. 10, 1981, 192–202.

23. J. Du, J. Y-T. Leung, *Scheduling tree-structured tasks with restricted execution times*, Inform. Process. Lett., Vol. 28, 1988, 183–188.

24. J. Du, J. Y-T. Leung, *Scheduling tree-structured tasks on two processors to minimize schedule length*, SIAM J. Discrete Math., Vol. 2, 1989, 176–196.

25. J. Du, and J. Y.-T. Leung, *Minimizing total tardiness on one machine is NP-hard*, Math. Oper. Res., Vol. 15, 1990, 483–495.

26. H. Emmons, *One machine sequencing to minimize mean flow time with minimum number tardy*, Naval Res. Logist. Quart., Vol. 22, 1975, 585–592.

27. M. Fujii, T. Kasami, K. Ninomiya, *Optimal sequencing of two equivalent processors*, SIAM J. Appl. Math., Vol. 17, 1969, 784–789, Err: SIAM J. Appl. Math., Vol. 20, 1971, 141.

28. H. N. Gabow, *An almost linear algorithm for two-processor scheduling*, J. Assoc. Comput. Mach., Vol. 29, 1982, 766–780.

29. M. R. Garey, and D. S. Johnson, *Scheduling tasks with non-uniform deadlines on two processors*, J. Assoc. Comput. Mach., Vol. 23, 1976, 461–467.

30. M. R. Garey, D. S. Johnson, Computers and Intractability: *A Guide to the Theory of NP-Completeness*. W. H. Freeman, San Francisco, 1979.

31. M. R. Garey, D. S. Johnson, B. B. Simons, and R. E. Tarjan, *Scheduling unit-time tasks with arbitrary release times and deadlines*, SIAM J. Comput., Vol. 10, 1981, 256–269.

32. M. R. Garey, D. S. Johnson, R. E. Tarjan, M. Yannakakis, *Scheduling opposing forests*, SIAM J. Algebraic and Discrete Math., Vol. 4, 1983, 72–93.

33. R. L. Graham, E. L. Lawler, J. K. Lenstra, A. H. G. Rinnoy Kan, *Optimization and approximation in deterministic sequencing and scheduling: a survey*, Ann. Discrete Math., Vol. 5, 1979, 287–326.

34. R. L. Graham, *Bounds for certain multiprocessing anomalies*, Bell System Tech. J., Vol. 45, 1966, 1563–1581.

35. W. A. Horn, *Single-machine job sequencing with tree-like precedence ordering and linear delay penalties*, SIAM J. Appl. Math., Vol. 23, 1972, 189–202.

36. W. A. Horn, *Some simple scheduling algorithms*, Naval Res. Logist. Quart., Vol. 21, 1974, 177–185.

37. D. S. Hochbaum, D. B. Shmoys, Using dual approximation algorithms for scheduling problems: *theoretical and practical results*, J. Assoc. Comput. Mach., Vol. 34, 1987, 144–162.

38. T. C. Hu, *Parallel sequencing and assembly line problems*, Oper. Res., Vol. 9, 1961, 841–848.

39. T. Ichimori, H. Ishii, T. Nishida, *Algorithm for one machine job sequencing with precedence constraints*, J. Oper. Res. Soc. Japan, Vol. 24, 1981, 159–169.

40. O. H. Ibarra, C. E. Kim, *Approximation algorithms for certain scheduling problems*, Math. Oper. Res., Vol. 3, 1978, 197–204.

41. R. M. Karp, Reducibility among combinatorial problems, in: R. E. Miller, J. W. Thatcher (eds.), *Complexity of Computer Computations*, Plenum Press, New York, 1972, 85–104.

42. H. Kise, T. Ibaraki, H. Mine, *A solvable case of a one-machine scheduling problem with ready and due times*, Oper. Res., Vol. 26, 1978, 121–126.

43. K. R. Kalra, K. Khurana, *Single machine scheduling to minimize waiting cost with secondary criterion*, J. Math. Sci., Vols. 16–18, 1981–1983, 9–15.

44. M. Kunde, *Beste Schranke beim LP-Scheduling*, Bericht 7603, Institut für Informatik und Praktische Mathematik, University Kiel, 1976.

45. J. R. Jackson, *Scheduling a production line to minimize maximum tardiness*, Research Report 43, Management Sci. Res. Project, UCLA, 1955.

46. E. L. Lawler, *Sequencing to minimize the weighted number of tardy jobs*, RAIRO Rech. Opr., Vol. 10, 1976, Suppl. 27–33.

47. E. L. Lawler, *A 'pseudopolynomial' algorithm for sequencing jobs to minimize total tardiness*, Ann. Discrete Math., Vol. 1, 1977, 331–342.

48. E. L. Lawler, *Sequencing jobs to minimize total weighted completion time subject to precedence constraints*, Ann. Discrete Math., Vol. 2, 1978, 75–90.

49. E. L. Lawler, *Sequencing a single machine to minimize the number of late jobs*, Preprint, Computer Science Division, University of California, Berkeley, 1982.

50. E. L. Lawler, *Recent results in the theory of machine scheduling*, in: A. Bachem, M. Grötschel, B. Korte (eds.), Mathematical Programming: *The State of the Art*, Bonn 1982, Springer-Verlag, Berlin, 1983, 202–234.

51. J. K. Lenstra, *Sequencing by Enumerative Methods*, Mathematical Centre Tracts 69, Mathematisch Centrum, Amsterdam, 1977.

52. J. W. S. Liu, K. J. Lin, W. K. Shih, A. C. Yu, J. Y. Chung, W. Zhao, *Algorithms for scheduling imprecise computations*, Report No. UIUCDCS-R-90-1628, Department of Computer Science, University of Illinois, 1990.

53. J. K. Lenstra, A. H. G. Rinnooy Kan, *Complexity of scheduling under precedence constraints*, Oper. Res., Vol. 26, 1978, 22–35.

54. J. K. Lenstra, A. H. G. Rinnoy Kan, *Complexity results for scheduling chains on a single machine*, European J. Oper. Res., Vol. 4, 1980, 270–275.

55. J. K. Lenstra, A. H. G. Rinnoy Kan, P. Brucker, *Complexity of Machine Scheduling Problems*, Ann. Discrete Math., Vol. 1, 1977, 343–362.

56. J. Y-T. Leung, G. H. Young, *Minimizing total tardiness on a single machine with precedence constraints*, ORSA J. Comput, to appear.

57. R. NcNaughton, *Scheduling with deadlines and loss functions*, Management Sci., Vol. 6, 1959, 1–12.

58. S. Miyazaki, *One machine scheduling problem with dual criteria*, J. Oper. Res. Soc. Japan, Vol. 24, 1981, 37–51.

59. J. M. Moore, *An n job, one machine sequencing algorithm for minimizing the number of late jobs*, Management Sci., Vol. 15, 1968, 102–109.

60. R. H. Möhrig, F. J. Radermacher, *Generalized results on the polynomiality of certain weighted sum scheduling problems*, Methods of Oper. Res., Vol. 49, 1985, 405–417.

61. C. L. Monma, J. B. Sidney, Optimal sequencing via modular decomposition: *characterization of sequencing functions*, Math. Oper. Res., Vol. 12, 1987, 22–31.

62. J. H. Muller, J. Spinrad, *Incremental modular decomposition*, J. Assoc. Comput. Mach., Vol. 36, 1989, 1–19.

63. K. Nakajima, J. Y-T. Leung, S. L. Hakimi, *Optimal two processor scheduling of tree precedence constrained tasks with two execution times*, Performance Evaluation, Vol. 1, 1981, 320–330.

64. M. E. Posner, *Minimizing weighted completion times with deadlines*, Oper. Res., Vol. 33, 1985, 562–574.

65. C. N. Potts, *A Lagrangian based branch and bound algorithm for a single machine sequencing with precedence constraints to minimize total weighted completion time*, Management Sci., Vol. 31, 1985, 1300–1311.

66. C. N. Potts, L. N. van Wassenhove, *An algorithm for single machine sequencing with deadlines to minimize total weighted completion time*, European J. Oper. Res., Vol. 12, 1983, 379–387.

67. S. Sahni, *Algorithms for scheduling independent tasks*, J. Assoc. Comput. Mach., Vol. 23, 1976, 116–127.

68. J. B. Sidney, *An extension of Moore's due date algorithm*, in: S. E. Elmaghraby (ed.), Symposium on the Theory of Scheduling and Its Applications, Springer-Verlag, Berlin, 1973, 393-398.

69. J. B. Sidney, *Decomposition algorithms for single-machine sequencing with precedence relations and deferral costs*, Oper. Res., Vol. 23, 1975, 283–298.

70. W. E. Smith, *Various optimizers for single-stage production*, Naval Res. Logist. Quart., Vol. 3, 1956, 59–66.

71. J. B. Sidney, G. Steiner, Optimal sequencing by modular decomposition: *polynomial algorithms*, Oper. Res., Vol. 34, 1986, 606–612.

72. F. J. Villarreal, R. L. Bulfin, *Scheduling a single machine to minimize the weighted number of tardy jobs*, AIIE Trans., Vol. 15, 1983, 337–343.

73. P. Bratley, M. Florian, P. Robillard, *Scheduling with earliest start and due date constraints*, Naval Res. Logist. Quart., Vol. 18, 1971, 511–517.

Engineering Predictable Real-Time Systems

Harold W. Lawson[*]

Lawson Publishing and Consulting Inc.
Torshammarsvägen 11, 3tr
18133 Lidingö
Sweden

1 Introduction

The demands placed upon real-time systems (or portions thereof) in respect to predictability continue to increase as these systems become integrated into a wide variety of safety critical applications. It is essential to be able to guarantee that all critical processing is accomplished accurately and on time. In this contribution, a point of view is established in respect to achieving predictability in combination with another vital ability, namely understandability. The argument is put forward that these two goals can be jointly attained; further, that understandability is the most important common denominator for achieving a variety of other important real-time computing abilities; for example, reliability, testability, verifiability, maintainability, and so on.

1.1 The Engineering of Real-Time Systems

It is important to remember that we engineer real-time systems and, in this regard, high level decisions are the same as for other branches of systems engineering; that is, risk analysis and management, allocation of various resources and trade-off analysis. However, the treatment of these high level decisions in the context of computer-based systems requires significant insight into a variety of factors including the nature and requirements of the applications, the methodologies and artifacts applied in creating system solutions, the life-cycle requirements as well as the human aspects of development and supporting processes.

This author has previously identified several significant problems in engineering computer-based systems and points to the importance of a unifying philosophy as a key to a successful project (see Lawson, 1990). One central project problem is artifact fixation; that is, the tendency to view an application or class of applications via specific artifacts (hardware and/or software). In this regard, we must

---

[*] The work has been supported by (FMV), the Swedish Defense Materiel Administration.

learn to apply the old adage; if the shoe fits, wear it. Artifacts (shoes) are all too often applied because they are known, available, and/or dictated, and not because they are the natural way to solve the problem. The result, unnecessarily complex solutions resulting in costly sore feet. Further, complex solutions place limitations on achieving essential real-time abilities such as reliability, testability, verifiability, maintainability, and so on.

As a parenthesis, it is interesting to note that in order to place emphasis upon the special properties of engineering complex embedded systems, the IEEE Computer Society has established a task force which is focusing upon Computer-Based Systems Engineering (see White, and others, 1992).

In this paper, we are primarily concerned with time and safety critical real-time system applications. Given the requirements and nature of such applications or set of applications, various solutions become more appropriate than others. Due to their time and safety critical nature, engineering risk and trade-off analysis typically points to the need for specific problem-oriented treatment of this class of computer-based system.

1.2 Predictability and Determinism

Various approaches to time and safety critical real-time systems provide predictability in various manners. For example, Locke, 1992 describes cyclic and fixed priority executives in this respect. Both of these solutions can be used to achieve predictability. That is, given purely periodic processing requirements, a proof can be provided which guarantees the ability of the system design to meet application timing constraints.

A harder but related demand on safety critical real-time systems is determinism. That is, that execution time as well as the order of execution is predetermined. Even more stringent, that within a specified time interval ti to tj, exact behavior can be reproduced from the state existing at ti. These further demands seem to be quite reasonable for almost all safety critical applications from the reliability, testability, verifiability, maintainability as well as the understandability point of view.

Stringent demands are being placed upon the design of safety critical real-time systems as legal requirements (safety licensing); as claims are brought to litigation due to real-time system failures, determinism, including reproducability, can become an essential means of legal proof in liability claims.

It is quite clear that any priority based solution which permits dynamically mixed processing order will never be able to meet stringent determinism nor time interval reproducability requirements. For example, the interesting and useful probabilistic rate monotonic results of Liu and Layland, 1973, concerning an arbitrary mix of periodic processes can only be utilized to prove predictability, not reproducible determinism.

1.3 Cyclic Approach

While criticism has been made of cyclic approaches in respect to being inflexible and difficult to maintain, they provide a known basis for achieving predictability and determinism; further, if properly designed, the reproducible behavior property can be achieved. Lawson, 1992a, has presented a philosophy, paradigm and model called Cy-Clone (Clone of the Cyclic Paradigm) which is aimed at removing the problems with cyclic approaches while providing deterministic properties for time and safety critical systems.

Cy-Clone is based upon a philosophy of resource adequacy; that is, there are sufficient resources to guarantee that all processing requirements are met on time. Given this philosophy, a processing paradigm has been established in which the programmed application logic is divided into short code segments (rules), each having the highly uniform and understandable structure denoted in Figure 1.

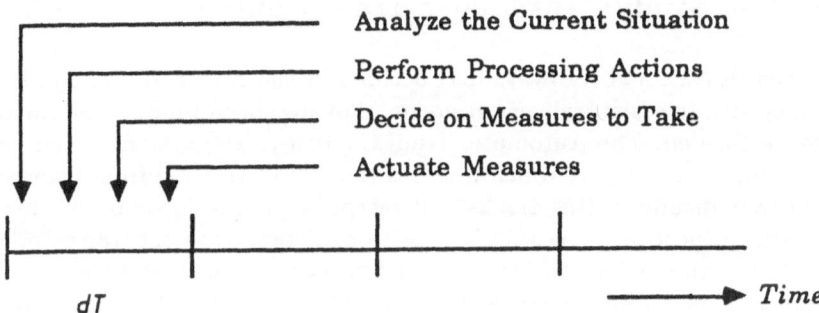

Fig. 1. The Basic Cy-Clone Cycle.

The most essential timing property is dT which establishes cyclic execution frequency. The dT time parameter must be long enough to permit all processing to be accomplished but sufficiently short to insure that stability is maintained in the external and internal environments. Rule processing may be conditional as indicated or unconditionally continuously executed by simply processing and actuating. Given the Cy-Clone philosophy and processing paradigm, various implementation models can be developed for centralized and distributed systems. Implementations can, if required and desirable, provide for mode shifts where the dT parameter varies in a controlled manner during execution.

By taking this view of time, the development of real-time applications becomes similar to the development of synchronous time-based hardware logic. In fact, within each dT, the short programmed logic sequences (rules) can be viewed as software circuits. The circuits, while executed sequentially within dT, are conceptually executed in parallel as in clock controlled hardware logic. This hardware analogy, in addition to providing understandable solutions, can be usefully exploited as means of transforming real-time software circuits into ASICs (Application Specific Integrated Circuits) and vice-versa.

The Cy-Clone approach has been established on the basis (If the shoe fits, wear it); that is, it is not claimed to be the best solution to all real-time systems. However, it is a proper and natural approach to achieving predictability, reproducible determinism, and understandability in time and safety critical real-time systems. Further, due to the continuing increases in computing power and decreasing hardware costs, engineering trade-offs in the direction of resource adequacy are well justified for a wide variety of applications. The Cy-Clone resource adequate approach has been verified in practice since the concepts upon which the approach rests have been successfully applied in time and safety critical applications, one of which we now briefly examine.

2 A Case Study: Automatic Train Control

The Swedish National Railways (SJ) decided in the mid-1970's to implement a control system to assist train engineers in following speed limits along the railway system in Sweden. The Automatic Train Control (ATC) system is composed of a telecommunication part which involves radio transmission from transponders located periodically on the tracks and reception in the locomotive. Read-only information concerning speed limits, position, distance to next transponder, and so on, is transmitted to the train as it approaches the transponder. Further, a computer control and operator part of ATC (located in the locomotive) implements the monitoring and control as well as communication with the train engineer. It is a time and safety critical "watchdog" system that advises the engineer and only reacts (autonomously stops the train or reduces speed) when the engineer should stop or reduce speed but fails to do so. Figure 2 illustrates the major components of the ATC system.

The transponder-telecommunication subsystem was developed by the Ericsson corporation and the on-board computer control and operator subsystem was developed by Standard Radio and Telefon; both corporations operating in Stockholm. The author was a consultant for the computer control part.

The on-board system is composed of triplicated microprocessors surrounded by sensors and actuators as well as operator communication. All three systems perform identical processing. Calculated results are checked by majority logic before they are delivered as system outputs. A simplified view of the computer system is provided in Figure 3.

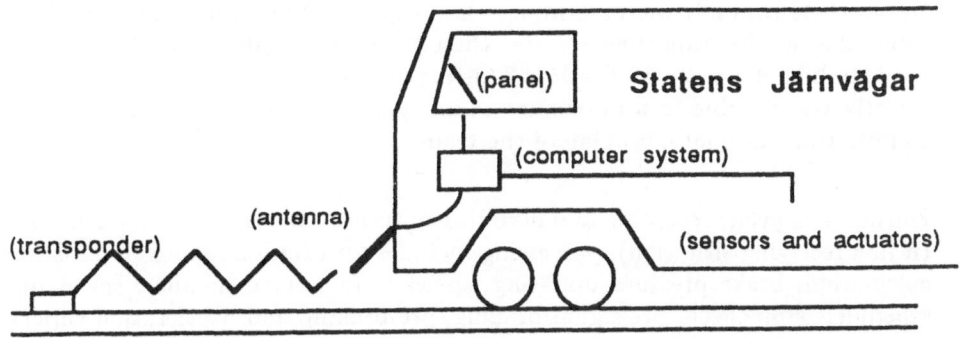

Fig. 2. Major "Components" of the ATC System.

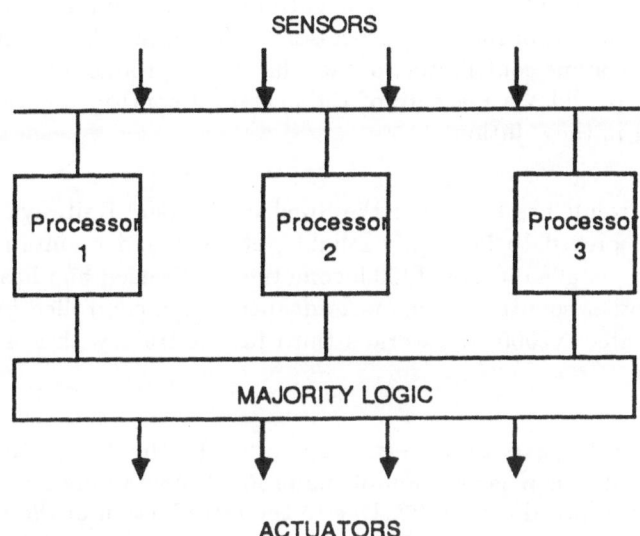

Fig. 3. View of the ATC On-Board Computer System.

After studying the problem, the environment in which development and testing would take place, and the problems for future updating, maintenance and so on, the author suggested an engineering philosophy for the real-time system that corresponds quite closely to the nature of the problem as well as to the fact that microprocessors of limited capacity would be utilized. The philosophy is grounded in the fact that the continuous system to be implemented is best viewed as cyclic precisely timed loops.

The basic cycle frequency (dT) was established in conjunction with the Swedish National Railways. It was determined that a cycle of 250 milliseconds was acceptable; that is, the train is never more than 250 milliseconds away from initiating the handling of a critical situation. This requirement, based upon train speed, is directly translatable to a maximum quantity of meters of track traversed prior to initiating automatic braking of the train.

During each cycle, reception and decoding of transponder information transpires (if in a receiving situation), processing includes for example, speed and distance calculation, brake pressure updating, speed limit button handler, speed limit scheduler, stop check, pre-signal braking, pre-braking and deceleration supervision, speed supervision and output calculations for the operator panel.

The resulting implementation yielded small understandable, testable and maintainable code segments for each application function which are written in Motorola 6800 assembly language. The entire system requires 8K of PROM memory, one copy in each of the three processors. In the late 70's, and even today, the low memory volume contributes to lower hardware production costs and reliability, but also provides a measure of the degree of control over product complexity achieved in the solution.

The net result has been that the Swedish National Railways received a system that has proved to be highly reliable, efficient and maintainable. The system has been installed in over 1400 locomotives in Sweden and has been exported to several other countries. The most advanced train controlled by ATC is the ABB Incorporated X2000, the world's third fastest train with speeds up to 300 km per hour.

After over 10 years of successful operation (without any PROM program modifications), a new generation of the product, containing several new functions, will be installed during 1992. Due to the introduction of the new functions, the more modern Motorola 68HC11 processor has been introduced and memory requirements have been extended to 32K PROM; very modest in these days of megabytes of software complexity. Further aspects of the ATC project have been reported in Lawson, 1990.

In conclusion, we can state that the cyclic approach taken has yielded a highly viable time and safety critical system. An interesting point is that due to the highly understandable robust solution, the system, in principle, functions as hardware and is rarely altered. I believe this characteristic is essential in the fundamental control loops of time and safety critical applications, for example, in automobiles, airplanes, ships, satellites, production automation, patient monitoring, and so on. Brooks, 1990, also points to the need for this hardware-like property at the lowest level of robotic systems.

3 Systolic Base Time

The most central issue for real-time systems is the view of time that is applied in the system solution. For Cy-Clone systems, like the ATC system, the time parameter (dT) is established on a rational application dependent basis. Other time and safety critical applications require proper engineering risk and trade-off analysis in order to determine appropriate execution frequency properties.

Given the highly useful analogy to the functioning of the human body as a real-time system, we utilize the notion of systolic base time. In systolic array technology, emphasis is typically placed upon incorporating homogeneous activities in order to optimize processing time. However, the human body as well as many time and safety critical real-time systems are characterized by heterogeneous activities, even multitudes of them operating in parallel. Cy-Clone provides a technology to deal with the systolic treatment of heterogeneous activities. Further, Cy-Clone can be applied in both centralized and decentralized environments.

Within a centralized single processing element or redundant fault-tolerant cluster such as ATC, all processing is performed within the limits of the systolic base time (dT). If processing resources are not sufficient to accomplish all processing, Cy-Clone defines two means of achieving resource adequacy; firstly, the obvious solution of employing faster processing elements or secondly, parallelizing and distributing functions to a multiple processing element cluster (see Lawson, 1992a).

In a distributed system, parallelism of cyclic execution is automatically obtained. However, we often find the need to operate nodes at varying frequencies. For example, in an automobile, engine functions may be monitored at 1000 Hz or higher, whereas, the fundamental control loop (systolic base time) required for safe automotive system operation is in the range of 60 to 100 Hz. In such environments, all parts of the system operating at higher or lower frequencies must "synchronize" around the systolic base time in order to assure proper system function.

3.1 Hard and Relaxed Synchronization

Based upon the application requirements, we may find the need to operate the entire system or portions thereof in a hard synchronized manner. For example, in controlling the coordinates of servo steering. In this regard, we can note that systems which operate on a probabilistic basis (without determinism nor well defined processing intervals) encounter the problem of jitter. That is, the timing tolerances applied in controlling the external environment are not sufficiently fine grain and regular to permit smooth operation.

A significant advantage of the Cy-Clone cyclic approach is that a well-defined timing discipline is employed which permits simultaneous hard synchronized control when required. This form of hard synchronization has been demonstrated in distributed fault-tolerant environments via the MARS system (see Kopetz, and others, 1989).

Note: MARS and Cy-Clone share the same resource adequate philosophy as well as exploiting the general advantages of triggering processing via time instead of via events (see Koptez, 1992). They vary somewhat in their processing paradigms.

Hard synchronization may even be required in respect to true time where the source of time can come, for example, from the satellite GPS (Global Positioning System). Overlaying systolic intervals over true timing sources not only produces a deterministic solution but results in highly accurate time driven systems.

Not all time and safety critical applications require hard synchronization. While their systolic base time (dT) provides for acceptable processing progress and system-wide stability, information may be communicated to and from the basic systolic cycle at varying points of time. In this case, relaxed synchronization can be utilized where results are utilized on a best available information basis. This relaxation of synchronization is very useful and can be neatly exploited in reducing scheduling complexity in distributed real-time system environments. We shall return to this aspect later in the paper.

3.2 Treatment of Faults

A strong advantage of applying a solution based upon timing intervals is the possibility to treat hardware and even software faults in a reasonable manner. This advantage accrues due to having simultaneous control over the continuous processing being done and the rate at which it is being performed. When operating in a cyclic manner, a fault may only have local time interval effects, but the system will automatically stabilize itself in succeeding time periods. This property is extremely difficult to achieve when a probabilistic processing (including event driven) approach is applied; especially when large quantities of state information are retained.

For potentially critical measurements, it is quite possible to build a time series for a suitable number of cyclic periods and apply interpolation in the presence of a fault in order to approximate a missing measurement. These projections may also be continually calculated and applied in determining the reasonability of measurements over time.

4 Holistic Point of View

In order to properly engineer time and safety critical real-time applications, a holistic point of view is essential. That is, the development and supporting engineering processes must be understood as well as the means of realizing the solution (that is, the artifacts). In Lawson, 1992b, a Behavior-Mapping-Resource model is introduced as a pedagogical means of understanding parallel and distributed real-time systems. Simultaneous control over all three parts of this BMR model is essential for achieving successful solutions to time and safety critical real-time systems (see Lawson, 1992a, as well as Halang and Stoyenko, 1991, for a related point of view).

Without control over the artifacts used for behavioral description and the resource structure, complex and potentially dangerous mappings may be required, especially when there is a significant semantic gap between the properties of the behavioral description artifacts and resource structure artifacts. Resolving semantic gap differences via program glue is dangerous in that it increases the life-long complexity and vulnerability of the real-time system by introducing non-productive code. By non-productive, I mean that the code does not directly contribute to accomplishing application functions but only exists for the purpose of adapting the solution to the properties of the behavioral description and/or resource structure artifacts.

Non-productive code is often introduced by the implementation requirements of general purpose programming languages, especially in the form of complex run-time systems. The program code for executives and operating system functions aimed at providing resource sharing also belongs to the non-productive code category.

All code, productive and non-productive becomes a part of the "final product". Thus, a goal for time and safety critical real-time systems must be to eliminate or at least minimize the quantity of non-productive code. The Automatic Train Control system functions without an executive and with only a very limited quantity of non-productive code. This fact has resulted in the very modest 8K PROM requirement. Any non-productive code that is introduced into real-time systems must be measurable, controllable, and maintainable.

Simultaneous control over Behavior, Mapping, and Resources in the context of the Cy-Clone approach provides a major step towards achieving the joint goals of predictability and understandability.

5 Application Domains and their Machines

In order to improve upon the understandability of computer-based systems in general, the author has introduced a means of describing and implementing application behavior based upon the notion of Application Machines (AMs) (see

Lawson, 1992c,d). An Application Machine is best described as a means of capturing the essential operations of an application domain in an abstract as well as in a refined concrete manner.

Within the domain of time and safety critical systems, applications predominantly deal with control and regulation based upon sensor and actuator data. Thus, an AM in this domain must be designed to provide control and regulation related operations that operate upon sensor and actuator data.

Significant advantages from the understandability as well as software technical view can be achieved by viewing sensors and actuators as being both physical and logical. That is, sensors supply measurements (actual from the environment or computed measurements via a software circuit). Actuators can be actual or be a software circuit which is initiated (actuated). Processing becomes Sensor/Actuator driven as well as systolic base time controlled.

The program structure of an AM is based upon the partitioning of application service functions (pre-programmed operations) and a control structure (connection schemata) which couples together operations thus building software circuits. We refer to the service functions as POPS (Programmed OPerationS). The direct and understandable "pseudo code" program structure that is derived for the time and safety critical application domain is portrayed in Figure 4.

There is no application relevant decision making within POPS; that is, they simply provide necessary transformations on S/A data. When required, the POPS can also be used to request service from a lower level. The POPS provide a well controlled set of primitives for constructing unconditional (purely time based) and conditional (time and predicate based) software circuits which can be separately tested, debugged and verified. Further, timing profiles can be extracted which can be used as the basis for planning during development as well as in mapping (that is, allocation and scheduling). Note that the basic structure of AM software circuits correspond to the fundamental Cy-Clone cyclic operations introduced in Figure 1.

Specific S/A values used in a block are identified, and it is possible to indicate the frequency of software circuits in a block (default is every dT). Thus, sufficient information is provided for allocation and scheduling of both processing and, when required, distributed communication. The software circuits can be grouped into modes, as illustrated, where the circuits of each mode provide an alternative dynamic cyclic schedule.

The straightforward structure of the AM can be exploited in the surrounding CAE (Computer Aided Engineering) system. Graphical means of constructing and testing software circuits can and should be provided.

Programmed Operations	Circuit Connection Schemata

Programmed Operations

procedure POP1( ) ... end;
procedure POP2( ) ... end;
procedure POP3( ) ... end;
procedure POP4( ) ... end;

.

.

.

procedure POPn( ) ... end;

Circuit Connection Schemata

DO forever
DO during dT
CASE
    cold mode:

           WITH S/A [EVERY Nth dT
           BEGIN

           PoPa( ), POPb( );

           IF situation-predicate THEN
           POPi( ), POPj( ), POPk( );

           .

           .

           IF situation-predicate THEN
           POPm( ), POPn( );

           END

    startup mode:

           WITH S/A [EVERY Nth dT]
           BEGIN

           .

           .

           .

           END

    etc.

ENDCASE

Fig. 4. Program Structure — An Application Machine.

In summary, the Application Machine notion provides a strong mechanism for focusing upon the essential issues of an application domain. It is, in abstract and concrete form, a focal point for establishing a common understanding amongst diverse vested interest parties such as product managers, systems engineers, application engineers, programmers (of POPS), system integration managers, systems maintenance personnel, and so on.

6 Distributed/Parallel Systems

As noted in Lawson, 1992a, there has been a lack of research (particularly
in the academic arena) in respect to exploiting the cyclic approach in paral-
lel/distributed real-time systems. This can be due to the fact that the simplifying fundamental properties seemingly do not provide a significant academic
research challenge. This is absolutely wrong, particularly in the area of distri-
buted/time based systems as demonstrated concretely in the MARS project (see
Koptez, 1989). That a time based approach is an essential ingredient in reducing complexity has also been noted in the general purpose computation field
by Valiant, 1990. He suggests the usage of a periodicity parameter as a means
of achieving mapping simplifications in the form of bulk synchronous processing.

In order to address the special issues related to complex real-time distributed/par-
allel real-time systems, but still be able to exploit the predictability and understandability properties of Cy-Clone, Lawson and Svensson, 1992, have introduced
Distributed/Parallel Cy-Clone as a basis for further research and development
(industrial and academic). A DP Cy-Clone system is surrounded by the external
environment in which it operates and is connected to real sensors and actuators,
even large quantities of them.

Each node within the system has a particular role based upon appropriate treatment of time granularity, data granularity and volume, homogeneity and hete-
rogeneity of processing, and processing granularity. Some form of Global Time
Base is assumed which may be obtained externally (for example, via GPS) and/or
internally based upon the clock frequency of the communication media that is
employed.

Each node contains a BB (BlackBoard) which is used for communication to and
from other nodes. The sum of all of the BBs defines the RTDB (Real-Time Data
Base). In principle, each node has a window into the RTDB. BBs most often
contain reduced information, that is, the volume of BB information is small by
comparison to potentially large quantities of information treated at the periphery of the system.

A generic DP Cy-Clone architecture is presented in Figure 5. A common characteristic of all processing elements in all nodes is that they provide well behaved
timing properties. Thus, in addition to time controlled processing as previously
described for Cy-Clone, SIMD PE-arrays, Digital Signal Processors and Systolic
Arrays are welcome members of the DP Cy-Clone family.

A few comments should be made in connection with Figure 5:

1. Every node in the system need not be able to access the BBs of all other
   nodes.

2. Not all nodes need be connected to external sensors and actuators. All nodes may refer to BB information in the same manner as referring to sensors and actuators. As considered above, it is useful from a conceptual as well as software technical point of view to treat the data contained in BBs as internal logical sensors and actuators. To a node, other nodes simply supply results (logical sensor data) periodically in the same manner as results are supplied periodically from external sensors. Further a node may, by periodically communicating to a BB available to other nodes, actuate processing in the other nodes.

The net result of viewing the system in this manner is that a node lives in an environment (both external and internal), however, the mechanisms for communicating and processing can be made largely identical.

3. A node may itself be composed of several sub-nodes, also of the DP Cy-Clone type. Such a node is a DP Cy-Clone cluster. The cluster concept permits hierarchical and other appropriate DP Cy-Clone architectures to be designed.

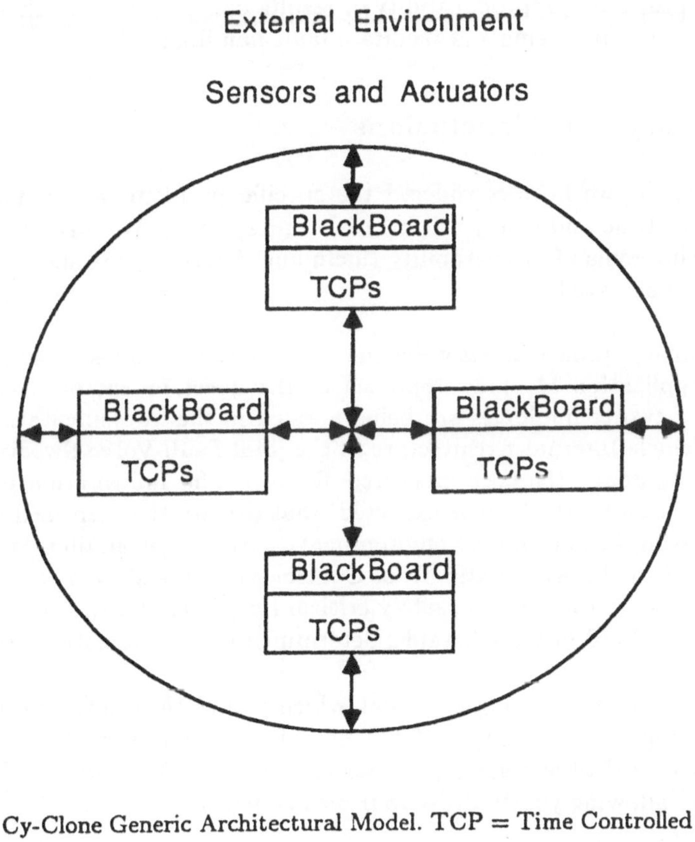

External Environment

Sensors and Actuators

Fig. 5. DP Cy-Clone Generic Architectural Model. TCP = Time Controlled Processor.

The DP Cy-Clone architecture may operate with hard or relaxed synchronization. Naturally, the relaxed mode, where the fundamental systolic base time is utilized in accessing best available information, is the most straightforward. However, within the basic systolic time it is also possible to exploit the "leading flank" of dT or locally managed sub dT time increments in order to simultaneously issue hard synchronized actuation. It is quite conceivable that a reasonably sophisticated DP Cy-Clone system will contain both hard and relaxed synchronization where the nodes dealing with hard synchronization requirements may be placed in separate clusters.

6.1 Systems Integration

As system complexity has grown, considerable attention has been given to the special problems of systems integration (for example, see Rossack and Ng, 1992). The Application Machine approach seems to provide a good building block for constructing and integrating systems. However, the properties of integrating time based systems like those based on Cy-Clone differ from integrating event based systems. Tools must be provided to verify the timing properties of the system at the time of system integration. From the system point of view, due to the time controlled properties, reproducability of results can be achieved, thus making it easier to localize problems and facilitate fault handling.

7 Summary and Conclusions

In this chapter, we have considered the specific problems associated with the treatment of time and safety critical real-time systems. We have demonstrated how the joint goals of predictability (including determinism) and understandability can be achieved.

The Cy-Clone approach to resource adequate systems has been described along with an Application Machine approach to the development of Cy-Clone software. These two technologies are being applied in the implementation of a distributed Vehicle Internal Architecture in the joint Saab-Volvo-Swedish National Development Board (Nutek) sponsored Road Traffic Information project (see Lawson and others, 1992). It is expected, that despite the increased complexity of multiplexing in automotive environments, advantages similar to those that have accrued in the Automatic Train Control project will be attainable within automotive environments. The safety critical functions of tomorrows automobiles must be realized in a predictable, deterministic and understandable manner.

Consider some sole searching questions which you as the reader must ask yourself concerning predictability and the need for understandability in time and safety critical real-time systems, and which places this contribution into proper perspective, allowing you to draw your own conclusions.

Do you want the critical functions of your future automobile to operate in a probabilistic (including event driven) or in a time-based deterministic manner?

Are you willing to pay an automotive mechanic to deal with the complexity of finding faults in a probabilistic (including event driven) automotive real-time system?

Are you willing to rely upon probabilistic (including event driven) solutions in other time and safety critical systems to which you are exposed such as trains, planes, and so on?

Do you feel comfortable knowing that non-productive code (often in large quantities) is being utilized in the systems upon which your safety relies?

As a final comment, we note the following relevant observation by Dijkstra, 1989.

"It is only too easy to design resource sharing systems with such intertwined allocation strategies that no amount of applied queuing theory will prevent the most unpleasant surprises from emerging. The designer who counts performance predictability among his responsibilities tends to come up with designs that need no queuing theory at all."

The End.

References

1. R.A. Brooks, *A Robust Layered Control System for a Mobile Robot*, in Winston, P.H. and Shellard, S.A. (Eds.), Artificial Intelligence at MIT-Expanding Frontiers, MIT Press, Cambridge, MA, 1990.
2. E.W. Dijkstra, *"The Next Forty Years"*, Personal Note EWD 1051, 1989.
3. W.A. Halang and A.D. Stoyenko, *Constructing Predictable Real-Time Systems*, Kluwer Academic Publishers, Boston-Dordrecht-London, 1991.
4. H. Koptez, *Time-Triggered versus Event-Triggered Systems*, Proc. International Workshop on Operating Systems in the 90s and Beyond, Lecture Notes in Computer Science, Springer-Verlag, Berlin, Vol. 563, 1992, 87–101.
5. H. Koptez, A. Damm, C. Koza, M. Mulazzani, W. Schwabi, C. Senft, and R. Zainlinger, *Distributed Fault-Tolerant Real-Time Systems: The MARS Approach*, IEEE Micro, February 1989, 25–58.
6. H.W. Lawson, *Philosophies for Engineering Computer-Based Systems*, IEEE Computer, Vol. 23, No. 12, 1990, 52-63.
7. H.W. Lawson, *Cy-Clone: An Approach to the Engineering of Resource Adequate Cyclic Real-Time Systems*, Journal of Real-Time Systems, Vol. 4, No. 1, 1992a, 55–83.
8. H.W. Lawson, *Parallel Processing in Industrial Real-Time Applications*, Prentice-Hall, Englewood Cliffs, NJ, 1992b.
9. H.W. Lawson, *Design for Understandability*, (submitted for professional publication), 1992c.

10. H.W. Lawson, *Application Machines: An Approach to Realizing Understandable Systems*, Proc. of the Euromicro 92 Conference, North-Holland, 1992d.

11. H.W. Lawson, and B. Svensson, *An Architecture for Time-Critical Distributed/Parallel Processing*, Proceedings of the Euromicro Workshop on Parallel and Distributed Processing, January, 1993.

12. H.W. Lawson, M. Lindgren, M. Strömberg, T. Lundqvist, K.-L. Lundbäck, L.-Å. Johansson, J. Torin, P. Gunningberg and H. Hansson, *Guidelines for Basement: A Real-Time Architecture for Automotive Systems*, Mecel, Inc., Göteborg, and Lawson Publishing and Consulting, Inc., Lidingö, Sweden, 1992.

13. C.D. Locke, Software Architecture for Hard Real-Time Applications: *Cyclic Executives vs. Fixed Priority Executives*, Journal of Real-Time Systems, Vol. 4, No. 1, 1992, 37–53.

14. C.L. Liu and J.W. Layland, *Scheduling Algorithms for Multiprogramming in a Hard Real-Time Environment*, Journal of the Association for Computing Machinery, Vol. 20, No. 1, 1973, 46–61.

15. W. Rossak and P.A. Ng, *System Development with Integration Architectures*, Proc. of Second International Conference on System Integration, June 1992.

16. L. Valiant, *A Bridging Model for Parallel Computation*, Communications of the ACM, Vol. 33, No. 8, 1990, 103–111.

17. S.M. White, M. Alford, B. McCay, D. Oliver, C. Tully, J. Holtzman, C.S. Kuehl, D. Owens and A. Willey, *Improving the Practice in Computer-Based System Engineering*, Proc. of National Council in Systems Engineering (NCOSE), July, 1992.

Real-Time Operating Systems: Can Theoretical Solutions Match with Practical Needs

Helmut Rzehak

University of the Federal Armed Forces Munich
Werner-Heisenberg-Weg 39
85579 Neubiberg
Germany

Abstract

Constructing real-time systems, which are predictable in a very restrictive sense, is a challenging task for scientists. On the other hand today's real-time operating systems do not meet these strong requirements. This paper gives an insight into sources of delays for application processes caused by the operating system. It follows from this analysis that most of the services of real-time operating systems insert unexpected delays to the application processes and worst case values are hardly to determine. Regarding the fact that real-time operating systems are used successfully certain deviations from the model of strict predictability seem to be tolerable for most applications. The paper presents some ideas to describe such tolerable deviations more precisely.

Keywords

Real-time operating systems, latency times, real-time performance metrics, concurrency control.

1 Introduction

A lot of papers has been published in the scientific community concerning real-time operating systems in general as well as special aspects about these. On the other hand off-the-shelf real-time operating systems are available and interface definitions are going to be standardized. At a first glance the various products differ in the scope of applications they support but within the same scope they look very similar. Much of the scientific work has influenced just a little bit the established solutions. The approved "good practice" as a prerequisite for standardisation seems to be somehow different from results achieved by scientific works.

This mismatch may simply come from the ignorance of some handy "experts" or may have some serious reasons. This paper tries to give an answer to this question taking into account some different application aspects of real-time operating systems.

2 Concepts for Real-Time Operating Systems

2.1 Critical View of some Definitions

The central point of most definitions for real-time computing is a required deterministic (or predictable) behaviour in the time domain. In contrast with this really existing systems contain many sources of nondeterminism. Among others we have arbitrary sequences of events to react on and generally it is hard to define how a system should react in a deterministic way on non-predictable input sequences. At the occurrence of the event the whole internal state of the system is usually unknown and this results in a non-predictable sequence of state transitions for performing the desired action. Having a close look to reality the very task in designing a real-time system is to reduce nondeterminisms in the overall system behaviour under an acceptable level because the complete elimination is impossible or at least too expensive. Basicly this means to describe the term "predictability" not by a binary value but by a fuzzy set using the membership function to determine if the level of predictability is sufficient. The conventional thinking about hard deadlines and mathematical proof of certain behavioural attributes is included as a special case. This new understanding of predictability gives a more realistic view of at least three aspects of real-time systems without leaving a solid basis for reasoning:

1. Certain deviations of the intended system behaviour may be acceptable if they occur very rarely. This is a realistic assumption for many (not to say for most) applications. Frequently worst case considerations are far to pessimistic and lead to oversized systems. E.g. an upper bound for the latency times introduced by the operating system, which will be discussed later on in this paper, may be considerably high, but the worst case situation will occur only under very special conditions. Perhaps these conditions will never be valid for an application.

2. Instead of describing the time constraints of a real-time task only by its deadline we can use a benefit function like in the Benefit Accrual Model proposed in the Alpha real-time operating system ([11], [12]). As a next step we can replace a certain benefit function by a fuzzy set of functions as shown in fig. 1.

3. We should take into account the limited resolution of the time scale. This is not due to the limited frequency of the clock ticks but due to arbitrary delays for event and message handling by the different subsystems. For distributed applications this aspect is particularly important ([25], [26]).

Our proposal is not covered by the classic distinction of hard and soft real-time systems. There exist only "soft" descriptions what a soft real-time system is. This means that we have no appropriate attributes describing the time constraints of a soft real-time system and as a consequence most of the scientific work concerns hard real-time systems. We would like to encourage people to consider not only classical hard real-time systems.

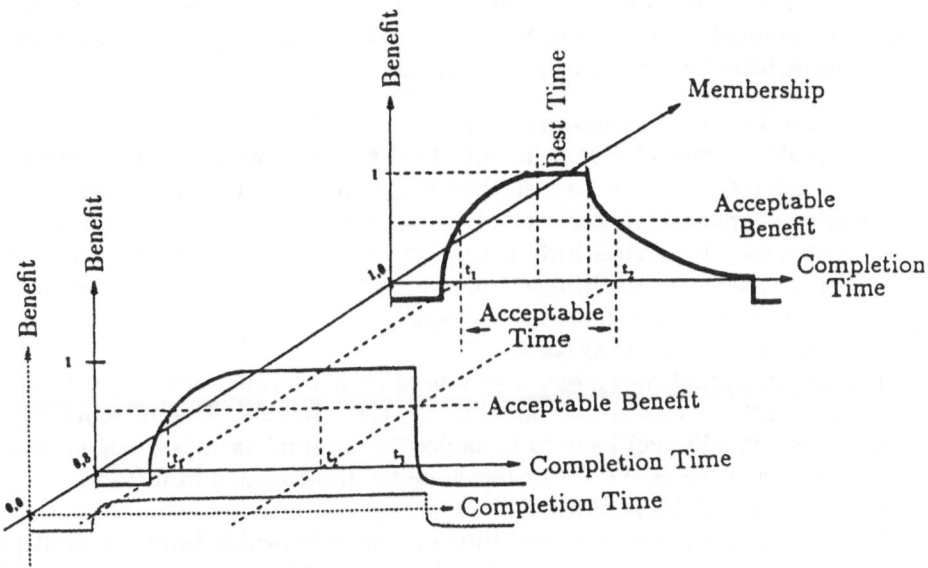

Fig. 1. Benefit as a Fuzzy Set of Functions

2.2 Functionality

Real-time operating systems are state of the art and have been used for a couple of years for many applications. The designers mainly highly agree upon functional requirements provided by system calls and differences in functionality mainly result from the scope of applications (e.g. whether an application requires a file system). Using the draft on real-time extensions for POSIX [20] as an example the traditional functionality of UNIX (multiprocessing, interprocess communication, file handling, standard input and output) will be enhanced by the following features for real-time applications (listed in the order of the draft):

- Realtime Signals Extensions
- Synchronized Input and Output
- Asynchronous Input and Output
- Semaphores

- Process Memory Locking
- Memory Mapped Files and Shared Memory
- Priority Scheduling
- Clocks and Timers
- Message Passing
- Realtime files

In order to tailor operating systems for applications not requiring the full functionality real-time profiles and their minimum hardware requirements are defined. The actual state of work on POSIX extensions for supporting real-time applications distinguishes between four profiles [23]:

- **Minimal real-time system:**
  This profile is typically used in embedded systems and somewhere else called an operating system kernel. The programming model is that of a single address space. This corresponds to a single POSIX process. Concurrent activities may be established through more than one POSIX threads [21]. Minimum hardware is a single processor with its memory, but no memory management unit or common I/O devices.
- **Real-time controller system:**
  The minimal real-time system is enhanced by a file system interface, character serial I/O and exception handling (POSIX Signals). One or more serial channels (RS-232-like) have to be added to minimal hardware but no mass storage device, since the file system may be implemented in memory.
- **Dedicated real-time system:**
  In addition to the minimal real-time system this profile supports multiple POSIX processes, a common interface for device drivers and a non hierarchical file system interface. For memory management hardware memory locking is provided. Minimal hardware assumes one or more processors with or without memory management unit.
- **Multi-purpose real-time system:**
  This profile supports full functionality of the POSIX real-time extensions. The hardware model assumes processors with memory management unit, high speed mass storage devices, network support and display devices.

We do not find elaborate concepts concerning scheduling, resource management or controlling real-time constraints. The functionality is based on fairly simple concepts like priority scheduling with preemption (dynamic priorities), synchronization by semaphores and message queues. There are some features allowing to implement more elaborate concepts in a special implementation and give support to the application through the standard interface.

Some problems need a new discussion of the relationship between the operating system and the programming environment. For some reasons information about the semantic context of a system call should be provided. An example is the problem of priority inversion using semaphores. Existing protocols for priority ceiling ([29], [24]) generally solve the problem. But there is assumed, that the semaphore will be released by the same process which has requested it. In other words: *the owner of the lock is well-known within the operating system.* If semaphores are used in some other ways the operating system is not able to determine the owner of the lock and a priority ceiling protocol fails. The problem may be left to the user, or the owner of the lock has to be made known explicitly to the operating system, e.g. by a semantic analysis performed by the programming environment.

2.3 Hierarchically Structured Systems

Powerful operating systems are no longer a monolithic entity. For reducing complexity the internal structure consists of a hierarchy of levels of which the lowest is the kernel (see fig. 2). It provides only a minimal set of functions from which the rest of the operating system can be constructed. The critical regions of the kernel can be kept short. Some user services may be performed by kernel functions directly, other services by functions on a higher level using kernel functions indirectly. Examples are file access and management services or network services.

A hierarchical structure has three advantages:

1. Latency times caused by higher levels (see next section) cannot affect processes only using kernel functions.
2. It is more adequate for providing extensions by the user. By this means more elaborate concepts can be implemented easier for gaining experience.
3. Tayloring systems for special needs is easier.

3 The Role of Latency Times

Unexpected delays caused by the operating system are commonly called latency times. Occasionally under certain combinations of conditions they occur with arbitrary length and have to be considered for applications with short response times. Many papers don't treat the kind how service requests arise in a real-time environment and therefore latency times are not discussed.

3.1 Origin of Latency Times

An external event is commonly signaled by an interrupt and we assume that the associated event reaction is part of a user task. Supposed that the interrupt has high priority to be immediately served and the currently running task has lower priority than the user task containing the event reaction, we define the time between the occurrence of the external event and the execution of the first statement of the associated event reaction within the user task as the Process Dispatch Latency Time (PDLT). If this first statement sets a bit in an externally

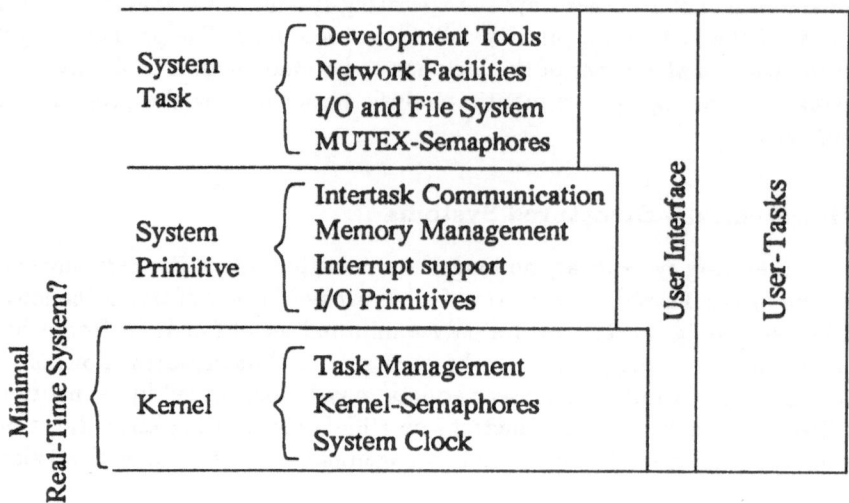

Fig. 2. Hierarchical Structure of an Operating Systems

observable register, the PDLT is easy to measure. For real-time applications we ask for the upper bound of the PDLT.

To give an answer we assume that just before the interrupt occurs the running task has executed a system call. If the called system function is not preemptable, the transfer of control to the task containing the event reaction is delayed until control is returned from the system function to user code. Fig. 3 gives a sketch of this situation.

In Fig. 4 the transitions of control are marked on the time scale. The PDLT is the time between point (1) and (2). Worst case is the dynamically longest system function. Generally this is unacceptable long for real-time applications. E.g. a traditional UNIX implementation with non-preemptable kernel functions is not suitable for real-time applications. To reduce the PDLT preemption of a kernel function should be possible, or in other words we need reentrant system calls.

For a better understanding we have to know why the preemption of kernel functions may be a problem. Generally kernel functions manipulate entries in data structures of the operating system kernel necessary to manage the various objects and resources of the operating system. Changes necessary to performing a function cannot be done in a single indivisible instruction and therefore during execution the contents may be temporarily inconsistent. If an interruption

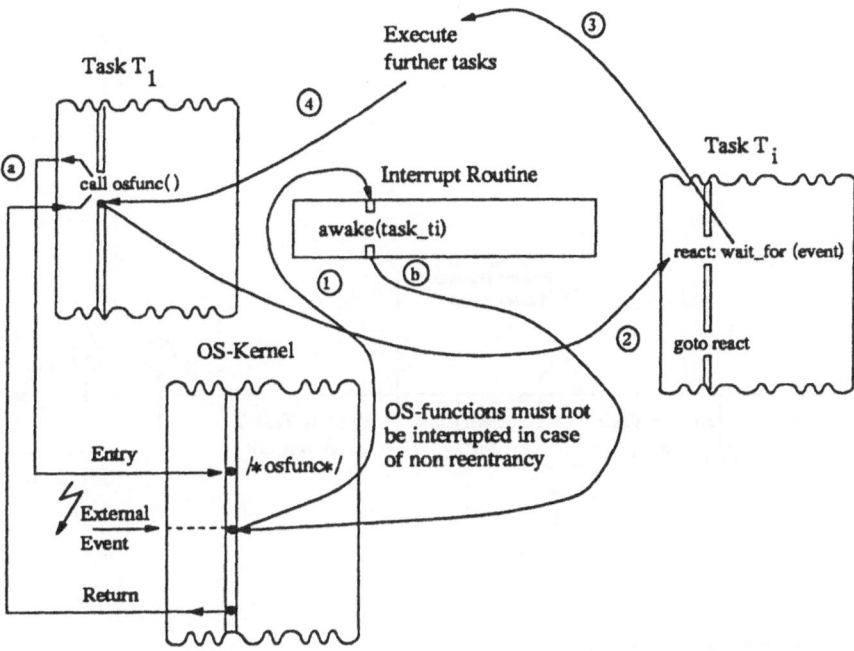

Fig. 3. Calling an Event Reaction

occurs in such a situation some or even all kernel functions are not executable because they operate on inconsistent data. The brute force way to overcome the problem is to forbid kernel preemptions. It is fairly simple and not so bad except for real-time applications.

Allowing preemptions to a certain extent it my happen that a kernel function may be called twice until returning from the first call. Therefore we need reentrant system calls. Summarizing, for kernel preemptions we have to maintain the following conditions:

- A sequence of instructions changing data from one consistent state to another consistent one, commonly called a critical region, must not be entered twice until the first entry call has reached the exit.
- If system data used by each of two critical regions have a common subset these two critical regions are called to be conflicting and must be entered as mutually exclusive.

Several concepts may be used to meet these conditions. With respect to real-time requirements the most elaborate one is constructing the kernel functions with critical regions and using semaphores for preventing reentrant execution of critical regions and to avoid conflicting concurrent execution. Such a kernel is sometimes called fully preemptable. Fig. 5 gives an example with three critical regions. It is shown how a preemption with a reentrant function call works.

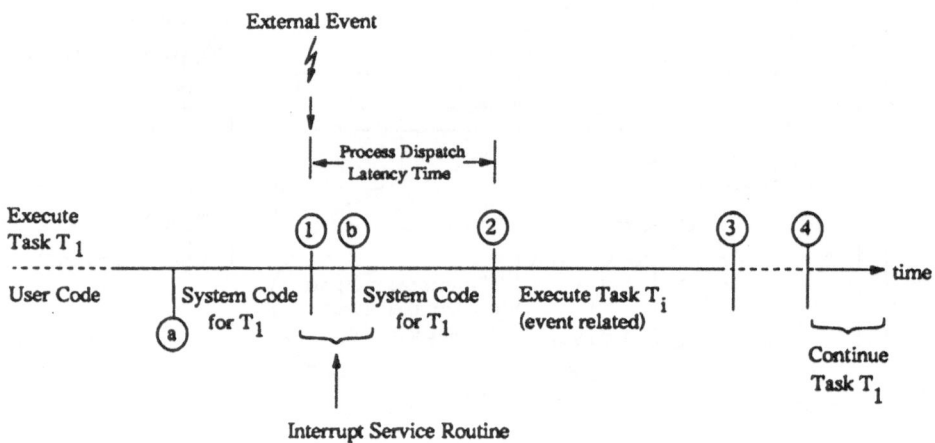

Fig. 4. Definition of the Process Dispatch Latency Time

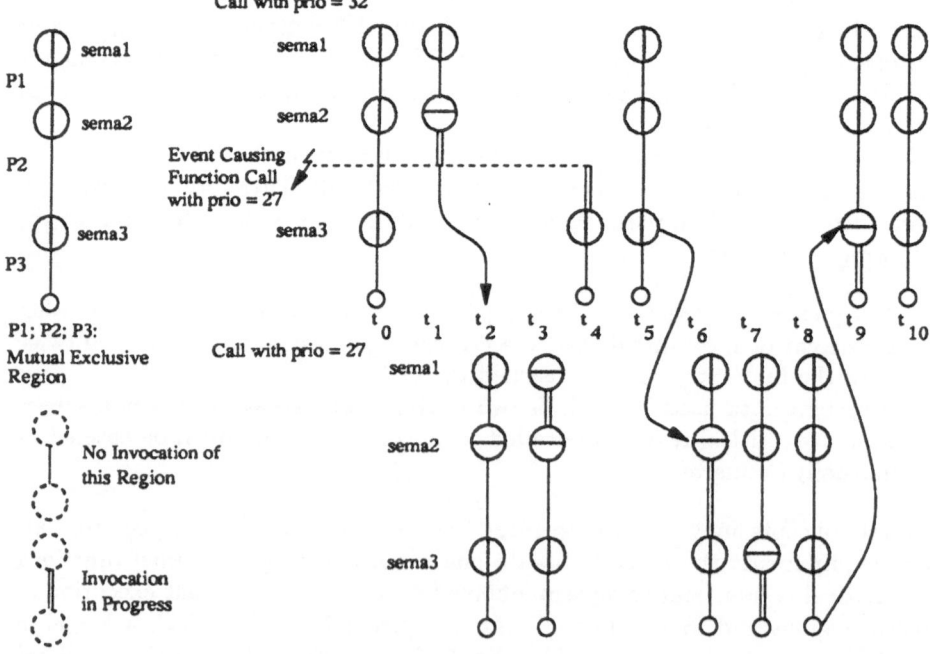

Fig. 5. Preemptive Execution of a Reentrant System Function

It should be noticed, that the construction of such a kernel is not an easy task. As we will see below, for good real-time performance the critical regions should be (dynamically) as short as possible. In so far as parts of device drivers are executed as kernel code they have to be included in the concept. E.g. this is important for using drivers with a real-time UNIX written originally for a traditional UNIX system, because their kernel level synchronization does not fit into the concept described here. Some compatibility modes may be offered for this purpose at the cost of real-time performance [6].

In the case of a fully preemptable kernel the PDLT does not depend on whether user or system code will be executed at the occurence of the external event. Therefore measured values are reasonably small. But as shown in Fig. 5 an unexpected delay may happen later on, if during the event reaction a system call invokes the interrupted kernel function. This is the time between the points $t3$ and $t6$ in Fig. 5 necessary to terminate the critical region. At a first glance the imposed latency time is at most the time necessary to execute the dynamically longest critical region. But this is not the worst case. Consider the situation at $t3$ in Fig. 5. If another external event happens causing the same function call with a higher priority (e.g. $prio = 22$) this call has to wait twice: for leaving $P1$ by $prio = 27$ and leaving $P2$ by $prio = 32$. We can continue this construction until a call has to wait for leaving all sections by other processes. The necessary nesting of system calls and events becomes more and more unlikely or even impossible.

Looking at the result of introducing kernel preemptions we are not sure if we have reduced the worst case value for the latency time because it depends on the application if a certain nesting of system calls and events is possible. Really we have gained that higher latency times have become much more unlikely using reentrant system calls. With respect to our remarks in section 2.2 we consider this to be an improvement.

We can sum up our results as follows:
For a fully preemptable kernel of an operating system with reentrant functions an arbitrary delay may be imposed into an event reaction. We call this the Maximum Kernel Latency Time (MKLT). It is not part of the Process Dispatch Latency Time. The MKLT depends on the application. An approximation is the execution time of the (dynamically) longest critical region of the kernel. Even this approximation is not easy to determine nor to measure without knowledge of the internal structure of the kernel. Sometimes reported statistical results may give a first glance but worst case values may be much higher than mean values.

There is another possible solution for implementing kernel preemptions:
If a second call takes place on a higher priority the first call (on a lower priority) will be aborted instead of reentering a function. For continuing the preempted process the first call has to be restarted. Compared with the usual solution of reentrant functions the latency time due to the restart of the function appears

on the lower priority. This is an advantage. On the other hand processor time is wasted and therefore latency times are imposed to all lower priority processes not only to the preempted one. For that reason aborting a kernel function seems a preferred solution only if we have a single very time critical process.

3.2 Some Published Results

Table 1 shows some measured values of the PDLT obtained from [6]. All systems claim to be real-time UNIX systems. Some seem to give a fairly good real-time performance.

OS	Hardware	Process Dispatch Latency	
		MIN μs	MAX μs
HP-UX	HP 9000/825	655	1991
CX/RT	Harris Night Hawk 3400	90	430
RTU	Concurrent/ Masscomp 6300	1605	11605
REAL/IX	AEG-MODCOMP Tri-D 9730 (MC 68030-25)	50	360

Table 1. Process Dispatch Latency Time for Some Systems

In contrast to the values for HP-UX in Table 1 Hewlett-Packard has published values for the kernel latency time of HP-UX ([2] and [3]). These values are shown in Table 2.

For HP-UX we see that the MKLT is 14.6 ms, whereas the maximum PDLT according to Table 1 is 1.991 ms. As described in [2] and [3] the kernel of HP-UX is not fully preemptable because the concept of critical regions guarded by semaphores (see section 3.1) is mixed with the concept of preemption points. This leads to a higher PDLT. Other available data ([14], [9] and [18]) underline the general supposition that the Maximum Kernel Latency Time is much higher than the Process Dispatch Latency Time. To compare real-time UNIX systems with specialized real-time operating system kernels Table 3 and Table 4 show

	Preemption OFF	Preemption ON
90 % of paths through the kernel	40 ms	1.4 ms
99 % of paths through the kernel	129 ms	3.4 ms
max. paths through the kernel	1127 ms	14.6 ms

Table 2. Kernel Latency Time for HP-UX

some application oriented characteristics for two operating systems measured on the same hardware (obtained from [9]). The considered UNIX system looks not so bad. Surely the results depend on the considered load (terminal I/O in Table 3 and Table 4). We expect less good results if network applications are included in the load.

As we have expected the results show that unexpected delays of considerable duration caused by the operating system may happen in user tasks. These delays are highly load dependent and it is not easy to give worst case values. Upper bounds derived from theory are far too pessimistic because they never may be reached by a certain application.

3.3 Latencies in Hierarchically Structured Systems

A close look on existing implementations shows that relatively long critical regions will be found exclusively in I/O-, file system- and network service-calls. For a hierarchically structured operating system (see section 2.3) these calls don't invoke kernel functions directly and in this case it is possible to keep critical regions of the kernel fairly short. This reduces latency times for those processes only using kernel functions but not in general because we have the problem of critical sections on higher levels too.

	RTOS-UH (Special Real-Time Kernel)	REAL/IX (Real-Time UNIX)
Max. Interrupt Frequency (kHz)	14.7	6.67
Interrupt Resolution Time (μs)	6.6	150.0
Process Dispatch Latency Time } [μs] Min. without Load Max.	55.2 63.9	128 171
Process Dispatch Latency Time } [μs] Min. with Load Max.	57.3 110	128.8 228

Hardware: MVME 147 with MC 68030-25 MHz

Table 3. Event Reaction Characteristics

Similar to the kernel, services on higher levels use internal data structures to manage their objects and resources. These internal data structures may be temporarily inconsistent too. Sharing services between several user tasks leads to the same problems as described in section 3.1. These problems are resolved in the same way establishing critical regions guarded by kernel semaphores. Clearly we have a latency time on a higher level if a preempted region should be entered again during a service call of a process with higher priority. Services on higher levels are not so closely linked together. They form classes with no common critical regions for any two classes and the latency on higher levels concerns only user tasks using the same service class. Especially tasks using only kernel services cannot be delayed by locked critical regions on higher level.

The problem of latency times on higher levels is weaker to some extent, but the problem still remains. We have seen that for the kernel latency time it is hard to get some figures by measurements without knowledge of the internal structure of the kernel. This is also true for latency times on higher levels. Information from vendors is quite unusual.

	RTOS-UH (Special Real-Time Kernel)	REAL/IX (Real-Time UNIX)
Intended Cycle Time T_0 [ms]	2.000	2.0833
Without Load: Deviation of T_0 [%] } Min. Max.	- 0.25 0.00	- 1.28 + 1.28
Mean Value [ms]	2.000	2.0833
With Load: Deviation of T_0 [%] } Min. Max.	- 11.75 + 11.75	- 4.96 + 4.96
Mean Value [ms]	2.000	2.0833

Hardware: MVME 147 with MC 68030-25 MHz

Table 4. Characteristics for Cyclic Tasks

4 Performance Evaluation

4.1 Performance Metrics

In general performance metrics for real-time operating systems should serve for

- calculating the overhead introduced by a service,
- calculating upper bounds for delays of running processes caused by the operating system, or
- serve for the user as a means of comparing different implementations.

Some methodologies and related metrics for measuring real-time performance have been proposed in the literature [6]. In addition to the defined functionality the draft on real-time extensions for POSIX defines performance metrics and a performance documentation option provides a document with measurements of these performance metrics.

Defining real-time performance metrics and corresponding measuring instructions we are faced with a couple of problems:

1. We have to decide if we will evaluate only by observing the operating system from the outside ("black box" evaluation) or if we can gather information

during execution of system calls, which means that we have knowledge about the implementation (white box evaluation) and that we can add some code to the system for measuring purpose. In the first case often we can evaluate only a sequence of functions and then can try to separate the influence of a single function by comparing some different sequences. Generally we have to think about what aspects are observable. In the second case we need support by the implementor.

2. Execution of some system calls depend on the context of other running processes (e.g. priorities or used semaphores) and we may have mode changes during service completion. For reproducible results we have to fix up this context considering realistic situations.

3. The execution of code necessary for gathering operating data has some influence on the measured object.

4. With respect to the load dependancy we would like to have data for different load situations. Therefore we need a unique description of the load to be offered for characterizing different realistic load situations by some parameters. A possible solution may be the use of a grammar-driven load generator [4].

Today vendors support some performance data, but it is difficult to compare them because mostly the metrics are not exactly the same or the operating conditions during measurement differ even if they are documented. Calculating upper bounds for delays of running processes caused by the operating system is more or less impossible.

4.2 "Black Box" Evaluation

For practical reasons a vendor-independent evaluation has to be based on the "black box" approach. According to their nature for some metrics, especially for latency times, we can only get statistical results. As we are interested in worst case values rather than mean values it may help to look for sophisticated test cases for producing long latency times. The general understanding of their origin and some knowledge about the implementation, possibly derived from other tests, should be used for constructing conditions for long latency times. Some work in this direction is at the very beginning.

A strong support of vendor-independent evaluation is the introduction of what I am calling reporting points. In a universal form this is the invocation of a user supported procedure if the control flow passes a reporting point during a system call. Some internal conditions of the operating system treated as formal parameters can be evaluated during execution of the procedure body. Some real-time operating systems offer such a feature in a very simple form for testing. By this means a trace of some events with time stamps can be recorded for off-line evaluation. This is a combination of "black box" and "white box" evaluation because from the outside we see the reporting points. A definition within the POSIX standard will really enable the user to compare different implementations.

5 Conclusions

Almost all real-time systems currently in operation are not predictable in a very strict sense. This is because all sources of nondeterminism are hard to eliminate and worst case estimations often are far beyond the intended time constraints. The exceptions are very simple systems mostly designed in conjunction with fault tolerance and work purely synchronous with a fixed cycle controlled by hardware. No interrupt handling is used. These systems do not use an operating system in the common meaning not only because of the latency times but with respect to program verification. Operating systems capable of handling asynchronous events necessarily have latency times and the difference between mean values and worst case values may have some degrees of magnitude, while worst case situations may happen extremely rarely. For the bulk of real-time applications deadlines are primarily used for describing an ideal situation from which deviations are acceptable to a certain extent. Scheduling based on dynamic priorities with preemption is commonly accepted, because deadlines can be mapped dynamically into priorities [16]. More attention should be paid on latency times with respect to the fact that they may appear only in the very late test phase under heavy load conditions or even at the first breakdown. For many applications an enhanced functionality of the operating system (e.g. like real-time POSIX) is mandatory and a pure but predictable one (in a very strict sense) is not an alternative.

At present open systems are coming up more and more introducing a new kind of nondeterminism: The change of hardware or software components by the end-user. As an example in [15] it is reported that by replacing an adapter card by another one claiming to be compatible the time behaviour has been drastically changed. The only solution is an on-line version control including the version of hardware components.

References

1. A. Burns and A. Wellings, *Real-Time Systems and their Programming Languages*, Addison-Wesley Publishing Company, 1990.
2. S.M. Doughty, S.F. Kary; S.R. Kusmer and D.V. Larson, *UNIX for Real Time*, Proceedings of the UniForum 1987, Washington D.C., January 1987, 219–230.
3. S.M Doughty, *Adding Real Time Capabilities to the UNIX Operating System*, Proceedings of the PEARL 87 Workshop über Realzeitsysteme, Boppard, 3.–4. Dez. 1987, 151–165.
4. W. Dulz and S. Hofmann, *Grammer-based Workload Modelling of Communication Systems*, Proceedings of the 5. Int. Conference on Modelling Techniques and Tools for Computer Performance Evaluation, Turin, 13.–15. Feb. 1991.
5. J. Fogelin, *The VxWorks Real-Time Kernel*, Wind River Systems, Alameda.
6. B. Furht et al., *Real-time UNIX Systems: Design and Application Guide*, Kluwer Academic Publishers, 1991.

7. B. Furht, *The Reality of a Real-Time UNIX Operating System*, Proceedings of the convention Echtzeit '91 (Ed: H. Rzehak), Sindelfingen, 11.-13. Juni 1991, Ludwig Drebinger GmbH, Munich, Germany, 281–296.

8. B.O. Gallmeister and Ch. Lanier, *Early Experience with POSIX 1003.4 and POSIX 1003.4a*, Proc. IEEE Real-Time Systems Symposium, San Antonio, Dec. 4–6, 1991, 190–198.

9. C. Gralla, *Quantitativer Vergleich von drei Echtzeitbetriebssystemen für die digitale Regelung*, Proceedings of the PEARL 91 Workshop über Realzeitsysteme, Boppard, 28.-29. Nov. 1991, Informatik-Fachberichte, Springer-Verlag, 141–155.

10. W.A. Halang and A.D. Stoyenko, *Constructing Predictable Real Time Systems*, Kluwer Academic Publishers, 1991.

11. E.D. Jensen, C.D. Locke and H. Tokuda, *A Time-Driven Scheduling Model for Real-Time Operating Systems*, Proc. IEEE Real-Time Systems Symposium, San Diego, Dec. 3–6, 1985.

12. E.D. Jensen, *Alpha: A Non-Proprietary Realtime Operating System for Mission Management Applications*, Proceedings of the convention Echtzeit '92 (Ed: H. Rzehak), Sindelfingen, 2.-4. Juni 1992, Ludwig Drebinger GmbH, Munich, Germany, 205–212.

13. N.I. Kamenoff and N.H. Weidermann, *Hartstone Benchmark: Requirements and Definitions*, IEEE Real-Time Systems Symposium, San Antonio, Dec. 4–6, 1991, 199–208.

14. W. Kriechbaum, *Adding Real-Time Capabilities to a Standard UNIX Implementation: The AIX Version 3.1.5 Approach*; Proceedings of the convention Echtzeit '91 (Ed. H. Rzehak), Sindelfingen, 11.-13. Juni 1991, Ludwig Drebinger GmbH, Munich, Germany, 63–71.

15. W. Kriechbaum, *Real-time Standards and Real-time Reality: a closer look at POSIX 1003.4*, Proceedings of the convention Echtzeit '92 (Ed. H. Rzehak), Sindelfingen, 2.-4. Juni 1992, Ludwig Drebinger GmbH, Munich, Germany, 199–204.

16. C.L. Liu and J.W. Layland, *Scheduling Algorithms for Multiprogramming in a Hard Real-Time Environment*, Journal of the ACM, Vol. 20, No. 1, Feb. 1973, 46–61.

17. S.T. Levi and A.K. Agrawala, *Real-Time System Design*, McGraw-Hill, 1990.

18. *REAL/STAR 1000 and 2000 Series Benchmark Report*, MODCOMP Benchmarking Group, Modular Computer Systems, Ft. Lauderdale, 1991.

19. *Portable Operating System Interface for Computer Environments*, ISO/IEC 9945-1: 1990 and IEEE Std 1003.1–1990 (POSIX.1).

20. *Realtime Extensions for Portable Operating Systems*, IEEE P1003.4/D12 Feb. 1992.

21. *Threads Extensions for Portable Operating Systems*, IEEE P1003.4a/D6 Feb. 1992.

22. *Realtime System API Extension*, IEEE P1003.4b/D1 Nov. 1991.

23. *Standardized Application Environment Profile-POSIX Realtime Application Support (AEP)*, IEEE P1003.13/D4 Nov. 1991.

24. R. Rajkumar, *Synchronization in Real-Time Systems: A Priority Inheritance Approach*, Kluwer Academic Publishers, 1991.

25. H. Rzehak, *Distributed Systems for Real Time Applications-Using Manufacturing Automation as an Example*, in: M. Schiebe, S. Pferrer (Eds.), Real-Time Systems, Engineering and Applications, Kluwer–Verlag, 1992.

26. H. Rzehak, *Distributed Real Time Systems for Manufacturing Automation*, IFAC Symposium on Intelligent Components and Instruments for Control Applications (SICICA'92), Malaga, May 20–22, 1992.

27. H. Rzehak, *Real-Time UNIX: What Performance can we expect?*, IFAC/IFIP Workshop on Real-Time Programming (WRTP '92), Bruges, June 23–26, 1992.

28. K. Schwan, A. Gheith and H. Zhou, *From CHAOSbase to CHAOSarc: A Family of Real-time Kernels*, IEEE Real-Time Systems Symposium, Lake Buena Vista, Dec. 5–7, 1990, 82–91.

29. L. Sha, R. Rajkumar and J.P. Lehoczky *Priority Inheritance Protocols: An Approach to Real-Time Synchronization*, IEEE Transactions on Computers, Vol. 39, No. 9, 1990, 1175–1185.

30. J.A. Stankovic and K. Ramamritham, *What is Predictability for Real-Time Systems?*, Real-Time Systems, Vol. 2, No. 4, 1990, 247–254.

31. J.A. Stankovic and K. Ramamritham, *The Spring Kernel: A new Paradigm for Real-Time Systems*, IEEE Software, May 1991, 62–72.

Real-Time Operating Systems*

John A. Stankovic

University of Massachusetts
Amherst, MA 01003
U.S.A.

Abstract

Real-time operating systems are an integral part of complex real-time
systems. Three general categories of real-time operating systems exist:
small, proprietary kernels, real-time extensions to commercial timesharing operating systems, and research kernels. This paper discusses each
of these areas focusing on how each of these classes deal with predictability. It is argued that the small, proprietary kernels are predictable,
but offer little help to the real-time systems designer and implementor
in producing predictable applications. Real-time versions of commercial
operating systems like UNIX and Mach offer greater implementation support, but are, *in general*, NOT predictable themselves nor offer enough
support to applications which require predictability. This, of course, does
not mean that there is *no way* to achieve predictability with these operating systems. It is possible to achieve predictability by very careful
design, by using a very limited subset of the overall features provided,
and by proving that the features being used for predictability cannot in
any way be impacted by any other part of the system. Finally, research
kernels are attempting to provide greater design, implementation and
evaluation support together with predictability for both the operating
system and the application.

1 Introduction

Real-time computing systems play a vital role in our society, controlling many
types of applications including simple ones such as laboratory experiments and
automobile engines, as well as very complex applications such as nuclear power
plants, flight control systems, manufacturing processes, and teams of robots working in hazardous environments [1], [19]. In real-time computing the correctness

* This work was funded in part by the Office of Naval Research under contracts
  N00014–85–K–0389 and N00014-92-J-1048, and NSF under DCR-8500332 and CDA-
  8922572.

of the system depends not only on the logical result, but also on the time at which the results are produced. Explicitly dealing with time (usually via direct control of equipment that is, in turn, controlling or operating in some larger environment) makes building and analyzing real-time systems difficult. If we can show that a task or set of tasks can meet their timing constraints we say that they are predictable. One important component in producing an effective, predictable real-time system is the *real-time operating system*. The operating system itself must be predictable. This means that the execution times of OS primitives in process management, memory management, IPC, etc. must be small and bounded. In addition, we believe that the real-time operating system should provide a significant amount of direct support for achieving application level predictability, not just operating system predictability. This direct support is missing from current commercial operating systems. There are many commercial and research oriented real-time operating systems. In discussing real-time operating systems it is possible to categorize them into three general groups: small, fast, proprietary kernels, real-time extensions of commercial operating systems, and research oriented operating systems. In this paper we discuss the current state of the art in each of these areas. We point out advantages, problems, and future needs in each of the areas with a particular emphasis on predictability. For tutorial purposes, we also present a more detailed description of one research oriented kernel — the Spring kernel.

2 Small, Fast, Proprietary Kernels

Existing practices for designing, implementing, and validating real-time systems are still rather *ad hoc*. Software engineering practices that advocate modularity and the use of abstract data types are not usually pursued throughout the real-time software production process due to their perceived conflict with real-time requirements. This attitude has permeated the small, proprietary kernels. These kernels are often used for small embedded systems when very fast and highly predictable execution time must be guaranteed [14]. To achieve speed and predictability, these kernels are stripped down and optimized versions of timesharing operating systems. To reduce the run-time overheads incurred by the kernel and to make the system *fast*, the kernel

1. has a fast context switch,
2. has a small size (with its associated minimal functionality),
3. responds to external interrupts quickly (sometimes with a guaranteed maximum latency to post an event but, generally, no guarantee is given as to when processing of the event will be completed; this later guarantee can *sometimes* be computed if priorities are chosen correctly),
4. minimizes intervals during which interrupts are disabled,
5. provides fixed or variable sized partitions for memory management (i.e., no virtual memory) as well as the ability to lock code and data in memory, and
6. provides special sequential files that can accumulate data at a fast rate.

To deal with timing requirements, the kernel

1. maintains a real-time clock,
2. provides a priority scheduling mechanism,
3. provides for special alarms and timeouts,
4. supports real-time queueing disciplines such as earliest deadline and jam a message into the front of a queue, and
5. tasks can invoke primitives to delay by a fixed amount of time and to suspend/resume execution.

In general, the kernels also perform multi-tasking and inter-task communication and synchronization via standard, well-known primitives such as mailboxes, events, signals, and semaphores. The kernels often provide very fast interrupt handling and context switches. While all these features are designed to be fast, fast is a relative term and not sufficient when dealing with real–time constraints. Nevertheless, many real-time system designers believe that these features provide a good basis upon which to build real-time systems. This is probably true where the proprietary kernels are most useful, that is, in small embedded applications such as instrumentation, communication front ends, intelligent peripherals and many areas of process control. Then because the application is so simple it is relatively easy to show that all timing constraints are met. Consequently, the kernels provide exactly what is needed[2]. However, as applications become more complex it becomes more and more difficult to *craft a solution* where all timing, computation time, resource, precedence, and value requirements are mapped to a single priority for each task. In these situations demonstrating predictability becomes very difficult. For example, a task may block when it attempts to access a semaphore, new tasks may be dynamically invoked at higher priorities, messages may not be available when a task begins execution, events may be posted very quickly but there may be no guarantee that the processing required to respond to the event will execute in time, etc. Given this large amount of asynchrony, concurrency, and blocking, the unfortunate implementor is required to assign the proper priorities that ensures the system always meets all of its deadlines. Because of these reasons, some researchers believe that current kernel features provide almost no direct support for solving the difficult timing problems, and would rather see more sophisticated kernels that directly address timing and fault tolerance constraints. Many research kernels are addressing these issues.

Recently there have been efforts to produce seamless real-time kernels that scale from the small, proprietary kernels to large kernels that support the full POSIX/UNIX interfaces (see Section 3). The idea is to let the user select tradeoffs in size, performance and functionality depending on the application. The lowest level of support is being called a nanokernel or alternatively a microkernel. However, it is still not clear if the larger of the seamless kernels will suffer from

---

[2] Examples of commercials kernels include LynxOS, PDOS, pSOS, VCOS, VRTX32, and VxWorks.

the same problems discussed in the next section, or if all these problems can be overcome.

3 Real-Time Extensions to Commercial Operating Systems

A second approach to real-time operating systems is the extension of commercial products, e.g., extending UNIX to RT-UNIX [5], or POSIX to RT-POSIX, or MACH to RT-MACH [22]. The real-time version of commercial operating systems are generally slower and less predictable than the proprietary kernels, but have greater functionality and better software development environments. For example, one advantage of RT-UNIX is that it is based on a set of familiar interfaces (standards) that speed development and facilitate portability. However, since many variations of UNIX have evolved, a new standards effort, called POSIX, has defined a common set of user level interfaces for operating systems. In particular, the POSIX P.1003.4, subcommittee is defining standards for real-time operating systems. To date, the effort has focussed on eleven important real-time related functions: timers, priority scheduling, shared memory, real-time files, semaphores, interprocess communication, asynchronous event notification, process memory locking, asynchronous I/O, synchronous I/O, and threads.

Various problems exist when attempting to convert a non real-time operating system to a real-time version. These problems can exist both at the system interface as well as in the implementation. For example, in UNIX interface problems exist in process scheduling due to the **nice** and **setpriority** primitives and its round robin scheduling policy. In addition, the timer facilities are too coarse, memory management (of some versions) contains no method for locking pages into memory, and interprocess communication facilities don't support fast and predictable communication. The implementation problems include intolerable overhead, excessive latency in responding to interrupts, partly but very importantly, due to the non-preemptability of the kernel, and internal queues are FIFO. These and other problems have been solved to result in a real-time operating system that is used for both real-time and non real-time processing. However, because the underlying paradigm of timesharing systems still exists users must be careful not to use certain non real-time features that might insidiously impact the real-time tasks. For example, in [5] they list over 60 RT-UNIX system calls that are not recommended to be used when running a real-time application. This is very disturbing because in converting from UNIX to RT-UNIX the following aspects were changed: scheduling, interrupt handling, IPC, the file system, I/O support, how the user controls resource use, timer facilities, memory management and the basic synchronization assumptions of the kernel. The juxtaposition of changing almost everything and then ending up with over 60 system calls that should *still* not be used, should lead one to question whether extending a commercial timesharing OS is the correct approach. We believe that it is not the correct approach because too many basic and inappropriate underlying assumptions still exist. This includes optimizing for the average case (rather than worst case), assigning resources on demand, ignoring most if not all semantic information about the application, independent cpu scheduling and resource allocation possibly causing unbounded blocking, etc. On the other hand, the trend to begin with a completely new implementation of UNIX based on microkernels may reduce or eliminate some of the above problems. Consider several more detailed examples from MACH.

MACH is heavily based on lazy evaluation, meaning that you never do anything until it is really needed. One example of this strategy is copy-on-write. Here either a message or part of an address space is not actually copied at the message send time or at address space create time, respectively, but delayed until that message (memory) is actually accessed. On the average this provides excellent performance. The problem is that large amounts of execution time may be required at the *wrong* time to finally perform the copy, causing a task to miss a deadline. Basically, it is unpredictable when slowdowns will occur. Can one eliminate all forms of lazy evaluation to push MACH towards predictability? Yes, but it is difficult because of the overpowering integration of this philosophy in the kernel. Virtual memory is another problem. It is possible to lock pages in memory to remove some of the unpredictability (except, it is nontrivial to decide when to lock and unlock, accounting for the cost of the lock and unlock, and ensuring that the pages are locked in time). Does locking pages, by itself, make the virtual memory part of the system predictable? What about unpredictabilities due to the memory map tables (lookup and maintenance), the MMU TLB entries (present or not), hash table entries used for quick lookup (access time in the table), and indirect problems such as how by locking many pages we might effect the performance of both real-time and non real-time threads needing pages now being drawn from a smaller pool?

Another fundamental problem is that most operating systems want to remove control over resources from the application. These operating systems consider it their prerogative to decide who should get resources for the best average case performance. For example, a multi-level feedback queue will modify the user specified priorities to balance I/O and CPU performance. If a real-time application designer went through torture to map all the complexities of his application into a set of priorities, and if the system adjusts these priorities, then the analysis and evaluation were for naught. Allowing fixed priorities or another real-time scheduling algorithm helps, but insidious interactions from the non real-time threads, through their resource use and scheduling policy, might slow down the real-time tasks (in some unanticipated way).

Given all these problems for RT-UNIX or RT-MACH can they be used in real-time applications? For real-time applications where missing a deadline has *no* severe consequences, priorities can be used. If deadlines must be guaranteed to be met, these operating systems can still be used *if* they are very simple systems and *if* the designers can hand craft a set of priorities that will always work. For example, given 5 independent periodic tasks with certain periods and deadlines, running only these at fixed priorities on these operating systems can easily be shown to work (it would be just as easy to use the proprietary kernels). However, as we add aperiodics, interrupts from the environment, shared data structures, precedence constraints between tasks, non real-time background processing, etc. assigning priorities such that it will always work becomes a nightmare and the designer is still not certain that lurking problems don't exist due to the underlying timesharing design. Such an approach typically has very high cost and is very difficult to maintain because any change requires a new mapping of priorities. New approaches are needed for real-time computing that challenge the basic assumptions made by timesharing operating systems and provide easy re-analysis upon modifications.

4 Research Operating Systems

While many real-time applications will be constructed with commercial real-time operating systems, as mentioned, significant problems still exist. In particular, the commercial offerings emphasize speed rather than predictability, thereby perpetuating the myth that real-time computing is fast computing [19]. Research in real-time operating systems is emphasizing predictability and argues that totally different approaches are required. In this section we will briefly mention two research projects: the MARS kernel which is based on a time driven model (rather than an event driven model), and the CHAOS system which is based on objects, and conclude with a more detailed description of the Spring kernel which is based on integrated, on-line, planning mode schedulers and global replicated memory to support predictable distributed computing.

The MARS kernel [4], [8] offers support for controlling an application based entirely on time events rather than asynchronous events from the environment. Emphasis is placed on an *a priori* design (including static scheduling) and analysis to demonstrate that timing requirements are met. An important feature of this system is that flow control on the maximum number of events that the system handles is automatic and this fact contributes to the predictability analysis. This system is based on a paradigm, i.e., the time driven model, that is different from what is found in timesharing systems.

The CHAOS system [15] represents an object based approach to real-time kernels. This approach allows easy creation of a family of kernels, each tailored to a specific hardware or application. This is important because real-time applications vary widely in their requirements and it would be beneficial to have one basic paradigm for a wide range of applications. The family of kernels is based on a core that supports a real-time threads package. This core is the machine dependent part. Virtual memory regions, synchronization primitives, classes, objects, and invocations all comprise additional support provided in each kernel. This system does not alter the basic paradigm presented by timesharing systems, but rather tries to work within that paradigm. This example system serves to show that some researchers do not agree that a new paradigm is necessary.

The Spring kernel [18] contains real-time support for multiprocessors and distributed systems. It uses on-line, dynamic planning and retains a significant amount of application semantics at run time. These features are integrated to provide direct support for achieving both application and system level predictability. A novel aspect of the work is the integration of real-time cpu scheduling and resource allocation. Another is the use of global replicated memory to achieve predictable distributed communication. The abstractions provided by the Kernel include guarantee, reservation, planning, and end-to-end timing support. Spring, like MARS, presents a new paradigm for real-time operating systems, but unlike MARS (to date), it strives for a more flexible combination of off-line and on-line techniques.

4.1 The Spring Kernel

In the remainder of this paper we focus on three main areas of the Spring kernel: process management, memory management and IPC, and stress how they relate to predictability.

4.1.1 Process Management

Processes are the conventional model seen by the programmer where such things as critical sections, shared memory, and synchronous and asynchronous communication can be used. Collections of processes may be grouped to form a process group with a single timing constraint. This approach enables programmers to use an approach to programming that they are comfortable with and enables the specification of end-to-end timing constraints. However, these programming language abstractions are not convenient for predictable execution because of the unpredictable use of resources and the resulting unbounded and unpredictable blocking that can occur. We use the compiler to transform processes into run time units of execution called tasks which are conducive to predictability. A task is a non-preemptable execution episode of a process with known worst case execution time, resource requirements, value, and timing constraints. A single process is decomposed into a set of tasks (called a task group) with precedence constraints [10]. A process group is transformed into a set of task groups. Once the transformation is complete, each task is completely predictable. The dynamic composition of *predictable tasks* is handled by the on-line planning scheduler [12]. It is important to note that as part of the transformation from processes to tasks, critical sections are eliminated. This is done by identifying resources protected by critical sections and associating those resources with non-preemptable tasks (pieces of a user level defined process). Then, the Spring scheduling algorithm works with these well defined, categorized, and predictable entities called tasks. The scheduler, by planning execution of tasks to avoid resource contention, supports the elimination of critical sections, minimizes context switches, and identifies deadlines that will be missed long before they are actually missed.

Another decision used in Spring is to retain significant application semantics about processes at run time. This enables more intelligent decisions to be made with regard to the actions to take, knowing in advance, that a deadline will be missed. Some of this semantic information is reflected in the information retained for each process.

Processes are characterized by:

1. C (a worst case execution time — this may be a formula that depends on various input data and/or state information pertaining to a specific process invocation)
2. D (Deadline) or period or other real-time constraint
3. preemptive or non-preemptive property
4. maximum number and type of resources needed (this includes memory, ports, etc.)
5. type: critical, essential, or non-essential
6. importance level for essential and non-essential processes
7. incremental process or not (an incremental task computes an initial answer quickly and then continues to refine the answer for the rest of its requested computation time)
8. location of process copies indicating the various nodes in the distributed system and on which processor of each node the process resides,
9. precedence graph (describes the required precedence among tasks in a process group)
10. fault model that indicates what action to take if this process is not guaranteed to make its deadline.

Scheduling is an integral part of the Kernel and the abstraction provided is one of a *currently* guaranteed task set. It is the single most distinguishing feature of the Kernel. Our scheduling approach separates policy from mechanism and is composed of 4 levels. At the lowest level multiple dispatchers exist; one type of dispatcher running on each of the application processors, and another type executing on the system processor. The *application dispatchers* simply remove the next (ready) task from a system task table (STT) that contains previously guaranteed tasks arranged in the proper order for each application processor. The *dispatcher* on the system processor provides for the periodic execution of systems tasks, and asynchronous invocation when it can determine that allowing these extra invocations will not affect guaranteed tasks, or the minimum guaranteed periodic rate of other system tasks. Asynchronous invocation of system tasks are ordered by importance, e.g., the local scheduler is of higher importance than the meta level controller (see below).

The three higher level scheduling modules are executed on the system processor. The second level is a *local scheduler*. The local scheduler on a node is responsible for dynamically *guaranteeing* that, given the current guaranteed task set, a new task or task group can be scheduled locally so as to meet its deadline. This algorithm dynamically composes predictable entities (tasks) into a predictable set of entities (the run time execution plan). It does this by ordering the tasks in the STT to reflect the order of their execution from the current time out into the future and in such a way that each task is guaranteed to meet its deadline (taking timing, resource and task value information into account).

The logic and implementation details involved in this algorithm are major innovations of our work and details can be found in [12], [13], [16]. In contrast, most other real-time scheduling algorithms are myopic and only decide the *next* task to execute. Such algorithms may fail catastrophically on overloads because they have no concept of total system state.

The third scheduling level is the *distributed scheduler* which (under certain conditions, e.g., the laxity of the task is large enough) attempts to find a node for executing any task or components of a task group that have to execute on different nodes [11], because they cannot be locally guaranteed. The fourth level is a *Meta Level Controller* (MLC) which has the responsibility of adapting various parameters or switching scheduling algorithms by noticing significant changes in the environment. These MLC capabilities support some of the adaptability and flexibility needs of next generation real-time systems. The distributed scheduler and MLC are not yet implemented in the Spring Kernel.

Process management primitives include creating a process which loads the executable image and sets up system data structures such as memory maps, PCB, etc. Currently, this is not done under strict time constraints because we would then require a predictable file system. However, once the process is created it then is eligible for hard real-time scheduling and it is predictable. In the current version, we restrict calling the primitive *create_process* to system initialization time and upon mode changes. Other primitives allow the activation (takes an initialized process and hands it to the scheduler) and deactivation (currently, this process is not to be executed but its image and system structures still exist) of a process. Using the activation and deactivation primitives allows periodic and aperiodic processes to be aynchronously scheduled. Two key aspects of the Spring Kernel are the retention of significant amounts of semantic information and flexibility. Use of the *set* primitive, applications can alter any information about a process contained in the PCB. For example, information that can be dynamically changed includes its value, deadline, or fault model. This and other information might vary as a function of system mode and allowing the dynamic updates supports a great degree of flexibility.

4.1.2 Memory Management

Many real-time systems use physical memory techniques in order to facilitate predictability as well as for speed. However, physical memory management has many disadvantages with respect to large, complex real-time systems including difficulty in handling dynamics and protection. The Spring Kernel uses logical memory management to allow for greater protection, dynamic loading, and sharing of portions of address spaces between processes. Logical memory can be implemented in a predictable fashion by using an MMU, but where there are no unexpected page faults (by having the used parts of the address space memory resident).

In Spring, each process has its own logical address space as does the Kernel. A logical address space is supported by using the MMU TLB, partitioned to include the current executing process and the Kernel. In other words, the entire Kernel is always mapped and new process maps are loaded at context switch time. All code and data is memory resident so there is never a page fault. Note that memory management techniques must not introduce erratic delays into the execution time of a task. Since page faults and page replacements in demand paging schemes create large and unpredictable delays, these memory management techniques are not suitable for real-time applications with a need to guarantee timing constraints. The Spring Kernel memory management has three main parts. First, allocating the memory resources is done in a careful manner to support predictability. Such resources are either preallocated or handled via the integrated cpu and resource allocation scheduler. More on this below. Second, memory management primitives exist to create memory pools of various types. For example, pools can contain physical pages, various Kernel data structures such as PCBs and ports, logical address spaces, and pools for variable sized blocks. Access to the pools is predictable. Third, there are a number of low level primitives to support the logical address space in a predictable manner. We now discuss each of these parts.

Using Memory Resources.

Except for the CPU, resources are modeled as memory resources. Many memory resources are created and preallocated at initialization time or mode change. For example, if two tasks of different processes share a data structure in exclusive mode, this data structure becomes a memory resource which is created at initialization time, the same as the tasks. Each of the two tasks is identified as requiring this resource in exclusive mode and the scheduling algorithm uses this resource requirement in its planning. This is a static allocation of resources and a run time guarantee approach. It is also possible to realize the scenario where the resource is not preallocated, but rather allocated at *scheduling* (guarantee) time. This is a dynamic allocation and run time guarantee approach. In this case if the allocation cannot be done due to shortage of the resources, then the task is not guaranteed. Finally, it is possible that a task dynamically creates a new resource. However, for such a task the worst case execution time must include the cost of invoking and executing the allocation primitive (which can execute with a bounded cost). If enough resources are not available, then it is an error and the task making the call should perform some appropriate action. Note that the task still completes by its worst case time, thereby not directly affecting the deadlines of other tasks. When a new resource is created it must be made visible to the scheduler and possibly other tasks. This approach is a dynamic allocation without guarantee for *new* resources. In a complicated hard real-time system, application semantics will require all three approaches to be supported. Initially, we are supporting the first approach. We hope to add the other approaches later.

We also point out that tasks are identified *a priori* to require a maximum number of memory resources of different types, but at activation time a task may request fewer resources. This feature potentially allows more tasks to be guaranteed.

Memory Pools.

Most memory pools are chunks of pre-allocated memory in the Kernel space consisting of a number of fixed-size blocks. Some pools require variable sized blocks, e.g., the graphs describing the process groups and task groups require a size that is dependent on the group size. The purpose of having pools is to support fast, predictable, and dynamic allocation/deallocation of Kernel objects such as PCBs, address translation maps, etc. Predictable primitives for fixed sized pool management include `get_block` and `free_block`. The `get_block` primitive takes a pool's starting address as input and returns a free block's starting address as output. Access time is essentially constant. The `free_block` primitive inserts a block at the head of a pool's free block list. Again, access time is constant. The `init_pool` primitive structures a pool of a particular type of memory resource. The input parameters to this primitive are the starting address of the pool, total number of blocks contained in this pool, the size of each block in bytes, and the alignment requirement of each block. This primitive then initializes the pool header accordingly, and links all the blocks together after aligning them appropriately.

Logical Address Space Support.

Using logical address spaces has a number of advantages including protection, case of supporting mode changes, and dynamic loading. The memory management primitives to support logical address spaces include those necessary to initialize memory maps, set page attributes, map and unmap pages, load maps, configure the MMU, make MMU TLB entries valid and invalid, and flush entries out of the TLB. We emphasize that all of these primitives are used to support logical address spaces, *not* virtual memory. Virtual memory with page faults is highly unpredictable and virtual memory where the application locks only certain pages in memory is still not completely predictable. See again the discussion of this fact in Section 3.

To support predictable logical address spaces our solution combines two basic and simple ideas.

1. Avoid page faults by preallocating, at process creation time, a physical page for every page in a program's address space, and loading that page in me-

mory. This eliminates unpredictability due to page faults.

2. Explicitly manage the contents of the TLB to ensure that all memory references experience TLB hits. This eliminates unpredictability due to TLB misses.

When a context switch occurs, the mappings for all the used pages in the logical address space of a process are loaded into the TLB. The TLB always contains the mappings for the portion of the operating system space required to support process execution; they are never flushed. This solution implies that we never make use of the main memory process maps during execution, again contibuting towards predictability. Of course, this approach increases the cost of a context switch. But, the cost is constrained to occur at the context switch time and is completely predictable. It should be noted that while our context switch time might be higher than is commonly expected, other approaches still pay for loading the TLB, however, that cost is not attributed to the context switch time but rather accumulated in a more dynamic fashion as pages are accessed.

Some of the other logical address space primitives are similar to those found in non real-time systems. This includes configuring the MMU which occurs at system initialization time, and initializing maps and setting page attributes which occur at process creation time. Page attributes can also be dynamically changed.

4.1.3 Interprocess Communication

In conventional systems, IPC is often unpredictable due to the potentially unlimited blocking time of applications synchronizing or waiting for messages. Complemented by our process to task mapping techniques and the scheduling approach, our IPC subsystem is distinct in that it provides predictable and bounded synchronous communication in a hard real-time environment. The Spring IPC mechanism provides a relatively conventional interface with message-passing using ports, but a significantly unconventional implementation that supports predictable real-time communication. Ports are kernel-protected memory objects (and their associated control information) that hold units of data called *messages*. Processes can communicate with each other by placing messages into ports and removing messages from ports. Ports have bounded capacity for predictability, and programmer-specifiable overflow and queueing policies. Messages have fixed sizes, and strict copy-by-value semantics. Messages can have *deadlines* that determine when they must be delivered to a port.

Ports and messages are *typed* in two ways, both based on the kind of communication employed.

The components of the type are:

1. *Task Type*. This mirrors the types available to tasks: critical, essential, soft real-time, or non real-time. This is in order to prevent non-guaranteed tasks from affecting guaranteed tasks' timing properties.

2. *Semantic Type.* This describes how messages in a port are to be used. These types are asynchronous, synchronous, request, and reply.

In distributed communication, a *connection* must be established between the sender and receiver, in order for two processes to communicate. The connection is the network bandwidth required to *send* to the port. Thus, it is the sending side that must provide the connection. We have identified two types of communication abstractions [2] to cater to the needs of the system.

Real-time virtual circuits (RTVC's) are dedicated channels that guarantee network access within a bounded amount of time. RTVC's are generally used by hard real-time tasks, and are allocated appropriately. Critical tasks have their RTVC's pre-allocated at system boot time; essential tasks have their RTVC's allocated at guarantee time.

Real-time datagrams (RTDG's) are communication channels that provide network access on a *best efforts* basis. RTDG's attempt to deliver a message within its deadlines, but no guarantee is made. RTDG's are used by soft and non real-time tasks, and are allocated at run time.

The primitives we provide to the programmer are the following:

1. *Asynchronous Send and Receive.* The sender does not wait for the receiver, and also does not wait to see if the message can be queued at the destination port; a receiver does not wait if no messages are available. Messages sent have a *deadline* that they *should* be delivered by.
2. *Synchronous Send and Receive.* The source process suspends after a send until the destination process performs a receive on the port and dequeues the message. The message sent has a *deadline* that it must be delivered by.

The sender of a message specifies a deadline — this is the time by which the IPC system should deliver the message. The delivery is guaranteed to arrive on time for synchronous communication involving hard real-time tasks. For asynchronous communication the system does its best to deliver the *message* on time. However, note that the deadlines of the individual hard real-time tasks are still guaranteed.

We also provide *request-response* primitives, but do not describe them here due to space limitations. It should suffice to say that request-response is a higher-level abstraction that can typically be constructed using synchronous send and receive.

Mapping Processes to Tasks.

The issue of mapping processes to tasks arises in interprocess communication. Synchronous communication conventionally implies that a task can be blocked for an indefinite period. For hard real-time tasks, unpredictable blocking can obviously not be allowed. To overcome this, we take advantage of the semantics of communication and the Spring system paradigm, mapping *processes* to *tasks*. To review, processes are the conventional process model abstraction seen by the programmer. Tasks are the units of execution that are scheduled and run by the Spring system. Synchronous communication in hard real-time tasks require recognition by the compiler and support in the scheduler.

A group of programs that cooperate and communicate among themselves form a *process group*. Each process is be decomposed into tasks that have precedence constraints attached to them. The precedence constraints allow the scheduler to construct a schedule that, if feasible, will guarantee that the entire process group will complete on time. In the distributed case, before any task of a process group is run, the local scheduler knows the execution plan of each task in the entire process group and their allocated communication channels.

Thus, at run-time, if a guaranteed task performs a synchronous receive, the scheduler knows *when* to schedule that task such that the message is *guaranteed* to be present. Thus, suspending a process defines a boundary between two tasks. The duration of the suspension time is determined by the scheduler when the process group as a whole is guaranteed.

In addition to compiling code, the Spring Compiler Environment, called The *Software Generation System* (SGS), identifies the correspondence between matching synchronous primitives within a process group. Information is passed between the SGS and the scheduler so that the scheduler can identify the precedence constraints between tasks.

Restrictions on Synchronous Communication.

Since synchronous communication affects scheduling decisions made for guaranteed tasks, we must maintain some restrictions on use of the synchronous IPC primitives. For example, we cannot allow a non-guaranteed task to communicate synchronously with a guaranteed task, as it would make the guaranteed task unpredictable. We cannot even allow a critical hard real-time task to synchronously communicate with an essential task. Because essential tasks are guaranteed dynamically, there is no *a priori* guarantee that any essential task will *ever* execute.

Thus, we must restrict synchronous communication in hard real-time tasks such that only tasks of the same type can synchronously communicate. In other words, critical tasks can only use synchronous communication with other critical tasks. Essential tasks may communicate synchronously only with other essential tasks. We do not need to restrict synchronous communication between soft and non real-time tasks, as they do not affect scheduling decisions.

We have implemented the IPC primitives using Systran's Scramnet distributed globally shared memory architecture [21] as a platform for our distributed system. Scramnet is a replicated global shared memory architecture that uses a fiber optic register insertion ring, running at 150 Mbits/sec. Each node has 2 MB of shared common memory, and writes to this memory are broadcast (circulated) about the ring by hardware. The main advantages of using a global shared memory architecture are that implementation of IPC primitives is easy (there are no levels of protocol stacks) and the resultant IPC is predictable. We are currently trying to exploit the global replicated memory for distributed scheduling and fault tolerance. It is also possible to scale the architecture for high performance computing by creating a 2-dimensional grid of rings where each node is connected to two rings [20]. We will not discuss this option here since our current configuration has only one fiber optic register insertion ring with 2 Mbytes of replicated memory.

5 Summary

Most critical, real-time computing systems require that many competing requirements be met including hard and soft real-time constraints, fault tolerance, protection, and security requirements [19]. In this list of requirements, the real-time requirements have received the least formal attention. We believe that it is necessary to raise the real-time requirements to a central, focusing issue. This includes the need to formally state the metrics and timing requirements (which are usually dynamic and depend on many factors including the state of the system), and to subsequently be able to show that the system indeed meets the timing requirements. Achieving this goal is non-trivial and will require research breakthroughs in many aspects of system design and implementation. For example, good design rules and constraints must be used to guide real-time system developers so that subsequent implementation and *analysis* can be facilitated. Programming language features must be tailored to these rules and constraints, must limit their features to enhance predictability, and must provide the ability to specify timing, fault tolerance and other information for subsequent use at run time. Execution time of each primitive of the Kernel must be bounded, and the operating system should provide explicit support for meeting application level requirements including the real-time requirements. More work is required in many areas of real-time operating systems including scheduling, I/O, predictable IPC, and robustness. The hardware must also adhere to the rules and constraints and be simple enough so that predictable timing information can be obtained, e.g., caching, memory refresh and wait states, pipelining, and some complex instructions all contribute to timing analysis difficulties. An insidious aspect of critical real-time systems, especially with respect to the real-time requirements, is that the weakest link in the entire system can undermine careful design and analysis at other levels. Research is required to address all of these issues in an integrated fashion.

6 Appendix — A Partial List of Research Questions

Although there are many research projects on real-time operating systems many open questions remain.

A partial list of such questions is as follows:

1. How deterministic can or should the OS be?
2. How can the OS support predictable distributed communication?
3. What support should be provided for end-to-end timing constraints, fault tolerance, safety, security, etc.?
4. How fault tolerant should the kernel itself be?
5. Can a timesharing interface to an OS be made suitable for hard real-time with proper implementation?
6. Should a real-time OS be seamless (from a micro-kernel all the way up to a large OS)?
7. What support is needed for monitoring, clock synchronization, etc.?
8. Is a local memory or shared memory model more suitable for multiprocessor architectures?
9. How can we exploit distributed shared memory and/or replicated global memory (sometimes called reflected memory)?
10. What are the correct interfaces to robotics, RTAI, Vision, high speed networking, multimedia, etc.?
11. Are standards appropriate for real-time OSs at this time?
12. Where is an OS (and architecture) impacted by the need to design for worst case rather than average case?
13. Where is an OS (and architecture) impacted by the need to design for the most important case rather than the most frequent [7]?
14. What functionality should be in the OS level and what in the application level?
15. Is a microkernel a good idea and if so what mechanisms and functionality should be in the microkernel?
16. What abstractions should be supported by a real-time kernel (e.g., real-time POSIX is considered unsuitable by many researchers, but what is missing? Do the correct abstractions include deadlines explicitly, guarantee, reservation, and fault tolerance?)?
17. Where is the dividing line between policy and mechanism and should the notion of separating policy and mechanism be applied to all functions in the kernel?
18. What should be the unit(s) of execution (independent tasks versus groups of tasks all at various granularities)?
19. Can object oriented real-time OSs be effective; are they the next generation operating system?

7 Acknowledgments

Many students have worked on various parts of the Spring Project including the Kernel. I wish to thank
K. Arvind, S. Biyabani, V. Cheng, M. Decao, E. Gene, M. Kuan, L. Molesky, E. Nahum, D. Niehaus, C. Shen, P. Shiah, F. Wang, W. Zhao, and G. Zlokapa.

I would especially like to thank Prof. Ramamritham for co-directing the project with me for many years.

References

1. L. Alger and J. Lala, *Real-Time Operating System For A Nuclear Power Plant Computer*, Proc. 1986 Real-Time Systems Symposium, December 1986.

2. K. Arvind, K. Ramamritham and J. Stankovic, *A Local Area Network Architecture for Communication in Distributed Real-Time Systems*, Real-Time Systems, Vol. 3, No. 2, May 1991.

3. S. Biyabani, J. Stankovic and K. Ramamritham, *The Integration of Criticalness and Deadline In Scheduling Hard Real-Time Tasks*, Real-Time Systems Symposium, December 1988.

4. A. Damm, J. Reisinger, W. Schnakel and H. Kopetz, *The Real-Time Operating System of Mars*, Operating Systems Review, July 1989, 141–157.

5. B. Furht, D. Grostick, D. Gluch, G. Rabbat, J. Parker and M. Roberts, *Real-Time Unix Systems*, Kluwer Academic Publishers, Norwell, Massachusetts, 1991.

6. V. P. Holmes, D. Harris, K. Piorkowski and G. Davidson, *Hawk: An Operating System Kernel for a Real-Time Embedded Multiprocessor*, Sandia National Labs Report, 1987.

7. D. Jensen, *The Kernel Computational Model of the Alpha Real-Time Distributed Operating System*, in Mission Critical Operating Systems, edited by A. Agrawala, K. Gordon and P. Hwang, IOS Press, 1992.

8. H. Kopetz, A. Demm, C. Koza and M. Mulozzani, *Distributed Fault Tolerant Real-Time Systems*, IEEE Micro, February 1989, 25–40.

9. L. Molesky, C. Shen and G. Zlokapa, *Predictable Synchronization Mechanisms for Real-Time Systems*, Real-Time Systems, Vol. 2, No. 3, September 1990, 163–180.

10. D. Niehaus, *Program Representation and Translation for Predictable Real-Time Systems*, Proc. Real-Time Systems Symposium, Dec. 1991.

11. K. Ramamritham, J. Stankovic and W. Zhao, *Distributed Scheduling of Tasks With Deadlines and Resource Requirements*, IEEE Transactions on Computers, Vol. 38, No. 8, August 1989, 1110–1123.

12. Ramamritham, K., J. Stankovic, and P. Shiah, *Efficient Scheduling Algorithms for Real-Time Multiprocessor Systems*, IEEE Transactions on Parallel and Distributed Systems, Vol. 1, No. 2, April 1990, 184–194.

13. Ramamritham, K. and J. Stankovic, *Scheduling Results in the Spring Project*, Chapter in Foundations in Real-Time Computing: Scheduling and Resource Management, editor Andre van Tilborg, Kluwer Academic Publishers, 1991.

14. J. Ready, *VRTX: A Real-Time Operating System for Embedded Microprocessor Applications*, IEEE Micro, August 1986, 8–17.

15. K. Schwan, A. Geith and H. Zhou, *From Chaos^{base} to Chaos^{arc}: A Family of Real-Time Kernels*, Proc. 1990 Real-Time Systems Symposium, December 1990, 82–91.

16. C. Shen, K. Ramamritham and J. Stankovic, *Resource Reclaiming in Real-Time*, Proc. Real-Time System Symposium, December 1990, 41–50.

17. J. Stankovic and K. Ramamritham, *The Spring Kernel: A New Paradigm for Real-Time Operating Systems*, ACM Operating Systems Review, Vol. 23, No. 3, July 1989, 54–71.

18. J. Stankovic and K. Ramamritham, *The Spring Kernel: A New Paradigm for Hard Real-Time Operating Systems*, IEEE Software, May 1991, 62–72.

19. J. Stankovic, *Misconceptions About Real-Time Computing*, IEEE Computer, Vol. 21, No. 10, October 1988.

20. J. Stankovic, *SpringNet: A Scalable Architecture For High Performance, Predictable, Distributed, Real-Time Computing*, Univ. of Massachusetts, Technical Report, 91–74, October 1991.

21. SYSTRAN Corporation, *Scramnet Network Reference Manual*, Dayton, Ohio, 45432.

22. H. Tokuda and C. Mercer, *ARTS: A Distributed Real-Time Kernel*, ACM Operating Systems Review, Vol. 23, No. 3, July, 1989.

Synchronization Techniques, Illustrated by the Concepts of the Dependable Distributed Operating System DEDOS

D.K. Hammer

Department of Mathematics and Computing Science
Eindhoven University of Technology
P.O. Box 513, 5600 MB Eindhoven, The Netherlands

Abstract

This article gives an overview of the most important synchronization issues in real-time systems in general and in distributed systems in particular. Special attention is paid to static (deterministic) methods and the role of distributed algorithms. Many of the concepts discussed are illustrated with concepts of the Dependable Distributed Operation System (DEDOS), which is presently under development at the Department of Computing Science of the EUT. It is shown that synchronization is one of the most important issues in concurrent and distributed real-time systems.

Keywords:
Atomic Objects, Dependability, Distributed Control Systems, Distributed Operating Systems, Distributed Systems, Hard Real-Time, Object-Orientated Systems, Static (deterministic) Scheduling, Synchronization.

1 Introduction

1.1 General

The first question to ask is: why is synchronization so important in modern real-time systems? The importance of synchronization has several reasons. First of all, many modern real-time systems are designed for the control of distributed processes and are usually distributed themselves: distribution, however, implies parallelism. Second, such systems usually have high dependability (for a definition see [16] requirements and dependability implies predictability. Finally, in order to build real-time systems with a high degree of parallelism and predictability, synchronization of the various activities is absolutely necessary. If we go one step further and consider also timeliness requirements, we see that the synchronization concepts must include time-boundedness, i.e. must be synchronous. The next question is how synchronization in parallel and distributed systems is implemented. The general approach is to achieve a certain type of consensus between the various participating peer entities like processors, processes, threads, executions, etc. If several objects (processors or processes) are involved, this has the big advantage that there is no single point of failure and the algorithm can be made resilient with respect to certain types of failures. The goal is always the handling of the various sources of non-determinism in order to achieve some global temporal ordering of events.

In order to make this point clear I would like to make a distinction between distributed control systems and distributed computer systems, as shown in figure 1. *Distributed control systems* focus on cooperation and coordination in order to achieve a common goal. Consequently, the synchronization is global and directly affects the application semantics. This is the class of systems considered in this paper. *Distributed processing systems* on the other hand, include all types of general purpose execution platforms, like the ones that can typically be found in an Open Systems Interconnection (OSI) environment. The various tasks are not necessarily related and the emphasis with respect to distribution is on connectivity and bandwidth. The various communication protocols only ensure a local ordering of events, i.e. an ordering that usually only affects the two communication partners. In addition, this ordering is often restricted to the communication subsystem and not necessarily visible at application level. In practice, of course, there is a large grey area between these two basic types of distributed systems.

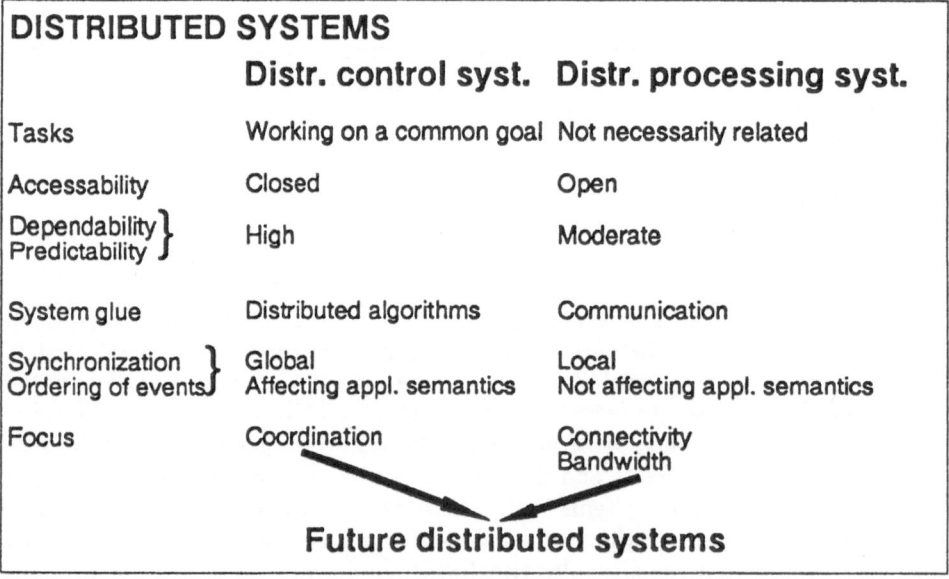

Fig. 1. The two basic types of distributed systems.

With respect to the level in the system where synchronization takes place, no particular distinction can be made. Figure 2 shows that synchronization is necessary at all levels of abstraction, i.e. at all levels of the system hierarchy. The layer structure of figure 2 is inspired by the DEDOS system summarized in chapter 1.2, but similar structures can be found in many other distributed systems.

The various synchronization facilities often have a hierarchical dependency themselves, i.e. higher-level constructs are implemented by means of lower-level ones. Standard examples are (1) the implementation of semaphores by means of interrupt disable commands in single-processor systems and by atomic instructions in multi-processor systems, (2) the implementation of monitors, (conditional) critical regions and rendez-vous by means of semaphores and (3) the distributed algorithm hierarchy described by Cristian [7], namely datagram/multicast service, clock synchronization, atomic broadcast, membership service and availability management service. Note that the DEDOS protocol hierarchy is implemented more efficiently, because the membership service is based on failure messages from lower-level facilities and the role of membership service and atomic multicast can be reversed. A detailed description of the DEDOS protocol hierarchy can be found in [25].

At the *hardware level* we find primitive hardware synchronization facilities, like logical gates, atomic, i.e. indivisible, instructions (e.g. atomic read/write registers, Test-and-Set instructions or Register-Swap instructions), priority interrupts, cache consistency algorithms, communication protocols (e.g. Medium Access Control (MAC) protocols), etc.. Up to the level of indivisible instructions, the synchronization times are so short that busy waiting (for the synchronization to take place) is the prevalent method. All higher level synchronization facilities are usually based on passive waiting, i.e. on some form of context switching between the various concurrent activities.

At the *Local Operation System (LOS) level* we find the typical synchronization facilities of a real-time kernel, namely (1) interrupt handling, performing the synchronization with the periphery and (2) semaphores and primitive Inter-Process Communication (IPC) services for the synchronization of concurrent tasks or activities. The latter usually is a form of a Data-Gram (DG) service.

The next three layers implement a Distributed Operating System (DOS). The main task of these layers is the management of distributed resources in such a way that the distributed nature of the system is transparent for the application in terms of resource location, concurrent resource access, resource migration, resource replication, resource failures and system size (scaling) (see [26]).

The *integration layer* contains the distributed algorithms that are necessary to glue the different processors or nodes of the system together. Clock synchronization is the first thing that is necessary to achieve a total ordering of events in time and to implement synchronous distributed algorithms. Once we have that, (1) a membership service can be implemented, based on the failure messages of lower-level facilities and (2) synchronous or asynchronous communication services can be provided, e.g. in the form of Remote Procedure Calls (RPC). Finally an Atomic Multi-Cast (AMC) service can be constructed, which is a necessity for the correct implementation of various systems services, like naming

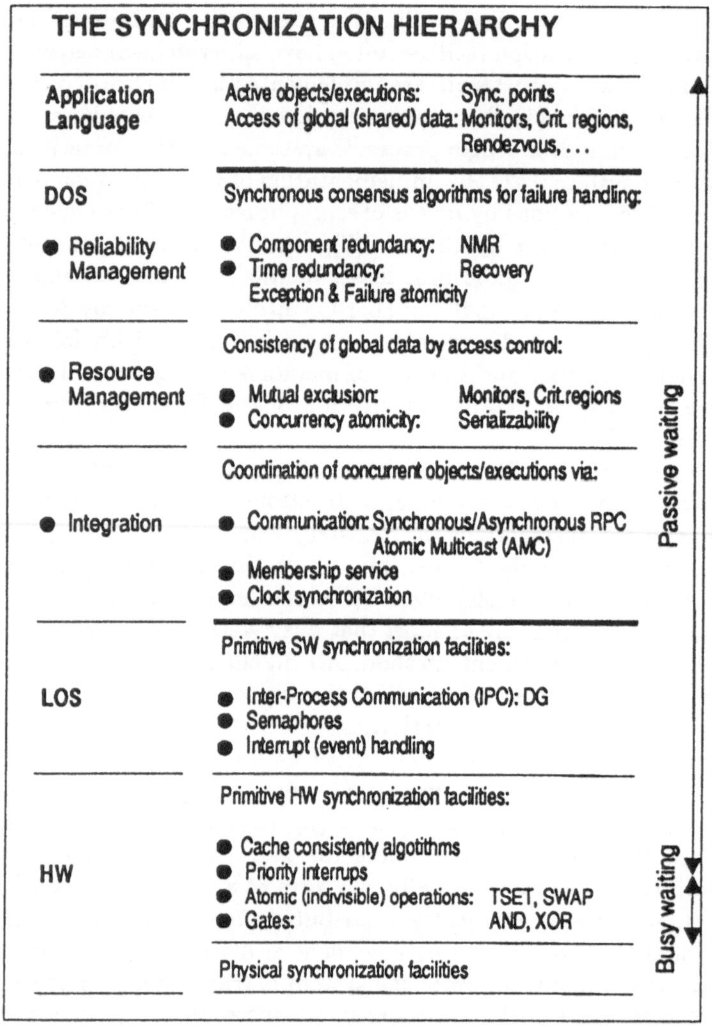

THE SYNCHRONIZATION HIERARCHY

Application Language	Active objects/executions: Sync. points Access of global (shared) data: Monitors, Crit. regions, Rendezvous, . . .
DOS	Synchronous consensus algorithms for failure handling:
● Reliability Management	● Component redundancy: NMR ● Time redundancy: Recovery Exception & Failure atomicity
	Consistency of global data by access control:
● Resource Management	● Mutual exclusion: Monitors, Crit.regions ● Concurrency atomicity: Serializability
	Coordination of concurrent objects/executions via:
● Integration	● Communication: Synchronous/Asynchronous RPC Atomic Multicast (AMC) ● Membership service ● Clock synchronization
	Primitive SW synchronization facilities:
LOS	● Inter-Process Communication (IPC): DG ● Semaphores ● Interrupt (event) handling
	Primitive HW synchronization facilities:
HW	● Cache consistenty algotithms ● Priority interrups ● Atomic (indivisible) operations: TSET, SWAP ● Gates: AND, XOR
	Physical synchronization facilities

Passive waiting ↑

Busy waiting ↕

Fig. 2. A typical synchronization hierarchy of a distributed system. The three main layers are shown, namely the Hardware (HW), the Local Operating System (LOS) and the Distributed Operating System (DOS) level, with examples of typical synchronization facilities belonging to the different sublayers.

(i.e. the translation of logical into physical names), fault tolerance by N-Modular Redundancy (NMR) and availability management.

The main synchronization problems to be solved at the *resource management layer* are related to the consistency of concurrently accessed global objects. The simplest mechanism, of course, is mutual exclusion by some form of locking. This method, however, has the danger of provoking deadlocks and restricts parallel resource accesses, because of its pessimistic concurrency control strategy. A more convenient way, however, is to tackle the problem at a higher level of abstraction. This can be done by supporting concurrency atomic objects (see capter 2.2) that serialize concurrent accesses by means of an optimistic concurrency control scheme, like multi-version time-stamping.

Finally, the *reliability management layer* implements various fault tolerance mechanism by means of synchronous distributed consensus algorithms. The redundancy necessary to tolerate failures has one of two forms:

- *Component redundancy* is used for *static fault tolerance* or failure masking by means of N-modular redundancy techniques. As already mentioned, the input messages are usually distributed between the replicated objects by means of an atomic multicast service. For the selection of, and the voting between the different input messages, various distributed algorithms exist, depending on the fault hypothesis. Another interesting problem is the synchronization of the replicated objects in the presence of various sources of non-determinism, like multi-receive statements in combination with variable message delays, preemption, scheduling delays and imprecise computations.
- *Time redundancy* achieves *dynamic fault tolerance* by means of failure recovery techniques. This is implemented by splitting executions into atomic transactions that operate on atomic objects. Two types of atomicity are relevant here: (1) exception atomicity that has relatively low implementation costs because it is assumed that the memory has no permanent failures and (2) failure atomicity that provides resilience against all types of crash failures, but depends on the availability of stable storage [17]. An introduction to the synchronization techniques and protocols used for atomic transactions can be found in [4], in [3], in [5] and in [17]. The synchronization aspects of atomicity are further elaborated in chapter 2.2.

As mentioned before, the services of a distributed operating system are provided in a more or less transparent way, i.e. the abstraction that is provided to an application is that of a virtual uni-processor system [26]. Although various types of synchronization are performed by the distributed operating system, the application needs its own synchronization facilities as well. If the abstractions provided by the distributed operating system are chosen well, these facilities can be relatively simple, like the atomic objects of the DEDOS system (see figure 9). The problems to be solved are essentially the same as in lower layers, namely the synchronization of concurrent objects or executions (activities) and the consistency of global (shared) data. The necessary facilities should, of course, be embedded into a high-level application language. Since many contemporary embedded real-time systems are, however, written in sequential languages, like C,

C++ and RTL, the synchronization facilities must be provided by the run-time system.

After heaving dealt with the question why synchronization is necessary and how it is implemented at the various levels of a distributed system, chapter 2 will treat a number of basic questions about synchronization. Namely: what are the right entities to be synchronized and what are the synchronization dimensions. Chapter 3 finally treats a number of important synchronization issues in more detail. There are, however, so many issues in this field that only some of them can be discussed. The choice of subjects represents the personal interest of the author. This choice is also inspired by the DEDOS system that illustrates many of the issues treated in this paper. The next paragraph gives a short overview about the most important design principles of DEDOS.

1.2 The DEDOS system

DEDOS (Dependable Distributed Operating System) [11] that is presently under development at the Eindhoven University of Technology (EUT), has the following aims:

- Provide a transparent execution platform for distributed embedded systems, as e.g. used in Computer Integrated Manufacturing (CIM), avionics, copying machines and telecommunication equipment.
- Support of dependability for critical applications. At the moment the effort is mainly concentrated on the support of timeliness and reliability.
- Support of an object-oriented programming model, that allows the specification of distribution as well as the specification of timeliness and reliability constraints.
- Provide an experimentation environment. Before a real system can be envisaged, many problems with the efficient integration of the various aspects must be solved. Among the most important issues are: integration of hard- and soft real-time facilities, hard/soft real-time synchronization, compatibility of the various distributed algorithms, efficient off-line scheduling algorithms and high-level language support.

Central to DEDOS is the so called *dual-dependability paradigm*, a statement about the combination of methods for the support of timeliness and reliability. As already mentioned above, DEDOS distinguishes two types of tasks[1], namely:

- *Hard real-time tasks* that must, within the fault hypothesis, meet their deadlines under all circumstances. In a typical system, only a small minority of all tasks (probably not more than 10%) will be critical.
  The predictability of these tasks is ensured because resource conflicts are avoided by means of static (deterministic) scheduling [29]. Of course, this strategy is only possible, if the number of executions is fixed and iterations

---

[1] This partition of DEDOS essentially coincides with the notion of an event-driven and a time-driven system as defined in [14].

are bounded: a requirement that is not difficult to meet for most real-time and safety critical control systems. The price for the predictability and static verifiability of the timeliness requirements is the bad resource utilization, i.e. the run-time inefficiency. In addition, this approach is very inflexible and not suited for systems whose configuration changes dynamically[2]. This stems from the fact that everything must be evaluated statically, while the event timings and the values of the guards are only known at run-time: a worst-case strategy must thus be used.

In order to ensure predictability, also in the presence of faults, static (component) redundancy (i.e. NMR-techniques) are used to achieve fault tolerance. As long as the fault hypothesis is met, i.e. as long as the redundancy is not exhausted, the system will continue to work. Note that this is a pessimistic approach, that causes unnecessary overhead for the normal case, i.e. when no faults occur.

– The inefficiency and inflexibility of the static approach is compensated by the ability of DEDOS to support also *soft real-time tasks*. The violation of a soft real-time deadline is not considered catastrophic and is either tolerated or causes a run-time exception.

The scheduling is performed on-line, according to well-known heuristic techniques, like priority scheduling and earliest-deadline-first scheduling. The soft real-time tasks are only allowed to consume resources if these are not utilized by the periodic hard real-time tasks and are preempted by the latter. Soft real-time tasks can be made fault tolerant by means of dynamic redundancy in the form of dynamic reconfiguration, followed by a recovery action. Recoverability is achieved by embedding all activities into transactions. In order to support dynamic reconfiguration, DEDOS supports dynamic process migration and location independent message communication [28]. Note that this approach is optimistic, because for the normal case the only overhead is writing checkpoints to stable storage. The drawback is that rather unpredictable delays can occur in case of a failure.

Note that in DEDOS hard and soft real-time tasks are horizontally integrated, i.e. they coexist on the same level of the system hierarchy and interact by means of the hard/soft real-time synchronization methods described in chapter 3.3. This is different from most other operating systems, like the Spring kernel [22] and the EMPS system [28]. These systems are based on vertical integration, i.e. lower-layer activities (like event and device handling) are supposed to be more critical and timely than higher-level ones. The advantage of horizontal integration is, that the programmer has full control over the timing properties of the system. As already mentioned above, the programming model [12] is object-oriented. At the moment, an extension of C++ , called DEAL (DEDOS Application Language), is used for pragmatic reasons. Based on this experience a high-level language will be defined in the future.

---

[2] One way to make static scheduling techniques more flexible, may be to work with a set of predetermined schedules for different system configurations.

C++ programs are enclosed in process classes, whose interface is defined in terms of import and export statements. Synchronous inter-process communication is supported by remote procedure calls. The communication stubs are derived from the import/export statements and automatically generated by a preprocessor. The programming model is independent from where a process is allocated. Whether remote procedure calls are local or must be sent via the network is thus determined by the global schedule, i.e. the process allocation scheme. As shown in figure 3, a global schedule is automatically generated for hard real-time tasks. At the moment, soft real-time tasks must be manually allocated, because no tools are available yet. Hard real-time executions are started during the initialization phase of the system. Because their number must be fixed, they are started in the main part of a process. Soft real-time executions, on the other hand, can also be dynamically created.

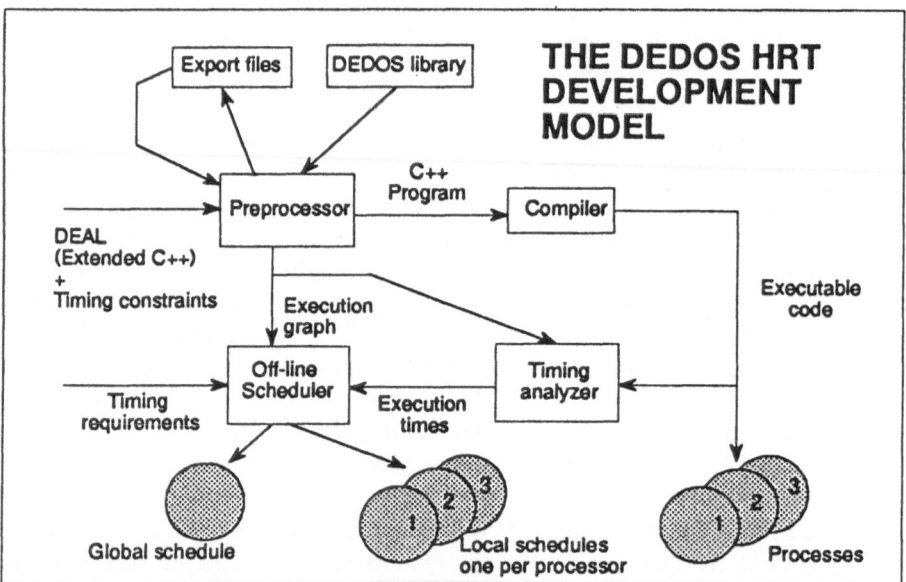

Fig. 3. The DEDOS hard real-time development model.

2 Basic synchronization issues

This chapter gives an overview of the most important synchronization issues. First, the synchronization of concurrent objects versus the synchronization of concurrent executions is discussed. Second, an overview is given about the different types of synchronization and the related synchronization constructs. In a practical system these synchronization types often are used in combination. I therefore prefer to talk about synchronization dimensions, rather than about types.

2.1 Which entities should be synchronized?

The most important choice that has to be made is which entities are subject to synchronization; the two basic possibilities are shown in figure 4. Traditionally, one always considers the synchronization of concurrent objects, like processes and threads [2]. Because these objects describe the static structure of the system and not its activities, this choice is essentially implementation oriented.

The alternative is to concentrate on the synchronization of concurrent dynamic entities or executions, that describe the run-time behavior of the system. Typical representatives of executions, or threads of control respectively, are traces, transactions and execution graphs. The advantage is, that the emphasis now lies on the dynamics of the system, i.e. the domain where synchronization actually takes place. Executions are the entities which actually cause parallelism (quasi-parallelism if they execute on one machine or true parallelism if processor boundaries are crossed), which consume resources and which must be timely. I, therefore, consider this choice to be more problem-oriented than the first one. After all, the user is not so much interested in the structure of the system but in the results of its activities. Of course, it is sometimes advantageous to assign synchronization attributes to static objects: typically, these are integrity constraints, like the atomicity attributes in DEDOS described below. This, however, does not change the fact that synchronization is only realized at run-time and should be made visible in terms of executions.

The choice of the synchronization entities is also important with respect to the specification, design, implementation and verification of the system. Especially for real-time systems, the design of the static and the dynamic system aspects should go hand-in-hand. The use of executions in addition to static entities also has the advantage that the resulting system is better to comprehend and to verify. Unfortunately, at the moment we do not have good methods for the support of such an approach. Most methods concentrate on the static structures of a system. Methods that support the design of the dynamic aspects either do not concentrate on executions (like the Yourdon dataflow analysis [33] and their real-time extensions [13] and [32]) or consider only the implementation level (like the various forms of schedulability analysis [10] and [27]). What we, however, need is top-down refinement of synchronization and timeliness issues by means of top-down refinement of executions. Because of their advantages with respect to software-engineering issues, object-oriented methods [19] are promising candidates for such an extension.

The advantages of synchronizing concurrent executions instead of concurrent objects have been acknowledged in the DEDOS system. According to the dual dependability paradigm outlined in chapter 1.2, a distinction is made between hard real-time and soft real-time executions. Another prominent example of an execution-based design is the Alpha kernel [6]. Figure 5 and figure 6 show some

SYNCHRONIZATION ENTITIES

	Concurrent objects (Processes, threads)	Concurrent executions (Traces, transactions)
Definition	Static	Dynamic
Orientation	Implementation	Problem
Design { comprehensibility verifyability }	Bad	Good { Visibility of: • (Quasi) parallellism • Crossing of boundaries of processes/processors }
Usability for synchronization	Bad	Good { Executions relate objects, consume resources and must be timely }
Design support	Good	Bad

Fig. 4. Synchronization entities.

execution related aspects of the DEDOS programming model. Processes merely define resource spaces (e.g. for addressing, open files and i/o devices) and are the units of protection. Threads are the units of concurrency and provide an environment for executions that enter a process space by means of a remote procedure call[3]. For efficiency reasons, threads are not dynamically created, but allocated from a pool of non-active execution environments. These pools are managed by the receive stubs of the remote procedure call facility, as shown in figure 11.

2.2 Synchronization dimensions

The next subjects of importance are the different sources of non-determinism and the appropriate synchronization techniques for the enforcement of a global event ordering. Since these synchronization techniques are often used in combination, we also talk about synchronization dimensions. The three basic synchronization dimensions are shown in figure 7. They can be characterized as follows:

- *Resource synchronization* is a local property, that assures the consistency of non-replicated common objects that are accessed by multiple executions

---

[3] When an execution temporally leaves an object because of a remote procedure call, the thread is blocked: it is continued when the result of the call is returned.

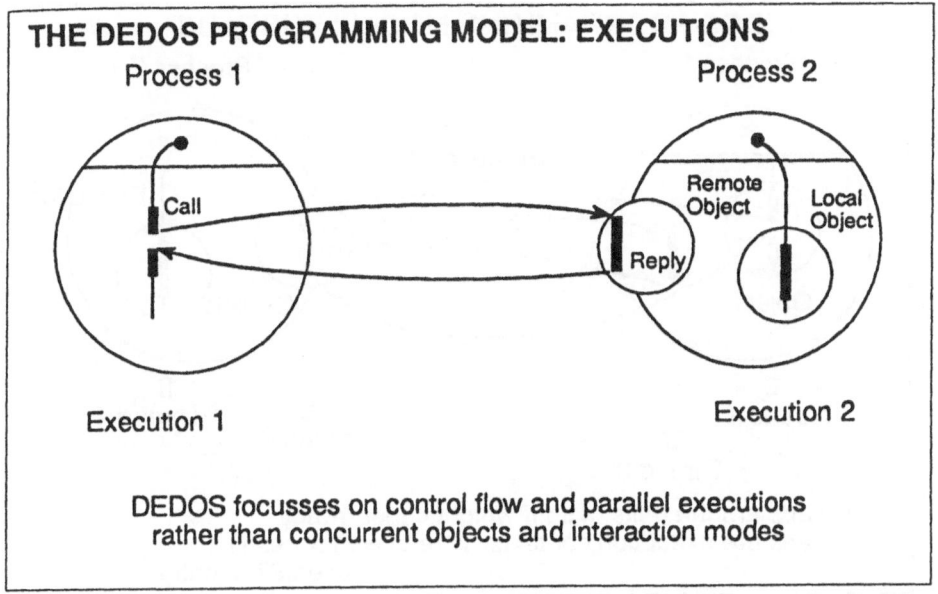

Fig. 5. The DEDOS programming model: Executions.

with particular resource demands and particular relative execution speeds[4]. The commonly used mechanisms to achieve this, like mutual exclusion and concurrency atomicity are exhaustively treated in the literature.

In addition, the consistency of objects must also be assured in case of failures. This is usually achieved by making an object failure atomic. A summary of the various types of atomicity is shown in figure 8.

- *Spatial synchronization* is a global property, that ensures that a distributed system shows predictable behavior despite of unknown remote event sequences and communication delays. Mechanisms like clock synchronization, object-group membership and replica consistency are normally realized with various forms of distributed consensus algorithms. In order to be suited for real-time systems, these algorithms must be synchronous, i.e. have bounded execution times.

- Finally, *temporal synchronization* is used to enforce certain temporal properties in the presence of unknown event timings, message delays and device delays. Typical examples are the obeyance of the timing constraints of executions (e.g. deadlines) and the activation or deactivation of activities

---

[4] For dynamic scheduling techniques, the resource demands and the execution speeds of executions must not necessarily be known. However, in order to use static scheduling techniques and schedulability analysis everything must be known in advance.

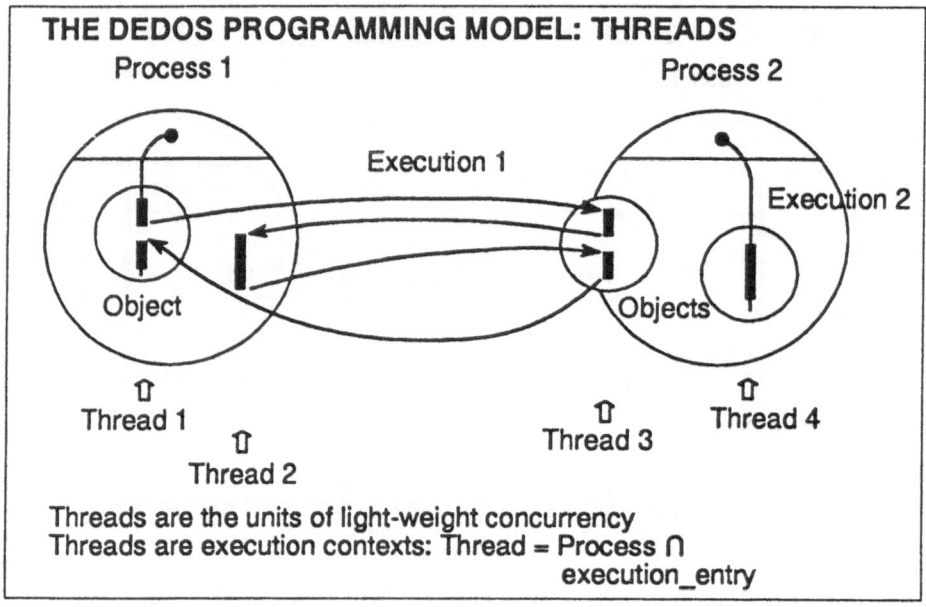

Fig. 6. The DEDOS programming model: Threads.

at particular absolute or relative times. This can be achieved by various forms of scheduling algorithms [23] and [27]. Well-known on-line scheduling strategies are priority scheduling, earliest-deadline-first and rate-monotonic scheduling.

Off-line scheduling techniques have the big advantage, that also resource synchronization properties can be statically enforced. This makes the run time system much simpler, because no extra facilities are necessary, like semaphores and various forms of atomic objects (see also chapter 3.2). In DEDOS, this property is not only exploited for critical applications. It is also used for the construction of system services, like clock synchronization, membership and hard/soft real-time synchronization [25].

The synchronization mechanisms can be either implicit or explicit. In the first case, common objects are atomic with respect to different types of failures. In the second case, various language constructs (like semaphores, monitors and critical regions) are known to ensure the desired properties. Implicit synchronization is performed at a higher level of abstraction, because it is expressed in terms of object attributes and does not need additional language constructs. This makes the program more comprehensive and less error prone. The various possibilities are summarized in figure 8.

```
THE SYNCHRONIZATION DIMENSIONS

Purpose:   Handling of different sources of non-determinism  }
           Ordering of events along different dimensions       } Usually in combination

Problem:   Algorithmic compatibility
           The combination of algorithms should be optimal or at least compatible
```

Type	Reason	Implementation
Resource	Unknown relative execution speeds, resource usage and failure events	Implicit or explicit
	E.g. Mutual exclusion Concurrency atomicity Exception/failure atomicity	E.g. Semaphore, Monitor Concurrency control algorithms Backward recovery
Spatial	Unknown remote event sequences and communication delays	Communication paradigms Synchronous distr. consensus algorithms
	E.g. Membership Replica consistency Clock synchronization	
Temporal	Unknown event timing	Scheduling algorithms
	E.g. obeyance of deadline (de)activation of activities	

Fig. 7. The synchronization dimensions.

Resource synchronization for common objects can come in three forms that ensure consistency under increasingly stronger fault assumptions:

- The handling of parallelism, respectively of non-deterministic execution speeds, can be either implemented by *concurrency atomic* (serializable) objects or by the usual explicit programming constructs, known from concurrent programming [2].
- If failures occur during the execution of an object-method, the object must be restored to a correct state. If these failures do not corrupt the primary memory, the object-state can be efficiently restored by means of checkpoints that have been previously stored in memory. The restoration of a previous consistent state can be hidden from the programmer by the notion of *exception atomic* objects. Otherwise, the programmer must provide an appropriate exception handler.
- The most severe cases are crash failures. The provision of fault tolerance for crash failures is expensive, because the checkpoints must be stored on stable storage [17]. Again, objects can either be made *failure atomic* or the programmer has to provide explicit forward or backward recovery algorithms.

The DEDOS object types and the various attributes that can be given to common objects are shown in figure 9. Of special interest are the scope and the lifetime of objects:

THE SYNCHRONIZATION OF COMMON OBJECT ACCESSES

Problem	Implicit	Explicit
	Atomicity as class attribute	Explicit mechanisms as language constructs
Concurrency	Concurrency atomicity Concurrency control algorithms to achieve serializability	Mutual exclusion Locks, semaphores Monitors, critical regions
Recoverable failures (No memory failures)	Exception atomicity Automatic restoration of a correct state	Exception handlers User programmed restoration of a correct state
Crash failures	Failure atomicity Use of stable storage	Fwd./Bwd. recovery

Fig. 8. The synchronization of global object accesses.

- *Local objects* are used by only one execution. Their lifetime is subject to the scope rules of the application language[5], i.e. the lifetime of a local object starts when an execution enters its scope and ends when the execution leaves the scope.
- *Global objects* are shared between several executions and have the lifetime of the embedding process (that created them and also owns them). In order to relieve the programmer from cumbersome details and to provide him with high-level facilities, all synchronization features are indirectly defined in terms of atomic objects. These can have one of the following attributes:

  - The *system attribute* denotes special system objects, like file descriptors, timers, communication ports, i/o devices and so-called synchronization objects. The latter allow the synchronization of several executions by means of *timed precedence constraints* [30]. System objects are always concurrency atomic.
  - The *atomic attribute* denotes objects that are concurrency atomic as well as exception atomic. These two attributes have been combined, because in a reliable distributed system most executions will be defined in terms of transactions. Transactions, in turn, imply both types of atomicity.

---

[5] For DEDOS at the moment this is extended C++ as described in chapter 1.2.

- Finally, the *recoverable attribute* denotes failure atomic objects that must be supported by stable storage. Failure atomicity has been combined with concurrency atomicity for the reasons given above.

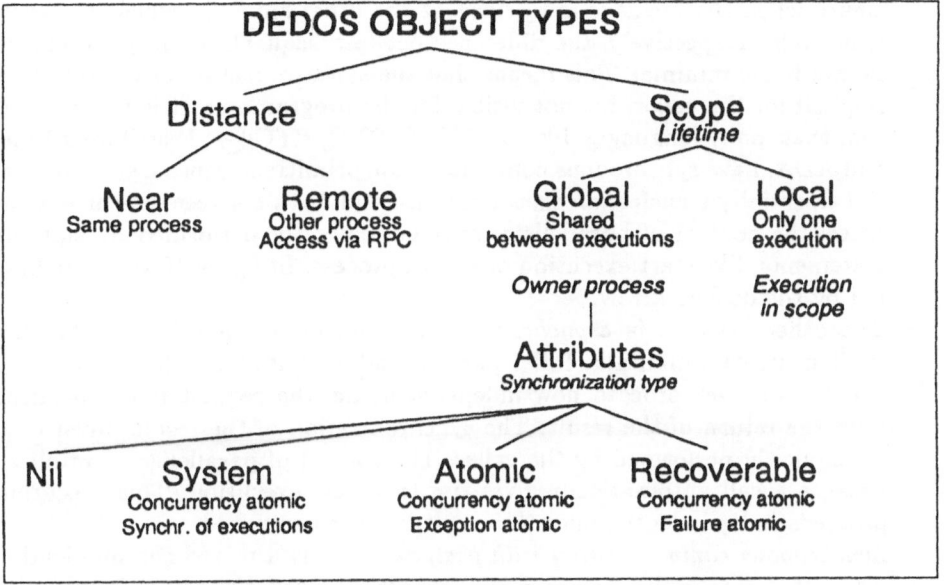

Fig. 9. The DEDOS object types.

3 Synchronization methods

This chapter discusses a number of issues that are important with respect to functional and temporal synchronization. Resource synchronization is well known and is therefore not explicitly treated here.

3.1 Spatial synchronization

Spatial synchronization has many aspects. In this context I will, however, only address two important ones: synchronization of concurrent objects or executions by means of communication and distributed consensus algorithms. These methods are used for the synchronization of two or several entities respectively.

Communication is the mechanism for the synchronization of two concurrent objects or executions. The communication paradigms that are available in a particular system are thus of prime importance. An overview of the basic possibilities is given in figure 10:

— The main advantage of *synchronous communication* primitives is, that they make programs simpler and more comprehensive. Since the sender only continues when the message is received at the other side[6], or when the result is available respectively, the difference between sequential and parallel programming is minimal. This means that the synchronization of the results is implicit for the caller, i.e. not visible for the programmer. It is for this reason, that many languages, like CCS/CSP, RPC, RTC++, Distributed Eiffel and ADA, have synchronous communication primitives. Since a synchronous call essentially transfers an execution back and forth between concurrent entities, the control of parallelism must be explicitly performed by suitable statements, like start execution or spawn process. In figure 10 this is indicated by the dashed arrow.
— The other extreme is *asynchronous communication*, that is available e.g. in Concurrent Smalltalk, Eiffel parallel and Distributed Eiffel. The caller and the receiver proceed now independent, i.e. the request is independent from the return of the result. The synchronization of the results must thus be explicitly performed by the caller. The control of parallelism is implicit, because a call automatically gives rise to a new execution. This execution proceeds independently, once the result has been returned.
— *Synchronous communication with postprocessing* is a mixed communication form, that implicitly spawns a new execution when the result is returned to the caller. The control of parallelism is thus implicit. As for synchronous communication, the synchronization of the result is not visible for the caller and is thus implicit.

Most languages support either synchronous or asynchronous communication. In the future, there might, however, be more languages that, similar to Distributed Eiffel, support several paradigms in order to allow the modeling of the controlled environment in a natural way. Typically, there are activities that are started while the starting entity continues with its current task: the results are only collected at some later point in time, whenever it is convenient. Other activities may depend on the results of a service and must thus wait until the service is finished and the results are returned.

Note that the synchronization of executions must always be performed via objects. In DEDOS this is done by calling a method of a special system object, called *synchronization object*. At the moment, DEDOS only supports synchronous communication via remote procedure calls. As shown in figure 11, the communication is performed via mailboxes in common memory in order to be location

---

[6] The precise semantic of received, i.e. whether the message is received by the network processor, buffered for processing or actually transferred to the application program, depends on the operating system.

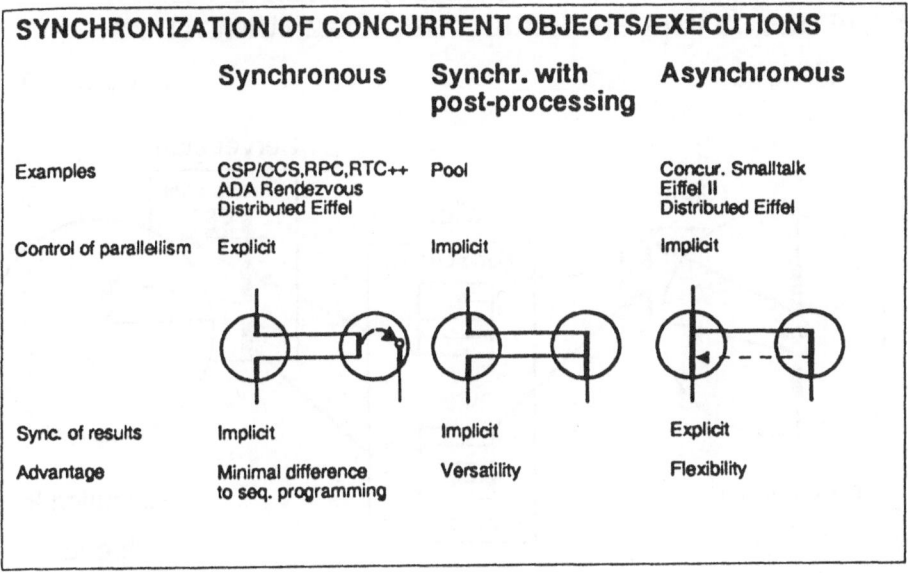

Fig. 10. Synchronization of concurrent objects or executions by means of communication.

independent and efficient. Details about the protocols and their implementation can be found in [28].

In real-time systems synchronization of several entities is performed by means of *synchronous distributed consensus algorithms*. It is beyond the scope of this article to give an overview of distributed algorithms. More details can be found in [20] and in [8]. It is, however, interesting to address some general issues that play an important role in distributed real-time systems:

– The most important problem is that distributed algorithms tend to be inefficient. Their performance typically is exponentially decreasing with the size of the membership group. There are several obvious ways to overcome this problem: It is possible e.g. to split the members (concurrent objects or executions) into overlapping subsets and to construct a hierarchy of algorithms. In broadcast networks, advantage can be taken of the possibility to send the result of a computation to several members.

The performance of distributed algorithms also critically depends on the fault hypothesis to be supported. Many algorithms are known that are resilient with respect to the most general type of faults, byzantine failures[7]: these algorithms, however, are very inefficient. One way to circumvent the

---

[7] Usually only hardware and environmental faults are considered, i.e. software failures are excluded. The underlying assumption is that the correctness of the software

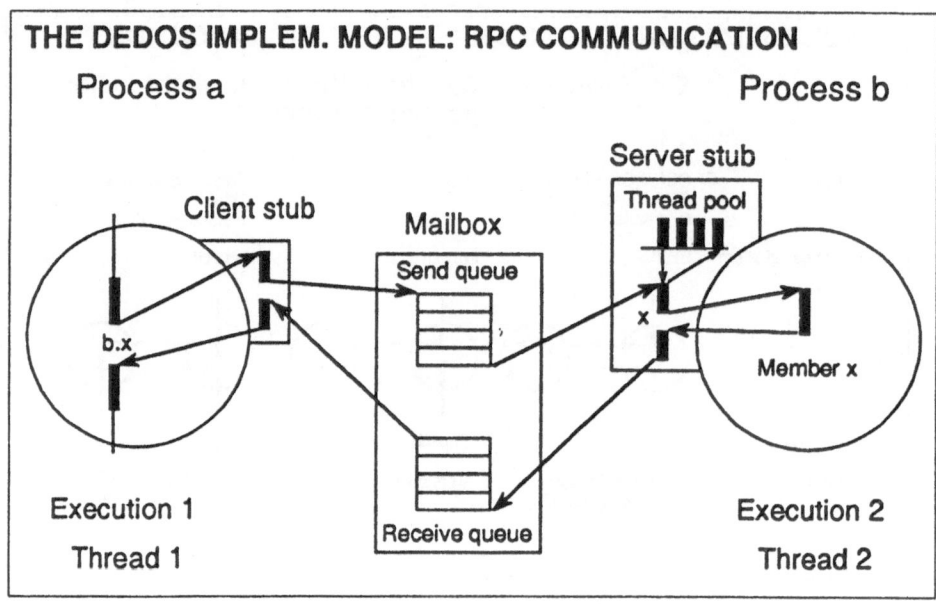

Fig. 11. The DEDOS implementation model: Synchronous communication via Remote Procedure Calls.

problem of byzantine hardware failures is the use of fail-stop memories and processors. Because this involves some form of self-checking, such a facility is, however, expensive to implement. Fortunately, there are many non safety-critical distributed real-time systems where the fault hypothesis can be relaxed to include e.g. only crash failures and timing failures[8]. An example of a family of synchronous atomic multicast protocols that support increasingly strong fault hypotheses, but not byzantine failures, can be found in [1].

– A general problem is what Le Lann calls the *algorithmic compatibility* issue [15]. Dependable systems must be designed in a multi-dimensional design space that goes beyond the traditional design dimensions like functionality, correctness and price. Therefore careful trade-offs between the different issues are required and especially between the various dependability requirements like performance (timeliness), fault tolerance and security. The problem is that up to now, distributed algorithms are designed for various specialized

---

should be ensured beforehand, e.g. by employing some form of failure prevention by means of formal specification and verification techniques.

[8] If an error detection mechanism is available, mutilation failures can be treated as omission failures, i.e. incorrect messages are discarded. Omission failures, in turn, can be treated as the extreme case of late timing.

purposes and not as a coordinated ensemble. This bears the danger that the algorithms compete rather than cooperate.

Typical examples of a suboptimal design are concurrency control algorithms (see e.g. [4], [3] and [5]) that stem from distributed databases and that do not support timeliness because their delays are long and rather unpredictable. Another example are the various forms of non-deterministic transmission and routing protocols that are standardized in open systems environments: these protocols only tolerate a restricted set of failures and usually do not support timeliness at all. An example of an impossibility result, that is also mentioned by Le Lann, is the fact that a distributed consensus cannot be reached in a system with crash failures in which the communication times are not bounded [9].

The DEDOS project tries to acknowledge the algorithmic compatibility problem by constructing a consistent set of protocols with high performance. First results are reported in [25].

3.2 Temporal synchronization

To construct timely systems, temporal synchronization is of prime importance. Temporal synchronization is achieved by means of scheduling methods. The two basic approaches are shown in figure 12. These approaches also constitute the basis of the time-triggered and event-triggered system construction approach as described in [14] and also used in DEDOS (see chapter 1.2).

Static temporal synchronization methods enforce timeliness and temporal synchronization by means of deterministic off-line scheduling methods. Based on an analysis of all possible execution graphs, their resource requirements[9] and their synchronization requirements (e.g. specified in terms of timed precedence relations) it is tried to construct a feasible schedule. Such a schedule, in principle, consists of a time-ordered list that allows the on-line scheduler to activate the appropriate activities (tasks) at the specified times. The implementation of the DEDOS on-line scheduler is described in [18].

The calculation of such a schedule boils down to interleaving the different activities in such a way that certain correctness predicates are met. The activities are usually defined as short non-preemptable pieces of code. An object-oriented design and programming model provides a natural way to decompose executions and to define the various activities in terms of method calls. This is one of the reasons why the object-oriented paradigm was adopted for DEDOS (see also [30]).

The solution of the combinatorial problem defined above involves at least two steps: first a global schedule must be constructed by allocating software entities (processes or objects) on hardware entities (processors or periperials). In the

---

[9] There is no difference between a request for the processor resource (usually expressed in terms of execution times) and any other resource. Note that in a distributed system the communication network can also be considered a resource that is indivisible insofar as messages that are transmitted over the same link must not overlap in time.

TEMPORAL SYNCHRONIZATION METHODS		
	Static (deterministic)	**Dynamic (heuristic)**
Execution	Off-line (in advance)	On-line (in situ)
Enforcement of features	All types of resource syncronizations	Usually restricted set
Implementation method	Construction of execution graph (Combinatorial)	Language constructs (Implemented by timers)
Based on	Correctness predicate	Heuristic function
Verification method	Implicit (by construction)	Explicit (analytical or simulation)
Complexity	NP-complete	Moderate
Predictability	High	Low
Flexibility	Low	High
	Small and simple periodic systems	Large and complex systems
	Predetermined configuration	Dynamic (re)configuration
	Specified environment	Unpredictable environment
Resource utilization	Low (worst-case analysis)	High (max. concurrency)
Suitable for	Hard real-time	Soft real-time

HRT/SRT Synchronization

Fig. 12. Temporal synchronization methods.

second step a local schedule is calculated for each hardware entity. If this is not possible, another allocation must be tried, i.e. some form of backtracking must be performed. Since backtracking can also occur at the local level, finding a feasible schedule is a NP-complete problem that can only be solved in a systematic manner for small problems. Practical methods are therefore based on heuristic search and pruning methods e.g. as described in [23] and [27]. In DEDOS it is tried to avoid global backtracking as much as possible (i.e. to make the scheduling algorithm more efficient) by defining for each scheduled activity a window. If the activity is scheduled within this window, activities on other processors are not affected [31].

As already mentioned in chapter 2.2, the advantages of deterministic scheduling techniques are:

- Finding a feasible schedule means that the timing properties of the system have been verified.
- Resource synchronization properties (see figure 7) can be statically enforced, i.e. no extra run-time constructs for resource synchronization are necessary. Typical resource synchronization properties are mutual exclusion, different types of atomicity and absence of deadlock. In addition, safety properties like termination, lifeness and security can also be automatically ensured at the expense of increased complexity of the off-line scheduler.

- The high predictability makes this method very suitable for safety critical hard real-time systems.

There are, however, several severe disadvantages:

- Since everything must be determined in advance, the resulting system is very inflexible. Static synchronization and scheduling techniques can e.g. not cope with changes of the configuration or the environment of the system[10]. In practice, this means that deterministic scheduling methods are restricted to rather small and simple systems.
- The resource utilization is very low since the static schedule must be constructed for the worst case that may rarely occur: data dependency and stochastic events are only known at run-time.
- Static scheduling is only suited for simple periodic problems. Fortunately, there are several types of safety critical hard real-time systems that can be based on cyclic polling of the environment. Typical examples are data acquisition systems, critical control loops and low-level device handling.
- Finally, up to now static scheduling is mainly used at the lowest level of abstraction, i.e. for analyzing and enforcing the timing properties of programs. What we, however, need are static scheduling techniques that support the stepwise refinement of the timing properties of a system. In this way the designer can already convince himself in an early stage that the system will meet the performance and temporal synchronization requirements. The problem with stepwise refinement of timing properties is, of course, that in an early stage of the design usually only rough estimates of the resource requirements are available.

Dynamic temporal synchronization methods in practice use rather simple heuristic on-line scheduling strategies to ensure the timeliness and the temporal synchronization properties of the system[11]. Typical heuristic functions are based on static priorities, dynamic priorities (deadline scheduling), earliest-deadlines and shortest-slack-times. The temporal synchronization is achieved by different types of language and operating system constructs in order to specify deadlines, periodicities, (de)activation of tasks, timed precedence constraints, etc. These constructs are implemented by various types of timers. Compared to static temporal synchronization methods that, in principle, allow the specification of all types of timing constraints, usually only a restricted set of constructs is available. Dynamic temporal synchronization methods have the following advantages:

- High flexibility and adaptability because everything is evaluated dynamically. For large and complex systems this property is essential in order to cope with all types of dynamic changes.

---

[10] In practice it should be feasible to calculate schedules for a small set of system configurations and environmental conditions in advance.

[11] The analytical solutions described in the literature are not realistic because they are based either on very simple models or on very restrictive assumptions.

- High resource utilization because the constructs are usually designed for maximum concurrency.
- Moderate combinatorial complexity compared to static methods. This is a consequence of the use of rather simple heuristic functions.

The disadvantages are:

- The verification of the system must be explicitly performed by other means like analytical proofs, simulations and tests.
- The predictability is usually low. Therefore dynamic methods are mainly suited for soft real-time problems.
- Finding schedules that ensure both timeliness and certain other properties might be difficult or even impossible. As pointed out in [15] earliest-deadline-first scheduling policies match with 2-phase locking plus deadline-based deadlock avoidance policies. On the other hand, common security policies may be incompatible with common concurrency control techniques like 2-phase locking, timestamp ordering and multi-version timestamp ordering.

3.3 Hard/soft real-time synchronization

In systems like DEDOS, where hard and soft real-time tasks coexist at the same level, the exchange of values between these two domains is important. A typical example is a control system where the data acquisition and the primary control loops are hard real-time, while the high-level supervision and the user interface are soft real-time. Obviously commands from the user interface and the supervisor must be passed to the hard real-time part, while results and alarms from the low-level data acquisition and control part must be passed higher up the system hierarchy. In an object-oriented design the data exchange will be performed via sets of common objects that are accessed by several hard and soft real-time executions. In order to support fault tolerance these objects may be replicated. The fact that the common objects may also be nested further enlarges the set of common objects.

The trouble stems from the requirements that (1) the set of common objects must be consistent when they are entered or left by executions or transactions (atomicity) and (2) that hard real-time executions must never be delayed because of resource synchronization for soft real-time tasks. Since the first requirement implies that hard real-time executions are not allowed to preempt soft real-time ones, one is faced with a problem. In addition, the interleaving of atomic read and write operations may cause unacceptable delays if many objects are involved.

As described in [24] the problem can be relaxed by realizing that in most cases it is not required that an access yields the latest values, as long as the data are correct and consistent. This allows the use of Multi-Version Time-Stamp Ordering (MVTSO) techniques as e.g. described in [4], [3] and [5]. This concurrency control technique is optimistic and has the advantage that a high degree of concurrency is allowed and that no deadlocks can occur.

As long as the latest value is not required, a further relaxation of the timing constraints is possible by allowing more concurrency. This is done by decoupling the write operations performed by hard real-time executions from the ones performed by soft real-time executions. This leads to the introduction of two types of common objects: (1) *hard write-objects* which can be read and written by hard real-time executions but which can only be read by soft real-time executions and (2) *soft write-objects* which can be read and written by soft real-time executions but which can only be read by hard real-time executions.

In a time sliced environment like DEDOS where soft real-time executions are performed in the gaps left by the hard real-time executions, this approach has another advantage. Write operations are more critical than read operations because (1) a new version (token) must be created for each update[12] and (2) the validity of the update must be checked at the end of the transaction by means of the timestamps. Hard real-time write operations on large sets of replicated and/or nested objects may thus seriousely jeopardize the throughput of soft real-time transactions. Obviously, the decoupling of these two types of write operations also helps in this case.

It is interesting to note that the hard/soft real-time synchronization algorithms can make use of periodic hard real-time executions themselves. This can be done in two ways: (1) in order to avoid unduly long delays for soft real-time transactions the latter can be transformed into hard real-time ones by a distributed request manager; (2) soft write-objects can be committed by a hard real-time execution in order to make the commit action efficient and atomic itself. In [24] these techniques are used for replicated and nested objects respectively. They have, however, a broader scope.

The protocols for distributed replicated objects and for distributed nested objects are described in [24]; the combination of these two cases must still be solved. These algorithms are only resilient against timing failures; the extension of the fault hypothesis with crash failures should, however, not be too difficult.

In order to demonstrate the concepts described above, figure 13 shows the most simple case: objects that are neither replicated nor nested.

For hard write-objects a hard real-time execution that wants to write an object either creates a new token[13] or converts the oldest version into a token, writes the value, writes a timestamp $T_n^w > T_{(n-1)}^w$ and finally converts the token into a version by committing it. A soft real-time execution that subsequently wants to read the data performs the following actions: a read timestamp T^r is generated, the value of the latest version (identified by the largest timestamp $T^w < T^r$) is read and a check is performed in order to detect whether this version has been updated meanwhile. If after the read operation $T^r < T^w$, the read transaction is aborted.

For soft read-objects the algorithm is similar. A soft real-time execution that wants to update an object either creates a new token or converts the oldest version into a token, writes the value, generates a timestamp $T_n^w > T_{(n-1)}^w$ and

---

[12] For efficiency reasons the number of versions is small and limited. This implies some form of version management for the recycling of old versions. This task can be conveniently managed by means of the timestamps.

[13] A token is a preliminary version that is not yet committed.

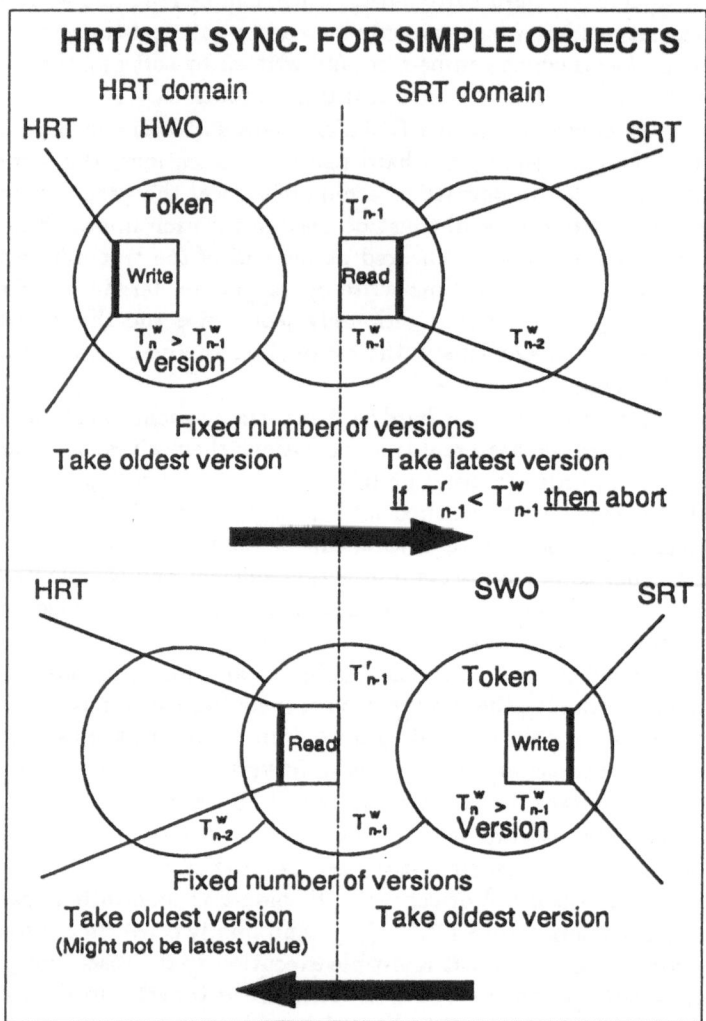

Fig. 13. Hard/soft real-time synchronization for simple objects. The following abbreviations are used: HRT and SRT stands for Hard Real-Time and Soft Real-Time respectively; HWO and SWO denote Hard Write-Objects and Soft Write-Objects respectively; Timestamps are denoted by T, their subscript gives the version of the corresponding object and the superscript denotes whether it belongs to a read or a write operation. Note that the version is only added to the figure for clarity. In reality the value of a timestamp is sufficient.

finally converts the token into a version. A hard real-time transaction that wants to read the data simply generates a timestamp T^r and reads the oldest version (identified by the largest timestamp $T^w < T^r$). No inference from a soft real-time transaction can occur because the hard real-time update is non-preemptable.

4 Conclusion

For distributed control systems, synchronization issues are important at all levels of the system hierarchy, from the hardware up to the application programs. In order to support rational design decisions it is important to clearly distinguish the different synchronization issues and their associated synchronization techniques. It is argued that the synchronization and timeliness aspects of a system can be better designed in terms of concurrent executions instead of concurrent objects.

From the three synchronization dimensions, resource, spatial and temporal synchronization, the latter two are the most interesting ones. Spatial synchronization in a distributed real-time system is achieved by means of synchronous distributed consensus algorithms. It is not only important that these algorithms are efficient themselves, but also that different algorithms cooperate rather than defeat each other. This problem is also known as the algorithmic compatibility issue.

To achieve temporal synchronization and timeliness, static scheduling methods have big advantages over dynamic ones. They can not only be used to enforce predictability of the system, but also to enforce all types of resource synchronization and safety features. In addition, by using these methods the emphasis is shifted from a posteriori verification by testing to a priori verification by construction and mathematical analysis. The drawback of static methods is their inflexibility and their bad resource utilization. The first argument is serious because many modern distributed real-time systems are increasingly large and operate in unpredictable environments. As explained below, the importance of the second argument will decline in future.

In future distributed real-time systems, the importance of optimal resource utilization will decrease considerably. This development has two reasons. First, the dependability requirements for this type of systems will steadily increase. This has to do with the fact that our society depends more and more on automatic control systems and failures have increasingly large and far-reaching consequences. Second, the economic and emotional costs of production stops, environmental accidents and injury of life are steadily increasing because we are no longer accepting such violations of normal service. Consequently the total costs of a service disruption may outweigh the initial system costs by several orders of magnitude. The costs of a system must therefore be seen in a broader context and it is no longer meaningful to optimize only the initial price of a system by optimizing its resource utilization. In this situation, the industry should take a serious look at advanced static methods in order to be able to construct predictable and safe systems for critical applications.

In order to achieve high flexibility and resource utilization in combination with predictability and safety, it is advantageous to combine deterministic off-line scheduling techniques with heuristic on-line ones. In this way, it is possible that hard real-time and soft real-time tasks coexist in the same system. The dual dependability paradigm of DEDOS goes one step further and combines these techniques for the achievement of timeliness with appropriate fault tolerance techniques. These integrative approaches are nice examples of the fact that dependable real-time systems that are practically usable cannot be based on a single paradigm. This argument certainly holds for large distributed systems.

If one combines soft and hard real-time tasks in one integrated system the question of hard/soft real-time synchronization arises. The problem stems from the fact that these two domains of operation have features that are quite different and not compatible. The algorithms presently known are extensions of well-known concurrency control algorithms and do not cover all circumstances. This subject therefore needs further investigation.

Finally, it can be concluded that our present design methods put too much emphasis on functional design and on the static (structural) properties of the system. There is therefore a need for an extension in two dimensions. First, the systematic design of dependability aspects like timeliness, reliability, safety and security must be supported. What we need are methods for the top-down refinement of these design dimensions, from the initial requirement specification down to the implementation. Second, our present design methods (like object-oriented design) must be extended in order to model also the dynamic properties of a system. It is argued that executions are the appropriate concept for such an extension. The reason is that executions show the synchronization requirements in a natural way: they relate distributed objects via the network, they consume resources and they must be timely.

Acknowledgements: The author thanks all members of the DEDOS group, and especially E.J. Luit, O.S. van Roosmalen and P.D.V. van der Stok, for many stimulating discussions and valuable remarks.

References

1. D. Alstein and P.D.V. van der Stok, *Reliable Multicast Protocols for Shared Memory Multiprocessors*, to be published as EUT Computing Science Note.
2. M. Ben-Ari, *Principles of Concurrent and Distributed Programming*, Prentice Hall, 1990.
3. B.K. Bhargava (ed.), *Concurrency Control and Reliability in Distributed Systems*, Van Nostrand Reinhold, 1987.
4. P.A. Bernstein. V. Hadzilacos and N. Goodman, *Concurrency Control and Recovery in Database Systems*, Addison-Wesley, 1987.
5. W. Cellary, G. Gelenbe and T. Morzy, *Concurrency Control in Distributed Database Systems*, North Holland, 1988.
6. R.K. Clark, E.D. Jensen and F.D. Reynolds, *An Architectural Overview of the Alpha Real-Time Distributed Kernel*, Nato Advanced Study Institute Conf. on Real-Time Computing, Sint Maarten, Dutch Antilles, October 1992.

7. F. Cristian, *Fault-Tolerance in the Advanced Automation System*, 20th Int. Symp. on Fault Tolerant Computing, June 1990.

8. *Int. Workshop on Distributeed Algorithms*, yearly.

9. M.J. Fischer, N.A. Lynch and M.S. Patterson, *Impossibility of Distributed Consensus with One Faulty Process*, J. ACM, Vol. 32, No. 2, April 1985.

10. W.A. Halang and A.D. Stoyenko, *Constructing Predictable Real-Time Systems*, Kluwer, 1991.

11. D.K. Hammer, E. Luit. P. van der Stok and O.S. van Roosmalen, *The Dependable Distributed Operation System DEDOS*, preprint EUT 1991, to be published as EUT Computing Science Note.

12. D.K. Hammer and O.S. van Roosmalen, *An Object-Oriented Model for the Construction of Dependable Distributed Systems*, Int. Workshop on Object-Orientation in Operating Systems (I-WOOOS), Paris, France, September 1992.

13. D.J. Hatley and I.A. Pirbhai, *Strategies for Real-Time Systems Specifications*, Dorset House, 1987.

14. H. Kopetz, *Event-Triggered versus Time-Triggered Real-Time Systems*, Int. Workshop on Operating Systems in the 90's and Beyond, Dragstuhl Castle, Germany, July 1991.

15. G. Le Lann, *Designing Real-Time Dependable Distributed Systems*, Computer Communications, Vol. 15, No. 4, May 1992.

16. J.C. Laprie, *Dependability: A Unifying Concept for Reliable Computing and Fault Tolerance*, Dependability of Resilient Computers (T. Anderson, ed.), Blackwell Scientific Publications, Oxford, 1989.

17. P.A. Lee and T. Anderson, *Fault Tolerance: Principles and Practice, Dependable Computing and Fault-Tolerant Systems*, Vol. 3, Springer, 1990.

18. E.J. Luit and V.A.P. Mombarg, *The DEDOS On-Line Scheduler*, Int. Workshop on Real-Time Programming, Bruges, Belgium, June 1992.

19. B. Meyer, *Object-Oriented Software Construction*, Prentice-Hall, 1988.

20. M. Raynal, *Distributed Algorithms and Protocols*, Wiley, 1988.

21. L.J.A.M. Somers, P.D.V. van der Stok and P.T.A. Thijssen, *Formal Specification and Simulation of a Real-Time Concurrency Control Protocol*, 2nd Int. Workshop on Responsive Computer Systems, (IWRCS-2), Tokyo, Japan, October 1992.

22. J.A. Stankovic and K. Ramamrithan, *The Design of the Spring Kernel*, 7th Int. Conf. on Distributed Computer Systems, 1987.

23. J.A. Stankovic and K. Ramamrithan (ed's), *Hard Real-Time Systems*, IEEE Computer Society Press, 1988.

24. P.D.V. van der Stok and A. Engel, *Shared Data Concepts for DEDOS*, 10th IFAC Workshop on Distributed Computer Control Systems, Semmering, Austria, 1991.

25. P.D.V. van der Stok, D. Alstein and E. Luit, *The Structure of the DEpendable Distributed Operating System (DEDOS)*, to be published as EUT Computing Science Note.

26. A.S. Tanenbaum, *Modern Operating Systems*, Prentice-Hall, 1992.

27. A.M. Tilborg and G.M. Koob (ed's), *Foundations of Real-Time Computing: Schedulingand Resource Management*, Kluwer, 1991.

28. G.J.W. van Dijk, *The Design of the EMPS Multiprocessor Executive for Distributed Computing*, EUT Thesis, March 1993.

29. J.P.C. Verhoosel, E.J. Luit, D.K. Hammer and E. Jansen, *A Static Scheduling Algorithm for Distributed Hard Real-Time Systems*, The Journal of Real-Time Systems, Vol. 3, 1991.

30. J.P.C. Verhoosel, *A Formal Deterministic Scheduling Model for Hard Real-Time Executions in DEDOS*, to be published as EUT Computing Science Note.

31. J.P.C. Verhoosel, *Deterministic Scheduling of Distributed Hard Real-Time Systems using Windows*, Nato Advanced Study Institute Conf. on Real-Time Computing, Sint Maarten, Dutch Antilles, October 1992.

32. P.T. Ward and S.J. Mellor, *Structured Development for Real-Time Systems*, Yourdon Press, 1985.

33. E. Yourdon, *Modern Structured Analysis*, Prentice Hall, 1989.

Communications for Real-Time Industrial Control: The Design Issues

M.G. Rodd

Dept. of Electrical & Electronic Engineering
University College of Swansea
Singleton Park
Swansea SA2 8PP
U.K.

1 Background to Industrial Communications

In most real-time automation applications we are required to control real-world, physical processes - processes which have their own intrinsic time-related properties. A chemical reaction, once started, proceeds according to its own dynamics, and the chemistry takes little notice of the controlling computer. Likewise, once a piece of metal is removed by a milling-machine, it cannot be replaced! These processes operate according to their real-time dynamics, and as a result, any controlling system must recognise these inherent real-time characteristics. A real-time computer control system is thus one in which the correctness of the system depends not only on the logical results of computations, but also on the time at which the results are produced. "Real-time" does not necessarily imply "fast", but does mean "fast enough for the chosen application".

It is important, therefore, to realise that in many stages of automation, two aspects of the control require real-time to be taken into consideration. In the first place, there are many situations in which the system must respond according to the requirements of the plant. One could consider, for example, a robot feeding a tool into a numerically-controlled milling machine. If, after the robot begins to move the tool towards the milling machine, the computer controlling the latter suddenly finds that it is not in a position to receive that tool, then the operation must be aborted. This means that a message must be sent back to the robot to halt its operation. In a situation like this, there is no way that a multitude of layers of communication protocols could be negotiated in the time available before that message needs to get through. Likewise, in an alarm situation, where something goes wrong, responses must take place at a very high rate, in order to cope with the situation.

In the second place, the question of real-time synchronisation of parts of the factory or process must also be borne in mind. Thus, for example, a robot picking up a component which is being conveyed by an automatic guided vehicle or by a conveyer belt, must know exactly when it is to undertake its picking task. Whilst current solutions require extensive interlocking between, say, the end effectors of the robot and an indexing system running on the conveyer belt, this does rather defeat the objective of having a communication channel between the intelligent controllers of these devices.

Finally, the question of real-time data consistency is important. The point here is that if operators (or, indeed, supervisory Artificial Intelligence systems) are to get a true picture of the total operation of their plants, then what they see on their screens (or blackboards) must correspond to what is actually happening on the plant. However, if the communication system requires a long time for messages to be passed up the various communication channels, then it is clear that operators simply cannot see a picture on their screens of what is actually happening at that moment in time. Basically, this all boils down to considering the question which is often referred to as "Reality in real-time control". Essentially, it must be emphasised that feedback control loops can be designed to operate successfully only if the time dynamics of the process to be controlled are sufficiently understood. This statement is just as true for continuous control as it is for discrete control aspects, where the dynamics of a cell, consisting of a variety of machine tools, are complex and probably non-linear. Fortunately, it all results in what has been referred to as "the first law of applied control". This simply says that the controller must respond to the speed of the plant! In other words, it is the plant which determines the pace of operation and not the computer. Thus, it must follow that control systems must be designed to match the requirements of the plant, and not necessarily those of an international communications standards organisation!

Arising directly out of these points is a fundamental philosophy in real-time control systems, which is that data has a meaning only when it is associated with time. This means that any communication system which cannot support time information is largely useless in many applications. It also indirectly implies that all nodes or computers in the distributed system must have a globally-agreed real-time clock. To provide a consistent picture of the plant to the operator or control system, all data must be linked to its time of creation, etc. It is essential that the real-time database is consistent in real time, and this can be achieved only by having all data stored together with the time at which it was created. It has also been found in many cases, that the length of time for which that data is valid — sometimes called the validity time of the data — also needs to be stated.

These points give rise to a consideration as to what structures are necessary to support communication systems which can respond in real-time. It is very clear, for example, that a maximum delay time through the communication system must be guaranteed. It is common experience that in most manufacturing and automation systems, a guaranteed maximum delay time across a network of 5 milliseconds appears to be reasonable, although in many new plants, 1 millisecond or better might well be required. In the process-control industry, it has often been estimated that a delay of up to 20 milliseconds is tolerable, but more recent information has shown that the lower this delay can be held, the higher the degree of control which can be applied.

A reasonable approach to the handling of data is thus one which is based on strict real-time, and assumes that all data is time-stamped and also has an explicitly defined validity time, during which the data is valid. Once this time has run out, the data can be discarded as it will be out of date. To support this, and meet the previously mentioned requirements, the underlying communication system must be truly deterministic.

2 Deterministic Communications

A communications system is deterministic if, when it is operating within its stated maximum load, all messages with a defined priority will be delivered within a maximum end-to-end message transfer time period.
From this important and somewhat provocative definition of a deterministic communication system, aspects of underlying considerations should be highlighted and these include the following:

Determinism: "... the doctrine that everything that happens is determined by a necessary chain of causation" (1986) — the Shorter Oxford Dictionary.

Deterministic: a system thus (from above) can be said to be deterministic if the performance of all components which comprise that system is fully defined — both logically and temporally.

Maximum load: a practical communication system will have a designed maximum possible load. Whilst average loading figures normally are of interest in non-time-critical applications, in areas where there are requirements of hard real-time performance, the maximum load permitted is an essential design parameter which could well determine the overall temporal determinism of the total resulting system.

Defined priority: with the exception of highly dedicated applications, most practical, industrial communication systems will (fundamentally for economic reasons) be required to carry a mixture of traffic — ranging from simple status reporting and general process statistics, through to the movement of data-files and programmes, right up to vital, time-critical control indications and instructions. As a result it will be pragmatic in all but very few applications to be able to define various priority levels for messages. (In simple terms, these priorities could well be in three categories — o hard deadlines: to be met in all circumstances, o soft deadlines: to be met whenever possible, o non-critical deadlines: a best effort service.

End-to-end performance: the performance of any single-layer of a defined communications protocol stack is almost irrelevant if not considered in a context of all the other layers. Remembering that the user is only interested in getting a message from point A to point B (where point A could be a sensor output and point B a control algorithm executing in a progress computer), it is the overall communication system performance which is important. (Thus, whilst academic debates about the best media access control protocols are of importance, in the end they could be largely irrelevant if the rest of the stack structure is inadequate).

Maximum transfer time period: as desirable as it might be for all messages to be delivered with a precisely defined, absolute and guaranteed transfer time, this does seem to be an unreasonable and somewhat impractical requirement. It is also not really necessary, especially when time-stamping and the defining of a validity time for messages is undertaken. As a result, it is acceptable to define only the maximum time taken — but it must be noted that this must be an absolute measurement and not a statistical one (as is the current common practice).

Based on the above set of observations and definitions, it will now be relevant to consider how communication systems that meet these requirements can be achieved — given, in particular, the real-world problems of the process industry.

3 Towards Real-Time Communication Systems

A critical component of any modern control system is clearly the communication system.
However, with industrial communication systems being a relatively small component of the total plant cost, the market available to producers of such communication systems is extremely small. It is not surprising, therefore, that industrial communication systems have to build upon those technologies which are utilised elsewhere in the communication field. As special as we might feel our applications are, we have to accept that we are addressing a small sector of the market and, in general, communications between our computers will be dominated by the needs of the larger data-processing and data-communications industry.

In the past, however, this reality did not seem to be a problem. After all, process engineers were used to using communication systems running at 110 bits per second, and now were being offered systems with bandwidths of 10 megabits per second! However, the mismatch between the actual application requirements and the available products is now increasingly becoming painfully obvious. Suddenly, we are being faced with situations in which we are utilising to the full the communication systems, and discovering that the available networking technologies, as elaborate as they might seem at first sight, simply cannot support our real-world time-critical control requirements.

The following section addresses some of the fundamental issues which must be considered in the designing communication systems for use in so-called real-time applications.

As we have moved towards distributed computer control structures, it has become evident that we need some form of hierarchy in order to structure these systems. We have to harness geographically related processes and, wherever possible, reflect the natural integration which results. We also find that as we develop an appropriate form of hierarchy in our distributed computer control systems, the various levels of automation define the information requirements. In practice, the so-called five-layer model, as illustrated in figure 1, seems to become relevant, reflecting as it does, most practical situations.

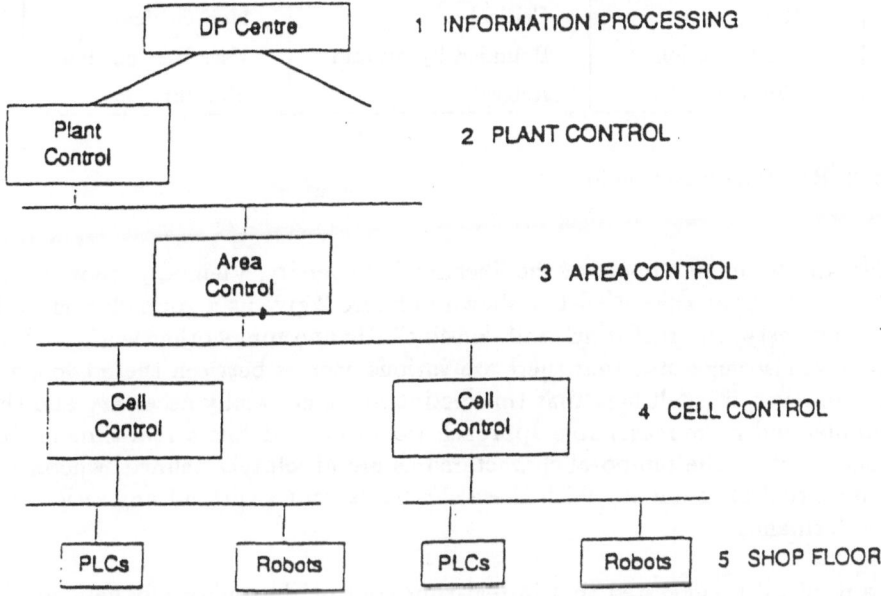

Fig. 1. The simplified model of a distributed computer control system

A further requirement of the distribution is to cope with the problem of system failure. During the early days of computerisation we learned, to our cost, the disasters which result from the "eggs in one basket" syndrome. The loss of an essential computer could be devastating. We have learned that the only way of tackling this is to distribute the system, so that the failure of any particular piece of software or hardware, or, communications equipment, will lead to a situation which at least can be contained.

It is self-evident that the data which flows around our distributed computer control system will, in many cases, be time-dependent and not merely value-dependent. It is important, therefore, that we look at the nature of the data in our system when we select methods of transmitting and storing that data.

Characteristic	Real-Time	On-Line
Response time	Hard	Soft
Pacing	By Plant	By Computer
Peak Performance	Must be Predictable	Degradable
Time Granularity	Less than 1 mSec	About 1 Sec
Data Files	Small-to-Medium	Large
Data Integrity	Short Term	Long Term
Safety	Critical	Non-Critical
Error Detection	Bounded by System	User Responsible
Redundancy	Active	Standby

Fig. 2. Real-time versus on-line.

Professor Hermann Kopetz of the Technical University, Vienna, proposed some years ago that the characteristics shown in figure 2 give us a good clue as to the difference between "real-time" and "on-line". He and many other workers in the area have also suggested that there are various degrees between these two extremes. However, it is felt here that this distinction is not really necessary and that a simpler and more reasonable approach would be to define a real-time process as one in which the temporal characteristics are absolutely defined, whereas an on-line situation is one in which these can be degraded without any serious loss of performance.

As a result, it is suggested that in real-time control, data normally has meaning only when it is associated with time. This implies, in the first place, that all data must be time-stamped at the time of creation in order to provide that time information. Of course, the direct consequence of this is that all nodes in a system must have access to a globally agreed real-time clock. Again, work by many authors has pointed to ways in which such clocks can be created. In essence, they require a good-quality local clock at each computing node, with some form of synchronisation — by means of frequently transmitted time messages, a separate timing channel, or access to some internationally transmitted standard [13].

Referring back now to Figure 1 it is important to investigate the data requirements at various levels, and from this one begins to see important patterns emerging [14]. At the higher levels, we see that the functions which are typically required include

- File transfer
- Electronic mail
- Remote file editing
- Status reporting to operators and higher levels of management
- Data acquisition from lower levels
- Supervisory control of lower levels, and
- Program transfer

In essence, at these levels, we are moving bulk data around, typically between relatively large computers. This could be between Computer Aided Design (CAD) systems, or sending plant status information through to management computers running production scheduling or manufacturing materials requirement planning. At this level we can see the need for efficient, but safe and reliable, transfer of bulk data. However, if we are, additionally, utilising this information for control decision-making, then it is necessary also to be able to send time-tagged information across this system, otherwise no useful control decisions can be made! However, we normally accept at this level of networking that delays will occur, particularly when large files are being transferred. It is clear also that we could almost consider this an on-line environment, provided that there is some form of access to time-stamped data where necessary.

Moving to the lower levels, we see a different collection of functions. Here we are really getting into the real-time control world, and the following characteristics emerge

- Minimal, defined message delay times
- Deterministic behaviour — particularly under crisis situations
- Real-time synchronisation
- Assured data consistency
- Inherent message redundancy
- Message broadcasting (single station sending information to many users), and
- Regular and frequent data updating.

Essentially, we are talking here about highly efficient data transmission. Speed is important, but only to the extent that it must match the response of the plant. Thus a very slow plant will not require very high transmission rates. However, what it will require are deterministic rates. Information which flows at this level is typically relatively small in quantity, but critical in terms of its determinism. Our communication systems are now truly part of the control loops!

Looking at our networking (or, in fact, inter networking) strategies in this way, gives us a clue as to how they may best be implemented, and what technologies are appropriate at which level. That there are different functions cannot be doubted, but a fundamental criterion has to be that where data is associated with time then the communication systems must inherently support this. However, a fundamental issue in the development of any interconnected computer structure is also that of incompatibility. Essentially, in a distributed computer system what we are really trying to do is to permit various computers from various manufacturers to share various pieces of data! Whilst from the point-of-view of the supplier it would be desirable for all our computers to be from their own company, and therefore be totally compatible, we soon realise that in the distributed computer control world we are at the mercy of a variety of suppliers, each of whom has particular strong points.

Thus, certain suppliers can provide very fine data processing hardware and software, whereas others specialise in hard-nosed, factory-floor compatible controllers. The difficulty in producing a distributed system is to bring all these bits and pieces together. The compatibility issue revolves around hardware, software and, of course, data.

In practice, solving the compatibility problem is extremely difficult and we are only beginning to make some impact on it. The key has to be standardisation — whether or not we or the suppliers acknowledge it. Naturally, at the upper data communication level much progress has been achieved of late in the move towards OSI-based protocols, and in other fields, too, the success of standardisation is evident — Ethernet and TCP-IP [14] are good examples of standards which have met their desired marks.

Of course in the hard world of process control standardisation is critical, but unfortunately, as was said previously, we are relatively small as an industry, when compared to the data communications field. Whilst we would like to set our own standards there is no way that we can economically go down this route and therefore we tend to be the "step-children" of the data communications industry.

Realising the problems of standardisation, General Motors initiated its MAP exercise some years ago [9] and at the same time Boeing Corporation developed its TOP initiative. In both cases the idea was to produce a profile of protocols which would be appropriate to their particular areas of application — in the case of MAP, manufacturing, and in the case of TOP, technical offices. It was realised right from the start that there was no point in going it alone, and that the way ahead would be to select an agreed, and internationally-acceptable protocol profile and within the various layers, to select certain protocols. It was also recognised that, where necessary, they would have to inject extra emphasis to direct the move towards the development of actual products.

Although MAP has attracted much criticism, it has undoubtedly been significant in that it has brought to the fore the need for standardisation. The exercise has also hastened the development of protocols which are appropriate (at least to some degree) to manufacturing and the process industry. It is clear, however, that the products which are resulting from this exercise are in many cases too expensive and too complicated to be of present value in the hard world of automation. Also, as will be highlighted later, the acceptance of the OSI-principles has resulted in protocols which are in direct conflict with the real-time application needs. However, at the same time, it must be acknowledged that certain aspects of the MAP exercise have undoubtedly proved to be extremely important.

Of particular significance is the development, through MAP, of MMS-Manufacturing Messaging Services [2]. MMS provides standardised mechanisms for sending messages around a process or manufacturing plant. The standard itself defines a core of services, and then it is left to specialised groups to provide so-called "companion standards", which expand on these services for particular application areas. It is probably fair to say that the MAP standardisation exercise should have started at the MMS level, leaving many of the lower-layer, and somewhat technologically-related issues for later, in that many of the lower layers, such as the physical layer, are highly influenced by technical achievements. Current issues, for example, whether MAP should use Ethernet or Token-passing might well eventually be rendered redundant.

The point is, though, that there can be little doubt that the standardisation exercises are extremely critical to the design of future distributed computer control systems and will have serious impacts on how we handle data within them. We cannot ignore them: they are economically critical and simply to neglect the MAP exercise, for example, would be extremely naive. To look closer at MAP, to take what is good out of it and then to assist in the development, or redevelopment, of some of the layers which are proving to be troublesome, makes eminent sense.

Another aspect of the trend towards standardisation fits in extremely closely with the idea of development hierarchies within integrated control systems. Exercises, such as MAP, have acknowledged that we will ultimately see a high-capacity data backbone running through the plant, fed by bridges or gateways from less-capable, cheaper networks, which in turn could well be fed by very low-cost, field-bus type networks. After much debate and academic discussion as to the ideal structure, there does appear to be an increasing consensus that our systems will ultimately move to a structure like that illustrated in figure 3.

Here we see the idea of having a powerful backbone LAN which can in turn talk, via gateways, to wide area networks. The backbone will also be able to communicate with more deterministic, high-speed networks - which we have chosen to call "Real-time LANs".

Whilst it is clear that current OSI proposals do not cope with the requirements of such real-time systems, there is no doubt that in the future they will. It is interesting to note also that many important companies operating in this area are envisaging models very similar to that proposed in figure 3. It is critical also to note that below the real-time LAN level, there is a move towards so-called "Standard" field-buses and here the current international attempts to standardise these low-level buses are particularly relevant.

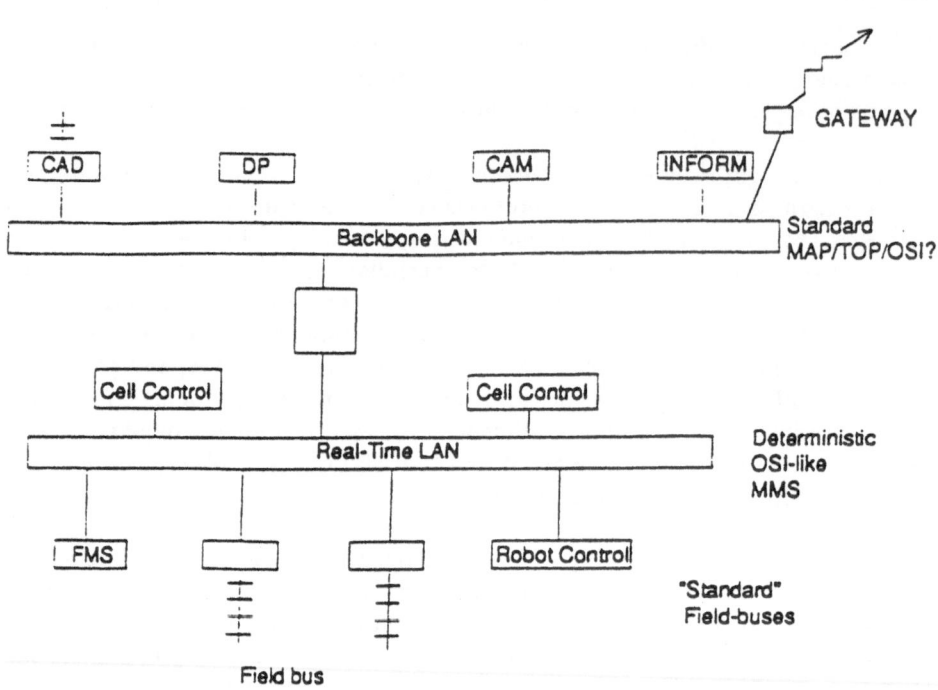

Fig. 3. Network hierarchy

4 Implementation Issues

As we mentioned previously, the drive for open computer communication systems provided the stimulus for much work in the standardisation of OSI protocols directed at a variety of applications. The ensuing development phases were, however, accompanied by disillusionment on the part of many users — the common grievances being that resulting products were:

- too expensive
- too complex
- too cumbersome, and
- too slow for time-critical applications.

Certain problems may be attributed to the fact that the OSI-based technologies have yet to mature; however, further restrictions are imposed by the inherent nature of the OSI 7-layer model and by the protocols which have emerged. Despite these, there are very good economic reasons to adopt, albeit in modified forms, the OSI concepts [4]. The reasons, we repeat, are simple — economics.

Just as MAP [9] and TOP looked towards OSI [3] for their selected profile standards, so must we, as we strive for systems which will cater for our real-time applications. We must reassess the OSI-based systems, using the very valuable work developed through the MAP initiative, to find real solutions. The key, though, is to appreciate fully the system requirements in supporting real-time process control.

4.1 System requirements in real-time applications

In real-time control there are some very important factors which must be considered and which, in the past, have been largely neglected, although well-discussed by such authors as Kopetz [5] and MacLeod [8]. Amongst the more critical factors are time, reliability and redundancy. As has been pointed out earlier, the adequacy of a control system to meet its requirements must be judged in terms of time concepts, and this is particularly the case when one is involved in high-speed digital control systems based on sampling techniques.

It is, therefore, recognised that communication systems (and their supporting structures, such as the messaging systems) which are to be used in real-time distributed systems, must be designed with time constraints always in mind. This section discusses some of the points which must be considered when designing such a system [4].

(i) **Autonomous operation**

   In order to implement fault tolerance and redundancy in a truly distributed system, the system controlling functions should be distributed. Consequently, every node on the network should be capable of working autonomously! It is, therefore, necessary to incorporate functions such as self-checking and emergency-handling at every node. This contradicts the well-accepted "master-slave" philosophy which is currently most common in distributed systems. In a typical "master-slave" situation, the failure of a "master" may be catastrophic since it may bring the whole system to its knees. Of course it is recognised that redundant "masters" may alleviate this short-fall to some extent. It is suggested, however, that the inherent benefits which distributed control systems provide, cannot be achieved with a "master-slave" approach. Indeed, it can be argued that it is impossible to obtain any real fault-tolerance in a system without inherently autonomous nodes!

(ii) **Data**

   As was emphasised earlier, in time-dependent processes data is judged not only on its actual value, but also on the time at which the value was obtained. Real-time data in any distributed network is thus valid only for a given period of time, and indeed has meaning only if the time of creation is specified! This forces designers increasingly towards the concept of atomic units of data, in which both the value and the time of creation are inseparable.

This implies that all data values in a real-time situation should be time-stamped at the source at which that data is created. Indeed, this concept goes further, and as has been pointed out [5], the accurate time-stamping of data provides many other advantages. It provides, for example, a way of handling distributed database consistency, as well as a means of removing data from a network in the case of late or invalid messages — thereby assisting in network management functions.

(iii) **Distributed global time information**

In order to support autonomy, fault-tolerance and the provision of time-stamping, it is evident that a global, physically-distributed, time reference is essential [7]. We suggest that every station on the network should contain a local clock which is periodically synchronised both to other local clocks as well as to a globally-agreed clock reference.

With the assistance of this distributed time reference, each node may be furnished with a system-wide view which provides the capability to execute functions across the network in real time! The availability of globally agreed time facilitates the synchronisation of operations as well as the execution of various error-detection/correction procedures [10].

(iv) **Guaranteed transmission time**

It is suggested that a fundamental requirement of a real-time distributed system is that all information should be transmitted within well-defined time parameters. It is unacceptable to design a control system based on, say, sampled-data theory, and then to support this by a communication system in which the period taken to transmit certain variables from one part of that control system to another is virtually undefined! Thus, it becomes essential to provide a communication system which can guarantee, at all times, an upper bound for the time taken for a message to go from one application process to another.

Also, the performance of the supporting communication system should be guaranteed under all conditions - particularly in emergencies. It is to realise that many protocols perform at their worst at times of heavy load — for example, when errors are detected.

Indeed, it is suggested that under critical or emergency conditions, the performance of the network must be absolutely deterministic in order to ensure orderly administration of the situation.

(v) **Primitives for real-time communication**

It is suggested that in a real-time environment many of the current, reliable, connection-oriented methods for communication are inappropriate. It can be seen, for example, that any PAR-based protocol (which involves Positive Acknowledgement with Re-transmission on time-out) is unacceptable since this can lead to messages actually arriving after being invalidated by the passage of time. Various aspects of the communication primitives which should be considered, include:

- The passage of time, as this may invalidate the information in the message.
- The question of where error detection should take place. If, for example, a temperature sensor is responsible for communicating its information back to the central processor, there is absolutely no point in that temperature sensor trying to handle the detection of any error — since there is nothing it can do about it anyway! Consequently, in many cases, error detection by the sender might be totally inappropriate.
- Communication traffic. This should neither be dependent on transmission error rates, nor become unpredictable in the case of high error conditions.
- Broadcast messages. In many real-time distributed control systems, the broadcasting of messages is of more importance than point-to-point communications! Error signals, system resets etc. are essential, as is the reception of common variable values by many users.

(vi) **Datagrams**

For many of the reasons mentioned above, it is suggested that a datagram service (often called "send-and-pray" since there is no intrinsic acknowledgement of message receipt) is appropriate for real-time communication systems. The rationale for this proposal is the following:

- No inherent acknowledgement is required, resulting in a lower overhead than a connection-oriented approach.
- Communication traffic depends totally on the message quantity and is determined at system design time.
- Services can easily handle multi-cast and broadcast.

(vii) **State-driven versus event-driven systems**

There is evidence to show that a state-driven approach to real-time control is increasingly being accepted as more appropriate than an event-driven system — despite the relatively constant heavy traffic which results [8]. In storing and transferring data within a distributed system, one can either use all the sampled values necessary to describe the data (i.e. the state) or only represent the changes (i.e. events) which result from transitions from some previous states. (Events, of course, represent changes of states, and states represent information during the intervals between events!)

In real-time distributed control, a state-driven approach seems to offer many significant advantages:

- State processes are never required to wait for inputs since they continue to use the states which have already been received, as long as they are still valid.
- Redundancy is intrinsic.
- Relatively loose synchronisation may be supported, since any data value available always contains a time-stamp.
- It appears easier to handle error recovery and error checking in a state-based approach, since one has a complete picture of the system.

- Finally, as we strive towards consistency in the distributed databases within a system, if one has the states of the critical processes constantly available, then every database in the distributed system can check its consistency against time.

4.2 OSI and real-time communications

From a first glimpse of the OSI structure and its mode of operation, one immediately identifies a rift between the open systems approach, and the characteristics we believe are fundamental to real-time distributed computer control systems. Of prime importance are the lack of facilities to support a "state"-based communication system and the costly and non-deterministic overheads incurred in implementing features which have limited uses in a real-time communication environment.

(i) **Broadcast and Multicast of Data**

A state-based data communication system involves the broadcasting of data which is frequently sampled at periodic intervals. Inherent in this communication mechanism are the features of a "fast as possible" datagram service which directly supports fault tolerance, and recovery of communication errors. Indeed, even the implementation of a simple PAR (Positive Acknowledge with Retransmission) protocol is seen as an unnecessary overhead in real-time environments. The very nature of OSI communications, with the creation of associations between peer entities at corresponding layers and the maintenance of a virtual circuit, inhibits the multicasting and broadcasting of messages in the system. Furthermore, the peer-to-peer layered structure implies a confirmed connection-oriented mechanism which is impractical — if not impossible — to support using a multicast communication scheme. Owing to this feature alone, it seems improbable that the OSI model in its current form will support the completely unacknowledged, connectionless broadcasting of data.

(ii) **The Express Transfer Protocol**

The emergence of the LAN protocol, XTP (eXpress Transfer Protocol), designed as a "real-time" replacement for the existing network and transport protocols, reveals the existence of a real need for functionality not currently met by OSI.

XTP is designed to enable data transmission at the high speeds supported by the emerging advanced local area networks — namely the 100 Mbits/s fibre distributed data interface (FDDI) and the new 16 Mbits/s token ring. The protocol supports confirmed multicast communications with a flexible addressing scheme which allows address formats to be specified by the implementor. Furthermore, protocol benchmark tests of XTP indicate that existing protocols such as OSI TP4 and TCP/IP (Transmission Control Protocol/Internet Protocol) require "five to ten times more processing power than XTP in order to attain equivalent transmission speeds.

Although XTP is by no means an ideal solution, it must be seen as a step in the right direction towards a standardized real-time communication system. The replacement of the network and transport protocols, however, does not address the problem of the connection-oriented service provided by MMS.

(iii) **Factors affecting OSI determinism**

The penalty incurred as a consequence of using a layered communication protocol is that the protocol processing requirements at every layer result in the formation of queues of messages awaiting service. This is compounded by the presence of multiple application associations (in a single system) with one or more receiving stations — these application associations require the establishment and maintenance of virtual circuits between the communicating entities, as well as the allocation of computer resources. The ramification of such a dynamic system is that it is inherently non-deterministic, in that the response time of any one message is dependent on the state of the communication system at the given instant in time. Furthermore, the number of associations maintained by any one station affects performance by reducing the number of buffers available per association for receiving data, thus making it necessary to use flow control on incoming data.

In order to increase the determinism — or place an "acceptable" upper bound on the non-determinism of the system — one must address the issues of reducing the message queues as well as the processing overheads associated with the virtual circuits.

(iv) **Restricting the number of associations**

One possible method of enhancing performance degraded by multiple associations could be to limit the number of active application associations at any one time.

Consider, for example, the extreme case of limiting the number of application associations to one per station — the implications are less than favourable. In the event that an application is required to transmit real-time data and if the destination is already involved in a transaction, the sender may not set up the required association, and as a result, the data may not be transferred in time to be of use. The situation is further compounded by the fact that the destination may not be able to close its current association until it holds the token. The sender would thus be required to wait at least as long as the token cycle time before the data may be transmitted. It is interesting to note that this scenario is not uncommon in current implementations, since the number of possible associations is implementation-dependent and directly related to the computing resources of the system.

Reducing the number of associations maintained at every node will, however, improve the performance of an individual association by making more buffers available per association.

(v) **Static Associations**

The overhead incurred by the negotiation and establishment of associations
may be reduced by setting up all the required associations (virtual circuits)
at the time of system configuration. These associations would remain static
for the lifetime of the particular configuration. Under these circumstances
it would be necessary to know all possible communicating entities during
operation of the system under all conditions — a rather complex task (if at
all possible).

A static configuration makes no assumptions regarding the frequency of message transmission and is still prone to the non-determinism of message queues
produced by "concurrent" associations.

(iv) **Real-time MMS**

An important aspect of matching OSI and, more particularly, the MAP profile to the requirements of real-time communications, will have to be the
adoption of a version of MMS, the manufacturing message service, which
can genuinely support real-time. This is dealt with in more detail in the
next section.

5 Real-Time MMS (RTMMS)

The dilemma which must be faced is that at least the back-bones of the communication systems used in automation installations are gradually migrating
towards MAP, or more generally, towards OSI-based systems. It is simply not
good enough, however, to suggest that MAP, MMS, etc. belong only at the higher
levels, and that as soon as one gets down to the real-time environment, one has
to use other standards. Commercial and technical success must lie in merging
these seemingly divergent approaches.

Current MAP and MMS have adopted point-to-point communication methodologies, and the services they provide are essentially event-driven, master-slave
structures. This approach can clearly be seen by investigating the types of objects and services defined in the MMS standards — for example, the use of
the client-server model, the concept of program invocation, and the availability of event-handling objects. Also, the basic underlying strategies of MAP
are point-to-point and connection-oriented, which, whilst appropriate to general data-communiction among ISO-supported systems, are unsuitable to support
datagram and broadcasting facilities.

By comparing the real-time requirements and the current MAP standards, it
is obvious that there is a gap, and work needs to be done to bridge this. Perhaps the most practical approach is to take as much as possible of the existing
standards, and modify the required services and protocols to meet the need of
real-time applications. Initial research has been undertaken to this end by the
Real-time Computing Network Group at the University of Swansea.

Real-time MMS (RTMMS) [11], has several fundamental characteristics which are necessary to support real-time messaging and system control. These facilities cannot be implemented through existing MMS without extremely complicated and lengthy procedures.

In contrast, with the introduction of these new features, it is believed that real-time problems can be solved in a consistent and economically-feasible fashion.

First, RTMMS has to be supported by datagram services: these are specifically used for handling real-time messages, because this is believed to be the appropriate communication protocol for state message handling. Secondly, RTMMS provides the necessary and sufficient services to support state-information transfer. Next, in order to support the principle that in a real-time application, every node should be capable of working autonomously, services emphasising "configuration", rather than direct control, have been included. These services will allow network users to inform other users how and when to do specific jobs, but not actually control the execution of the jobs — hence, supporting autonomous operation. Finally, and most importantly, RTMMS inherently supports the basic idea of the atomic nature of value and time by considering data and its origination time (i.e. time-stamping) as atomic elements of real-time information. Therefore, wherever the data is, it can be confidently examined and utilised.

To give a flavour of RTMMS, one of the new objects defined in RTMMS, and the services related to it, will be briefly discussed. Full discussions can be found in the reference. The example here is that of a "State Variable" object. This is defined as:

    Object State Variable
    Key Attribute State Variable Name
    Attribute: MMS Deletable
    Attribute: TYPE Description
    Attribute: Creation Time
    Attribute: Life Time
    Attribute: Work Mode

The importance here is that this object inherently includes the data value together with time information. Wherever real-time data is created, it must be time-stamped.

Therefore, on receiving the data, users can judge the value in the light of its cration time and predefined life time.

Apart from normal MMS services which are necessary to support various object management functions, such as "define" and "delete", a new service, "State Variable Report" has been defined. This is unlike a conventional MMS service; rather, it is broadcast-based and variable-name adressed. This means that data senders do not know, or even care, who will receive the message. Receivers will check the variable name first, in order to decide whether to accept the variable or ignore it.

It should be evident that the aim of introducing such a state variable object is to handle real-time state values and their transmission. Together with another new object, a "Configuration" object (an object which supports autonomous operations in a node) and its related services, communication in real-time state driven systems can be adequately handled.

One thing which should be mentioned, however, is that RTMMS cannot be used as an isolated element in a conventional MAP stack. RTMMS requires additional support from all the layers within the stack. The most obvious example is the need for a broadcast facility, which will involve functions of, at least, all the network-related layers (Layers 1, 2 and 3).
Also, implementing global time, which is critical to RTMMS, requires support from both the communication stack and the computing environment. Thus, to build an appropriate real-time environment, it is essential to consider architectural aspects which directly affect RTMMS and also the related environment.

6 EPA/Mini-MAP/FAIS: Are these the Solution(s)?

Much interest has been expressed in EPA/Mini-MAP — and certainly several vendors are claiming products in this area. The Enhanced Performance Architecture (EPA) is a reduced-protocol profile providing limited services to the application process in an attempt to improve the speed of communication [14]. The architecture comprises a 3-layer stack consisting of the physical, data link and application layers, incorporating MMS as the main application service element. Any additional functionality (usually found in layers 3 to 6) must be implemented by the user in the application processes of the system.
(As a point of clarification it should be noted that a MAP/EPA node provides both the full and reduced protocol profiles, whereas a node with only the EPA is called Mini-MAP.)

There are, however, several critical issues yet to be resolved in EPA. For example, the use of MMS (Manufacturing Messaging System) in EPA necessitates a Logical Link Control mechanism different from that used in MAP. Owing to the fact that MMS is a connection-oriented protocol, the reduced services offered by the EPA protocol profile require the logical link control to provide additional functionality before MMS may be used. MAP specifies LLC Type 1, whereas the EPA specifies LLC Type 3.

It is obvious, therefore, that LLC is a significant area of incompatibility between MAP and EPA. Furthermore, the reduced stack does not conform to the OSI 7-layer model which defines the interaction between adjacent layers. Since Mini-MAP normally uses 5 Mbits/s carrier-band transmission media, as opposed to 10 Mbits/s broadband in the MAP backbone, a bridge or router is required for their interconnection, resulting in additional latency and potential congestion. Consequently, an application process on a full MAP stack requiring information exchange with an application process on a Mini-MAP stack, requires the use of a MAP/EPA node as an interface.

A very significant recent development, though, has been the acceptance, at least in part, by the MAP Users Group of the proposals from Japan referred to as FAIS — Factory Automation Interconnection System [1]. For some years now the Japanese have been working on their proposal which to some extent matches the requirements of Mini-MAP but also appears to rival work being undertaken elsewhere in the development of the so-called Fieldbus standard. Whilst the latter has dragged on for several years and is now limping slowly towards some degree of acceptance (resulting in a Standard which will probably be redundant and out-of-date before implementation), FAIS has made much progress and following recent discussions, FAIS has now been equated to Mini-MAP.

FAIS is important in that it offers a much higher bandwidth than the original fieldbus specification, and closely matches the Mini-MAP specification, i.e. transmission at 5 megabits per second. Of importance, also, is that the Japanese have been working on a version of MMS for incorporation into FAIS, which will allow for the rapid transfer of messages. It is evident that, when observed against the background both of Mini-MAP and of the fieldbus, there will be a version of MMS emerging which will match the requirements of the low-level networking in the model shown in Figure 1. This so-called "fieldbus messaging service" (FMS) should, however, also include ingredients of RTMMS, as outlined in Section 5 above.

7 Conclusions

It is evident that limiting the operation of the OSI stack, as well as using static associations, etc., leads to a "proprietary" system that comes close to negating the very aim of open systems: additionally, even under a restricted stack, the real-time requirements would not necessarily be met.

However, we should return to the fundamental issue — we will, by necessity, have to use OSI-based communication systems. It is a question now of bending the standards to fit our real needs — and, of course, bending the ears of the standards-making representatives [11]!

References

1. FAIS Implementation Specification - Mini Mop Subset, Version 2.0/Draft 1, IROFA, 1991.
2. ISO DIS 9506, Manufacturing Message Specification, 1988.
3. ISO IS 7498, Information Processing Systems — Open Systems Interconnection — Basic Reference Model, American National Standards Association Inc., 1984.

4. I. Izikowitz, M.G. Rodd and G.F. Zhao, *A Real-time OSI-Based Network Is it possible?*, Proc. IFAC Workshop on DCCS, Pergamon Press, 1989.

5. H. Kopetz, F. Lohnert, W. Marker and G. Panthner, *The Architecture of Mars*, Report sc ma82/2, Technical University of Berlin, 1982.

6. H. Kopetz and W. Ochsenreiter, *Clock Sychronization in Distributed Real-time Systems*, IEEE Transactions on Computers, Vol. C–36, No. 8., 1987.

7. L. Lamport and P.M. Melliar-Smith, *Synchronizing Clocks in the Presence of Faults*, Journal of the ACM, Vol. 32, No. 1, 1985.

8. I.M. MacLeod, *Using Real-time to Achieve Coordination in Distributed Computer Control Systems*, Proceedings of the IFAC World Congress, Budapest, 1984.

9. Map 3.0 Specification, May 1987.

10. J. Wensley et al., *SIFT: Design and analysis of a fault-tolerant computer for aircraft control*, Proceedings of the IEEE, Vol. 66, No. 10, 1978.

11. M.G. Rodd, I. Izikowitz and Guo Feng Zhao, *RTMMS — An OSI-based Real-time Messaging System*, Int. Journal on Real Time Systems, Vol. 2, 1990, 213–234.

12. M.G. Rodd, *Real-time Issues in Distributed Databases for Real-time Control*. Proceedings IFAC Workshop on Real-time Distributed Databases, Pergamon Press, 1989.

13. H. Kopetz and W. Ochsenreiter, *Clock Sychronization in Distributed Real-time Systems*, IEEE Transactions on Computers, Vol. C–36, No. 8, 1987.

14. M.G. Rodd and F. Deravi, *Communication Systems for Industrial Control*, Prentice Hall, 1989.

Safety Engineering and Assurance for Real-Time Systems

John A. McDermid

Dependable Computing Systems Centre
University of York
York Y01 5DD
U. K.

1 Introduction

Many real-time systems are also safety-critical, that is they are used in applications where their inappropriate behaviour, or failure, could lead to loss of life, or severe environmental damage. Examples include the flying control systems for aircraft[1], reactor protection systems, and anti-lock braking systems for cars. The primary difference between the development of non-critical real-time systems and safety-critical real-time systems is that we are concerned with failures, both of the computer system and the wider system in which it is embedded. Our discussion will focus on the issue of identifying failure modes and showing that safety requirements are met, despite the fact that failures can occur.

More specifically, our primary aims are two-fold:

- to describe some of the more widely used engineering techniques for analysing failure behaviour;
- to set out the beginnings of the development of a scientific underpinning for these engineering techniques which enables them to be better understood and improved by being better automated, and linked to the design process.

Thus this paper should serve to explain current practices, and to indicate ways in which they can be related to standard (academic) concepts of software and systems engineering.

We assume a general understanding of the concepts of safety and safety-critical systems, but stress a few key points regarding the specification and analysis of safety-critical systems. The most important point is that safety is a systems issue, and that we have to analyse software in a systems context. Traditional safety engineering techniques do not address real-time issues, although they are concerned, inter alia, with time domain failures.

We will, however, give a temporal bias to our presentation in order to link the safety engineering concepts to the real-time issues. To avoid confusion we need to introduce a few terms, but we eschew definitions as far as is possible. Any

---

[1] These systems are often erroneously referred to as "fly-by-wire".

unqualified use of system is intended to be generic, and the following distinctions between different sorts of system are made for clarity:

- **real-time system** — a computer system subject to real-time requirements;
- **embedding system** — an engineered system, usually containing a mixture of technologies, of which a real-time system forms a part, e.g. a computer controlled, hydro-mechanically actuated braking system on an aircraft;
- **platform** — a system containing one or more embedding systems, e.g. an aircraft containing a braking system, a flying control systems, etc.;
- **environment** — system in which the platform is embedded, e.g. controlled airspace and airports for an aircraft.

These are not rigorous definitions, but hopefully they are adequate to give clarity to what follows, and to avoid ambiguity in the use of the term system.

The rest of the paper is structured as follows. In section 2 we briefly describe the most important safety engineering and analysis techniques, and indicate their primary strengths and weaknesses. Whilst the description is broad, it is influenced by the author's experience and knowledge of aircraft systems. Section 3 outlines a conceptual framework for describing and "underpinning" the safety engineering techniques. These ideas represent a "snapshot" of an evolving understanding of the conceptual basis of the techniques. Section 4 considers the links between the analysis techniques and the design process. Finally Section 5 presents conclusions about the utility of the current techniques, and ways in which they can be developed and improved.

2 Engineering Techniques

Many industries, e.g. aerospace and nuclear power, have a long tradition of developing safety critical systems, although it is relatively recently that computers have formed a major part of these systems. These industries have developed techniques for analysing safety critical systems and, in particular, their behaviour in the presence of failure. As these techniques are concerned with systems they are still relevant when computers are used, although some adaptation is needed for dealing with software. The purpose of this section is to give an overview of these techniques, and to illustrate the strengths and limitations of the techniques, especially when applied to real-time systems. We start by briefly considering requirements.

2.1 Requirements for Failure Behaviour

The requirements for a real-time, safety-critical system obviously depend on the application of the system (its purpose), however there is commonality in the requirements, and in the techniques used to define the requirements. We focus on these common features which are primarily concerned with failure behaviour.

2.1.1 Categorisation of Failures

Real-time systems are only safety-critical if their failure (or normal behaviour[2]) could lead to an accident. More specifically we identify:

- **accident** — a situation we wish to avoid, typically involving loss of human life (usually a state of the environment, or an interaction between the platform and the environment);
- **hazard** — a state of the platform which will (is likely to) lead to an accident, barring unplanned recovery action (usually a state of the platform or the embedding system if the state can be localised);
- **failure** — a state or behaviour of a real-time system which will (is likely to) lead to a hazard, and hence an accident (a state of the real-time system, given our interest in this paper).

There are no "hard and fast" boundaries between these categories, but they are representative of the concepts used in practice. We use the term "is likely to" because we will, for example, view a state as hazardous if there is a significantly increased risk of an accident, even if the accident does not necessarily follow. We can illustrate the use of the concepts by considering a commercial aircraft:

- **accident** — loss of passengers and crew due to aircraft running off the end of the runway whilst attempting to take off;
- **hazard** — application of wheel brakes between V1 and VR (the points where a commitment is made to take off, and where the wheels leave the ground, respectively);
- **failure** — the brakes and steering control unit (BSCU) computer issuing a "brake" command, between V1 and VR, with no input from the pilot. Safety requirements for real-time systems arise from analysis of such sequences of events or states. The requirements arise from an analysis of the hazards, and common generic requirements for safety critical systems, as we shall now explain.

2.1.2 Hazard Analysis

In most industries developing safety critical systems, the nature of potential accidents are well-known, and the development process therefore starts with a hazard analysis. Again hazards associated with particular embedding systems are usually well-known[3] — in the case of an aircraft BSCU the manufacturers

---

[2] Throughout the rest of this paper we will assume we are concerned with failures, although this is something of a simplification. In some cases normal behaviour is hazardous; in many cases the combination of normal behaviour of one system and a failure in another can combine in a manner which is hazardous. This will become rather clearer when we consider failure analysis methods.

[3] Hazard analysis for new classes of system is difficult, and there are few guidelines.

will have a list of known hazards which they will use as a basis for analysing a proposed new system. The set of hazards is unlikely to be modified unless some new technology or a major change in operating philosophy (of the embedding system or platform) indicates that new forms of accident, or ways of causing an accident, are likely to be encountered. Hazard analysis is usually judgmental, although the chemical engineering industry have developed a set of techniques known as HAZOPS which give a systematic approach for analysing hazards.

A second aspect of hazard analysis is concerned with the severity of the accidents, and hence of the hazards. Typically this is done by analysing the accidents, or the sequence of accidents that might follow from a particular hazard. Again this form of analysis is often experience based, although there are techniques, e.g. event tree analysis (ETA) [2], which can be used for modelling such sequences. The severity is then assessed according to some quantitative or qualitative, scale. The scale might simply be number of deaths.

In qualitative terms distinctions will be made between minor injury, a single death and multiple deaths. Usually there are standards for particular industries that determine the scales to be used, e.g. IDS 00-56 for defence applications in the UK [12]. It is quite common to combine some measure of the expected frequency with which the hazard may arise and the severity of the hazard to arrive at a measure for risk. Where quantitative information is available, risk may also be expressed in numerical terms, e.g. expected number of deaths per operational hour. Where qualitative analysis is carried out, often risks are divided into a small number of levels, as is done, for example, in DefStan 00–56 [12]. Much has been written about hazard analysis. The topic is crucial to the study of safety-critical real-time systems, but it is rather outside the scope of this paper. Hence, for the rest of this paper, we shall assume that the identification of hazards is unproblematic.

2.1.3 Generic Requirements

There are two "generic requirements" which are frequently encountered:

- no single point failure shall lead to a hazard;
- the probability of a given hazard arising, regardless of the cause and how many failures are involved, shall not exceed a figure derived from an assessment of the severity of the accident which might arise from the hazard;

In practice the probability might be expressed per unit time, or per demand, depending on the nature of the system. For real-time systems it is likely that the requirements will be expressed per unit time, although arguably a distinction should be made between periodic (time-triggered) and aperiodic (event-triggered) systems.

Thus, in practice, it is common to have safety requirements expressed as probabilistic bounds on the frequency of occurrence of particular failures. The aim of the design process is to ensure, so far as possible, that these requirements are met. The aim of the design analysis is to demonstrate that the requirements have been met.

2.2 Design Analysis

In practical developments of real-time safety-critical systems there is iteration and interaction between the design and analysis processes. For the sake of simplicity in presentation we describe the analysis techniques as if the designs were fixed, then discuss the relationships between design and analysis in section 4. We first consider types of analysis, then discuss three of the most important techniques.

2.2.1 Types of Analysis

All the analysis techniques are concerned with identifying and assessing the propagation of failures through the system, and this clearly depends on the design. This analysis is difficult both philosophically and practically: it is very difficult to know when all possible failure modes have been considered and the number of failure modes to consider is vast. Complementary techniques have been developed to try combat these difficulties. A common classification of techniques is:

- **top-down** — working from hazards down toward failure modes of elementary components;
- **bottom-up** — working up from component failure modes towards hazards.

In practice the techniques also consider the physical structure of the platform and the way this affects propagation of failures, see Section 2.2.4.
It is common also to distinguish two uses of the techniques:

- **logical** — concerned with the possibilities for failure propagation;
- **quantitative** — concerned with the likelihood of failures propagating. Logical analysis usually serves as a pre-cursor to quantitative analysis, although the uses may be more strongly linked (see below).

Most practical safety analysis processes involve the use of three techniques:

- **fault-tree analysis (FTA)** — a top-down technique used to assess probability of hazards arising;
- **failure modes and effects analysis (FMEA)** — a bottom-up technique used to assess the effects of individual failure modes (there is a variant known as FMECA, see Section 2.2.3);
- **zonal analysis** — used to assess the interaction between the embedding systems, basing the analysis on the failure propagation within the physical zones of the platform.

Other techniques may be used, but these are the most important, and the most widely used. We discuss each in turn.

2.2.2 FTA

Fault-trees [15] are widely used for system and hardware analysis, and can be applied to software. They are used at all levels, from platform down to embedding and real-time system (and on sub-systems constructed using non-computing technologies). We illustrate the general principles and the application to real-time systems.

2.2.2.1 Basic Concepts

Fault-trees are used to represent the propagation of failures, particularly combinations of failures, through a system. A single tree will relate to a single hazard. The trees are usually represented vertically on a page, with the single "top event", i.e. the event at the top of the tree, representing the hazard, and more primitive (partial) causes of the hazard appearing at lower levels in the tree. The events in the tree are combined at nodes.

Each node is referred to as a gate, and there is a strong analogy with digital logic. The meaning of an and gate is that all input events have to occur in order that the output event occurs. The meaning of an or gate is that at least one input event has to occur in order that the output event occurs. There is no restriction on the arity of gates, i.e. the number of inputs that they may have. The notation used is quite conventional.

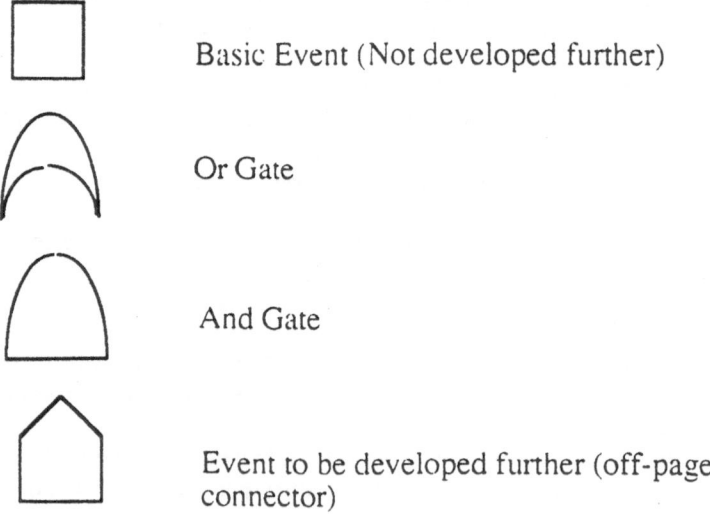

Basic Event (Not developed further)

Or Gate

And Gate

Event to be developed further (off-page connector)

Fig. 1. Basic Fault-Tree Symbols

It is common for fault-trees to be large, and for them to be split across many pages, hence the need for off-page connectors. It is also fairly common to have other forms of gate — exclusive or, majority (m out of n) and inhibit, where one particular input can prevent failure propagation. Obviously these are just convenient ways of simplifying trees, and to make their meaning more immediate, as these logical gates can be constructed from the more primitive gates (and negation).

We can give a simple illustration of a fault tree:

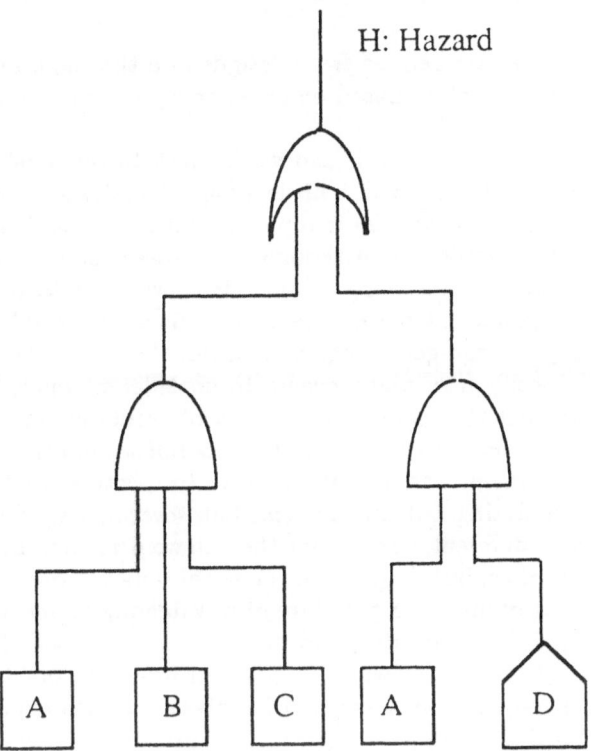

Fig. 2. Simple Example Fault Tree

In this simple example the hazard arises if events A, B and C occur simultaneously, or if events A and D (which will be expanded elsewhere) occur simultaneously. It is common for intermediate events (the output of the and gates above) to be unlabelled. In the example related to the aircraft braking system illustrated above, the hazard and the events might be:

H application of wheel brakes between V1 and VR;
A aircraft is between V1 and VR;
B pilot issues a "brake" command;
C faulty mode logic in BCSU fails to override the command from the pilot;

D the brakes and steering control unit (BSCU) computer issuing a "brake" command, between V1 and VR, with no input from the pilot.

We can see that the "events" actually represent a mixture of events and states. This is common in practical application of fault trees. It is also common for one event (or state) to be part of more than one combination which could lead to a hazard, as in the case above.

2.2.2.2 Derivation of Fault-Trees

In practice fault-trees are derived from designs in a thorough manner, although the design "analysis" is often based on experience, not on any mechanically applicable set of rules.

The analysis starts with a hazard, and works back through the design, looking for possible causes of that hazard. This is a logical analysis, and it produces the first level of the tree. The process is repeated until the tree is complete (hence the use of the term top-down). Although this process sounds simple there are some important judgements being made. First, we need to decide how many failure modes to consider at once, because it is usually possible for some event to occur if enough things go wrong. Sometimes the requirements (or relevant standards) will specify how many events to consider at once, but often there is simply a judgement that some combination of events is "incredible" and can be discounted. Note, however that there is probabilistic information being taken into account in producing the logical structure (cf. section 2.2.1).

Second, we are analysing not one system, but several, i.e. when a failure has occurred we have a different system, not the one we designed. In some cases this may be a trivial change, but, in general, the set of failure modes will change once the first failure has occurred, e.g. failure of a watchdog timer will (potentially) allow new timing failures to arise, and perhaps other classes of failure as well. Although this may sound somewhat trite it is of profound practical significance and is one of the reasons why this sort of analysis requires experience and judgement.

Third, we need to decide when to stop, i.e. when we have gone to enough detail. Is this when we have gone down to individual integrated circuits, gates, or transistors? In practice the answer is partly governed by the use of information from the FMEA, and partly governed by practicality, regarding the cost of the analysis, and the degree of risk associated with missing out the next level of analysis. It is also influenced by the use of redundancy, as we may be able to show that failures from particular sources will be masked, and hence do not require further analysis.

2.2.2.3 Manipulation of Fault-Trees

The logical structures constructed by considering hazards can now be analysed to remove certain impossibilities. Specifically the trees are analysed to determine circumstances where some combination of events is infeasible, i.e. a sensor has to give a valid reading and an invalid one at the same time. These infeasible sub-trees are known as cut-sets, and are removed from the trees. Thus logical analysis yields a reduced tree containing all possible causes of a hazard, up to some assumptions about the number of coincident events to consider.

In principle the logical structures can be used for quantitative analysis, simply by adding the failure probabilities of the root nodes of the tree, and propagating the probabilities through the tree. However it is normal to do a further stage of manipulation on the tree — to produce the so-called minimal cut-set form. This involves reducing the tree to a disjunct of conjuncts, i.e. a tree with an or gate at the top, fed by a set of and gates. The combination of events at the input to each and gate represents an unnecessary, but sufficient, cause of the hazard. Quantitative analysis can be carried out much more easily in this form — the hazard probability is the sum of products of the probabilities of the leaf failure modes [4] (the inputs to the and gates)[4]. The tree of figure 2 is in minimal cutset form.

2.2.2.4 Application to Real-Time Systems

The application of the above to hardware systems where we can evaluate failure probabilities is fairly unproblematic — but what of real-time systems containing software? We need to consider both the use of fault-trees to analyse software, and the use of quantitative analysis. We consider probabilistic issues first. It is now well-understood that probabilistic evaluation of failure probabilities is infeasible, given the failure rates demanded for safety-critical applications [3]. The only realistic approaches are:

- to assume the software failure probability is zero, i.e. that it is correct vis a vis the hazards[5];
- to assume that the software failure probability is one, and engineer the system so that no reliance is placed on the software.

This latter approach is impractical in many applications, e.g. unstable fighter aircraft, hence the former approach is (perhaps implicitly) adopted. Much could be said about the validity of the first approach, but the debate is really outside the scope of this paper. However it is worth noting that, in effect, this is what is done in other branches of engineering. It is assumed, when carrying out fault-tree analysis, that the design is correct. Considerable effort, using established design and analysis (or testing) principles, goes into ensuring that this assumption is as well-founded as possible. Whether or not this is an acceptable approach for software is a socio-technical issue which we do not broach here.

Some work has been carried out on the application of fault-tree analysis to software. A set of "templates" has been produced for deriving fault-trees from Ada programs [9]. This approach seems to be bottom up, not top-down, but

---

[4] There is an isomorphism between the boolean algebra underlying the fault-tree and arithmetic on probabilities.

[5] This "special case of correctness" is sometimes referred to as safety integrity.

it is possible to apply it in a top-down manner (but see section 3.3). Fault-trees applied in this way are very strongly analogous to Dijkstra's wp-calculus, although they focus on hazards, not the "normal" post-condition of the program [5]. In practice, fault-trees are rarely applied to software although they were used in the assessment of the Darlington reactor protection system in Canada.

2.2.2.5 Summary

Fault-trees are the primary analytical technique for demonstrating that a design satisfies the second class of safety requirement — that a given hazard is (acceptably) unlikely to arise.

Fault-trees are really a system analysis tool, but they can be applied to software, and are certainly applicable to systems containing software. The basic data for fault-trees is the set of failure modes for the system components. This data comes from FMEAs and, to a lesser extent, from zonal analysis.

2.2.3 FMEA

FMEA [1] is another widely used technique, again being general in its applicability. Like FTA it is most properly viewed as a systems analysis technique, although it can be applied to systems developed using particular technologies, e.g. analogue electronics.

We discuss general principles, and the application of FMEAs to real-time systems.

2.2.3.1 Basic Principles

In contrast with FTA, FMEA is a bottom up technique, concerned with the effects of single failure modes on the rest of the system. Specifically the components of a system are analysed to determine their failure modes. The effects of these failure modes are then deduced by consideration of the design. The results of this "analysis" are then set out in tabular form.

The tables represent both the failure modes of components, and the effects of those failure modes on the system containing the components. The technique is applied hierarchically to deal with the fact that a complete embedding system, or platform, is too complex to analyse in one stage (i.e. a system at one level is treated as a component at the next). This is the essence of the technique, although the application is rather more complex[6].

A fragment of a typical FMEA table is illustrated below. Again we use an aircraft brakes and steering system as an example:

---

[6] An analogy with Go seems appropriate: the rules are trivial, yet it takes a lifetime to learn to play the game (use the analysis technique) with maximum effect — and its hard for a computer to play (automate)!

Failure Mode	Phase	Probability per hour	Effect	Symptoms
Loss of one hydraulic supply	Ground	10-6	None as dual supply	Indicator on Secondary Panel

This simple fragment shows the component failure mode on the left, and the effect in the fourth column from the left. The additional columns show:

- **phase** — this is added to simplify the analysis, as the effects (and perhaps the probability) will be different in the air to on the ground;
- **probability per hour** — this is the likelihood that the failure mode will arise, based on historical data, or calculations (see below);
- **symptoms** — these are the way in which the failure mode will manifest itself — in this case there is an explicit indication to the pilot.

Even this illustration is simplistic — FMEAs may have nearer twenty columns, but the example serves to show the basic ideas. As with FTA, there are a number of points to consider.

2.2.3.2 Important Characteristics of FMEA

First, the FMEAs are the primary means of demonstrating satisfaction of the first generic requirement — that no single point failure can lead to a hazard. This is obviously straightforward when we can say that a particular failure mode has no effect at that level. In general the situation is more complex. It may be that the failure mode has an effect at the level analysed, but that it does not cause an overall failure of the platform. In many cases there will be some effect from the failure, but the effect is controllable, e.g. the loss of the computerised flying control system on an A320 is controllable due to the presence of mechanical control over trim FMEA[7]. In the above circumstances it is still very likely that the system would be deemed to have satisfied the "no single point failure" requirement, at least in this respect.

Second, there is the difficult issue of what we consider to be a single point failure, and the associated issue of when to stop the analysis. FMEAs are developed hierarchically (see below) so we need to determine what is a "single point" at the level of abstraction at which we are working in the design process. This is somewhat judgmental, and it is hard to substantiate the judgements, even via fault-injection experiments on real equipment, as it is very hard to monitor and isolate failures. The decision of when to stop the analysis is usually taken pragmatically. It is common to go down to the level of complete electronic components, e.g. a CPU chip, but not below that level. A decision to go further would result in massive analyses (e.g. there are 1.2M transistors on an M68020, each of which can fail in more than one way!) and probably little improvement in the

---

[7] Strictly speaking, this is not a valid example, as the flying controls could not be lost due to a single point failure; the example was chosen for ease of description.

quality of the safety analysis. In practice when analyses are truncated in this way it is important to ensure that the failure modes assumed for the component are "pessimistic enough" to cover all the real failure modes (although there is a penalty of being too pessimistic).

Third, we need to consider possible sources for the failure rate data. In many cases accurate figures are available for the basic components, e.g. valves, or electronic components, based on extensive historical use of the components. In some cases the reliability data is published in handbooks and there are programs for evaluating the failure probabilities of complex electronic circuits or assemblies. For less familiar components other techniques are used, and the best figures that can be produced may be derived from comparisons with other similar components. The environment of the components is crucial and, for example, in an aircraft engine electronic systems have to withstand lightning strike inducing fields of about 1000V/m, and this may be the limiting factor in the reliability (failure rate), not the intrinsic failure rate of the components.

Fourth, FMEAs are developed in hierarchies to help master the bulk of the analyses.

The hierarchies often relate to real physical boundaries in equipment, rather than some idealised abstractions. Whilst this approach is effective, it is often the case that effects at one level are not treated as failure modes at the next — the effects are re-grouped to simplify analysis. Whilst this doesn't invalidate the approach, it indicates the extent to which it is judgmental.

This is another reason why it is not entirely straightforward to (fully) automate FMEA, although of course it is possible to give automated clerical support to FMEA[8].

Fifth, there are strong links to FTA, but not as clear as one might expect. The "bottom level" failure modes in the FMEA ought to be the leaf nodes in the fault-tree[9], although many of these leaves will relate to normal states of the system, not failures, as illustrated above.

There usually is a clear mapping at this level, but there is not a strong correlation at higher levels — the intermediate nodes on the FTA do not correspond to effects in the FMEA as the FTA considers multiple failures. Again, this does not invalidate the approaches, but it makes it harder to use them as means of validating each other.

Sixth, it is quite common to use FMECA [1] — failure modes effects and criticality (or consequences) analysis. This is an extension of FMEA, which ranks the effects according to their severity. This is used to focus the analysis and to reduce the burden of producing tables for effects which are of low criticality (even if they are fairly probable).

---

[8] Many practical applications of FMEA are carried out simply with a combination of a database and text processing software.

[9] Strictly, they should be the events of entering a given failure mode.

2.2.3.3 Application to Real-Time Systems

Finally, we should consider software, especially that in real-time systems. FMEA is not normally applied to software, although it is arguable that Leveson's templates for Ada are rather more like FMEA templates than FTAs (albeit based only on logical failure modes). So far as the author is aware there has only been one attempt to apply FMEA to software at a detailed level — and this simply showed that the software potentially had lots of failure modes and effects, especially if the underlying hardware failed. The general conclusion seems to be that it is not appropriate to apply FMEA at this level. Raheja however argues that it is possible to use FMEA as a "reliability growth" tool for systems containing software [14]. We return to this point in section 3.

2.2.3.4 Summary

FMEA and FMECA are the basic means of showing satisfaction of the first generic requirement. In practice they are very voluminous and may run into thousands of pages for a complex electro-mechanical system. They complement FTA, but are not normally applied to software.

2.2.4 Zonal Analysis

FTA and FMEA are focused on specific systems (usually embedding systems in the terms introduced above) although they consider issues such as loss of power supply, etc. As mentioned above it is also necessary to consider the interaction between systems. This is the role of zonal analysis, sometimes known as zonal hazard analysis.

In performing zonal analysis a platform is divided into zones which correspond to physical sub-divisions of the platform (physical fault-containment structures). The interaction of systems (real-time and other sub-systems of the embedding system) within the zone are then considered, by analysing the way in which their behaviour, or failure modes, might affect the other systems. For example, the effect of the leak of hydraulic fluid on electronic systems would be considered, as would EMC[10] effects. Other examples would be the effect of a rotor burst in an aero engine leading to blades going through a wing. The results of zonal analysis are, again, represented in a tabular way and they are very similar in concept to FMEAs, except that the failure mode and effects cross systems, rather than being hierarchically related within systems. Consequently we do not amplify on issues of representation, but consider a few important properties of zonal analysis.

First, zonal analysis is important. Many accidents involving real-time systems have involved unanticipated combinations of events. There is also a risk of common mode failures, that is a single failure source which induces effects in many components or systems at once, producing failures which were thought to be "in-

---

[10] Electro-Magnetic Compatibility, which is concerned with the effects of electromagnetic radiation from one set of electronic/electrical circuits on another.

credible". Zonal analysis will tend to detect such possibilities, e.g. by identifying ways in which logically independent systems can interact through physical proximity. Zonal analysis is intrinsically interdisciplinary, and one of the aims is to get representatives of different disciplines to communicate in order to determine "cross-discipline" failure propagation. The author is aware of failures (which adversely affected availability, not safety) that have occurred due to inadequate communication between hydraulic and electrical engineers when modifying a protection system. The aim of zonal analysis is to detect these omissions, and to ensure that they are taken into account in FMEA.

Second, in principle zonal analysis should be applied hierarchically, as with FMEAs. (The zones are always decomposed hierarchically.) However if the zones are identified systematically the likelihood of there being significant effects in a parent zone from a failure in a child zone should be very low, and it may be possible to carry out zonal analysis in a much "flatter" way. However an aircraft engine fan burst is an example where one failure (or its effects) may propagate through several zones.

Third, zonal analysis provides input to FTA in a similar way to FMEA. The effects of one system on another should form leaf nodes in the fault-trees for the second system. This sort of relationship is found in practice. In the case of software we would expect the effects of certain sorts of failures to appear as "erroneous" inputs, e.g. corrupted data from a sensor, and to be taken into account accordingly in the software fault-trees. Results of zonal analysis, i.e. the effects of one system on another, may also appear as failure modes in FMEAs.

Finally, zonal analysis is not normally applied to software — however there may be a need so to do. Typically software functions which are intended to be independent are kept in separate processors — the implicit zonal analysis being that a failure of one software function cannot affect another. The validity of this point is questionable, especially where we have communicating processes which may lock resources. Further, if supposedly independent software functions share a processor and are kept apart by a "safety kernel" then there may indeed be a need for a zonal analysis — where the zones are the "containment areas" enforced by the kernel.

Zonal analysis can perhaps most readily be thought of as an adjunct to FMEA, concerned with system to system failure effects, not the effects within one system. It can also be thought of as the link from physical structure to failure modes. Zonal analysis is keyed to the physical structure of the platform, whereas FTAs and FMEAs are more (but not entirely) concerned with logical (design) structure.

2.3 Strengths and Limitations

The first thing that should be said about these techniques is that they work — that is they have been applied in many industries, e.g. civil aerospace, and have helped produce remarkably safe artefacts. This is not a trite observation. The systems and problems the techniques deal with are very complex, and it is quite an accolade that the techniques do scale up to be used on such systems. However, they are not without their limitations — at least seen from an academic, or scientific, perspective[11].

The techniques introduced above are systematic in the sense that they are based on (fairly) well-defined procedures, but not in the sense of having a strong "scientific" basis[12].

One obvious manifestation of this is the weak link between design and the analyses, e.g. FMEA and FTA. This is a problem both in deriving the FMEA or FTA in the first place, and in updating them when the design changes. In practice experienced engineers can derive FMEAs and fault-trees from designs, but there is no genuine analytical basis for the derivation, except in a few specific cases, e.g. "sneak circuit analysis" which addresses certain failure modes of electronic circuits. Our aim in section 3 is to indicate the beginnings of (what is believed to be) a "scientific" basis for these analyses.

This is the main limitation in principle, but there are also a number of pragmatic problems, in addition to the issue identified above. The use of the techniques, e.g. FMEA, often produces pessimistic results, so the analysis is often followed by "engineering judgement" in adjusting the figures. The difficulties can easily be seen by considering modern electronic circuits. For a simple electronic circuit almost all component failures will lead to a circuit failure. With more complex components, the designs often (deliberately and as a side-effect of complexity of the state space) mask failures, and the straightforward use of reliability formulae will give pessimistic results.

Strictly, these problems should be approached by careful design analysis and the use of Markov (or semi-Markov) models to calculate reliability. Further, these analyses should be focused on failure modes which are potentially hazardous. At the present "state of the art" Markov analysis tools are incapable of handling the most complex systems, so safety engineers are forced back on engineering judgement. Again the aim here is not to be critical, merely to point out some of the difficulties of applying what seem to be straightforward techniques.

We have already hinted at the relationship between design and analysis. Strictly speaking design and analysis should be carried out in a highly integrated way — the identification of too high a probability of failure using a fault tree should result in a design modification, and hence the reduction of the probability of some leaf event, or perhaps the introduction of an inhibit gate into the tree. In practice the links are much weaker — indeed the division between the groups doing the design and analysis is often formalised in the company organisation. We return to the technical aspects of this relationship in section 4.

The final comment we must make is on the bulk of the analysis documentation. The safety documentation for modern systems such as civil aircraft run into hundreds of thousands of pages[13]. This is a major impediment to understanding,

---

[11] This is not to say that the techniques are without foundation. As is often the case the engineering practice has preceded the science, and part of my aim here is to draw out the scientific underpinnings of the analyses.

[12] Perhaps engineering or systematic would be a better term.

[13] Perhaps there is an optimisation to be made here between the safety of air travel, and the damage to the environment and people caused by destruction of rain-forests!

and producing effective and appropriate analyses. Our only intellectual weapons
here are abstraction — finding effective abstractions which do not reduce the
quality of the analysis, and structuring. However we believe it is possible to give
some more structured and systematic underpinnings to the analyses, and hence
to provide some degree of automation, see section 4.

3 Underlying Concepts and Their Use

As should be clear from the above descriptions, the underlying basis of the failure analyses is a causal model of the system of interest, primarily focused on
events which we might term "failures". This realisation seems fairly unsurprising
— many safety engineers have appreciated this fact for many years. The crux,
however, is how to exploit it. The aim here is to indicate an approach which,
hopefully, represents the beginning of a "scientific underpinning" for these safety
analyses in a form which can also be linked with the design process, and also
lead to partial mechanisation of the analyses.

We first amplify on the nature of causal models of systems, then consider the way
in which the modelling of failures can be systematised, before addressing the key
issue for making the approach practical and powerful — (semi-)automatically
deriving the causal models from the design. It should be stressed, at this point,
that we have moved from describing current industrial practice to research hypotheses, albeit hypotheses supported with a modicum of data (non-refutation).

3.1 Causal Models

The nature of causality, and hence the building of causal models, is very subtle
and complex. However we take a pragmatic view and present here a set of views
about the way in which causal structures can usefully be modelled for the analysis
of safety critical real-time systems, without going into philosophical details. We
first discuss the basis of the causal models which we believe underly methods
such as FMEA and FTA, then illustrate the links to these methods.

Fairly obviously, the causal model must contain at least two components:

- a causal relation;
- a set of events (or states).

We discuss each of these aspects of the model in turn.

3.1.1 Causal Relations

In producing models we need to decide on a number of properties which we
require these components of our models to possess, the most important being
whether the basic causal relation represents necessary cause or sufficient cause.
Note that this is an issue of modelling, not metaphysics. In the real world only
sufficient causes cause anything!

Intuitively it seems sensible that we should demand that the causal models show sufficient cause, i.e. event A is sufficient to cause event B, as this gives a simple and unequivocal model which is easy to interpret. Arguably we should further require that the causal relations shown are necessary and sufficient — this implies that we have then given a complete description of the cause of some effect. However this implies that we (may) have to write very complex causal descriptions, often involving modelling large quantities of physics — things that we would rather "take as read" rather than having to spell them out explicitly.

More pragmatically, these are not the sort of structures we see in fault-trees, and we need to treat fault-trees as a special case of the causal models.

After reducing a fault-tree to the minimal cutset form (see figure 2) the outputs from the and gates are sufficient but unnecessary causes of the hazard (sufficient, because any one of them can cause the hazard, unnecessary, because none of them have to occur for the hazard to occur). Similarly, the inputs to the and gates represent insufficient but necessary parts of an unnecessary but sufficient condition to cause the hazard. These insufficient but necessary parts of an unnecessary but sufficient condition, known as INUS conditions have been studied by philosophers as they are the most common form of causal description found in practice[14].

Before the fault-tree is reduced to this form the causal relationships are less uniform.

In FMEAs the causal relationship between failure mode and effect is also an INUS relation, but there is no explicit representation of the unnecessary but sufficient condition. This condition really is the combination of the failure event with the design of the component or system being analysed. In practice we need to build models where we explicitly state the nature of the causal dependencies, and where we can have necessary, sufficient, etc. causal relations as appropriate. For pragmatic reasons many of the causal descriptions will reduce to an INUS form.

3.1.2 Representing Events, States and Conditions

A further important issue concerns the basic units in the model, i.e. the states and events. In the examples of FTA and FMEA we have discussed both events and states and used them almost interchangeably. This is not sloppiness. In practice they are used fairly interchangeably — for example a failure mode in an FMEA may be a state, but entry into the failure mode may be the event which appears in an associated fault-tree. (Even though these are conceptually different they are often given the same description.) The interchangeability of these notions reflects a need to be flexible in modelling. Consequently we introduce a notion of a condition which encompasses both states and events, i.e. states and events are seen as special cases of conditions, and build the causal structures between

---

[14] See Mackie[10] for a full, if somewhat philosophical, treatment of the nature of causal descriptions. This "sweeps up" issues such as non-determinism, etc. which bedevil such analyses.

conditions[15].

The next issue is the selection of the level(s) of abstraction, and physical bases, which are appropriate for producing such models. This depends on the purpose of the model. For very early models, e.g. to be used in hazard analysis, we may be happy to model conditions as uninterpreted names (predicate or function symbols if we represent the models in some form of logic). Later we might find utility in having an explicit model of the physical artefact being analysed and to define the conditions as predicates over the model (or descriptions using the terms of that model if using natural language). For hazard analysis this may be a physical model of the environment and the platform; for a real-time system it may be a form of computational model.

In fact, for real-time systems we need (at least) two computational models for different purposes:

- an architectural computational model (ACM) — concerned with the broad-level process and communication (data flow) structures, together with scheduling;
- a concrete (implementation level) computational model (CCM) — concerned with processors, peripherals, the run-time kernel, and the like.

The ACM is the basis for analysis at high level design, and the CCM is the basis for analysing implementations. Clearly these models should be related, in the sense that properties in the ACM should be abstractions of the CCM. Similar relationships should exist between the causal models, and that brings us on to their content.

3.1.3 Content of the Causal Models

For "normal behaviour" a causal model would follow the design structure fairly directly. For failure behaviour this is not the case, as physical issues affect the causal structures (cf. zonal analysis) and failures can, in effect, result in changes to the design structure anyway. Thus what we need is the causal relations to represent "failure propagation" through the design. In part this will reflect the design structure. For example the emission of a message on a LAN unintentionally will (may) cause a failure in the recipient — here the failures propagation preserves (and observes) the design structure. Simplistically we can view failures as falling into two classes — structure preserving, and structure modifying. Thus a causal model used to represent the propagation of failures through a system contains representations of failures which propagate according to the design structure, and those which violate, and/or modify, it as will often be the case for those relations which correspond to zonal analyses.

Causal models based on the principles outlined above can be used as the basis for deriving the results of the standard failure analyses. More precisely, if the

---

[15] It is possible to give quite a good set of rigorous definitions of the differences between state, event and condition, but it seems inappropriate to consider such issues here.

models contain all possible combinations of failures[16] then the FTA, FMEA and zonal analyses are special cases of the causal model. The FMEA is an abstraction from the causal model being concerned with "one to one" causal relations, restricted to conditions concerned with a particular system. Note that this is an information losing abstraction — the information about the design and its part in the causal model is hidden when producing the FMEA. The zonal analysis is a similar abstraction, here concerned with causal relations where the related conditions are associated with different systems. The FTA is a more complex abstraction, where the causal relations are "many to one", and the cardinality of the domain of the relation depends on what are deemed to be credible combinations of failures. For future reference we refer to a causal model which represents failure propagation as a failure propagation model, or FPM.

3.1.4 Summary

In summary, an FPM is a generalisation of the standard failure analyses (or rather the results of applying those analyses). In itself, the observation is interesting, but not very useful. Utility comes if this observation enables us to gain some analytical power. It seems possible that these analyses could be generated semi-automatically from design descriptions, given knowledge of the relevant computational or physical model. In order to see how this might be done we need to consider ways of classifying failures, and recovery techniques, as these may give us the basis for automating the analysis. We return to the issue of automation in section 3.3.

3.2 Failure and Recovery Models

The relationship between the design and the FPM arises through the way that the components of the design fail, and the ways in which they can detect and recover from failure.
We consider ways of systematically modelling such properties, in order to help bridge the gap between Ted design and the FPM. For brevity we "lump together" the failure detection and recovery mechanisms, although we recognise that they are distinct concepts.

3.2.1 Classification of Failures

It has long been recognised that it is possible to classify failures. Probably the most widely used classification is due to Ezhilchelvan and Shrivastava [7], and this is relevant to the architectural level (ACM). Expressed simply, their model is:

- **omission** — an output (action) is omitted (does not occur);
- **timely** — an output (action) occurs when it should, but with the wrong value (effect);

---

[16] Conceptually — clearly we cannot construct this model in its entirety.

– **timing** — an output (action) occurs, but not when it should;
– **commission** — an output (action) occurs even though it should not.

The model is exhaustive, i.e. it covers all cases, but it is subtle and it requires interpretation in terms of a particular computational model. The classes of failure are all related, in the sense that an omission failure is an extreme case of a timing failure, and so on. We use this model in the following discussion for illustrative purposes, but note that different models are needed at different levels of abstraction, and for different technologies.

The interpretation in terms of a computational model is important, for two reasons.

First, the meaning of the terms is rather different in the different computational models. Our attempt to formalise these concepts [6] shows that a precise model of computation, e.g. of the relationships between inputs and outputs of processes, is needed to properly distinguish the above classes of failures. Second, the propagation of the failure (i.e. it's consequences) depends on the computational model. For example, an omission failure in a data flow system might lead to timing errors, or further omission failures. An omission error in a shared memory system might lead to timely errors (wrong values processed) or perhaps deadlock, if access to the shared memory is protected by locks. Thus, the failure classification can be used in conjunction with the computational model as a way of deriving the consequences of failures. As indicated above, other categories are needed for the CCM.

Before we illustrate this more fully, however, we need to consider two other aspects of failures: their permanency, and the way they are detected and treated, i.e. the recovery mechanisms.

Failures may be permanent or transitory. More precisely, failures may fall anywhere on a spectrum of permanence, where the end points, or extremes, of the spectrum can be characterised as:

– permanent (irrecoverable);
– momentary (transient).

These definitions are intended to be interpreted relative to the mission of the platform.

Obviously the permanence of the failure affects the way that it propagates (consider for example the propagation of the effects of a permanent short circuit), but is has more influence on the way that it is handled. This leads us on to forms of recovery.

3.2.2 Classification of Recovery Mechanisms

Again it is possible to classify recovery techniques, but this is somewhat more difficult than with failures [6]. In general recovery techniques depend very much on the design of a specific system, and the difficulties of detecting erroneous states. However it is useful to think of the recovery techniques from the point of view of the way in which they transform failures. For example, using replicating redundancy most classes of (single point) failure will be transformed to null, i.e. they will be masked. Using a watchdog timer, a timing failure can be trapped and, via the substitution of an estimated value, transformed into a timely failure (a value domain failure, but the value is delivered on time). Recovery techniques can therefore be categorised in terms of the failure transformation which they effect. Clearly this form of concept underlies FMEAs, as they show a transformation from failure modes to effects, including null (this represents the case where a single point failure cannot lead to a hazard). Note that this means that the FPM is a forest, not a tree, as there are many "null" events with quite complex causes!

In general the set of transformation classes is defined by the failure classification — in principle it is possible to convert any form of failure into any other, or null. Thus with N failure classes there are $N + 1$ transformation classes, allowing for the fact that a failure may be unchanged by a component. In practice failure detection will not be perfect, and this is an area where failure (or error) detection probability might be introduced in order to generate (say) a Markov model to estimate the probability of an effect in an FMEA given knowledge of the probabilities of the basic failure modes. This is an important possibility, but space doesn't allow us to investigate it further.

3.2.3 Summary

The categorisation of failure modes and recovery techniques gives us a basis for deriving and structuring FPMs (or the standard analyses) from designs. We make no claims that we have given an adequate set of failure classifications for the relevant computational models, but hope that we have illustrated the concepts. In practice specific models may be needed for particular real-time systems architectures, see section 3.4 below. There is a further possible way of categorising failures, but we leave this to the discussion of derivation of causal models from the design, as it affects the practicality of automating this process.

3.3 Derivation of Causal Models from the Design

It is clear that causal models of failure are derived from the design in that FTAs and FMEAs are developed by safety engineers using the design as their starting point. As we indicated above there is a certain measure of "black art" in doing this, and the FPM is only of utility, as opposed to scientific interest, if it can be (semi-)automatically derived from designs. Our aim here is to provide some evidence that this is possible, even if the process is not yet fully understood. We start by considering an existing approach to safety analysis, and then draw out some more general principles.

3.3.1 An Existing Approach

Our first simple example of a derivation technique, is the use of "templates" for code level FTA of Ada programs [9]. Leveson and her colleagues have produced a set of templates which can be applied mechanically to derive fault trees from Ada code. (Indeed we have implemented a tool which carries out part of the derivation [8].) Here the design model is the Ada code (implicitly the CCM is the semantics of Ada) and there is only one class of failure — a logical error in the program, excluding errors in the control structure[17]. This design representation, plus the fault assumption, is enough to generate the fault-tree. But what of the more general causal model, i.e. the FPM?

We commented earlier that this use of templates appears to be bottom-up, whereas fault-trees are applied top-down. More specifically, they derive the structures from consideration of failures, not working back from hazards. The templates actually generate the underlying FPM for the program, from the given fault assumption. This is a (very small) subset of the complete FPM. The "genuine" fault-trees can then be derived from the FPM, once the hazards have been identified, by pruning away that part of the structure which does not relate to the hazard. Note that this clarifies the basis of the Ada "fault-trees" and illustrates that the FPM can be generated from a design, at least in some circumstances. This is an important observation, as our experience is that safety engineers find the notion of the fault-tree templates somewhat confusing, as they run counter to the principles of normal fault-trees.

We also note that, in this case, the failures considered are logical — that is concerned with the design, rather than physical failure modes. As the analysis is carried out in terms of program structure, this is, in fact, a form of program verification, albeit one which is directed towards hazards, rather than partial or total correctness. We have previously explored the relationship between fault-trees and Dijkstra's wp-calculus [5], but the realisation that the templates generate an FPM post-dates that paper.

3.3.2 Further Examples

Whilst we have shown one example where an FPM can be generated from a design we need to show that the approach is general if we are to prove its utility. It is easiest to address this question by considering the architectural stage, specifically the ACM, as this is an important abstraction for analysing the behaviour of a real-time system. We can again best do this by means of some (contrasting) examples. We consider three superficially similar cases where a sensor emits time-stamped data to a processor which makes some calculations and passes on the data. Let us call the sensor S and the processor P, we then have:

- event triggered architecture (1) — omission failure from S leads to P not being triggered, and hence an omission failure from P;
- event triggered architecture (2) — omission failure from S leads to P not being triggered; this is detected by a watchdog W and an estimated value is returned, thus P has a timely failure;

---

[17] This is not made explicit in the paper, and it has not been checked with Leveson, but all the templates appear to have exactly this characteristic.

- time triggered architecture — omission failure from S does not affect the triggering of P, but P detects stale data (using the timestamp) and an estimated value is returned, thus P has a timely failure;

Other examples could be given, but the above indicates how the failure modes interact with the computational model to determine the failure propagation and transformation, i.e. the contents of the FPM. It should be noted, however that the failure propagation path will not always be the same as that of the program/system data or control flow.

It seems clear that FPMs can be generated from designs, given an adequate representation of the computational model and knowledge of the relevant failure classes[18]. The main practical issue is whether or not enough in formation is present in the design representation to facilitate this analysis. We raise one more point of principle, then consider pragmatics.

3.3.3 The Feasibility of FPM Derivation

It seems very much easier to generate FPMs from designs where the failures do not change the structure of the system. If the structure does change, then the number of possibilities to consider increases enormously. In principle this is "just another modelling issue" but in practice it is likely to be very difficult to produce system or computational models which reflect the change in structure that can arise from a failure. We can thus categorise the causal relations associated with particular failure modes in terms of their ease of automated (mechanised) generation, taking the simplest first:

- causal structures follow data and control flow structure;
- causal structures do not entirely follow logical design structure, but are not contingent on the particular failure mode;
- causal structures do not follow data and control flow structure, and vary with the failure modes.

This notion needs to be generalised for other technologies, but the expression of these concepts is appropriate for real-time systems where we are concerned with computational models.

An example of this third class would be a hardware "stuck at" fault in a memory address register which causes software units to corrupt one another, but where the causal structures are determined by a mixture of the dynamic properties of the programs, which bit in the address register was stuck, the mapping of programs to memory, and so on. There is no reason, in principle, why all three cases could not be handled automatically, but it is much easier to handle the first two cases. Also, in practice, there needs to be a role for the human in determining when the failure modes are too improbable to be worth considering, so complete automation is not necessarily a panacea.

Clearly the approach implied above will only work if the design contains enough

---

[18] And probably failure sources.

information to allow the causal structures to be generated. Typically they do not — specifically design notations such as Yourdon, Ward-Mellor, etc. do not contain adequate information for the example above to be analysed. It is obviously possible to seek to improve the design representation (see section 4), but it is also possible to introduce a notation to explicitly model the flow of failures through the system, as an "intermediate step". To this end we have developed a failure propagation and transformation notation (FPTN) [8] which bridges the gap between automatic generation of the FPM from a design, and explicit definition of the FPM (more strictly FPM fragments from which the whole model can be generated). The gain here is that the system level FPM can be derived from "local rules" describing part of a design.

There is a further example system which lends corroboration to our approach. The IFME (integrated fault management environment) project[19] undertaken by BAe and the Turing Institute is primarily concerned with analysing failure behaviour of electronic systems for aerospace applications to facilitate the design of automated fault detection and reconfiguration equipment. However they have also discovered that they have enough information to be able to generate FMEAs automatically.

4 Conclusions

We have set out some basic ideas leading towards (what is hoped will become) a "scientific underpinning" for the standard failure analyses. It appears that we have produced a useful conceptual basis for such analyses, and have also provided some evidence that the ideas are of practical utility, in the sense that they can be used to automate, at least in part, the generation of FPMs and hence FTAs and FMEAs (by focusing on particular hazards or failures). Zonal hazard analyses can also be derived in a similar manner. We are not proposing that there is no room for human skill and judgement in performing these analyses — rather that some tedious and error-prone activities can be mechanically supported.

In order to make the ideas truly useful for real-time systems we need adequate computational models, and knowledge about the failure modes and their propagation through the system. We have not yet shown that this is feasible for a complete system design, and much more practical and theoretical work is needed before we can demonstrate the utility (or otherwise) of the approach. One of the important factors, however, will be the way that the analysis techniques link into the design process. As indicated earlier, the relationship between the analyses and the design process is normally rather weak. We now consider what can be done to rectify this problem.

---

[19] To the author's knowledge there are no public domain papers describing this project, although there is demonstrable software which includes a FMEA tool.

5 Relationships to the Design Process

In normal systems engineering projects, design and safety analysis are treated as distinctly separate activities. Indeed there are often organisational boundaries separating the designers and the safety engineers. Whilst this separation does give some increased confidence that there is independence in the design assessment, it can lead to inefficiencies.

Specifically there is often a need to adjust the design in the light of the safety analysis, and a tighter integration of the groups would lead to faster iteration and (probably) higher productivity. Thus there are technical and managerial reasons for wanting tighter integration between design and analysis, and these lead to technical requirements on the methods and tools used in design and analysis. Space doesn't permit a full discussion, but we can draw out a few important points.

There are many properties of a "good" design method or notation. One class of properties relates to our ability to analyse the design representation — for functionality, timing behaviour, failure behaviour, and the like. In the case of failure behaviour we need to be able to represent the causal conditions identified above, and to have enough information about the failure propagation to generate the FPM, and hence to do the analysis in terms of the FTAs and FMEAs (and zonal analysis) which we can derive from the FPM. This means that the design notation must have a strong enough underlying semantics (the semantics will amount to a computational model at many levels in the design process) to generate the FPMs, at least in the simpler cases identified above. This would then give us the basis for a quick iteration around the design, safety analysis, re-design ... cycle.

The above might sound far-fetched, but it is only the equivalent in the failure domain of system level scheduling analysis — although perhaps the analogy hints at some of the computational difficulties which will have to be overcome to make the approach tractable.

In practice safety analysis is carried out at multiple stages in the development process, starting with requirements, and working through the stages of design towards the implementation, where the failure properties can finally be established. In theory there is some form of "refinement relation" between the failure modes identified at each level, although (so far as the author is aware) no attempt is made in practice to relate failure modes at the different levels. However one can envisage using the FPM concepts hierarchically, and one could analyse the internal structure of some design unit to see how the failure modes are propagated and transformed, then use the resultant "summary" FPM as a basis for more abstract analysis.

Thinking in "bottom up" terms this is analogous to verifying the pre-post specification of a procedure, then using the resultant predicate in higher level verification, i.e. for verification of the calls of the procedure.

In practice one would proceed at least partially top-down, and produce "specifications" of the failure behaviour (FPM) for the design units. Failure behaviour is, to some extent, an emergent property, i.e. one that one cannot partition and design into a system, so these specifications would have to be viewed as guidelines, not hard specifications. Nonetheless there is the basis for a managed approach to achieving the required failure properties.

To make the above approach work, there is a need for suitable representations at all the stages of the development process, supported by appropriate semantics. There seem to be two basic approaches:

- develop a (set of) design notation(s) which is (are) sufficiently rich that FPMs can be derived from the design specifications;
- add an FPTN[20] component to existing design representations to provide an explicit, declarative, model of the failure propagation and transformation.

The basic trade-off here is between analytical power and ease of development of the design notations.

There are several possible starting points for either approach, depending on the level in the development process of interest. We briefly consider the levels associated with the ACM (architectural computational model). In practice we would expect to have a number of different architectural models, e.g. separating the application process architecture from the underlying infrastructure, but we eschew such detail in order to give a simple exposition of ideas.

At the ACM level, there are a number of candidate process algebras. However few of these have the necessary properties for hard real-time systems, and they do not seem well-suited to modelling the variety of causal conditions identified above. On the other hand, more practically derived notations such as MASCOT3 [13], and its derivatives, have more of the necessary semantics (if not the formal basis) to support the derivation of FPMs. For example inter-process communication and triggering of one process by another is explicit — so some of the examples indicated above could be modelled. However these notations have some limitations too. It is not possible from MASCOT3 diagrams to determine whether an input on one channel (a communication link) will produce output on one or several of its output channels. Thus enhancement of MASCOT3 with a set of state transition tables, or diagrams, such as StateCharts, would render the model more complete. Of course weak points in the model can be strengthened by the explicit use of FPTN style notations, or this can be used as an initial specification, to be refined at a later stage. Indeed our FPTN notation was made to look like structured design notation so that it fits in naturally with this style of design representation.

This simple illustration enables us to consider more fully the relationship between the design and the failure analysis. Assume that an FPM is derived from a design description for a particular process (task in MASCOT3 terminology), and then FMEAs and FTAs are derived from the FPM by specifying the failure modes and hazards of concern. Assume further that the design was unsatisfactory, in that there was a single point failure which could lead to a hazard.

This could then be dealt with by introducing a mechanism for detecting the

---

[20] Or a suitable enrichment of this notation, e.g. to be more explicit about the probability of detecting various failure conditions.

failure, and recovering from it. Depending on the source of the failure this could lead to an extra process operating in parallel with the process being analysed, and some voting logic. Alternatively it could lead to internal detection and recovery mechanisms within the process which would be represented by additional state transitions within the tables or StateCharts.

To realise the above in practice would require a reflection of the failure modes of the underlying infrastructure in the terms of the design representation, in other words the conditions representing the failure modes would need to have an explicit representation. This might restrict the notation to a particular class of architecture and infrastructure, but this is a trade-off we may be willing to make if we are developing a safety critical system.

We could amplify further on these ideas — but it seems inappropriate to do so, as much still needs to be done to substantiate the basic concepts, so we now draw some general conclusions.

6 Conclusions

We have tried in this paper to span both long-established industrial practice, and current research ideas, or speculation.

Safety engineers have established an effective set of techniques for safety analysis, which are applicable to real-time systems, but they are very time-consuming in use and highly judgmental. The techniques are focused on particular sorts of requirement: showing the absence of hazardous single point failures, and showing that certain hazards will not arise (are sufficiently unlikely to arise that they can be tolerated). The techniques are tabular or graphical in nature, and are implicitly based on causal models of failure propagation through systems.

Whilst these techniques are effective, they are onerous in use and produce voluminous documentation. They are difficult to update and maintain, and often bear less strong a relationship to design than might be expected. The aim of our research speculation has been to show how the underlying causal basis of the analyses might be made more explicit, and exploited to systematise, or even automate, some of the analysis. We have also discussed ways in which the analysis might be linked more tightly with the design process. It is hoped that this "formalisation" of the causal basis for safety analysis might lead to a greater ability to automate certain of the analyses, and hence address some of the problems of maintenance and mapping to design, indicated above.

Whilst these ideas are speculative, they are not without foundation. Some existing projects and tools have provided "existence proofs" that, at least part of, the process of safety analysis can be automatically supported, by exploiting (albeit implicitly) the ideas of failure and recovery models (FPM), set out above. We are carrying out a number of projects on safety analysis in York, e.g. SSAP which developed the FPTN notation [8] and SAM [11] which is concerned with support for the development of large scale safety cases. One of the aims of these projects is to improve the lot of safety engineers by giving automated support to safety analysis, without constraining them unduly and preventing them from applying engineering judgement, when this is appropriate. It is hoped that the principles described above can be exploited in meeting this aim.

If the FPM ideas turn out to be sound and effective, then hopefully this paper will have lain some of the first seeds of a new "scientific underpinning" for safety analysis.

7 Acknowledgements

My understanding of safety analysis techniques has been derived from interactions with various systems and safety engineers, most notably in BAe Warton and Filton. A number of people have been helpful in explaining the arcane arts of safety analysis, and clarifying my ideas: Benita Hall, Sandy Drysdale, Brian Jepson and Gerry Southcombe deserve especial mention. In so far as the descriptions of the techniques reflect industrial realities, they deserve credit, although I must take the blame for any inaccuracies and infelicities.

The more novel ideas described herein have evolved over some time, and have resulted from discussions with a number of academic and industrial colleagues. I am particularly grateful to two of my research staff with whom I worked in developing these ideas: Stephen Clarke who carried out much of the work on the relationship between fault-trees and wp-calculus, and Peter Fenelon who developed many of the ideas of failure propagation and transformation, and the FPTN notation. Discussions with Steve Mallon of BAe Dynamics have also been very useful.

References

1. *Design Analysis Procedures for Failure Modes*, Effects and Criticality Analysis (FMECA), Aerospace Recommended Practice (ARP) 926, Society of Automotive Engineers, Detroit, USA, 1967.

2. P.A. Bennett, *Safety*, Software Engineer's Reference Book, J.A McDermid (ed), Butterworth Heinemann, 1991.

3. R.W. Butler, G.B. Finelli, *The Infeasibility of Experimental Quantification of Life-Critical Software Reliability*, Proceedings of ACM SigSoft Conference on Software for Critical Systems, New Orleans, 1991.

4. *Reliability Computation using Fault Trees*, Technical Report NASA–CR–124740, NASA Jet Propulsion Laboratory, 1971.

5. S.J. Clarke, J.A. McDermid, *Weakest pre-conditions and fault trees: a comparison and analysis*, SEJ (to appear), 1992.

6. S.J. Clarke, J.A. McDermid, *A Failure and Recovery Algebra*, YCS 168, 1992.

7. P.D. Ezhilchelvan, S.K. Shrivastava, *A classification of faults in systems*, Technical Report, University of Newcastle upon Tyne, 1985.

8. P. Fenelon, J.A. McDermid, *Safety CASE: An integrated toolset for software safety analysis*, submitted for publication, 1992.

9. N.G. Leveson, J.L. Stolzy, *Safety analysis of Ada programs using fault trees*, IEEE Trans. on Reliability, Vol. 32, No. 5, 1983.

10. J.L. Mackie, *Causes and Conditions*, in Causation and Conditionals, ed. E. Sosa, Oxford, OUP, 1975, 15–38.

11. J.A. McDermid, *Safety Cases and Safety Arguments*, CSR Conference on System Safety, Luxembourg, 1992.

12. *Interim Defence Standard 00–56*, MoD, 1991.

13. *Special Edition on MASCOT3*, SEJ, Vol. 1, No. 3, 1986.

14. D. Raheja, *Software System Failure Mode and Effects Analysis (SSFMEA) — A Tool for Reliability Growth*, IRSM 90, Tokyo, 1990.

15. W.E. Vesely, *Fault Tree Handbook*, US Nuclear Regulatory Commission, Washington DC, USA, 1981.

Safety Licensing and Formal Correctness of High Integrity Embedded Systems

John Cullyer

Dept. of Engineering
University of Warwick
Coventry CV4 7AL
U.K.

Abstract

This paper describes techniques for applying formal mathematical methods to the specification and design of high integrity embedded control systems which are implemented using microprocessors and real-time software. For reasons of public policy, including preservation of human life and protection of the environment of the Earth, certain classes of control systems in industries such as aviation and nuclear power are subject to independent analysis and certification, before operational use is permitted. The techniques described in this paper are intended to provide a practical route for the development of such highly critical systems. By combining the specification language Higher Order Logic (HOL) with the disciplined use of annotated subsets of the computer programming languages such as Ada, a framework has been developed for the development of the operational software for practical safety-critical equipment. A worked example, of an electronic speed control mechanism for road vehicles, is used to illustrate some of the steps.

1 The Global Problem

By "embedded systems" we mean those applications of computer hardware and software in which the equipment is hidden from public view, within the electronics bays of aircraft, deep inside the protection mechanisms of nuclear reactors, within the engine compartments of cars and trucks and in hundreds of similar real-time control systems. Many of these regimes involve the independent certification of the plant or vehicle before operation or use is attempted. No nation will allow a civil aircraft to fly without a Certificate of Airworthiness and no nuclear reactor is allowed to operate without independent assessment of its design, protection and operating procedures.

If hardware or software malfunction places the lives of the general public at risk, or threatens serious damage to the environment of the Earth, we describe the system as "high integrity". Special procedures are then invoked which cover the specification, design, verification and operation of the electronic equipment. This paper provides an introduction to this area of real-time computing for those who may not have encountered the scientific and engineering principles which have been adopted internationally. Clearly safety-critical computing is a matter of international concern: aircraft may crash in countries distant from their home base and the plume of radioactivity released after a nuclear accident will not respect any geographical boundary.

The material in this review has been collated from recent work in the University of Warwick, UK, which was supervised by the author. Conclusions are presented from two doctoral theses, [22], [19], published in mid-1992. These results are combined with material from a recent report to NASA, written when the author was working as a Distinguished Visiting Scientist at the Jet Propulsion Laboratory, Pasadena, California [8].

This paper is intended to provide an insight into the specification design, verification and licensing of high integrity systems, using formal mathematical techniques. It is assumed that the reader is thoroughly conversant with modern control system design, using hardware architectures which involve microprocessors or microcontrollers and modern software engineering methods. A tutorial approach has been adopted, in that a single formal specification technique (Higher Order Logic) is described and then used in a detailed example, of an electronic throttle for a road vehicle.

2 Major Steps in Specification and Design

By "formal methods" we mean those techniques for specification, verification and design which rely on discrete mathematics (set theory, predicate calculus etc.) and are supported by automated tools. The practical methods include those which are listed in subsection 3.2 of this paper. All the methods which are in use in industry have an excellent mathematical basis and viable sets of computer tools, running on standard workstations. Such methods avoid the ambiguities implicit in plain language specifications and design documents.

Enhancing the proposals in [19], the technique which should be adopted when specifying and designing high integrity equipment consists of a number of consecutive stages, which differ somewhat from those listed in conventional "textbook" approaches to system design:

1. **Safety criteria selection:**
   The safety criteria are established in discussion with the civil or military user. These are the criteria on which the certification of the system for use will depend.

2. **Determination of criticality levels:**
   For each hazard foreseen a specific criticality level is established after discussion with the user. A commonly used scale is one running upwards from Level 0, "low criticality", to Level 4, "critical to a large proportion of the population".

3. **Requirement extraction and specification:**
   From the plain language requirement created by the customer, the designers

extract a formal, mathematical engineering specification, which is mutually agreed to be necessary and sufficient.

4. **Implementation:**
The safety-critical hardware will be implemented as some mixture of sensors, processors, RAM, ROM, data highways and actuators, whilst the software is developed subject to the constraints considered later in this paper.

5. **Verification and validation:**
For each perceived hazard, the system will be assessed as conforming to the formal specification or will be found to be deficient in some way.

6. **Certification:**
Based on steps 1 to 5 above, the statutory authority either will grant a license for operation or will require modifications to the specification and design. In the latter case, fresh validation and verification tests will be required.

Formal mathematical techniques are directly applicable to steps 3, 4 and 5 above, but have little place in the other phases of development. Specifically, formal techniques have the greatest impact at step 3, when extracting a rigorous specification from a mass of plain language text, which from its very nature will be incomplete and inconsistent.

As the design proceeds, the formal specification derived at step 3 above is transformed into more detailed specifications of software and hardware components. Figure 1 shows a broad view of the steps involved. At each design transformation, the abstractions of the parent document are transformed into lower level abstractions, such as the description of a single real-time process [15].

3 Techniques Proposed

3.1 Overview

This section does not offer a critical comparison of available techniques. Rather, a particular doctrine is described which has proved to be valuable and cost effective in various projects, ranging from the autopilots of robot spacecraft, nuclear power plant and avionics to the high integrity software needed for railway interlocking and signalling [7]. Some of the material below has been summarised from a NASA report, dealing with high integrity control systems for spacecraft [8].
The methods proposed are based on:

1. The use of Higher Order Logic (HOL) for specifications, at several levels.
2. The production of emulators, written in Ada, which "animate" these specifications.
3. The writing of the operational software in a carefully constrained subset of Ada, with embedded "annotations", which are essential for subsequent automated verification against the HOL specifications.
4. The use of automated static code analysis to check the control flow, data use, information flow and semantic behaviour of each module of software.

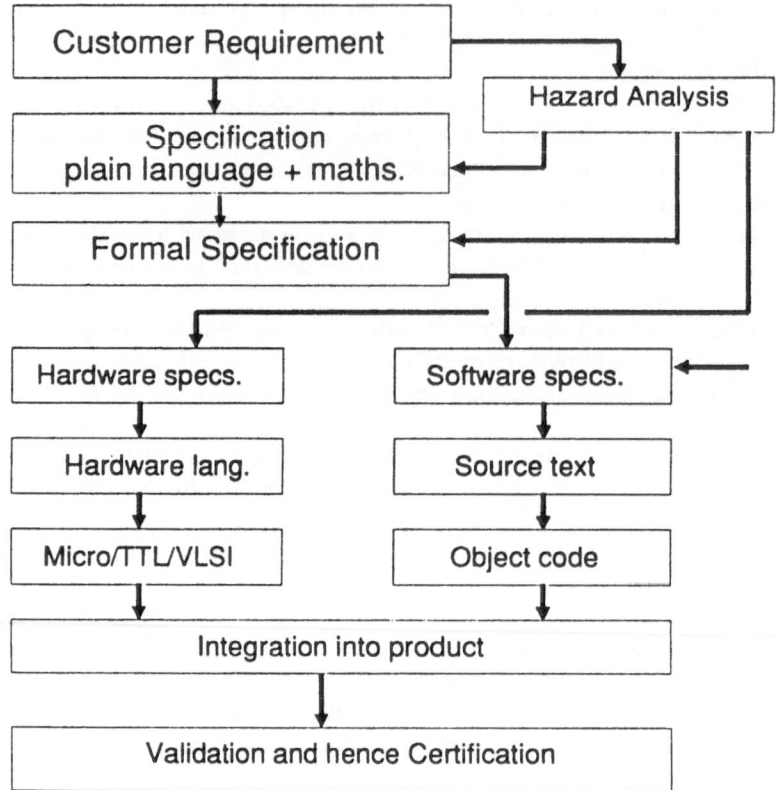

Fig. 1. Steps in the Development of a High Integrity System.

5. The dynamic testing of the operational software, guided by the outputs from the static analysis.

If such techniques are adopted, the Formal Specification will be produced in response to a Statement of Requirements from the end-user of the system in question. Ideally, this Formal Specification should be developed by close collaboration between the Design, Software Reliability, Hardware Reliability and System Safety team, if such teams exist as separate managerial entities. In a small project team, this division of responsibility is unlikely.

The main purpose of the specification is to define precisely the intended operation of the system. It will include clauses covering factors such as functional descriptions, details of asynchronous interfaces with other systems (including human operators) and safety invariants, which must be preserved in particular modes of operation of the embedded system. Such a specification provides the basis for a demonstration of the fitness for use, and must therefore support an objective assessment of whether the system meets the specification (and hence the original requirements), as a basis for subsequent certification.

At present most teams involved in high integrity control produce such specifications in natural language, which may be interspersed with control laws or similar mathematics. Such documents are ambiguous and it is at this point that formal techniques potentially can reduce project costs, without sacrificing the reliability of the control system.

3.2 Specification Languages

The behaviour of computer systems can be satisfactorily modelled with discrete mathematics [21]. This mathematical base means that designers can construct formal system models whose consistency can be demonstrated [5], and from which implementations can be derived. In other words, the formal specification can act as a template for the subsequent design of the critical software.

Three formal specification languages favoured in the United Kingdom are HOL [11], Z [17] and VDM [13]. All invoke a rigorous mathematical approach to specification, in which a system model is constructed from abstract data types and associated functions. Formal specification is carried out at varying levels of abstraction. As the system is decomposed, further details will emerge and the formal specification may be extended. In principle, each such refinement can be proven correct [14], but cost and manpower constraints mean that this is rarely done across a whole plant or vehicle. Instead, a Project Manager may require some key areas of the specification to be checked mathematically, but rely on the other disciplines to ensure the consistency of much of the specification material.

3.3 Emulation of Specification

A "prototyped" or "emulated" specification helps the design team and safety specialists to assess the adequacy and correctness of the specification. It can also be used to help with safety assessment, by experimenting with various input conditions. A prototype may be maintained throughout the spacecraft development to evaluate proposed changes in the Requirement [2].

Since specification languages such as HOL are not programming languages and are therefore not executable, we cannot "run" the specification in any dynamic sense and check its properties. Typically, we should like to emulate the state machines which are described by the formal specification, using a SUN workstation or possibly a fast PC. This provides substantial additional confidence in the formal mathematics. To do this we must convert the text of the specification manually into a programming language, such as Ada.

In taking this step it is imperative that we use the language which will be employed for the operational software and we should obey all of the Codes of Practice mandated by the Project Manager. It may seem curious to adopt such a rigorous style when writing an emulator, which probably will be discarded later in the design cycle. The reason for taking so much care is that experience has shown that design teams find it helpful to remove parts of the emulator code, for example highly trusted functions, and use these software components in the operational system. Therefore, all emulators of this class should be written with the same rigor as the real-time high integrity software and the packages and modules should be subject to Configuration Management, just as if they were planned initially to be part of the critical operational load.

3.4 Programming Languages

When deciding on a programming language for the emulation of our formal specification and subsequently for the design of the operational computer programs, we have to take account of recent work on safety-critical software [6]. According to Carré and Clutterbuck [1] there are six essential considerations for a high-integrity programming language:

a) Unambiguous Definition
   The programming language needs to be logically coherent and unambiguous, with a formally defined semantics.
b) Simplicity of Definition
   The language definition should be short, of the complete Ada language runs to many volumes.
c) Expressive Power
   There must be sufficient descriptive power in the language to allow the user to represent all aspects of the specification.
d) Security
   There must not be features in the programming language whose presence makes it very difficult (or impossible) to detect violation of the language rules other than by execution. All standard programming languages suffer from insecurities.
e) Verifiability
   For high integrity applications we must be able to show that the implementation matches its specification.
f) Bounded Space and Time Requirements
   In real-time control applications we must ensure that adequate memory is available. In addition, strict timing requirements demand finite bounds on the number of times any loop may be obeyed.

Considering some of the flaws in commonly used programming languages in the light of the above list [7]:

1. Ada is extremely complex and contains many insecurities;
2. Pascal's support for data abstraction is limited;
3. C is so poorly defined that it should never be used in high integrity systems, although it does have uses in systems of very low criticality;
4. MODULA-2 is sound but has little commercial support;
5. Assembly languages are very informally defined and are too permissive.

A comparative study giving more details on these points can be found in a recent paper by Cullyer, Goodenough and Wichmann [6], [20].
Research and development has produced some answers to the above problems. By using a subset of the Ada language and adding appropriate annotations,

(viewed as comments by the Ada compiler), we can produce a reliable means of developing high integrity software, as discussed in [3]. In referring to subsets of languages, we do not mean to imply that a restricted form of compiler should be used, since this would violate the doctrines of the Ada language, as defined by the United States DoD. We refer here to the use by design teams of a small subset, with compilation being carried out via a full Ada compiler, capable of supporting the whole language.

When considering the boundaries of a safe subset of Ada, we find that we have to delete a great deal of the language which is accepted internationally; notably the use of generics and all references to real-time processes (tasks) have to be avoided if we are to work in a safe software regime [4]. This indicates the widespread nature of the insecurities in the parent language.

3.5 Implementation of Emulators

The technique advocated for emulator software is to write each major part of the formal specification as an Ada package and then partially verify these packages using static code analysis tools, as discussed below. When we need even more confidence, we can explore the semantic behaviour of each package, generate verification conditions and maybe satisfy ourselves of the correspondence of the Ada software with the original specification using a theorem prover. The latter step is rarely done for emulator software, because of the cost.

3.6 Design of Operational Software

Following on from the specification, or in parallel with this activity, there will be the architectural and detailed design activities. Prototyping (emulation) may be used to assess the effectiveness of different design approaches, as well as checking their conformance with the original prose requirements. If the specification is formally stated it is possible in principle to show by logical reasoning that system requirements have been maintained by the design [15]. However, this is a difficult task, and a formal approach which instead concentrates on the safety and reliability invariants is more practical. In other words "prove the safety-critical properties".

3.7 Software Verification

3.7.1 Combination of Techniques

The material in this sub-section is a summary of the work by Clutterbuck in the BCS Monograph referred to earlier [1]. He has proposed that code verification should comprise three complementary techniques (program walkthrough, static analysis and dynamic testing), all of which should be used for the assessment of highly reliable software. Omission of any limb is very unwise.

It should be possible to relate every line of source code to the design and hence to the specification with little or no difficulty. The UK STARTS Guide gives a comprehensive list of the software tools available in Europe which aid such correspondence checks [18].

3.7.2 Code Reviews

In a code review [9], the code reader should not have to refer to the programmer for clarification. If clarification is required, then this should be made through additional program comments (or perhaps design changes in severe circumstances) and not verbally. At the end of the review, the reviewer's comments must be recorded and the resulting actions followed through by the design team.

3.7.3 Static Code Analysis

Secondly, the reviewers should use the output of static analysis tools to guide their judgment of the integrity of the software. Static analysis does not require the execution of the program being analyzed. It can be used to determine properties of the program which are universally true for all possible execution conditions. In addition, static analysis can be used to check adherence to Codes of Practice. It may encompass more sophisticated checks such as language restrictions, control structure, data usage, etc. For reliable application of these checks, automated tools are required.

The most effective use for static analysis is the demonstration of a program's good structure, and its functional behaviour with respect to its specification. Such analyses are performed for all paths through the program and for all input data over a defined range. These techniques are in day-to-day use in many design centres in Europe for both civil and military projects, but have rarely been adopted in the USA [3].

3.7.4 Code Proofs

The most rigorous technique for showing conformance between implementation and specification is that of formal program verification [3]. Although labour intensive and requiring considerable skill, such analyses may be justified for highly critical software, where dynamic test cannot by itself be relied upon to show that the software will operate correctly in all circumstances. However, program verification is not a substitute for dynamic test; timing constraints for example cannot easily be verified in this way and hardware and compiler errors may be revealed under dynamic test.

To perform a proof of an Ada function or procedure, the detailed specification for the module must define the function of the module in an appropriate logical notation, such as HOL. The module specification may in turn be derived from a more abstract formal specification (for example, HOL at a higher level of project documentation).

Then "assertions" (pre-conditions, post-conditions and loop-invariants), will have been embedded in the program as formal comments (annotations) during coding. From these assertions, verification conditions are generated which if proven to be true, verify conformance of the code to the specification. To assist with these proofs, an automated theorem checker should be used.

As already mentioned, static code analysis tools can generate verification conditions from suitable code. Such tools also include an interactive theorem prover to assist in the proof of these theorems. The theorem prover generates a proof script, providing valuable Quality Assurance support when the costs of proofs are justified.

Formal program proof is not easy. It is currently undertaken for only the most critical systems and by highly trained personnel [7]. However, tool support is gradually improving, and the use of such a technique can be expected to become a requirement for critical digital control systems in the near future. Its scope can be limited, for example we may attempt to prove that the safety-invariants hold, and nothing else.

3.7.5 Dynamic Test

Dynamic test is the conventional method of checking programs. The developer's test strategy for safety-critical software should be defined during the specification and design phases, and must include module functional tests for normal and error conditions and module integration tests.

A program under test is executed with differing combinations of input data and the results are analyzed to see if they are as expected. This requires the creation of tests, an environment (test harness) to apply the tests to the software being tested, the definition of expected results, a comparison of the actual results to the expected results, a procedure for correcting discrepancies and a demonstration of test data adequacy [16].

Although each of the above is a subject in its own right, the most difficult areas are the generation of test data and the demonstration of the adequacy of the test data set. Ideally one would like to say that all possible inputs have been applied to the system. For even a relatively simple program this is impractical. A number of commercially available test systems do attempt to provide metrics for test coverage. Even with such automated aids, determining an acceptable level of coverage for software of a given criticality is difficult, but the task can be eased if the output of static code analysis is used as a template for the test vectors.

4 Formalism Used in this Paper

The only way to gain an impression of the power and utility of formal methods is to consider a specific language and its applications. This paper uses Higher Order Logic (HOL), since this is the discipline employed by the author's team in the University of Warwick. We will discuss the issues of the verification and certification of high integrity systems by applying HOL to an automated subsystem for controlling the speed of road vehicles, as discussed in Section 5.

4.1 Basis of Higher Order Logic

The HOL system was developed by Gordon and his team at the University of Cambridge [11]. It implements a version of Church's Simple Type Theory and uses standard predicate logic notation. We will make use of the functions negation (**NOT**), conjunction (**AND**), disjunction (**OR**), and implication (==>) to form the functions we need. In addition we shall need to use the idea of Universal Quantification (**FOR ALL**) which will appear in the text as ! and Existential Quantification (**THERE EXISTS**), typed as ?. Table 1 gives the list of the primary constructs used.

The primary way in which the HOL logic differs from first order predicate calculus is by allowing higher order variables to range over functions and predicates. We can write down safety properties which are True over a wide class of functions of a given signature.

Notation	Meaning
P(x)	x has the property P
R(x, y)	Relation R holds between x and y
~ t1	Negation of t1
t1 \/ t2	t1 OR t2
t1 /\ t2	t1 AND t2
t1 ==> t2	t1 IMPLIES t2
t1 = t2	t1 if and only if t2
! x.t[x]	t[x] is True for all x
? x.t[x]	t[x] is True for some value of x
(t => t1 | t2)	if t is True then t1 else t2

Table 1. HOL Notation

4.2 HOL Types

The HOL logic is strongly typed. Everything we write down must have a type. For example, the type **bool** denotes the set of Booleans and **num** the set of natural numbers. In addition, we can build up compound types by using operators such as **list** and **#**. For example, the function signature

:(num# num) → bool

specifies a function which takes two **num** parameters and delivers a **bool** result. As another example, a real (decimal) number can be modelled in HOL as 3-tuple of (bool#num#num) where the first and second **num** fields denote the integer and decimal part respectively, and the boolean value indicates the sign (with negative being True to correlate with computer arithmetic).

We shall make extensive use of lists, which are defined in a HOL library in the following terms:

NIL	: (*)list	% an empty list
CONS	: * – > (*)list – > (*)list	% list constructor
HD	: (*)list – > *	% head of list
TL	: (*)list – > (*)list	% tail of list
NIL	: (*) list – > bool	% detect empty list
APPEND	: (*)list – > (*)list – > (*)list	% append lists

In the signatures above, the symbol * indicates a "polymorphic" type, that is any legal type in the logic. Usually when discussing such functions it is referred to as "alpha" and if there are other distinct polymorphic types in the analysis then these are written as ** ("alpha2"), *** ("alpha3"), and so on. Application of these library functions to lists is easy, for example:

HD [F; T; T; F] ==> F
TL [F; T; T; F] ==> [T; T; F]

Obviously we need some way of "indexing" lists to pick out a particular member and this is done with **EL**, which is defined by recursion to be:

EL |- (! l. EL 0 l = HD l) /\
      (! l n. EL (SUC n) l = EL n (TL l))

In words, if we call **EL** with the index 0, we obtain the head of the list (i.e. the 0th element). Otherwise, for all lists and indices we apply **EL** to the tail of the list, until the entry we want becomes the head of the list. We have introduced a new concept above, namely the use of the "turnstile" symbol |- to indicate a function definition which has been stored already.

Lists have other important properties. In particular, we can apply the same predicate (test) to every member of a list, using the library function **EVERY**:

EVERY |- (!P. EVERY P [ ] = T) /\
(! P h t. EVERY P (CONS h t) = P h /\ EVERY P t)

Describing this informally, the predicate **P** applied to the empty list delivers True, (which is used to end the recursion) and for all lists of finite length made up from a head h and a tail t, we obtain the answer by applying the test **P** to the head of the list and forming the **AND** with the recursive call of **EVERY** applied to the tail. Eventually, the tail will become the empty list and the recursion will halt.

With a little practice, writing functions in this style becomes straightforward, but it is accepted that this type of logic is not familiar to most engineers. If we use languages such as Z or VDM the problems of perception are different, but it seems to be true that we can only argue rigorously about safety (or security) properties if we adopt one or more such mathematical disciplines.

4.3 Temporal Logic in HOL

Time will be defined using the HOL type :num, which represents the semi-infinite set of natural numbers. Since we are dealing with real-time systems we need to find some way of embedding ideas about temporal properties into our overall strategy for verification and certification. The resulting theory will allow us ultimately to make some generic statements about safety properties.

Using results from [12], we can define four temporal operators, **henceforth**, **eventually**, **next** and **until** in HOL and give an informal description of each in plain English. At this stage in the discussion we give the full text of each function, as needed for input to the HOL tools.

HOL Definition 1
let henceforth = new_definition
('henceforth',
"!(p :time − > bool) (t :time). henceforth p t =
(! (t1 :time). (t <= t1) ==> p t1)");;

Informally: henceforth p delivers True if p holds from now on.

HOL Definition 2
let eventually = new_definition
('eventually',
"!(p :time − > bool) (t :time). eventually p t =
(? (t1 :time). (t <= t1) /\ (p t1))");;

Informally: eventually p delivers True if at some future time p holds.

HOL Definition 3
let next = new_definition
('next',
"!(p :time − > bool) (t :time). next p t = p(SUC t)");;

Informally: next p evaluates to True on an interval if p evaluates to True on the next interval, t + 1.

HOL Definition 4
let until = new_definition
('until',
"!(p1 p2 :time − > bool) (t :time). until p1 p2 t =
(? (t1 :time). (t <= t1) /\ (p2 t1) /\
(! (t2 :time). ((t <= t2) /\ (t2 < t1)) ==> (p1 t2)))");;

Informally: The term **p1 until p2** delivers True if **p2** holds at some time and **p1** holds at least until that time.

To understand these statements more clearly, imagine that the predicate **p** in henceforth, eventually and next is a function with HOL signature:

check_safety :time — > bool

Here check_safety is assumed to be a function which delivers True if the system is in a safe state and False if it is in an unsafe state. Then, henceforth (check_safety t) is a way of expressing the need to remain in a safe state at all times from t onwards. The application of next (check_safety t) shows how we can try and describe the safety of a system in a transitive manner. If the high integrity equipment is in a safe state at some time t and next (check_safety t) holds, then the system will continue to be safe, at least until we perturb the situation in some way, such that next is no longer valid.

We must be concerned about the utility of these temporal operators. Establishing the correctness of statements about temporal logic is a time-consuming matter. Fortunately, a great deal of the basic work has been done by Hale, using the HOL theorem proving system [12]. He has established that the following lemmas are valid in this world of linear temporal logic:

HOL Definition 5
let Not = new_definition
('Not',
"!(p :time — > bool) (t :time). Not p t = ~(p t)");;

HOL Definition 6
let Imp = new_definition
('Imp',
"! (p1 p2 :time — > bool) (t :time).
Imp p1 p2 t = ((p1 t) ==> (p2 t))");;

HOL Definition 7
let And = new_definition
('And',
"! (p1 p2 :time — > bool) (t :time).
And p1 p2 t = ((p1 t) /\ (p2 t))");;

HOL Definition 8
let Or = new_definition
('Or',
"! (p1 p2 :time — > bool) (t :time).
Or p1 p2 t = ((p1 t) \/ (p2 t))");;

Now we can apply familiar results such as De Morgan's Theorem and carry out related algebraic manipulations in this temporal logic.

There seems to be adequate evidence from the formal methods literature [7] that temporal logic plays a considerable part in safety analysis, alongside the verification of algorithmic properties. The crucial point is that any decision to employ temporal logic must be accompanied by axioms for that logic within the primary formal language we are using (HOL in this paper). We cannot afford to work in two disparate languages, with their own type definitions and proof rules. Hence the need to embed these temporal operators in HOL libraries, before we go any further.

4.4 HOL Theories

The result of producing a HOL text which defines the functionality of a given subsystem is called a "theory". A HOL theory is very similar to a logician's theory. Like a logician's theory, a HOL theory contains types, constants, definitions and axioms. The most important difference is that a HOL theory also contains an explicit list of theorems which have been proved from the axioms and definitions using a theorem prover, whereas a logician's theory implies all theorems that could be proved.

A HOL theory is stored in a number of files called the theory files. Each theory file contains some types, constants, axioms and theorems, together with pointers to other theory files called its "parents". The collection of reachable files is called the "ancestry" of the theory. When the HOL system starts, the initial theory is the theory HOL itself. The ancestry of the theory HOL contains all types, axioms, constants and theorems of the HOL logic. All new theories (specifications) created during a HOL session are extensions of the theory HOL either directly or via some other theories such as those provided as HOL libraries.

4.5 Proving Theorems

A theorem is the result of a proof. When we have crucial properties of safety and reliability at stake, we may choose to establish correspondence between a top level specification and the next lower level of specification by proving theorems and delivering these results to our colleagues for Peer Review. Such work is expensive and time-consuming, but does lead to a higher degree of confidence.

On those occasions when the Project Manager requires mathematical proofs, they can be carried out in two different manners: "forward proof" and "goal-directed proof". A technical description of these options is outside the scope of this paper. All proofs are costly in terms of the manpower and computer resources used. Normally, we will only conduct formal proofs using HOL or a similar discipline when the consequences of the risk of failure of computer software or hardware could be catastrophic. Reasons for conducting proofs range across loss of human life, serious damage to the environment, and so on.

5 Example of "Drive-by-Wire" Throttle

This example is summarised from a recent doctoral thesis [19] and the complete mathematical treatment can be found in that document. The application is a specific need in automotive electronics, namely the requirement for a microprocessor based control system for replacing the mechanical linkage between the throttle pedal (accelerator) and the carburettor. In the jargon of the times, the subsystem is regarded as a "Drive-by-Wire" (DBW) throttle, by analogy with "Fly-by-Wire" (FBW) aircraft. The controller has been specified in HOL, and from that specification a prototype system has been implemented and tested. In his thesis Tran describes the development of a formal specification for the DBW controller in three major steps:

1. External interfaces to the controller; i.e. electronic signals from the brake pedal, engine, and so on.
2. A formal specification of the controller.
3. Verification problems, including proof of temporal properties.

5.1 System Description

This controller is to govern the operation of a valve in a car's carburettor which in turn controls the air/fuel mixture. It interacts with the environment through a number of external interfaces:

- **Accelerator pedal:** the system interacts with the accelerator via a position sensor unit, which is basically a linear potentiometer and an idle switch to calibrate the pedal demand when the system starts up. The idle switch provides a binary signal, namely **idle**, which is true when the pedal demand is zero and false otherwise.
- **Brake:** the brake input is also a binary switch, designated **brake**, which is true when the brake is applied and false otherwise.
- **Gear:** the system senses the status of the gearbox by an input signal **gear**, which is set to true when the car is in top gear and false otherwise.
- **Control buttons:** different functions of the controller can be activated by buttons on the driver's control panel. For example, the button to request cruising is denoted by the Boolean signal **cruise**. When this button is pressed, **cruise** is set to true if and only if the engine is running and the transmission is in top gear. When the cruise control is activated, the system stores the current speed, and holds the car at that speed.
- **Actuator:** the system controls the car through an actuator attached to the throttle valve. This actuator is mechanically in parallel with the accelerator pedal mechanism, such that whichever one is demanding greater speed controls the throttle. The control system drives the actuator by means of an electrical signal having a linear relationship with throttle deflection, with 0 volts setting the throttle valve closed and 16 volts setting it fully open.
- **Speed sensor unit:** the controller measures road speed by counting pulses it receives from a sensor on the drive shaft. The pulse rate from this sensor corresponds to vehicle miles per hour, through a proportional constant.

5.2 Safety Requirements

The safety and operational requirements include a number of algorithmic and timing constraints.

1. The system should never fail with the throttle actuator being stuck open. This safety property requires us to prove that the system is "safe" in this sense in all modes of operation.
2. When the system senses that the speed is above the selected cruise speed, it must completely release the throttle (this situation would occur when driving downhill). At any speed below the selected cruise speed, it must drive the throttle to a deflection proportional to the speed error. For smooth and stable servo operation, the system must update its outputs at least once every second.
3. To avoid rapid increases in acceleration, the actuator must never traverse its full range to fully open in less than 10 seconds. It may close at any rate, however, since the car just coasts when the throttle is closed.
4. When the car is accelerating, the control system must measure the acceleration and clamp it at 1 mph/sec. The throttle setting will be affected by the gradient. If the acceleration reaches 1.2 mph/sec, the throttle should be closed; at 0.8 mph/sec, it should be fully open. Between these limits, the opening is to be linearly related to acceleration.

It will be seen that the points above are typical of the demands from automotive engineers when writing the requirements for a new electronic subsystem. The primary safety property, that the throttle must never jam fully open is somewhat masked by a plethora of other requirements.

5.3 Design of System

Figure 2 shows an overview of the DBW throttle and its interfaces. The rest of this subsection formalises this view. The design follows these steps:

1. Model the system using finite-state machine theory. This is not a formal step in the sense that it relies on the intuition of the designer and is used mainly as a means of communication with the automotive engineers.
2. Write HOL formulae specifying the required control algorithms. The specification may refer to any of the events, data variables, and activities of the car and its speed control.
3. The specification then must be verified to ensure that it satisfies the required safety and timing constraints.
4. Write an emulator in a "safe" subset of Ada to animate this specification.
5. Develop the operational software in the chosen subset of Ada.
6. Verify this software against the formal specification, using a mixture of static code analysis and dynamic testing and validate its overall behaviour against the orginal requirement from the automotive engineers.
7. Submit the equipment to an independent test house for certification and hence sale and subsequent use in road vehicles.

The balance of this paper concentrates on steps 1, 2 and 3 above. The specification of the DBW throttle is defined by predicates which express relations

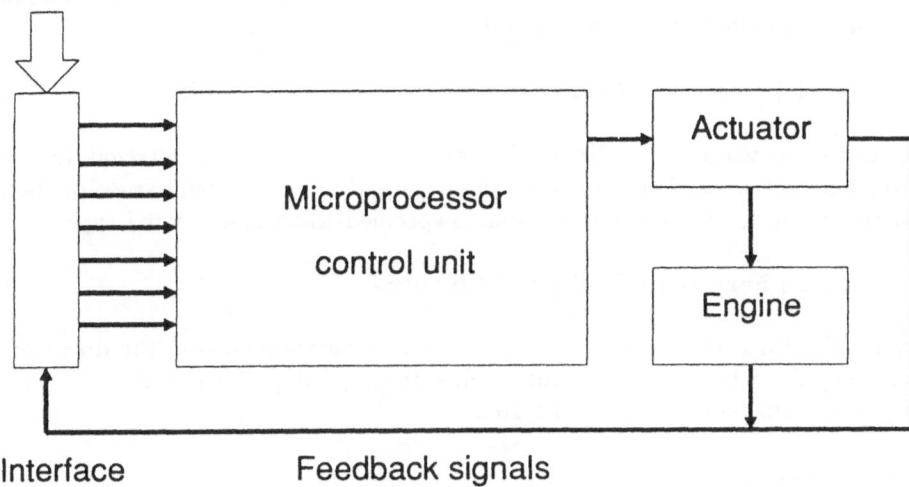

Fig. 2. Schematic Diagram of the Throttle Control Unit.

on time-dependent signals. These predicates are based, in part, on variables representing physical input and output signals. They also are functions of other signals representing the internal state of the DBW throttle. Time-dependent signals are modelled as functions from discrete time to signal values. As discussed already in subsection 4.3, discrete time is represented by the natural numbers.

The top level specification for the DBW controller is based on the transformation of a state vector:

(s, state)

where s represents a set of thirteen individual control signals, represented by the HOL type sig_ty, which run from the interface unit to the controller, as indicated in Figure 2. It is convenient to view these signals as a single input to the controller. Once inside the system, this bundle of inputs is separated into the thirteen individual electronic signals. The term state represents the state of the DBW throttle, and will be expanded later.

Then the total behaviour of the system can be defined by a function NextState, which will be called repeatedly in the following manner:

..NextState(s2, NextState(s1, NextState(s0, state0)

where s0, s1, s2, ... are the successive sets of asynchronous input signals and state0 is the state of the control system at time zero.

In the formal specification there is a variable **mode** which defines the system operating modes corresponding to the transition diagram shown in Figure 3. There are six discrete states which the FSM can reach. Hence **mode** is defined as an enumerated variable of the type,

Reset | Idle | Traction | Shutdown | Manual | Cruise

Other state variables, **valid_cruise** and **pwm_act** are the internal variables which keep tracks of the cruise status flags and the directional sense of the actuator respectively. The latter signal is specified as an enumerated type:

Close | Forward | Backward | Neutral

Since the throttle actuator must come to rest before changing the direction of motion, the following constraint applies to the pulse-width-modulated (pwm) signal output by the DBW subsystem:

HOL definition 9
let pwm = new_definition
('pwm_def',
"pwm pwm_act angle demand =
((demand = 0) => Close |
((demand > angle) =>
((pwm_act = Forward) => Neutral | Forward) |
((angle > demand) =>
((pwm_act = Backward) => Neutral | Backward) |
Neutral)))");;

5.4 Overall Behaviour

This controller is built up from six functions, namely reset, manual, traction, cruise, shutdown, and idle control. The behaviourial specification is modelled as the finite-state machine shown in Figure 3, which reads the current status of the input vector s and then delivers its next state. The decision making algorithm is based on a set of pre-defined conditions which correspond to different system operating modes.

5.4.1 Manual Control
The manual control is the normal working mode of the controller where the position demand which is interpreted from the pedal sensor, is directly output to the actuator. The required input validity conditions are specified by the relations:

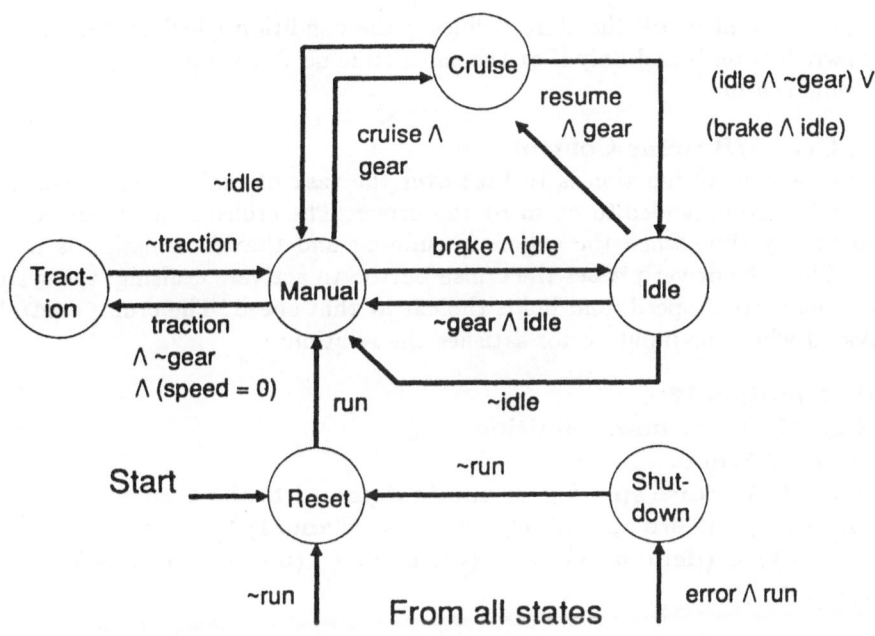

Fig. 3. State Transition Diagram for the DBW Throttle.

HOL definition 10
let ILLEGAL = new_definition
('ILLEGAL_def',
"ILLEGAL (b :time − > bool) (p :time − > bool) (t :time) =
~XOR2 (b t) (p t)");;

HOL definition 11
let Zero = new_definition
('Zero_def',
"Zero (b :time − > num) (t :time) = ((b t) = 0)");;

The function **ILLEGAL** is a temporal construct which takes predicates b and
p of the type :time → bool and returns true if b and p occur simultaneously.
For example,

HOL definition 12
let stop_ok = new_definition
('stop_ok_def',
"stop_ok idle demand t = ILLEGAL idle ~(Zero demand) t");;

The predicate **stop_ok** therefore defines a the condition which states that the **idle** switch is on if and only if at the same time no **demand** is requested from the pedal sensor.

5.4.2 Cruise/Resume Control

The cruise control function is to take over the task of maintaining a constant speed when commanded to do so by the driver. The cruise control can be operated at any time when the engine is running and the transmission is in top gear. When the driver presses the cruise button to activate cruising, the system stores the current speed, and holds the car at that speed. The cruise control is activated when the input vector satisfies the relation:

HOL definition 13
let C_COND_1 = new_definition
('C_COND_1_def',
"C_COND_1 cruise speed gear mode demand brake t =
(cruise t) /\ ~(Zero speed) /\ (mode = Manual) \/
~((speed t) < (demand t)) /\ ~(brake t) /\ (mode = Cruise)
/\ (gear t)");;

The driver should be able to increase the speed at any time by depressing the accelerator pedal, or reduce the cruising speed by depressing the brake pedal. Thus, driver can go faster than the cruise control setting simply by depressing the accelerator pedal far enough. When the pedal is released, the drive-by-wire system will regain control.

At anytime when the brake pedal is depressed or the transmission shifts out of top gear, the cruise function must be deactivated. Following this, when the brake is released, and the transmission is back in top gear, and the control button **resume** is pressed, the system must return the car to the previously selected speed. However, if the cruise function has been deactivated during the intervening interval, **resume** has no effect. Thus, an internal flag **valid** is needed to keep track of the cruise status and this flag can only be set if cruise mode is valid.

The complete requirement for the **cruise** and **resume** controls can be defined as follows:

HOL definition 14
let CRUISE_COND = new_definition
('CRUISE_COND_def',
"CRUISE_COND cruise speed resume valid gear mode
demand brake t =
(((cruise t) /\ ~(Zero speed) /\ (mode = Manual))
\/
(~((speed t) < (demand t)) /\ ~(brake t) /\ (mode = Cruise))
\/
((resume t) /\ valid /\ (mode = Idle))) /\ (gear t)");;

5.4.3 Other Modes of Operation

The above definitions cover only one of the modes of the DBW throttle, but this level of detail should be sufficient for the reader to follow the general process of deriving these functions from the plain language Requirement for this control system. The details of the other auxiliary functions needed can be found in [19].

5.4.4 Complete Finite State Machine

The form of the overall finite state machine definition is shown below. Despite the lengthy nature of this function, its structure is simple. Notice that the HOL statements beginning with **let** simply define local variables, to be used in the main body of the function. Fundamentally, the function **NextState** is a six limb case clause, with one limb for each of the machine states illustrated in Figure 3.

HOL definition 15
let NextState = new_definition
('NextState_def',
"Nextstate s mode valid_cruise pwm_act (t :time) =

let running	= RUNNING s in
let gear	= GEAR s in
let brake	= BRAKE s in
let watchdog	= WATCHDOG s in
let failed	= FAILED s in
let overtemp	= OVERTEMP s in
let idle	= IDLE s in
let traction	= TRACTION s in
let cruise	= CRUISE s in
let resume	= RESUME s in
let demand	= DEMAND s in
let speed	= SPEED s in
let angle	= ANGLE s in
let stop_ok	= (ILLEGAL idle (Zero demand) t) \/ failed \/(mode = Shutdown) in
let reset_ok	= RESET_COND running t in
let cruise_ok	= ~reset_ok /\ (CRUISE_COND cruise speed resume valid_cruise gear mode demand brake t) in
let traction_ok	= ~reset_ok /\ (TRACTION_COND mode traction speed gear idle t) in
let shutdown_ok	= SHUTDOWN_COND watchdog overtemp stop_ok t in
let idle_ok	= ~reset_ok /\ (IDLE_COND mode idle brake gear t) in
let valid	= ((mode = Cruise) => ~reset_ok | valid_cruise) in
let pwm_base	= pwm pwm_act (angle t) in

```
    (reset_ok      => (Reset, valid, (pwm_base zero_demand))     |
    (shutdown_ok => (Shutdown, valid, (pwm_base zero_demand)) |
    (idle_ok       => (Idle, valid, (pwm_base idle_demand))       |
    (cruise_ok     => (Cruise, valid, (pwm_base (speed t))        |
    (traction_ok   => (Traction, valid, (pwm_base (demand t)))    |
                        (Manual, valid, (pwm_base (demand t)))
    )))))")„
```

The function **NextState** specifies the overall mechanism for determining what happens at any instant of time. In the definition of **NextState** input vectors are used to select the next state and determine the current output of the machine, hence the function is specified in such a way that the state vector only includes all internal variables. Thus a sequence of applications of the function be represented as a Finite State Machine, where values **s0, s1, ...** represent the input vector at time **0, 1, ...** as explained in subsection 5.3.

Finally we use the function NextState to define a predicate **BEHAVIOUR**, shown on the next page, which specifies the intended behaviour of the controller as a relation on time-dependent signals **s, mode, valid_cruise,** and **pwm_act**. Let the time-dependent signals corresponding to these state variables be **st, modet, valid_cruiset,** and **pwm_actt,** respectively.

HOL definition 16
let **BEHAVIOUR** = new_definition
('**BEHAVIOUR_def'**,
"**BEHAVIOUR** sigt modet valid_cruiset pwm_actt t =
NextState (sigt t) (modet i) (valid_cruiset t) (pwm_actt t) t =
((modet (t + 1)), (valid_cruiset (t + 1)), (pwm_act (t + 1)))");;

5.5 Method of Verification

This section describes the method used to investigate the correctness of operation and safety of the DBW controller and some of the basic proof techniques which are used to carry out this plan in the HOL system. Although the terms "correctness" and "verification" may be understood in an informal context to mean different things to different people, these terms have a precise, technical meaning when formal logic is used to verify a design. The formal verification (or proof of correctness) for the DBW throttle system refers to the derivation of a theorem by formal proof in the HOL formulation of higher-order logic. This theorem relates the specification of the intended behaviour, given by the predicate **BEHAVIOUR** to some safety and timing constraints.

The bulk of the formal proof of the DBW controller is organised into three main steps:

1. Prove that the design is safe at all time and in all possible states (that is, that the throttle actuator cannot be driven fully open by malfunction of the control system).

2. Prove that each state transition is correctly interpreted. That is, establish the correctness of the state transition diagram shown in Figure 3.
3. Prove that the temporal properties listed in subsection 5.2 are satisfied, using embedded temporal logic.

The most important safety rule which applies to the controller design is that, at any instant of time t, the system should never fail with its throttle fully opened. Thus, a state is considered to be safe if and only if it satisfies the predicate:

!s m v p t. State_safe (s, m, v, p) t =
~(FAILED s t) \/ (p = Close)

Here the abbreviation s is used for st, m is used for modet, v is substituted for valid_cruiset and p for pwm_actt. Following this, the system is safe if it delivers a next state which belongs to a safe operating mode, which can be expressed by the predicate:

!s m v p t. SAFE (s, m, v, p) t =
State_safe (s, (NextState s m v p t)) t

It is intuitively clear from the specification of NextState and SAFE that if the system is working normally and receives an input vector which is safe at time t then it delivers an operating state which is also safe at time t + 1. However, it is not obvious how the controller gets into a safe state at the beginning. Therefore, the following constraint defines the initial or startup mode of the system:

!s m v p t. INIT (s, m, v, p) t =
~RUNNING s t /\ (DEMAND s Eq 0) t

This definition asserts that the controller is initialised whenever the engine is not running and there is no demand from the accelerator pedal. Now we face the challenging task of proving that:

1. The initial state is safe.
2. By induction, that if the system is safe at any time t, then it is safe at time t + 1.
3. That the temporal constraints are satisfied.

Details of the completion of these steps, using the HOL theorem prover, can be found in [19]. One interesting result is that the specification of the finite state machine, HOL definition 15, was found to be safe but over-cautious, leading to potentially poor performance of the car in some circumstances. In his research, Tran succeeded in improving the top level specification, such that safety was preserved whilst simultaneously enhancing the performance of the vehicle.

It would have been possible to create an emulation of the HOL definitions 1 to 15 in subset Ada and deduce further properties of the DBW throttle by emulation. This was not done for this particular problem, since the problems could be perceived via the HOL text alone. However, it would have been easy to write such an emulator, to increase certainty in the specification. A study of this paper will show any competent programmer how such an emulator can be derived.

6 Conclusions

The techniques described in this paper are known to work effectively in application regimes such as the design of spacecraft autopilots, civil and military avionics, nuclear power, automotive electronics, and railroad signalling.

Based on this experience, we should be able to map formal methods of specification onto existing industrial techniques, without undue changes to the conduct of design work. The bonus should be much clearer definitions of needs, backed up by exploration using emulators. Designers can do a great deal to build up confidence early in the project life cycle by studying the needs for subsystems through the medium of animated specifications.

When developing high integrity software and hardware, there appears to be international acceptance that extra steps have to be taken at system level to protect human life and the environment. The current debate centres on whether or not formal methods can help at a lower level of design, such as software module specifications and hardware subsystem specifications, including the design of ASICS.

This is not answered directly by any material in this paper, because the discussion has not been taken that far. However, supposing that designers adopt both mathematical specifications and a trusted subset of Ada for highly critical software, then verification can proceed via static code analysis, compilation on a host machine, transfer to the operational hardware and dynamic testing guided by the results of automated static analysis.

The judgement on these issues will be made by senior managers, based on many decades of collective experience. The primary conclusion of this paper must be that there is no scientific barrier to the adoption of formal methods in industry, when developing critical systems which are subject to independent scrutiny and certification.

Acknowledgements

The author is indebted to the formal methods community on both sides of the Atlantic for many of the concepts in this paper. Particular thanks are due to Dr Michael Gordon and his team in the University of Cambridge, UK, Dr John Kelly and the Formal Methods Team at the NASA Jet Propulsion Laboratory, Pasadena, USA, and the author's two immediate past research assistants, Wai Wong and Sang Tran in the University of Warwick, UK.

References

1. British Computer Society *Monograph on the Specification, Design and Verification of Safety- Critical Software*, edited by B.A. Wichmann, 1991.
2. Bromell, J.Y., Sadler, S.J., *A Strategy for the Development of Safety-critical Software*, in: Achieving Safety and Reliability with Computer Systems, ed. B.K. Daniels, Elsevier Applied Science, 1987.
3. Carré, B.A., *Reliable Programming in Standard Languages in High Integrity Software*, edited by C. Sennett, Pitman Publishing, 1989.
4. Carré, B.A., *SPARK — The SPADE Ada Kernel*, Program Validation Limited, Southampton, UK, 1989.
5. Cohen, B., Harwood, W.T., Jackson, M.I., *The Specification of Complex Systems*, Addison-Wesley Publishing Company 1989.
6. Cullyer, W.J., Goodenough, S.J., Wichmann B.A., *The Choice of Computer Languages for Use in Safety-Critical Systems*, Software Engineering Journal, Vol 6, No 2, 1991, 51–58.
7. Cullyer, W. J., *Safety-Critical Control Systems*, Computer and Control Engineering Journal, Vol. 2, No. 5, September 1991, 202–210.
8. Cullyer, W.J., *Application of Formal Methods to Highly Reliable Software for Spacecraft and for the DSN*, NASA Jet Propulsion Laboratory Report, May 1992.
9. Fagan, M., *Design and Code Inspections to Reduce Errors in Code Development*, IBM Systems Journal, Vol. 15, No 3, 1976.
10. Goodall, R.M., *High Speed Digital Controllers Using an 8 Bit Microprocessor* Software and Microsystems, Vol. 4, 1985, 109–116.
11. Gordon, M. J., *A Proof Generating System for Higher-Order Logic*, Kluwer Academic Publishers, 1987.
12. Hale, R.S., *Programming in Temporal Logic*, Computer Laboratory, University of Cambridge, Report No. 173, July 1989.
13. Jones, C.B., *Systematic Software Development Using VDM*, Prentice Hall International, 1986.
14. Leveson, N.G., Harvey, P.R., *Analyzing Software Safety*, IEEE Transactions on Software Engineering SE–9, No.9, 1983.
15. McDermid, J., *Assurance in High-Integrity Software*, in: High Integrity Software, edited by C. Sennett, Pitman Publishing 1989.
16. Parnas, D.L., van Schouwen, J., Kwan, S.P., *Evaluation of Safety-Critical Software*, Communications of the ACM, Vol. 3, June 1990.
17. Spivey, J.M., *The Z Notation*, Prentice Hall International, 1988.
18. *A Guide to the Methods and Software Tools for the Construction of Large Real Time Systems*, STARTS Guide, 2nd edition, Vol. 1-2, UK National Computing Centre, Manchester, UK, 1987.
19. Tran, S.C., *Applications of Formal Methods in Engineering*, Ph.D. thesis, Department of Engineering, University of Warwick, UK, May 1992.
20. Wichmann, B.A., *Insecurities in the Ada Language*, National Physical Laboratory, Teddington UK, report DITC 137/89, 1989.
21. Woodcock, J., Loomes, M., *Software Engineering Mathematics*, Pitman Publishing, 1988.
22. Wong, W., *Application of Higher Order Logic to Railway Signalling and Interlocking*, Ph.D. thesis, Department of Engineering, University of Warwick, UK, March 1992.

Formal Specification and Timing Analysis of High-Integrity Real-Time Systems

Miguel Felder, Carlo Ghezzi, Mauro Pezzé *

Politecnico di Milano
Dipartimento di Elettronica
Piazza Leonardo da Vinci 32
20133 Milano
Italy

Abstract

We motivate the need for formal specification and verification of specifications in the case of high-integrity real-time systems. After a review of sample approaches, we concentrate the attention on Petri nets augmented to support timing requirements. We illustrate a very general formalism and an associated timing analysis procedure. We then illustrate a restriction of the general model and a specialized analysis procedure. Concepts are mainly illustrated via examples and informal descriptions. The reader is directed to the published literature for formal details.

1 Introduction

Real-time computer systems are increasingly being used in safety-critical applications, where the effect of failures can have unacceptable costs. Examples of such applications include computerized control systems that manage comlex applications, such as critical industrial plants, patient monitoring systems, defense systems, and air traffic control systems. The need for such applications to be characterized by high integrity is evident.

Most such critical real-time applications display a combination of complexity and critical requirements that cannot be tamed by simply applying good common sense. Moreover, most existing informal or semi-formal methods [35, 60, 32] are unable to provide acceptable levels of assurance that the final product behaves as expected. We claim that the best way to improve systems quality is to develop these systems formally.

Unfortunately, if in principle formal methods are capable of providing higher assurance levels, many existing formal methods are still in their infancy. In particular, they either lack adequate tool support, especially if the notation is highly

---

* This material is based upon work supported by the Esprit project IPTES, and by the Progetto Finalizzato Sistemi Informatici e Calcolo Parallelo (CNR).

expressive, or they lack expressive power, if they are fully automated. Moreover, existing well-established formal methods, such as VDM or Z, do not traditionally address the special requirements of real-time systems.

In this paper, we concentrate our attention on the specification phase at the requirements and design stages, i.e., before the system is implemented. Specification formalisms are therefore evaluated in terms of how expressive they are (how naturally and easily specifications can be provided) and how verifiable specifications are. Specification verification is indeed a major aspect of the specification activity. If we want to ensure that the application we are going to implement faithfully reflects the real requirements, so that no errors are inadvertently transferred from the specification down to the implementation and the delivered system, special care must be paid to assessing the specification before starting an implementation. Otherwise, the only way to capture incorrectly specified requirements would occur much too late, maybe even after the application has been delivered and is being executed in real life. But at that point, not only the cost of (part of) the development effort would have been wasted, but also the costs of failures would bear on the costs of the project.

In this paper, we concentrate on specification and specification verification. In particular, since we are deliberately restricting our attention to real-time systems, we discuss how timing properties can be verified at the specification level. We concentrate on timing issues since they are critical for real-time systems that operate under strict time constraints, whose violation may have severe consequences. For example, as a reaction to an incoming alarm signal, one might require that an action be undertaken at least after a certain time t_1 and before another time t_2. A failure to meet this requirement might be a serious flaw in the application.

The paper is organized as follows. Section 2 provides an overview of existing approaches to formal specification and verification of timing properties at the specification level. The rest of the paper will then provide case studies of specification formalisms and verification approaches. Since existing approaches are too many to be analyzed in depth here, Section 3 introduces as a case study a specification formalism based on Petri nets and outlines how timing properties can be verified. Section 4 considers a subclass of the formalism and shows how the reduced expressiveness of the formalism can be traded for the existence of a simpler analysis algorithm. Both Sections 3 and 4 are highly based on examples to introduce the methods, rather than relying on formal definitions and theorems. Section 5 contains some conclusions and draws the directions for future work.

2 Review of selected existing approaches

Formal specification for real-time systems has recently drawn the attention of many researchers. The main approaches being pursued may be broadly classified

in two categories: operational approaches and descriptive approaches. Operational approaches include specification formalisms based on different kinds of automata while descriptive ones are mainly based on algebra or different temporal
logics.

In this section we select some of the existing approaches and discuss their contribution. Our goal, however, is not to provide an exhaustive survey of existing
approaches, but rather to focus on some relevant work that is being done in the
two approaches, and relate them to the work reported here. Most of the formalisms proposed in the literature to cope with real-time systems specifications
are extensions of already existing non-timed formalisms. Let us mention, among
others:

- Extensions of process algebras, like Timed CCS [72], Timed Lotos [19], ATP
  [65].
- Extensions of temporal logics. Classical temporal logics [59] deal with time
  in a qualitative way, which makes them not suitable to deal with real-time
  systems. To overcome this drawback, extensions were proposed where time
  is treated in a quantitative way: In some cases, time is a derived concept:
  it is derived on the basis of the *next* operator, which allows specifications
  to deal with a discrete time domain [50]. Other approaches introduce an
  explicit clock variable or function (e.g., see RTL [42] and RTTL [58]). Instead,
  TRIO [56], MTL [48] and TCTL [2] are examples of temporal logics based on
  bounding the temporal operators [4].
- Extensions of finite state machines. This is generally done by imposing timing
  constraints on the transitions, like in Timed Transitions systems [38] or in
  EMS [58]. Another approach is taken in [2], where the automata are extended
  with timer variables.
- Extensions of Petri Nets. Two main techniques for representing time in Petri
  nets have been proposed in the literature: attaching time to transitions [53,
  61, 39] or, alternatively, to places [69, 16]. In both cases, time constraints are
  imposed to the next firing of the transitions. A more general model including
  and extending most of the timed models is presented in Section 3.

As far as verification is concerned, we concentrate here on two main classes
of well-known properties: *safety* and *liveness* properties [23]; we show that this
distinction can be imprecise and propose a better classification in terms of universal, existential, and general properties. A safety property specifies that certain
undesirable behaviors never occur. A liveness property specifies that some desirable state is eventually reached. In our case, we assume that both safety and
liveness are stated with regard to a certain time limit: The undesirable behavior
does not occur within a giving time (*timed safety*); the desired state is reached
within a certain time limit (*timed liveness*). A timed safety property specifies
an invariant property that must hold until a certain lower bound for time is
reached. Instead, a timed liveness property asserts that a property eventually
holds, before an upper bound for time is reached. Hence, they are also called
in the literature *bounded invariance* and *bounded response*, respectively [4]. In

order to prove a safety property it is thus necessary to explore the entire state
space up to the time limit. On the other hand, a liveness property requires to
prove that a given desired state can be entered.

For example, in a railway system specification, one might wish to prove that it
is possible to reach station B from station A in less than X minutes (bounded
response) and that the train never enters an intersection before X seconds have
elapsed since the barriers are down (bounded invariance). It is often claimed that
almost all critical properties required for real-time systems are safety properties.
In fact, under the assumption that time progresses, both classes of properties,
bounded response and bounded invariance, are safety properties [52, 4, 37]. Next,
we briefly review a sample of the languages that have been proposed in the literature along with their verification methods.

RTL [42] is an extension of first-order logic allowing one to specify systems in
terms of the event/action model and to impose temporal constraints on the possible system evolutions. RTL extends first-order logic by introducing particular
operators to express sequential and parallel composition of events, the start, the
end, and the number of occurrences of a given event. The temporal domain adopted in RTL is isomorphic to natural numbers. The descriptions of events, actions
and temporal constraints are then translated into a set of first-order formulas
and arithmetic relations describing the time instants at which the modeled system evolves. A procedure controls the consistency of the specification, written
in a higher level language that is translated into RTL, and its compatibility with
any safety property expressed in RTL.

TRIO [56, 29] and Metric Temporal Logic [48] are extensions of linear temporal logic where the classical temporal operators can be derived from the basic
operators such as Dist or Futr and Past. These operators state the distance between events. TRIO and MTL have similar expressive capabilities; but they were
designed by intending different uses of the specification. [48] provides a sound
axiomatization of MTL and a deductive derivation theory. Instead, TRIO was
defined by providing model-theoretic semantics, and special care was paid to
providing mechanisms supporting constructive verification of properties. In particular, the emphasis is on validating specifications by directly executing them.
TRIO's validation mechanisms are based on the tableau-method [22]. A recent
work [23] also provides a sound axiomatization for TRIO. This axiomatization
is enriched with a proof system, which is used in [23] to specify and prove properties of real-time systems modeled in terms of Timed Petri nets [53]. TRIO
has been extended into TRIO+ [57] and TRIO* [17], introducing modularity and
higher level mechanisms, which provide better support to cope with complex
systems specifications. ASTRAL [26] is also a high level assertional language based on ASLAN [6] and TRIO. Its semantics was defined in terms of a translation
schema into TRIO. Thus, any ASTRAL specification can be translated into a
TRIO formula, and then TRIO's validation methods can be applied to analyze
the specification.

[3] defines a real-time logic based on propositional calculus rather than on first order predicate calculus, namely Timed Propositional Temporal Logic (TPTL). Since in TPTL quantification over time is not allowed, the language is decidable and thus a suitable proving mechanism can be defined. A tableau-based decision procedure has been developed.

[73] defines Asynchronous PTL (APTL), which extends TPTL by explicitly introducing local clocks, whose values cannot be directly compared. An underlying asynchronous distributed model is introduced in order to interpret timing inequalities involving different clocks. APTL is still decidable, and decision procedures have been defined for it. While TPTL is an extension of linear temporal logic, TCTL [2] is a similar extension of branching propositional temporal logic CTL [15].

[2] describes an approach based on the verification of systems modeled with timed graphs, by model-checking their temporal operational specification [15]. Model-checking is a technique in which a state graph model of the system behavior is verified with respect to a temporal logic formula describing either a bounded response property or a bounded invariance property. The operational language used, timed graphs are an extension of the finite state machines where timers are added. A timer is a variable, whose values uniformly increase. A timer can be set to zero with any transition occurrence and its value corresponds at any instant to the time elapsed since it was last reset. Guards are also added to transitions to impose timing constraints on the occurrence of the transitions. The transitions are instantaneous. An important result claimed by the authors is that the model-checker's complexity *does not blow-up* when dealing with dense time.

A different approach to extending temporal logic for real-time is adopted in Real Time Temporal Logic (RTTL) [58]. [58] divides the system specification into two layers: an operational part and a descriptive one. Extended State Machines (EMS) are used as an operational language, while RTTL is used as a descriptive specification language. EMS consists of a finite state automaton, augmented with variables with arbitrary domains. Transitions are labeled with a *guard* (a first order formula on state variables) and an *operation* (a value assignment to state variables). A transition can occur if its guard evaluates to true, and then the global state is updated by executing its operation. The specification of real-time properties is possible by considering a particular component of the automaton as a "clock", i.e., by introducing a discrete variable, called time or T, whose value monotonically increases as the system evolves. RTTL, is a standard first order logic using an explicit clock variable T. The clock variable T assumes the value of the corresponding time for each state. RTTL provides a proof system for safety properties and decision procedures for finite state cases.

A similar approach is taken in [38, 36] with timed transitions systems. A timed transition system is an extension of state machines, where timing constraints are imposed on the transitions. A pair $[l_v, u_v]$ is associated with each transition v, representing the minimum and maximum delay for its occurrence. A property proof system is provided for timed transitions systems. A visual representation can be obtained by extending the notation of Statecharts, by annotating each transition with the respective pair [46]. This approach is also extended to cope with hybrid systems where system behaviors are decomposed into two time phases, one discrete and the other dense.

Like Statecharts, other synchronous programming languages have been proposed, notable examples are Lustre [12] and Esterel [9]. Lustre is a declarative language, while Esterel is an operational one. A discrete global clock rules the behavior of all the components. This assumption and the fact that it is only possible to deal with deterministic specifications make the analysis of the whole system much simpler. In fact, there are verification tools and compilers that translate the code into the form of an extended finite automaton. This automaton can be executed and some validation and analysis techniques can be applied. Model-checking techniques are applied to verify whether the implementation meets safety requirements.

The last mentioned synchronous approach, i.e., compiling specifications into automata in order to execute them and apply verification techniques, is extended in [64] to cope with asynchronous systems with both discrete and dense time. [64] proposes a specification formalism which consists of a timed process algebra, ATP, augmented with watchdog and timeout constructs. Specifications are compiled into timed graphs [2] and properties expressed with TCTL can be verified with model-checking techniques [2].

[24] suggests a Petri net-like formalism called Hierarchical Multi State Machine (HMS) to describe a real-time system operationally. The operational formalism is coupled with an assertion language used to state preconditions and postconditions. Time is implicitly incremented by 1 by the firing of a single transition or by the concurrent firing of several transitions. Given an execution path of a HMS and the set of pre- and postconditions, a set of inequalities, is derived representing the time conditions for the feasibility of the path. Thus, solving the inequalities determines whether a potential plan can be scheduled.

[52] uses mapping techniques to prove timing properties of systems with timing constraints. The technique is based on representing the system as an automaton whose states include predictive timing information. The formal model used is a *timed automaton*. A timed automaton is an Input/Output automaton enriched with a boundmap describing the timing assumptions for the components of the system (e.g., the timing conditions stating the lower and upper bounds between the occurrence of events). Timing assumptions and timing requirements are both represented by these automata. Then, the method involves the construction of a mapping from the *assumption automata* to the *requirements automata* in order to show that the system meets the safety requirements. [5] provides a sample of analysis of time bounds.

In this paper, we are mainly concerned with the operational formalism of Petri nets, which will be discussed in the next sections. Hereafter, we briefly mention the different proposals to introduce time in Petri nets.

In [53] a time interval $[l_v, u_v]$ is associated to each transition v, representing the minimum and maximum time delay that must elapse between the enabling of v and its firing. [61] and [39] essentially propose to associate a firing *duration* Δ to each transition. In this case, a transition *starts firing* as soon as it is enabled and its firing takes Δ time units. [16] and [69] suggest to attach a waiting time to places. A token must wait the time associated to the place before it can contribute to the enabling of any transition. A transition fires as soon as enabled. [14] proposes to translate the reachability graph of a bounded Timed Petri net into a Moore machine, on which net properties are analyzed by using a model-checker. The Timed Petri nets used in [14] are a slight modification of Merlin and Farber's nets. Yet another Real Time Temporal Logic (RTTL) is used as an assertional language. This RTTL is an extension of CTL [15], by adding ad-hoc operators to describe operational behaviors. Another technique for analyzing Merlin and Farber's nets will be introduced in Section 4.1.

Several other formal approaches to specify real-time systems and prove timing properties have been developed that we did not describe here; for instance, see [1, 40, 43, 7].

3 TB nets

Time Basic nets (TB nets) [28] are an extension of Petri nets. We assume that the reader is familiar with Petri nets; otherwise he or she can refer to [63] for a comprehensive description. TB nets have been introduced in [28]. In this paper, we introduce them rather informally by using a slightly different notation than in [28]. In TB nets, each token is associated with a *timestamp*, representing the time at which the token has been created by a firing. Each transition is associated with a *time-function*, which describes the relation between the timestamps of the tokens removed by a firing and the timestamps of the tokens produced by the firing.

Definition 1 (TB nets). A TB net is a 6-tuple $< P, T, \Theta; F, tf, m_0 >$ where

1. P, T, and F are, respectively, the sets of places, transitions, and arcs of a net. Given a transition t, the preset of t, i.e., the set of places connected with t by an arc entering t, is denoted by $^{\bullet}t$; the postset of t, i.e., the set of places connected with t by an arc exiting t, is denoted by $t^{\bullet}$.
2. Θ is a numeric set, whose elements are the timestamps that can be associated with the tokens. The timestamp of a token represents the time at which it has been created. For instance, Θ can be the set of natural numbers, or the set of non-negative real numbers. In the following, we assume $\Theta = \Re^+$ (the set of non-negative real numbers, i.e., time is assumed to be continuous).

3. tf is a function that associates a function tf_t (called time-function) with each transition t. Let en denote a tuple of tokens, one for each place in the preset of transition t. Function tf_t associates with each tuple en a set of values θ ($\theta \in \Theta$), such that each value in θ is not less than the maximum of the timestamps associated with the tokens belonging to tuple en. $\theta = tf_t(en)$ represents the set of possible times at which transition t can fire, if enabled by tuple en. When transition t fires, the firing time of t under tuple en is arbitrarily chosen among the set of values θ. The chosen firing time is the value of the timestamps of *all* the produced tokens.

4. m_0, the *initial marking*, is a function associating a (finite) multiset of tokens with each place. In general, we use function m to denote a generic marking of nets, i.e., $m(p)$ denotes the multiset of tokens associated with place p by marking m.

In order to define the rule by which new markings of the net may be generated, starting from the initial marking m_0, we need to define the concepts of *enabling tuple*, *enabling*, *firing time*, and *enabling time*.

Definition 2 (Enabling tuple, enabling, firing time, enabling time). Given a transition t and a marking m, let en be a tuple of tokens, one for each input place of transition t. If $tf_t(en)$ is empty, there exists no time instant at which transition t can fire under tuple en; i.e., transition t is not enabled under tuple en. If $tf_t(en)$ is not empty, en is said to be an *enabling tuple* for transition t and the pair $x = < en, t >$ is said to be an *enabling*. The triple $y = < en, t, \tau >$ where $< en, t >$ is an enabling and $\tau \in tf_t(en)$, is said to be a *firing*. τ is said to be the *firing time*. We refer to the maximum among the timestamps associated with tuple en as the *enabling time* of the enabling $< en, t >$.

The dynamic evolution of the net (its semantics) is defined by means of firing occurrences, which ultimately produce firing sequences.

Definition 3 (Occurrence of a firing in a marking). Given a marking m and a firing $y = < en, t, \tau >$ such that en is contained in m, the firing occurrence of y in m produces a new marking m', that can be obtained from m by removing the tokens of the enabling tuple en from the places of $^\bullet t$, and producing a new token with timestamp τ in the places of $t^\bullet$. If x is a firing that produces marking m' from m we write $m[x > m'$.

Definition 4 (Firing sequence). Starting from the initial marking m_0, a firing sequence σ is a finite sequence of firings x_i, $1 \leq i \leq n$, such that $m_{i-1}[x_i > m_i$ where m_{i-1} is the marking produced by the occurrence of the first $(i-1)$ firings, starting from m_0.

Example 1 (Bus stop). Figure 1 shows a simple TB net representing a bus stop. Place p_1 represents a passenger waiting for the bus. Place p_2 represents the bus at the stop. Place p_3 represents the bus after having left the stop. Transition t_1 represents the bus leaving the stop with the new passenger on board. Transition

t_2 represents the bus leaving the stop without the new passenger on board. Time-functions associated with transitions are represented by the sets of firing times associated with the enabling tuples. The timestamps associated with the tokens in the input places are referred in the time-functions through the names of the places. Time function tf_{t_1} associated with transition t_1[2] is a function with two arguments p_1 and p_2, namely the timestamps associated with the tokens in places p_1 and p_2, respectively. Transition t_1 cannot fire at a time less than the time of the token in p_1, i.e., a passenger can get on the bus only after the bus has arrived at the stop. Transition t_1 can fire between 5 and 30 time units after the token arrives in place t_2 (all units are assumed to be given in seconds in this example). The time needed for opening the doors is 5 sec; and the maximum delay after which the doors are closed and the bus leaves the stop is 30 sec. If the passenger does not get on the bus at the stop, e.g., because he/she is late (place p_1 is not marked), the bus continues its route (transition t_2). Transition t_2 fires immediately if the driver decides not to stop because there are no passengers waiting for the bus. It fires later if the driver decides to stop because there are passengers willing to get off the bus.

It should be noticed that according to the original Petri nets' semantics transition t_1 may not fire although enabled. This represents the passenger waiting for the bus, but deciding not to get on the bus because, say, it is too crowded, or the bus not opening the doors because, say, it is already full and stops only for letting people get off.

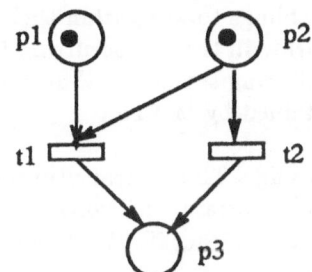

$$tf_{t_1}(p_1, p_2) = \{\tau \mid max(p_1, p_2 + 5) \leq \tau \leq p_2 + 30\}$$
$$tf_{t_2}(p_2) = \{\tau \mid p_2 \leq \tau\}$$

Fig. 1. A TB net representing a bus stop.

According to Petri net semantics, an enabling does not necessarily produce a firing occurrence: the enabling states whether a firing can occur, but does not force a firing to occur. If a firing does not occur at some point, it may occur at some later point (unless some other firing occurrence disables it). As a consequence, it may happen that the firing times of the firing occurrences in a firing

---

[2] In the following, we always indicate the time-function associated with a transition t with the subscript notation tf_t.

sequence are not ordered in ascending order. In order to restrict the systems that may be specified using TB nets to the set of feasible systems, we constrain the net behavior by requiring that:

a1. no firing occurs at a time that is less than any of the timestamps of the tokens of the initial marking, and

a2. the firing sequences are restricted to a subset of firing sequences whose firing times are monotonically non-decreasing with respect to their occurrence.

The set of all firing sequences that satisfy these two constraints defines the semantics of net. More precisely, according to [31], we define this semantics as Monotonic Weak Time Semantics (MWTS). MWTS is not the only kind of useful semantics that may be defined for TB nets. Another important kind of semantics is called Strong Time Semantics (STS).

STS is defined by restricting the set of firing sequences to the subset of MWTS firing sequences where

b1. no enabling tuple exists in the initial marking m_0 whose maximum firing time is less than the maximum of the timestamps associated with the tokens in m_0, and

b2. for each marking m_i produced by a sequence of i firings representing the prefix of a STS firing sequence $\sigma = <x_1, x_2, \ldots x_n>$, there exists no tuple en enabling a transition t in m_i such that the time of the firing x_{i+1} is greater than the maximum firing time of t under tuple en.

Intuitively, STS requires enablings to fire within their maximum firing time unless disabled by any other firing in the net occurring before the maximum firing time has expired. The set of firing sequences that may be obtained by STS is a proper subset of the set obtained by MWTS.

When a system is specified using a TB net, transitions represent events or actions that can (or must) occur under certain time constraints. If STS is used, then the events *must* occur as specified. Instead, if MWTS is used, the time function specifies when the events *can* occur.

According to the above definitions, the time of a firing may be equal to the enabling time of the tuple that belongs to the firing. Intuitively, this means that an effect (the firing) can occur with no delay after the cause that enables it is fulfilled. Therefore, it is possible to have sequences of firings where the time does not change. In practice, it is useful to restrict the attention to a subclass of TB nets, such that there exist no infinitely long firing sequences which take a finite amount of time. This constraint, that represents a *feasibility constraint* on firing sequences, is implicitly assumed to hold in the rest of the paper.

TB nets generalize time Petri net models presented in the literature in two ways:

c1. by defining MWTS, in addition to STS, the only semantics traditionally considered for timed Petri nets, c2. by providing a general mechanism for describing time evolution (time-functions).

Example 2 (Factory). Figure 2 shows an example of a TB net with STS. It represents part of the assembly line of a plant, where machine tools move through processing areas (cells) to perform automation steps. The machine tool modeled in the example of Figure 2 is a varnisher. The whole system is composed of three main comonents: the *varnisher*, the *doors* that isolate the varnisher during the operations in a cell for safety reasons, and the *slide*, that moves the varnisher through the assembly line and locks it in correspondence to the cell containing the object to varnish.

The states of the varnisher are represented by places p_1, p_2, and p_3. Place p_1 represents the varnisher ready for operating, place p_2 represents the varnisher operating, and place p_3 represents the varnisher after the varnishing of the object has been completed. The operations of the varnisher are represented by transitions t_1, t_2, and t_3, that represent the load of the varnish in the machine, the start, and the end of the varnishing respectively. Places p_4 and p_5 represent the state of the doors, closed and open respectively. Transition t_4 represents the doors closing, and transition t_5 represents the doors opening.

The slide is only partially represented. In particular it is only represented the part of the slide of a single cell. The complete slide can be represented by replicating the description of a single cell for the number of cells in the plant. Place p_6 represents the slide entering cell i. Place p_7 represents the slide locked in cell i. Place p_8 represents the slide ready to exit cell i. Transition t_6 represents the locking of the slide in cell i, transition t_7 represent the unlocking of the slide, and transition t_8 represents the slide moving to the next cell.

Places p_9, p_{10}, p_{11}, p_{12}, p_{13}, and p_{14} represent control signals that synchronize the operation in order to guarantee a correct behavior of the whole system. Places p_{10} and p_{11} represent the slide controller signaling to the door controller and the varnisher, respectively, that the slide has been successfully locked, and thus the doors can be safely closed and the slide is in a safe position for starting the varnishing. Place p_{12} represents the door controller signaling to the varnisher that the doors are closed and thus the varnishing can start without risks for operators. Places p_9 and p_{13} represent the varnisher signaling to the door controller and the slide controller, respectively, that the varnishing has been completed and thus the doors can be opened again and the slide can be unlocked. Finally, place p_{14} represents the door controller signaling to the slide controller that the doors are open and thus the slide can be unlocked without risks.

Time function tf_{t_1} describes the time for loading the varnisher (20 to 30 seconds[3] after the last operation). The varnishing (transition t_2) cannot start earlier than

---

[3] In this example time is expressed in seconds.

10 seconds after loading the varnisher and earlier than 30 and 20 seconds after receiving the signals from the slide and the door controller, respectively. It must start within 60 seconds after all preconditions are fulfilled. The varnishing operation (transition t_3) takes from 120 to 180 seconds. The doors are closed between 15 and 20 seconds after the signal from the slide controller (transition t_4) and they are open with the same delay after the signal from the varnisher is received (transition t_5). The locking of the slide takes from 60 to 90 seconds (transition t_6). The unlocking of the slide occurs between 60 and 90 seconds after being enabled (transition t_7). Finally, the slide moves from one cell to the next in 210 to 240 seconds (transition t_8).

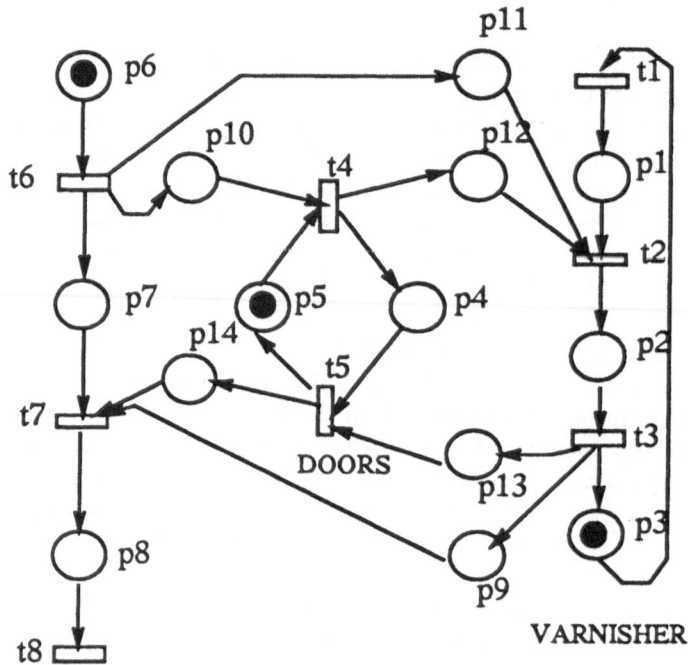

$$tf_{t_1}(p_3) = \{\tau \mid p_3 + 20 \le \tau \le p_3 + 30\}$$
$$tf_{t_2}(p_1, p_{11}, p_{12}) = \{\tau \mid max(p_1 + 10, p_{11} + 30, p_{12} + 20) \le \tau \le max(p_1, p_{11}, p_{12}) + 60\}$$
$$tf_{t_3}(p_2) = \{\tau \mid p_2 + 120 \le \tau \le p_2 + 180\}$$
$$tf_{t_4}(p_5, p_{10}) = \{\tau \mid max(p_5, p_{10} + 15) \le \tau \le max(p_5, p_{10} + 20)\}$$
$$tf_{t_5}(p_4, p_{13}) = \{\tau \mid max(p_4, p_{13} + 15) \le \tau \le max(p_4, p_{13} + 20)\}$$
$$tf_{t_6}(p_6) = \{\tau \mid p_6 + 60 \le \tau \le p_6 + 90\}$$
$$tf_{t_7}(p_7, p_9, p_{14}) = \{\tau \mid max(p_7, p_9 + 60, p_{14} + 60) \le \tau \le max(p_7, p_9 + 90, p_{14} + 90)\}$$
$$tf_{t_8}(p_8) = \{\tau \mid p_8 + 210 \le \tau \le p_8 + 240\}$$

Fig. 2. A TB net representing a varnishing automation plant.

TB nets are themselves a special case of a more general formalism, called ER nets [28]. ER nets are a class of high-level Petri nets that can specify data (as values associated with tokens), functionality (as relations associated with transitions), timing, and control. [30] discusses verification via symbolic execution for ER nets without timing constraints. [23] describes how to prove properties of ER nets by reasoning in terms of a real-time temporal logic. Hereafter we concentrate on timing and ignore data and functionality; the resulting formalism is thus a TB net. The next subsection presents a method to prove temporal properties of TB nets.

3.1 Analysis of TB nets

TB nets may be analyzed by constructing the *Time Reachability Tree (TRT)*, as described in [31]. A TRT is a (generally infinite) tree that describes all possible reachable markings. The procedure that builds it is based on symbolic execution. A symbolic state is defined by symbolic values for the token timestamps and by a predicate specifying a constraint on the symbolic values. The symbolic state stands for all actual states where the timestamps satisfy the constraint. These concepts are illustrated by the following example.

Example 3 (Transmission link). Figure 3 shows a TB net representing the transmission of packets on a Communication link. Packets are of three different lengths and the time taken for the transmission depends on their length. In particular, the transmission of packets of length l_1 takes from $\delta_{1_{min}}$ to $\delta_{1_{max}}$ time units, starting from the time the packet is ready to be transmitted (place p_1 marked) and the station is ready for transmission (place p_2 marked), the transmission of packets of length l_2 takes from $\delta_{2_{min}}$ to $\delta_{2_{max}}$ time units, and the transmission of packets of length l_3 takes from $\delta_{3_{min}}$ to $\delta_{3_{max}}$ time units[4].

A symbolic marking μ representing a packet ready for transmission at time τ_1 and the station ready for transmission at time τ_2 associates a symbolic value τ_1 to place p_1 and a symbolic value τ_2 to place p_2. The constraint

$$0 \leq \tau_2 - \tau_1 \leq \theta$$

expresses the fact that the station became ready at most θ time units after the packet.

Nodes of the TRT represent symbolic markings. If no confusion arises, in the following we use the words *node* and *symbolic marking* interchangeably. Arcs of the TRT represent *symbolic firings*, i.e., sets of *actual firings* enabled in at least one of the actual markings represented by the source node of the arc. The target node of an arc can be seen as the union of all the possible actual markings produced by the actual firings represented by the symbolic firing corresponding

---

[4] Using ER-Nets [28], it would be possible to associate the packet's length as an attribute to the tokens of place p_1. It would also be possible to make the value of the time-function dependent on the value of the tokens (i.e., the packet's length).

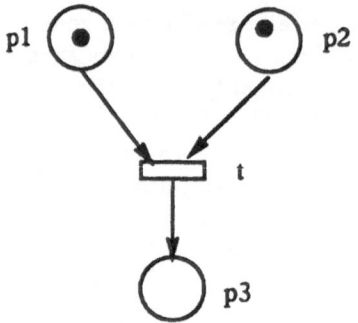

$$tf_t(p_1, p_2) = \{\tau \mid max(p_1, p_2) + \delta_{1_{min}} \leq \tau \leq max(p_1, p_2) + \delta_{1_{max}} \text{ or}$$
$$max(p_1, p_2) + \delta_{2_{min}} \leq \tau \leq max(p_1, p_2) + \delta_{2_{max}} \text{ or}$$
$$max(p_1, p_2) + \delta_{3_{min}} \leq \tau \leq p_1 + max(p_1, p_2) + \delta_{3_{max}}\}$$

Fig. 3. A TB net fragment representing the transmission of packets on a Communication network.

to the considered arc. Building the TRT consists of identifying symbolic enablings and building the target nodes for all the symbolic firings corresponding to the symbolic enablings. The rules for identifying symbolic enablings and symbolic firings depend on the chosen time semantics. Moving from MWTS to STS requires new rules to be added.

For example, let us consider the net of Figure 3 under MWTS, with the initial symbolic marking μ. The symbolic values τ_1 in place p_1 and τ_2 in place p_2 represent pairs of tokens that can concur to enabling transition t. In order to verify if the pair ofsymbolic values $< \tau_1, \tau_2 >$ enables transition t, we must verify if there exists at least one substitution of actual values for τ_1 and τ_2 that represents an actual enabling in one of the actual markings represented by the symbolic marking μ. In general, this can be verified by examining the constraint C and the time-function associated with the considered transition. In the example, the set of firing times produced by time-function tf_t is non-empty for any pair of values in the preset of t. This set contains only elements greater than the values associated with the tokens in the preset of transition t. Being such tokens the only tokens in the net fragment of Figure 3, the monotonicity constraint, i.e., the requirement that the next firing time is not less than the time of the last firing in the net, is also satisfied. Thus, we can conclude that the pair $<< \tau_1, \tau_2 >, t >$ is a symbolic enabling.

Given a symbolic enabling, the corresponding symbolic firing produces a new symbolic state $S' = < \mu', C' >$, that represents all the actual markings that can be produced by the actual firings represented by the considered symbolic firing. μ' can be obtained from μ by simply removing the symbols in the symbolic enabling from the preset of transition t (τ_1 is removed from place p_1 and τ_2 is removed from place p_2) and adding a new symbolic value to each place of the postset of transition t (τ_3 is associated with place p_3). C' can be obtained by adding to C a constraint on the new symbolic value τ_3, so that it only represents firing times corresponding to the enabling tuples according to the time-function associated with transition t, and it is no less than the last firing in the net. The additional constraints can be easily obtained by substituting the place identifiers occurring in the time-function tf_t with symbolic values of the enabling tuple, and by adding a term that requires the new symbolic value being greater than the symbolic value corresponding to the last firing in the net.

In this case the additional constraints are

$$max(\tau_1, \tau_2) + \delta_{1_{min}} \leq \tau_3 \leq max(\tau_1, \tau_2) + \delta_{1_{max}} \ or$$
$$max(\tau_1, \tau_2) + \delta_{2_{min}} \leq \tau_3 \leq max(\tau_1, \tau_2) + \delta_{2_{max}} \ or$$
$$max(\tau_1, \tau_2) + \delta_{3_{min}} \leq \tau_3 \leq \tau_1 + max(\tau_1, \tau_2) + \delta_{3_{max}} \ and \ \tau_3 \geq \tau_2.$$

The constraint C' is thus given by the following expression:

$$0 \leq \tau_2 - \tau_1 \leq \theta \ and \ (max(\tau_1, \tau_2) + \delta_{1_{min}} \leq \tau_3 \leq max(\tau_1, \tau_2) + \delta_{1_{max}} \ or$$
$$max(\tau_1, \tau_2) + \delta_{2_{min}} \leq \tau_3 \leq max(\tau_1, \tau_2) + \delta_{2_{max}} \ or$$
$$max(\tau_1, \tau_2) + \delta_{3_{min}} \leq \tau_3 \leq \tau_1 + max(\tau_1, \tau_2) + \delta_{3_{max}}) \ and \ \tau_3 \geq \tau_2.$$

For STS the symbolic enabling must satisfy a further constraint: the set of firing times smaller or equal to the maximum firing time of any other symbolic enabling must be non-empty. Such a constraint must be also explicitly added to the constraint characterizing the new symbolic state.

For the simple net fragment of Figure 3 MWTS and STS, do not differ. We will see the differences between them for the example of Figure 2.

The analysis procedure we outlined before, builds a finite portion of the TRT[5], since we are interested in proving bounded invariant and bounded response properties, as we said in Section 2. The portion of the TRT corresponding to a TB net that we need to build for proving bounded invariance and bounded response properties is finite since the properties can be expressed by referring to a finite amount of time and the net is guaranteed not to present infinitely long firing sequences taking a finite amount of time by definition.

Let us consider the assembly line of Figure 2. There are several interesting bounded invariance and bounded response properties that we would like to prove. For instance, we would like to prove that once the slide arrives at cell i, the varnishing is completed successfully within a given deadline. We would also like to prove that once the slide arrives at cell i, the varnisher does not operate with the doors open or the slide unlocked before leaving successfully cell i, i.e., unsafe states are not entered within the time the machine-tool is operating in cell i.

For the sake of space, in this section, we only consider one bounded response property. In particular we would like to show how to prove that once the slide arrives at cell i, the varnishing is completed successfully within a given deadline. More precisely, we would like to prove that if, at a given time, the varnisher has successfully completed the last operation (place p_3 marked), the doors are open (place p_5 marked), and the slide has arrived at cell i (place p_6 marked), then the varnishing is completed within 6 minutes (360 seconds).

This can be proved by building the portion of the TRT with a root corresponding to places p_3, p_5, and p_6 marked with the same timestamp, and each leaf

---

[5] Assuming that the feasibility constraint on firing sequences holds.

corresponding to either one of the two cases:

1. a successful operation (place p_3 marked within 360 seconds);
2. a symbolic marking with a timestamp greater than 360 seconds.

If all the leaves of the portion of the TRT correspond to case (1), the property holds; if at least one of the leaves corresponds to case (2), the property does not hold.

The initial symbolic marking associates to places p_3, p_5, and p_6 the same symbolic value τ_0, with the only constraint requiring τ_0 to be greater than or equal to zero.

The initial symbolic state $S_0 = < \mu_0, C_0 >$ can be thus described as
$\mu_0(p_3) = \{\tau_0\}, \mu_0(p_5) = \{\tau_0\}, \mu_0(p_6) = \{\tau_0\}, C_0 = (\tau_0 \geq 0)$.

In the initial state S_0 two transitions have one tuple of tokens in their preset (transitions t_1 and t_6) and a non-empty set of associated firing times; thus both are enabled according to MWTS.

However according to STS (which is required here), only transition t_1 can fire. In fact, the possible firing times for transition t_1[6] are the values in the interval $[\tau_0 + 20, \tau_0 + 30]$, while the possible firing times of transition t_6 are the values in the interval $[\tau_0 + 60, \tau_0 + 90]$. According to STS, transition t_6 cannot fire before transition t_1 since it cannot fire before $\tau_0 + 60$ while transition t_1 is required to fire no later than $\tau_0 + 30$. Notice that the computation of the symbolic enabling requires the ability to manipulate expressions, which turns out to be easy in this example, but may be unsolvable in the general case.

The firing of transition t_1 leads to a new symbolic state $S_1 = < \mu_1, C_1 >$, where:
$\mu_1(p_1) = \{\tau_1\}, \mu_1(p_5) = \{\tau_0\}, \mu_1(p_6) = \{\tau_0\}$,
$C_1 = (\tau_0 \geq 0 \ and \tau_0 + 20 \leq \tau_1 \leq \tau_0 + 30)$.

The reader should notice that C_1 has been simplified using suitable algebraic rules. Thus the monotonicity constraint ($\tau_1 \geq \tau_0$) that requires the time of the current firing (τ_1) to be greater than or equal to the time of the previous firing (only τ_0 in this case) has been simplified, since it is implied by the other constraints. The STS constraint, requiring the time of the firing to be less than or equal to the maximum firing time of any other enabling, does not produce any new term, since there is only one symbolic enabling.

In the symbolic state S_1 only transition t_6 is enabled. Its firing leads to the symbolic state $S_2 = < \mu_2, C_2 >$, where:
$\mu_2(p_1) = \{\tau_1\}, \mu_2(p_5) = \{\tau_0\}$,
$\mu_2(p_7) = \{\tau_2\}, \mu_2(p_{10}) = \{\tau_2\}$,
$\mu_2(p_{11}) = \{\tau_2\}$,
$C_2 = (\tau_0 \geq 0 \ and \ \tau_0 + 20 \leq \tau_1 \leq \tau_0 + 30 \ and \ \tau_0 + 60 \leq \tau_2 \leq \tau_0 + 90)$.

In the symbolic state S_2 only transition t_4 is enabled. Its firing leads to the symbolic state $S_3 = < \mu_3, C_3 >$, defined as follows:
$\mu_3(p_1) = \{\tau_1\}, \mu_3(p_4) = \{\tau_3\}$,
$\mu_3(p_7) = \{\tau_2\}, \mu_3(p_{12}) = \{\tau_3\}$,

---

[6] If there is only one enabling tuple for each transition, as in this case, we use the name of the transition to indicate the enabling.

$\mu_3(p_{11}) = \{\tau_2\}$,
$C_3 = (\tau_0 \geq 0 \text{ and } \tau_0 + 20 \leq \tau_1 \leq \tau_0 + 30 \text{ and }$
$\tau_0 + 60 \leq \tau_2 \leq \tau_0 + 90 \text{ and } \tau_2 + 15 \leq \tau_3 \leq \tau_2 + 20)$.

The expression derived from the evaluation of the time-function tf_{t_4} has been simplified by considering that the value of τ_0 is constrained to be less than or equal to τ_2.

In the symbolic state S_3 only transition t_2 is enabled. Its firing leads to the symbolic state $S_4 =< \mu_4, C_4 >$, where:

$\mu_4(p_4) = \{\tau_3\}$,
$\mu_4(p_7) = \{\tau_2\}$, $\mu_4(p_2) = \{\tau_4\}$,
$C_4 = (\tau_0 \geq 0 \text{ and } \tau_0 + 20 \leq \tau_1 \leq \tau_0 + 30 \text{ and }$
$\qquad \tau_0 + 60 \leq \tau_2 \leq \tau_0 + 90 \text{ and } \tau_2 + 15 \leq \tau_3 \leq \tau_2 + 20 \text{ and }$
$\qquad \tau_3 + 20 \leq \tau_4 \leq \tau_3 + 60)$.

Finally, in S_4 only transition t_3 is enabled. Its firing leads to the symbolic state $S_5 =< \mu_5, C_5 >$, where:

$\mu_5(p_4) = \{\tau_3\}$,
$\mu_5(p_7) = \{\tau_2\}$, $\mu_5(p_3) = \{\tau_5\}$,
$\mu_5(p_9) = \{\tau_5\}$, $\mu_5(p_{13}) = \{\tau_5\}$,
$C_5 = (\tau_0 \geq 0 \text{ and } \tau_0 + 20 \leq \tau_1 \leq \tau_0 + 30 \text{ and }$
$\qquad \tau_0 + 60 \leq \tau_2 \leq \tau_0 + 90 \text{ and } \tau_2 + 15 \leq \tau_3 \leq \tau_2 + 20 \text{ and }$
$\qquad \tau_3 + 20 \leq \tau_4 \leq \tau_3 + 60 \text{ and } \tau_4 + 120 \leq \tau_5 \leq \tau_4 + 180)$.

The construction of the TRT can stop here since we reached a leaf where place p_3 is marked and no other branch of the TRT is still open.

With a simple algebraic computation it is possible to derive the firing set of possible values for τ_5 (the timestamp of the token in place p_3 relative to τ_0: $\tau_0 + 215 \leq \tau_5 \leq \tau_0 + 350$. It is thus possible to conclude that starting from any initial marking corresponding to the symbolic state S_0, we always reach a marking where place p_3 is marked within 350 seconds, i.e., the varnishing is completed within the required deadline. The computation of the time relative to the initial marking is easy for this example, but can turn out to be undecidable, depending on the comlexity of the predicates which define time-functions.

4 Special cases of TB nets

TB nets generalize the time Petri net formalisms[7] presented in the literature [27, 28]. For example, the formalism proposed in [53], hereafter referred to as MF nets, is a TB net with strong time semantics, where time-functions associate each enabling tuple with an interval, relative to the enabling time of the transition. Figure 4(a) describes an MF net fragment. The corresponding TB net fragment is shown in Figure 4(b).

Other formalisms surveyed in Section 2, such as [61], [39], [16], and [69] can also be easily described by using TB nets, as shown in [27].

---

[7] We exclude from this stochastic time Petri net formalisms.

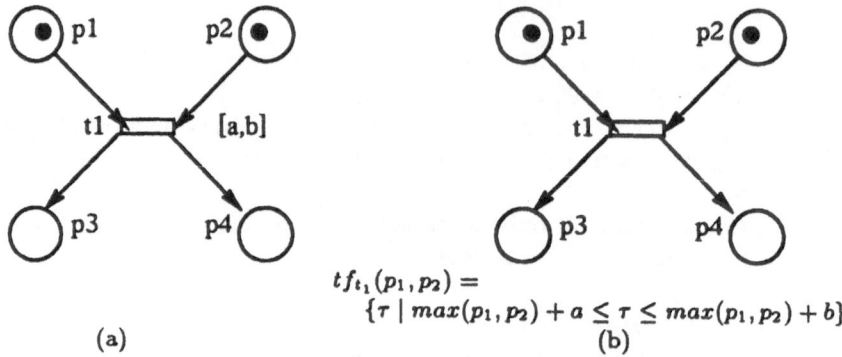

$$tf_{t_1}(p_1, p_2) =$$
$$\{\tau \mid max(p_1, p_2) + a \leq \tau \leq max(p_1, p_2) + b\}$$

(a)   (b)

Fig. 4. A MF net fragment and the corresponding TB net fragment.

4.1 Analysis of MF nets

In this section we show how MF nets can be analyzed, following the method proposed in [10] and [11] on a simple example. We refer the reader to [11] and [10] for a complete description of the method.

The method is enumerative and is strongly based on reachability analysis. As the behavior of a Petri net is represented by its set of reachable markings, the behavior of a MF net is represented by the set of states. A *state* is a pair (M,I) where M is a reachable marking, and I is a function that associates to each transition enabled by M a time interval in which the transition is allowed to fire. Then, it is possible to check liveness and safety properties by building the corresponding state graph.

The method allows one to analyze bounded nets by considering the time domain as either natural or rational numbers. Since transitions may fire at any time of the interval defined by I, the states have in general an unbounded number of successor states. Hence, the authors propose a method which builds a graph of state classes. A state class is the set of all states reachable from the initial state. The nodes of the graph represent state classes. A node — or a state class — consists of a pair (M,D) where M is a marking reachable from an initial marking after a sequence of firings without considering time; and D is a set of inequalities constraining the firing time values for transitions enabled by M. Arcs are labeled with *firable* transitions from the source node. A transition is *firable* from a node s, if the marking M_s enables it and its minimum firing delay is less than the maximum firing delay for all the transitions enabled by M_s. This condition is necessary to ensure STS. The target node represents the state of the net after the firing of the transition labeling the arc occurred; i.e., it is comosed by the resultant marking and the updated timing constraints. The values are relative to the last firing. Any solution to the inequalities in a node means that there exists at least one feasible firing schedule from the the initial class.

Consider the net in Figure 5; it is a simplified description of a video game about a missile S and an anti-missile P responsible to shoot down S. A token in place *S_launched* represents that S has been launched. The player radar detects the missile within 2 seconds (transition *detected*). Transition *P_launch* represents the launching of the anti-missile P. The meaning of the net is that if a player is able to launch an anti-missile P while the missile S is still flying, the missile is shot down (transition *shoot_down*); otherwise S hits the target.

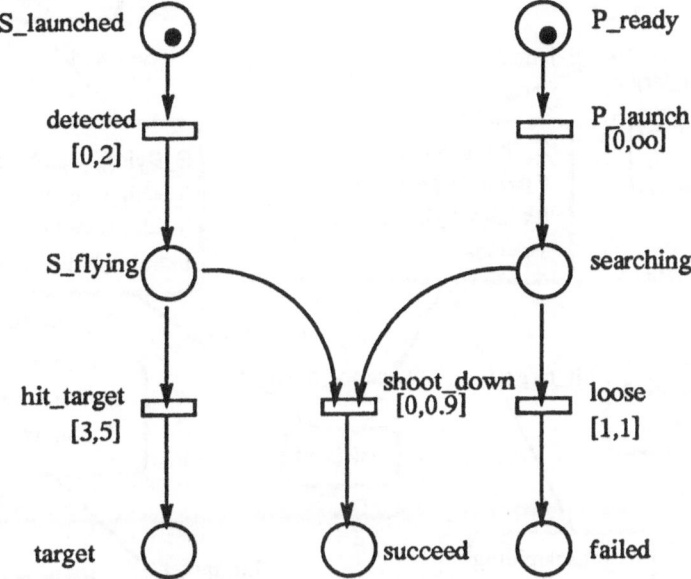

Fig. 5. MF net describing the missile/anti-missile game.

The graph of states for the net in Figure 5 is represented in Figure 6. The graph describes all possible behaviors of the net. Therein, any solution to the inequalities in which *detected* precedes *P_launch* by at most 2 time units causes the immediate firing of *shoot_down*; any solution where *P_launch* comes more than 5 time units after *detected* causes the anti-missile to fail the target. On the other hand if the launching comes after 2.1 and before 5 seconds, the result is non-deterministic. Reasoning on reachability graph, one can also realize that there are some possible schedulings where *P_launch* precedes in time the missile detection, and even that S is shot down (e.g., the following firing time sequence is feasible *P_launch:0, detected:0.5, shot_down:0.9*).

On the other hand, Figure 5 shows that MF cannot comletely capture some subtle system aspects. For instance, if a more realistic model is desired, the success of the anti-missile P should depend on the time elapsed since S was launched and its speed. Such systems aspects would be adequately described using ER-nets.

[51] extends this method to deal with the analysis of safety, recoverability and fault-tolerance properties, by adding hazard states to MF nets.

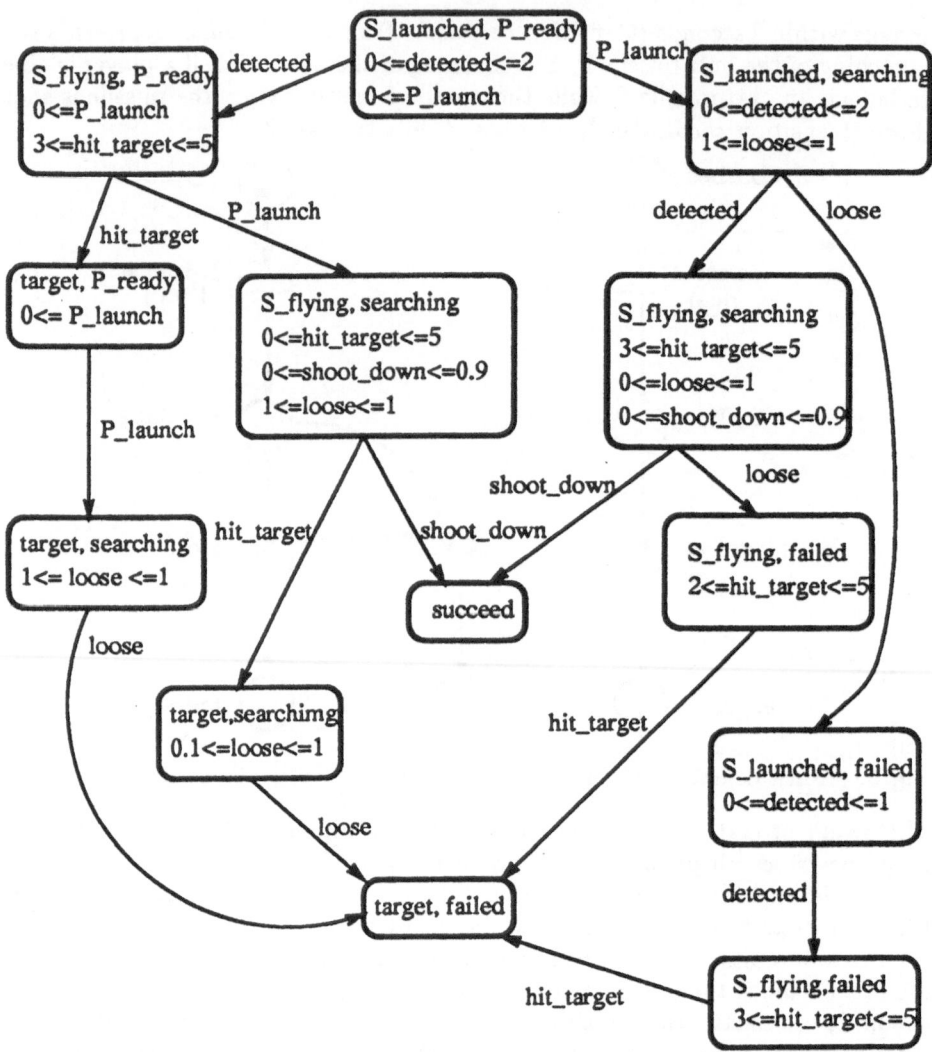

Fig. 6. The reachability graph corresponding to Fig. 5.

5 Conclusions

Formal specifications should be used in the early stage of development of critical real-time systems. Formal specifications can then drive the application development on safe grounds. But formal specifications themselves should be verified, in order to avoid error propagation from specification down to the implementation. In this paper we provided a motivation for these issues. We then reviewed a number of proposed specification formalisms and discussed their approaches to specification verification. As we pointed out, the field is still in rapid evolution. It is therefore impossible to provide an exhaustive analysis of existing proposals and conclusive comparisons of mutual advantages and disadvantages.

A large part of the paper was then devoted to discussing formal specification and verification of timing properties for time Petri nets. The reason for our choice is twofold: On the one hand, we wanted to provide a case study of a specification formalism for real-time systems and a description of the approaches available for verification. On the other, the choice reflects our personal bias: we have been working on Petri nets as a specification formalism for real-time applications [28], and we are currently working on the development of a specification environment for critical real-time applications based on this approach [44]. Petri nets are a powerful operational formalism, which is well known for being able to support simulation (i.e., specification testing); in this paper we concentrated on verification of timing properties. Other on-going work in our group is providing a framework for proving properties of Petri nets, where not only timing information is taken into account, but also data and functionality aspects are considered. In particular, [23] presents a proof theory for ER nets [28], a class of high-level Petri nets that generalizes TB nets. The approach is based on the use of TRIO, a real-time temporal logic notation developed by our group [29], to express properties of nets. [23] is a first step towards integrating an operational approach — based on Petri nets — and a descriptive approach — based on temporal logic — to specify and verify real-time systems. Different formalisms, based on different specification styles, should in fact be viewed as complementary, rather than competing, approaches.

The potential benefits of a multi-formalism approach are now being recognized by many researchers. We strongly believe that the ability to handle multiple formalisms and integrate them in an open, extensible environment should play a central role in the future specification environments for high-integrity real-time systems. This will be the focus of our future research.

References

1. M. Abadi, L. Lamport, *An Old-Fashioned Recipe for Real-Time*, Real Time: Theory in Practice, LNCS 600, Springer Verlag, 1992.

2. R. Alur, C. Coucorbertis, D. Dill, *Model-Checking for Real-Time systems*, Proceedings of the 5th IEEE lics 90, 1990.

3. R. Alur, T. Henzinger, *A Really Temporal Logic*, Proceedings of the 30th Annual Symposium on Foundations of Computer Science, IEEE Computer Science Press, 1989, 164–169.

4. R. Alur, T. Henzinger, *Logics and Models of Real Time: A Survey*, Real-Time: Theory in Practice, LNCS 600, Springer Verlag, 1992.

5. H. Attiya, N. Lynch, *Time Bounds for Real-Time Process Control in the Presence of Timing Uncertainty*, MIT, Report MIT/LCS/TM–403, July 1989, appeared in RTSS'89.

6. B. Auernheimer, R.A. Kemmerer, *ASLAN: User's Manual*, TRCS84–10, Department of Computer Science, University of California, Santa Barbara, March 1985.

7. Auernheimer B., Kemmerer R.A., *RT-ASLAN: A Specification Language for Real-Time Systems*, IEEE Transactions on Software Engineering, Vol. SE–12, No. 9, September 1986.

8. H.E. Bal, J.G. Steiner, A.S. Tanenbaum, *Programming Languages for Distributed Computing Systems*, ACM Computing Surveys, Vol. 21, No. 3, September 1989.

9. G. Berry, P. Couronné, G. Gonthier, *Synchronous Programming of Reactive Systems, an Introduction to ESTEREL*, INRIA Report No. 647, 1987.

10. B. Berthomieu, M. Menasche, *An Enumerative Approach for Analyzing Time Petri Nets*, Proceedings of IFIP Congress, September 1983.

11. B. Berthomieu, M. Diaz, *Modeling and Verification of Time Dependent systems Using Time Petri Nets*, IEEE Transactions on Software Engineering, Vol. SE–17, No. 3, March 1991, 259–273.

12. P. Caspi, et al., *LUSTRE: A Declarative Language for Programming Synchronous Systems*, Proceedings of the 14th Annual ACM Symposium on Principles of Programming Languages, Munich, 1987.

13. K.M. Chandi, J. Misra, *Parallel Program Design: A Foundation*, Addison-Wesley, 1988.

14. C. Chang, H. Huang, C. Song, *An Approach to Verifying Concurrency Behavior of Real-Time Systems Based on Time Petri Net and Temporal Logic*, Proceedings of InfoJapan 90, 1990.

15. C. Clarke, E. Emerson, S. Sistla, *Automatic Verification of Finite-State Concurrent systems Using Temporal Logic Specifications*, ACM–TOPLAS, Vol. 8, No. 2, April 1986.

16. C. Coolahan, N. Roussopoulos, *Timing Requirements for Time Driven Systems Using Augmented Petri Nets*, IEEE Transactions on Software Engineering, September 1983.

17. E. Corsetti, A. Montanari, E. Ratto, *Dealing with Difference Time Granularities in Formal Specifications of Real Time Systems*, The Journal of Real-Time Systems, Vol. 3, 1991, 191–215.

18. B. Dasarathy, *Timing Constraints of Real-Time Systems: Constructs for Expressing Them, Methods for Validating Them*, IEEE Transactions on Software Engineering, Vol. SE–11, No. 1, January 1985.

19. D. Daniels, T. Dillon, *The Notion of Time in Distributed Systems*, Proceedings of the 5th Australian Software Engineering Conference, IREE, Sydney, 1990.

20. L.K. Dillon, G.S. Avrunin, J.C. Wileden, *Constrained Expressions: Toward Broad Applicability of Analysis Methods for Distributed Software Systems*, ACM Transactions on Programming Languages and Systems, Vol. 10, No. 3, July 1988, 374–402.

21. S.R. Faulk, D.L. Parnas, *On Synchronization in Hard Real-Time Systems*, Communications of the ACM, Vol. 31, No. 3, March 1988.

22. M. Felder, A. Morzenti, *Specification Testing for Real-Time Systems by History Checking in TRIO*, Proceedings ICSE 14, Melbourne, Australia, May 1992.

23. M. Felder, D. Mandrioli, A. Morzenti, *Proving Properties of Real-Time Systems Through Logical Specifications and Petri Nets Models*, Dip. di Elettronica-Politecnico di Milano, Report 91–072, December 1991.

24. A. Gabrielian, M. Franklin, *Multilevel Specification of Real-Time Systems*, Communications of the ACM, Vol. 34, No. 5, May 1991, 51–60.

25. C. Ghezzi, R.A. Kemmerer, *ASTRAL: An Assertion Language for Specifying Real-Time Systems*, Report No. TRCS 90–25, Department of Computer Science, University of California,Santa Barbara, California, November 1990.

26. C. Ghezzi, R.A. Kemmerer, *ASTRAL: An Assertion Language for Specifying Real-Time Systems*, Proceedings of the Third European Software Engineering Conference, Milano, Italy, October 1991.

27. C. Ghezzi, D. Mandrioli, S. Morasca, M. Pezzé, *A General Way to Put Time in Petri Nets*, Proceedings of the 4th International Workshop on Software Design and Specifications,Monterey, California, April 3–4, 1987.

28. C. Ghezzi, D. Mandrioli, S. Morasca, M. Pezzé, *A Unified High-Level Petri Net Formalism for Time-Critical Systems*, IEEE Transactions on Software Engineering, Vol. SE–17, No. 2, February 1991.

29. C. Ghezzi, D. Mandrioli, A. Morzenti, *TRIO: A Logic Language for Executable Specifications of Real-Time Systems*, Journal of Systems and Software, June 1990.

30. C. Ghezzi, D. Mandrioli, S. Morasca, M. Pezzé, *Symbolic Execution of Concurrent Programs Using Petri Nets*, Computer Languages, April 1989.

31. C. Ghezzi, S. Morasca, M. Pezzé, *Timing Analysis of Time Basic Nets*, submitted for publication.

32. H. Gomaa, *Software Development of Real-Time Systems*, Communications of the ACM, Vol. 29, No. 7, July 1986.

33. D. Harel, *Statecharts: A Visual Formalism for Complex Systems*, Science of Computer Programming, Vol. 8, No. 3, June 1987, 231–274.

34. D. Harel et al., *STATEMATE: A Working Environment for the Development of Complex Reactive Systems*, Proceedings 10th International Conference on Software Engineering, Singapore, April 11–15, 1988, 396–406.

35. D.J. Hatley, I.A. Pirbai, *Strategies for Real-Time System Specification*, Dorset House, 1988.

36. T. Henzinger, Z. Manna, A. Pnueli, *Temporal Proof Methodologies for Real Time systems*, Proceedings of the 18th ACM Symposium on Principles of Programming Languages, 1991, 353–366.

37. T. Henzinger, *Sooner is Safer than Later*, Department of Computer Science, Stanford University, 1991.

38. T. Henzinger, Z. Manna, A. Pnueli, *Timed Transitions Systems*, REX'91, Presented also in School on Formal Techniques in Real-Time and Fault-Tolerant Systems, Nijmegen, Netherlands, January 1992.

39. M. Holliday, M. Vernon, *A Generalized Timed Petri Net Model for Performance Analysis*, IEEE Transactions on Software Engineering, December, 1987.

40. J. Hooman, *Specification and Compositional Verification of Real-Time Systems*, Ph.D. thesis, Eindhoven University, 1991.

41. M.S. Jaffe, N.G. Leveson, *Comleteness, Robustness, and Safety in Real-Time Software Requirements Specification*, Proceedings 11th International Conferenceon Software Engineering, Pittsburgh, Pennsylvania, May 15–18, 1989.

42. F. Jahanian, A.K. Mok, *Safety Analysis of Timing Properties of Real-Time Systems*, IEEE Transactions on Software Engineering, Vol. SE–12, No. 9, September 1986.

43. F. Jahanian, A.K. Mok, *A Graph-Theoretic Approach for Timing Analysis and Its Implementation*, IEEE Transactions on Computers, Vol. C–36, No. 8, August 1987, 961–975.

44. The Journal of Real-Time Systems, Special issue on the Esprit IPTES project, to appear.

45. R.A. Kemmerer, *Testing Software Specifications to Detect Design Errors*, IEEE Transactions on Software Engineering, Vol. SE–11, No. 1, January 1985.

46. Y. Kesten, A. Pnueli, *Timed and Hybrid Statecharts and Their Textual Representation*, School on Formal Techniques in Real-Time and Fault-Tolerant Systems, Nijmegen, Netherlands, January 1992.

47. R. Koymans, R. Kuiper, E. Zijlstra, *Specifying Message Passing and Real-Time Systems with Real-Time Temporal Logic*, ESPRIT'87 Achievement and Impact, North Holland, 1987.

48. R. Koymans, *Specifying Message Passing and Time-Critical Systems with Temporal Logic*, Ph.D. Thesis, Eindhoven University of Technology, 1989.

49. R. Koymans, W.P. de Roever, *Examples of a Realtime Temporal Logic Specification*, LNCS 207, Springer Verlag, Berlin, 1985.

50. F. Kroger, *Temporal Logic of Programs*, EATCS Monographs on Theoretical Computer Science, Springer Verlag, 1987.

51. N.G. Leveson, J. Stolzy, *Safety Analysis Using Petri Nets*, IEEE Transactions on Software Engineering, Vol. SE–13, No. 3, March 1987, 386–397.

52. N. Lynch, H. Attiya, *Using Mappings to Prove Timing Properties*, MIT, Report MIT/LCS-TM412.b, December 1989, appeared in PODC'89.

53. P.M. Merlin, D.J. Farber, *Recoverability of Communication Protocols: Implications of a Theoretical Study*, IEEE Transactions on Communications, Vol. COM–24, September 1976.

54. R. Milner, *Calculi for Synchroni and Asynchroni*, Theoretical Computer Science, Vol. 25, 1983.

55. A. Morzenti, D. Mandrioli, C. Ghezzi, *A Model Parametric Real-Time Logic*, Politecnico di Milano, Dipartimento di Elettronica, Report 90.010, 1990, to appear in SCM Transactions on Programming Languages and Systems.

56. A. Morzenti, *The Specification of Real-Time Systems: Proposal of a Logic Formalism*, Ph.D. Thesis, Dipartimento di Elettronica,Politecnico di Milano, 1989.

57. A. Morzenti, P. SanPietro, *An Object Oriented Logic Language for Modular System Specification*, ECOOP'91, LNCS 512, Springer Verlag, July 1991.

58. J. Ostrof, *Temporal Logic For Real-Time Systems*, Research Studies Press LTD., Advanced Software Development Series, Taunton, Somerset, England, 1989.

59. A. Pnueli, *The Temporal Semantics of Computer Programs*, Theoretical Computer Science, Vol. 13, 1981.

60. W.J. Quirk, *Verification and Validation of Real-Time Software*, Springer Verlag, Berlin, 1985.

61. C. Ramamoorthy, G. Ho, *Performance Evaluation of Asynchronous Concurrent Systems Using Petri Nets*, IEEE Transactions on Software Engineering, September 1980.

62. C. Ramchandani, *Analysis of Asynchronous Concurrent Systems Using Petri Nets*, MIT, February, 1974.

63. W. Reisig, *Petri Nets: An Introduction*, Springer Verlag, 1985.

64. X. Nicollin, J. Sifaki, S. Yovine, *Compiling Real-Time Specifications into Extended Automata*, Transactions on Software Engineering, Special Issue on Real Time Systems, to appear.

65. X. Nicollin, J. Richier, J. Sifakis, J. Voiron, *ATP: An Algebra for Timed Processes*, Proceedings IFIP Working Conference on Formal Description of Programming Concepts, North-Hooland, Tiberias, Israel, 1990.

66. R.M. Smullyan, *First Order Logic*, Springer Verlag, Berlin, 1968.
67. IEEE Software, *Special Issue on Formal Methods*, Vol. 7, No. 5, September 1990.
68. J.A. Stankovic, *Misconceptions About Real-Time Computing: A Serious Problem for Next-Generation Systems*, IEEE Computer, Vol. 21, No. 10, October 1988.
69. P. Stotts, T. Pratt, *Hierarchical Modeling of Software Systems with Timed Petri Nets*, Proceedings of the 1st International Workshop on Timed Petri Nets, Torino, Italy, July 1985.
70. I. Suzuki, *Formal Analysis of the Alternating Bit Protocol by Temporal Petri Nets*, IEEE Transactions on Software Engineering, Vol. SE–16, No. 11, November 1990.
71. IEEE Transactions on Software Engineering, Special Issue on Formal Methods in Software Engineering, Vol. SE–16, No. 9, September 1990.
72. Y. Wang, *Real-Time Behaviour of Asynchronous Agents*, LNCS 458, Springer Verlag, 1990, 502–520.
73. F. Wang, A. Mok, E. Emerson, *Formal Specification of Asynchronous Distributed Real-Time systems by APTL*, Proceedings ICSE 14, Melbourne, Australia, May 1992.
74. J.M. Wing, *A Specifier's Introduction to Formal Methods*, IEEE Computer, Vol. 23, No. 9, September 1990, 8–24.
75. J.M. Wing, M.R. Nixon, *Extending Ina Jo with Temporal Logic*, IEEE Transactions on Software Engineering, Vol. SE–15, No. 2, February 1989.
76. P. Zave, *PAISLey User Documentation Volume 3: Case Studies*, Computer Technology Research Laboratory Report, AT&T Bell Laboratories, Murray Hill, New Jersey, 1987.
77. W. Zuberek, *Timed Petri Nets and Performance Evaluation*, Proceedings of the 7th Annual Symposium on Computer Architecture, May 1980.
78. J. Zwiers, *Compositionality, Concurrency, and Partial Correctness*, LNCS 321, Springer Verlag, Berlin, 1989.

Predictability and Techniques for Schedulability Analysis

Alexander D. Stoyenko[1], *Thomas J. Marlowe*[2]

[1] Dept. of Computer and Information Science
New Jersey Institute of Technology
Newark, NJ 07102
U.S.A.

[2] Dept. of Mathematics and Computer Science
Seton Hall University
South Orange, NJ 07079
U.S.A.

A typical real-time application involves the use and control of expensive equipment, possibly in situations where a missed deadline may well lead to substantial damage, including loss of human life. For many real-time systems it is thus of paramount importance that they adhere *predictably* to their critical timing constraints. A real-time system must be tested, analysed and checked to adhere to its critical timing constraints *before* the system is put in place.

A real-time system consists of hardware and software components. In most cases, the hardware components are composed of a relatively small number of subcomponents. It is uncommon to develop new hardware for a real-time application. Thus, considerably more effort is usually invested in the development of the software components of the system. The software components are typically programmed in a high level language with some lower level functions possibly written in assembly. As the software is written, the programmer attempts to follow the timing specifications of the system to the best of his or her ability. The resulting code is subjected to analysis for adherence to its critical timing constraints. This form of analysis, introduced by Stoyenko [32, 33, 34, 36] is commonly referred to as **schedulability analysis**.

Naturally, schedulability analysis can be done by hand or through ad hoc techniques. However, this approach is not desirable. Consider the following analogy with compilation. The earliest programs were hand-assembled, or even written directly at machine-level. As application software size grew, the need for high level language programming became apparent, such languages were developed, and compilers were written. It is still possible to hand-assemble any program. However, hand-assembly is extremely time-consuming, error-prone, and produces code that is not inherently better than that generated by a compiler. Assuming that automated, accurate schedulability analysis technology can be made available to the real-time system developer, there is no excuse for the continuing wastage of the developer's time on ad hoc analysis activities.

Practical schedulability analysis should not be confused with what has been traditionally understood by scheduling (even though, often a study of a formal scheduling discipline includes a rudimentary schedulability analysis of abstract, "perfect" tasks). Indeed, in simple, theoretical task models (such as with a set of pure-computation tasks, a single preemptable CPU and no other shared resources, contention, communication and no overhead whatsoever), some scheduling disciplines are known to be "better" (typically in the sense of meeting deadlines) than others [3, 19, 31, 10]. In practice, however, one neither can *choose* (provably, there are no optimal disciplines) nor *needs* a better or best discipline — any reasonable one can be used (such as for instance Earliest-Deadline-First, Rate-Monotonic, or Best-Effort). On the other hand, schedulability analysis *is* needed in practical systems (since timing is part of their requirements). Thus, in our opinion to provide *practical* schedulability analysis is a problem that is not only exceedingly hard but one that is considerably harder than that of providing practical scheduling.

In what follows, we discuss a number of schedulability analysis issues that we consider relevant, and present our view on how these issues may be addressed. The accuracy of schedulability analysis depends on the knowledge of accurate timing information at a number of levels in a program. For all programs, we are concerned with machine- or assembly-instruction-level timing. This timing — whose accurate determination is often very hard due to unpredictable timing features of the hardware — is discussed briefly in Section 1. The next type of timing deals, naturally, with high-level statements, which compose compilable units (tasks, subprograms). The accurate determination of this timing — presented in Section 2 — is made difficult by loops (for all programs) and conditional statements (for parallel programs mainly). Next, we address, in Section 3, task-level timing which is relevant and difficult for parallel programs. In discussing schedulability analysis, we need to not only identify its inherent difficulties — such as the classic tradeoff between its accuracy and efficiency (the problem of accurate analysis is NP-complete) — but also to provide solutions for overcoming them. Thus, we discuss, in this Section, such techniques as program transformations and conditional linking that very substantially reduce the number of cases accurate analysis has to consider. Finally, we briefly outline, in Section 3.3, the issues of multi-task interactions, focussing on the case of assigning real-time software components in parallel systems — where less accurate (the problem of optimal assignment, even with perfect knowledge of per component timing, is NP-complete as well) analysis suffices.

1 Instruction-Level Timing

While determining instruction-level timing is conceptually very straightforward, in practice the problem is notoriously difficult. The difficulties stem from insufficient predictability in the hardware and system software run-time platform on which the instructions execute.

On the surface, it may appear that instruction times are predictable and duly provided in hardware and system software manuals. For example, given an instruction, its parameter types, and the addressing mode for each parameter, a software manual may specify how many cycles are required to execute the instruction, and a hardware manual may readily translate the number of cycles into the number of CPU cycles and the amount of physical time required. However, computed this way, accurate and predictable the instruction times are not. Instructions with seemingly fixed CPU timing vary in time due to bus and other contention delays. Hierarchical memories can lead to unpredictable variations in process execution timing. Cycle stealing slows down the processors in an unpredictable way. Consequently, DMA operations in a real-time computer system are a source of difficulty when determining process execution timing. Knowing the maximum flow rates from DMA device controllers allows calculation of a worst-case bound on process slow-down. However, it is difficult to use this bound in other than a very pessimistic way, unless the relative amount and relative positioning of DMA activity is known. Network communications — done over varying speed and contention interconnected media — lead to even greater variance in execution times.

To facilitate accurate instruction-level timing (and the consequent analysis), the hardware and system software clearly need to satisfy certain predictable execution criteria. As uncommon as these criteria may seem, not only can realistic systems closely fitting these assumptions be assembled from existing components, a number of sources indicate that entire such system software and hardware systems used in time-critical real-time applications can, should be and are being designed this way [2, 6, 7, 8, 27, 29, 30, 43, 44].

A number of techniques exist that deal with various sources of unpredictable timing. Busses and network links can be configured scheduled as token rings with uniform token propagation and message buffering. DMA and other asynchronous requests can be buffered and time-sliced, similarly to memory refreshes. I/O operations can be precisely-timed and buffered (if early). Time differences due to jumping and pipeline breaks can be eliminated by swapping and pipelining post-branch instructions optimistically. Clock granularity and instruction cycles can be benchmarked. Secondary storage operations can be measured predictably through swapping by unit of activity or pre-paging scheduling blocks (which is a de facto state-of-the-art in many existing time-critical applications, see for instance [1]). However, clearly all these techniques operate at the hardware or system software level, and consequently their detailed discussion is beyond the scope of this Chapter. The reader is referred to [8], among other sources, for these details.

2 Statement-Level Timing

In short, a schedulability analyser (as pioneered in [33, 34, 36]) consists of two parts: a partially language-dependent front-end and a (mostly) language-independent back-end. Statement-level timing is ascertained in the front-end. The front-end is embedded in the code generating/storage allocating back-end of a high level language compiler. As instructions are generated, the front-end computes the amount of time they will take to execute and builds program trees of segments (a tree per compilation unit, such as a subprogram or a task), keeping track of intra- and inter-procedural and modular dependencies, concurrency control, and control flow. At this level, it is assumed that there is a reliable method for determining instruction-level times (that is, the hardware and system software predictability assumptions are needed, as discussed in the previous Section). In addition, given a reasonably predictably platform, it is often the case that the execution times needed for schedulability analysis are for blocks of instructions which are long enough that small variations in execution times of individual instructions tend to average out within a block [9].

As statements are translated into assembly instructions in the coder, the front-end of the analyzer builds a tree of segments for each procedure or task. The various types of segments are as follows. **Simple segment** contains the amount of time it takes to execute an explicit section of code. As each assembly instruction is generated in the straight-line section, the front-end of the schedulability analyzer adds its execution time to the segment time. (Subject to predictability assumptions, instruction execution time is computed, in a table-driven fashion, as a function of the opcode(s), the operands and addressing modes.) All times are recorded in processor clock cycles instead of in absolute time for some implementation of the architecture. **Internal-call segment** contains the name of a called internal routine, and will eventually be resolved by substituting the amount of time it takes for that routine to execute. **External-call segment** and **System-call segment** are similar to an internal-call segment. If the call attempts to enter or exit a critical region (see below), the identifier of the region, and a pointer to the region state descriptor are stored in the segment record. Furthermore, if the call has a timeout, then the time after which to time out is recorded. **If segment** splits a tree into two subtrees where one subtree corresponds to the then-clause, and the other one to the else-clause of the corresponding if-statement. The segment will eventually be resolved, and only the subtree which takes longer to execute will stay. Case-statements result in a multi-way generalization of two-way if-segments.

A loop does not by itself cause a tree sub-branching. If the body of the loop is all pure explicit code, then the loop just results in a simple segment incorporating the amount of time it takes to execute a single iteration times the number of iterations. If the body of the loop contains a call segment or an if segment, then the loop is unwound into a segment chain, i.e., its body is repeated the number of iterations times.

As an assembly instruction is generated, the front-end of the analyzer records its execution time. The time is computed as a function of the operation code, the operands, and the addressing modes. A procedure explaining how to compute such timing information for a particular machine architecture is typically given in a machine instructions manual. The time is added to the current simple segment being built.

Apart from building segment trees, the front-end of the analyzer also records information on the organisation of critical regions as well as calling information. For every critical region its start and end are recorded, as well as which routines and tasks use it. For every routine it is recorded who calls it, whom it calls, what critical regions it uses, and what I/O operations it executes. Finally, for each task its frame (minimal activation period — for instance a sensor may be probed once per second) and activation information are recorded, as well as whom the task calls, what critical regions it uses, and what I/O operations it executes.

To demonstrate how segment trees are built, let us consider the example of Figures 1, 2 and 3.

H_1 $x := y + z$
H_2 $y := 2 * y$
H_3 $B\ (x,y)$
H_4 if $y > x$ then
H_5 $z := z + 5$
H_6 else
H_7 enter-critical-region (R)
H_8 end if
H_9 $z := x * y$

Fig. 1. A block of high-level language statements.

A_{01} *<Add y and z and assign to x>*
A_{02} *<Shift y left one bit>*
A_{03} *<Push x,y on stack; Jump to B>*
A_{04} *<Restore stack>*
A_{05} *<Compare y and x>*
A_{06} *<If greater, jump to A_{09}>*
A_{07} *<Add 5 to z>*
A_{08} *<Jump to A_{11}>*
A_{09} *<Push R on stack; Jump to Kernel.EnterCriticalRegion>*
A_{10} *<Restore stack>*
A_{11} *<Multiply x and y and assign to z>*

Fig. 2. The corresponding block of assembly statements.

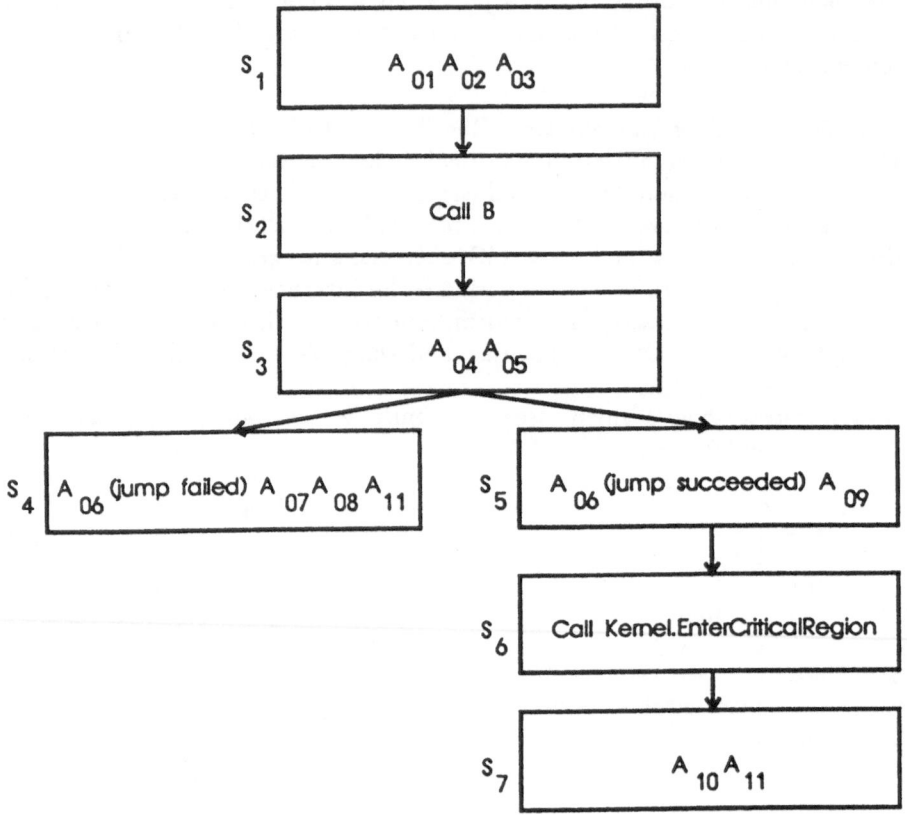

Fig. 3. The corresponding tree of segments.

High-level statements H_1 and H_2 translate into assembly sections A_{01} and A_{02} respectively. H_3, a call to a procedure B, generates sections A_{03} and A_{04}. The procedure execution will take place right after A_{03}, a section comprising a push on stack of the variables x and y and a jump to B, and before A_{04}, a stack restore section. The if-test of H_4 results in a compare A_{05} and a conditional jump A_{06}. The assignment H_5 maps to A_{07}. The else H_6 becomes the unconditional jump A_{08}. The enter-critical-region H_7 generates A_{09}, an assembly section encompassing a push on stack of the region identifier R and a jump to $Kernel.EnterCriticalRegion$, the kernel routine supporting the enter-critical-region operation, and A_{10}, a stack restore section. The last assignment statement, H_9 generates section A_{11}.

The segment tree corresponding to the high-level code block is formed as follows. A_{01}, A_{02} and A_{03} form a contiguous section of straight-line code. Thus, they comprise a single simple segment S_1. The amount of time A_{01}, A_{02} and A_{03}

take to execute is recorded in the segment. The call to B forms S_2, an internal-call segment.[3] A_{04} and A_{05} form a simple segment S_3. Now we must form two branches. If the conditional jump A_{06} fails, then the sections A_{07}, A_{08} and A_{11} will be executed. The amount of time it takes to execute A_{06} if the test fails is thus combined with the times of A_{07}, A_{08} and A_{11} to form a simple segment S_4. If the test succeeds, then the sections A_{09}, A_{10} and A_{11} will be executed. The right branch is therefore formed as a list of three segments: a simple segment S_5 encompassing A_{06} (if it succeeds) and A_{09}, a kernel-call segment S_6 corresponding to the enter-critical-region, and S_7, a simple segment comprising A_{10} and A_{11}. For simplicity, in this example we proceeded as if enter-critical-region were a native language construct, and we omitted a discussion of how the region identifier name and other supplementary information are stored.

The front-end of the schedulability analyzer provides the following statement-level timing information. The statistics for each statement involved consists of its line number coupled with the worst amount of time, in clock cycles, the statement may take to execute. The information is produced for the following statements: (1) each language-level expression or non-iterative statement (such as assignments, asserts, binds, returns and exits), (2) each selector (if- or case-) statement consisting of straight-line code, on the basis of which it is possible to determine the longest (timewise) clause, and (3) each iterator-statement consisting of a body of straight-line code. The programmer can use this statement-level information to determine which statements and groups of statements run longer than he or she expects. The information can also be used at a later stage, when the rest of schedulability information, such as guaranteed response times, becomes available. Then the programmer can decide which process parts have to be re-written to increase their speed.

3 Task-Level Timing

Task-level timing is ascertained in the back-end of the schedulability analyzer. The back-end is a separate program, whose task it is to resolve all information gathered by the front-end, and to predict guaranteed response times and other schedulability information and diagnostics for the entire real-time application. The back-end constructs a map from a high-level language program, or more precisely, from the corresponding segment trees built by the front-end, to an instance of a schedulability analyzable model. The instance is then solved (analyzed) for guaranteed schedulability. The back-end of the analyzer is largely independent of the compiler, the machine architecture and so on.

3.1 Resolving and Analyzing Segment Trees

The back-end of the analyzer starts off by resolving segment trees built by the front-end. All individual segment trees and critical region, routine, and task records are concatenated into one file, including the segment trees and records

---

[3] or an external-call segment. It does not really matter for the purpose of the example.

pertinent to predefined kernel and I/O routines. All non-kernel calls are recursively resolved by substituting the corresponding routine segment tree in place of each call segment. As many if segments as possible are resolved.

After all non-system calls are resolved, only task segment trees are left. The trees are converted to different segment trees, where each possible segment is one of the following. **Regular segment** is one containing the amount of time it takes to execute a section of code that is not in a critical region in the absence of contention. **Critical region** segment is one containing the amount of time it takes to execute a critical region of code in the absence of contention. **Specified-delay segment** corresponds to a delay specified in any execution time bound clause or in a schedule in the program. **Queue-delay segment** corresponds to a delay while waiting to enter a critical region, and is implicitly present in the segment tree just before every critical region segment. **If segment** has the same semantics as before.

We now demonstrate how front end segment trees are converted continuing with the example of Figures 1, 2 and 3. Figure 4 has the corresponding converted subtree, now a part of a process tree. The simple segment S_1 maps to a regular segment N_1. The call to B is resolved and N_2, the tree of B, is substituted. We now form two branches (the new if segment is implicit). Since one branch of the subtree involves a kernel call, both branches are kept. The segment S_3 is combined with the first regular segment of each branch. Thus, S_3 and S_4 together form N_3, a regular segment corresponding to the failed jump case, and S_3 also becomes a part of the first regular segment of the right branch. The way $Kernel.EnterCriticalRegion$ operates is as follows: interrupts are turned off, queues are updated, interrupts are restored. The regular segment N_4 thus comprises S_3, S_5 and the interrupt disabling code of the signal. The queue-updating code of $Kernel.EnterCriticalRegion$ forms a critical region segment N_5 (preceded by an implicit queue-delay segment). The return from $Kernel.EnterCriticalRegion$ is combined with S_7 to form a regular segment N_6. Each leaf of the tree of B is extended with the two branches we just formed.

When segment tree conversion is complete, the tasks are ready to be mapped to an instance of a schedulability analyzable model. The exact form of the model depends on the topology of the system on which the real-time application is intended to be run. Once mapped to the model (represented as sets of equations), the model is solved for intermediate (such as queue sizes) and ultimate (such as guaranteed response times) schedulability metrics using *frame superimposition* [33, 34]. Frame superimposition simply means fixing a single task's frame at its starting time and positioning frames of other tasks along the time line in such a way as to maximize the amount of resource contention the task incurs. Frame superimposition uses relative positions of segments and distances between segments on the time line. The algorithm shifts frames exhaustively, for every time unit, for every task, for every combination of frames possible.

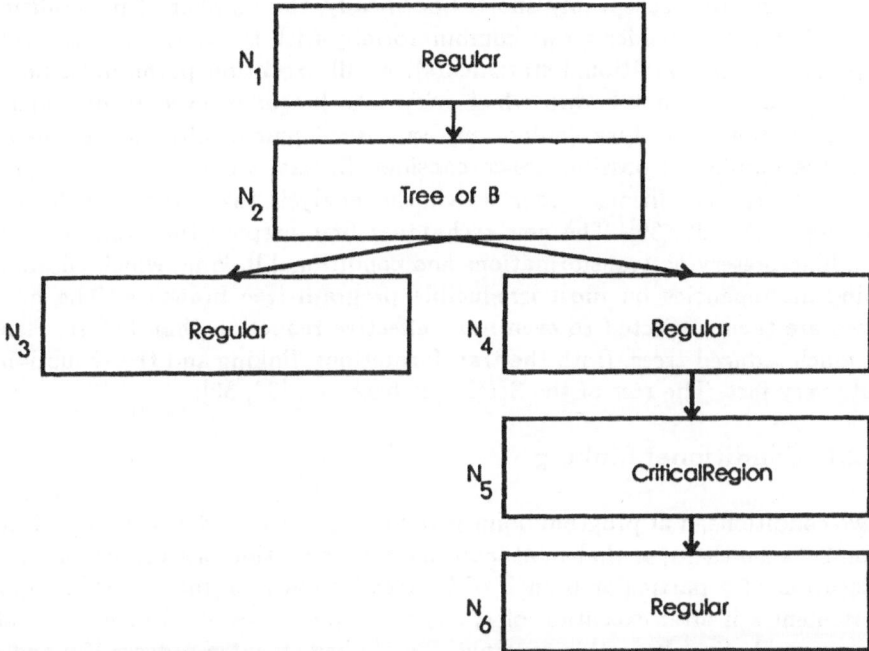

Fig. 4. The corresponding converted subtree of segments.

The frame superimposition algorithm is clearly of exponential complexity. In fact, finding the optimal worst-case bound for resource contention in the presence of deadlines is NP-complete, given that even the most basic static deadline scheduling problems are [46, 5]. However, this part of the analysis operates on a small number of objects (segments, each combining a great many statements), in a relatively small number of arrangements. Moreover, it has been demonstrated that considerably better delay bounds are derived by this algorithm, than by closed-form or polynomial complexity algorithms [33, 34, 36, 26, 45].

Once the metrics are available, they are reported to the programmer. The programmer then studies these metrics (detailing, if need be, the timing of the performance of every routine, call, critical region access, even every statement), and decides whether the program should be run as it exists, or whether it should be modified. Should the program need to be modified, the metrics are of great help in determining where and how.

3.2 Facilitating Fast Analysis

While the predicted response times derived by the analysis through frame superimposition are very accurate, the analysis may take very long to execute on some programs. Consequently, care must be taken to keep the execution time of

the analyzer tool acceptably short. Specifically, the number of possibilities the
analysis has to consider grows combinatorially with the number of control flow
alternatives (in conditional statements), as all execution paths must be considered where it is not known which may take longer to execute or which may
generate more inter-task contention. Each such pair of alternatives then doubles the number of possibilities to consider. Special techniques which virtually
eliminate the conditions under which the analysis takes too long have been
developed [37, 38, 39]. The new techniques first prepare the program through
deadline-preserving transformations and conditional linking, which eliminate timing discrepancies on most irreducible program tree branches. The program
trees are then subjected to even more effective reduction than before, resulting
in much reduced trees. Both the transformations, linking and the reduction execute very fast. The rest of the Section is based on [38, 39].

3.2.1. Conditional Linking

Two conditions, a at program point p and b at q, are *linked* if there is an implication between them, so that in at least one case execution of a branch of a implies
execution of a particular branch of b. A condition p is *linked* with assignment
statement s if after execution of s, any subsequent execution of p will evaluate
to a compile-time knowable constant. The linkage is intra-process if p and q (or
s) are points in the same process, and inter-process otherwise. (There is a third
case, in which some procedures or critical sections have not been inlined, and p
and q lie in different procedures, which will be considered in future work.)

General linkage of conditions is undecidable, due to dependence on input values.
Even simple cases may be difficult, in part because of loops and recursion; the
restricted syntax of real-time languages is an advantage here. An identifiable
subset of conditional expressions in typical real-time programs will be amenable
to linking; depending on application area and code development style, this can
provide a significant reduction in the path space considered by the analyzer. In
particular, the conditions involving simple expressions on run-time constants,
boolean or enumerated variables (especially tags of variant union types or variables used repeatedly in case statements), or variables used in tests in loops
(especially those varying slowly or in predictable ways), will be amenable to
linking. While it may seem that highly tuned code should contain few linkages,
potential links may arise (1) in the original code, in the repeated use of the same
case statement or tag variable of a union type, or via code reuse without specialization, (2) through instantiation of architecture or application constants, as
for partial evaluation [22, 23], or (3) through unwinding of loops and inlining
of procedure calls, a standard technique in schedulability analysis. Many if not
most of these potential links can be expected to involve sibling conditional expressions, and to relate conditions involving scalar variables.

In addition to lowering the complexity of schedulability analysis for real-time
programs, linking of conditionals can improve estimates for resource usage and

for critical path length. Actual run-time critical path length can be decreased by transforming the code when adjacent conditionals are shown to have an equivalence linkage, since the second conditional need not be executed. The static estimate of critical path length, provided by schedulability analysis, can also be improved through discovery of a linkage of the long branch of one conditional with the short branch of another, or through discovery of dead code, independent of transformation of the actual code. This can significantly reduce bounds on execution time: in these cases, a program which the analyzer would have rejected may pass after linking, more time can be devoted to imprecise computation, or frames can be shortened if desired.

Static estimates of total usage of a resource can also be sharpened considerably, if, for example, two instances of use of resource R will provably never occur in the same execution; interprocess linking can be quite valuable here. Linking can also result in better inclusion of sporadic processes, if, for example, there are links between conditions in periodic processes and the stimulus of a sporadic process, or among such sporadic process stimuli.

Our approach to linkage involves backward propagation of assertions generated by a condition p until an implication is discovered relating p to a previous condition q, or until p is satisfied or falsified by a previous assignment statement s, or until a suitable inference can no longer be propagated (at which point the approach assumes no linkage is possible). Assuming that the last case has not occurred, one may be able to transform the code, depending on the relative positions of p and q (or s) in the the program — q or s will always be a control flow predecessor of p; distinctions arise from conditional nesting. These cases are most easily understood in terms of a *conditional nesting tree* for the program — essentially, the program dependence graph (PDG [4, 14]) of the loop-free program. (Recall that p is a conditional, q an antecedent conditional, and s an antecedent assignment statement.)

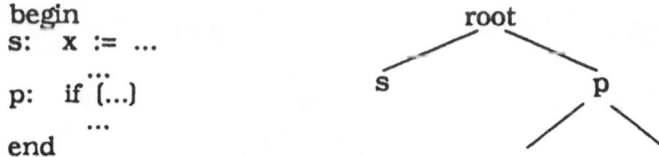

Fig. 5. p and s are siblings.

1. If s is a sibling of p (for example, s is not included in any conditional, and p is a top-level conditional—see Figure 5), then p will be constant, and one of the branches of p can be pruned.

2. If q is a sibling of p (or s is a child of a sibling q) (see Figure 6), then transform:

   - If $q \leftrightarrow p$, then replace

$$\textbf{if } q \textbf{ then } s_1 \textbf{ else } s_2;$$
$$s_3;$$
$$\textbf{if } p \textbf{ then } s_4 \textbf{ else } s_5$$

   by

$$\textbf{if } q \textbf{ then } \{s_1; \ s_3; \ s_4;\}$$
$$\textbf{else } \{s_2; \ s_3; \ s_5;\}$$

   (see Figure 7); likewise if s in s_1. The transformation if $\sim q \leftrightarrow p$ is analogous.

   - If $q \rightarrow p$, then

$$\textbf{if } q \textbf{ then } s_1 \textbf{ else } s_2;$$
$$s_3;$$
$$\textbf{if } p \textbf{ then } s_4 \textbf{ else } s_5$$

   can be transformed into

$$\textbf{if } q \textbf{ then } \{s_1; \ s_3; \ s_4;\}$$
$$\textbf{else } \{s_2; \ s_3;$$
$$\textbf{if } p \textbf{ then } s_4$$
$$\textbf{else } s_5\}$$

The remaining one-way implications result in analogous transformations.

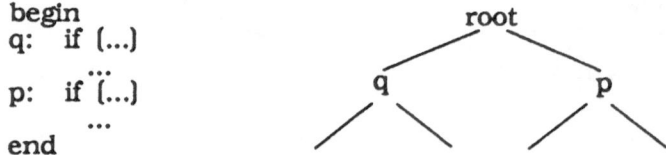

Fig. 6. p and q are siblings

3. If p is a descendant of q, and p lies on the appropriate branch of q (or $q \leftrightarrow p$), then one branch of p can be pruned.

4. If q is a descendant of a sibling of p, or p and q are each descendants of siblings, then ordinarily no transformation will be performed.

5. If p is a descendant of a sibling r of q, then there is an option of duplicating r (and intervening code) on each branch of q, simplifying p on one or both of the resulting paths as appropriate, but most often it is preferable not to transform.

Note, in the absence of constructs such as instruction caches, that this duplication of r cannot interfere with worst-case timing properties. Note also that in the case in which p and q (or p and s) are in different branches of some conditional, information will never be propagated from p to q (or s), and no potential link will be reported.

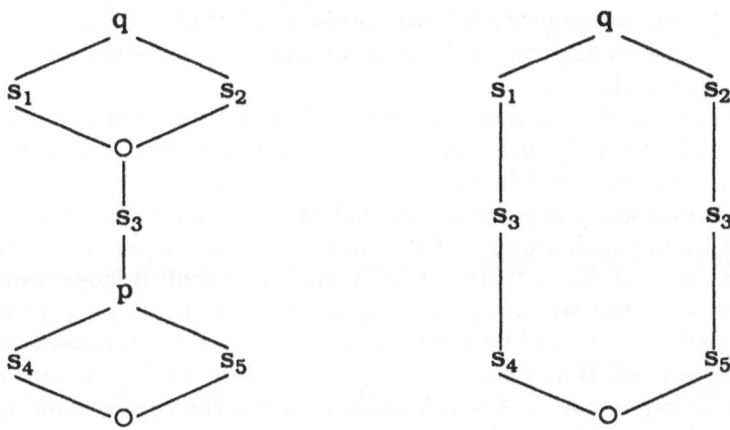

Fig. 7. Transformation for equivalent conditionals.

In the last three cases, program transformations analogous to loop transformations for parallelization (e.g., exchange, splitting, fusing) [25, 48, 49] may apply to the conditional nest, allowing the linked conditionals to be brought to the top of the nest. However, the applicability of these transformations requires not only that semantics be preserved, but also that they do not interfere with timing constraints [20].

The general approach for detecting intra-process linked conditions is as follows:

– Define syntactic sets C, A, R of, respectively, tests in conditional statements, assertions (intuitively, preconditions — not necessarily weakest preconditions — implying a given truth value for a test), and assignment statements. (These sets are usually closely related. For example, C could be tests of the form x relop c, for x a variable and c a constant or variable, A the set of assertions $\{x \in I\}$, for I a set of integers expressed as a disjoint union of (possibly unbounded) intervals, and R $\{x := c$ and $x := y\}$.) In general, C will have to be a subset of A.

- Determine all tests (a, p), where a is a test and p its program point, in C.
- Use static condition slicing to slice each process backward [14, 47] from the program points in C, on all variables, along control and data dependence edges. This is closely related to condition slicing [28]. The set of variables occurring in the slice forms the set of "interesting" variables; all others may be ignored. Backward propagation of the slice will terminate if it encounters an assignment not corresponding to R, or (in most cases) a system or critical section call.
- In the sliced graph, for each condition (a, p) in C, form two **expectations**, $\langle a, p, T \rangle$ and $\langle a, p, F \rangle$ (where p here is considered as a location, rather than a condition). Propagate each assertion backward, modifying the first component as for Hoare logic [11, 12, 13][4], until one of the following occurs:
  1. At some assignment, the first component becomes **true**.
  2. At some conditional test, the condition or its negation implies the first component.
  3. The current statement is a **read** statement, a system or critical section call (but see the subsequent discussion of external procedure calls), or an assignment not in R.
  4. At some assignment or conditional, the first component becomes **false**.
  5. Resolving with the current statement is impossible, or an assertion which is not in A. Since there are no condition-controlled loops, this last case typically happens when expectations such as $\langle b, p, T \rangle$ and $\langle c, p, T \rangle$, propagating backward on the branches of a conditional, cannot be resolved at the head. It may also occur for certain choices of C, A, and R, if there is no expression in A which safely captures the effects of an assignment on the current assertion.
  6. The root of a flow graph is reached.

  In the first two cases, the transformations discussed earlier may apply; in the next three, abandon the search for linkage. In either of these cases, continue to propagate a value (**true** or **bottom** ($\perp$), respectively), in order to correctly and precisely resolve conditionals in which q or s nests. In the final case, which should never occur, there is a possibly uninitialized variable.
- If conditions at appropriate nesting levels have been linked, then transform the code as outlined earlier.

Examples. Consider first simple sets C, A, R. The set C of conditions is

$$\{x \; relop \; t \mid t \text{ a variable or constant } \};$$

the set A of assertions is $\{x \; relop \; y\} \cup \{x \in S \mid S \subset \mathbf{Z}\}$, where all variables are in V, the set of interesting variables, and S is represented as a disjoint union of intervals. If there are v variables of interest, there are $O(v^2)$ assertions of the first type, but the number of possible assertions of the second is determined by the cardinality of the set of possible S (which is finite and a priori boundable since the program by assumption has all loops unwound—compare [42]). Finally,

---

[4] See also the following examples, and discussion in [24].

the set R of right-hand sides of assignments is $\{y, c, y\ plusop\ c\}$. For each condition p at program point a, two expectations $\langle a, p, T \rangle$ and $\langle a, p, F \rangle$ are established.

What remains is to specify how to propagate assertions, and in particular how to infer assertions at both the bottom and the top of a test node given the assertions at the top of its **true** and **false** branches. For simplicity, rules are given only for assertions $x > 0$ and $x = y$; the others can easily be inferred by analogy.

Figure 8 shows how each of these two assertions are resolved with statements in the slice other than tests. The first two columns classify the statements; the third gives the assertion in the expectation at the top of the node resulting from the assertion at the top of the table coming in at node bottom. Figure 9 shows how assertions on the two arms of a conditional can be resolved. The first table shows the results for a test of the form $x > 0$, the second for a test $x = y$, and the third results which follow for any test. There may be additional rules not presented here. Throughout, x, y, and z are assumed to be distinct variables. WRITE represents the write-set of a procedure or system call, that is, the set of caller variables possibly modified by execution of the called procedure (see subsequent discussion).

An example follows in Figure 10, whose assertion propagation is shown in Figure 11. Note that

- **true** and $\bot$ values are retained until a condition tree sibling of the original condition is reached, at which point the information will no longer be needed to allow proper resolution of information on the other branch.
- Additional progress may be possible after an initial linkage (see also the experiments below).

Even in this simple framework, most particularly in dealing with tests of the form $x = y$, there is sometimes a choice of assertion to propagate. For example, if the assertion on the **true** branch is $x = z$ and on the **false** branch is **true** (that is, execution of the **false** branch of q will cause the given branch of p to execute), either $x = z$ or $y = z$ can be propagated; the first of these is captured in the rule base. (In either case, suppose further propagation indicates that (WLOG) the **true** branch of conditional r can link with (again WLOG) the **true** branch of p. Then in having taken the **true** branch of r, either the **true** or the **false** branch of q will be taken. If the **false** branch of q, then the **true** branch of p will execute by assumption; if the **true** branch of q, either of the assertions given will result in the expectation $\langle p, T, x = y \rangle$ being satisfied at the head of that branch, so again the **true** branch of p will execute. Thus the linking of (r, T) with (p, T) is correct.)

Since in such cases one choice may lead to linking, and another not greater precision and more linkage may result from propagating more than one expectation per condition, at the cost of an additional factor of number of interesting variables v in number of assertions, and of v^2 in complexity. The choice among possible assertions hints that the framework need not be not a lattice, nor the

statement	statement	result
	assertion $x > 0$	
assign	$y := exp$	no change
	$x := c$	true if $c > 0$, $\perp$ else
	$x := y$	$y > 0$
	$x := x + c$	$x > -c$
	$x := y + c$	combine previous cases
	$x := other$	$\perp$
read	x in read	$\perp$
	other	no change
system	x in WRITE	$\perp$
calls	other	no change

statement	statement	result
	assertion $x = y$	
assign	$z := exp$	no change
	$x := y$	true
	$x := z$	$y = z$ if $z \in V$, else $\perp$
	$x := y + c$	$\perp$
	$x := x + c$	$\perp$ (since $x = y - c \notin A$)
	$y := c$	$x = c$
	$y := z$	$x = z$ if $z \in V$, else $\perp$
	$y := x$	true
	$y := x + c$	$\perp$
	other	$\perp$
read	x or y in read	$\perp$
	other	no change
system	x or y in WRITE $\perp$	
calls	other	no change

Fig. 8. Resolving assertions and statements.

propagation functions necessarily distributive, or even monotone [21]; there are straightforward examples to show that this is indeed the case. Thus each rule must be individually shown to be correct, safe, and robust; it may however be conservative, and fail to detect linkage even where linkage is theoretically deducible within the current framework. However, it can easily be seen that each of the rules presented here preserves logical implication, whence any linkages detected by use of these rules are in fact valid.

Implementation to date has used this first framework. For a more complicated example, take C and R as above, but let A be

$$\{x \in S \mid S \subset \mathbf{Z}\} \cup \{(x \in S_x) \wedge (y \in S_y)\}$$

(for S, S_x and S_y sets of integers as above); any operation which would in princi-

true branch a_T	false branch a_F	result	note
		test q: x > 0	
$x \in S$	any	true if $(0, \infty) \subset S$	link (p, T) and (q, T)
any	$x \in S$	true if $(-\infty, 0] \subset S$	link (p, T) and (q, F)
$x \in S_T$	$x \in S_F$	$x \in (S_T \cap (0, \infty)) \cup (S_F \cap (-\infty, 0])$	
$x \in S_T$	$y \in S_F$ or $\perp$	$x \in S_T \cap (0, \infty)$	unless linked above
$y \in S_T$ or $\perp$	$x \in S_F$	$x \in S_F \cap (-\infty, 0]$	unless linked above
$y \in S_T$	$z \in S_F$	$\perp$	
other	other	$\perp$	except as below
		test q: x = y	
$x = y$	any	true	link (other branch similarly)
$x \in \{c\} \cup S$	$x \neq c$	$y = c$	
any	$x \in S$	$\perp$	except previous cases
other	other	$\perp$	except as below
		any test	
any	true	same	unless linkage
true	any	same	unless linkage
any	same	same	unless linkage
$z \in S_T$	$z \in S_F$	$z \in S_T \cap S_F$	unless linkage

Fig. 9. Resolving assertions and tests.

ple result in a more complicated assertion will instead terminate propagation without conclusion. (A trivial extension could again include variable equality.) Again, up to ranges S for each variable, there are $O(v^2)$ different types of assertion.

Costs and benefits of linking. Successful linkage will always reduce the number of paths considered by the schedulability analyzer. If, in the earlier general notation for transformations, each of the s_i are straightline code, then, in Figure 7 (the equivalence of conditionals), the reduced form at worst somewhat less than doubles in size (if s_3 is very large), and the number of paths decreases by a factor of two. In the implication of conditionals, the code again doubles at worst, and the number of paths decreases from 4 to 3.[5]

Doubling of the reduced form only appears to be a large price, as the following indicates. The reduced form is already highly condensed for condition-linking analysis, with unimportant statements discarded, and will be further reduced

---

[5] If there are n_i paths through s_i, then the number of paths decreases from $n_3 (n_1 + n_2) (n_4 + n_5)$ to $n_3 (n_1 n_4 + n_2 n_5)$ in the equivalence, and to $n_3 (n_1 n_4 + n_2 (n_4 + n_5))$ in the implication; the resulting reduction can range from negligible to almost total depending on the values of the n_i.

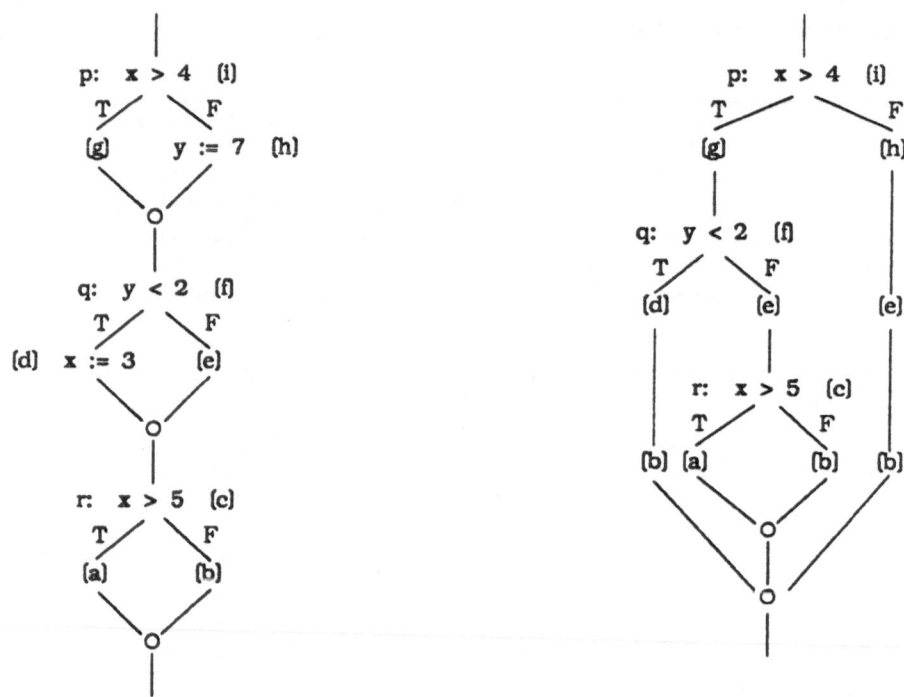

Fig. 10. An example of linked conditions.

for schedulability analysis, where only timing information, critical section access, and resource usage remain. The doubling affects only the schedulability analysis, and *not the resulting executable code*. The degree of code expansion versus the simplicity of the result is the determining factor in deciding whether to apply a semantically safe transformation to the executable code rather than just to the analysis. Further, the doubling can be eliminated at little cost by using jumps or a parameterless procedure call around s_3, resulting in the addition of at most a constant number of statements per transformation. Even using naive doubling, doubling is local. The number of times a given statement will be doubled depends on the number of condition links across it, and the number of one-way links in which it appears. Detection of a constant test, and in some cases detection of an equivalence link, will actually shrink the reduced form, and may also shrink the executable code. Finally, the linking analysis can be safely terminated, or a given linkage unperformed, at any time. Thus conditional linking will not cause an explosion of executable code, and cannot even expand the reduced form code unacceptably relative to the cost of schedulability analysis.

The above analysis presumes some prior static analysis of the program: the

node	expectation number	expectation	note
a		none	
b		none	
c	1	<x > 5, r, T>	
	2	<x ≤ 5, r, F>	
d	1	< ⊥, r, T>	
	2	true	link ((q,T),(r,F))
e	1	<x > 5, r, T>	
	2	<x ≤ 5, r, F>	
f	1	< ⊥, r, T>	from d1 and e1
	2	<x ≤ 5, r, F>	from d2 and e2
	3	<y < 2, q, T>	
	4	<y ≥ 2, q, F>	
g	1		abandon
	2	<x ≤ 5, r, F>	
	3	<y < 2, q, T>	
	4	<y ≥ 2, q, F>	
h	2	<x ≤ 5, r, F>	
	3	< ⊥, q, T>	
	4	true	link ((p,F), (q,F))
i	2	< ⊥, r, F>	abandon
	3		abandon
	4	<y ≥ 2, q, F>	from g2 and h2
	5	<x < 4, p, T>	
	6	<x ≥ 4, p, F>	

second pass

h	1	<x > 5, r, T>	since h now reaches only e
i	1	true	link ((p,F), (r,F))

Fig. 11. Propagation of assertions in Figure 10.

language is strongly typed and type checking has been performed; aliasing is handled satisfactorily by inlining or by static analysis; static analysis has been performed to extract live variables and def-use chains used in slicing; loop unrolling and procedure inlining have already occurred. These analyses do not add appreciably to the cost overhead of schedulability analysis. Live variable and def-use information is already being used to eliminate dead code, and in any case is not particularly expensive once procedures have been inlined. Aliasing should not occur after inlining in the absence of pointers or dynamic data structures, which are forbidden in Real-Time Euclid. The cost of slicing is more than recovered in the decrease in the cost of the analysis. Finally, while inlining and unrolling may be costly, they are in any case needed for schedulability analysis. Moreover, the discovery of even one linkage resulting in a transformation will, by the above, cut the cost of schedulability analysis by a factor of at least 4/3, more than enough to pay for the entire linking analysis, even if that analysis uses a fairly robust set of assertions and conditions.

3.2.2. Program Transformations

Conditional linking can be integrated with the deadline-preserving transformations [38]. The semantics of real-time programs must include deadline satisfaction. We say that a program transformation is: **Deadline-isomorphic** if the transformed program will meet deadlines if and only if the original program did; **Deadline-preserving** if the transformed program will meet deadlines if the original program did; **Deadline-extending** if the original program would have met deadlines whenever the transformed program does; **Deadline-destroying** if it satisfies none of these properties.

We employ a number of deadline-preserving transformations of conditional code, subject to a number of standard symbolic executions and other assumptions. Essentially, we can view a sequence of delay-free (meaning, the statements do not request a shared service) statements as a single statement taking as long to execute as the sum of the lengths of the individual statements. Likewise, a conditional with two delay-free branches will certainly not take longer than the longer branch, and by above assumptions, could take that long. We can also condense a loop without delays into a node taking as long as the loop would have, i.e., approximately, the size of the range times the sum of the length of the loop body and the time for incrementing the range variable. In a loop with delays, the delay-free tail of an iteration of the loop can be merged with the delay-free head of the next iteration.

We can, however, do more: we can insert fixed delays into flow branches to make accesses to a critical region happen at the same time as on other branches. The critical region will then start and finish at the same time on both branches. Inserted delays that are needed to balance a non-critical region node only block the task they are inserted in. On the other hand, inserted delays that are needed to balance a critical region node extend the shorter critical region and, thus, do not only block the task they are inserted in, but also other tasks seeking entry to a critical region.

Moreover, we can insert varying delays into a shorter branch that does not access a critical region to mimic the critical region access done in a longer branch. The insertion of delays requires that, during schedulability analysis as well as at run-time[6], when an inserted delay is reached, the task acts and has the same effect on other tasks as if it were trying to execute a critical region of the size of the delay. The insertion of appropriate delays is our principal deadline-preserving transformation. The transformation does two things: first, it makes the resulting flow graph smaller and simpler (and thus faster to analyze); second, the transformed program is easier to pre-schedule at compile-time.

We can easily either (a) compare two delay-free branches, or (b) take any branch in place of an empty branch. A small extension of (b) is (b') to take a branch with arbitrary structure and time T in place of a delay-free branch with smaller time T'. In either case, we can insert delays; in the first case, the delays are constant, but in the second they can be symbolic, but still cannot result in a program which fails to satisfy a deadline if the original program (subject to the symbolic execution assumptions) would. Otherwise, our system will compare branches only if neither contains a conditional or loop statement which itself contains a delay, i.e., if both branches are effectively linear. Observe that it is acceptable to have requests to multiple critical resources along the same branch, for as long as the requests follow a static resource hierarchy, as defined for instance in HI-PEARL [35]. In this case, we may be able to select one branch and insert delays in the other, to constrain calls to the critical region to occur exactly at times when calls would be made on the other branch, without violating a deadline.

We use two versions of such tests. The first (c) applies to branches of the same length, and compares the sequences of execution times. We say that one sequence *dominates* another one, if its elements are pairwise greater than or equal to the other's. If the sequence for the branch with greater total execution time dominates the other branch sequence, then delays can be inserted in a deadline-isomorphic manner. The second (d) applies to branches of different lengths: if the longer also has the greater total execution time, and if the sequence of times for that branch can be partitioned (by adding consecutive elements together) so as to dominate the other sequence, then we can still insert delays in a deadline-isomorphic manner.

The four tests ((a), (b'), (c) and (d)) are illustrated — left to right — in Figure 12 (the fifth conditional will be explained very shortly). For simplicity, there is only a single critical section. The ith non-critical section straight-line node is represented as a label x, where *clock(node)=x*. The ith critical section straight-line node is represented as a square labeled x on the inside, where *clock(node)=x*. The ith delay prior to entering the critical section is not drawn explicitly but is present before the critical section. Without loss of generality, the sizes of all fork and join nodes are immaterial — these nodes are represented as circles. All resulting delays are generated and inserted in the right branches. In (a), a fixed delay of 2 is prepended to the node labeled 3. In (b'), a fixed delay of 4 is prepended to the node labeled 4, and a varying delay of $4+d$ is inserted between

---

[6] That is, during both symbolic and real execution.

that and the join nodes (or in other words, a critical section of size 4 is introduced
there that will time-wise simulate the execution of the genuine critical section
in the left branch). In (c), a fixed delay of 3 is prepended to the node labeled 1,
another fixed delay of 2 is prepended to the critical section node (labeled 2), and
yet another fixed delay of 2 is prepended to the node labeled 3. Finally in (d), the
node labeled 4 is split into two: one labeled 2 and the consequent representing
a critical section of 2; this critical section is prepended with a fixed delay of 3;
another fixed delay of 3 is introduced between the newly created critical section
and the original critical section, the original critical section is prepended with a
fixed delay of 1, and the node before the join node (labeled 2) is prepended with
a fixed delay of 2.

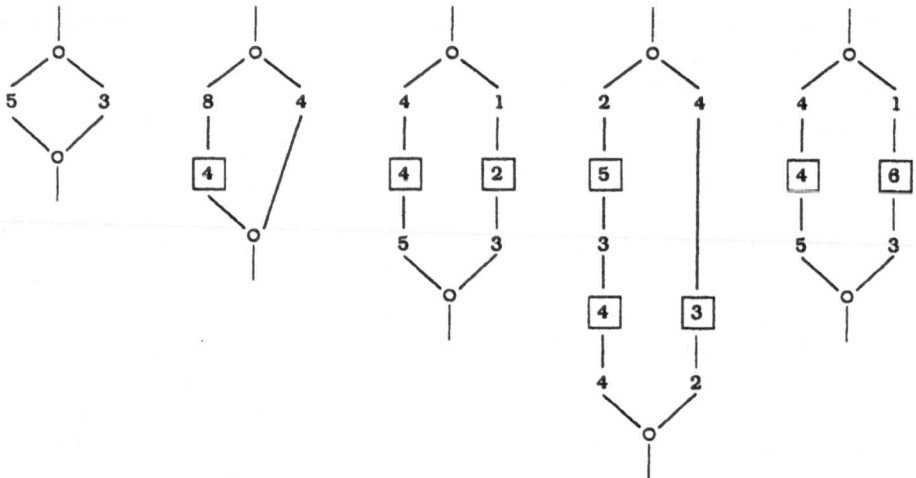

Fig. 12. Four conditional clustering tests and an irreducible conditional.

Although these tests can insert delays and eliminate conditionals from schedulability analysis, some simple conditionals may remain *irreducible*, resistant to
clustering. Consider, for instance the fifth graph in Figure 12. The graph was
obtained by taking the third graph and setting the right branch's critical section
size to 6. Now, the two branches remain different, but neither dominates the
other. Thus, clustering delay insertions are no longer guaranteed to be deadline-
preserving. However, prepending the nodes labeled 1 and 3 with fixed delays of 1
and 2 makes the conditional reducible (by moving the trailing 2 units of the node
labeled 4 into its branch's critical section). Unfortunately, the effect of the two
insertions is not deadline-isomorphic or preserving, but is deadline-extending.
Of course, should the program resulting from these transformations still meet
deadline, the static schedule it generates can be used. Whether this happens will
depend on how much slack exists, on how many deadline extensions are required,

and how much they extend the time of the process(es) in which they occur, and whether their critical section accesses are in fact time-critical.

In general, deadline-extending transformations involve delay insertions on multiple branches. A possibly useful class of transformations introduces only a part of a complete deadline-extending transformation. In the same example, a simpler (than the original) graph with a partially-reduced conditional results if only the delay of 2 is prepended to the node labeled 1 (but the node labeled 3 is not prepended with a delay of 2. This transformation, while potentially deadline-destroying, preserves more of the original conditional structure. Future work will consider incremental techniques for analysis of such partially-reduced graphs in polynomial time, that is, carrying reduction to completion, possibly extending deadline, and then undoing particular transformations one at a time (or one part at a time) until deadline is satisfied. Another possibility is to restrict the source of the exponential explosion in the analysis of irreducible graphs, although necessarily in a potentially deadline-extending way. Such a restriction on resource contention, and an associated efficient and accurate analysis and transformation algorithm, are considered in [38]. The key idea is for a critical section to hold on to all the requesting processes until the end of a busy interval; this reduces the consequences of variation in request arrival order, and thus localizes the analysis.

3.2.3. Interaction of Transformations and Linking

Transformations and linking can be used in concert to reduce the complexity of schedulability analysis. Not only does linkage of conditionals reduce the amount of path exploration needed in the schedulability analyzer, it can enable further pruning of branches by the program transformer. While it appears that combination of irreducible conditionals cannot result in reducibility, Figure 13 shows an example where even the one-way linkage ($q \leftrightarrow p$) of a reducible and an irreducible block can yield a single, completely reducible block (following the linking the right subgraph has been "unrolled" into two paths originating at the root fork node — this graph structure is identical to the linked one for the purposes of transforming).

Thus linking can enable transformations, and performing one link can make another easier to detect. Neither transformation nor linkage, however, can create additional links, since, in the former case, the shorter branch may still have a semantic effect affecting the branch chosen in the later conditional, and in the latter, the implication will still hold along all executable paths. To enable transformations to interact with linking, the analysis can retain a virtual header node with zero time cost, the condition, and the WRITE set of the suppressed branch; the branch can be re-expanded, if its condition is linked with another, or if propagation of assertions past the virtual node depends on the nature of assignments in its WRITE set. The ordering of linkages linking distant code regions is a subject of current research.

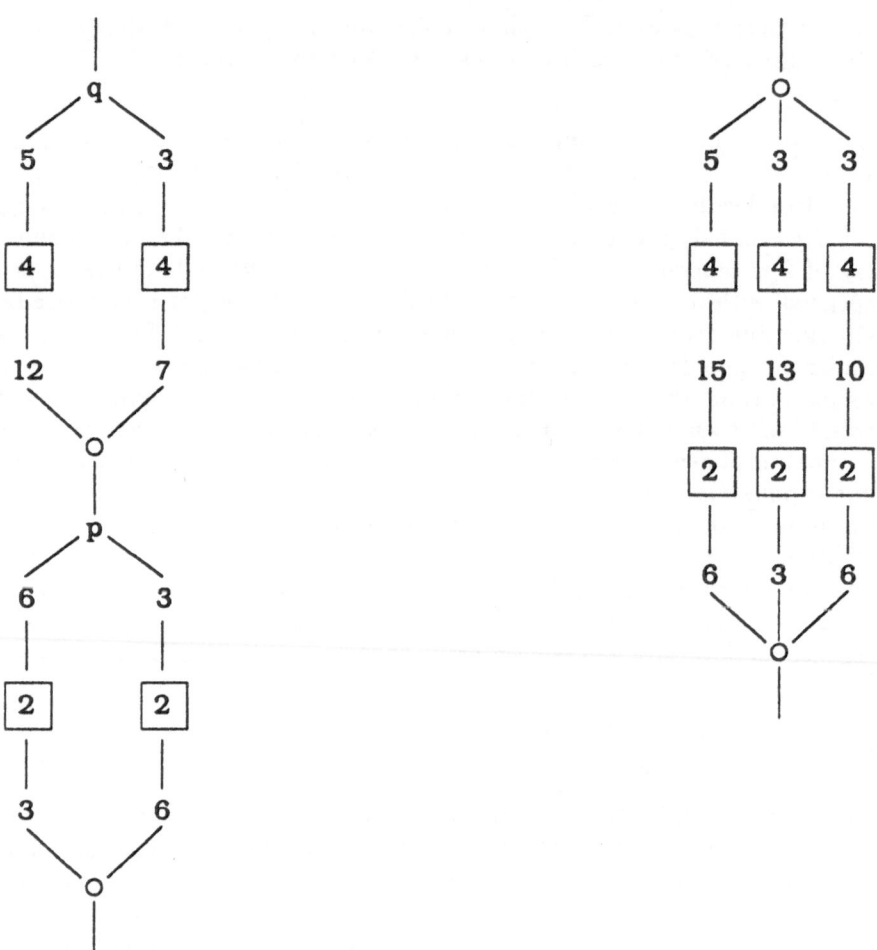

Fig. 13. Linking of conditions results in reducibility.

3.3 Inter-Task-Level Timing

While traditional real-time systems have often taken the form of either a cyclic executive or a relatively small number of independent, coarse processes, executed on a small number of processors, today's and future systems consist of large numbers of processes and software components used by the processes, and are expected to run on modern computer architectures, which often are (highly) parallel. Consequently, techniques are needed to map these processes and components to the processing elements (PEs), while facilitating such high-performance real-time objectives as meeting deadlines, keeping response times reasonably short, and balancing the workload over the PEs. Furthermore, as more and more modern systems, such as the C^3I or embedded applications, are expected to adapt in a timely, rapid and correct fashion to frequently changing environment variables and conditions,[7] it is very important that real-time systems be able to adapt predictably to new workloads even when the exact nature of these workloads cannot be anticipated.

We have developed assignment evaluation metrics used in a simple assignment algorithm for real-time processes and abstract data objects (called by the processes). The details of these metrics are beyond the scope of this Chapter, but can be found in [40, 41]. The programming and execution models allow for asynchronous calls. The metrics are based on demands and utilizations of PEs and communication links. Each demand (or utilization) consists of two parts: one due to the processes and objects already assigned, and the other due to those yet unassigned. Based on these demands and utilizations, service rates are projected for each PE and link. The rates are used in turn to project process response times. Next, the amount of parallelism due to calls is estimated and used to adjust the projected response times of the processes.

The assignment algorithm is applied in a bottom-up, breadth-first order to the nodes of a directed acyclic call-graph (DAG) of the program (of processes and objects). At every application, a constant number of least-utilized PEs are considered, each of process response times is projected, and the overall laxity of each process is computed. Projected assignments are considered only if they violate no projected deadline and cause no projected utilization to exceed 100%. The PE with the largest overall laxity for processes is chosen for the assignment.

A preliminary quantitative evaluation of the assignment algorithm and its evaluation functions has shown that the assignment projected response times and laxities are very close to those actually observed. Moreover, the response times and laxities are considerably better than those in the case of identical programs assigned according to the assignment that chooses the best of five random tries.

What makes this work applicable to the problem of assigning real-time software components are the facts that:

1. the metrics are both accurate and fast to compute, with the overall assignment algorithm complexity of $O(\#PE(\#P + \#O)^2)$, where $\#PE$, $\#P$ and $\#O$ are the numbers of PEs, processes and objects, respectively;
2. the metrics consider deadlines, load-balancing, and parallelism;
3. the metrics predict performance on the basis of projected service rates of PEs and links;
4. the metrics treat PEs and communication links in an integrated, uniform way.

---

[7] For instance, a fighter plane may encounter enemy aircraft and anti-aircraft fire, with little warning and independently of the pre-existing flight plan.

Unlike response times projected by worst-case analyses (such as frame superimposition [33, 34, 36] or the analysis of Leinbaugh [16, 17, 18]), the response times projected by the metrics are not worst-case times in the sense of being upper bounds on all conceivable response times. Rather, the response times are upper bounds on the expected or average response times. In guiding the assignment of real-time processes and objects, we are cautious to be neither overly optimistic nor pessimistic. At the same time, we cannot afford to engage in overly expensive, frame-superimposition-like, analysis, *at every assignment step*. Once the processes and objects have been assigned, it is possible to run exact schedulability analysis given the assignment and compute accurate worst-case response times.

4 Conclusion

Schedulability analysis is an integral part of developing predictable real-time systems. It has been stressed strongly at one of this ASI's panels, predictability does not imply being static or inflexible, only being analyzable. Thus, all real-time systems should be predictable and for every one there is an applicable form of schedulability analysis. In this Chapter we have discussed briefly analysis and techniques that have been applied in systems of the Eighties and early Nineties. (More details can be found in [33, 34, 36, 37, 38, 39, 40, 35, 41, 8] and elsewhere.) We have seen how schedulability analysis is done at instruction-, statement-, task- and inter-task-levels of real-time programs. We have discussed related issues, such as reducing the number of possibilities accurate analysis has to consider and applying fast heuristics to facilitate assignment of real-time software components.

While since introducing schedulability analysis, we have gained significant experience and have done extensive evaluations of our techniques, great many questions remain unanswered. For instance, even though Real-Time Euclid [33, 15] included a well-defined model of hierarchical exception handlers, we do not really know how to incorporate exceptions into real-time computation and how to predict timing properties accurately in the *possible* presence of these exceptions. We believe that future efforts in schedulability analysis should address not only exceptions and faults, but also parallelism, varying system configurations, adaptability, conflicting non-functional requirements in addition to time-criticalness (such as fault-tolerance, security, dependability and so forth), and megaprogramming. We hope that some of these will have been addressed before the requirements of the next generation of real-life real-time systems leave all state-of-the-art "research" solutions firmly behind.

Acknowledgements

This work is supported in part by the U.S. ONR Grant N00014-92-J-1367, by the NATO Grant CRG-90-1077, by the AT&T UEDP Grant 91-134, by grants from Siemens Corporate Research, and by the NJIT SBR Grant 421250. The author has also been supported by grants from Honeywell, DEC, Bailey Controls, AT&T Foundation, the Center for Manufacturing Systems at NJIT, and the State of New Jersey.

Much of what has been presented here is based on joint work with Mehmet Akşit, Wolfgang Halang, Tom Marlowe and Lonnie Welch. Moreover, all members of the Real-Time Computing Laboratory at NJIT have participated in many aspects of this work. The author is indebted to all his fellow ASI participants, and especially Andy Bernat, Giovanni Cantone, Carlos Cardeira, Rod Chapman, Özer Ciftcioglu, Matjaz Colnariz, John Cullyer, Aldo Esposito, Borko Furht, Carlo Ghezzi, Dieter Hammer, Connie Heitmeyer, Günther Hommel, Steve Howell, Doug Jensen, Kane Kim, Werner Kriechbaum, Phil Laplante, Harold Lawson, Jane and David Liu, Imad Mahgoub, Mirek Malek, Steve Masticola, John McDermid, Ulrich Schmid, Rick Sheldon, Kang Shin, Marco Spuri, Jack Stankovic, Hartwig Steusloff, Ken Tindell and Janusz Zalewski for their many excellent comments.

References

1. T.P. Baker and G.L. Scallon, *An Architecture for Real-time Software Systems*, IEEE Software, May 1986, 50–59; reprinted in tutorial "Hard Real-Time Systems", IEEE Press, 1988.

2. G. Chroust, *Orthogonal Extensions in Microprogrammed Multiprocessor Systems — A Chance for Increased Firmware Usage*, EUROMICRO Journal, Vol. 6, No. 2, 1980, 104–110.

3. K. Ecker, *Organisation von parallelen Prozessen*, Bibliographisches Institut, Mannheim, Germany, 1977.

4. J. Ferrante, K. Ottenstein, J. D. Warren, *The Program Dependence Graph and its Use in Optimization*, ACM Transactions on Programming Languages and Systems, Vol. 9, No. 3, 319–349.

5. M. R. Garey, D. S. Johnson, *Complexity Results for Multiprocessor Scheduling under Resource Constraints*, SIAM Journal on Computing, Vol. 4, No. 4, December 1975, 397–411.

6. W. A. Halang, *On Methods for Direct Memory Access Without Cycle Stealing*. Microprocessing and Microprogramming, 17, 5, May 1986.

7. W. A. Halang, *Implications on Suitable Multiprocessor Structures and Virtual Storage Management when Applying a Feasible Scheduling Algorithm*, in "Hard Real-Time Environments, Software — Practice and Experience, Vol. 16, No. 8, 1986, 761–769.

8. W. A. Halang, A. D. Stoyenko, *Constructing Predictable Real-Time Systems*, Kluwer Academic Publishers, Dordrecht-Hingham, 1991.

9. M. Harmon, T. Baker and D. Whalley, *A Retargetable Technique for Predicting Execution Time*, Proceedings of the IEEE Real-Time Systems Symposium, IEEE, December 1992.

10. R. Henn, *Deterministische Modelle für die Prozessorzuteilung in einer harten Realzeit-Umgebung*, Ph.D. Thesis, Technical University Munich, 1975.

11. C. A. R. Hoare, *An Axiomatic Basis for Computer Programming*, Communications of the ACM, Vol. 10, No. 12, 1969.

12. J. Hooman, W.-P. de Roever, *Design and Verification in Real-Time Distributed Computing and Introduction to Compositional Methods*, Proceedings of the Ninth International Symposium on Protocol Specification, Testing, and Verification, North-Holland, 1989.

13. J. Hooman, *Specification and Compositional Verification of Real-Time Systems*, Ph.D. Thesis, Eindhoven University of Technology, Eindhoven, the Netherlands, 1991.

14. S. Horwitz, J. Prins, T. Reps, *Integrating Non-Interfering Versions of Programs*, Conference Record of the Fifteenth Annual ACM Conference on the Principles of Programming Languages, 133–145.

15. E. Kligerman, A. D. Stoyenko, *Real-Time Euclid: A Language for Reliable Real-Time Systems*, IEEE Transactions on Software Engineering, Vol. SE–12, No. 9, September 1986, 940–949.

16. D. W. Leinbaugh, *Guaranteed Response Times in a Hard-Real-Time Environment*, IEEE Transactions on Software Engineering, Vol. SE–6, No. 1, January 1980, 85–91.

17. D. W. Leinbaugh, M.-R. Yamini, *Guaranteed Response Times in a Distributed Hard-Real-Time Environment*, Proceedings of the IEEE 1982 Real-Time Systems Symposium, December 1982, 157–169.

18. D. W. Leinbaugh, M.-R. Yamini, *Guaranteed Response Times in a Distributed Hard-Real-Time Environment*, IEEE Transactions on Software Engineering, Vol. SE–12, No. 12, December 1986, 1139–1144.

19. C. L. Liu, J. W. Layland, *Scheduling Algorithms for Multiprogramming in a Hard-Real-Time Environment*, JACM, Vol. 20, No. 1, January 1973, 46–61.

20. T. J. Marlowe, S. P. Masticola, *Safe Optimization of Hard-Real-Time Programs*, Proceedings of the Second International Conference on Systems Integration, June 1992.

21. T. J. Marlowe, B. G. Ryder, *Properties of Data-Flow Frameworks: A Unified Model*, Acta Informatica, Vol. 28, No. 2, 1991, 121–164.

22. V. Nirkhe, W. Pugh, *Application of Partial Evaluation to Hard Real-Time Programming*, Proceedings of the IEEE/IFAC 1991 Workshop on Real-Time Operating Systems and Software, 74–79.

23. V. Nirkhe, W. Pugh, *Partial Evaluation of High-level Imperative Languages, with Applications in Hard Real-Time Systems*, Conference Record of the Nineteenth Annual ACM Conference on the Principles of Programming Languages, 269–280.

24. J. S. Ostroff, *Survey of Formal Methods for the Specification and Design of Real-Time Systems*, Tutorial on the Specification of Time, IEEE Press, 1993

25. D. Padua, M. J. Wolfe, *Advanced Compiler Optimizations for Supercomputers*, Communications of the ACM, Vol. 22, No. 12, 1986, 1184–1201.

26. G. Parnis, *Simulation of Packet Level Handshaking in X.25 Using the Real-Time Euclid Programming Language*, Student Project Report, Department of Computer Science, University of Toronto, April 1987.

27. *KE-Handbuch*, Periphere Computer Systeme GmbH, Munich, 1981.

28. E. Schatz, B. G. Ryder, *Directed Tracing to Detect Race Conditions*, Rutgers University Laboratory for Computer Science Research Technical Report No. LCSR-TR-176, 1990. (To appear, Proceedings of the 1992 International Conference on Parallel Processing).

29. K. Schleisiek-Kern, *Private Communication*, DELTA t, Hamburg, 1990.

30. G. Schrott, *Ein Zuteilungsmodell fuer Multiprozessor-Echtzeitsysteme*, Ph.D. Thesis, Technical University, Munich 1986.

31. P. G. Sorenson, *A Methodology for Real-Time System Development*, Ph.D. Thesis, Department of Computer Science, University of Toronto, 1974.

32. A. D. Stoyenko, *Turing goes Real-Time ...*, Internal Programming Languages Report, Department of Computer Science, University of Toronto, May 1984.

33. A. D. Stoyenko, *A Schedulability Analyzer for Real-Time Euclid*, Proceedings of the IEEE 1987 Real-Time Systems Symposium, pp. 218–225, December 1987.

34. A. D. Stoyenko, *A Real-Time Language with A Schedulability Analyzer*, Ph.D. Thesis, Department of Computer Science, University of Toronto, 1987.

35. A. D. Stoyenko, W. A. Halang, *High-Integrity PEARL: A Language for Industrial Real-Time Applications*, to appear in: IEEE Software in 1993; a longer version available as "High-Integrity PEARL and its Schedulability Analyzer: Transferring State-of-the-Art Real-Time Software Technology from University Laboratories to Industry," Department of Computer and Information Science Technical Report CIS-91-16, New Jersey Institute of Technology, July 1991.

36. A. D. Stoyenko, V. C. Hamacher, R. C. Holt, *Schedulability Analysis of Hard-Real-Time Programs*, IEEE Transactions on Software Engineering, Vol. 17, No. 8, August 1991.

37. A. D. Stoyenko, T. J. Marlowe, *Schedulability, Program Transformations and Real-Time Programming*, Joint IEEE and IFAC/IFIP Workshop on Real-Time Systems, Atlanta, Georgia, USA, May 1991, 33–41, also in *Real Time Programming*, Pergamon Press, 1992, 33–41.

38. A. D. Stoyenko, T. J. Marlowe, *Polynomial-Time Transformations and Schedulability Analysis of Parallel Real-Time Programs with Restricted Resource Contention*, *Real-Time Systems* Vol. 4, No. 4, November 1992, 307–329.

39. A. D. Stoyenko, T. J. Marlowe, W. A. Halang, M. Younis, *Enabling Efficient Schedulability Analysis through Conditional Linking and Program Transformations*, Control Engineering Practice, Vol. 1, No. 1, January 1993.

40. A. D. Stoyenko, L. R. Welch, *Analysis of Timing Behavior of Software Components in Complex Systems*, in revision for IEEE Software, 1993.

41. A. D. Stoyenko, L. R. Welch, *Metrics for Assigning Components of Complex Real-Time Systems*, a working paper, 1993.

42. R. Strom, D. M. Yellin, *Extending Typestate Checking Using Conditional Liveness Analysis*, IEEE Transactions on Software Engineering, to appear.

43. T. Tempelmeier, *A Supplementary Processor for Operating System Functions*, 1979 IFAC/IFIP Workshop on Real-Time Programming, Smolenice, 18–20 June 1979.

44. T. Tempelmeier, *Operating System Processors in Real-Time Systems — Performance Analysis and Measurement*, Computer Performance, Vol. 5, No. 2, June 1984, 121–127.

45. S. A. Thurlow, *Simulation of a Real Time Control System Using the Real-Time Euclid Programming Language*, Student Project Report, Department of Computer Science, University of Toronto, April 1987.

46. J. D. Ullman, *Polynomial complete scheduling problems*, Proceedings of the 4th Symposium on OS Principles, 1973, 96–101.

47. M. Weiser, *Program Slicing*, IEEE Transactions on Software Engineering, Vol. SE-10, No. 4, 1984, 352–357.

48. M. J. Wolfe, U. Banerjee, *Data Dependence and its Application to Parallel Processing*, International Journal of Parallel Processing, Vol. 16, No. 2, 1987, 137–178.

49. M. J. Wolfe, *Supercompilers for Supercomputers*, The MIT Press, Cambridge MA, 1989.

A Distributed, Fault-Tolerant Real-Time Language*

Günter Hommel

Technische Universität Berlin
Institut für Technische Informatik
Franklinstr. 28/29
1000 Berlin 10
Germany

1 Introduction

Early programming languages used for the implementation of real-time systems did not include language constructs to cope with modularity, concurrency, synchronization, communication, time control, and dependability. The only way to integrate some of that functionality was to allow for assembler language insertions and operating system calls. Programs of that type are extremely non-portable.

An important step to overcome the portability problem of real-time programs was the development of the programming language PEARL [7]. Essential concepts included in PEARL are modularity, concurrency, synchronization, time control, and exception handling. There are quite a few papers (e.g. [12]; [10]; [23] that classify and describe the concepts of this language in comparison to other programming languages.

With the event of microprocessors it was possible to economically realize automation systems as distributed real-time systems. At that time, available real-time languages did not include language concepts to describe the distribution of program units to the distributed processors. A distributed program was therefore realized by distributing sequential programs to the various processors. The communication between those programs was realized by calling the appropriate functions of a real-time operating system.

Consequently, the next step in the development of real-time languages was the attempt to integrate language constructs for distributed programs. In order to realize distributed real-time systems, language constructs are needed to define entities that can be distributed to various computers — we call those entities *distribution units* — and constructs that allow the communication between those distribution units. As global memory is not available in distributed systems, communication must be realized by message passing.

Concepts like virtual shared memory, as discussed in computer architecture for the design of massive parallel systems, are not appropriate for real-time systems.

---

* This work has been supported by Deutsche Forschungsgemeinschaft (DFG) under grant Ho 1257/2-1

The time for communication cannot be determined in a deterministic way and thus, upper bounds for the time to access an object cannot be guaranteed. This problem is comparable to timing considerations in paging systems.

Language constructs for the description of distribution units and their physical mapping to various computers have been defined already very early for an extension of PEARL [22]. Another important programming language that allows to describe the distribution of programming units to various computers is CONIC [15]; [17]. A short comparison of the concepts of both languages can be found in [12].

The possibility to describe distribution units and the possibility to dynamically change their physical distribution, i.e., to reconfigure the system, allows to implement fault-tolerant systems. Language constructs for the realization of fault-tolerant systems have also been described in the extension of PEARL mentioned above and in CONIC. An extended combination of concepts from those two developments finally resulted in an extension of PEARL for distributed systems [8]. A description of the relevant new language constructs can be found e.g. in [11]. Another important real-time language for practical industrial use is Ada [6]. Ada allows to describe concurrency using process declarations (*tasks*). The communication between processes is message based using the rendezvous concept. As Ada allows the access to task-global objects, however, it is — in general — impossible to use Ada tasks as distribution units. An extension of Ada for the construction of distributed systems is therefore not possible without restrictions of the standard language.

As the most realistic real-time applications are realized as distributed systems today, there has been much effort to define extensions for Ada in order to allow the implementation of distributed systems [2]; [5]; [9]; [14]; [18]; [24]; [25]. In some of those extensions [5]; [14]; [18] also the aspect of constructing fault-tolerant systems with Ada has been addressed.

In the following sections one of those extensions of Ada is discussed in detail. The programming language GranAda [18] has been designed in an ongoing research project at the Technische Universität Berlin. GranAda allows to construct distributed, fault-tolerant real-time systems.

The remainder of this paper is organized as follows: In the next section the design criteria for GranAda and a comparison with related work are presented. Section three describes those additional language concepts important for the construction of distributed, fault-tolerant programs. Section four gives an idea on how to use those language constructs to design fault-tolerant systems with GranAda. Section five describes the implementation of GranAda. Conclusions and acknowledgments complete the paper.

2 Design Criteria for GranAda

There are different approaches to implement distributed real-time systems. One approach mostly used in industrial environments is to apply standard programming languages like FORTRAN or C. Aspects of concurrency, communication, synchronization, time control, error recovery, and distribution are coped with using primitives of real-time operating and communication systems. The problem of this approach is that programs are not portable and highly rely on machine-specific services as there is still no agreement on standards for (distributed) real-time operating systems.

A second approach most computer scientists would prefer is to design a new programming language integrating all concepts for distributed real-time systems. This is of course tempting but usually results in nice academic languages nobody is going to use in industrial applications.

The third approach is a compromise: We try to find a programming language that is accepted for industrial applications and includes as many machine-independent concepts as possible for concurrency control, communication, synchronization, time control, error recovery, and distribution. The missing concepts are integrated in a way that leaves the original programming language untouched.

We adopted this third approach and chose Ada [6] as the basic programming language. Ada is a quite modern language, fulfilling many requirements needed for real-time programming. Nevertheless, the design of complex distributed systems is not supported directly and requires some enlargement.

In common, distributed real-time applications are designed as interacting tasks or processes. Accordingly, GranAda extents Ada with language constructs that allows the specification of logical distribution, i.e., distributable software units, consisting of Ada tasks. (Such distribution units are also called *logical* or *virtual* nodes, thus being an abstraction of the physical distribution, i.e., the processing nodes of a computer network.) The *Virtual Node* approach was also adopted in DIADEM [2].

A quite opposite view was taken in APPL [5]. APPL is a separate language, which is used to form distribution units from entities (e.g. variables, procedures, tasks, etc.) of a conventional Ada program. APPL has the advantage that every Ada program may become distributed, however, APPL programs possess *all-or-nothing* semantics [14], i.e., resulting distributed systems are not degradable.

In general, complex software systems are not error-free and hardware faults cannot be ruled out. Therefore, subsystems may fail and it is especially crucial to provide fault-tolerance and/or degraded services within distributed real-time systems. We believe that a programming language should offer suitable constructs and mechanisms in order to simplify this task. This is also true with respect to system maintenance. Long-lived distributed real-time systems are subject to evolutionary changes (e.g. hardware rearrangements or software upgrades). They have to be carried out on-line while unaffected parts of the system continue to operate [17].

Although GranAda simplifies software development and system maintenance, it requires some programming guidelines and some programming discipline. Nevertheless, the linguistic support offered by a distributed real-time language should maintain ease of use and expressiveness, with corresponding run-time support being as efficient as possible. The success and acceptance of a distributed, fault-tolerant real-time programming language will depend on how these partially contradictory goals are met.

3 Language Constructs of GranAda

Within GranAda the basic real-time language constructs of Ada for

- concurrency (tasks)
- synchronization and communication (rendezvous)
- time control (delays)
- error recovery (exceptions)

are also available. Furthermore, GranAda defines these constructs in a distributed sense anew (see also section 3.2). In addition, distribution units can be specified in GranAda using the keyword **grain** (see section 3.1).

Besides these intra-program language constructs a separate configuration language is used to express the mapping of distribution units onto the processing nodes of the underlying network. Basically, a separate configuration language enhances configuration flexibility. In GranAda, the configuration language is also used for change management as well as accomplishing requirements of fault-tolerance. Redundancy, reconfiguration, and graceful degradation policies (see section 3.3) can thus be realized.

3.1 Specification of the Logical System Structure

The specification of the logical system structure is an aspect of *programming-in-the-large*, i.e., a top-down, prior to the implementation, design methodology. A distributed real-time system may be partitioned into logically independent top-level software components (e.g. representing real objects, as machines, devices, etc.), each consisting of one or more concurrent tasks. Therefore, a GranAda application consists of an arbitrary number of distribution units, so called *grains*. Each grain comprises one or more Ada tasks. The specification of grains is expressed by a strictly block-oriented language construct, encapsulating Ada task specifications and declarations. Single tasks and task objects may be grouped to a grain specification as below (keywords are shown in bold typeface):

```
grain EXAMPLE_GRAIN is
    task TASK1 is ...
    task TASK2 is ...
    TASK3 : TASK3_TYPE;
end EXAMPLE_GRAIN;
```

Virtual nodes and task types (which are not part of a grain specification since they can be used in different grains) are specified within package specifications. The implementation parts of single tasks are grouped to a grain body similarly:

```
grain body EXAMPLE_GRAIN is
    task body TASK1 is ...
    task body TASK2 is ...
end EXAMPLE_GRAIN;
```

The distribution specification is at the outmost level in the view of traditional Ada program structures. Tasks within grains depend on library packages only. Dependent tasks or data objects may be declared locally to the tasks of a grain. An important aspect of grain specifications additionally to other Ada program structures is to further enforce modern software engineering concepts, such as modularization techniques and object-oriented data-encapsulation. Employing such concepts is an essential criteria for building large but easily maintainable systems.

Of course, there are no global objects accessible to different grains. Currently, there are still two restrictions that will be removed in future releases of GranAda. First, it should be possible that grains propagate exceptions. In this case they will be specified within grain specifications. Second, task access types will be incorporated to realize dynamic systems with a flexible communication pattern [2].

When designing the logical system structure, it has to be taken into account that we recommend some general programming guidelines: entry calls between two and only two tasks should always be implemented in the same direction. The application should also refrain from implementing nested rendezvous, although supported by GranAda. Both restrictions help to design transparent flow control and to prevent deadlocks.

3.2 Communication in GranAda

The specification of the logical system structure, more precisely GranAda's grain concept, does not impose a specific communication mechanism. For example, we could have implemented a non-Ada like procedural communication package, allowing asynchronous message passing via ports, as in Cnet [9], or with datagrams as in DARK [24].

Instead, we define a straightforward Ada extension: the remote rendezvous. That means that communication and synchronization is always achieved by entry calls and accept statements. Thus, the Ada rendezvous is a uniform language construct in GranAda, no matter whether it is local or remote. Of course, GranAda comprehends the full rendezvous concept, e.g., timed and conditional calls, selective waits, or nesting of rendezvous in the usual way. However, the semantics of remote rendezvous is restricted in that way that addresses or references, passed as rendezvous parameters, may not be dereferenced in a remote address space.

Remember, a rendezvous effects a synchronous control transfer between two and only two tasks. Ada's rendezvous mechanism is based on an asymmetric direct naming scheme, i.e., the calling task names the called task as well as an associated entry, whereas the identity of the calling task is anonymous to the called task.

Obviously, Ada's direct naming scheme restricts configuration flexibility with respect to communication patterns [17]. One could use task access types, in order to achieve flexible communication patterns; however, there is no way to express a one-to-many pattern. Nevertheless, the rendezvous mechanism of Ada has been found to provide a level of abstraction superior to solutions using ports and send/receive primitives [13]. On the other hand, asynchronous message passing employing send/receive statements seems to be necessary for reasons of efficiency, since there may be multiple transactions in progress concurrently. Asynchronous message passing may be emulated in Ada by an additional task [3]; [11].

Another problem of Ada's rendezvous mechanism is that a called task is not affected by an abort of a calling task. Thus, Ada does not guarantee failure atomicity of rendezvous [3]. Note that another fundamental problem within current Ada implementations is the priority inversion [21], where a high-priority task can be prevented from executing by a low-priority task, if they are blocked within the same first come first served entry queue.

3.3 Configuration of the System

In distributed real-time applications where computers are mostly dedicated to peripheral devices, application-transparent configuration would often be inappropriate. Therefore, it is possible to explicitly map distribution units onto physical nodes of the underlying network using configuration statements.

In GranAda, the specification of distribution units is expressed within the GranAda program, whereas the configuration is described separately by a special configuration language. The subsequent steps of specifying and configuring a GranAda application are illustrated in Fig. 1.

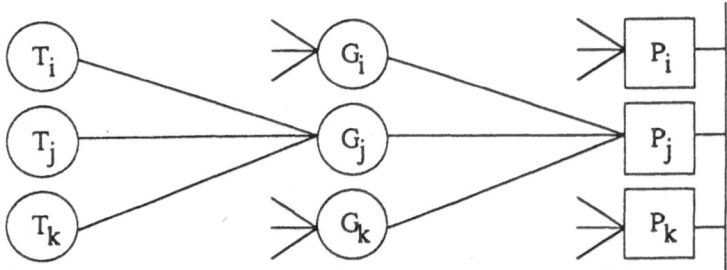

Fig. 1. Specification and configuration (T: Ada tasks, G: grains, P: processors)

Conceptually separating configuration from specification and implementation is an important aspect [15]. A separate configuration language enhances configuration flexibility, so configuration changes may be enforced on-line without rebuilding the entire system. Portability is another important aspect, since the configuration within distributed real-time systems mainly depends on the structure of the physical equipment, while an algorithmic software solution, e.g. a device driver, remains identical, no matter to which processor the device is connected. Moreover, a configuration language is also necessary for change management, since evolutionary changes of long-lived distributed real-time systems, e.g., rearranging hardware or exchanging software components, cannot always be predicted at the time the system is designed [17]. Of course, such changes should

be possible while the system continues to operate without disrupting unaffected parts of the system. Since maintaining a running application is a runtime
aspect, GranAda uses an on-line configuration management utility to execute
statements, i.e., commands, of the configuration language. The use and the semantics of these operations are described in the following two sections.

In GranAda, the configuration language is also used to implement fault-tolerant
systems. Configuration language constructs are employed to describe the configuration of redundant backup software components and their reconfiguration
and graceful degradation policies. Distribution units (grains) are the smallest
replaceable units (SRUs).

The operations of the configuration language are also provided as a procedural interface for the programmer. Therefore, it is also possible to dynamically
control the system configuration by the running system itself. Grains may be
migrated from one processing node to another, or grains may be replaced. This
is especially useful for unmaintained systems or program driven (and more sophisticated) reconfiguration strategies.

3.3.1 Creating and Loading Distribution Units

A GranAda application consists of one or more grains, which are specified within the program. After having built a GranAda application, executable images,
derived from those grain specifications, are available in a program directory. To
configure a system, the configuration management utility (called *gm*, which is
a shorthand for GranAda Manager) has to execute *create* commands. The syntax of the *create* statement is shown below (as usual, keywords are shown in
bold typeface, non-terminals are enclosed in <>. [and] indicate optional items,
whereas | denotes alternatives):

```
create [warm | cold backup]
   grain(<number>) <actual name>
   [is <specified name>]
   at <physical node name>
   [priority is <number>]
   [parameter is <string literal>]
   [reconfiguration is upward | demand]
```

The *create* statement introduces a grain with its actual name to the system,
i.e., makes it known to the system. The specified name of a grain is the grain
name introduced in the grain specification within the program. If grains are not
derived from grain templates, the actual name is the same as the specified grain
name, which may be omitted in this case. Thus the most simple create command
could be e.g.:

create grain ROBOT at NODE1

Different actual names are used to derive several grain instances from one specified grain. The following example shows the creation of two grain instances from
one specified grain:

create grain ROBOT1 is ROBOT at NODE1
create grain ROBOT2 is ROBOT at NODE2

A grain is either a primary grain (grain(1)) or a warm or cold backup grain with an higher order number (grain(2..N)) and carries the same actual name as the corresponding formerly created primary grain. Every (backup) grain has to be created and configured explicitly. Furthermore, it is possible to additionally specify a string parameter. This parameterization may be especially useful in the context of derived grain instances.

Whether an executable image is loaded onto a target processor is determined automatically. Warm backup grains are loaded at system initialization time, whereas cold backup grains are loaded only in the case of failures.

In addition, load priorities can be assigned to grains. This is useful, e.g., in the case of a reconfiguration when one node fails and the grains of this node have to be shifted to another node. If this node is not able to load all of those grains additionally, it has to be decided which services will have to be dropped. This decision is based on the specified priorities.

3.3.2 Starting Distribution Units

After the creation of grains, the *gm* utility has to execute *start* commands to launch the application. The *start* command has one parameter which is the actual name of a formerly *created* grain. Only primary grains have to be started explicitly, whereas backup grains remain in a passive state. If a primary grain fails, a backup grain is activated automatically, taking on the primary grain's role.

Note that primary and backup components may be created as instances of different grain implementations. Provided the interfaces are identical, this is useful for implementing alternate services [14].

3.3.3 Stopping and Deleting Distribution Units

Opposed to the *create* and *start* operations, there are the *stop* and the *delete* operation. The stop operation halts the execution of a grain, where the grain has to agree to this request. A running grain can handle this request by accepting an entry call and subsequently performing an orderly shut-down possibly preserving its internal state. Deleting a grain removes it from the system. The corresponding image is unloaded if it is not used by another grain.

4 Constructing Fault-Tolerant Systems with GranAda

Within distributed real-time systems services may become unavailable due to hardware failures (processors, communication media, peripheral devices, etc.) as well as due to erroneous software. Therefore, (sub-)system failures cannot be ruled out. In general, the probability of failures increases with the complexity of the distributed real-time system.

The concept of distribution units has two important properties with respect to these considerations. First, distribution units are abstract entities that can survive physical node failures. Second, distribution units can restrict error propagation beyond their boundaries.

Since the failure of a component performing essential or critical tasks can not be tolerated, software-implemented fault-tolerance, i.e., redundant software components, can be applied in order to increase the availability of a distributed real-time system. First, GranAda applications should be degradable, and second, they should be able to tolerate N component faults, depending on the number of backup components. For the rest of this paper, we restrict our argumentation to processor failures only, where we assume fail-stop behavior of processors [19]. In GranAda, processor failures may be treated in different ways. The first possibility is to allow the system to degrade, disabling some services and disregarding failed components until they are repaired and re-integrated. This is useful, if redundancy cannot be achieved. The second possibility is to provide hot redundancy of software components and appropriate forward error recovery at the application level. The third possibility is to replicate software components and reconfigurate the system in the event of failures. Systems constructed in accordance with the two latter alternatives are also known as gracefully degradable system. While the second approach is application-dependent, the third approach requires backward error recovery in order to continue the service in a consistent system state.

Failures of real-time systems can be tolerated most efficiently at application-level by means of forward error recovery strategies. On the other hand, an increased availability of software components despite of processor failures can only be achieved by software replication and backward error recovery mechanisms. In this case, failures are treated as unanticipated asynchronous events.

4.1 Fault Detection and Error Processing

Most languages for distributed programming, e.g., CONIC [17], Argus [16], SR [1], etc., provide failure detection mechanisms in conjunction with their communication facilities. In GranAda, the predefined exception TASKING_ERROR is raised at the site of the calling task if a rendezvous fails. Therefore, remote rendezvous, reveal at-most-once semantics, which is a straightforward extension of conventional Ada semantics.

If a component fails and the calling tasks gets informed via the propagation of the predefined exception TASKING_ERROR, an appropriate forward error recovery can be implemented as part of a corresponding exception handler.

In Ada a calling task can detect the failure of a called task, but a called task is unaware of the failure of a calling task. This can cause problems in situations where more than one rendezvous is necessary to achieve proper synchronization or resource management. GranAda provides a configuration change notice mechanism (see the following section), which also allows the detection of a component's failure even in the absence of application-level communication, especially the failure of a calling task within a called task.

4.2 Configuration Change Notice

In degradable and long-lived distributed real-time systems the configuration is subject to changes. This means that software components may become temporarily unavailable between failure and repair, or have to be replaced by new ones. In order to maintain the current configuration of the system, GranAda provides a predefined generic package called CONFIGURATION_CHANGE_NOTICE. This is specified as follows:

```
generic
   with procedure BIRTH(GRAIN_NAME : in STRING);
   with procedure DEATH(GRAIN_NAME : in STRING);
package CONFIGURATION_CHANGE_NOTICE is
end CONFIGURATION_CHANGE_NOTICE;
```

The problem that a called task is unaware of the failure of a calling task can be illustrated by an example similar to the one given by Cmelic et al. [4]. If a client failed before releasing an allocated resource, the failed client would block the corresponding server forever. This problem can be resolved using a death-notice mechanism [20]; [4]. Upon a death-notice of the failed client, the server is able to release the resource. As an example, a robot server is chosen, assuming this common resource to be synchronized and controlled within the same grain (string operations are incorrect in order to avoid stilted Ada code sequences):

```
grain ROBOT_GRAIN is
   task ROBOT is
      entry BIRTH(GRAIN_NAME : in STRING); -- birth-notice
      entry DEATH(GRAIN_NAME : in STRING); -- death-notice
      entry LOCK(GRAIN_NAME : in STRING); -- synchronization
                                                operation
      entry UNLOCK; -- synchronization operation
      entry MOVE(); -- robot operation
      ...
   end ROBOT;
end ROBOT_GRAIN;
```

```
-- library package implementation
with CONFIGURATION_CHANGE_NOTICE;

procedure BIRTH(GRAIN_NAME : in STRING) renames ROBOT.BIRTH;
procedure DEATH(GRAIN_NAME : in STRING) renames ROBOT.DEATH;

-- instantiation of predefined GranAda package,
-- enabling interactions of the run-time system with the application
```

```
package MY_CONFIGURATION_CHANGE_NOTICE is new
CONFIGURATION_CHANGE_NOTICE(BIRTH, DEATH);

grain body ROBOT_GRAIN is
  task body ROBOT is
    LOCKED : BOOLEAN := FALSE; -- state of synchronization
    LOCKING_GRAIN : STRING; -- grain which has allocated the resource
  begin
  loop
    select
      when not LOCKED => -- resource is available
        accept LOCK(GRAIN_NAME : in STRING) do
          LOCKING_GRAIN := GRAIN_NAME; -- remembering grain
        end LOCK;
        LOCKED := TRUE; -- remembering state of synchronization
    or
      when LOCKED =>
        accept UNLOCK;
        LOCKED := FALSE; -- remembering state of synchronization
    or
      when LOCKED =>
        accept DEATH(GRAIN_NAME : in STRING) do
          if GRAIN_NAME = LOCKING_GRAIN
          then -- release resource, because client has failed
            LOCKED := FALSE; -- changing state of synchronization
            -- recover robot, if necessary
          end if;
        end DEATH;
    or
      when LOCKED => -- accept robot operations
    end select;
  end loop;
  end ROBOT;
end ROBOT_GRAIN;
```

Based on this mechanism the *death* of a calling task could be detected. This might be implemented as follows:

```
-- allocate resource, identifying yourself
ROBOT.LOCK(GRAIN_NAME => GRANADA_SYSTEM.GRAIN_NAME);
loop
  ROBOT.MOVE(); -- exclusive resource operations
  ...
end loop;
ROBOT.UNLOCK; -- deallocate resource
```

The proposed generic configuration change notice mechanism works as a call-back mechanism known from object-oriented languages, which enables interaction between the run-time support system and the application. We assume that (rare) *births* and *deaths* are detected by the run-time system within a given worst-case deadline. After detection, the previously instantiated procedures are called.

The exact semantics of this mechanism are as follows: should the run-time system be able to activate a backup component, the procedure DEATH is not called, i.e., the failure is handled transparently to the application. Only, if the run-time system is not able to activate a backup component, the procedure is called as noted above. If all spare grains are exhausted finally, the system may, however, degrade, losing its "gracefulness".

In order to achieve proper synchronization between the application and the run-time system, these procedures should be implemented as entry procedures (as shown in the example). Nevertheless, the application is free to renounce any notifications, i.e., to implement an empty procedure, or to accept the notification conditionally, i.e., to use timed entry calls or guarded accept statements.

The knowledge about the current logical configuration provided by this mechanism may also be used for implementing service changes with respect to the current system configuration. As an example, we consider some device server which normally controls the access to some specific device. If the original device is not available, the server is able to change the configuration in such a way that another device could take over the service.

A birth-notice can be used at the site of a calling task to synchronize with a reintegrated, temporarily unavailable server:

```
loop
  INNER_LOOP: loop
    if ROBOT_SERVER_UP
    then -- some necessary beforehand operations which should not be
              executed
      -- on each iteration while the robot server is unavailable,
      -- e.g., requesting another resource
      NORMAL_WORK: begin -- doing normal work
        ROBOT.LOCK;
        ...
      exception
        when TASKING_ERROR => -- "ROBOT_GRAIN" has failed
          ROBOT_SERVER_UP := FALSE;
          exit INNER_LOOP; -- normal work is not possible any more
      end NORMAL_WORK;
    else -- try to resynchronize or doing something else
      select
        accept BIRTH(GRAIN_NAME : in STRING) do
          if GRAIN_NAME = "ROBOT_GRAIN"
          then -- normal work is possible again after reintegration
```

```
            ROBOT_SERVER_UP := TRUE;
            exit INNER_LOOP;
          end if;
        end BIRTH;
      else
        -- doing something else
      end select;
    end if;
  end loop INNER_LOOP;
end loop;
```

4.3 Failures with Degradation

If redundant components are not provided or if there are no more redundant components available, a component failure will lead to system degradation. As noted in section 4.1, a component failure can be detected via the predefined exception TASKING_ERROR or via the DEATH procedure of the configuration change mechanisms.

The reaction is application-dependent. A fail-safe behavior might be to ring an alarm clock or to stop the train. The detecting component could also implement some form of fail-stop functionality, e.g. switch off some machines. Another compensation would be to resynchronize a detecting component with the reactivation of the failed component. An example for the implementation of a system with degradation in the case of failures has been shown in section 4.2.

4.4 Gracefully Degrading Systems with Redundancy

In order to retain high availability, a distributed real-time system may be implemented with redundant hardware and software components. In the following sections, we will give some example scenarios to illustrate, how a gracefully degradable system can be designed with GranAda.

4.4.1 Hot Redundancy

Suppose, for example, that two robots are connected to one computer each. The control software on each computer may be different as the hardware of the robots is not identical. The control software for each robot is realized as a grain:

```
grain ROBOT1 is
  task ROBOT1_TASK is
    entry MOVE(FRAME:FRAME_TYPE);

    ...
  end ROBOT1_TASK;
end ROBOT1;

grain ROBOT2 is ...
  task ROBOT2_TASK is
```

```
    entry MOVE(FRAME:FRAME_TYPE);
    ...
  end ROBOT2_TASK;
end ROBOT2;
```

The two grains are mapped to the two different computers:

create grain(1) ROBOT1 at NODE1
create grain(1) ROBOT2 at NODE2

Suppose, the two robots could access the same working space. In this case a (hot) redundant move operation could be implemented such that after the failure of one robot, a client task could engage in a rendezvous with the other robot. Anticipating the failure of NODE1, for example, a client task may be programmed as follows:

task body ROBOT_CLIENT is
  ...
  ROBOT1_TASK.MOVE(ACTUAL_FRAME);
  ...
  exception
    when TASKING_ERROR =>
      ROBOT2_TASK.MOVE(ACTUAL_FRAME);
    ...
end ROBOT_CLIENT;

4.4.2 Warm Redundancy

Suppose each of the both robots is connected to two computers. In this case identical backup grains can be created on both computers:

create grain(1) ROBOT1 at NODE1
create warm backup grain(2) ROBOT1 at NODE2
create grain(1) ROBOT2 at NODE2
create warm backup grain(2) ROBOT2 at NODE1

The provision of backup components has the effect of hiding the failure of a primary grain from the application. As opposed to the example given in the previous section, in this case, the remote rendezvous of a client task exhibits at-least-once semantics. Thus, instead of raising the predefined exception TASKING_ERROR, the run-time system performs a backward error recovery. The backup component is activated and the entry call is retransmitted. If we assume that a MOVE operation is idempotent, this is no problem, even if the previous move operation has been executed partly. Note that if the requirement of idempotent remote rendezvous is not satisfied, backup grains should not be considered.

Since processor failures causes the loss of data located in volatile memory, GranAda provides a basic checkpointing scheme. This permits to preserve the current state of a grain within its backup component. To achieve this, the application may define essential variables and may checkpoint these variables at arbitrary points of the computation:

```
essential ESSENTIAL_VAR : ESSENTIAL_TYPE;
begin
   ...
   checkpoint_essential;
   ...
end
```

With this mechanism the amount and frequency of checkpointing is fully under application control. Since our checkpointing mechanism is based on asynchronous message transmission, it is quite efficient. Nevertheless, fault-tolerance mechanisms may be applied to critical tasks within a real-time system only if their execution within a given deadline can be guaranteed. In distributed systems, however, this mainly depends on the access scheme of the medium access layer and the upper layer protocols necessary to achieve end-to-end communication, checkpointing, error detection, and error recovery.

4.4.3 Cold Redundancy

There are two differences between warm and cold redundancy, although the example from the previous section holds also for cold redundancy. First, cold backup grains will be loaded in the case of failures only. Second, for cold backup grains the checkpoint mechanism is inactive. Those two differences yield less processor and memory utilization and less run-time overhead. On the other hand, reconfiguration time is much longer and a cold backup grain is started from the scratch.

Note that in any case of redundancy, timed entry calls can be implemented, thus, a client may withdraw from a request if the current reconfiguration time cannot be tolerated.

4.5 Reconfiguration Strategy after Repair

The *create* allows to specify the reconfiguration strategy as *demand* or *upward*. This is used to determine whether the system has to switch back to a previous configuration or whether it has to remain in the current configuration, after a previously failed component has been repaired and reintegrated into the system. Normally, reconfiguration in GranAda takes place on demand, i.e., when a currently active grain fails. Obviously, this demand reconfiguration strategy always applies to primary grains. An anticipatory *upward* reconfiguration strategy can be specified if it is desired that after a failure and the corresponding repair of a component the system is reconfigured immediately to the previous configuration (thus leaving a possibly degraded system state). In this case it is always the goal to run a configuration of grains with minimal order numbers. If the reconfiguration strategy is omitted, the default is on *demand*. So backup grains may act as primary grains, although grains with a minor order number have been reintegrated. If subsequently an active backup grain fails, an *upward* reconfiguration strategy is used whenever possible.

Based on the specified reconfiguration strategy, it is the responsibility of the run-time system to deactivate warm backup grains or to unload maybe unneeded images of cold backup grains.

5 Implementation

The programming language GranAda consists of two parts: a pre-compiler and a distributed run-time system. In addition, the management utility *gm* constitutes the GranAda support environment. The pre-compiler is implemented with the utilities **FLEX** and **BISON**, which are GNU's equivalents to UNIX's standard utilities **LEX** and **YACC**, respectively. The run-time system and the *gm* utility are implemented in Ada.

A prototype implementation of GranAda is available that currently does not provide the full functionality described in the previous chapters. However, it is possible to implement and execute distributed real-time applications in a heterogeneous environment. Our target environment is a VAXcluster consisting of several VAX nodes running the operating systems VAX/VMS and VAXELN. The pre-compiled Ada code and the interface of the run-time system are independent of the operating system being used.

Communication within our current target environment is based upon the standard DECnet communication system. DECnet uses a CSMA/CD medium access scheme, which does not satisfy the requirement of worst-case message delivery times. GranAda's remote rendezvous mechanism uses a Transport Service, which is recommended within DECnet. Although we provide an efficient implementation on top of the Transport Service (communication links are established and broken at the begin and at the end of each calling task), we are examining the use of a reliable Datagram Service.

6 Conclusion

GranAda, an extension of Ada, was designed to simplify the design of fault-tolerant and degradable distributed real-time systems. Grain specifications were introduced to impose a strictly block-oriented distribution specification on top of Ada. Inside grain implementations the full Ada language is applicable.

GranAda offers linguistic support for different configuration requirements. It is possible to implement hot, warm, and cold redundancy in dynamically configurable systems. Redundancy and dynamic reconfiguration is essential for tolerating system failures, i.e., retaining system availability. In order to allow evolutionary changes during continuous system operation, GranAda offers operations and appropriate generic interfaces to the application program.

Additional work is necessary to implement full GranAda. Further extensions of the pre-compiler as well as of the library management support are needed. The run-time support system needs to be enhanced, in order to fully support error detection and recovery. Future work will also concentrate on the performance and availability analysis of gracefully degradable systems written in GranAda.

Acknowledgments

The author would like to thank Peter Müller for his continuous commitment in the GranAda project and his helpful support during the preparation of this paper. He and Uwe Wolfgang Brandenburg gave valuable comments on earlier versions of this paper. Thanks are also due to Ralf Guido Herrtwich, who participated in GranAda's design phase. The author is also grateful to Andreas Renner for implementing the prototype pre-compiler and to Norbert Steingräber for enhancing GranAda's run-time system and support environment.

References

1. Andrews, G.R., Olsson, R.A., *The Evolution of the SR Language*, Distributed Computing, Vol. 1, No. 1, 1986, 133–149.
2. Atkinson, C., Moreton, T., Natali, A., *Ada for Distributed Systems*, The Ada Companion Series, Cambridge University Press, 1988.
3. Burns, A., Lister, A.M., Wellings A.J., *A Review of Ada Tasking*, LNCS, Vol. 262, 1987.
4. Cmelik, R.F., Gehani, N.H., Roome W.D., *Fault Tolerant Concurrent C: A Tool for Writing Fault Tolerant Distributed Programs*, FTCS-18, 1988, 56–61.
5. Cornhill, D.T., Rakesh, J., Kamrad II, J.M., *Ada Program Partitioning Language: A Notation for Distributing Ada Programs*, IEEE Trans. Software Eng., Vol. 15, No. 3, 1989, 271–280.
6. DoD *Reference Manual for the Ada Programming Language*, ANSI/MIL-STD-1815A, 1983.
7. DIN, *Programmiersprache PEARL*. DIN 66253, Beuth-Verlag, Berlin, Köln, 1980.
8. DIN, *Informationsverarbeitung – Programmiersprache PEARL – Mehrrechner-PEARL*, DIN 66253, Teil 3, Entwurf, Beuth-Verlag, Berlin, Köln, 1987.
9. Fantechi, A., Inverardi, P., Lijtmaer, N., *Using High Level Languages for Local Computer Network Communication: A Case Study in Ada*, Software-Practice and Experience, Vol. 16, No. 8, 1986, 701–717.
10. Halang, W.A., Mangold, K., *Real-Time Programming Languages*, in M. Schiebe, S. Pferrer (eds.): *Real-Time Systems Engineering and Applications*, Kluwer Academic Publishers, Boston, 1992, 141–200.
11. Herrtwich, R.G., Hommel, G., *Kooperation und Konkurrenz*, Springer-Verlag, Berlin, 1989.
12. Hommel, G., *Language Constructs for Distributed Programs*, in M. Paul, H.J. Siegert (eds.): *Distributed Systems – Methods and Tools for Specification*, LNCS, Vol. 190, 1985, 287–341.
13. Ichbiah, J.D., Barnes, J.G.P., Heliard, J.C., Krieg-Brueckner, B., Roubine, O., Wichmann, B.A., *Rationale for the Design of the Ada Programming Language*, ACM SIGPLAN Notices, Vol. 14, No. 6, Part B, 1979.
14. Knight, J.C., Urquhart, I.A., *On the Implementation and Use of Ada on Fault-Tolerant Distributed Systems*, IEEE Trans. Software Eng., Vol. 13, No. 5, 1987, 553–562.
15. Kramer, J., Magee, J., *Dynamic Configuration for Distributed Systems*, IEEE Trans. on Software Eng., Vol. 11, No. 4, 1985, 424–436.

16. Liskov, B., Scheifler, R., *Guardians and Actions: Linguistic Support for Robust Distributed Programs*, ACM TOPLAS, Vol. 5, No. 3, 1983, 381–404.

17. Magee, J., Kramer, J., Sloman, M., *Constructing Distributed Systems in Conic*, IEEE Trans. on Software Eng., Vol. 15, No. 6, 1989, 663–675.

18. Müller, P., Hommel G., *GranAda: A Programming Environment for Implementing Distributed Real-Time Applications*, Proc. 1992 Int. Symp. on Artificial Intelligence in Real-Time Control (to appear).

19. Schlichting, R.D., Schneider, F.B., *Fail-stop processors: An approach to designing fault-tolerant computing systems*, ACM TOCS, Vol. 1, 1983, 222–238.

20. Schlichting, R.D., Purdin, T.D.M., *Failure Handling in Distributed Programming Languages*, SRDSDS-5, 1986, 59–66.

21. Sha, L., Goodenough, J.B., *Real-Time Scheduling Theory and Ada*, IEEE Computer, Vol. 23, No. 4, 1990, 53–62.

22. Steusloff, H., *The Impact of Distributed Computer Control Systems of Software*, Digital Computer Applications to Process Control, Pergamon Press, 1981, 529–536

23. Stoyenko, A.D., *The Evolution and State-of-the-Art of Real-Time Languages*, Journal of Systems and Software, Vol. 4, 1992.

24. Van Scoy, R., Bamberger, J., Firth, R., *An Overview of DARK*, Ada Letters, Vol. 9, No. 7, 1989, 91–101.

25. Volz, R.A., Mudge, T.N., Naylor, A.W., Mayer, J.H., *Some Problems in Distributing Real-Time Ada Programs across Machines*, Ada Letters, Vol. 5, No. 2, 1985, 72–84.

An Overview of Real-Time Database Systems

Ben Kao[1,2] *and Hector Garcia-Molina*[2]

[1] Princeton University
Princeton, NJ 08544
U.S.A.
[2] Stanford University
Stanford, CA 94305
U.S.A.

1 Introduction

Traditionally, real-time systems manage their data (e.g. chamber temperature, aircraft locations) in application dependent structures. As real-time systems evolve, their applications become more complex and require access to more data. It thus becomes necessary to manage the data in a systematic and organized fashion. Database management systems provide tools for such organization, so in recent years there has been interest in "merging" database and real-time technology. The resulting integrated system, which provides database operations with real-time constraints is generally called a real-time database system (RTDBS) [1].

Like a conventional database system, a RTDBS functions as a repository of data, provides efficient storage, and performs retrieval and manipulation of information. However, as a part of a real-time system, whose "tasks" are associated with time constraints, a RTDBS, has the added burden of ensuring some degree of confidence in meeting the system's timing requirements.

Example applications that handle large amounts of data and have stringent timing requirements include telephone switching (e.g. translating an 800 number into an actual number), radar tracking and others. Arbitrage trading, for example, involves trading commodities in different markets at different prices. Since price discrepancies are usually short-lived, automated searching and processing of large amounts of trading information are very desirable. In order to capitalize on the opportunities, buy-sell decisions have to be made promptly, often with a time constraint so that the financial overhead in performing the trade actions are well compensated by the benefit resulting from the trade. As another example, a radar surveillance system detects aircraft "images" or "radar signatures". These images are then matched against a database of known images. The result of such a match is used to drive other system actions, for example, in choosing a combat strategy.

Conventional database systems are not adequate for this type of application. They differ from a RTDBS in many aspects. Most importantly RTDBSs have different performance goals, correctness criteria, and assumptions about the applications. Unlike a conventional database system, whose main objective is to provide fast "average" response time, a RTDBS may be evaluated based on how often transactions miss their deadlines, the average "lateness" or "tardiness" of late transactions, the cost incurred in transactions missing their deadlines, data external consistency (how current the values of data are in reflecting the state of the external world), and data temporal consistency (values of data in the database should be taken from the external world at similar times) [37].

As a real-time system, specifications related to timing constraints are usually supplied by the application designers. For most cases, these timing requirements are expressed as deadlines for transactions. Transactions of this sort, with which explicit time constraints are associated, are termed real-time transactions.

As mentioned above, a RTDBS can be viewed as a value-added database system that supports real-time transactions. A real-time transaction has to be completed by its deadline to be of full benefit to the system. Such guarantees are usually hard to ensure. In case a transaction's deadline is not met, the transaction is called a tardy transaction.

Real-time database systems differ in the way tardy transactions are handled, and this issue is generally referred to as the overload management problem. A tardy transaction may carry positive, zero, or negative residual value to the system. For the positive case, even though the benefit obtained by completing the tardy transaction is usually less than its full fledged value, the system should still complete it, if possible. The system may, however, choose to lower the transaction's priority so that non-tardy transactions are given preferential treatment, for example, in accessing system resources. When a tardy transaction completely loses its value (zero residual value case), it should be dropped to free system resources for the benefit of other transactions. Finally, when a tardy transaction carries negative value, the system may choose to raise the transaction's priority so that it can be completed as soon as possible to diminish the cost incurred due to it tardiness. On the other hand, the system may lower the transaction's priority or even drop it so that other transactions have a better chance of meeting their deadlines. The decision is dependent upon the application semantics. In the extreme case that a system cannot afford having a tardy transaction (e.g. in nuclear power plant control), the system is said to be a hard real-time database system; otherwise, if tardy transactions are tolerated even though they may be undesirable (e.g. arbitrage trading), we say that the system is a soft real-time database system.

It is argued in [38] that with current technology, it is very hard to provide an absolute guarantee on meeting transaction deadlines, and therefore, RTDBSs are mostly limited to soft real-time systems. There are several factors that make it hard for a RTDBS to meet all deadlines. Firstly, the executions of database transactions are usually data and resource dependent. To guarantee satisfaction of transaction deadlines requires enormous excess resource to accommodate for the highest system load. Secondly, full transaction support involves many database protocols which are highly unpredictable in their execution times. Concurrency control protocols, for example, often introduce blocking and restart of transactions over resource contention. Thirdly, disk-based database systems interact heavily with the I/O subsystem. Problems such as disk seek time variation, buffer management and page faults, cause the average case and worst case execution times to differ widely. All these add to the unpredictability of transaction execution.

While difficulties for ensuring transactions meet their deadlines certainly exist, since most RTDBSs are used for highly specialized applications, special techniques may be applied to improve the system's real-time behavior. For example, if the database is small enough to fit into main memory, most of the I/O operations can be eliminated. This in turn, gets rid of the problem of page faults and I/O scheduling. We will discuss main memory database systems later in this chapter.

Also, in some real-time systems, "tasks" or transactions can be preanalyzed. Semantic properties of transactions and data may be known a priori. The knowledge of transaction runtime and resource requirements may lead to more effective scheduling and concurrency control protocols. As an example [30], in a conventional database system the number of constraints is assumed to be large. Checking them individually may be impractical, so instead serializability is used as the correctness criterion. However, "since real-time systems may have a fixed number of processes and the databases are statically structured, it may be feasible to specify a small set of integrity constraints which are most critical for the system's correctness." [30] Specialized protocols may then be designed that allow non-serializable but consistent schedules.

In the rest of this chapter, we will discuss some problems concerning the design of a RTDBS. We will present some solutions as proposed by the research community. We will also examine the various components of a database system and discuss what features should be added to support real-time transactions.

2 Transaction Model

In this section, we look at the attributes of real-time transactions and discuss how they affect transaction design. In particular, we will discuss the issue of deadline assignment, and how semantic information can be used to help meeting the system's timing constraints.

The following types of information about transactions may be available and may be of use in scheduling and concurrency control:

1. Timing constraints — E.g. deadlines.
2. Criticalness — It measures how critical it is that a transaction meets its deadline. Different transactions may have different criticalness. Note that criticalness is a different concept from deadline. A transaction may have a very tight deadline but missing it may not cause great harm to the system.
3. Value function — Related to a transaction's criticalness is its value function. A value function of a transaction measures how valuable it is to complete the transaction at some point in time after the transaction arrives. Some typical value functions are shown in Fig. 1.
4. Resource requirements — This includes the number of I/O operations to be executed, expected CPU usage, etc.

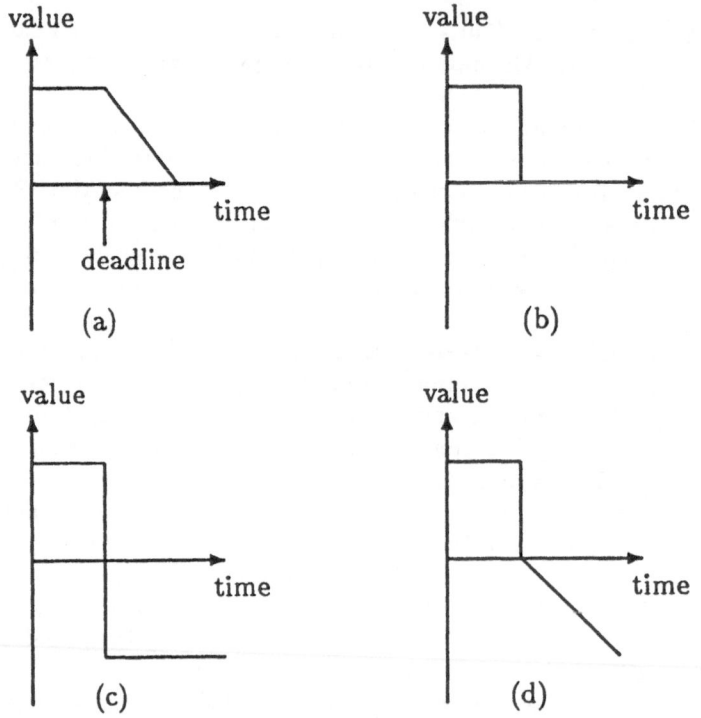

Fig. 1. Example value functions. Tardy transaction has (a) diminishing positive value, (b) zero value, (c) negative value, (d) increasingly negative value.

5. Expected execution time — This is usually hard to predict (see Sect. 3).
6. Data requirements — Read sets and write sets of transactions.
7. Periodicity — If a transaction is periodic, what its period is.
8. Time of occurrence of events — At what point in time will a transaction issue a read/write request?
9. Other semantics — Is the transaction read only? Does it conflict with any other transaction? If so, will they ever be executed at the same time? How up-to-date the data is required by the transaction?

There are many ways that this information can be used to help the design of real-time transactions. We demonstrate its use by the following examples.

One example concerns database consistency. In a conventional database system, as long as transaction atomicity, consistency, isolation and durability (the ACID properties) are enforced, transactions can be executed concurrently to increase throughput without jeopardizing correctness. However, insurance of the ACID properties does not come cheap. Special protocols for concurrency control, transaction commitment, and database recovery have to be exercised. Very often, such protocols hamper the system's real-time performance through blocking, transaction abortion, deadlock, and additional I/O due to logging.

Since full transaction support is costly, it has been suggested [38] that real-time data and transactions be categorized into classes depending on their timing, synchronization, consistency, and atomicity properties. Then using the supplied semantic information, devise special minimal transaction supports that are sufficient for the classes.

Another example use of semantic information as suggested in [12] is to analyze transactions and construct contingency plans for each transaction type. Contingency plans are alternate actions that can be invoked whenever the system determines that it cannot complete a task in time. A contingency plan is usually economical to execute less than the original transaction. It provides useful but not optimal results. A related idea on imprecise computations can be found in [10].

Among the attributes of a real-time transaction, deadline is the most important one. This piece of information is used in many aspects of a RTDBS, be it concurrency control, scheduling, or the use of contingency plans and imprecise computations. Usually the deadline of a transaction is specified by the application designers. However, if the transaction model supports nested transactions or subtransactions, there is the question of how time constraints are assigned to individual subtransactions based on the parent transaction's deadline.

To illustrate this problem, let's consider a transaction T with deadline d. Further assume that T consists of two subtransactions T_1 and T_2 to be executed in order. Since T_2 is executed last, its deadline should be d, the deadline of its parent transaction. But what about T_1's deadline? If we set it to be d minus the expected execution time of T_2, T_2 is left with no slack[3] and the system runs the risk of missing T's deadline. A probably better but more complicated solution is to assign a tighter deadline to T_1. If T_1 misses it, its deadline is incremented gradually until it is completed. A problem with this scheme is that transactions with "soft" but tight deadlines (e.g. T_1) will interfere with the execution of others that have "harder" deadlines (e.g. T_2).

So far we have assumed that real-time constraints are specified on the transactions. Korth et. al. [26] propose a different model with which deadlines are associated with consistency constraints. In addition to transactions that maintain correct database states, in their model, transactions may be invoked to record the effects of some external event that is generated outside the system (e.g. sensor reading). The ensuing change in the database state may render a consistency constraint invalid (e.g. room temperature $< x°F$), and that constraint may need to be restored within a specific deadline (e.g. the room temperature has to be raised within 30 seconds). Once an inconsistency is detected, a "patch-up" transaction is invoked to attempt to correct the violation. The patch-up transaction, however, may cause other consistency constraints to be violated. This leads to a possible chain of transaction triggering.

In [26], three types of transactions, which have *different atomicity and consistency requirements*, are considered:

---

[3] The slack time of a transaction is the amount of time that the transaction can be delayed in its execution but still be able to meet its deadline. We will have a more precise definition of slack time later in this chapter.

1. External-input transactions: These transactions are executed to record relevant events that occur in the external world into the database. They are often simple, write-only transactions with short duration. In order to keep the database externally consistent, external-input transactions should be able to execute promptly without waiting or blocking. They may cause a consistency violation.

2. Internal transactions: These transactions are similar to standard database transactions. They are also invoked to restore consistency of the database. Their execution could be of long-duration.

3. External-output transactions: These transactions cause actions to be performed in the external world. Just like the external-input transactions, they are often of short-duration.

Their approach to consistency restoration works as follows: First of all, by analyzing the underlying real-time system, a predicate-priority graph (PPG) is constructed. A PPG is a bipartite graph consisting of two kinds of nodes representing transactions and consistency constraints. An edge emerging from a transaction node, T_1, to a constraint node, C_1, means that the execution of T_1 may cause C_1 to be violated. The fanout of a transaction node may be larger than one, meaning that a transaction can potentially violate several consistency constraints. An edge from a constraint node, C_2, to a transaction node T_2 symbolizes that by executing T_2, C_2 will be restored. Again, a constraint node may have multiple outgoing links. In that case, *any one* of the transaction nodes that are pointed to by a constraint node is capable of restoring the constraint. A choice is thus possible in selecting a "patch-up" transaction.

Now, when a constraint is violated, a "patch-up" plan is constructed by analyzing the PPG. A "patch-up" plan is represented by an inconsistency-resolution subgraph (IRS) of the PPG, which provides a strategy for resolving any inconsistencies. Intuitively, an IRS gives a partial ordering of transaction execution so that consistency constraints are restored.

Since a constraint violation may be fixed by more than one internal transaction, there may be more than one IRS choice for restoring an inconsistency. Korth's paper suggests several strategies for selecting an IRS. For example, choose an IRS such that:

1. the total execution time of the transactions involved is minimum.

2. the IRS involves the least number of transactions.

3. the IRS violates the least number of consistency constraints.

4. the slack time for restoring consistencies is maximum.

These strategies are engineered towards different system performance metrics. Complexities of problems related to the implementation of these strategies are also studied in [26]. Some of these problems are found to be NP-hard.

3 Transaction Scheduling

A major part of real-time system research concerns scheduling of jobs (of which transactions are one kind) in a multiprogramming environment. Following Liu and Layland's paper [31], numerous others have been published on the subject. Among these is a series of work done by Lehoczky, Sha et. al. [27] [28] [29]. For a survey on scheduling algorithms in a hard real-time environment readers are referred to [9].

Much of the work done on real-time job scheduling focuses mainly on CPU scheduling. Transaction scheduling, however, involves not only the CPU. In fact, due to the extensive data processing requirements of a database system, resources such as data, I/O, and memory are also subjects to severe competition among concurrently running transactions. Careful scheduling on the use of these resources are very important to the performance of RTDBSs.

In this section, we discuss some general issues of transaction scheduling. Since most of the real-time scheduling protocols revolve around the use of priority, we will discuss how priority is assigned to transactions. We also discuss CPU scheduling and its database related problems. Algorithms for scheduling other system resources such as data, I/O, and memory will be discussed in the following sections on concurrency control, I/O scheduling, and buffer management respectively.

As a major asset of a computer system, efficient use of CPU cycles is very important.

Conventional scheduling algorithms [33], as employed by most of the existing operating systems, aim at balancing the number of CPU-bound and I/O-bound jobs to maximize system utilization and throughput. They are also designed to treat processes fairly, each one gets its fair share of the system resource. Other performance criteria include small job turnaround time, small waiting time, and fast response time. However elaborated, these algorithms are not adequate for real-time transaction scheduling. This is because in a RTDBS, transactions should be scheduled according to their criticalness and the tightness of their deadlines, even if this means sacrificing fairness and system throughput.

Real-time scheduling algorithms should therefore be based on the "inequalities" of transactions. They should give preferential treatment to transactions which are very critical and with stringent timing constraints.

A popular method is to assign a numeric priority to each transaction which reflects their relative urgency. Transaction with higher priority is given an upper hand in gaining access to system resource.

A transaction has many attributes that may affect its priority. Below is a list of those attributes that are most relevant to a RTDBS. The parenthesized variables next to each attribute represents the individual quantitative measure of each concept.

1. Criticalness (γ) — the more critical a transaction is, the higher is its priority.
2. Deadline (d) — the earlier its deadline, the higher is the transaction's priority.

3. Amount of unfinished work (l) — a transaction with less amount of unfinished work may be given a higher priority than a transaction with a large amount of unfinished work. In the extreme case when a transaction has begun its commit phase[4], its priority could be raised to a higher value. This enables a committing transaction, which requires minimal computation, to finish fast. Resources held by the committing transaction can thus be released sooner to reduce blocking of other transactions [19].

4. Amount of computation already invested (c) — a transaction that already has a large amount of computation done may be given a higher priority. Preempting a transaction in a database system requires not only the release of resource but also careful rollback of the transaction. It is sometimes easier and less wasteful of system resource to rollback a transaction that has only run for a short time.

5. Age (a) — a transaction that arrived early should be given a higher priority than those that arrived late. This scheme reduces turnaround time and helps keep data externally consistent.

6. Slackness (s) — slackness measures how long a transaction's execution can be delayed while still making it possible to meet the transaction's deadline. If we denote the arrival time of a transaction by t_a, then slackness can be expressed as:

$$s = d - t_a - c - l.$$

The tighter the slackness of a transaction is, the higher should be its priority.

It is generally hard to capture the idea of urgency by only one of the items discussed above. Consequently, it is suggested in [38] that a combination be used to compute a priority value function ($pr()$). In particular, the following formula is suggested as an example:

$$pr(T) = \gamma(w_1 a - w_2 d + w_3 c - w_4 l)$$

where the $w_i's$ are weights reflecting the relative importance of the various factors.

We note that when priority computation is based on the amount of unfinished work and slackness, a good prediction of transaction execution time is needed. We have discussed in Section 1 the factors which make a precise prediction hard to achieve.

As an attempt, we can generally decompose the execution time (t_{exec}) into three components as follows [6]:

$$t_{exec} = t_{fault} + t_{db} + t_{nondb}$$

where t_{fault}, t_{db}, and t_{nondb}[5] denote the times spent in page fault, data-processing operations, and non-data-processing operations respectively. We look at these

---

[4] A transaction is in its commit phase after it finishes all the computation. Any data it updates are being written to disk in this phase.

[5] This notation is adapted from [6].

terms one by one.

The term t_{fault} represents the amount of time spent in paging data from disk to memory. For periodic transactions, if data prefetching is possible, a memory resident database can be assumed. This removes any uncertainty on t_{fault} by essentially setting it to zero. Otherwise, t_{fault} includes all the time for I/O operations. Due to the wide gap between memory access time and disk access time, in a disk-based database, the use of a deterministic worst-case bound on t_{fault} is too pessimistic. A probabilistic model on estimating t_{fault} may be more effective in this case. Scheduling algorithms which are based on execution time prediction, therefore, have to take into account the fact that the estimates are not precise.

The variable t_{nondb} measures the execution time of non-database related operations while t_{db} measures database related ones. It is generally harder to estimate t_{db} than t_{nondb}. The reason being that the amount of data processing usually depends on the state of the database itself. It is suggested that metadata be kept describing the size of each object class [6]. Execution time on data processing is then estimated dynamically with the help of these metadata.

Before we end this section, we briefly discuss various scheduler properties and compare their relative merits with respect to RTDBSs. These properties include on-line vs. off-line, conflict-avoidance vs. conflict-resolving, and preemptive resume schedulings.

Due to the unpredictable job arrival pattern, conventional scheduling algorithms are usually on-line. That is, the order of transaction execution is not pre-computed. However, in RTDBS, if information about the transactions' data access patterns, periodicities, deadlines etc. is available, transaction preanalysis should be carried out off-line [6]. Transaction execution order is thus scheduled before transactions arrive. Since off-line schedulers are given more information, and sooner, they are more flexible and usually produce better schedules.

When there are concurrently running tasks in a system, there are potential conflicts on resource access. These resources include data, I/O, memory and others. When given a job, a conflict-avoidance scheduler detects and resolves conflicts among jobs over resources before the job is released for execution [6]. For conflict-avoidance be applicable, all resource requirements must be known in advance. A conflict-resolving scheduler, on the other hand, handles conflicts when they actually occur. A conflict-resolution protocol, for example, may decide that a resource requester aborts a resource holder, if it is determined that the requester has a higher priority over the resource. The penalty of using a run-time conflict resolution strategy is the uncertainty it introduces in transaction execution time [6].

Finally, we note that preemptive resume CPU scheduling may not be suitable for database systems [8]. Under this scheme, a high priority transaction preempts a low priority one for CPU. The low priority transaction is not aborted and does not relinquish any lock held. It simply sleeps and then resumes processing when the high priority transaction completes. If the low priority transaction is holding lock on a hot item, a convoy of waiting transactions will be formed due to the extended period of locking. This convoy, once formed, tends to persist for a long time [5]. The convoy phenomenon causes long waits for locks and should be avoided in a real-time system. A solution based on priority-based round-robin CPU scheduling is suggested in [8], where the length of a CPU slice is determined by the priority of a transaction.

4 Concurrency Control

Concurrency control refers to the control of interaction among concurrent transactions in such a way that database consistency is not destroyed [25]. Transactions interact with each other mainly through reads and writes of data items. Careful access control on data therefore needs to be exercised. A good deal of work has been done on this subject for conventional databases (see, for example, [32]). The purpose of this section is to discuss the properties of concurrency control protocols that are pertinent to RTDBSs.

Serializability is the most popular correctness criterion in concurrency control. A sequence of database operations is considered serializable if its effect is *equivalent* to a serial transaction schedule. This condition, however, often limits the degree of multiprogramming, and introduces blockings and restarts of transactions.

An argument which supports sacrificing serializability to improve performance in a RTDBS is that data are often short-lived in some real-time applications [36]. The claim is that any inconsistency introduced by concurrent transactions does not spread too much over the database. Since the content of the database does not get corrupted badly, techniques like compensating transactions as discussed in Sect. 2 may be useful.

However, depending on the application semantics, serializability may be a better choice for maintaining database consistency. In this case, the prevalent approaches to concurrency control are lock-based protocols and optimistic concurrency control protocols.

Two phase locking (2PL) is the most common locking protocol in conventional database systems. With 2PL, a transaction execution consists of two phases. In the first phase, locks are acquired but may not be released. In the second phase, locks are released but new locks may not be acquired. In case a transaction T_R requests a lock that is being held by another transaction T_H, T_R waits.

Conventional locking protocols, like 2PL, are unsatisfactory for RTDBSs. The two main problems encountered are the possibility of priority inversion and deadlock. Let's take a look at the problem of priority inversion first.

Consider the example given above which involves a lock requester T_R and a lock holder T_H. If the priority of T_R is higher than the priority of T_H, then a high priority transaction waits for a low priority one to finish. We call this phenomenon *priority inversion* [2], [4], [34], [22].

Priority inversion is very undesirable in a RTDBs because a high priority transaction is blocked by a low priority one. Since the low priority transaction is discriminated against in its use of system resources, the blocked high priority transaction is essentially running at an effective priority equal to that of the low priority transaction. This renders the real-time scheduling algorithms ineffective.

One solution to this problem is to hoist the priority of the lock holder to that of the requester. Referring to our earlier example, T_H will be executed at an elevated priority equal to $pr(T_R)$. This priority lift truly reflects the urgency of completing T_H, whose progress means progress of T_R. We call this strategy *Wait Promote* [34].

> Wait Promote:
> IF $pr(T_R) > pr(T_H)$ THEN
> $\quad$ T_R waits;
> $\quad$ T_H inherits the priority of T_R;
> ELSE
> $\quad$ T_R waits;
> ENDIF

We note that the property of priority inheritance, as exhibited by the Wait Promote strategy, should be transitive. It means that if T_H is itself blocked by some other transaction X, then we should set $pr(X) = \max \{pr(X), pr(T_R)\}$. Also, if a lock holder is blocking more than one lock requester, the priority of the lock holder should be set to the maximum of the requester's priorities.

The problem with Wait Promote is that we still let a low priority transaction block a high priority transaction. If aborting a transaction is not too expensive, we may choose to abort the low priority lock holder and let the high priority lock requester proceed. This strategy is called *High Priority* [2].

> High Priority:
> IF $pr(T_R) > pr(T_H)$ THEN
> $\quad$ T_R aborts T_H;
> ELSE
> $\quad$ T_R waits;
> ENDIF

The use of High Priority eliminates the problem of priority inversion. However, a problem arises if the priority function chosen (e.g. least slack) is such that a restarted transaction may have a higher priority than its previous incarnation. In such cases, when the restarted transaction tries to acquire locks, it may abort the transaction that killed it before because the restarted transaction is now running at a higher priority. This leads to the problem of cyclic restart.

To avoid this problem, before a lock requester T_R aborts a lock holder T_H, the scheduler should make sure that the next incarnation of T_H, T_H^A, also has a lower priority than T_R. This modified *High Priority* algorithm *without cyclic restart* is shown below [2]:

> High Priority without Cyclic Restart:
> IF $pr(T_R) > pr(T_H)$ AND $pr(T_R) > pr(T_H^A)$ THEN
> $\quad$ T_R aborts T_H;

> **ELSE**
> T_R waits;
> **ENDIF**

The High Priority strategy, although simple, may abort transactions too liber-
ally. This wastes system resources and results in lower throughput, and should
be avoided unless it is necessary. For our example, if it is estimated that the slack
time of T_R is longer than the remaining running time of T_H, then T_H may be
allowed to finish without missing T_R's deadline. In that case, T_H is not aborted
to save system resources. This strategy, called *Conditional Restart* [2], is shown
below:

> Conditional Restart:
> E_H := estimated remaining running time of T_H;
> S_R := estimated slack time of T_R;
> **IF** $pr(T_R) > pr(T_H)$ **AND** $pr(T_R) > pr(T_H^A)$ **THEN**
>   **IF** $S_R \geq E_H$ **THEN**
> T_R waits;
> T_H inherits the priority of T_R;
>   **ELSE**
>   aborts T_H;
>   **ENDIF**
> **ELSE**
> T_R waits;
> **ENDIF**

There are two complications of Conditional Restart. First, if there is a non-trivial
probability that the chain of blocked transactions involves more than one transaction, the strategy needs to be modified. For example, if T_H is itself blocked
by a transaction X, then instead of comparing E_H and S_R, we ought to compare
the sum of the expected execution times of H and X with S_R instead. Second,
estimations of E_H and S_R have to be available.

The above discussion shows that no single strategy excels. The choice is dependent upon the applications, the availability of resources, and the cost of
transaction restart.

As mentioned earlier, the second problem of locking protocols is the possibility
of deadlock. Whenever a set of transactions get involved in a circular wait, a
deadlock occurs [33]. In such a situation, a transaction involved in the deadlock
is chosen to be aborted. This victim transaction should be picked such that
the largest number of remaining transactions can meet their deadlines. Example
strategies for choosing a victim in deadlock resolution include [19]:

1. Abort a transaction that already passed its deadline.
2. Abort a transaction with the longest deadline.
3. Abort a transaction that is least critical.

Finally, empirical studies have shown that when deadlock occurs, it usually involves only two transactions [13]. There are thus not many choices for a victim. Hence, it may not be wise to use a sophisticated but expensive deadlock breaking protocol.

Most commercially available database systems use lock-based concurrency control protocols. Optimistic concurrency control, however, has the advantages of being non-blocking and deadlock free. These properties are very desirable for a real-time system. We devote the rest of this section to a discussion of optimistic concurrency control as applied to RTDBSs [18], [21], [35].

With optimistic concurrency control, the execution of a transaction can generally be divided into three phases:

(1) Read phase,
(2) validation phase, and
(3) write phase.

During the read phase, data items are read into memory. Computations based on the values of these data items are performed. New values are computed, but are not written into the database until the write phase. In general, if the concurrency control scheduler has decided that a transaction T_i be serialized before a transaction T_j, the following conditions have to be satisfied [21]:

1. R/W rule. Data items to be written by T_i should not have already been read by T_j.
2. W/W rule. T_i's writes should not overwrite T_j's writes.

When a transaction finishes its computation, it enters its validation phase in which the R/W and W/W rules are tested. If any one of the rules is violated, conflict resolution, which usually involves aborting one or more transactions, is invoked. One scheme for validating the rules is to check if any one of the following conditions hold:

1. T_i completes its execution before T_j started (no interleaving).
2. The write set of T_i does not intersect with the read set of T_j (thus enforcing the R/W rule), and T_i completes its write phase before T_j starts its validation phase (this enforces the W/W rule).

Readers are referred to [25] for details on this validation scheme.
When validation fails, a conflict resolution scheme is invoked. Several schemes are suggested in [21]. We quote three examples here:

1. Broadcasting Commit. Always let the validating transaction commit and abort all the conflicting transactions. This strategy guarantees that as long as a transaction reaches its validation phase, it will always finish.
2. Abort the validating transaction only if its priority is less than that of all the conflicting transactions.

3. If the priority of the validating transaction is not the highest among the conflicting transactions, wait for the conflicting transactions with higher priority to complete.

Simulation experiments have been carried out in [17] comparing 2PL with High Priority and optimistic concurrency control with Broadcasting Commit. Their results show that under an overload management policy of discarding tardy transaction, optimistic concurrency control can outperform 2PL. An independent study by Huang and Stankovic [21] also compares an optimistic concurrency control algorithm (OCCL_SVW) with 2PL. Their results show that the performance difference between OCCL_SVW and 2PL is sensitive to the amount of data contention, but not to the amount of I/O resource contention. In particular, the optimistic concurrency control protocol performs better than 2PL when data contention is low; otherwise, 2PL has a better performance.

5 I/O Scheduling

In a disk-based database system, disk I/O occupies a major portion of transaction execution time. As with CPU scheduling, disk scheduling algorithms that take into account timing constraints can significantly improve the real-time performance. CPU scheduling algorithms, like Earliest Deadline First and Highest Priority First, are attractive candidates but have to be modified before they can be applied to I/O scheduling. The main reason is that disk seek time, which accounts for a very significant fraction of disk access latency, depends on the disk head movement. The order in which I/O requests are serviced, therefore, has an immense impact on the response time and throughput of the I/O subsystem. To illustrate, let's consider the following example as shown in Fig. 2.

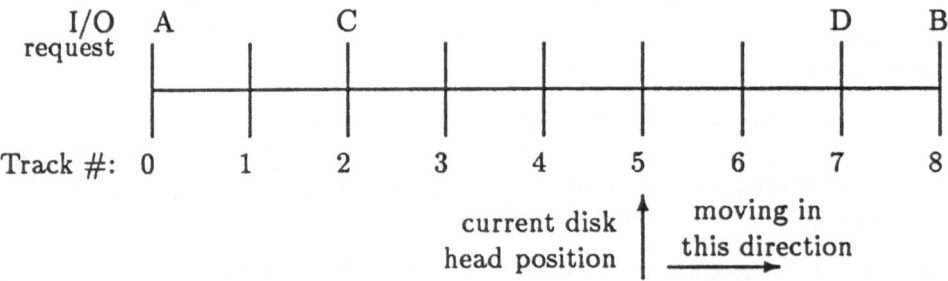

Fig. 2. Disk scheduling example.

Suppose we have four requests A, B, C and D in the I/O queue with their priorities in the following order:

$$pr(A) > pr(B) > pr(C) > pr(D).$$

The position of the data needed by each request is shown in Fig. 2. If Highest Priority First (HPF) scheduling is employed, the servicing order would be:

$$\text{HPF:} \quad A, B, C, D.$$

We note that in this case, the head sweeps the disk back and forth four times, or 32 tracks. Considering that the requests can be satisfied in only 11 track movement (in the order of D, B, C, A), apparently HPF is not a very smart way of scheduling the disk head if response time or throughput is a concern.

Algorithms for shortening disk head movement have been devised [39]. The Elevator Algorithm, for example, moves the head from one end of the disk to the other and then back, servicing whatever requests are on its way, and changing direction whenever there are no more requests ahead in its direction. Referring to the example in Fig. 2, the Elevator Algorithm will produce the following servicing schedule:

$$\text{Elevator:} \quad D, B, C, A$$

which takes three times less disk head movement than Highest Priority First does.

The problem with the Elevator Algorithm, as applied to real-time systems, is that the priority of requests is not considered. In our example, the highest priority request A is serviced last. There is thus a trade-off between maximizing throughput and meeting system's timing constraints. Methods that combine the properties of HPF and the Elevator Algorithm are very desirable. In what follows, we describe two middle-ground I/O scheduling algorithms: one that puts the Elevator concept on Highest Priority First scheduling, and another which adds the flavor of HPF to the Elevator Algorithm.

When Highest Priority First scheduling is used, the disk head may pass through tracks for which there are other low priority requests. The Elevator principle says "do pick them up because the disk head is already there!" In [3], [4], Abbott presents the FD-SCAN[6] algorithm. Simply stated, FD-SCAN follows HPF in always "targetting" the disk head towards the track with the highest priority request, but also services whatever requests are on its way. Consider the earlier example, the servicing order under FD-SCAN would be:

$$\text{FD-SCAN:} \quad C, A, D, B.$$

We note that in this example, the disk head moves a similar distance as the Elevator Algorithm but the highest priority request A is served sooner.

In Abbott's studies, FD-SCAN is tested against other disk scheduling algorithms including First Come First Served, the Elevator Algorithm, Shortest Seek Time

---

[6] In [3] and [4], deadline is used as a priority measure. FD-SCAN stands for "Feasible Deadline SCAN." Any request whose deadline is determined to be impossible to meet is discarded.

First, and Earliest Deadline First. Simulation results show that FD-SCAN performs best among the algorithms tested in terms of the ability to meet deadlines. This property is most prominent when the load of the I/O subsystem is high. Also, this advantage of FD-SCAN is persistent through a wide range of system parameter settings.

In [8], the problem of long seek time for the Highest Priority First scheduling is addressed. It is argued that the use of fine grain priority gives the HPF scheduler a FCFS-like average seek time (with possibly even worse response time). Their idea (which we will call the Highest Priority Group First (HPGF)) is to blur the boundaries of priority. Disk requests are grouped into a small number of priority levels even though the transactions issuing the I/O requests may have distinct priorities in other parts of the system. Once these groups are formed, the disk is scheduled to service the highest priority group first. In case there is more than one request in the highest priority group, the Elevator Algorithm is used for the intra-group scheduling. Referring to our example, if requests A and B are in a high priority group, and requests C and D are in a low priority group, the service order under HPGF would be:

$$\text{HPGF:} \qquad B, \ A, \ C, \ D.$$

We note that in the example, the disk movement is much less than what HPF would require, while the higher priority requests are served before the lower priority ones.

Through a series of experimental studies [8], it is found that HPGF performs better than the Elevator Algorithm in meeting deadlines. This benefit is achieved at a cost of a prolonged *average* response time. However, the study shows that the response time degradation mainly affects low priority requests. High priority requests, on the other hand, experience response times which are very close to what the Elevator Algorithm provides.

6 Buffer Management and Memory Resident Database

In the last three sections, we have discussed various issues concerning access to CPU, data, and disk I/O in a real-time database system. In this section, we turn our attention to yet another system resource — main memory. We will discuss how memory is managed and how it can be used efficiently to improve the performance of RTDBSs.

This section is divided into two parts. The dividing issue is whether memory space is tight or plentiful. If a real-time system has only limited amount of memory, *buffer management*, which concerns the allocation of memory space among concurrent transactions, has to be specially designed. The goal here is to ensure that the execution of high priority transactions is not hindered by the lack of memory. On the other hand, if memory is plentiful, much of the data can reside in main store[7] forming what is called a *memory resident database system*

---

[7] We use the word "store" as a synonym of "memory".

(MRDBS). An MRDBS has many features, such as fast and predictable access time, which make it particularly suitable for real-time applications.

6.1 Buffer Management

The availability of memory affects transaction response time in two ways. First, before a transaction starts its execution, buffers (memory pages) have to be allocated to the transaction. These buffers are used to store the execution code, copies of files and data paged in from disk, and any temporary objects produced. Depending on the transaction, a certain number of buffers have to be allocated in order to prevent the transaction from *thrashing*[8]. When memory is running low, a transaction may be blocked from execution. The amount of memory available in a system thus limits the number of concurrently executable transactions. Second, some applications, such as image processing, have high demands on memory. Their executions will be significantly slowed down if memory is tight and frequent memory swapping is done.

The job of a buffer manager is to allocate memory buffers to transactions intelligently such that high priority transactions enjoy shorter response times. A buffer manager is usually specified in terms of its admission policy and buffer replacement policy. We briefly explain each policy in turn below. We will also give examples on how transaction priorities are used to improve the manager's real-time behavior [20].

When a transaction T is issued, the buffer manager will decide whether to admit it for execution. This decision is called the transaction admission policy. We assume that transactions be able to supply the buffer manager with the number of buffers it needs for proper execution. If enough free space is available, transaction T is admitted. Otherwise, T is blocked or else a number of running transactions can be suspended[9] and their buffers reallocated to transaction T. For the latter case, the decision of which transactions to suspend can be determined by their priorities. A simple solution would be to suspend transactions with the lowest priorities until either:

1. enough number of buffers have been freed up for T to execute, or
2. there are no more unsuspended transactions with priority less than that of T.

In the first case, the freed-up buffers are allocated to T and T is admitted. For the second case, T is blocked due to a lack of memory.

When a transaction references a data item which is not already in memory, a free buffer has to be allocated to page in the data. If no more free buffers are available, some buffer has to be flushed out to disk (if it was dirty) and its content replaced by the needed data. The choice of a buffer for replacement is called

---

[8] In our context, thrashing refers to the phenomenon in which a transaction spends most of its time swapping data to and from disk [33].

[9] A suspended transaction is swapped out to disk and its execution is halted.

the buffer replacement policy.

Traditional replacement policies include Least Recently Used (LRU), Least Frequently Used etc. [33]. In [8], a new policy, Priority-LRU, is proposed which considers transaction priority as well as buffer recency. This algorithm groups transactions into m priority classes. All buffers which are being used by some transaction in the ith class is put into a list L_i and are said to be of priority i. The buffer pool is thus organized into m lists: $L_1, L_2, \ldots, L_m$ according to buffer priority. The Priority-LRU algorithm can be succinctly described by the following pseudo code:

```
Priority-LRU(W_R):
S := φ;
(* put the least recently used buffer of each list into S *)
FOR i := 1 TO m DO
      x := least recently used buffer in L_i;
      S := S ∪ {x};
END FOR
(* pick the lowest priority buffer in S that is not one of the W_R
   most recently used buffers *)
WHILE S ≠ φ DO
      x := lowest priority buffer in S;
      (* test if x has been referenced recently *)
      IF x is one of the W_R most recently accessed buffers THEN
         S := S - {x};
      ELSE
         RETURN(x);
      ENDIF
END WHILE
RETURN(no suitable page);
```

The Priority-LRU algorithm takes one parameter, W_R, which controls the relative importance of recency and priority. For example, when W_R is set to zero, the least recently used buffer in the lowest priority group is chosen. A low priority buffer is always chosen in favor of higher priority ones. Conversely, if W_R is set high, then low priority buffers will get a break if they are referenced recently enough.

6.2 Memory Resident Database System

As discussed in Sects. 1 and 3, one of the major difficulties encountered in designing a RTDBS is the long and often unpredictable disk access delays. As the price of memory continues to drop, one possible remedy is to put data directly into memory, thus eliminating I/O accesses. In this subsection, we give a brief account on memory resident database system design. Interested readers are referred to [7], [14], [15], [16], and [36] for further reading.

Compared to disk, main memory access time is much faster (1000–10000 times), and is more predictable (no disk seek). These features are very desirable in RTDBSs, and may even be necessary if transactions have extremely tight time constraints.

However, putting all the data in memory is not without its disadvantages. Above all, an MRDBS is more costly than a disk-based system. Even though technology for high density memory chips is improving and the cost dropping, currently there is still a limit on how much data can be memory resident. For large databases, storing data in main memory has to be done selectively. In a real-time environment, if transaction data requirement is relatively stable and known, data items that are referenced by high priority transactions should have preference over low priority ones in claiming memory residency.

Another problem with main memory is its volatility. Data stored in main memory usually do not survive through a power failure, nor a CPU failure. An MRDBS, therefore, still requires disks to provide a stable backup storage. Conventional recovery protocols that load the entire database to memory from the disk backup copy, and then apply the transaction log to bring the database up-to-date may be too slow for real-time applications. Mechanisms which allow quick restart and the database to function (partially) during recovery have to be employed [23]. For example, in [14], a recovery technique for MRDBS is proposed. Their method assumes that a small part of main memory is made stable by separate battery backup. This stable memory is used to store log records of "pre-committed" transactions. Schemes for check-pointing the database and compressing the transaction log for fast restart are also discussed.

A third MRDBS issue is that their design goals are different from a conventional disk-based system. Data structure and query processing algorithms for traditional database systems are optimized to reduce the number of disk accesses and to enhance data clustering [25], [41]. These goals are no longer valid[10] in an MRDBS. When data are memory resident, query optimization and data structure should be designed to minimize CPU processing time and the amount of memory space used. Conventional access methods and database structures have to be revised. A B-tree [11], for example, is found to be less efficient than hashing for MRDBS index search. This is due to the additional space a B-tree needs to store all the keys and pointers [7]. The sort-merge join algorithm [24], which was designed to reduce the number of disk I/O, is also found to be inferior in performance than the hash-merge algorithm when memory is plentiful [7].

Finally, small data access time also affects the choice of a concurrency control mechanism [36]. Without I/O delay, transaction execution time will be small in an MRDBS. Blocking delays due to data locking will also be reduced. We can thus afford to have a coarser granularity for data lock to reduce memory and processor overhead. Moreover, since memory is an important asset, optimistic

---

[10] Clustering may still improve data access time in an MRDBS by putting data that are often referenced together in the same "cache line". This increases the cache hit probability. The impact is, however, not as dramatic as data clustering on disk.

concurrency controls that create temporary data objects, and those which store multiple versions of data, may not be attractive in an MRDBS [36].

7 Conclusion

In this chapter, we have discussed the various issues concerning the design and implementation of real-time databases and transaction processing. We distinguished a RTDBS from a database system and a real-time system by its more demanding goals. We also looked at application semantics and showed how they can be used to improve RTDBSs performance. CPU, data, I/O, and memory scheduling were also discussed. Furthermore, some desirable features of memory resident databases as applied to a real-time environment were also mentioned. Due to space limitation, some other aspects of RTDBS which deserve special attention are not covered by this chapter. These topics include fast and incremental recovery protocols [23], database architectures that support predictable transaction execution, programming languages that provide constructs for timing specifications [40], query processing and optimization techniques that are based on real-time performance goals, scheduling methods that improve data external and temporal consistency [37] and distributed real-time databases [30]. Finally, we note that appropriate deadline assignment to subtransactions is very crucial to the success of many real-time database protocols. Relatively little work has been done on this subject. As real-time databases evolve, however, we expect to see more work on this, and many other RTDBS problems.

References

1. R. Abbott, H. Garcia-Molina, *What is a Real-Time Database System?*, Abstracts of the Fourth Workshop on Real-Time Operating systems, IEEE, July 1987, 134–138.
2. R. Abbott, H. Garcia-Molina, *Scheduling Real-Time Transactions: A Performance Evaluation*, Proceedings of the 14th VLDB Conference, August 1988, 1–12.
3. R. Abbott, H. Garcia-Molina, *Scheduling I/O Requests with Deadlines: A Performance Evaluation*, IEEE Real-Time System Symposium, Dec. 1990, 113–124.
4. R. Abbott, *Scheduling Real-Time Transactions: A Performance Evaluation.* Ph.D. Dissertation, Princeton University, 1991.
5. M. Blasgen, J. Gray, M. Mitoma, T. Price, *The Convoy Phenomenon*, Operating Systems Review, Vol. 13, No. 2, 1979, 20–25.
6. A. P. Buchmann, D. R. McCarthy, M. Hsu, U. Dayal, *Time-Critical Database Scheduling: A Framework for Integrating Real-Time Scheduling and Concurrency Control*, IEEE, 1989.
7. M. J. Carey, T. J. Lehman, *Query Processing in Main Memory Database Management Systems*, Proceedings of ACM SIGMOD, 1986, 239–250.
8. M. J. Carey, R. Jauhari, M. Livny, *Priority in DBMS Resource Scheduling*, Proceedings of the 15th VLDB conference, 1989, 397–410.

9. S. C. Cheng, J. A. Stankovic, K. Ramamritham, *Scheduling Algorithms for Hard Real-Time Systems — A Brief Survey*. Hard Real-Time Systems, IEEE, 1988, 150–173.

10. J. Chung, J. Liu, W. Shih, *Fast Algorithms for Scheduling Imprecise Computations*, IEEE Real-Time System Symposium, December 1989, 12–19.

11. D. Comer, *The Ubiquitous B-Tree*, ACM Computing Surveys. Vol. 11, No. 2, June 1979.

12. U. Dayal et. al., *The HiPAC Project: Combining Active Databases and Timing Constraints*, SIGMOD Record, Vol. 17, No. 1, March 1988, 51–70.

13. C. Devor, C. R. Carlson, *Structural Locking Mechanisms and Their Effect on Database Management System Performance*, Information Systems, Vol. 7, No. 4, 1982, 345–358.

14. D. Dewitt, R. Katz, F. Olken, L. Shapiro, M. Stonebraker, D. Wood, *Implementation Techniques for Main Memory Database Systems*, Proceedings of ACM SIGMOD, 1984, 1–8.

15. H. Garcia-Molina, R. J. Lipton, J. Valdes, *A Massive Memory Machine*, Technical Report No. 315, Dept. of EECS, Princeton University, 1983.

16. H. Garcia-Molina, K. Salem, *Crash Recovery Mechanisms for Main Storage Database Systems*, Technical Report CS-TR-034-86, Dept. of Computer Science, Princeton University, 1986.

17. J. Haritsa, M. Carey, M. Livny, *An Being Optimistic about Real-Time Constraints*, Proceedings of the 9th ACM symposium on Principles of Database Systems, April 1990.

18. J. Haritsa, M. Carey, M. Livny, *Dynamic Real-Time Optimistic Concurrency Control*, IEEE Real-Time Systems Symposium, December 1990, 94–103.

19. J. Huang, J. Stankovic, D. Towsley, K. Ramamritham, *Real-Time Transaction Processing: Design, Implementation and Performance Evaluation*, University of Massachusetts COINS TR, May 1990, 90–43.

20. J. Huang, J. Stankovic, *Buffer Management in Real-Time Databases*, University of Massachusetts COINS TR, July 1990, 90–65.

21. J. Huang, J. A. Stankovic, *Experimental Evaluation of Real-Time Concurrency Control Schemes*, Proceedings of the 17th VLDB Conference, September 1991, 35–46.

22. J. Huang, J. Stankovic, *On Using Priority Inheritance In Real-Time Databases*, IEEE Real-Time Systems Symposium, December 1991, 210–221.

23. B. Iyer, P. Yu, Y. Lee, *Analysis of Recovery Protocols in Distributed On-line Transaction Processing Systems*, IEEE Real-Time Systems Symposium, Dec 1986, 226–233.

24. D. Knuth, *The Art of Computer Programming: Sorting and Searching*, Addison-Wesley, 1973.

25. H. F. Korth, A. Silberschatz, *Database System Concepts*, McGraw Hill, 1986.

26. H. F. Korth, N. Soparkar, A. Silberschatz, *Triggered Real-Time Databases with Consistency Constraints*, Proceedings of the 16th VLDB Conference, 1990, 71–82.

27. J. P. Lehoczky, L. Sha, R. Rajkumar, *Solutions for some practical problems in prioritized preemptive scheduling*, Proceedings of IEEE Real-Time Systems Symposium, 1986, 181–189.

28. J. P. Lehoczky, L. Sha, J. K. Strosnider, *Enhanced Aperiodic Responsiveness in Hard-real-time Environment*, Proceedings of IEEE Real-Time Systems Symposium, 1987, 261–270.

29. J. P. Lehoczky, L. Sha, B. Sprunt, *Aperiodic Task Scheduling for Hard-real-time Systems*, The Journal of Real-Time-Systems, 1989, 27–60.

30. K. Lin, M. Lin, *Enhancing Availability in Distributed Real-Time Databases*, ACM SIGMOD Record, March 1988, 34–43.

31. C. L. Liu, J. W. Layland, *Scheduling Algorithms for Multiprogramming in a Hard Real-Time Environment*, Journal of the ACM, Vol. 20, No. 1, 1973, 46–61.

32. C. H. Papdimitriou, *The Theory of Database Concurrency Control,,* Computer Science Press, 1986.

33. J. L. Peterson, A. Silberschatz, *Operating System Concepts*, Addison-Wesley, 1985.

34. L. Sha, R. Rajkumar, J. P. Lehoczky, *Priority Inheritance Protocols: An Approach to Real-Time Synchronization*, Dept. of Computer Science, Carnegie-Mellon University, CMU-CS–87–181, December 1987.

35. L. Sha, R. Rajkumar, J.P. Lehoczky, *Concurrency Control for Distributed Real-Time Databases*, ACM SIGMOD Record, March 1988, 82–98.

36. M. Singhal, *Issues and Approaches to Design of Real-Time Database Systems*, ACM SIGMOD Record, March 1988, 19–33.

37. X. Song, J. Liu, *How Well Can Data Temporal Consistency be Maintained?*, Proceedings of IEEE Symposium on computer-Aided Control System Design, March 1992.

38. J. Stankovic W. Zhao, *On Real-time Transactions*, ACM SIGMOD Record, Vol. 17, March 1988, 4–18.

39. T. J. Teorey, T. B. Pinkerton, *A Comparative Analysis of Disk Scheduling Policies*, Communications of the ACM, Vol. 15, No. 3, March 1972, 177–184.

40. P. van der Stok, *The Feasibility of a Relational Database Programming Language in Process Control*, IEEE Real-Time Systems Symposium, December 1984, 105–113.

41. G. Wiederhold, *Database Design*, McGraw-Hill, 1983.

Is Time a Real Time?
An Overview of Time Ontology in Informatics *

Fabio A. Schreiber

Dipartimento di Elettronica e dell'Informazione
Politecnico di Milano
Piazza L. da Vinci 32
20133 Milano
Italy

Abstract

Aim of this paper is to introduce several aspects of time in the heterogeneous world of Informatics and define ontologies for time in different
domains of computers and their applications. Some philosophical and
physical backgrounds are given, to show how, from the richness of often
contrasting ideas developed in the framework of these disciplines, many
useful concepts have been derived also for computer science. Architectural aspects of computer systems, Information Systems applications, and
Real-time systems, are considered as temporally problematic domains.

Keywords

clock, information system, philosophical theories, real time system, relativity
theory, synchronization, temporal logic, time ontology, time skew.

1 The Nature of Time

Time drives our lives in a pervasive and convulsive way. It was not always so;
people, today as in the past, have very different feelings about time. Lunch-time
seems to be a synchronous, clock driven, event for the employees of a large city,
but it was absolutely asynchronous for the stone-age men, who were driven only
by hunger stimuli.

For a long time and in many different environments, men thought of time as
something periodical, strictly connected to natural events; therefore in many
ancient cultures, the Greek and Roman classical world included, time was mainly
conceived with a *cyclic* structure. However, the first appearance of the modern
conception of time dates back to the oldest "best-seller" ever written: the Bible!

---

* This work was partially supported by CNR-CSISEI and MURST

Bereshit — in the beginning, the first word in the book of Genesis (Fig. 1) — marks the start of a flow of events which go on through the history in a *linear* way towards the messianic era [26]. Even if the idea of an open structure of time seems to have been present also in other ancient civilizations, such as the Zoroastrian Iranians [68], it was through the Jewish/Christian thought that the western world got its view of time. Anyhow, periodic phenomena still retain their importance in the *measurement* of time, whatever it means, as we shall later see.

Fig. 1. *Bereshit* (Soncino, Italy, 1488)

Things do not become easier even when we limit ourselves to give only a scientific connotation to time. On this ground, every high-school student could tell you that "time is the independent variable used to describe the laws of motion of mechanical systems", but we all know that modern physics is deeply rooted in the critique of the space and time concepts to such a point as theories and models, both at atomic and cosmological levels, are challenged today on the ground of the definition of time itself [48].

In Computer Science and Engineering, time has always been of major concern, owing to the need of synchronization among the different functional units in the computer; the clock has always been the heart of any digital system. However the first problems which required a deep understanding of temporal issues came in with the birth of distributed computing systems, where the definition of a *global time* has to cope with finite propagation delays [32]. We shall see that today, thanks to the widening of the dimensions of silicon devices achieved with Wafer Scale Integration, and with the very high switching rates attainable with ballistic transistor technologies, the notion of a single definite time is questionable even for a single circuit!

However, time is a concern not only for computer systems architects, but, during the eighties, it became increasingly relevant in many application fields, such as real-time control systems, information systems, automatic reasoning systems, planning systems, etc. .... Accordingly, new kinds of time have been introduced such as calendar (wall-clock) time, execution time, simulation time, etc. ...

Aim of this paper is to introduce several aspects of time in the heterogeneous world of Informatics and define ontologies for time in different domains of computers and their applications, and not to discuss the very nature of time by itself, a philosophical problem which is to remain open forever. However, in sections 1.1 and 1.2 we are going to give some philosophical and physical background, because, from the richness of often contrasting ideas, developed in the framework of these disciplines, many useful concepts have been derived; we shall leave the reader to confront himself against them, following his personal belief. Section 2 deals with architectural aspects, and section 3 with information systems applications.

1.1 Philosophical Theories

Since the oldest times and in the common sense feeling space and time have been perceived as something different from the other objects and processes; they have been considered either as some kind of structured containers of events in the natural world (absolutistic view) or just as some kind of abstraction to represent the relations among objects and processes (relational view). These views correspond to the different conceptions about the reality of the physical world and about the classical concept of "substance".

However, while the modern conception gives space and time the same dignity, philosophers in the classical times — noticeably those of the Eleatic school — gave space a greater attention, while considering time just as a "disturbance" in their conceptual systems. Time, in particular, was given mainly a practical role, being connected to the changes evidenced by astronomical phenomena and by the problem of motion. Therefore its metrical properties were considered, while no clear distinction was made between events happening in time and time itself. This conception explains also the cyclical structure attributed to time since the most archaic thinkers, which survived up to the modern era. Typical of this conception is the Heraclitus doctrine of "transmutation" — later recalled by the Stoic school — in which the world was endlessly involved in a birth and death cycle, the substance remaining essentially unchanged. The links of time to the celestial phenomena is further pushed by Plato, for whom time is being produced by the revolution of the celestial sphere and was created with it.

The first to perceive the problem of differentiating time from movement was Aristotle [4]; he thought that time was the numerable aspect of motion, in the ordering of "before" and "after" (IV, 11)[2], time and motion defining each other, while distinguishing between them since time cannot cease or change its speed like ordinary motions do. He also perceived that the uniform circular motion

---

[2] The numbering in parenthesis refer to book and chapter of [4]

can be used to measure time (IV, 12)(IV, 14) and he raised the problem of the nature of "present" as a separating instant between "past" and "future" (IV, 10). However he arrives at seemingly contradictory conclusions since in (VIII, 1) he claims an infinite, open, and continuous structure of time, while in (VIII, 8) he states that infinity and continuity are only possible on the circle, thus — in this fact following Plato — linking time to the perfect circular and uniform motion of heavens.

It was the Atomistic school, mainly with Democritus and Hepicurus, the first who abandoned the cyclic view of time while retaining its infinity: time was not created, hence there is no beginning for time; however for them the future is still closed since evolution is but a transformation of states.

The relation of time to modal logic was another topic which concerned ancient thinkers; temporal quantifiers such as *sometimes, never, always, etc.* were directly connected to the notions of *possibility* and of *necessity* by the Megarians and the Stoics. Their views diverged on the inclusion of the present time in the definition of necessity and of possibility: Stoics — namely Diodorus Chronus — considered as possible that which is realized at *some present-or-future time* and as necessary that which is realized at *every future time*; Megarians, on the other hand, did not admit the *now-relativization* and defined as possible that which is realized at *some time* and necessary that which is realized at *all times* [54].

We must make a jump of nearly a millennium before time is considered again as a philosophical issue; with St. Augustine the linearity of time is definitely assessed on the basis of theological arguments [5] (even if the circular view survived for a long time). Another important issue is risen by Augustine, although the problem had already been pointed out by Aristotle [4] (IV, 14): time is presented as a *subjective feeling*; only present is real, past is identified with memory and future with expectation, both memory and expectation being present facts *connected with the human mind* [6].

In Middle Age also temporal modalities had a great success thanks to the Arabic logician Avicenna, to St. Thomas Aquinas, and to the British school (William of Ockham, Albert of Saxony, and John Buridan) [54]. We shall come back to this subject in section 3.

Therefore we can say that by the beginning of the 5th century A.D., and even well before, some major issues in the nature and in the structure of time had been identified:

- linearity vs. circularity;
- finiteness vs. infinity;
- openness vs. closure;
- discreteness vs. continuity;

- absolute {past, present, future} vs. relative {before, concurrent-with, after} ordering;
- objectivity vs. subjectivity;
- definition of temporal modalities.

During the 17th century a separation process begins between the natural sciences and philosophy, mainly due to methodological issues, but still we find the same topics (and often the same authors) going on in parallel on the two sides. In this period other major discussions on the nature of time were carried on by Newton and Leibnitz dealing with the foundations of mechanics, we are going to mention in section 1.2, and, after them, a few other contributions were made by philosophers of the rationalistic and of the empiricist schools, respectively supporting an *absolute* against a *relative* view of time, until the work of E. Kant.

Kant adds to the traditional components of knowledge — the empiric sensations and the rational intellect — a new component, he calls *intuition*, which is present, in its primary form, with two modalities: space, the form of external sensibility, and time, the form of the internal sensibility. Space and time allow the formulation of *a priori* synthetic judgments which put together the experience from the real world with the necessary universality of the pure reasoning [28].

After Kant, physics and philosophy tend to concentrate on different goals, and space and time become definitely **scientific objects** themselves [48]. Time comes again as a philosophical topic in the second half of the twentieth century, in the frame of logic and linguistics, as we shall discuss in section 3.

1.2 Physical Theories

The birth of modern Mechanics, thanks to Copernicus and Galilei, and its great development due to Kepler, Newton and others, puts time in a privileged, central position as *the independent variable* in the observation and description of the motion and the formulation of the physical laws.

Newton looks at time as a container of events, which homogeneously flows independently of anything else. It is an **absolute mathematical entity**, which can also be called *duration*. Relative time is the sensible measure of the duration we perceive by means of motion.

Leibnitz, on the other hand, can be considered the father of relativism. Space and time only represent **relative order relations** and they do not possess any objective substantiality.

The debate between the two opposite conceptions marks the following centuries until the fundamental work of A. Einstein [13]. The logical foundation of the restricted theory of relativity is the discovery that many statements, whose truth

or falsity was thought to be demonstrable, were only conventional definitions
[53]. The major consequence of this consideration is the *relativity of the simultaneity*; we can say that two events are simultaneous only if they happen under our
direct perception. Otherwise we must observe the local clocks of each of them and
stipulate — by convention — a procedure which tells us if the two clocks mark
the same time. However, to do that, we must exchange information and, as it was
experimentally proven, this can be done only at a finite speed, the speed of light.

Without going into the details of the theory of relativity, for which we refer to [13]
or to the tutorial exposition [14], we mention here two results which are relevant
from the ontological point of view: first, time looses its privileged position as
the independent variable for describing natural phenomena, while only a *four
coordinate space-time continuum* is used to express the physical laws; second,
each event (a point in space-time) is the vertex of a twofold cone which contains
the past and the future of the event itself. Points which belong to trajectories
(*world lines*) lying within the cone are related to the vertex event by a precedence
relation, which express **causality**. Points outside the cone are simply "elsewhere"
and cannot be causally related to the event; they are independent of the event
or *concurrent* with it. Therefore any interaction between two events can only
occur within the intersection of their *light cones* as shown in Fig. 2.

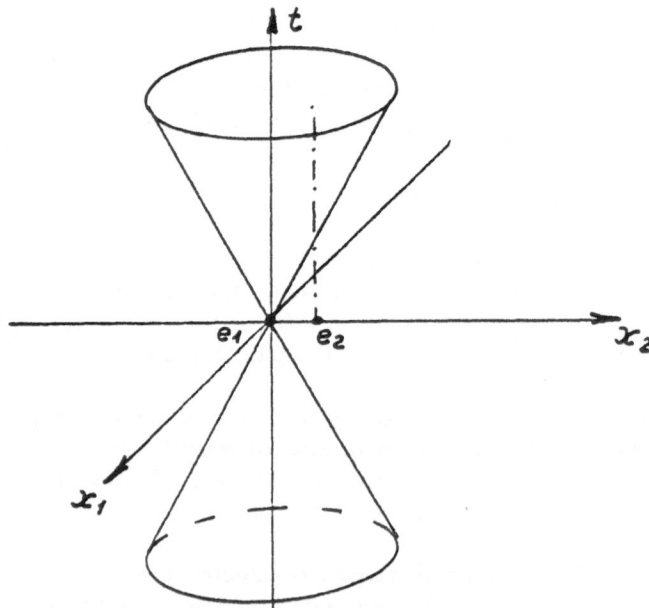

Fig. 2. A three-dimensional picture of the *light cone* of event e_1 and a *world line* of
event e_2

The reality of *becoming*, a problem which also bothered some philosophers in ancient times, was risen during the 19th century by the discovery of irreversible processes in thermodynamics. The temporal precedence relation is asymmetric, but is it also unidirectional? In other words, is there a **time arrow**? While a great difference is empirically and psychologically observable between past and future (e.g. we can remember the past, but not the future and we can determine the future, but not the past), physicists still harshly debate whether there is a scientifically provable theory in support of an anisotropy of time or not [53, 24].

The concepts of space and time discussed up to this point are the result of our perception of the world of the "middle dimensions"; when we enter in the world of microphysics, ruled by the laws of quantum mechanics, or in the deep spaces of relativistic cosmology we are not sure of the meaning itself of time. At the cosmological level we should define a *cosmic time*, to which all local clocks should synchronize, and this has been made through a set of very complex geometrical assumptions on the space-time [48]. As to the quantum theory, the non-deterministic nature of the micro-objects forces to extrapolate to the micro world, in an analogical way, the time concept used in the macro world [25]; even if the empirical results are very good, this makes the theory inconsistent from an ontological point of view. The situation then is the following: the Universe is made by progressive aggregations of objects of increasing size, but no general definition can be given of time which encompasses all the dimensions of it, from elementary particles to galaxies and quasars. Only sophisticated mathematical theories, mostly inconsistent with each other, support the different views of today theoretical physicists.

So the question is legitimate: **is time a real time?**

2 Time in Computer Systems

Computers, as a class of very complex digital systems, have always been deeply concerned with timing problems. Digital signals in fact are discrete both in space (the space of their values) and in time (the sampling instants). Therefore, a circuit generating well defined periodical signals – *the clock* – has always been fundamental in many types of digital circuits and components.

Moreover, communication between different functional components inside the computer, for exchanging both control and data signals, need some information to synchronize their operations. This information is provided by the distribution of the clock signal around the chip, the board or the backplane of the computer.

A common abstraction which is made dealing with electronic circuits, consists in considering that the value of a signal is identical at all points along a given conductive path. The largest region for which this condition holds is called *equipotential region* [57]. As long as the propagation delay of the signals is much smaller than their frequency, the equipotential region is as large as to include the whole machine; in this case we can consider the clock as an **absolute reference signal** and build synchronous devices relying on it. However the progress in electronic technology in recent years has been such as to increase device speeds up to 1 ns delay per logical gate, while reducing conductor sections and crowding devices on the chip. The result is that, owing to the increase in resistance and capacitance of the paths, propagation delays did not improve at the same rate. Therefore even a single chip cannot be considered anymore an equipotential region, not to say of Wafer Scale Integration components [18].

The presence of a *clock skew*, that is a difference of phase of the global clock signal at different circuit locations, poses the designer of digital circuits problems similar to those faced by the distributed computing systems designer; the circuit must be divided into several equipotential regions, which communicate with each other following some **precedence constraints**, thus abandoning the notion of an absolute time and assuming a **relativistic** attitude.

On the other hand, in distributed computing systems the partial ordering of events, induced by the precedence relation, is not enough if we want to obtain fault-tolerance, performance, or hard real-time properties, and synchronization with physical time becomes necessary [32, 44]. In [47] it is reported how a clock drift in a Patriot missile software prevented it from adequately tracking the incoming Scud that hit the Dhahran barracks during the Gulf war.

In the following, we shortly examine the problems of generating clock signals in logic networks, and in section 2.2 those related to an ordered and reliable exchange of information in distributed systems.

2.1 The Clock

The simplest way to model a clock is to use a boolean signal (a square wave) whose transitions between the two voltage levels mark the clock ticks. This abstraction, however, does not take into account some important phenomena occurring in real circuits: *metastability, finite rise time,* and *jitter.*

While metastability is an important issue, related to the nature of cross coupled circuits, that should be avoided by designers since it can delay the next tick forever, here we are more concerned with the other two problems since they influence the clock's precision. A finite rise time influences the definition of the exact instant at which the transition occurs, phase jitter consists in small variations of the intervals between transitions. Therefore a general model of a clock signal is [41]

$$x(t) = p(((f + \Delta f)t + \Phi(t)) \text{ modulo } 1) \tag{2.1}$$

where:

- $p(t)$ is a 50% duty cycle square wave;
- f is the *nominal frequency*;
- Δf is a possible *frequency offset*;
- $\Phi(t)$ is the *instantaneous phase variation*.

$\Phi(t)$ can represent a deterministic signal, a random process (e.g. white noise), etc. If we assume that $\Phi(t)$ be a deterministic, continuous, and differentiable function, then – for a clock to be "good" – the following conditions must hold:

$$\begin{cases} \Phi(t) \leq \Phi_{\max} \\ \overline{\frac{d\Phi(t)}{dt}} = 0 \end{cases} \tag{2.2}$$

i. e. the phase must be bounded and its derivative must have a time average equal to zero.

The *instantaneous frequency* is defined as

$$f(t) = f + \Delta f + \frac{d\Phi(t)}{dt} \tag{2.3}$$

If the *average frequency* $(f + \Delta f)$ is a constant (i.e. the *instantaneous frequency deviation* $d\Phi(t)/dt$ averages to zero) the clock is **isochronous**, while if $\Delta f = \Delta f(t)$ the signal is **anisochronous** and its phase is not bounded. The jitter induced by a time-varying phase, with components greater than 10 Hz, is a very disturbing effect in digital communications and it must be neutralized by the use of *elastic store* registers.

The best clocks available today are based on transitions in the orbital states of an electron; the Hydrogen Maser has a *frequency stability* of $2 * 10^{-14}$ per day, with a maximum offset of $1 * 10^{-12}$ per year. These devices are used by national administrations to keep a standard reference time; the quartz oscillators used in computer systems show stabilities in the order of 10^{-6} per day.

It is out of the scope of this paper to go into the details of the structure and implementation of physical clocks, for which we address the reader to [43, 12]; however we must mention the fact that the use of clocks in logic networks puts some constraints on the shape and duration of the pulses generated by the local clock and the clock period must be adjusted so that there is a *certainty period* during which the output signal is guaranteed to be correct [42]. Then the simple boolean (one phase) clock and the combinational logic must obey the following rules (Fig. 3a) [57]:

- the delay of the combinational logic must be
  - greater than the clock width;
  - less than the clock period;
- the clock width must be
  - greater than the time for charging the present state combinational inputs;
  - less than the minimum combinational delay.

If such a scheme could work with discrete components circuits, the satisfaction of all the constraints, in spite of the possible environmental changes, becomes unfeasible today for large systems, unless the clock is included on the integrated system chip.

Therefore multiple phase clocks have been defined, in order to simplify the constraints and to provide a region of reliable operation in any working condition (Fig. 3b) [57]. It should be noted that, when a clock skew is present, it is not always possible to choose the clock period large enough to fall into the certainty region and an additional delay must be added, so reducing the system throughput [42].

2.2 Synchronization in Distributed Systems

A distributed computing system is one in which computational units are spatially separated and communicate between each other by exchanging messages. More generally, we can say that a system is distributed if *the message transmission delay is not negligible compared to the time between events in a single process* [32]. In distributed systems we often find as many independent clocks as the number of computational units; this is the common case of a set of loosely connected processors. Therefore, in large computer networks the *Internet Network Time Protocol (NTP)* is adopted as a standard to synchronize the clocks of a number of *Time Servers* and to automatically organize and maintain a *Time Synchronization Subnet* to keep their accuracy with respect to the *Coordinated Universal Time (UTC)* provided by the national standards. The synchronization subsystem in Internet is *plesiochronous*, since there are several master oscillators which are closely synchronized in frequency, but not phase-locked to a single frequency standard [43].

We can say in general that *synchronization is the action of making different processes in a computer network or different parts of a circuit or different clocks to agree on a same time reading.*

In the context of multiprocessors and of distributed systems, where processes are executed in a real concurrent environment, synchronization insures that operations occur in the logically correct order, and it allows the establishment of causal implications between events in different computational units. In fact, the *happened before* relation, which is implicit in any sequential computation, is meaningful and systemwide consistent only if events are referred to a single clock, otherwise it can only establish a *partial order* for the set of events happening under the same local clock, as we saw in section 1.2. As an example, such considerations are essential in many concurrency control and recovery algorithms for distributed transaction management.

Leslie Lamport was the first to recognize this fact, rising – within the computer scientists community – the **duality between a relative and an absolute time** [32]. Partial ordering of events, in fact, can be obtained getting rid of any physical "real" time, by just relying on local *logical clocks* which are but a *non*

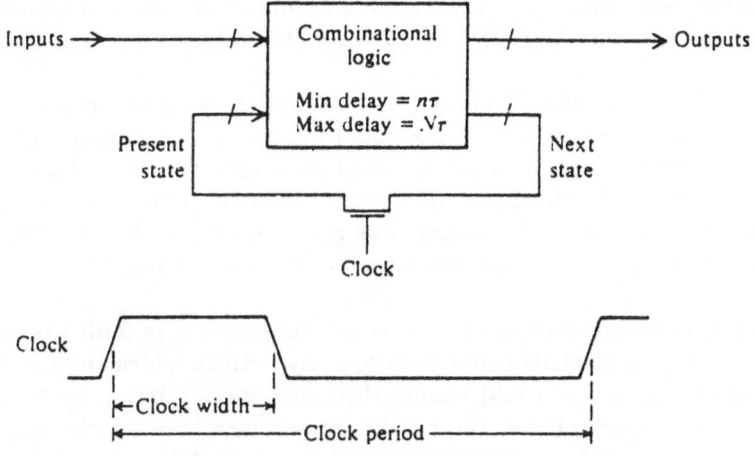

$(R_{on}C_{in})_{max} <$ clock width $< n\tau$
$N\tau <$ clock period $<$ refresh period

a) One-phase clock

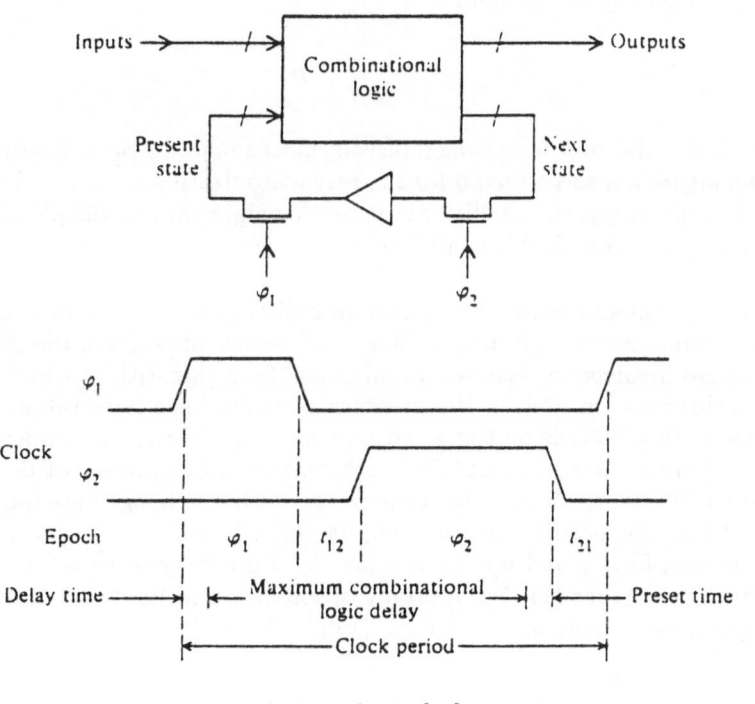

b) Two-phase clock

Fig. 3. Clock schemata

decreasing monotonic function mapping events on the set of integers; any such a
logical clock can be implemented by a counter without any link to actual time.

In an isolated distributed system, i.e. one which does not interact with an external environment, it is even possible to get a total ordering built on a set of
partially ordered logical clocks; a distributed algorithm, based on the exchange
of "time stamped" messages among the different processes, which achieves a
somehow arbitrary total ordering was given in [32]. Rules to obtain a "causal
ordering" from partially ordered logical clocks appear in [17].

However, in many cases, such as in real-time systems, in fault-tolerant systems,
and to avoid anomalous behaviours (e.g. by actions which bypass the system's
normal operation and could violate the cause-effect relation by "making holes"
in the "light cone" of the events), the interactions between the system and the
environment must be explicitly taken into account. This is possible recurring to
physical clocks [32, 34, 58]; therefore we must deal again with the precision and
the drift of physical clocks and with the propagation delay occurring in message
transmission [3]. In his paper [32], Lamport gives a limit for avoiding anomalous
behaviours when using physical clocks: be $\kappa \ll 1$ the *frequency drift* of a physical
clock, ϵ the *greatest (small) difference between two clocks readings* at the same
time, μ the *shortest transmission time* for interprocess communication, then the
following inequality should hold

$$\frac{\epsilon}{(1 - \kappa)} \leq \mu \tag{2.4}$$

To keep (2.4) valid over long time intervals, clocks must be periodically synchronized; an algorithm and a bound for the resynchronization period is also given in
[32]. Not surprisingly, the conditions set by this algorithm on the physical clocks
behaviour closely match those in (2.2).

Anomalous behaviour however can arise in a distributed system not only due to
shortcuts through the environment, but also because of faults in the clocks or in
the processes involved in their synchronization. Some algorithms which maintain
clock synchronization even in the presence of faults have been proposed in the
literature setting bounds on the worst-case skew, on the total number of clocks
necessary (and sufficient) to obtain synchronization in presence of m malicious
(Byzantine) faults, on the number of messages to be exchanged among the partners to obtain synchronization, etc. [66, 34, 30]. Moreover, since the topic is an
intriguing one, formal and mechanical proofs of their correctness (or of flaws in
them) have been given [11, 58]; a survey of software and hardware fault-tolerant
synchronization in distributed systems is provided in [51].

---

[3] And we are lucky that, for the time being, space vehicles housing Earth-connected
computing systems fly at speeds which are well below the speed of light, so we can
use Newtonian space-time without requiring relativistic corrections!

Other very interesting points about synchronization in *natural* systems can be found in [23, 67].

Looking back at this section from an ontological point of view, we notice that, in the generation and dissemination of a time-reference signal, the following questions are addressed:

- **physical clocks are continuous** while **logical clocks are discrete**, therefore an optimal granularity must be chosen, based on application constraints;
- **absolute time vs. relative time** is resolved in favor of the first, but at the price of establishing complex communication protocols for synchronizing local clocks;
- absolute time is used for establishing **causal** relations, which are essential in many applications to obtain reliability.

3 Time Representation in Information Systems

After dealing with the *nature* of time in section 1 and with its *materialization* in section 2, we are going to present here the different *representations* of time which have been used in information systems.

Philosophers began to consider time again in the middle forties, in the frame of cognitive sciences and linguistics. The first approaches [55, 50] regarded time just as a variable in first order predicate calculus. *Tense Logic* was defined by Prior [49] as a particular kind of modal logic, for reasoning about the modalities of the discourse; a systematic exposition of *Temporal Logic* was given by Rescher and Urquhart in [54] and by Van Benthem in [65].

In the logicians' community there is a strong debate on the need of creating a non standard *Temporal Logic*. Scholars having mathematical and physical background and interests claim that times can be designated by terms in a first order theory, which is more than adequate for time modeling. Besides Russell and Quine, these authors — referred often to as *detensers* — comprise Allen, McDermott, Kowalski and others. People interested in linguistic aspect of logic, on the other hand, feel that time is tightly woven into languages, under the form of different tenses of the verb, and they relate modal to temporal notions, as we saw in section 1.1; Prior and Von Wright belong to this *tensers* school. Just to show how things become complicate, we only mention that, in his theory of tense, Reichenbach defines three different times for each tense: an *utterance* time, at which the sentence is expressed, a *reference* time, which we refer to in the sentence, and an *event* time, which is the object of the sentence; with such a scheme he can explain structures like the future perfect tense [52]. We do not insist on this point because we think it has a technical more than a substantial nature; after all, the two approaches are not in contrast with each other since the first order approach can be used as an interpretation for the modal one [20].

In the meanwhile, Temporal Logic arose the interest of computer scientists both for its capability of expressing the needs of temporal description in knowledge engineering applications and for providing a rigorous formalism for specification and verification of concurrent and Real-Time software. As Galton points out, in the first field "... temporal logic is used to *enable computer programs to reason about the world ...*", while in the second it is used "*... to enable the world to reason about computer programs ...* " [20]. In the following, we shall review the fundamental ontological issues common to both fields, then the choices made for the different applications will be presented.

Primitive Time Entities

One of the most fundamental questions in the whole ontological issue, which raises a sort of "chicken-and-egg" problem, is the choice of the primitive time entity. Three options are found in the literature:

- **points of time** (instants);
- **segments of time** (intervals);
- **occurrences in time** (events).

Obviously these concepts can be derived from each other [64], however the choice is not trivial as far as the application world modeling is concerned. Instants can be viewed as the limit of intervals shrinking to zero duration, while intervals are defined by a beginning and an ending point. Events are considered differently whether an **absolute** or a **relative** view is taken. In the first case, **time ontologically precedes events** since it is a container of events and it is used to distinguish among them; in the second case **events ontologically precede time** since events are used to identify time instants! Moreover events are spatio-temporal entities, as we saw in section 1.2, therefore their role as basic temporal entities is questionable.

Time Topology

Since time has a dynamic nature, it comes spontaneous to define trajectories in time so that any two time entities can be related by an **order relation**; the question at issue is if the order is a *total* or a *partial* one. In the first case, each time entity has at most one predecessor and one successor; this property can be mapped on the infinite line — thus producing a true **linear** time — or on a closed (circular) line — thus producing a **periodic** time [4]. If only a partial order is allowed, one speaks of a **branching** time, in the sense that each time entity can have many predecessors (*branching in the past*) and many successors (*branching in the future*).

While the linear time model is the standard in natural sciences (e.g. physics), the **linear past** — **branching future** model has gained popularity among

---

[4] To be rigorous, periodic time can be defined only after a *metric* has been defined; see later.

computer scientists because it allows the representation of a deterministic past (what happened did happen) together with an open future (all that could happen). The semantics regarding the topology of time is usually reflected by the temporal modalities provided for describing events [39, 7, 15, 40, 38].

Branching time raised a dispute on whether it should be interpreted as *branching of time* or *branching in time*, i.e. if branching is a structural property of time, or it is the *course of events* which branches in a linearly structured time. The second view has been generally accepted because of its simplicity and conceptual clarity (how could we establish precedence relations between divergent courses of time?). On the other hand, the distinction only makes sense in an absolutistic conception, while the relativistic point of view clears out the duality since events constitute time [54].

Temporal Relationships

One of the first consequences of an instant based against an interval based description emerges when we consider the relationship between any two entities. With a point description, a simple precedence relation is all that we need; with intervals we need a set of 13 different relations (Fig. 4): **before(x y)**, **meets(x y)**, **overlaps(x y)**, **during(x y)**, **starts(x y)**, **finishes(x y)**, their inverses and **equal(x y)** [1].

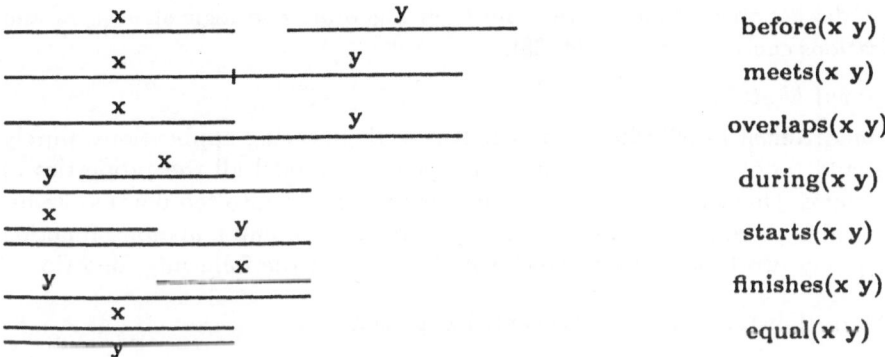

Fig. 4. relationships between two intervals

Boundedness

The relationship between time entities exhibits some problems as far as the boundary conditions are concerned. We can ask whether every time has a *successor (predecessor)* or if there is a last (first) moment in time. Notice that boundedness does not imply that time is *finite* or *infinite*, which is a metrical property.

If no beginning and no ending times exist, we can define a **homogeneous** time structure, where the local environment of any temporal position is temporally equivalent to any other. This makes simulation possible by compressing a long *real time* into a shorter *simulation time* on the continuous time line [5].

Speaking in terms of intervals, the question is whether they are **open (closed)** at one or at both ends. This property is especially relevant for the **meets(x y)** relation, where a *dividing instant* exists when some variable which is **true** in x becomes **false** in y (or viceversa), i.e. a state change intervenes between the two intervals. If we remain in a classical logic context, symmetric models of the kind **closed-closed** or **open-open** must be ruled out in the description of physical systems, because it is impossible that p and $\neg p$ be both false (Excluded Third principle) or both true (Non Contradiction principle) at the same instant; in other terms, we should choose between contradiction and indeterminacy!

Time Structure

The problem above is closely connected to the kind of structure we use to represent time. Many authors feel time is **continuous** in the sense that time points can be mapped on the set $\mathcal{R}$ of real numbers and time intervals are totally covered by a set of subintervals. Others think that a **dense** structure, i.e. one that maps time entities on the set $\mathcal{Q}$ of rationals, is enough to represent all real life situations. Finally a strong claim is made in many software engineering applications for a **discrete** time structure, mapping points or intervals on the integers set $\mathcal{Z}$. Obviously, choosing $\mathcal{Q}$ or $\mathcal{Z}$ makes the problem of the dividing instant to vanish, while $\mathcal{R}$ and $\mathcal{Q}$ rule out finiteness.

A deep discussion on time entities and their algebraic and logic structures and implications can be found in [64, 65].

Temporal Metric

Both in Artificial Intelligence and in Software Engineering applications, purely logical and topological features are not enough to model all the properties of real systems. Quantitative concepts must be introduced into temporal systems, transforming them into **chronological** systems, by defining a *distance* function between any two time entities, which satisfies at least the following conditions:

a) the **null** distance between two entities is defined

$$d(t, t') = 0 \text{ iff } t = t';$$

b) distances among any three entities obey the triangular inequality

$$d(t, t') + d(t', t'') \geq d(t, t'').$$

Therefore, the set of values for the temporal variables constitute a **metric space** in which it is possible to correlate an arbitrary time entity with a unique number, which represents the distance of the entity itself from a *reference element*. Usually this is assumed to be the identity element of the additive group formed by the set of the time values together with the (relative) addition operation; in

---

[5] This is also possible with circular time, but not with branching time [54]

this case the identity element is the *zero* and distances add up in the usual arithmetic way [54, 29]. Such groups have an intrinsic linear ordering relation which is symmetric with respect to past and future, the identity element behaving as the *present time*.

In true branching time structures the notion of a metric time becomes tricky. In fact one could measure distances between the projections of the elements on an underlying (linear) time axis, but simultaneity could bring to a violation of condition *a*); moreover *we are not assured* that clocks in different branches behave in the same way, thus granting the comparability of the measures [54].

The introduction of a metric entails the definition of *metric units*, which define the **granularity** of the time structure, e.g. *year, day, minute, etc..* Moreover, we can express a temporal proposition in terms of a chronologically *stable* time specification, i.e. a **date** such as "April 26th 1992", or in terms of a chronologically *unstable* one, i.e. a **pseudo-date** such as "the day after tomorrow".

Finally, it is the introduction of metric time which allows us to define periodic (circular) time and its representation as a sequence of intervals of equal length on the time line. Such a representation is useful to clearly distinguish between past and future of repeating events, whereas on the circle they coalesce. More complex spatial topologies, such as *helix*, which can account both for periodicity and evolution in time, are seldom mentioned in the literature.

A compact and structured summary of the axioms and rules of temporal logic most relevant to the ontology of time can be found at the end of [56]; implications of special relativity and thermodynamics on tense logic are discussed in [8].

3.1 Applications in Reasoning and in Planning Systems

If natural language understanding was the first application area which moved researchers in Artificial Intelligence to deal with time representation, it was the possibility of building systems which could reason about temporal facts which stimulated the most fruitful practical approaches. The application domains to which time reasoning has been applied are: planning [40, 10], Decision Support Systems [9], Fault Diagnosis [35], office systems [36], deductive and temporal databases [31, 60].

The work of J. F. Allen must be acknowledged for its attempt to set the foundations for time reasoning systems [1, 2, 3]; he is concerned with *properties* of objects which *HOLD* in *every subinterval* of an interval, with *events* which define the interval in which they *OCCUR*, and with *processes OCCURRING* during *some subinterval* of an interval.

From the ontological point of view, the only thing on which authors agree is the use of *first order calculus against modal logic* (although time modalities are trea-

ted in [36] and some mixed approaches are presented in [19]). With respect to all
the other aspects the choices have been different and strongly debated [21, 63];
while Allen favors intervals as basic time entities against point based descriptions, Galton, Mc Dermott and others use instants, and Kowalski uses events.
Discrete time structures are often preferred, unless continuous phenomena are to
be described, but this does not seem a critical issue, while authors contend again
on the matter of linear vs. branching time. Table 1 shows a comparison of the
ontological features of some interesting proposals; a clear survey and comparison
of several time reasoning systems appears in [35].

Table 1. Reasoning systems comparison

Author	Allen [1]	McDerm. [40]	TSOS [36]	EC [31]	TMM [10]
Time Primitive	interval	point	point	event	point
Time Reference	relative	relative	abs/rel	relative	relative
Time Topology	linear	R-branch.	linear	linear	R-branch.
Time Bounds	[–)	∞	[–) ; ∞	(–)	[$\to \infty$
Time Structure	continuous	continuous	discrete	discrete	discrete
Time Metric	no	no	yes	no	yes

[–) means left-closed, right-open interval

Another controversial point in reasoning systems is in the possibility of establishing a *causal relation* between events related by a pure precedence relation. As
we saw, causation is the source of a millenary debate among philosophers and
scientists, who support or deny a cause-effect relation; a proof that things are
far from being settled is given by the work of Shoham [59] and by the critical
reviews of it [46].

As a last point, I remember Temporal Databases as a complex form of time
management in information systems. Traditional Database systems are static
representations of the last updates performed on the stored information. However sometimes it could be necessary to keep the history of the updates to the
database and also to update retroactively the information in the Database, on
the base of data which have been known only recently. These operations require
the addition of a temporal dimension to the DBMS and the definition of a *transaction time*, i. e. the time the information was stored in the Database, and of
a *valid time*, i. e. the time when the relationship in the enterprise being modeled was valid [60, 62]. These two times, together with the *query time*, i. e. the
time the query is done, closely resemble the Reichenbach triad [52], mentioned
before, query time being analogous to utterance time, valid time to event time,
and transaction time to reference time. The last of a series of comprehensive
bibliographies on all the different aspects of Temporal Databases appeared on
ACM SIGMOD Record [61].

3.2 Applications in Software Engineering

The interest of software engineers for timing problems first arose in the context of formal techniques for program verification, when methods successfully used with sequential programs failed to work with *concurrent* programs. In fact, the input-output relations computed by a program composed of two parallel processes cannot be inferred by combining the input-output relations computed by the two processes running independently, since they can be altered by possible interference between the processes themselves [37]. Standard propositional or first-order calculus has been used to model the static part, while the dynamics is modeled by modal logic.

Very quickly the study was generalized to *reactive* systems, i. e. those programs whose role is to maintain an ongoing interaction with their environment, which include - besides concurrent programs — Real-time programs, and Operating Systems [38]. Many reactive programs do not even terminate (e. g. Operating Systems and Real-time process control systems), therefore the traditional verification techniques must be directed toward new classes of properties; Manna and Pnueli define them as follows [37]:

- **Invariance (Safety)**: program properties that hold continuously throughout the execution; they assure that *nothing bad will happen*. They are expressed through the **always** (necessity) modal clause $\Box p$.
- **Eventuality (Liveness)**: program properties that guarantee that some event will finally be accomplished; they assure that *something good will happen*. They are expressed through the **sometimes** (possibility) modal clause $\Diamond p$.
- **Precedence (Fairness)**: program properties stating that a certain event always precedes another; they are expressible using the **until** operator Up.

In these classes all the interesting properties of reactive systems are included, e. g. partial correctness and deadlock freedom (invariance), total correctness and responsiveness (eventuality), absence of unsolicited response and fair responsiveness (precedence).

We shall only mention that, together with the standard boolean connectives, the first-order universal $\forall$ and existential $\exists$ quantifiers, the modal clauses (necessity having a universal nature and possibility having an existential one), and the **until** operator introduced above, many other temporal operators have been introduced and utilized in the literature; noticeably: **next** $\bigcirc p$, **unless** Wp, **since** Sp. The $\Box p$ (always p) and $\Diamond p$ (sometimes p) operators, including the present instant as part of the future, are the reflexive counterparts of the Priorean strict operators Gp (it will always be the case that p) and Fp (it will be the case that p).

Another distinction was made between the two operators **sometimes** $\leadsto p$ and **not never** $\Diamond p$ whose meanings are equivalent in linear time, but differ in branching time [33, 15].

From an ontological point of view, it is interesting to notice that *a temporal logic with the* until *operator and restricted to the future fragment* is sufficient to express all the first-order properties of reactive systems [20, 38], other operators for future and past being useful, but not necessary. This can be explained with the fact that proving programs properties requires reasoning from a program step onwards and not viceversa.

The need of formal specification languages comes out as a logical consequence of the possibility of formally proving program properties, since formal proofs need a formal statement of functional as well as of performance requirements. Several proposals have been made, mainly in the frame of Real-time process control applications, where timing constraints are an explicit requirement in assuring system integrity.

Table 2 shows a comparison among some well known proposals of verification and specification systems. We can notice that all of them, except RTL, use modal logic (against reasoning systems, which prefer standard logic), systems applied to verification of concurrent programs preferring propositional calculus, while Real-time specification languages prefer 1st order calculus. The two application domains differ also as to the adoption of a metric, which is necessary for real-time, whereas relative ordering is enough for concurrency. Other ontological issues common to most proposals are:

— the *discreteness* of the time model (except Koymans, who is interested in continuous process control) ;
— the choice for *points* or instantaneous events as basic time entities (except ITL).

Once again, time topology requires a special consideration, since in software engineering, as well as in reasoning systems applications, it is a major source of debate among the different proposals. Contrasting with the simplicity of linear time logics, very complex branching time structures have been defined. In branching time models two kind of formulas can be defined: *state formulas*, which are valid at each time point, and *path formulas*, which hold over an entire path spanning many branches. In [7] quantification over possible futures and quantification over individual times are tightly combined into six non decomposable modalities, while in [15] the path quantifiers ∀ (for all paths) and ∃ (for some path) can be applied to expressions containing state quantifiers F, G, U, etc. to convert path formulas to state formulas and viceversa. Expressive power of the resulting model is the goal of branching time advocates [15] and really they succeed in providing it, however for most practical applications linear time models are sufficient.

Besides linear and branching time, a third interesting topology is related to periodic phenomena; we saw above that circular time has been a very popular model in the past and that periodic time can be represented on the line by

Table 2. Formal verification and specification systems proposals

Author	Lamport [33]	Ben Ari [7]	Manna [37]	Emerson [15]
Scope	conc. ver.	conc. ver.	conc. ver.	conc. ver.
Approach	modal propos.	modal propos.	modal propos.	modal propos.
Primitive	point	point	point	point
Reference	–	–	–	–
Topology	linear	branch/circ	linear	branching
Direction	future	future	future	future
Bounds	$[\to \infty$	∞	$[\to \infty$	$[\to \infty$
Structure	discrete	discrete	discrete	discrete
Metric	no	no	no	no

$[\to$ means left-closed, right-open interval

Author	Koymans [29]	RTL [27]	ITL [45]	TRIO [16]
Scope	RT spec./ver.	RT spec./ver./synth.	conc. spec./ver.	RT spec./ver.
Approach	modal 1st ord.	non modal 1st ord.	modal 1st ord.	modal 1st ord.
Primitive	point	event (point)	interval	point
Reference	relative	abs/rel	relative	relative
Topology	linear	helix	linear	linear
Direction	past/future	–	future	past/future
Bounds	∞	$[\to \infty$	$[\to \infty$	∞
Structure	continuous	discrete	discrete	cont./discr.
Metric	yes	yes	no	yes

$[\to$ means left-closed, right-open interval

the series of the repeating events. A topology that integrates both aspects of periodicity and evolution in time is the *helix* in a three-dimensional space, where the base plane projection describes periodicity and the third coordinate axis describes evolution. A practical example of such a coordinate scheme is given by the "@" function in RTL, where the value of @(e,i) is the time of occurrence of the ith instance of the event e, as shown in figure 5.

4 Conclusions

So, can we answer the question: "Is time a real time?" Quoting St. Augustine [6], we could say: "... I know well enough what it is, provided that nobody asks me about; but if I am asked what it is and I try to explain, I am baffled". Fortunately, the problems computer engineers are faced with do not ask for metaphysical answers on the very nature of time, but they need a set of pragmatic guidelines which could assist designers and programmers in the realization of architectures and applications.

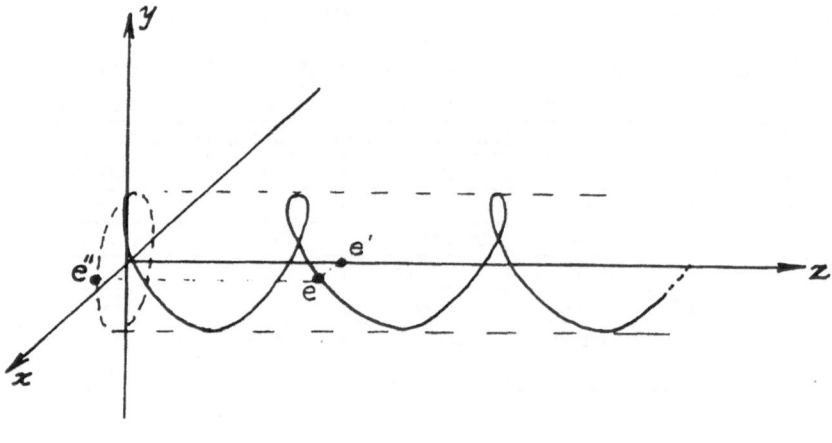

$$helix \begin{cases} x = A \cos \frac{2\pi}{T}(t + t_0) \\ y = A \sin \frac{2\pi}{T}(t + t_0) \\ z = h\frac{2\pi}{T}(t + t_0) \end{cases}$$

$$@(e, i) = iT + t_0$$

Fig. 5. Topology of the @ function in RTL

We saw that the fundamental issues are the same both for hardware and for software, therefore a distinction on this ground does not seem useful, while a classification of temporal models based on the *realistic* requirements of the different applications seems much more fruitful. In this sense we can conclude that yes; everybody can have his "real" time!

As a last thing, I want to thankfully mention Angelo Morzenti, Massimo Pauri and Barbara Pernici for the time spent in helpful discussions on time.

References

1. J.F. Allen, *Maintaining Knowledge about Temporal Intervals*, Communications of ACM, Vol. 26, No. 11, 1983.
2. J.F. Allen, *Towards a General Theory of Action and Time*, Artificial Intelligence, Vol. 23, 1984, 123–154.
3. J.F. Allen, *Time and Time Again: The Many Ways to Represent Time*, Int. Journal of Intelligent Systems, Vol. 6, 1991, 341–355.
4. *Aristotle — Physica — Laterza*, Bari 1991.
5. St. Augustine, *The City of God*, Book XII, Ch. XIII.

6. St. Augustine, *Confessions*, Book XI, Ch. XXX.

7. M. Ben-Ari, A. Pnueli, Z. Manna, *The Temporal Logic of Branching Time*, Proc. 8th ACM Symp. on Principles of Progr. Lang., 1981, 164–176.

8. J.P. Burgess, *Basic Tense Logic*, in D. Gabbay, F. Guenter (Eds.), Handbook of Philosophical Logic, Reidel Dordrecht, Vol. II, 1984, 90–133.

9. S. De, S. Pan and A. Whinston, *Temporal Semantics and Natural Language Processing in a Decision Support System*, Information System, Vol. 12, No. 1, 1987.

10. T.L. Dean and D. McDermott, *Temporal Data Base Management*, Artificial Intelligence, Vol. 32, 1987, 1–55.

11. D. Dolev, J.Y. Halpern and H.R. Strong, *On the Possibility and Impossibility of Achieving Clock Synchronization*, Journal of Computer and System Sciences, Vol. 32, 1986, 230–250.

12. C.E. Dyreson and R.T. Snodgrass, *Time-stamp Semantics and Representation*, TempIS Technical Report No. 33, Dept. of Computer Science, Univ. of Arizona, Tucson 1992.

13. A. Einstein, *The Meaning of Relativity*, 5th ed., Princeton Univ Press, Princeton 1955.

14. A. Einstein, *Relatività: esposizione divulgativa* (Transl. from "Über die spezielle und allgemeine Relativitaetstheorie: gemeinverstaendlich, 16th ed.), Boringhieri, Torino 1960.

15. E.A. Emerson and J.Y. Halpern, *"Sometimes" and "not never" Revisited: on Branching vs. Linear Time*, Journal of ACM, Vol. 33, No. 1, 1986, 151–176.

16. M. Felder, D. Mandrioli and A. Morzenti, *Proving Properties of Real-time Systems Through Logical Specifications and Petri Net Models*, Dip. Elettronica Politecnico di Milano, rep. No. 91–072, 1991.

17. T. Fidge, *Logical Time in Distributed Computing Systems*, IEEE Computer, Vol. 24, No. 8, 1991.

18. J. Fried, *An Analysis of Power and Clock Distribution for WSI Systems*, in G. Saucier, J. Trilhe (Eds), Wafer Scale Integration, North-Holland, Amsterdam 1986.

19. A.P. Galton, *Temporal Logics and their Applications*, Academic Press, London 1987.

20. A.P. Galton, *Temporal Logic and Computer Science: an Overview*, in [19].

21. A.P. Galton, *A critical Examination of Allen's Theory of Action and Time*, Artificial Intelligence, Vol. 42, 1990, 159–188.

22. C. Ghezzi, D. Mandrioli and A. Morzenti, *TRIO a Logic Language for Executable Specification of Real-time Systems*, Journal of Systems and Software, Vol. 12, No. 2, 1990.

23. B.C. Goodwin and M.H. Cohen, *A Phase-shift Model for the Spatial and Temporal Organization of Developing Systems*, Journal of Theoretical Biology, Vol. 25, 1969, 49–107.

24. S.W. Hawking, *A Brief History of Time*, Bantam Books, New York 1988.

25. W. Heisenberg, *I pricipi fisici della teoria dei quanti* (Transl. from "Die physikalischen Prinzipien der Quantumtheorie"), Boringhieri, Torino 1963.

26. A.J. Heshel, *The Shabbath: Its Meaning for Modern Man*, Farrar, Straus & Giroux Inc., New York 1951.

27. F. Jahanian and A. Mok, *Safety Analysis of Timing Properties in Real-Time Systems*, IEEE Transactions on Software Eng., Vol. SE–12, No. 9, 1986.

28. E. Kant, *Critica della ragion pura* (Transl. from "Kritik der Reinen Vernunft"), Laterza, Bari 1949.

29. R. Koymans, *Specifying Real-Time Properties with Metric Temporal Logic*, Real-Time Systems, Vol. 2, 1990, 255–299.

30. H. Kopetz and W. Ochsenreiter, *Clock Synchronization in Distributed Real-Time Systems*, IEEE Trans. on Computers, Vol. C–36, No. 8, 1987.

31. R.A. Kowalski and M.J. Sergot, *A Logic Based Calculus of Events*, New Generation Computing, Vol. 4, 1986, 67–95.

32. L. Lamport, *Time, Clocks and the Ordering of Events in a Distributed System*, Communications of ACM, Vol. 21, No. 7, 1978.

33. L. Lamport, *"Sometimes" is sometimes "not never": on the Temporal Logic of Programs*, Proc. 7th. sc acm Symp. on Principles of Progr. Languages, Las Vegas 1980, 174–185.

34. L. Lamport and P.M. Melliar-Smith, *Synchronizing Clocks in the Presence of Faults*, Journal of ACM, Vol. 32, No. 1, 1985.

35. R. Maiocchi and B. Pernici, *Temporal Data Management Systems: A Comparative View*, IEEE Transactions on Knowledge and Data Engineering, Vol. 3, No. 4, 1991.

36. R. Maiocchi, B. Pernici and F. Barbic, *Automatic Deduction of Temporal Information*, to appear in ACM Transactions on Database Systems.

37. Z. Manna and A. Pnueli, *Verification of Concurrent Programs: the Temporal Framework*, in R.S. Boyer, J. Strother Moore, The Correctness Problem in Computer Science, Academic Press, London 1981.

38. Z. Manna and A. Pnueli, *The Temporal Logic of Reactive and Concurrent Systems: Vol. 1, Specification*, Springer-Verlag, New York 1992.

39. R. McArthur, *Tense Logic*, Reidel, Dordrecht 1976.

40. D. McDermott, *A Temporal Logic for Reasoning about Processes and Plans*, Cognitive Science, Vol. 6, 1982, 101–155.

41. D.G. Messerschmitt, *Synchronization*, in T.H. Meng, Synchronization Design in Digital Systems, Chap. 2, Kluwer Academic Publishers, Boston 1991.

42. D.G. Messerschmitt, *Isochronous Interconnect*, in T.H. Meng, Synchronization Design in Digital Systems, Chap. 6, Kluwer Academic Publishers, Boston 1991.

43. D.L. Mills, *On the Chronometry and Metrology of Computer Network Timescales and their Application to the Network Time Protocol*, ACM Computer Communication Review, Vol. 21, No. 5, 1991.

44. A.K. Mok, *Towards Mechanization of Real-Time Systems Design*, in A.M. van Tilborg, G.M. Koob, Foundations of Real-Time Computing: Formal Specifications and Methods, Kluwer Academic Publishers, Boston 1991.

45. B. Moszkowski, *Executing Temporal Logic Programs*, LNCS 164, Springer-Verlag, Berlin 1984.

46. P. Naur and J. Delgrande, *Reviews of Y. Shoham*, ACM Computing Reviews, Vol. 30, No. 1, 1989.

47. P.G. Neumann, *Survivable Systems*, Communications of ACM, Vol. 35, No. 5, 1992

48. M. Pauri, *The Universe as a Scientific Object*, in E. Agazzi, A. Cordero (Eds.), Philosophy and the Origin and Evolution of the Universe, Kluwer Academic Publishers, Boston 1991.

49. A.N. Prior, *Diodorean Modalities*, The Philosophical Quarterly, Vol. 5, 1955, 202–213.

50. W.V. Quine, *Elementary Logic*, Harper & Row, New York 1965.

51. P. Ramanathan, K.G. Shin and R.W. Butler, *Fault-Tolerant Clock Synchronization in Distributed Systems*, IEEE Computer, Vol. 23, No. 10, 1990.
52. H. Reichenbach, *Elements of Symbolic Logic*, Macmillan, New York 1947.
53. H. Reichenbach, *The Philosophical Meaning of the Relativity Theory*, in P.A. Schilpp (Ed.), Albert Einstein: Philosopher-Scientist. The Library of Living Philosophers, Evanston 1949.
54. N. Rescher and A. Urquhart, *Temporal Logic*, Springer-Verlag, Berlin 1971.
55. B. Russel, *Principles of Mathematics*, George Allen and Unwin, London 1903.
56. F.A. Schreiber, *A Breviary to Time Concepts for Information Systems*, Rivista di Informatica, Vol. XX, No. 1, 1990.
57. C.L. Seitz, *System Timing*, in C. Mead, L. Conway, Introduction to VLSI Systems, Chap. 7, Addison-Wesley, Reading (Mass.) 1980.
58. N. Shankar, *Mechanical Verification of a Generalized Protocol for Byzantine Fault Tolerant Clock Synchronization*, in Vytopil J. (Ed.), Formal Techniques in Real Time and Fault Tolerant Systems, LNCS No. 571, Springer-Verlag, Berlin 1992.
59. Y. Shoham, *Reasoning about Change, Time and Causation from the Standpoint of Artificial Intelligence*, MIT Press, Cambridge 1988.
60. R. Snodgrass and I. Ahn, *Temporal Databases*, IEEE Computer, Vol. 19, No. 9, 1986.
61. M.D. Soo, *Bibliography on Temporal Databases*, ACM SIGMOD Record, Vol. 20, No. 1, 1991.
62. A. Tansell, R. Snodgrass, J. Clifford, S. Gadia and A. Segev (Eds.), *Temporal Databases: Theory, Design and Implementation*, Benjamin-Cummings, Reading 1993.
63. R. Turner, *Logics for Artificial Intelligence*, Ellis-Horwood, Chichester 1984.
64. J.F. Van Benthem, *Time, Logic, and Computation*, in J.W. De Bakker, W.P. de Roever, G. Rozenberg (Eds.), Linear Time, Branching Time and Partial Order in Logics and Models for Concurrency, LNCS 354, Springer Verlag, Berlin 1989.
65. J.F. Van Benthem, *The Logic of Time*, 2nd edition, Reidel, Dordrecht 1991.
66. J.L. Welch and N. Lynch, *A New Fault-Tolerant Algorithm for Clock Synchronization*, Proc. Third ACM SIGACT-SIGOPS Symp. on Principles of Distributed Computing, 1984.
67. A.T. Winfree, *The Geometry of Biological Time*, Springer-Verlag, Berlin 1990.
68. G.J. Withrow, *Reflections on the History of the Concept of Time*, in J.T. Fraser et Al. (Eds.), The Study of Time, Springer-Verlag, Berlin 1972.

An exhaustive list of bibliographical references on time could take an entire volume by itself. Therefore we urge the interested reader to follow, like a pointers chain, the references included in the items above.

A Consensus-Based Framework for Responsive Computer System Design*

Miroslaw Malek

Department of Electrical and Computer Engineering
The University of Texas at Austin
Austin, Texas 78712
U.S.A.

Abstract

The concept of responsive computer systems is presented. The emerging discipline of responsive systems demands fault-tolerant and real-time performance in both parallel and distributed computing environments. The responsiveness measure is discussed and a new design framework for responsive systems is introduced. The new framework is based on the fundamental concept of consensus and on application specific responsiveness. It is shown that consensus is crucial in responsive synchronization, communication, diagnosis, and reconfiguration.
It is also illustrated how these tasks form a part of the consensus-based operating system, and, when combined with application specific methods, handle fault-tolerance and real-time issues germane to a given application. This approach seems to be the most appropriate for the design of fault-tolerant, real-time, parallel/distributed systems.

1 Introduction

Until recently, the disciplines of parallel/distributed computing, fault-tolerant computing, and real-time systems have, to a large extent, evolved separately. As computer users increasingly demand timeliness and dependability, there is an urgent need to integrate the theory and practice of real-time systems, fault-tolerant computing, and parallel/distributed computing. We call such integrated systems responsive [2], since they must respond to internal guiding programs or external inputs in a timely, dependable, and predictable manner.

The researchers in fault-tolerant computing may define a responsive system as a fault-tolerant system with timing constraints, in which a timing violation is perceived as a timing fault; the real-time research community may define a responsive system as a real-time system that guarantees real-time behavior even

---

* This work was supported in part by the Office of Naval Research Contract No. N00014-88-K-0543, Grant No. N00014-91-J-1858 and the Texas Advanced Technology Grant 386.

in the presence of faults. Whatever perspective we take, we may easily conclude that responsive systems raise a significant number of fundamental issues of theoretical and practical relevance.

Responsive computer systems are crucial in many applications. Communication, control, avionic systems, robotics, multimedia, decision support systems, banking, air traffic control, and even point-of-sale terminals are just a few examples of systems that require responsiveness.

The objective of this paper is to introduce a concrete design framework for optimizing both dependability and timeliness in the multicomputing environment. We outline the foundations for responsive systems design and define a measure of responsiveness that could be used in the specification and design of responsive systems.

Our philosophy is based on the observation that high responsiveness can only be achieved by developing an ultrareliable kernel, whose correctness is provable, and combining it with application-specific responsive system design techniques. This is due to the diversity of applications and environments that make universal, highly responsive systems extremely difficult to design.

Our approach focuses on the identification of the fundamental tasks that must be incorporated in a responsive system kernel and the development of application specific techniques for maximizing responsiveness. This approach is based on two further observations: the omnipresence of consensus[2] and the inevitability of probability. We view synchronization, communication, data access and storage protocols, diagnosis, scheduling, replicated data management, and reconfiguration as consensus problems. Therefore, the consensus concept is fundamental in any multicomputer environment. The inherent complexity of the system combined with the random occurrence of faults implies that probability cannot be avoided, and, even in so called "hard" real-time systems, only probabilistic guarantees can be given.

The paper is divided into the following parts. In Section 2, we discuss a consensus-based framework for responsive computer systems. Next, a proposal for a measure of responsiveness that should be easily specified, analyzed, and measured is presented. Section 4 introduces the concept of responsive consensus and outlines plans for implementing it in a distributed computing environment. Section 5 focuses on a responsive scheduler design that gives probabilistic guarantees of timely and efficient schedules even in the presence of faults. Section 6 proposes a framework for application-specific methods for achieving high responsiveness, which we support with our results for fault-tolerant, parallel algorithms design. Section 7 presents the conclusions and reiterates our ideas regarding responsive computer system design.

---

[2] In this case, consensus is defined as an agreement among computers.

2 The Consensus–Based Framework

The consensus-based framework for responsive systems aims to define the core concepts and the functions that will lead to comprehensive design methods for responsive computer systems. We propose a Consensus-based Operating system for REsponsive computing (CORE) that may become the bedrock for systems such as UNIX, MACH and CHORUS in order to improve their responsiveness.

Any successful design requires quantitative and/or qualitative goals that can be verified through measurement. The most successful designs are based on particular models that are accurate abstractions of reality. Of course, the ultimate model is a copy of the given system itself; however, with the high complexity of today's systems, such a model is frequently unattainable. Therefore, models for these systems tend to focus on a specific aspect of system behavior or a specific layer of system design. We propose a definition of responsiveness, which combines availability and timeliness (a specific proposal for this measure is outlined in the next section), and introduce a layered model in which characteristics such as synchronicity, message order or lack of it, and bounded or unbounded communication delay are well defined for a specific environment. This layered model [1] is based on the consensus problem [3] and is, in our opinion, fundamental to the design of responsive multicomputer systems. In multicomputer systems, the consensus problem is omnipresent. It is necessary for handling synchronization and reliable communication, and it appears in resource allocation, task scheduling, fault diagnosis, and reconfiguration. Consensus tasks take many forms in multicomputer systems.

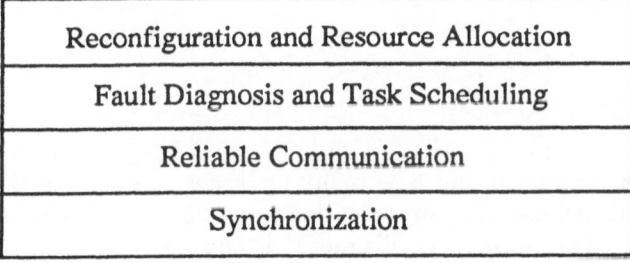

Fig. 1. Consensus problems in fault and time management.

Figure 1 is a preliminary model for fault and time management in a multicomputer environment in which each layer represents a separate consensus problem. At the base of the model is the synchronization level. For a system to be responsive (i.e., fault tolerant and real time), there must be an agreement about time for fault detection and task execution. The next layer represents the requirement for reliable communication. Responsive computers must agree on how and when

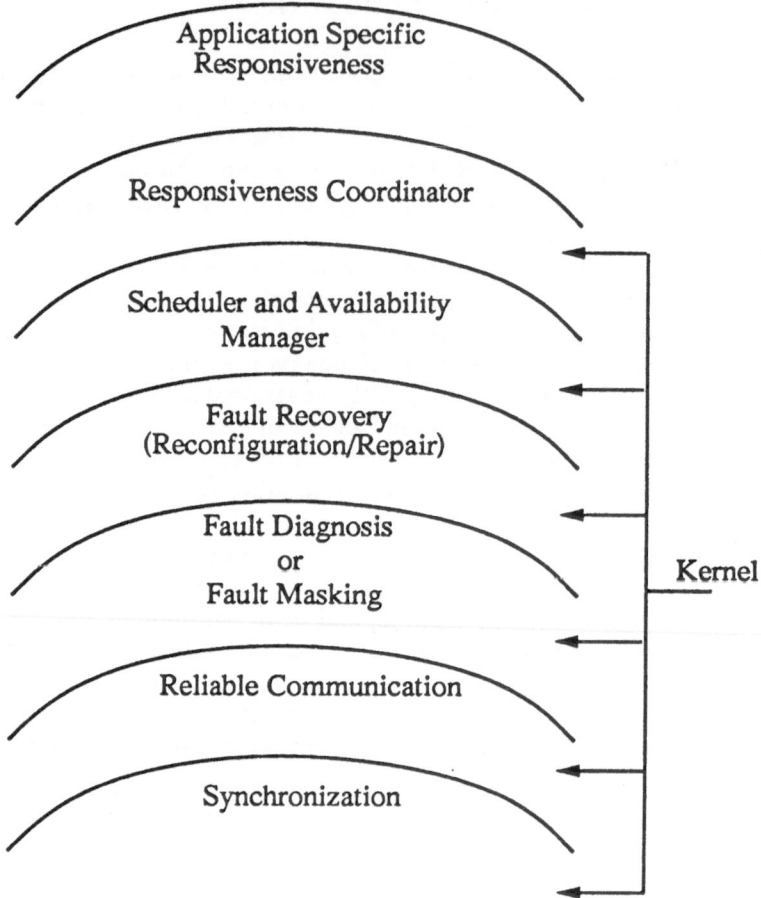

Fig. 2. A framework for responsive systems design.

information is exchanged and how many messages can be considered delivered or lost. Also, timeliness of communication is crucial in achieving a high level of responsiveness. The third layer, diagnosis, is equally fundamental to both real time and fault tolerance, for agreements must be reached on task scheduling and on who is faulty and who is not. Finally, the fourth layer illustrates the need for agreement on resource allocation and reconfiguration for efficient task execution and recovery from potential faults. In addition, we add a scheduler that manages space (resources) and time, and an availability manager. The scheduler and availability manager are in turn managed by the responsiveness coordinator, which is responsible for maximizing responsiveness and, therefore, coordinating reconfiguration in the presence of faults. Application specific responsive design methods are placed on top of the kernel functions in our responsive system design framework, which is shown in Figure 2. Another view of this framework is illus-

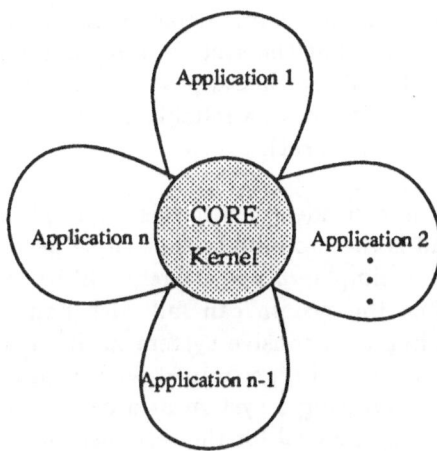

Fig. 3. Another perspective on a responsive systems design framework.

trated in Figure 3, in which functions in the CORE kernel support applications armed with application specific techniques for responsive system design.

With the variety and complexity of the numerous applications in multicomputer systems today, we insist on this approach as it is our belief that general techniques have some limitations and, when used alone, cannot assure a high level of responsiveness. We believe that, although the small generic kernel may be proved to be correct, the correctness of real-world applications, in most cases, cannot be proven. Hence, application specific techniques are necessary.

In responsive system design, all of the consensus problems should be accomplished in a timely and reliable manner. To design a responsive system, we need responsive synchronization, responsive communication, responsive task scheduling, responsive fault diagnosis, responsive resource allocation, and responsive reconfiguration. This means each layer should incorporate timeliness and dependability measures, as well as the various classes of faults. This requirement opens a number of research issues, and only a few of them have been studied from the perspective of responsiveness, which is discussed in the next section.

3 The Responsiveness Measure

In order to quantify a system's ability to perform responsively, a probabilistic measure of responsiveness is introduced. The responsiveness measure combines the traditional measures of fault tolerance and real time, namely availability and the ability to complete a task set by some deadline, with the objective of co-optimizing these dependent system qualities. This is done by examining the system from the task's perspective. Consider that a system consists of a set of tasks, each having a particular execution deadline that may or may not be met.

Whether or not a task's deadline is met depends on the ability of the system to perform the task set, given that the system hardware and software have some probability of failing. By taking this approach, we acknowledge that responsiveness is the ability to perform, in a reliable and timely manner, the system's required functions (i.e., its task set).

Responsiveness, then, is dependent on the user's needs, which are ultimately the system's goals, and is the probability that these needs will be fulfilled. Unless these needs are very simple, responsiveness will be less than one. The user must balance how often the system can fail with how much the system will cost. This makes building a responsive system an iterative process of the user specifying what task set must be performed with a particular responsiveness, and the system designer creating a system at a certain cost that will meet the user's requirements. Thus, the goal for the responsiveness measure is that it be sufficiently intuitive so the user may easily use it to specify his requirements, and sufficiently rigorous so the designer may analytically evaluate the system's responsiveness.

In general, one may assume that the system responsiveness is a function of availability and timeliness, which are time dependent, and can be defined as $r(t) = f[a(t), p(t)]$. Deriving a precise responsiveness criterion for a multicomputer environment, as well as methods for evaluating and measuring responsiveness, is still an open issue.

If a single-processor system is required to run a single task, its responsiveness $r(t)$ is the probability $a(t)$ that the processor performs the task without error (i.e., the instantaneous availability, or reliability, of the processor) multiplied by the probability $p(t)$ that the processor can complete the task before its deadline (i.e., the task is schedulable at a given time t). In short, $r(t) = a(t)p(t)$. If this system is required to perform n tasks, the probability that a particular task is completed is related to its governing scheduling policy and the other tasks in the system.

In addition, if multiple tasks are executed on a single or multiple processor system, the responsiveness measure could be defined as

$$r(t) = \frac{1}{n} \sum_{i=1}^{n} a_i(t)p_i(t),$$

where a_i is the lifetime availability of task i and p_i is the probability that task i will be completed before its deadline [2]. a_i is calculated using the standard availability evaluation techniques for the configuration of equipment performing task i and the duration of task i. p_i is the probability that task i will complete before its deadline, given that it is part of some task set scheduled on the system. Note that responsiveness $r(t)$ varies between zero and one with higher values of $r(t)$ indicating a greater likelihood that the task set will be completed within its deadlines.

For a gracefully degradable system, such as a consensus-based system, a_i and p_i may be calculated to any desired precision by computing a weighted average of these probabilities over the various configurations. For example, a four-processor, single-fault-tolerant, consensus-based system would have a_i and p_i calculated for the two cases when there are four and three fault-free processors (two, one or zero fault-free processors amounts to a system failure and $a_i = 0$), then weighted and averaged depending on the expected time the system will spend in these various configurations.

We view the proper definition of responsiveness as the key to any optimization that might be done in responsive systems design. Only experience will show whether $r(t) = f[a(t), p(t)]$ is a measure that can accurately portray a system's ability to satisfy the user's needs, yet can still be useful to the system designer. It should be noted that responsiveness is a function of the current time t, a task set T (with its timing characteristics), the available time to deadline $(d = t_d - t)$, and an execution strategy (replication in time or replication in space).

One of the principal goals in responsive system design is to accurately define responsiveness and make it useful, easily modeled, and easily measurable. Complete and accurate evaluation of responsiveness may require sophisticated models that can cross the bounds of the design hierarchy without the usual state space explosion. We are currently studying system and service models that focus on responsiveness. Since it seems that no existing modeling paradigms are suitable, we adopt Rainbow Nets [9], and limit the state explosion by incorporating the concept of model projections based on the protocol projection idea [19].

4 Responsive Consensus

As mentioned in Section 2, consensus is a fundamental and pervasive problem in distributed systems, and it permeates every layer of the fault and time management framework of the multicomputer environment. Responsive consensus is a general approach to the consensus problem in which consensus is treated as a single, generic problem with multiple manifestations. Our aim is to bring these manifestations into a single framework that is applicable to any consensus situation.

In the proposed responsive system framework (see Section 2), consensus tasks make up the basic functions of the responsive kernel. Therefore, a consensus algorithm is required that is simple and efficient, since it will be used often, versatile, since it has many functions, and flexible, since it must operate at many levels in various systems that may have different fault models. Since the consensus tasks determine what types of faults and how many faults may be tolerated, they are closely related to the system responsiveness measure.

The time needed to execute the consensus protocol must be strictly limited. Moreover, the protocol must execute in a fault-tolerant manner. In other words, consensus itself must be responsive. Sophisticated methods are needed to ensure timeliness, correctness, high availability, and universality of consensus protocols. Since many consensus protocols are able to operate correctly in the presence of faults, a primary concern is to guarantee the timeliness of responsive consensus. In addition, we envision a need for two types of consensus, global and application specific. Global consensus protocols should produce information on the status of the entire system; application specific consensus should provide status information on a subset of the processing elements involved in the execution of a given application. To handle the timeliness issue in a large processor population, we developed the Hierarchical Partitioning Method (HPM) [4], which is briefly described in the next section.

4.1 The Hierarchical Partitioning Method (HPM)

In a large network, there will be groups of processors that, to a large extent, operate independently from other processors, thus greatly diminishing the usefulness of global diagnosis and global consensus. It is desirable, then, to create a mechanism that allows the formation of local consensuses, the reconfiguration of local consensuses, and the efficient dissemination of the results of other local consensuses. Hierarchical partitioning provides such a mechanism.

The HPM is a proposed design for an implementation of responsive consensus because of the choices a designer has in tailoring the HPM to a particular system. This flexibility includes selecting a particular consensus algorithm or set of algorithms that meet the needs of the system fault model. For example, the HPM has been studied using system diagnosis techniques, which are consensus protocols designed to identify which processors are faulty and which are fault free, and Byzantine agreement algorithms, which are consensus protocols whose goal is to allow the fault-free processors to agree on some set of information [4].

The Hierarchical Partitioning Method (HPM) has been shown to reduce the effects of reaching consensus in large, distributed systems [4], and it has also been shown that the HPM uses many fewer messages than a global consensus algorithm, which implies that the HPM takes less time. Because consensus tasks will be executed at the same time as other system tasks, they must not disrupt the network with large bursts of communication. The HPM divides the consensus into many independent tasks and keeps the consensus information distributed, thus avoiding the large message bursts that can occur in global consensus algorithms.

The HPM is a strong base on which to build a complete responsive consensus algorithm; it has an availability that is adjustable by the system designer, it reduces the time needed to reach consensus by reducing the required number of messages (thus increasing the system's ability to produce timely results), and it may incorporate any number of existing consensus protocols, which makes it flexible enough to suit the system's fault model.

4.2 Consensus Algorithm Selection

The HPM is flexible because it allows the system designer to choose the particular consensus algorithm that best suits the system's fault model and requirements. Recognizing which consensus implementation is the correct one for the job is not simple, though, as many algorithms have been presented.

A survey of the existing consensus protocols [3] was done and revealed that basically every area of consensus research addresses the problem of providing a mechanism that produces correct results in a multiple processor environment when that environment contains some number of faulty processors. There are three main directions in this research: system-level diagnosis [5], processor membership [6], and Byzantine agreement [8, 7]. Despite the similarity of purpose, these areas were developed in isolation from each other. Together, though, they form a spectrum of solutions for many different situations.

For an environment that has different fault models and priority schemes, the development of a universal, responsive consensus protocol to handle synchronization, reliable communication, diagnosis, and configuration is needed. In fact, it is possible to introduce a single algorithm that works for all four of these tasks under different fault assumptions and for a variety of timeliness requirements. A single algorithm forms the foundation for our CORE operating system.

5 The Responsive Scheduler

The scheduler plays a critical role in the operation of a real-time system. Scheduling in real-time systems is the process of allocating resources to tasks so the task timing constraints are not violated. The reason that scheduling is widely studied is because, in general, it belongs to the class of NP-complete problems. Thus, a perfect solution to scheduling does not exist and forces the use of scheduling policies or heuristics. Since future responsive systems will be complex, static scheduling might not be feasible, and, instead, dynamic scheduling, in which scheduling is performed "on-the-fly" as the tasks arrive, or mixed scheduling, in which both static and dynamic scheduling are used, should be employed. Also, situations in which the task arrival instants, execution times, and timing constraints are non-deterministic must be considered. A good design for the scheduler is essential because it plays a central role in a responsive system. Not only is it relied on to arrange for the timely execution of application tasks, but even fundamental system level tasks, such as executing programs to achieve synchronization or consensus on who is faulty and who is not, may have to be handled by the scheduler. Therefore, a scheduler that meets the responsiveness criterion is an important and integral part of a responsive system.

5.1 Design Issues for a Responsive Scheduler

Two important goals for a responsive scheduler are scheduling for timeliness and scheduling for fault tolerance. The first goal of a responsive scheduler is to schedule the tasks using the available resources so each of the tasks can complete within its given deadline. As defined earlier in Section 3, the responsiveness of a system is a product of its availability and its timeliness, i.e., its ability to complete the tasks on time. The timeliness of a system is dependent on the number of processors, their speed, and the existence of a schedule to execute that task. It is the role of a scheduler in a responsive system to fulfill the last requirement, that is, to arrange for the timely execution of the task. Each task has a task execution window during which the results of the execution of that task must become available.

Scheduling for fault tolerance is a novel aspect that must be incorporated in all responsive systems. Unlike schedulers used in traditional systems or in real-time systems operating today, the scheduler will have to handle the issue of task fault tolerance. In a responsive system, we would expect the dependability requirement of all tasks to be specified. The system will attempt to fulfill that requirement by adding redundancy to task execution when a processor cannot directly meet the specified goals. In our view, this will be achieved by close interaction between the scheduler and the availability manager. The availability manager will, at periodic intervals, update the scheduler about the status of all processors (whether they are faulty or fault-free) and their dependability, such as their reliability or availability measure. This information will be used by the scheduler to schedule the task to the appropriate location. However, if a critical task requires a dependability that cannot be met directly by a single processor, the scheduler will attempt to form a processor group that meets this need through task execution redundancy based on the processors dependabilities and fault models.

There are three ways to add redundancy to a system, space redundancy, time redundancy, and a combination of space and time redundancy. Space redundancy is achieved by replicating the task over the processor group. Assume that a task demanding an availability $a_i(t)$ arrives.
Let us say that its execution time has been estimated as τ and its time to deadline is d. In this case, the scheduler will create a processor group that will have an availability of at least a_t over the time interval $0-d$, and it will schedule the replicas of the task on each of the processors of that group for τ time units in the interval $0-d$. This information will be then passed on to the availability manager, which will be responsible for forming a consensus about the result of the tasks and handling any faults in the replicas. Note that other tasks may also be scheduled on those processors over the remaining time.

Time redundancy is achieved by repeating the execution of a task. Let us assume that a task has the same timing requirements as before. Then, the task may recover from a temporary fault if its execution is repeated. We can evaluate availability of such a task as $a_{12} = a_1 a_2 + a_1(1 - a_2) + a_2(1 - a_1)$. Note that $a_1(t_1)$ and $a_2(t_2)$ may vary as they are executed at different times.

In the case of space-time redundancy, the availability manager reports the availabilities of various processors. The scheduler selects the processor or processor group with availability of a_{pg}. This means that the processor or processor group is likely to be down for $1 - a_{pg}$ percent of the time d. Thus, the scheduler will schedule the task for $\tau + (1 - a_{pg})d$ instead of τ time units, and, if a failure occurs and the processor group is down, there is still enough time for it to recover from the fault and execute the task successfully.

A scheduler is itself a part of the responsive system and as such should have the two basic features of responsiveness, namely, timeliness and fault tolerance. Since dynamic scheduling of tasks with non-deterministic characteristics on multiprocessors is NP-complete, the time it will take to obtain an optimum solution, if one exists, might be prohibitive. A scheduling policy or a scheduling heuristic would have to be used instead. However, one has to guarantee that the scheduler itself would obtain a schedule in a timely fashion. A scheduling policy, such as First-come-first-serve, Earliest-deadline-first, Least-laxity-first, etc., has the advantage of having deterministic times to schedule tasks, but a generic search-technique such as tabu, we believe, may be able to obtain acceptable schedules with a much lower development cost and a greater simplicity in design. In a complex system, several scheduling algorithms may need to be employed to achieve schedules of acceptable quality. It may also turn out that a generic search heuristic gives quality solutions while being simple and robust (in the sense of being able to solve any scheduling problem).

The scheduler, because it is at the core of an operating system, must be protected from faults. Since a scheduler failure is catastrophic, it is necessary that the scheduler be fault tolerant. This means that there will be multiple locations where a scheduler is executing so a single point failure cannot affect the entire system. Another issue is whether the scheduler is centralized or distributed. A fault-tolerant centralized scheduler would consist of multiple replicas that cooperate to obtain a schedule. Each of these replicas could be identical, or each may execute a different scheduling algorithm, which would result in a hybrid search technique [17, 18]. In case of a distributed scheduler, each processor should have its own local or global scheduler with the provision that the scheduler of another processor will take over in case of a failure. The local scheduler scheme would also require a load-sharing strategy to handle additional load at a processor in case of transient overloads. This could be achieved by consensus. Global schedulers would need a consensus on choosing the best schedule among fault-free processors.

5.2 Estimating the Number of Required Processors

An important issue that must be addressed while designing a responsive system is to determine how many processors are required. One approach to solving this problem is the probabilistic determination of the number of processors required in a responsive system based on the task characteristics — specifically, the inter-arrival time distribution, the execution time distribution, and the distribution of the time to deadline of the task. Assuming that none of these task characteristics are likely to be deterministic in a complex responsive system, one would have to accept probabilistic estimates of how many processors are needed. A method of finding probabilistic estimates for an infinite-server queueing system that sets an upper bound on the actual number of processors can be used. However, the choice of a scheduling policy has a direct bearing on the number of processors that need to be employed. We can effectively estimate the number of processing elements required in a system based on a scheduling policy, the fault models, the probabilistic distribution of task characteristics (load), and the dependability (namely the availability and reliability) of the processing units.

6 Application-Specific Responsiveness

As discussed in Section 2, responsive systems are composed of a hierarchy of consensus tasks (see Figure 2), which includes synchronization, reliable broadcast, fault diagnosis, and reconfiguration. At the top of this hierarchy is application specific responsiveness. That is, a responsive system can be viewed as a system in which there is a responsive kernel that supports many different responsive applications. We believe that application-specific properties facilitating low-cost fault tolerance should be incorporated in the design process along with other complementary techniques at the hardware or system level, such as self-checking or replicated logic, error detecting/correcting codes, checkpointing and process/processor replication.

The basic framework we pursue is one that considers an ultrareliable kernel with responsive services, such as consensus (synchronization, communication, diagnosis, reconfiguration) and scheduling. Besides that, we exploit application-specific properties to achieve efficient fault detection and recovery. By efficient we mean fault detection and recovery methods that incur low space and time overheads.

Previous research in application-specific responsiveness has focused so far on issues in fault tolerance. It is now our goal to expand and integrate these ideas with issues in real-time system design. Previous results include the NEST scheme for fault tolerance [10], naturally redundant algorithms [11], and a study of the cost (in terms of space and time overheads) and benefits (in terms of fault coverage) of various techniques for fault tolerance [16].

6.1 The NEST Scheme for Fault Tolerance

The NEST scheme for fault-tolerant application design described in [10] is based on a formal study of fault-tolerant algorithmic properties. These fault-tolerant properties may be applied at the hardware, system, or application level, but they are exploited at the application level. The formalization of fault-tolerant properties provides a common ground for studying fault-tolerant systems. In this context, redundancy is studied as a safety property and recovery is studied as a progress property. As a result, it is possible to define in a rigorous way what it means for an application to be fault tolerant.

Another consequence of this study is an outline of formal techniques that add fault-tolerant properties to applications when they are not present. This way, NEST provides both a model and a design methodology for fault-tolerant applications. Two algorithmic transformations, superposition and concatenation, are defined. Superposition can be used to add safety properties, such as redundancy, and concatenation can be used to insert progress properties, such as recovery, to applications. The insertion of redundancy is called invariant embedding, and the addition of recovery properties is called progress securing.

Based on the rigorous framework proposed in NEST, a comprehensive design methodology for responsive parallel applications can be achieved in three steps:

1. The definition of system fault tolerance, timing requirements, and limitations.
2. An investigation of whether the application (or an existing version of the algorithm) has inherent characteristics that cause some (or all) of the desired fault tolerance and timeliness properties to be met.
3. The application of general techniques through which the existing version of the application may be transformed to acquire the missing properties and meet the desired responsiveness related requirements.

A complete description of NEST, including the formalization of fault-tolerant properties, a formal definition of what it means for an application to be fault tolerant, and the full description of a methodology for fault-tolerant parallel application design, is presented in [10].

6.2 Evaluation of Techniques for Fault Tolerance: Cost/Benefit Relation

We evaluated a number of existing fault-tolerance techniques [16] for their space and time overheads and the kinds of faults that they are able to tolerate. The results of this work are summarized in Table 1 in which N is the number of processors, T is the number of supersteps, and I_{CP} is the number of supersteps in the interval between the checkpoints. The techniques evaluated were replication and voting, checkpointing and rollback [12], algorithm-based fault tolerance [13], self stabilization [14], inherent fault tolerance [15], and the natural redundancy approach [11].

6.3 The NEST Scheme for Responsiveness

The NEST scheme, which was primarily designed for fault tolerance, should address real-time issues. A formal framework that incorporates concepts related to

TYPE OF TECHNIQUE	REDUNDANCY				FAULTS TOLERATED
	SPACE		TIME		
	# of processors		# of supersteps		
	needed	extra	needed	extra	
Triplication with Voting	$3N$	$2N$	$T+1$	1	multiple temporary and permanent
Checkpointing and Rollback	N	—	$T + I_{CP}$	I_{CP}	multiple temporary
Algorithm-based Fault Tolerance	$N+2$	2	$T+1$	1	single temporary
Self Stabilization	N	—	?	?	multiple temporary
Inherent Fault Tolerance	N	—	$\frac{T*N}{N-1}$	$\frac{T}{N-1}$	multiple fail-stop
Approach Based on Natural Redundancy	N	—	$T+1$	1	single temporary and permanent

Table 1. Necessary space and time redundancy and faults tolerated by different fault-tolerance techniques.

system fault-tolerant properties and system real-time properties at the application level is the basis for application specific responsiveness. Our focus here is the study of the conditions and the probability that a given application will be able to meet timing constraints in the presence of faults. Ultimately, the system should be intelligent enough to be able to dynamically choose the appropriate fault tolerance technique depending on the criticality of a task, on the nature of the faults that affect the system (permanent or temporary, single or multiple), or on the amount of time that is available for recovery before a deadline is missed.

7 Conclusion

As computer systems proliferate and our dependence on them increases, responsiveness will be the most sought after quality in computer and communication systems. In this paper we developed the foundation for such responsive systems using consensus and scheduling as the basic constructs.

In our framework, the concepts of responsive consensus and responsive scheduling are fundamental. The universal consensus algorithm for synchronization, reliable communication, diagnosis, and reconfiguration was described, and a scheduler that works in a reliable and timely manner even in the presence of faults was presented.

This universal consensus forms the basis for our responsive operating system called CORE.

In addition to CORE, application specific methods, such as those presented here, are essential, because high responsiveness can only be achieved by combining an ultrareliable kernel with application specific techniques.

Acknowledgment

I would like to acknowledge my students Mike Barborak, Mihir Pandya, and Luiz Larenjeira for contributing to responsive consensus, responsive scheduling, and application specific responsiveness, respectively.

References

1. M. Malek, *Responsive Systems: A Marriage between Real Time and Fault Tolerance*, Keynote Address, Proceedings of the 5th International GI/ITG/GMA Conference on Fault-Tolerant Computing Systems, Nürnberg, Germany, Springer-Verlag, Informatik-Fachberichte 283, September 25, 1991, 1–17.
2. M. Malek, *Responsive Systems: A Challenge for the Nineties*, EuroMicro 90: Microprocessing and Microprogramming, August 30, 1990, 1–5.
3. M. Barborak, M. Malek and A.T. Dahbura, *Consensus Problem in Fault-Tolerant Computing*, Department of Computer Sciences, The University of Texas at Austin, November 1991, No. TR-91-40.
4. M. Barborak and M. Malek, *Partitioning for Efficient Consensus*, Technical Report, Department of Electrical and Computer Engineering, The University of Texas at Austin, May 1992.
5. F. Preparata, G. Metze and R. Chien, *On the Connection Assignment Problem of Diagnosable Systems*, IEEE Transactions on Electronic Computers, EC-16, No. 6, December 1967, 848–854.
6. F. Cristian, *Reaching Agreement on Processor-Group Membership in Synchronous Distributed Systems*, Distributed Computing, Vol. 4, 1991, 175–187.
7. M. Pease, R. Shostak and L. Lamport, *Reaching Agreement in the Presence of Faults*, Journal of the ACM, Vol. 27, No. 2, April 1980, 228–234.
8. M. Fischer, N. Lynch and M. Paterson, *Impossibility of Distributed Consensus with One Faulty Process*, Journal of the ACM, Vol. 32, No. 2, April 1985, 374–382.
9. A. Johnson and M. Malek, *Rainbow nets for system analysis*, IBM Systems Technology Division, Austin, Texas, IBM Technical Report, No. TR 51.0565, September 1989,
10. L. Laranjeira, M. Malek and R. Jenevein, NEST: *A Nested Predicate Scheme for Fault Tolerance*, to appear in IEEE Transactions on Computers.
11. L. Laranjeira, M. Malek and R. Jenevein, *An Tolerating Faults in Naturally Redundant Algorithms*, The 10th Symposium on Reliable Distributed Systems, Pisa, Italy, September 1991, 118–127.

12. R. Koo and S. Toueg, *Checkpointing and Rollback-Recovery for Distributed Systems*, IEEE Transactions on Software Engineering, Vol. SE–13, No. 1, January 1987, 23–31.

13. K.H. Huang and J.A. Abraham, *Algorithm-Based Fault Tolerance for Matrix Operations*, IEEE Transactions on Software Engineering, Vol. SE–33, No. 6, June 1984, 518–528.

14. E.W. Dijkstra, *Self-Stabilizing Systems in Spite of Distributed Control*, Communications of the ACM, Vol. 17, No. 11, November 1974, 643–644.

15. F.B. Bastani, I. Yen and I. Chen, *A Class of Inherently Fault-Tolerant Distributed Systems*, IEEE Transactions on Software Engineering, Vol. 14, No. 10, October 1988, 1432–1442.

16. L. Laranjeira, M. Malek R. Jenevein, *Space/Time Overhead Analysis and Experiments with Fault-Tolerant Techniques*, The Third IFIP Working Conference on Dependable Computing for Critical Applications, Palermo, Italy, September 1992.

17. M. Malek, M. Guruswamy, H. Owens, M. Pandya, *A Hybrid Algorithm Technique*, Department of Computer Sciences, The University of Texas at Austin, No. TR–89–06, 1989.

18. M. Malek, M. Guruswamy, H. Ownes and M. Pandya, *Serial and Parallel Search Techniques for the Traveling Salesman Problem*, Annals of Operations Research, Vol. 21, 1989, 59–84.

19. S.S. Lam and A.U. Shankar, *Protocol Verification via Projections*, IEEE Transactions on Software Engineering, July 1984, Vol. SE–10, No. 4, 325–342.

Static Models and Simulation Engine for Time-Analysis and Verification of Mission-Critical Distributed Systems

*Giovanni Cantone**

Universita di Roma "Tor Vergata"
Laboratorio di Informatica
Dipartimento di Ingegneria Elettronica
Via della Ricerca Scientifica
00133 Roma
Italy

Abstract

A method and a simulation engine for predicting temporal behaviours of time-life critical distributed processes are suggested in the following. Dynamic systems and the maximum parallel model are specially considered while the concept of local time is emphasized. The proposed method is based on timed concurrent direct graphs as a model for representing task objects and types. Some arcs of such a graph are labelled by duration values. These values depend on both the assumed behaviour paradigm and the hard/soft execution platforms. The proposed simulation engine is a tool for extracting timeliness from a system of timed concurrent d-graphs. For this aim, graphs are concurrently explored by the simulator and a virtual local time is associated with each graph exploration. Duration labels of explored arcs are then used to update local times and to predict the expected behaviours of the application system. Relevant information produced by the simulator includes timing of events, and the partitioning of the application behaviours into initial, periodic, transient and completion phases (both in the worst and the best behaviour paradigms).

1 Introduction

Real-time systems include time critical environments or plants which have to be controlled. The plant processes are implemented by the same environment which executes them virtually in parallel. The control sub-system is composed by software processes and their underlying machines or system (US), i.e. the hardware platforms and the run-time supports. The task of real-time controllers is to control the plant behaviour by receiving data and signals, processing them, and taking actions or returning results sufficiently quickly to affect the functioning of the environment at that time [37], [38]. The control sub-system of a special

---

* This work was partially supported by the "Progetto Finalizzato Sistemi Informatici e Calcolo Parallelo" of CNR (I) under grant No. 90.00705.PF69

class of real-time systems, the hard-real-time (HRT) systems, is strictly required to meet demands on time, with no failures being tolerated [35]. In order to
tolerate faults, especially in life-critical systems, both time/space and hard/soft
redundancies can be included [9]. A human operator may be charged with the
responsibility of interacting with the system, following some procedures, and
implementing some error recovery mechanisms, which should be activated only
in certain stated situations. Depending on the plant organization and, possibly,
on the Certification Authority guide-lines, a real-time system can be arranged
in some independent applications.

Parallel computation represents a viable solution to expanding computational requirements and a promising vehicle for improving both timeliness and
fault-tolerance of HRT controllers. While there is no universal agreement about
parallel computation models, a growing body of theories and a number of experiments are involved in the comparative analysis of parallel/concurrent computations in global processing environments, that can be immediately implemented
by shared memory multi-processors, with respect to parallel computations in
local processing environments, as immediately implemented by private memory
distributed multi-computers [33]. However, when HRT systems are taken into
consideration, the evaluation of computation models has to be driven mainly by
model predictability [36].

While a coming paper is expected to treat the predictability of parallel/ concurrent processes in global environments, the present one takes the predictability
of distributed processes in the maximum pure parallel model into consideration
[40]. This model argues for the introduction of computational resources at every
level of the control system, and for the assumption that the underlying processing system has enough power for executing each ready task in parallel, i.e. for
immediately activating a new process, running ready-to-run processes, proceeding ready-to-communicate partner-tasks, if any couple of partner tasks is ready
to, and so on.

These lecture notes are the result of on-going research aimed at extending
both static reasoning, models, methods, techniques and tools for mission critical
systems from sequential [11], [12], [15], [8], to concurrent [5], [7] fault-tolerant
[9], [10] processing environments. Such an extension is specified to be easily
transposed into tools and to support software engineering concepts, such as
iterative development, maintainability, direct and reverse engineering, reuse of
components and related experiences [3], temporal experiences included [6], [13].

At the present state of the art, principles and paradigms for predictability
[19], [39], [22], and methods for computing time bounds of sequential systems
are largely known [34], [31]. Moreover, the life-cycle of a sequential HRT product
is supported by specific tools [1]. Furthermore, schedulability analysis concepts
were extended to systems which include global memory synchronization mechanisms like semaphores, and prototypes were implemented [35]. Finally, industrial
tools for performance assessment included some forms of concurrency [18].

Time properties which are investigated in the following are best and worst
response times, initial, periodic, transient, and completion behaviours of application systems. Clock sharing is not assumed and the concept of time locality is

emphasized.

The formal closure [32], [25] of the worst (best) timeliness and other properties of parallel processes that could exchange messages by un-restricted schemes [26], with non-deterministic ones included, is known to be a complex analytical task [40]. Consequently, a lot of practical problems arise even when very few messaging processes are taken into consideration [40], regardless which intermediate model is chosen to represent a system of tasks. So in these lecture notes some heuristics are considered together with automatic static analysis. In particular, an approach including deterministic simulations and interactions with an expert operator is followed, as sketched in Figure 1.

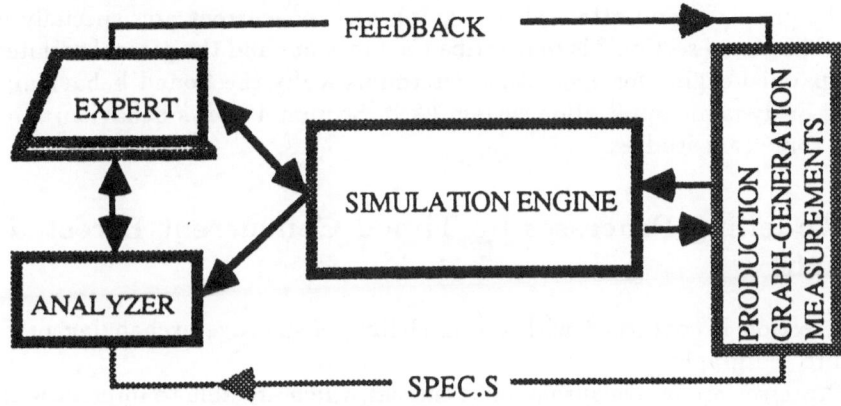

Fig. 1. Environment of the simulation engine.

The simulation engine extracts information on the timing of events — like task creations, communications and completions — from a model of the application. The analyzer and the expert check the timing information in order to characterize behaviours of the application. Results from comparisons of simulated behaviours and temporal specifications are used to feedback the production. A major challenge, besides the simulation technology itself, was to approach modelling notations that can easily include sequential models and could be comfortable both to system and software engineers, and to develop methods that support a smooth transition from system-level modelling to hardware and software implementation, with traceability along the way [18].

In these lecture notes, processes are modelled by "Timed Concurrent Directed Graphs", TCDGs. Arcs and/or nodes of such a graph are augmented by some time information. In order to manage changes in the software architecture of dynamic systems, TCDGs include both actual and potential arcs (as, for instance, in the UCLA graph model [30]). Moreover, the concept of graph-history of an application system is introduced. Timed Regular Expressions (TREs) or Timed Petri Nets (TPNs) rather than TCDGs could be used to model tasks. TCDGs of a regular system [2] and related temporal properties can be easily expressed by a system of TREs. Moreover, the use of some Timed Petri Net model only [16],

[29], [17] is in the author's perspective work; in fact, Timed Petri Nets include TCDGs. Finally, the proposed simulation engine could be easily modified to explore TPNs or scan TREs, and extended to handle hybrid systems, i.e. systems possibly made by a combination of TREs, TPNs, and TCDGs.

The main goal of the next section is to show that behaviours of max-par higher level language (HLL) distributed processes can be deterministically predicted, once some HRT constraints are met by the software processes and the underlying system. For this purpose it shows the timed concurrent d-graph as an intermediate model for representing a task object or type. It introduces concepts like d-graph structure of an application system, reasons about the temporal properties of structures of d-graph objects, and recalls [7] that time stamp sequences can be predicted and attached to d-graph arcs, concurrent arcs specially included. The aim of section 3 is to describe the functions and the general architecture of a parallel engine for generating deterministically the bound behaviours of a static or dynamic application system (AS). Section 4 shows behavioural results from some case-studies.

2 Modelling Processes by Timed Concurrent Directed Graphs

This section is concerned with the modelling of message exchanging processes by directed graphs.

Processes are active autonomous entities which are able to interact with one another. We assume

- both static processes and dynamically instanceable task types;
- static channels;
- static behaviour of processes;
- message passing only, as model of interaction;
- pure maximum parallelism, as model of computation;
- asymetric extended rendezvous, as model of synchronization.

Requests to exchange messages with tasks to be created in the future are excluded by this version of the paper. Primitives which could dynamically modify the behaviour of processes, like "Become" in the Actors model, are not considered.

Similarities of some of the points above to the Ada communication and programming model are obvious and, to provide focus, the discussion in the remainder of these notes will be with respect to Ada [41], [28]. However, we are reasoning on a conceptual level while Ada is used as the meta-language of our expressions; so the lack of time predictability and other well-known limits shown by the present Ada standard (like semantics of the Delay statement, common time because of the Package Calendar, possibility to share data), and problems related to the implementation of true distributed Ada compilers are not taken into consideration. Moreover, some concurrent primitives will also be discussed that Ada does not provide or provides with different semantics. Our proposals were easily applied to CSP-like symmetric synchronous communication models, as briefly sketched in the "Thinking/eating philosophers" case-study herein included. Finally, our proposals hold for "many to/from many" synchronous communication models, as shown in the included "Client pool/Server pool" case-studies.

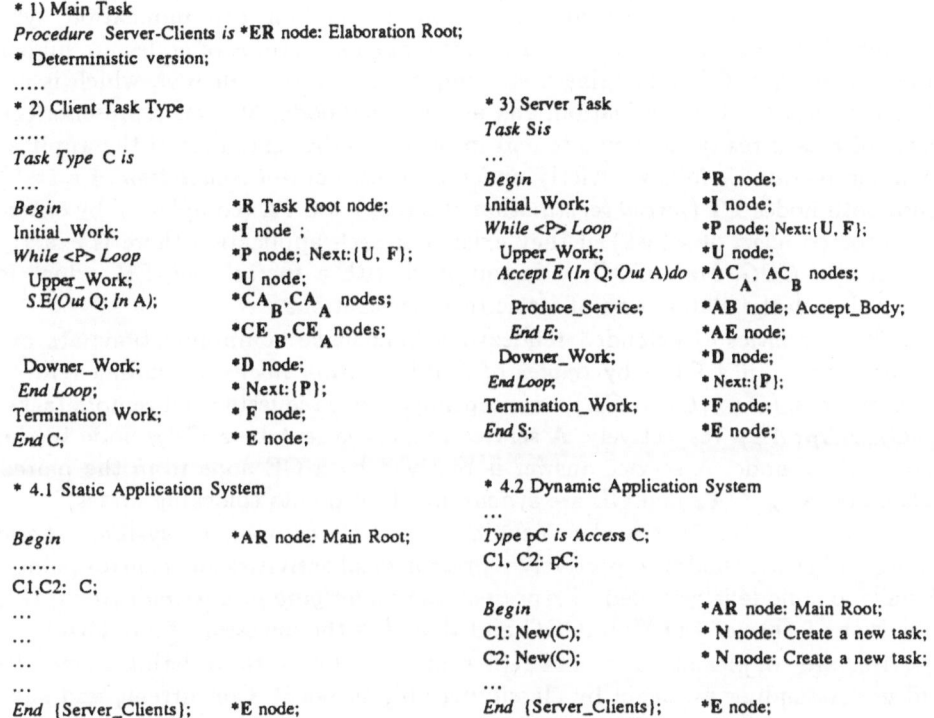

Table 1. Static/Dynamic application systems consisting of a Main task, some Clients, and one Server.

Table 1 recalls two Ada-like coded classic examples that will be extensively considered throughout the paper. Both examples include a main task (Server_Clients), a Server task (S), and a set of Client tasks. They are different from one another by the static or dynamic techniques the main task used to create Client tasks, respectively. Tasks are assumed to be run remotely. Initializations and producing/consuming messages are supposed to be local activities or to depend on fully embedded (lower nesting level) tasks. Both deterministic and non-deterministic versions of similar examples will also be considered with multiple servers, each server being able to perform multiple services (the programs are not shown for the sake of brevity.)

2.1 Concurrent Directed Graphs

The "Concurrent Directed Graph", CDG(P), is assumed in the following as a model for representing a task P (see Figure 2). The CDG of a task is a static object which is derived from the task text. As usual, such a direct graph is based on finite sets of nodes and arcs.

Nodes represent task activities, creation, completion, communication, synchronization, or control points. Nodes that embed structures of nodes are higher level nodes. Any CDG contains a starting node, say R as in *root*, which is associated with the task activation, and an *anti-root* node, X. This represents the state of a task ready to complete and implements the semantics of the application completion. X follows strictly nodes E (End: *natural completion* of a task) and, both nodes FT (*forced termination* of a task) and FA (completion by externally forced *abort* of a task), if they exist. For each application there is exactly one *special CDG*, Main_CDG. It is equipped with a *special root*, ER, which is charged with the elaboration of static task declarations.

The semantics of extended rendezvous handshake communications are explicitly shown in a CDG by *triples of (sub)operation nodes* for calling remote task services, (CA_B, CA_A, CE), or accepting service requests from remote tasks, (AC_A, AC_B, AE), respectively. A service request is sent by a CA_B node to the paired AC_B node. A service answer is received by a CE node from the paired AE node. AC_A, CA_A and CE are synchronization points (blocking nodes).

Creation nodes, N, are also included by CDGs of dynamic systems. *Local* nodes and *control* nodes respectively represent local activities and control points. Finally, one node is assumed to represent the *underlying processing system*, US; this is the father of any Main_CDG and thus it is the ancestor of any CDG.

Arcs are couples of nodes and represent partial or total ordering items. To aid understanding we begin by classifying arcs as Local, Concurrent, and sub-classifying Local arcs as Properly_Local, Application_System_Dependent_Local and Concurrent arcs as Actual, Potential. A further useful classification of arcs as in Normal, Exception was used. However, for the sake of brevity, the Exception flows will not be further taken into consideration [20].

Concurrent arcs are couples of nodes in different task-graphs (or include US). In the enclosed figures, dotted arrows were used to draw concurrent arcs. Both nodes of an *Actual concurrent arc* are included by graph objects, i.e. CDGs of task objects. At least one node of a *Potential concurrent arc* is included by a graph type, i.e. the CDG of a task type which could be possibly referred to at run time. R and ER (X) nodes are only entered (exited) by concurrent arcs. Such an arc (or edge) is denoted by e_0 (e_X) and is called starting arc of a CDG (completion arc of an application system). A node ER is exited by a number of concurrent arcs, one arc for each remaining static task. A potential concurrent arc exits a dynamic Creation node. Such a potential arc is linked to the CDG type to be possibly dynamically instanced rather than connected to a CDG object (see Figure 3a). Concurrent arcs exit Abort nodes; such arcs are connected to the nodes of the graph-task which could be possibly aborted. Three concurrent arcs, (CA_B, AC_A), (AC_B, CA_A) and (AE, CE), are associated with a rendezvous

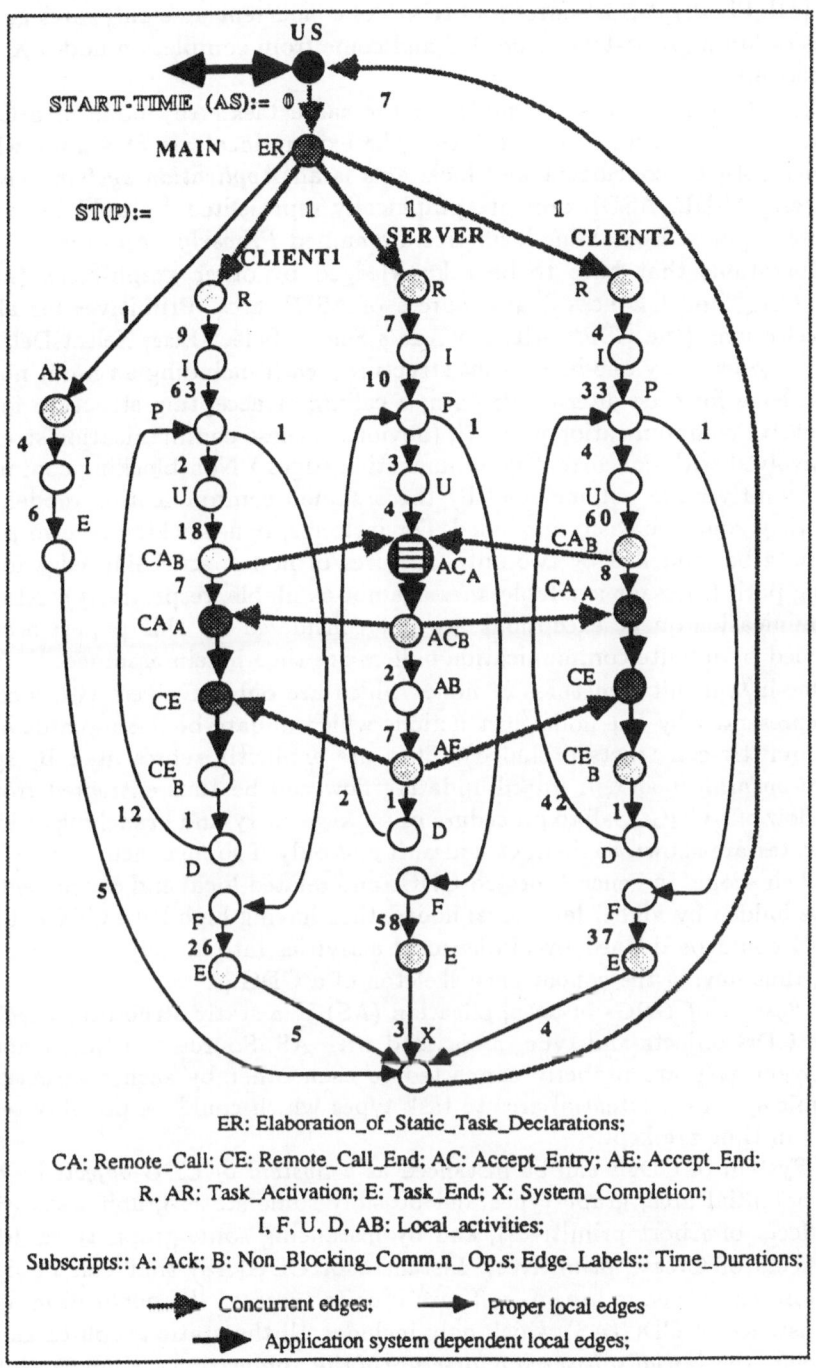

Fig. 2. Concurrent d-graphs of a static application (see text in Table 1).

[28], [41]. Finally, US is source and target of concurrent arcs only; arcs go to ER nodes of Main graph-tasks from US and come from completion nodes X to US, respectively.

Local arcs are couples of nodes in the same task. Any node of a CDG is involved at least with some local arc. The exiting local arc of a node which is entered both by concurrent and local arcs is an *Application system dependent local arc*, ASDL. ASDL arcs are graphically represented by bold lines in the enclosed figures. Remaining local arcs are named *Properly local arcs*.

Operations that have to be acknowledged by other graph-tasks (namely, AC_A, CA_A, and CE nodes) are sources of ASDL arcs. Primitives for alternative selections (the CSP's Alt, the Ada's Select, Select-Else, Select-Delay) are locally modelled by one-in/one-out structures, each including an n-out node, an ASDL edge for each alternative path, a calling or accepting structure for each alternative communication path [7]; (obviously, these communication structures are involved with concurrent communication edges.) Non-blocking communication primitives are not included by the assumed communication model. However, they could be easily modelled. For instance, non-blocking receive primitives could be modelled by two out-structures of nodes, an ASDL edge for each exiting path (message available, message not-available, respectively). Also, full-communication-queue exceptions are not considered by this paper; acceptors equipped by infinite communication buffers are thus herein assumed.

One-in/one-out structures of nodes which are only involved with local arcs are represented by one node (instructions which update boolean guards of non-deterministic constructs excluded). They are explicitly represented by specific *Guard-updating nodes*. A guard-updating flow can be thus extracted from the local flow of a CDG. Call to procedure or package entry and branching or looping predicates are shown as distinct nodes, if and only if some concurrent primitive is in their scope. In general, nested CDGs and related local and concurrent flows can be hidden by higher level local nodes, thus having high level CDGs. Finally, a CDG could be defined by hiding local activities into an adjacent concurrent node, thus having the concurrence skeleton of a CDG.

A *System of CDGs* of an application (AS) is a static structure, CDG(AS), of the CDG objects and types associated with AS. Source and target nodes of concurrent arcs are properly connected to each other by such a structure. In dynamic systems, potential arcs to task types which could be possibly referred to at run-time are kept.

A System of CDGs can be instanced as a *System of CDG objects* by hiding both potential arcs, graph-types and possibly some static graph-tasks (due to the effects of Abort primitives), and by instancing some graph types (due to the effects of Create primitives). Instances of CDG(AS) that can be derived one from the other represent *software architectures of the application system*. The instance of CDG(AS) which only includes all the static graph-tasks of AS represents the *initial software architecture* of the application system, Arch0(AS). Later on, Curr_Arch(CDG(AS)) will be used to denote the current software architecture of the application system, and consistent sequences of architectures will be implicitly referred to.

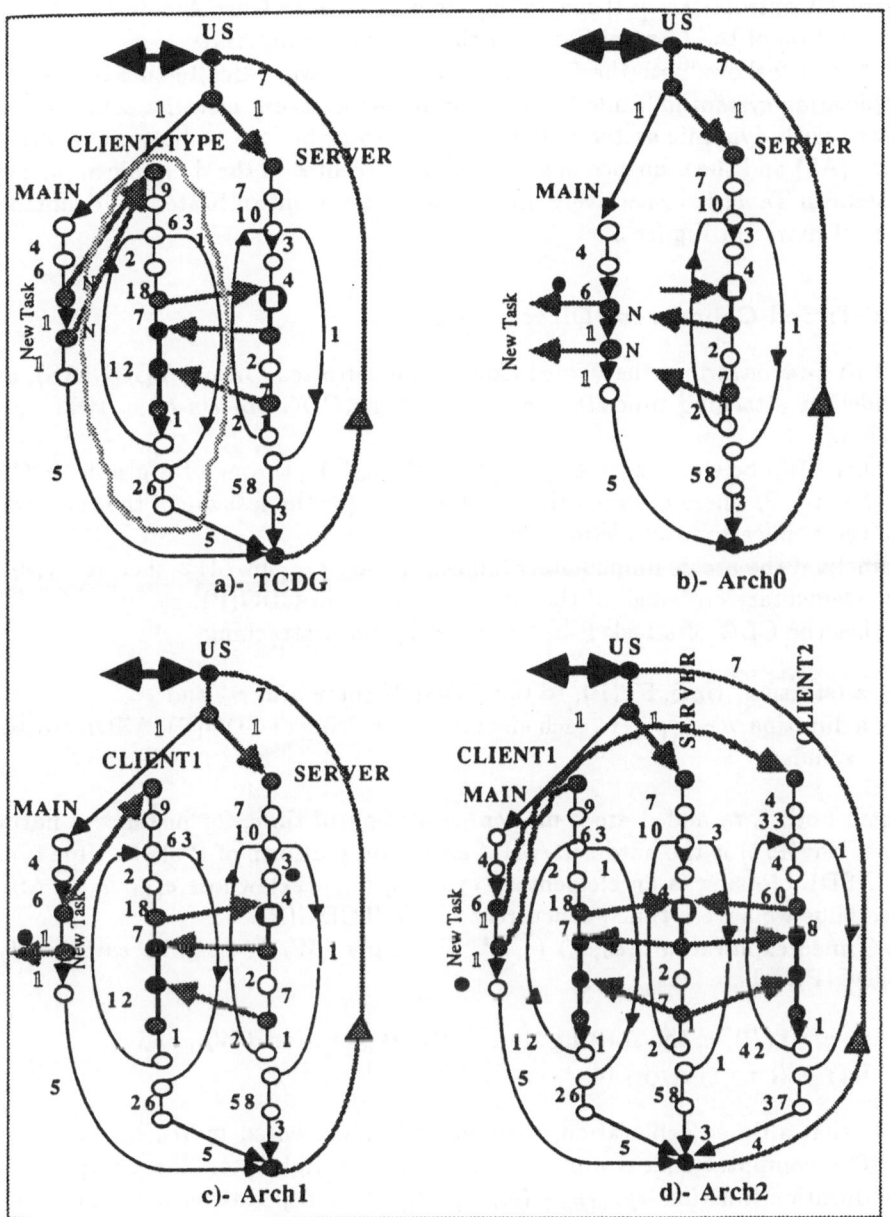

Fig. 3. TCDG and software architectures of the dynamic application in Table 1.

A Control_State can be associated with a CDG object. It assumes values in the set of the CDG's nodes and is also named Current_Node of the CDG. A Concurrent_Control_State [41] can be thus associated with Curr_Arch(CDG(AS)), as a collection of the Control_States of the current architecture.

Figure 2 shows both the CDG(AS) and the software architecture of the static application system in Table 1. One or more architecture histories could be associated with dynamic systems. Figure 3, left to right, top to bottom, shows the CDG(AS) and the sequence of software architectures of the dynamic application system in Table 1, respectively. Instances of task Control_States are denoted by special marks in Figure 3.

2.2 Timed Concurrent Directed Graphs

Let us now introduce the Timed Concurrent Directed Graph, TCDG(AS), as a model for attaching time stamps to arcs of the CDG objects of an HRT application.

Let LW_P be a partial (total) "local" walk, $e_0(e)^*$, through the graph CDG(P) of the task P, where e is a local arc of CDG(P) (or the last arc of the total walk, i.e. the application completion arc, e_X).

Namely, if the arc e_i immediately follows the arc e_{i-1} in LW_P then (e_{i-1}, e_i) is an "elementary crossing" of the node $(e_{i-1} \cap e_i)$ in CDG(P).

Let the CDG of a task P be extended by both attaching

- a (starting) time, ST(P), to the CDG(P) entry arc, e_0, and
- a duration, $d_{Env(P,t)}$, to each elementary crossing of CDG(P), ASDL crossings excluded,

where both t, t_0 and d are some representation of time, for instance a natural type, Env(P, t) is the hard-soft/plant execution platform of P at the time t, and an ASDL crossing is an elementary crossing (e_i, e_{i+1}) whose e_{i+1} is an ASDL arc. Thus we have a timed concurrent CDG, TCDG(P).

Timed exploration, $(e_0, t_0) (e, t)^*$, or simply $LW_P{}^{ST}$, can be associated to TCDG(P), where

- $t_0 = ST(P)$, is the starting time of the exploration LW_P, and
- $t_{i+1} = t_i + d_{Env(P,t_i)} (e_i, e_{i+1}, t_i), (e_i, e_{i+1}) \in LW_P$.

Note that a timed exploration is equivalently represented by $(e_0, t_0) (e, d)^*$.

The computational complexity of t depends tightly on the complexity of the duration function $d_{Env(P,t_i)} (e_i, e_{i+1}, t_i)$. This depends on both the current execution environment of P and the content of the elementary crossing (e_i, e_{i+1}). Moreover, it depends on both the state and the possible non-determinism of any element of the global system by the argument t_i.

In order to compute statically the duration of (some) elementary crossings, let us begin by excluding dynamic migration of control tasks from one execution platform to another, different one.

Once both the worst (best) behavioural paradigm is assumed [21], and assumptions of predictability [34], [31], [35] are met by the executing platforms and locally by any task, the restriction of d to elementary local crossings, (i.e. (e_i, e_{i+1}) whose e_{i+1} is a properly local arc), can be easily implemented as a static map, $\text{Worst}(e_i, e_{i+1})$ $(\text{Best}(e_i, e_{i+1}))$ [14]. In fact, for each path that crosses a local activity, the worst (best) crossing time, or an upper (lower) bound of such a constant time, can be deterministically predicted. Moreover, similar results can also be extended to elementary crossings of primitives like Create and Abort, if deterministic behaviours are assumed for distributed run time support. Also response times can be predicted for asynchronous (non-blocking) communications, in the assumption of a deterministic network. Finally, the duration of an ASDL crossing depends on the behaviour of the global system.

For the sake of simplicity, $\text{Worst}(e_{i+1})$ rather than $\text{Worst}(e_j, e_{i+1})$ is used to label arcs in the enclosed figures, where $\text{Worst}(e_{i+1})$ is the maximum of $\{\text{Worst}(e_j, e_{i+1}), \forall e_j \in \{\text{Input\_Arcs}(e_{i-1} \cap e_i)\}\}$, (respectively, $\text{Best}(e_{i+1})$, i.e. the minimum of $\{\text{Best}(e_j, e_{i+1}), \forall e_j \in \{\text{Input\_Arcs}(e_{i-1} \cap e_i)\}\}$,) where Input_Arcs(n $\in$ CDG) denotes the set of the CDG's arcs whose target is the node n. Consequently, d is reduced to a mapping from arcs to duration time. For instance, arcs of the CDGs in Figure 2, communication arcs and the application system dependent local arcs excluded, were labelled by the worst durations.

In order to handle migrating control tasks, a number of maps are needed for each task P. For each behavioural paradigm, this number equals the number of processor max-groups, which show the same time performances and could be charged to execute P.

Finally, consistent sequences of time stamps can be associated with the arcs of Curr_Arch\{TCDG(AS)\}s, ASDL arcs and concurrent arcs included, while exploring the graph-system associated with a HRT application. For any TCDG(P) in Curr_Arch\{TCDG(AS)\}, let the pair (Curr_Edge(P), Curr_Time(P)) be the element that was the most recently walked through by $LW_P{}^{ST}$. Let us also assume that the remaining arcs of $\{TCDG(P)\}$ are labelled by the Null time value. In order to attach time stamps to arcs, a graph exploration is needed for each alive task. If an explorer, $LW_P{}^{ST}$, is associated to each exploration, then it is requested to behave as a not intruding task which takes charge of i) initiating a local time-counter by the starting time of P, $t_0(\text{TCDG}(P))$; ii) moving the time-counter along the worst (best) local path of TCDG(P), starting from $e_0(P)$; iii) increasing the time-counter by the proper duration at each elementary crossing and, cooperating to event generation by iv) producing counter copies whenever a node is walked through which is the source of concurrent arcs and v) consuming counters, the last one excluded, whenever a node is walked through which is the source of an application system dependent local arc or of e_X [7].

3 Simulating the Behaviour of Distributed Processes

This section describes the organization and the implementation of a simulation engine to characterize the history of events which occur in a max-par distributed system.

3.1 Simulated Events

In the following, only the communication events and the events which affect the software architecture of the application system are considered. Other kinds of events could be easily considered.

Let an event be the tuple (EQ, SO, TG, ET), where EQ is the event qualifier and, SO and TG identify the event's source and target respectively; (utility functions to return the identifiers of the source or target explorer (SO_ID, TG_ID), graph (G_ID), or node (N_ID), are implicitly assumed.) ET, as in event time, is the current local time of SO or TG, as shown in the following sub-section.

The event qualifier type, Event_Type, follows by enumeration:

- *Creation*: SO creates TG as (the explorer of) a new TCDG object and ET equals SO.Curr_Time by such an event. Also, this forces the TG's Curr_Time to equal ET and the TG's Curr_Edge to equal $e_0(TG)$.
- *Termination*: SO terminates normally or abnormally. The event time equals SO.Curr_Time by such an event and TG equals SO.
- *Abort*: SO forces TG to terminate. ET equals SO.Curr_Time;
- *Communication*: a rendezvous between the caller SO and the acceptor TG occurs. In order to cope with rendezvous interrupting messages (see [7]), we split the Ada unique communication event in three (sub)events: *Rendezvous_Request*, *Rendezvous_Start*, and *Rendezvous_End*. The occurrence time of a communication (sub)event generally equals Maximum(Curr_Time(SO), Curr_Time(TG)) and both SO and TG are forced to assume the event time, where SO and TG are the (sub)event's source and target, respectively.

3.2 The Simulation Engine

With the goal of predicting the timeliness of HRT application systems by using related TCDGs, the simulation engine shown in Figure 2 is expanded to that in Figure 4.

3.2.1 General Architecture of the Engine

The general architecture of the simulator engine in Figure 4 includes:

1. A Data-base G of TCDGs whose elementary crossings, arcs or nodes are quoted by the worst (best or other) durations. It is assumed that a TCDG can be accessed by its identifier, G_ID.
2. A task type Graph_Explorer, *LWT* (as in Local Walker Type). It is instanced one or more times during a simulation session, one time for each static or dynamic creation of a graph object. An explorer is assumed to be able to
   - Look at G by G_ID for a TCDG;
   - Walk through a TCDG;
   - Exchange messages with, and receive commands from a monitor **M**.
3. A Monitor **M** which is assumed to be able to
   - Exchange messages with the Expert **E** and send messages to the analyzer **A**;

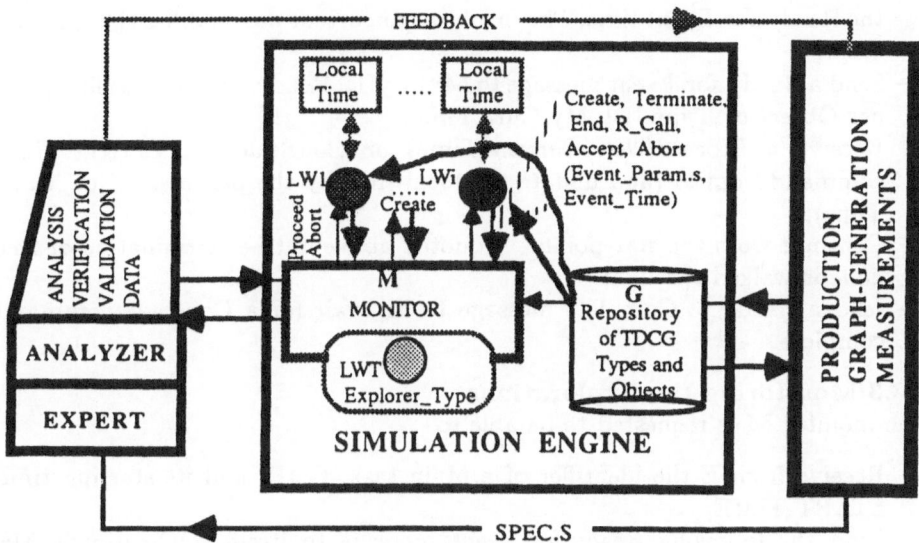

Fig. 4. Simulation engine for dynamic systems of messaging tasks.

- Create, command and, delete explorers;
- Pair Waiting_for_Rendezvous explorers.

4. An Expert **E** which, assisted by an Analyzer **A**, is assumed to be able to

- Start a simulation session;
- Exchange messages with **M**,
- Detect and show periodic or erroneous behaviours (e.g. attempts to couple with un-born or dead tasks; deadlock, livelock or starvation);
- Abort Explorers and Stop the simulation session.

Note that **M** and the alive instances of *LWT* cooperate to generate architecture histories of the application systems.

3.2.2 Exploration of Timed Directed Graphs
Any instance **LW** of *LWT* is assumed to be able to

- Identify itself (or accept an identifier), My_ID;
- Accept a task-graph identifier (G_ID) and starting time (t_0);
- Load a copy of an identified graph, TCDG:= **G** (G_ID);
- Assume (e_0, t_0) as an initial timed arc and t_0 as an initial local time of a TCDG exploration;
- *Proceed to explore the next arc of the TCDG(G_ID)'s worst (best or other) execution path, and to increase the current time by the elementary crossing duration;
- Continue from the "*" point quoted above up to cross a node which is involved with some concurrent arc. At such a point the graph explorer is ready for a simulated event. The simulated local time, Curr_Time, constitutes

the Ready_for_Event time. The involved concurrent arc qualifies the expected event;

- Send a Ready_for_Event message to M: (MyID, Ready_Event_Qualifier, [Partner_Object_or_Type_ID], My_Curr_Time);
- Receive a Proceed(New_Current_Time) or Conclude(New_Current_Time) command from M (and update the local time by the parameter New_Curr_Time);
- Continue from the star point "*" quoted above until a Termination or End node is walked through;
- send a Ready_to_Complete message to M; wait for a Conclude command; complete.

3.2.3 Monitoring the Explorations
The monitor M is requested to be able to

- Receive from E the identifier of a Main task, G_ID, and its starting time, START_TIME;
- Send the following Ready_for_Event message to itself: (OCreationO, US, G_ID, START_TIME);
- *Accept the next Ready_For_Event message: (Ready_Event_Qual, Left_ID, Right_ID, Ready_Time); *Case* Ready_Event_Qual *of*
- CREATION: Instance a new Explorer, LWID, and send the identifier of the son-graph (Right_ID) to it. Include LWID into the table of Awake explorers (note that static and dynamic graph-tasks are created similarly). Proceed LWID and Left_ID with Ready_Time, i.e the simulated current time of the father explorer (Left_ID), as time parameter.
- TERMINATION: Conclude Left_ID with the parameter Ready_Time. Move the descriptor of Left_ID from the table of the Awake explorer to the table of the Ready_to_Complete explorers.
- END: Conclude Left_ID with the parameter Ready_Time. Move the descriptor of Left_ID from the table of the Awake explorers to the table of the Ready_to_Complete explorers.
- ABORT: Conclude Right_ID with the parameter Ready_Time. Move the descriptor of Right_ID from the table of the Awake explorers to the Ready_to_Complete table.
- RENDEZVOUS_START_REQUEST: move the descriptor of Left_ID from the table of the Awake explorers to the Waiting_for_Rendezvous_Start table; save the message Ready_for_Event.
- RENDEZVOUS_START: Proceed both the involved explorers with the parameter Ready_Time. Move the descriptors of the involved explorers from the Waiting_for_Rendezvous_Start table to the Awake table.
- RENDEZVOUS_END: Proceed both the involved explorers with the parameter Ready_Time. Move the descriptors of the involved explorers from the Waiting_for_Rendezvous_End table to the Awake table.
- RENDEZVOUS_END_REQUEST: move the descriptor of Left_ID from the table of the Awake explorers to the Waiting_for_Rendezvous_End table; save the message Ready_for_Event.

- CONCLUSION: check the table of Ready_to_Complete explorers by Left_ID and possibly detect exceptions. If the table of the Alive explorers is empty, then arrange to finish.
- STOP: Send to E the messages that are still enqueued, if any, and the tables of the Alive, the Ready_for_Rendezvous, and the Ready_to_Complete explorers; arrange to finish; complete.
- Forward the message Ready_For_Event to E and A, so passing information about the occurrence of an event, the RENDEZVOUS_REQUEST cases obviously excluded;
- Repeat from the star point "*" quoted above up to obtain an empty Ready_for_Event queue;
- Pair ready for calling and ready for accepting explorers by using the saved Ready_for_Rendezvous_Start messages and applying proper temporal rules. Send to M (self) the message ("RENDEVOUS_START", SO, TG, Max(Curr_Time(SO), Curr_Time(TG)). Also, pair each acceptor (SO) which is ready to complete a rendezvous with the associated caller (TG) which is ready for such a (sub)event and, send to M the message ("RENDEVOUS_END", SO, TG, Max(Curr_Time(SO), Curr_Time(TG)). Due to the space tyranny, the proper temporal rules that M should apply can't be extensively shown within this paper. They can be found in [7]. Briefly, they charge the Monitor to select, among the waiting callers and the waiting acceptors, the matching pair (SO, TG), if any, which shows the max available priority and the best potential event time. Also, [7] shows that if ready deterministic communications are not available, the Monitor tries with non-deterministic ones and selects the matching pair, if any, which addresses some alternative open service, say the one which shows the worst duration.
- Repeat from the star point "*" quoted above until the arc e_X is walked through (i.e. each alive explorer sent a Ready_to_Complete message) or a STOP command is received from E. Send to M (self) a CONCLUSION or a STOP message, respectively.

4 Test Cases and Results

Concepts shown in the above Sections were partially implemented by some pre-prototype tools, whose validation results are partially shown in this section. The pre-prototypes were specified to include the "many to/from many" communication model (A^2S). They were initially implemented in single processor environments by using both a sequential coding language, Pascal, and a concurrent one, Ada. Test case results from static systems both with some Servers and some Clients, and without an intermediate buffering Mailbox, or with a deterministic or non-deterministic Mailbox, respectively, are orderly shown by this section. At the present time, a platform of multiple Transputers [24] is also used to run an initial version of the simulator pre-prototype. This was coded in Occam [23], a language based on static tasking, static channels, task interactions only by message exchange both through memory or physical links. This Section shows also test case results from max-par implementations of the N thinking/eating philosophers with limited number of forks.

Event histories of the simulated cases were observed to be generally characterized as in the following, as expected:

– Initial phase: at least one task that is expected to exchange messages was never engaged in a rendezvous (periodic rendezvous excluded; see next phase);
– (Periodic phase: a frame of timed rendezvous, concerning all tasks which are expected to message again, repeats until the termination of a task (or an interrupting message, see [7]) makes the phase to complete;
– Transient phase: during this phase the application system effects the transition from a periodic phase to the next one)*;
– Termination phase: completion of the application system.

Table 2 shows results from an A^2S test case made by one Server and two clients and characterized as in Figure 2.

RV_NO.	EV_START_TIME	EV_END_TIME	CURRENT_CLIENT
01	100	110	C1
02	120	130	C2
03	150	160	C1
04	200	210	C1
05	245	255	C2
06	265	275	C1
07	315	325	C1
08	365	375	C1
09	385	395	C2
10	415	425	C1
11	465	475	C1
12	510	520	C2
13	530	540	C1
14	580	590	C1

```
. . . . . . . . . .
APPLICATION SYSTEM   VIEW: START_TIME = 0;
   PERIOD DETECTED: PERIOD = 265;
                        DETECTION_TIME = 590;
   APPLICATION SYSTEM ENTERED A STEADY CONDITION AT TIME 60.
CLIENTS VIEW: SERVICE_WORST_DURATIONS: C1=10; C2=10;
   MAXIMAL DISTANCE BETWEEN CONSECUTIVE SERVICES:
      C1   65              C2   140
```

Table 2. Results from the deterministic case study in Figure 2.

Figure 5 and Figure 6 show dimensions and simulation results from two A^2S classes of Deposit_Mailbox_Withdraw test cases. Both classes are made by multiple Deposit tasks, multiple Withdraw tasks and one Mailbox intermediate task. The Mailbox of the second class of cases is controlled by a Select construct. For the sake of brevity, results from systems equipped with relatively fast, one slot Mailbox tasks, only are considered.

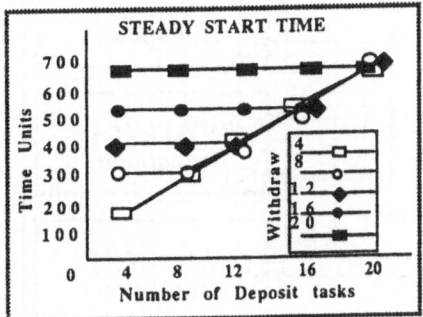 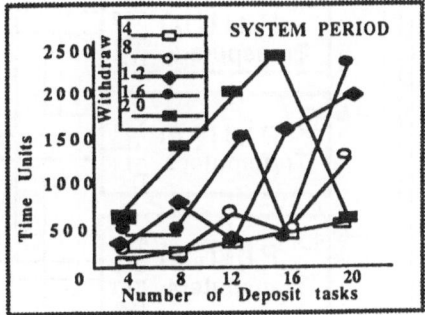

Fig. 5. Results from a case-study with both multiple Deposit and Withdraw tasks, and a deterministic Mailbox task.

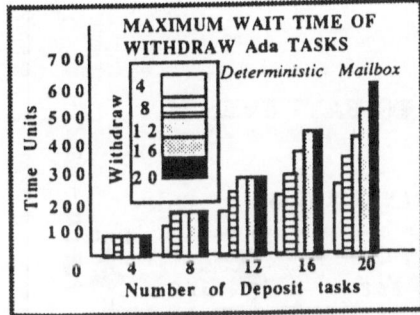 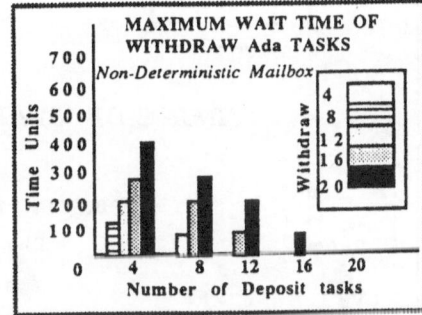

Fig. 6. Results from deterministic (left) and non-deterministic (right) case-studies, both with multiple Deposit and Withdraw tasks, and one slot Mailbox task.

In the first class of systems (see Figure 5 and Figure 6 left), both the Deposit and the Withdraw tasks were characterized by similar time performances. The application system joined the steady status after a time threshold plus some time: the greater the number of tasks, the greater the threshold; the more the number of depositors exceeded the number of the withdraw tasks, the greater was the steady start-time. The application system period was observed to depend on the least common multiple between the number of Withdraw tasks and the

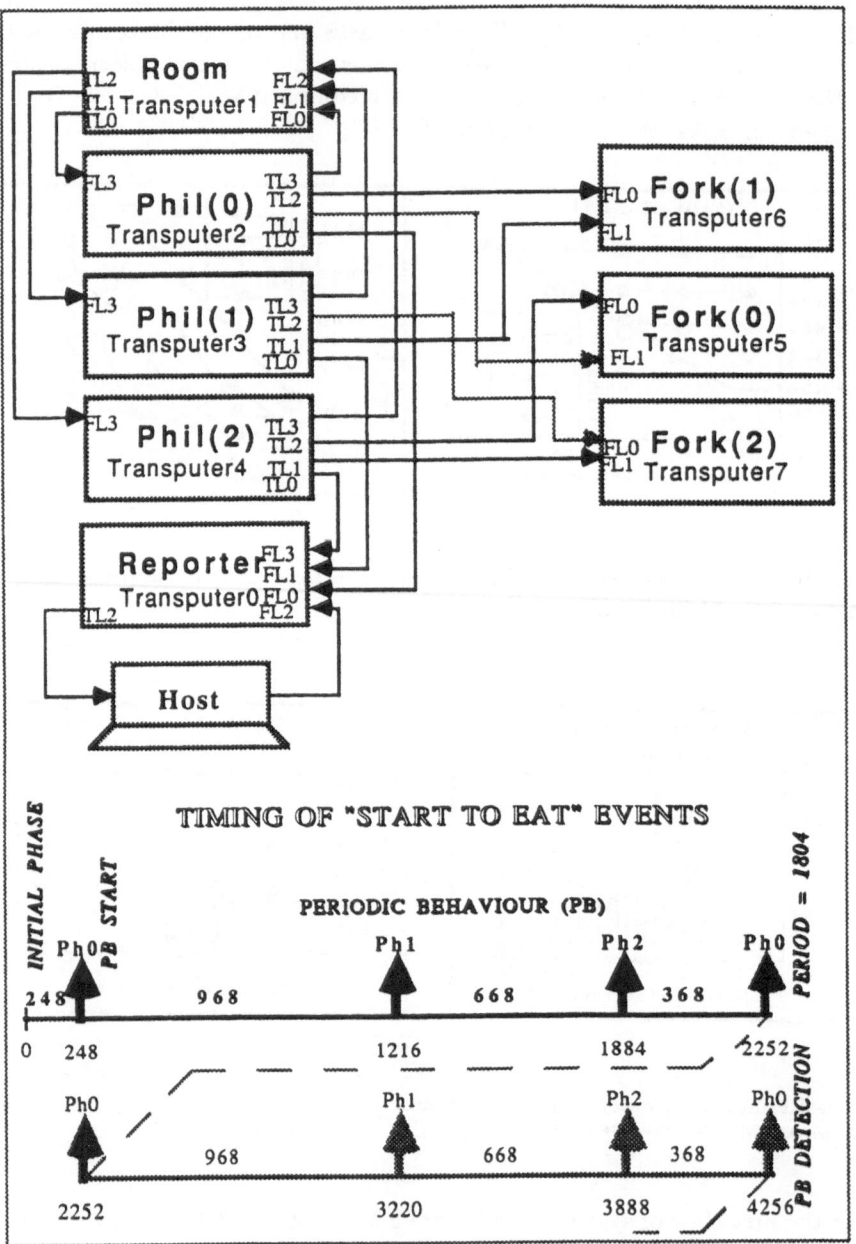

Fig. 7. Thinking/eating philosophers: Transputer platforms and instances of results.

number of Depositors, as it was expected, due to the internal determinism and the equality between timeliness of local activities.

In the second class of systems (see Figure 6 right), cyclical local-works of the Deposit tasks were assumed to show less duration than the paired works of the Withdraw tasks. The maximum waiting time of the Withdraw tasks was observed to be null when the number of Depositors was greater than the number of consumers, as it was expected due to the internal non-determinism of the intermediate task.

Finally, the max-par Transputer platforms used for the simulation of three Occam eating/thinking philosophers with limited number of forks, are shown in Figure 7 together with some initial results. Here within, one of the processes (Room) performs a waiting room, where at most one ready_to_eat philosopher waits for available forks. It is used to prevent deadlock or starvations. Finally, the Reporter detects events and shows them to the operator desk Host.

5 Conclusions

Static prediction of max-par time-life critical message exchanging processes was investigated by this paper. The author is involved with the comparative evaluation of the complexity of the proposed method with respect to the known ones, the extension of the model to cope with communications involving tasks to be created in the future, the extension of the prototype to treat with interrupting messages and, last but not least, the reuse of software components and their temporal properties in the HRT domain.

Acknowledgments

My gratitude to Professor Bruno Fadini which, early in the seventies, led his graduated students at the University of Naples "Federico II", including myself, to perform an engineering approach toward graphs as software modelling tools. Moreover, from the late 80's up to now, he beneficially advised, and spent some of his efforts,among others, toward funding this kind of research. I also wish to thank Francesco S. Gragnani for his help with the implementation of simulation software and time measurements. Last but not least, many thanks go to my under-graduate students of Operating Systems at the University of Naples "Federico II", for their help with the production, collection and analysis of program response-time data.

References

1. C. Andre, M. Peraldi, *Hard Real-Time System Implementation on a Microcontroller*, Proc. of IFAC-IFIP Int. Workshop Real-Time Programming, Bruges, Belgium, June 1992.
2. L. Bic, A.C. Shaw, *Logical Design of Operating Systems*, Prentice Hall, 1988.

3. V.R. Basili, G. Caldiera, and G. Cantone, *A Reference Architecture for the Component Factory*, ACM-TOSEM, Vol. 1, No. 1, 1992.

4. G. Bruno, M. Marchetto, *Process-translable Petri Nets for the Rapid Prototyping of Process Control Systems*, IEEE-TSE, Vol. 12, No. 2, 1986.

5. G. Cantone, *Predicting Timeliness of Distributed Processes*, Technical Report RI-90.12, DIE-University of Rome at Tor Vergata, Italy, December 1990.

6. G. Cantone, *Reusing Temporal Properties of Real-Time Software*, Proc.s of the 3rd IEE Int. Conf. on Software Engineering for Real-Time Systems, Cirencester, UK, September 1991.

7. G. Cantone, *Reasoning about Time Properties and Simulation of Hard Real-Time Distributed Dynamic Processes*, Technical Report RI-92.08, DIE-University of Rome at Tor Vergata, Italy, October 1992.

8. G. Cantone, E. Ciancamerla, M. Minichino, *A Method for Computing HOL SW Time Response and its Validation*, Proc. of IFAC/IFIP SAFECOMPO91 Symposium, Trondeim, Norway, October 1991.

9. G. Cantone, B. Ciciani, *Inserting State Restoration Requests in Systems of Distributed Processes*, Microprocessing and Microprogramming, Vol. 19, No. 1-5, December 1987.

10. B. Ciciani, G. Cantone, *Comments on "Design and Evaluation of a Fault-Tolerant Multiprocessor Using Hardware Recovery Blocks"*, IEEE TOC, Vol. 38, No. 9, 1989.

11. G. Cantone, A. Esposito, *An Initial Approach to Response Time Verification of Critical Programs*, Proc. of CSCI-CNR Int. Conf. on Massively Parallel Systems, Naples, Italy, December 1987.

12. G. Cantone, A. Esposito, *A D-Graph based Approach for Verifying Response Times of Critical Programs*, Microprocessing and Microprogramming, Vol. 27, No. 1-5, 1989.

13. G. Cantone, F.S. Gragnani, *A Reuse Based Environment to Develop and Verify Hard Real-Time Distributed Applications*, Proc. of the 2nd Eurospace Int. Symposium "Ada in Aerospace", Rome, Italy, November 1991.

14. G. Cantone, F.S. Gragnani, *Software Methods for the Assessment of the Temporal Behaviours of Programs and Fragments. An Approach Based on the Theory of Measurement Errors*, TR-92.09, DIE-URMTV, University of Rome at Tor Vergata, Italy, October 1992.

15. G. Cantone, C. Iapicca, *Temporal Properties of Ada Critical Applications*, Proc. of the 1st Eurospace Int. Symposium on "Ada in Aerospace". Barcelona, Spain, January 1991.

16. F. Fuggetta, C. Ghezzi, D. Mandrioli, *Some Consideration on Real-Time Behavior of Programs*, IEEE-TSE, Vol. 15, No. 3, 1989.

17. M. Felder, D. Mandrioli, A. Morzenti, *Proving Properties of Real-Time Systems trough Logical Specifications and Petri Net Models*, Rep. No. 91-072, DIEI-Politecnico di Milano, Italy, 1991.

18. G. Forte, *Tools Fair: Out of the Lab, Onto the Shelf*, IEEE Software, May, 1992.

19. W.A. Halang, *On Real-Time Features Available in High-Level Languages and Yet to be Implemented*, Microprocessing and Microprogramming, Vol. 12, 1983, 79–87.

20. W.A. Halang, *Predictable HRT Software*, Proc. of the 1st Euromicro RT Workshop, Como, Italy, September 1989.

21. T.A. Henzinger, Z. Manna, A. Pnueli, *An Interleaving Model for Real Time*, Proc. of Jerusalem Conf. on Information Technology, Jerusalem, Israel, October 1990.

22. W.A. Halang, A.D. Stoyenko, *Real Time Systems*, Kluwer Acad. Press, 1991.

23. INMOS Limited, *Occam 2 Reference Manual*, Prentice-Hall Int, Hertfordshire, UK, 1988.

24. INMOS Limited, *The Transputer Application Notebook*, Redwood Burn Ltd., Trowbridge, UK, 1989.

25. F. Jahanian, A.K. Mok, *A Graph Theoretic Approach for Timing Analysis and its Implementation*, IEEE-TC, Vol. 36, No 8, 1987.

26. H. Kopetz, R. Zainlinger, G. Fahler, H. Kantz, P. Puschner, W. Shutz, *An Engineering Approach Towards Hard Real-Time System Design*, Proc. of ECSE '91, Milano, Italy, LNCS 550, Springer Verlag, 1991.

27. E. Kligerman, A.D. Stoyenko, *Real-time Euclid: A Language for Reliable Real-Time Systems*, IEEE TSE, Vol. 12, No. 9, 1986.

28. D. Mandrioli, R. Zicari, C. Ghezzi, F. Tisato, *Modeling an Ada Task System by Petri Nets*. Computer Languages, Vol. 10, No. 1, 1985.

29. T. Murata, *Petri Nets: Properties, Analysis and Applications*, Proc. of the IEEE, Vol. 77, No. 4, 1989.

30. J.L. Peterson, *Petri Net Theory and the Modeling of Systems*, Prentice-Hall, 1981.

31. P. Puchner, C. Koza, *Calculating the Maximum Execution Time of Real-Time Programs*, Real-Time Systems, Vol. 1, No. 3, Kluwer Acad. Press, 1989.

32. A. Pnueli, *Specification and Development of Reactive Systems*, Information processing 86, H. Kugher (Ed.), 1986.

33. A.A. Rizzi, L.L. Witcomb, D.E. Koditschek, *Distributed Real-Time Control of Spatial Robot Juggler*, Computer, May 1992.

34. A.C. Shaw, *Reasoning about Time in Higher Level Language Software*, IEEE-TSE, Vol. 15, No. 7, 1989.

35. A.D. Stoyenko, V.C. Hamacher, R.C. Holt, *Analyzing Hard-Real-Time Programs For Guaranteed Schedulability*, IEE TSE, Vol. 17, No. 8, 1991.

36. J.A. Stankovich, K. Ramamritham, *What is Predictability for Real-Time Systems?*, Real-Time Systems, Vol. 2, No. 2, 1990.

37. J.A. Stankovich, *Real-Time Computing Systems: The Next Generation*, TR 88-06, Dep. of COINS, Univ. of Massachusetts, January 1988.

38. J.A. Stankovich, *Misconceptions about Real-Time Computing*, IEEE Computer, October 1988.

39. A.D. Stoyenko, *Analyzing PEARL Programs for Timely Executability and Schedulability*, Unpubl. Rep. UCLA, April 1990.

40. R.K. Shyamasundar, L. Yuhsiang, *Static Analysis of Real-Time Distributed Systems*, IEEE-TSE, Vol. 16, No 4, 1990.

41. R.N. Taylor, *Steps to an Advanced Ada Programming Environments*, IEEE-TSE, Vol. 11, No. 3, 1985.

Asynchronous Decentralized Realtime Computer Systems

E. Douglas Jensen

Digital Equipment Corporation
129 Parker St., PKO3-1/22D
Maynard, MA 01754
U.S.A.

Abstract

Realtime computer systems which perform physically and logically de-centralized mission management such as collaborative direction within a team of autonomous entities conducting manufacturing, maintenance, or combat must accommodate significant run-time uncertainties in the application environment and system resource state, by being dynamically adaptive. In particular, such systems have mission-critical time constraints which must be satisfied acceptably as specified by the application given the current circumstances.

Thus, they violate the static, deterministic, synchronous premises on which most conventional realtime computing concepts and techniques are founded. A different paradigm for non-deterministic asynchronous realtime scheduling is being developed. The Benefit Accrual Model is a framework that generalizes the traditional special cases of deadline time constraints, and unanimous optimum as the scheduling criterion, to encompass a wide spectrum of realtime *hardness* and *softness* in a unified way. Best-Effort scheduling algorithms exploit this generality. The progenitor of this scheduling paradigm was publicly introduced in the Alpha decentralized realtime OS kernel; and the current version is being incorporated into a new realtime version of the Mach 3.X kernel by Digital Equipment Corp.

1 Introduction

Realtime computing as we normally think of it arose in a historical context having two formative characteristics: first, the applications have been relatively small, simple, centralized subsystems for low-level, synchronous, sampled-data monitoring and control; and second, the machines suffered from a chronic insufficiency of hardware resources due to restricted cost, size, weight, or power. Both of these defining characteristics are now changing so much in degree that they are changing in kind.

An increasing number of realtime computing applications are larger, more complex, more decentralized, strategic systems. These are characterized by the interaction of a multiplicity of autonomous entities cooperating adaptively to perform a mission-critical realtime task as best as they are able, given their individually inaccurate, incomplete views of an inherently dynamic and uncertain application and system state e.g., decentralized realtime mission management, as discussed in the next Section.

Microprocessor execution speed and memory size are growing in performance and dropping in cost at an extremely fast pace which is expected to continue into the foreseeable future [1]. As in non-realtime computing systems, increased supply normally releases pent up demand. Higher processor speed is expanding (rather than diminishing, as might be imagined) the need for realtime resource management technology at the application level e.g., realtime rule-based applications, such as synthetic operator assistants for combat platforms and industrial plants, and realtime sensor fusion-based applications, such as *virtual reality* trainers/simulators, CAD tools, and entertainment systems. The same is true at the OS levels, where greater processor performance enables universally desired improvements in survivability, adaptability, safety and security.

These changes in application and hardware violate the premises underlying many concepts and techniques of traditional realtime computing. In particular, the conventional realtime scheduling dichotomy of *hard* and *soft* realtime is too oversimplified to be applicable to this new regime (at least): *hard* as being *deterministic* is an unrealistic special case; and *soft* as being all other cases is imprecise and ad hoc.

This paper describes a more general, realistic, and careful model for expressing realtime constraints and scheduling criteria, particularly motivated by the distinctive requirements of asynchronous decentralized realtime computing systems, which encompasses a wide spectrum of realtime *hardness* and *softness* in a well-defined and uniform manner.

To prepare for describing this model, first Section 2 provides an overview of certain fundamental problems raised by asynchronous decentralized realtime computing in mission management applications, then Section 3 briefly discusses a basic limitation of traditional realtime concepts and techniques in this new environment. Section 4 describes the Benefit Accrual Model, and Section 5 summarizes some Best-Effort scheduling algorithm research using (an early version of) that model.

2 Asynchronous Decentralized Computing Systems

2.1 Physical and Logical Decentralization

Decentralized realtime computing is called for by an application most frequently because: application resources e.g., factory or plant machinery, combat platforms are inherently spacially dispersed; and survivability, in the sense of graceful degradation for continued availability of situation-specific functionality, is usually more cost-effective by replication and partitioning than attempting physically centralized functionality which is infallible or indestructible. Decentralized realtime computing is implied by technology most frequently because: multiple smaller processors are now very often more cost-effective than a single larger one; and the high performance of current processors compared to that of memory subsystems necessitates multicomputers with message-passing over a backplane bus.

Decentralization may be physical or logical. The physical and logical decentralization of a computing system is generally different for different computations and at different levels of the system.

We argue that a trans-node computation's degree of physical decentralization is the extent to which the ratio between nodal computing rate and internodal communication latency is significantly high with respect to the nature of the computation, as manifest in the need for that computation to explicitly accommodate this ratio when performing trans-node resource management [2]. High degrees of physical decentralization are not necessary if this ratio is insignificant: when either the nature of the computation does not involve much trans-node resource management, commonly the case in network-style distributed systems (e.g., [3]); or the computation's trans-node resource management is performed on its behalf at some other (lower) level in the system, such as by a distributed operating system or distributed execution environment.

Resource management generally is more difficult when it is highly physically decentralized than when not. Allocating the degrees of decentralized resource management to levels of a computing system is affected by its realtime characteristics. Because realtime computing systems are mission-oriented, application-specific information can limit and even eliminate some of these difficulties; but the need to meet time constraints can exacerbate others.

We regard a computation's logical decentralization to be the degree to which it is performed multilaterally, determined by: consentaneity-the extent to which the participating entities must contribute to the computation before it is complete; equipollence-the functional parity of the participating entities; and the number of participating entities [4]. A quintessential form of utmost logical decentralization is negotiated consensus among autonomous peers. Intermediate forms are exemplified by succession where all activities of a computation are performed for a period of time by one entity, and then by another, in some serial sequence and partitioning where each entity performs a different activity of the computation, whether consecutively or concurrently.

Physical and logical decentralization tend to interact. High degrees of physical decentralization at some level imply significant logical decentralization of at least some resource management at that level is valuable or essential. High degrees of logical decentralization at some level, such as the application, in a multi-node context imply high degrees of physical decentralization at that or lower levels. High degrees of both logical and physical decentralization can easily have extremely complex dynamics which result in chaotic behavior; avoiding chaos while maintaining high performance and adaptivity in such systems with many degrees of freedom requires sophisticated control techniques which are as yet nascent (e.g.,[5]). The very strong coupling among nodes (such as global synchrony) sometimes employed to construct highly predictable realtime computer systems for low-level applications, that are both logically and physically decentralized to significant degrees at the expense of adaptability (e.g., [6],[7]), is sufficient but not necessary for the avoidance of chaotic behavior.

2.2 Mission Management Applications

Some (including the earliest) modestly decentralized realtime applications are low-level, synchronous, sampled data communication, monitoring, and processing (e.g., process control, sonar) subsystems. But the decentralized realtime applications of interest here are those strategic ones now emerging for the purpose of managing the entire system's mission (e.g., coordination of multiple entities which are manufacturing a vehicle, repairing a damaged reactor, conducting an air engagement) they are in addition to, and employ and control, the constituent lower-level (centralized and decentralized) realtime subsystems.

Realtime mission management that is highly physically and logically decentralized is distinctive in the extent to which it is subject to substantial execution-time uncertainties at the application levels. The computations are predominately asynchronous (mutually and globally) e.g., event driven, aperiodic; they have dynamic dependencies e.g., resource conflicts, precedence constraints; they are co-evolving i.e., each computation's behavior depends on that of others; and the computations routinely constitute an overload. As in any system, faults, errors, and failures occur; but mission management systems are permitted little or no downtime for repairs or reconfiguration. Computing system physical distribution per se also generally introduces considerable additional uncertainties e.g., variable, unknown computing and communication latencies.

Dependably maximizing mission success — including timeliness, survivability, safety and security — despite all these multifarious exigencies of the current application and system resource situation, can require that the system adapt on-line not only its approach to performing the mission, but occasionally even its goals (the *fog of war* [8] is a clear, albeit extreme, example).

Virtually all such realtime reconciliation of uncertainty and dependability at the system and mission levels has historically been based solely on the talent and expertise of the system's human operators e.g., in the factory control rooms and aircraft cockpits. Increasingly, the complexity and pace of the systems' missions, and the number, complexity, and distribution of their resources, cause cognitive overload which requires that these operators receive more support in this respect from the computing system itself.

Such support cannot be relegated entirely to the application level in realtime computing systems (cf. the DARPA/USAF Pilot's Associate program [9]), because realtime acceptability requires management of computer resources not (or not sensibly) under the control of applications. Under such circumstances, both the application and computing system software (e.g., OS) must make a best effort to accommodate dynamic and non-deterministic mission and resource conditions in a robust, adaptable way so as to undertake that as many as possible of the most important computations are as acceptable, in the time and other domains, to the application as possible.

Best effort resource management is generally heuristic a familiar approach at the application levels (most conspicuously in artificial intelligence, pattern recognition) and less visibly at the system software levels. Because heuristics are essentially foreign in traditional realtime systems, we employ the term *best effort* to more clearly evoke our intended departure in philosophy analogous to the utilization of the term *guess* [10] for inferences performed by certain intelligent user interfaces, e.g., [11].

Heuristics in general, and best effort realtime resource management in particular, involve trade-offs of risk management and situational coverage. Best-effort on-line realtime scheduling heuristics currently offer empirically-based high confidence that acceptable computational timeliness will be achieved over a broad range of conditions; but with no or low formal bounds on guaranteed timeliness (note that this is necessarily always true of the humans currently performing best-effort resource management). Conversely, traditional *hard* realtime scheduling algorithms provide formal guarantees of optimal computational timeliness under extremely restricted-generally unrealistic-conditions, but behavior which is unknown or known to be pathologically wrong outside those conditions. Examples of applications which seem to call naturally for each of these extremes come immediately to mind but in making the trade-offs and compromises to find an application- specific appropriate middle ground, one must beware of the human trait to undervalue the reduction, as opposed to the elimination, of risks [12].

Present realtime resource management, e.g., scheduling, technology does not offer the opportunity for such application-specific trade-offs between situational coverage and optimality. A new, more general realtime resource management paradigm is needed to better accommodate the special requirements of asynchronous, decentralized realtime computing systems. Paradigm shifts are rather uncommon in computing e.g., parallel processing and virtually unprecedented in realtime computing.

3 Realtime Computing Systems

3.1 The Definition of 'Realtime'

We consider a computing system or operating system to be a realtime one to the extent (this is not a binary attribute) that: time-physical or logical, absolute or relative is part of the system's logic (analogous to errors being states in a fault tolerant system); and in particular, that resources are managed explicitly to satisfy the completion time constraints of the applications' (and thus its own) computations, whether statically or dynamically.

Time constraints, such as deadlines, are introduced primarily by natural laws e.g., physical, chemical, biological which govern an application's behavior and establish acceptable execution completion times for the associated realtime computations.

Real fast is often confused with *realtime*. A computing system or operating system may satisfy its applications' computation completion time constraints implicitly (by good luck) or by hardware brute force (e.g., MS-DOS on a 200 MIPS computer). Such systems may successfully operate in realtime and (in the latter case) could be rational, cost-effective solutions for certain applications — but by our definition they are not realtime systems, because they do not employ realtime (time constraint driven) resource management.

Deterministic computation in the realtime context literally means that the computation's timing is known absolutely, in advance [13] there is no uncertainty about any parameters of the computation (e.g., arrival time, execution duration) and its future execution environment (e.g., resource dependencies and conflicts due to other computations) which could affect its timing (at least barring faults, and preferably within acceptable fault coverage premises). Thus, deterministic scheduling can indeed, must [14] be done off-line. There are very few actual realtime applications and systems which (inherently or forcibly) meet this determinism criterion of absolute timing certainty — most are subject to some inevitable dynamic fluctuations and variabilities of computation and communication timing, due to input data arrivals, resource dependencies and conflicts, overloads, and hardware and software exceptions (not to mention faults, errors, and failures outside the presumed coverage).

We consider that a computation's timeliness may be non-deterministic but predictable in the sense that it can be estimated acceptably (with determinism being the maximum, ideal, case [15] which can only be asymptotically approached in practice). Predictability implies that all parameter values of the computation (e.g., arrival time, execution duration) and its future execution environment (e.g., resource dependencies on, and conflicts with, other computations) are known sufficiently well, and that the computation's timeliness is governed by processes (particularly the scheduler) whose time evolution is sufficiently well controlled. The degree of predictability is then established according to the application-specific interpretation of *acceptably* e.g., it may be desired that the estimate be extremely precise in most instances at the expense of being less so in the remainder, versus being less but equally precise in every instance.

The timing estimations may be obtained by formal analysis, simulation, empirical measurement, or code examination. The resulting predictability of timeliness (e.g., response or completion time) may be expressed in a variety of ways e.g.: an assured upper bound (a lesser or least upper bound since any system's timing could be said to be predictable by the choice of one high enough); or in terms of discontinuous rules which relate various execution contexts to estimated, bounded, or even certain timeliness values (those contexts being ones which are most likely, or most important, or just most readily relatable to timeliness estimations); or a probability distribution function of timeliness values.

When the parameters of the computation and its future execution environment are known in the form of random variables so that their uncertainty is characterized by probability distribution functions (a reasonable presumption in many cases), the computation's timeliness may be amenable to stochastic analysis e.g., the probabilities of execution completion at different times can be derived for certain situations (but as with deterministic scheduling, many of the most interesting cases are either known to be intractable or still defy explicit solution). However, the contexts and thus approaches of stochastic scheduling are predominately oriented toward non-realtime objectives, such as makespan or flowtime [16], which are analytically and computationally easier than stochastic scheduling to meet due times [17] (and for which there is greater application demand than from the realtime community).

The parameters of many realtime systems, especially in higher level and larger scale contexts such as mission management (whether centralized or decentralized), are often too asynchronous i.e., intermittent, irregular, and interdependent to have known or tractable probability distribution functions; thus, these systems must be treated as non-stochastically non-deterministic.

Independent of the computation and environment parameters, a computation's timeliness predictability also depends on the time evolution characteristics of the scheduler. It is normally taken for granted that realtime scheduling algorithms per se are deterministic even if the parameters are not. Nevertheless, algorithms in general and scheduling algorithms in particular sometimes take advantage (e.g., for simplicity) of making non-deterministic decisions: stochastic schedulers have proven to be successful in certain distributed systems (e.g., [18], [19]); and non-stochastic decision making occurs not only in Petri Nets and certain programming languages, but even in realtime scheduling algorithms (e.g., [20]). Most significantly, however, is the strong tendency for highly physically and logically decentralized schedulers to enter chaotic regimes [5].

Both determinism and predictability are independent of timeliness (e.g., deadline, response time) magnitudes. A system may be deterministically, or highly predictably, too slow with respect to some particular timeliness magnitude requirement. Thus, a realtime performance specification must include both dimensions of timeliness.

3.2 Traditional Realtime Resource Management Responsibilities

Every realtime computer system divides the responsibility for satisfying application completion time constraints between the application software and OS software. In most cases, the responsibility for satisfying application time constraints is primarily that of the application software. Small, simple subsystems make it possible for the application programmers to perform most of the realtime resource management, and limited hardware makes it necessary.

The realtime application programmers normally perform an off-line (static) mapping of their computations' completion time constraints (and other attributes such as relative functional criticality) into *priorities* in some way which is often ad hoc, but sometimes methodological e.g., frame-based or rate-monotonic, for periodic computations. The application may also adjust some priorities on-line. Application programmers usually conduct some time constraint-driven resource management dynamically by employing clocks and counters provided by the hardware and OS. Application programmers also use time constraints explicitly and implicitly for managing other resources, both off-line and on-line, to reduce sharing and contention.

A realtime OS's share of the time constraint satisfaction responsibility is normally to perform priority-based scheduling i.e., seeking to keep the processor(s) executing the highest priority ready computation(s). Because priorities convey much less information than actual time constraints, OS resource management is thereby simplified.

Much realtime OS resource management is intended to be *real fast* as opposed to realtime: a principal goal is to minimize the execution time of OS services and internal operations. An instance of this which receives particular attention as a performance metric is changing execution from one computation to another e.g., interrupt response and context switching.

Some OS resource management is realtime by our definition in that it seeks to satisfy completion constraints on some of its service and internal operation times. These time constraints are usually not based on the or even any particular application completion time constraints; but different realtime applications imply different requirements for the magnitudes and constraints of these service and internal operation times.

A tiny minority of realtime OS's have used application completion time constraints, in the form of deadlines, directly for on-line processor scheduling. Their success has been limited because deadline-based (including slack time) scheduling was often independently re-discovered without the benefit of knowing and understanding the prior theory and experience. Thus, each re-discoverer had to learn by experience that deadline-based scheduling exhibits behavior which is non-intuitive (e.g., deadline scheduling minimizes the maximum lateness) and counterproductive (e.g., instability when overloaded, or when preemption is allowed in multiprocessors), and may have premises which do not match the application and computing system contexts; deadline-based scheduling can also be processor cycle intensive. All but the last of these reasons have also adversely affected the practice of off-line deadline-based scheduling of computer systems. This traditional division of responsibilities between the application programmers and the OS can be counterproductive in the emerging non-traditional realtime contexts.

3.3 Scalable Realtime Capability

According to our definition of realtime, many computing systems are realtime to some relevant degree: slightly e.g., a payroll system which automatically generates the checks on time (not early or late); a little more so — e.g., disk driver software; considerably more so e.g., an OLTP system which automatically performs financial trading based on dynamic market parameters; highly most (but not all) computing normally thought of as realtime.

Unfortunately, there has never been a comprehensive conceptual or technological framework which can coherently encompass all these degrees of realtime. Consequently, realtime computing concepts and techniques for different systems are ad hoc and largely disjoint from each other, which causes these differences in degree to become differences in kind. In particular, this incoherence impedes the construction of computing systems which are scalable in degree of realtime, and thus in size, complexity, asynchrony, and decentralization.

Traditional realtime systems are informally dichotomized as *hard* versus *soft* primarily according to their *determinism* or *predictability* (these terms are popularly misused synonymously) in meeting their computation deadlines. *Hard* realtime conventionally is defined as being *deterministic* in the sense that the only critical computations are those with deadlines, and the scheduling objective is that all these computations must always meet their deadlines, otherwise the system has failed catastrophically. *Soft* realtime conventionally is defined as being *non-deterministic* in the sense that missing a deadline is not necessarily a catastrophic system failure i.e., *soft* means *not hard*: in some cases, missing certain deadlines under certain conditions may be acceptable; in other cases, the time constraints are not really deadlines but preferred times or time ranges. The *predictability* of timeliness is popularly regarded as the metric for hardness and softness, although the term is rarely described, much less defined.

Instead of viewing both determinism and predictability as being independent of timeliness magnitude, *hard* and *soft* realtime are also usually associated with *shorter* and *longer* timeliness metrics such as deadlines (typically, interrupt response times on the order of 10 to 100 versus 1000 microseconds), respectively. Because the traditional realtime viewpoint and its terminology is imprecise, oversimplified, and unrealistic, it can — and does — limit the kinds of realtime systems that can be built, and the cost-effectiveness of those that are built. Asynchronous decentralized realtime computer systems for mission management are a conspicuous instance of suffering from both these limitations.

The developing paradigm of realtime scheduling described here, viz. the Benefit Accrual Model, offers a more systematic, general, and realistic framework which can reduce such limitations. It provides a comprehensive method for expressing time constraints and scheduling objectives that encompasses a wide spectrum of realtime *hardness* and *softness* in a unified way. In addition to conventional realtime scheduling algorithms, this framework accommodates Best-Effort algorithms which seek to better satisfy the requirement in asynchronous decentralized systems for robust adaptivity to dynamic system and application conditions.

4 The Benefit Accrual Model Of Realtime Scheduling

4.1 Introduction

We consider a realtime computation to be a segment of a computational entity (such as a thread, task, or process) subject to a completion time constraint (such as a deadline).

We define a time constraint to be the specification of: a time period during which completion of the realtime computation's execution affects the temporal component of its acceptability; and that effect (e.g., completing before the deadline is acceptable, and otherwise is unacceptable).

A time constraint is manifest in the computation program as a demarcated region of code whose execution completion time is subject to the time constraint. A computational entity may include multiple realtime computations sequentially or concurrently (i.e., nested), as shown in Figure 1.

Fig. 1. Time constraints manifest as demarcated code regions.

The classical deadline imposes a binary partitioning of a computation's completion time range into either acceptable (prior to the deadline), or not (after the deadline), as illustrated in Figure 2. The semantics of *not acceptable* are specific to the computation and application e.g., non-productive or counter-productive in some way.

Often non-deterministic execution-time variabilities make it very useful to have *softer* in the sense of non-binary-relationships between when a realtime computation completes execution, and the temporal acceptability of that computation. A realistic example of such a softer time constraint is that if a particular computation cannot be completed at an optimum time i.e., before its *deadline* then: completing it a little tardy is suboptimum, but better than not completing it at all; however, completing it very tardy is worse than not completing it at all. See Figure 3.

The description of this example indicated that the *deadline* was redefined to be the end of the optimum, rather than the acceptable, completion time zone. The normal definition of deadline (Figure 4) would cause popular realtime scheduling algorithms to complete more computations in the suboptimum zone than was intended by the example soft time constraint. Thus, such non-binary completion time/acceptability relationships raise questions such as: which time is best considered the *deadline*, and what the other completion delimiting times are; how are these specified times used for scheduling.

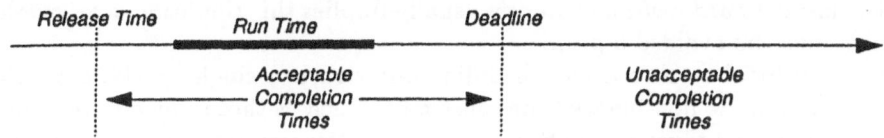

Fig. 2. The classical deadline.

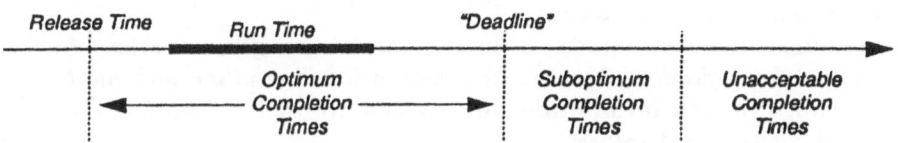

Fig. 3. A "softer" time constraint.

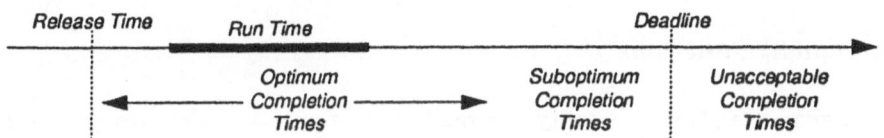

Fig. 4. Combination deadline and softer time constraint.

The execution of each realtime computation is not necessarily scheduled to maximize its individual temporal acceptability. A realtime system (normally) has a multiplicity of realtime computations which are executed in a partial order according to a scheduling criterion: a collective temporal acceptability criterion for a set of realtime computations, in terms of their individual time constraints-e.g., the classical *hard realtime* criterion that all realtime computations meet all their deadlines. In some cases such as the classical *hard realtime* one there is an equivalence between the individual and collective temporal acceptability criteria (e.g., *each* and *all*).

A particular scheduling criterion applied to a particular set of realtime computations may result in a subset of them whose individual time constraints will/would not be optimally satisfied; how and when this is resolved is situation-specific (the classical *hard realtime* criterion usually implies this condition is an overload which must be avoided a priori).

The traditional *hard realtime* scheduling criterion is a single special case which does not apply to non-binary time constraints, such as those which have multiple completion time zones or redefined *deadline. Softer* time constraints in the sense of non-binary completion time acceptability necessitate associated *softer* in the sense of non-unanimous and non-optimum-scheduling criteria. In the context of our example, the softer criterion is that the maximum possible number of computations complete in the optimum zone, and all the remainder complete in the suboptimum zone.

Traditional *soft* realtime scheduling criteria are disparate, ad hoc, and imprecise; thus, they do not offer a basis for systematically expressing scheduling criteria for non-binary time constraints.

In the Benefit Accrual Model, a time constraint is a generalization of the conventional *hard deadline* because the conventional *deadline* and *hard realtime* scheduling criterion involve time directly and are well-defined (contrary to the state of conventional *soft* realtime).

The Benefit Accrual Model is based on two concepts: a benefit function, which generalizes the classical *deadline* of a realtime computation; and a benefit accrual predicate, which generalizes the classical *hard realtime* scheduling criterion that a set of computations always meet all its deadlines.

This model generalizes the author's earlier concept of *time-value function* resource scheduling [21], [22], which was first employed in the Alpha realtime decentralized OS kernel [23], [24].

4.2 Benefit Functions

The urgency i.e., time criticality of a realtime computation is expressed in terms of the benefit it provides to the system as a function fB of the time at which the computation is completed (see Figure 5). The benefit metric is application-specific and defined system-wide. Benefit functions are derived by the programmers directly from the requirements and behavior of the realtime computation (usually an application activity); this is subject to a system-wide engineering process (just as are assignments of classical priorities).

The function fB is unimodal if it is concave downward (we will define that linear functions are so) i.e., any decrease in value cannot be followed by an increase otherwise it is multimodal. A multimodal function has at least one instance of a monotonic decrease in value followed by a monotonic increase, and thus there are multiple non-contiguous time intervals when it is better to complete the computation than during the times separating them (see Figure 6). A multimodal function involves non-linear optimization which is often intractable on-line, so we do not discuss multimodal functions further here.

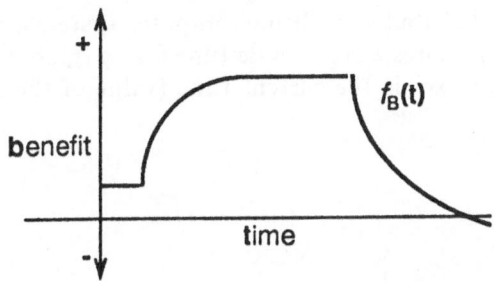

Fig. 5. Benefit function.

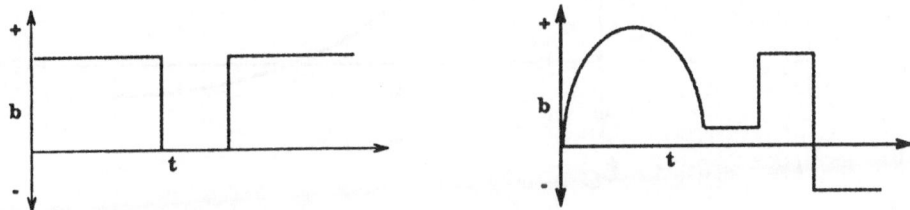

Fig. 6. Multimodal benefit functions.

A computation's benefit function can be changed each time it is released for execution, as illustrated in Figure 7.

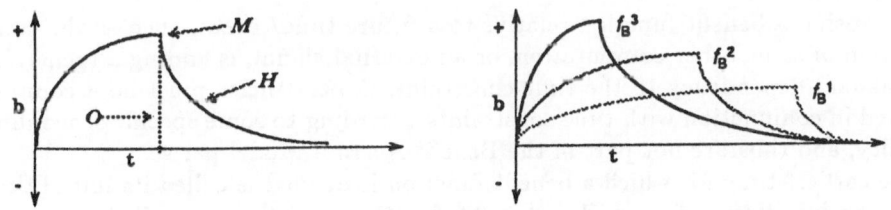

Fig. 7. A computation changing benefit functions each release.

The benefit function time axis is the one the scheduler uses. It may be physical, either absolute (*calendar/wall clock*) time i.e., year, month, date, hour, minute, second, msec or relative to (since) some past event. Alternatively, it may be logical e.g., a number which monotonically increases, but not necessarily at regular intervals. In some distributed realtime computer systems, time constraints can span nodes, which requires a trans-node time frame (global clock). The origin of the benefit function axes is the current time (value of the system clock) tC, as seen in Figure 8.

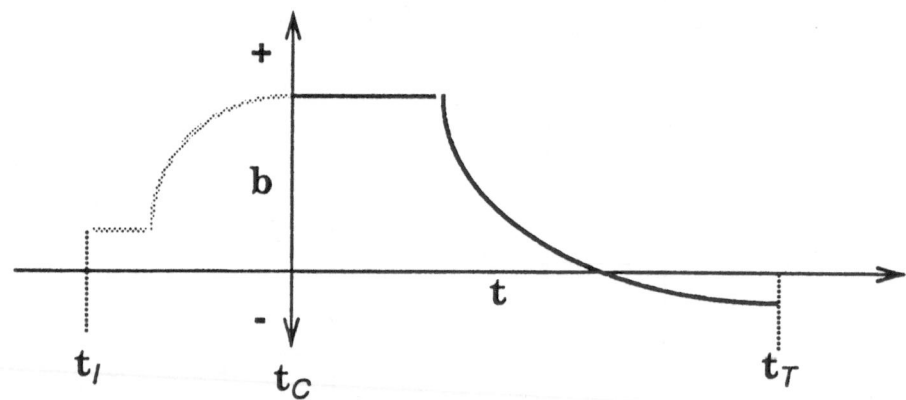

Fig. 8. Initial and terminal times.

It may be preferable for an application programmer to express some benefit functions in terms of a time parameter different from that of the global time axis e.g.: a computation's deadline being incremental time units from now, regardless of the axis metric; or a particular physical absolute time, though the axis is physical relative time but these differences must subsequently be translated for scheduling. Translations between physical and logical time frames are ordinarily infeasible.

Expressing a benefit function relative to a future time/ event, such as the completion of some other computation, or an external signal, is adding a (generally dynamic) dependency to the time constraint. Dependencies must be accommodated in conjunction with time constraints according to some specific scheduling policy, and thus are not part of the Benefit Accrual Model per se.

The earliest time for which a benefit function is defined is called its initial time tI; the latest time for which a benefit function is defined is called its terminal time tT (see Figure 8). Some systems and scheduling algorithms call for the specification of an indefinitely extended terminal time. A benefit function is evaluated only for values of its time parameter between the current time and its terminal time. If the terminal time is reached (tT = tC) and execution of the realtime computation has not begun or has begun but not completed, the realtime computation is aborted and the time constraint is removed from scheduling consideration. If a realtime computation is sufficiently likely to complete execution after its initial time, a scheduling algorithm could choose to begin it before the initial time.

The later time tL (see Figure 9) is that after which the benefit function value is (monotonically) non-increasing; thus, completing the realtime computation at or after this time is better. A benefit function always has a later time. The sooner time t is that after which the benefit function value is (monotonically) decreasing; thus, completing the realtime computation at or before this time is better. A benefit function need not have a tS < tT. If its value becomes zero or negative at time tE > = tS, a benefit function has an expiration time.

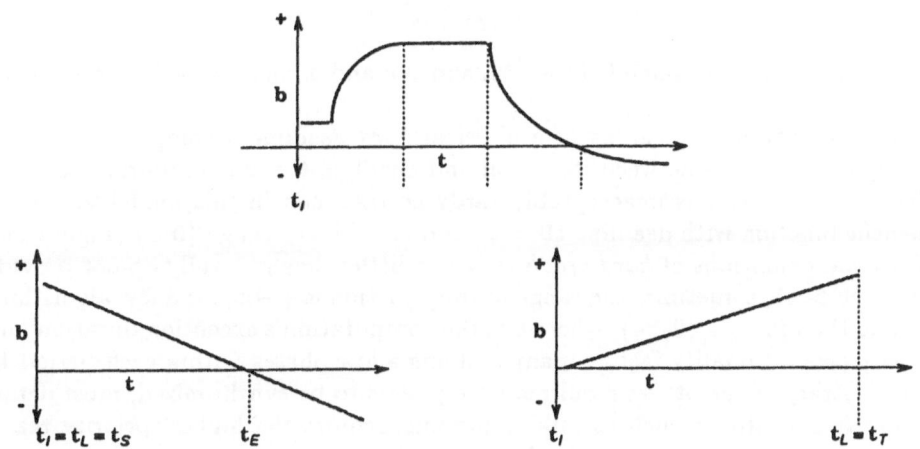

Fig. 9. Later, sooner, and expiration times.

It can be necessary for a realtime computation to be completed at a time yielding zero or negative benefit: early, rather than delaying execution until the greatest positive benefit is expected; or tardy, rather than terminating (or not initiating) execution after there is no expectation of positive benefit. Such cases arise due to dynamic dependencies, when a computation: has been initiated and cannot be stopped (preempted or aborted) or undone (such as one related to a physical activity in the application environment); or would block another if not completed, despite its consequential zero or negative benefit.

A special case of a sooner time tS is a due time tD, distinguished by the benefit function's first derivative having an infinite discontinuity at tS = tE (shown in Figure 10). A deadline is a due time subject to a collective temporal acceptability criterion which does not allow the due time to be missed.

A benefit function is defined as hard if it has: a zero or constant negative value before tL; an infinite discontinuity in its first derivative at tL if tL > tI; a due

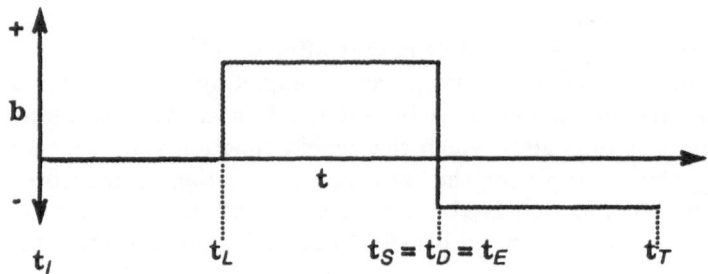

Fig. 10. Example hard benefit function.

time tD; a constant value between tL and tD; and a constant value between tD and tT.

The most common meaning of a classical *hard deadline* a computation which completes anytime between its initial and deadline times is uniformly acceptable, and otherwise is unacceptably tardy corresponds in this model to a hard benefit function with deadline tD = tT and unit binary range {0, 1} (Figure 11). Classical definitions of *hard deadline* vary a little: they generally do not provide for a tL > tI; sometimes the range of this function is {−∞, 1}; a few algorithms define the range as {0, ke}, where e is the computation's execution duration and k is a proportionality factor; many systems allow phases within each period to be arbitrary, while others require all the phases to be synchronized; most deterministic algorithms, such as rate-monotonic, require the highest priority ready activity to execute, thus disallowing phase shifts.

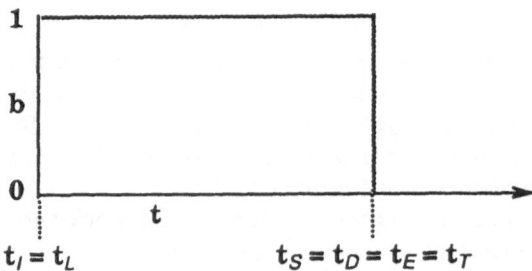

Fig. 11. Hard deadline benefit function.

All benefit functions which are not hard are soft. Soft benefit functions can have arbitrary values before and after the optimal value at tS (Figure 12); they need not have constant values on each side of tL and tD, or expiration times (Figure 13).

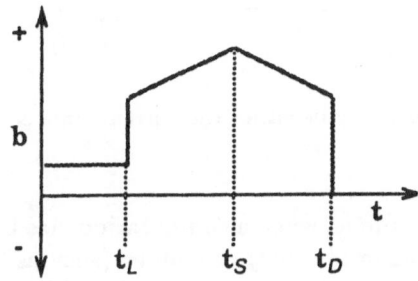

Fig. 12. Example soft benefit function.

Fig. 13. Example soft benefit functions.

A time constraint and thus benefit function is made known to the scheduler at its release time (which is usually a scheduling event).

When the benefit function is released, its initial time may be either the current time the time constraint is released at the time it is to take effect (i.e., at $tI = tC$) or a future time the time constraint is released in advance (i.e., $tI > tC$) to improve scheduling (but $tI \leq tC$ is a necessary condition for the computation to complete, if not also begin, execution). See Figure 14.

Expressing or releasing a benefit function relative to a future time/event, such as the completion of some other computation or an external signal, is adding a (generally dynamic) dependency to the time constraint. Dynamic dependencies can require a realtime computation to be completed at a time yielding zero or

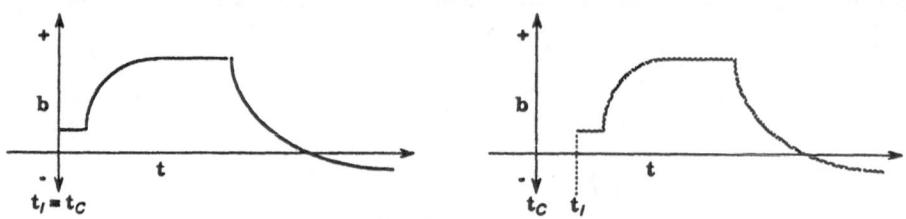

Fig. 14. The initial time may be either the current time or a future time.

negative benefit for example, when a computation: has been initiated and cannot be stopped (preempted or aborted) or undone (such as one related to a physical activity in the application environment); or would block another if not completed, despite its consequential zero or negative benefit. Dynamic dependencies can require indefinitely extended function terminal times. Dependencies must be accommodated in conjunction with time constraints according to some specific scheduling policy, and thus are not part of the benefit accrual model per se.

4.3 Importance

Each computation generally also has a relative importance i.e., functional criticality with respect to other computations contending for completion. Importance is orthogonal to urgency: a computation with high urgency (e.g., a near deadline) may not be highly important; or a computation with low urgency (e.g., a far deadline) may be very important.

Importance may be a function fI of time and other parameters that reflect the application and computing system state, and can be represented and employed similar to urgency (Figure 15).

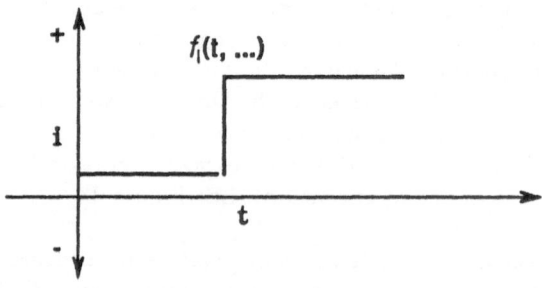

Fig. 15. Importance function.

In simple cases, importance may be a constant, and urgency (benefit) may be simply scaled by importance e.g., by multiplication, addition, or concatenation. In more general cases where importance needs to be a variable, fB and fI must be evaluated together dynamically to determine the benefit e.g., as some function of the fB and fI functions, g(fB, fI). See Figure 16.

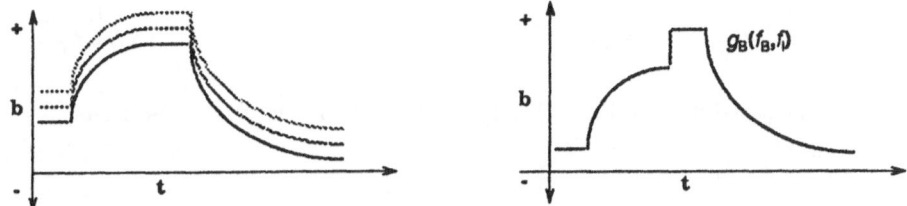

Fig. 16. Scaled and functional combination of benefit and importance.

4.4 Execution Duration

A realtime computation has an execution duration of which the scheduler usually has some information about prior to execution. This information can be either known deterministically (the most common presumption), or estimated. Most estimates are stochastic (known in expectation), but alternatively may be non-stochastic e.g., bounds or rules. Execution duration information may or may not take into account a forecast of dynamic dependencies. Non-deterministic durations may be estimated dynamically (during the computation's execution) e.g., conditional probability distributions, or execution-time knowledge-driven rules.

4.5 Benefit Accrual Predicates

The scheduler considers all released time constraints between the current time and its horizon tH the future-most terminal time (Figure 17). It assigns the estimated execution completion times, and consequently the initiation times and ordering, for those computations using an algorithm which seeks to sufficiently satisfy the scheduling (collective temporal acceptability) criterion (such as earliest-deadline-first for the classical *hard realtime* criterion of all computations meeting their deadlines). The algorithm should also take into account dependencies and importances.

It is feasible to schedule a particular set of realtime computations if its collective temporal acceptability criterion can be sufficiently satisfied. A particular set of realtime computations is schedulable if there exists at least one algorithm which

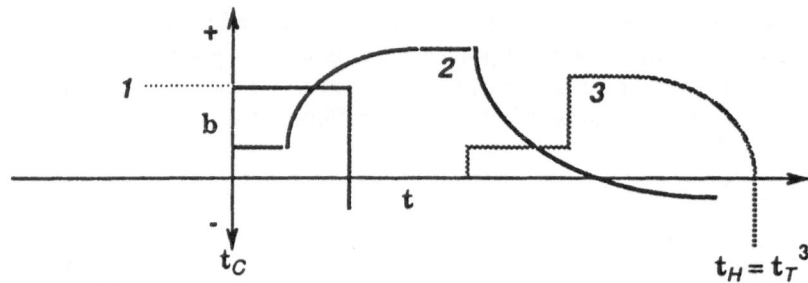

Fig. 17. The scheduler considers all released benefit functions to its horizon.

can feasibly schedule it. A scheduling algorithm is optimal if it always produces a feasible schedule whenever: in the static case, any other algorithm can do so; in the dynamic case, a static algorithm with complete a priori knowledge would do so.

The ideal case of every computation always completing execution at an optimum time is unrealistic in general. Even though the traditional *hard realtime* cases are intended and commonly imagined to achieve this ideal, physical laws (especially in asynchronous decentralized systems) or the intrinsic nature of the applications (especially at mission management levels) generally make it non-cost-effective or even impossible.

Most actual realtime systems desire a sufficient number of computation completion times to be sufficiently likely to be sufficiently acceptable (perhaps optimal) under the current application and computer system circumstances.

For the special case of any collective temporal acceptability criterion defined to be a unanimous optimum of the individual temporal acceptabilities, there is an equivalent criterion defined in terms of individual, rather than collective, optimums e.g., meet all deadlines means meet each deadline, and maximize all benefits means maximize each benefit.

In general, collective temporal acceptability is not defined as necessarily unanimous or optimum with respect to the individual computations' temporal acceptability e.g., minimize the number of missed deadlines, or maximize the sum of the benefits.

In the Benefit Accrual Model, collective temporal acceptability criteria are based on accruing benefit from the individual computations in a set, in a manner specified by a benefit accrual predicate for that set. This is general enough to encompass a wide range of temporal acceptability criteria e.g.: the optimum cases such as traditional *hard realtime*, for which the predicate is the product of the individual benefits (assuming the usual range of $\{0, 1\}$); potentially sub-optimum cases, for which example predicates are to maximize the sum (mean, etc.) of the individual benefits; the number of computations during a time frame T which achieve at least P percent of their maximum possible benefit; the probability that at least P percent of the computations during a time frame T will achieve their maximum benefits.

5 Best-Effort Scheduling

5.1 Introduction

Scheduling principles and practices which are realtime by our definition (i.e., based on satisfying completion time constraints) have until recently been focused exclusively on guaranteeing that a unanimous optimum scheduling criterion will be met (e.g., the classical *hard realtime* case of guaranteeing that all deadlines are always met). Even though the traditional *hard realtime* cases are intended and commonly imagined to achieve this ideal, physical laws (especially in decentralized systems) or the intrinsic nature of the applications (especially at mission management levels) generally make it either non-cost-effective or impossible (there are only a few exceptions).

In general, realtime systems need a sufficient number of computation completion times to be sufficiently likely to be sufficiently acceptable (perhaps optimal), given the current application and computer system circumstances (perhaps over a wide range of such circumstances) where each instance of *sufficient* is application-specific.

The Benefit Accrual Model provides a framework for expressing *softer* time constraints in the sense of non-binary completion time acceptability and scheduling criteria in the sense of non-unanimous and non-optimum. It accomplishes this in addition to and in the same manner as the conventional *hard* time constraints and scheduling criteria. These softer needs are realized with Best-Effort scheduling algorithms

Best-Effort (BE) realtime scheduling algorithms seek to provide the *best* as specified by the application computational timeliness they can, given the current application and computer resource conditions.

5.2 Overview of Best-Effort Realtime Scheduling Work

This concept, and the Time-Value Function progenitor of the Benefit Accrual Model as a framework for expressing time constraints, were originated by Jensen [21], [22]. The first generation of BE-on-line (at execution time)-scheduling algorithms emerged from Jensen's Archons Project at CMU [23], for the Alpha realtime decentralized OS kernel [24]: Locke's algorithm [19] and Clark's algorithm [20].

Locke's algorithm allows a wide variety but not all forms of Time-Value Functions (TVF's). Locke intends that importance be reflected by scaling the TVF values. The scheduling optimality criterion is the special (but reasonable) case of maximizing the sum of the job values attained. Execution times are defined stochastically.

The algorithm schedules jobs Earliest-Deadline-First (EDF) since that is optimal when underloaded. If a job arrival, or execution time overrun, results in a sufficiently high probability of overload, jobs are set aside in order of minimum expected value density (expected value/expected remaining execution time) until the probable overload is removed.

Locke's algorithm does not address dependencies (e.g., precedence, resource conflicts).

Locke used simulations to demonstrate that his algorithm performed well in comparison to others for a number of interesting overload cases, but provided no formal performance characterizations. Versions of Locke's algorithm have been implemented and experimentally verified to be superior and cost-effective with respect to traditional realtime scheduling algorithms for a number of interesting cases. In the Alpha realtime distributed OS kernel, these included: a battle management application for air defense, by General Dynamics and the Archons Project at CMU [25]; and a ball-and-paddle realtime scheduling evaluation testbed by the Archons Project [26]. Locke's algorithm was implemented in the Mach 2.5 OS kernel, and measured on a synthesized realtime workload by the Archons Project [27].

Clark's algorithm makes a major contribution by dealing with dependencies (e.g., precedence, resource conflicts) which are not known in advance. It employs the same scheduling optimality criterion as Locke's. Clark permits only rectangular TVF's, whose value is the job's importance. Job execution times are both fixed and known.

Clark's algorithm selects jobs to be scheduled in decreasing order of value density (VD), and then selected jobs are scheduled EDF for the TVF's he allows, this both meets all deadlines and maximizes summed value. When each job is scheduled, so are those on which it depends. If necessary, precedent jobs are aborted or their deadlines are shortened (whichever is faster), to satisfy the deadline of the dependent job.

Clark used formal analysis and simulations to show that when overloaded, if the algorithm can apply all available cycles to jobs that complete, no other algorithm can accrue greater value given the current knowledge; but since future jobs are unknown, there is no performance guarantee. Clark's algorithm is being implemented in both the Alpha and Mach 3.X OS kernels.

A second generation of on-line BE algorithms is being devised as part of a recent multi-university effort to establish formal performance bounds for on-line algorithms in general and certain BE ones in particular [28], [29], [30]. Their work is focused on the competitive factor, which measures the value an algorithm guarantees it will achieve compared to a clairvoyant scheduler.

Like Clark's, their algorithms allow only rectangular TVF's, and (mostly) require both fixed and known execution times.

The principal result is that if all values are proportional to execution time, an on-line algorithm can guarantee a competitive factor of no more than 1/4. The performance bound is lower when value is not proportional to execution time, or the ratio of maximum to minimum VD increases, or execution times are not fixed and known.

This confirms the intuition that realtime performance guarantees are impossible if workload characteristics are unknown. However, the most recent research suggests that acceptable performance assurances may be possible when limited, reasonable, workload information is known; learning and understanding such trade-offs is one of the most important advances still to be made for BE algorithms.

The most closely related work to Best-Effort realtime scheduling is Cost-Based Scheduling for queueing and dropping network packets [31]. In this context, a cost function specifies the cost per unit length of queuing delay for a packet as a function of time. Packets are limited to non-decreasing cost functions.

Unlike Best-Effort processor scheduling, which create a whole schedule, the cost-based network algorithm queues the next packet which it estimates would cost the most to delay. Cost is calculated using a estimation of future cost that would be incurred, which is the same for all packets. The optimization objective is to minimize the average delay cost incurred by all packets. Dependencies are not considered, but explicitly recognized as critical.

Their simulations show that the algorithm performs well compared to the standard packet queuing algorithms, and to Locke's algorithm, for packets averaging unit length, in near fully loaded conditions. The premises of this work do not correspond well to the workload characteristics of interest for best-effort realtime computation scheduling.

In addition to this on-line research, a first generation of off-line BE algorithms is being devised in France [32], [33].

Benefit functions employ more application-supplied information, and thus exact a higher computational price than when little such information is used (e.g., by static priority) or no information is used (e.g., by round robin). Best-Effort realtime scheduling algorithms utilize more application-supplied information than is usual, and place specific requirements on the kind of scheduling mechanisms that must be provided (i.e., in the OS kernel cf. those of the Alpha kernel).

These prices can be minimized by good engineering, and then paid in different ways, including with inexpensive hardware: higher performance processors; a dynamically assigned processor in a multiprocessor node; or a special-purpose hardware accelerator (analogous to a floating-point co-processor) in a uniprocessor or multiprocessor node.

Acknowledgments

This work is funded in part by the USAF Rome Laboratories and the USN Surface Warfare Center, as well as by Digital Equipment Corporation.

The author gratefully acknowledges his helpful discussions with Ray Clark, Mike Davis, Alan Downing, David Maynard, and John Peha.

References

1. A.W. Wieder, A. Neppl, *CMOS Technology Trends and Economics*, IEEE Micro, August 1992.

2. R.K. Clark, E.D. Jensen, F.D. Reynolds, *An Architectural Overview of the Alpha Real-Time Distributed Kernel*, Proc. of the USENIX Workshop on Microkernels and Other Kernel Architectures, April 1992.

3. D.P. Anderson, D. Ferrari, P.V. Rangan, S.-Y. Tzou, *The DASH Project: Issues in the Design of Very Large Distributed Systems*, report No. UCB/CSD 87/338, U. of CA/Berkeley EECS Department, January 1987.

4. E.D. Jensen, Decentralized Control, *Distributed Systems: An Advanced Course*, Springer-Verlag, 1981.

5. T. Hogg, and B.A. Huberman, *Controlling Chaos in Distributed Systems*, IEEE Transactions on Systems, Man, and Cybernetics, November/December 1991.

6. A. Damm, J. Reisinger, W. Schwabl, H. Kopetz, *The Real-Time Operating System of MARS*, Operating System Review, ACM, July 1989.

7. S.-T Levi, S.K. Tripathi, S.D. Carson, A.K. Agrawala, *The MARUTI Hard Real-Time Operating System*, Operating System Review, ACM, July 1989.

8. C. von Clausewitz, *On War*, tr. by J.J. Graham, N. Trubner & Co. (London), 1873.

9. Ab Hugh, Dafydd, *The Future of Flying*, AI Expert, January 1988.

10. B.A. Myers, *Demonstrational Interfaces: Step Beyond Direct Manipulation*, Computer, IEEE, August 1992.

11. K. Huff, V. Lesser, *Knowledge-Based Command Understanding: An Example for the Software Development Environment*, TR 82-6, Computer and Information Sciences, U. of MA, 1982.

12. D. Kahneman, P. Slovic, A. Tversky (Ed.), *Judgement Under Uncertainty: Heuristics and Biases*, Cambridge University Press, 1982.

13. E.L Lawler, J.K. Lenstra, A.H.G. Rinnoy Kan, Recent Developments in Deterministic Sequencing and Scheduling: A Survey, *Deterministic and Stochastic Scheduling*, M.A.H. Dempster et al. (eds), D. Reidel, 1982.

14. J. Xu, D.L. Parnas, *On Satisfying Timing Constraints in Hard-Real-Time Systems*, Proc. ACM SIGSOFT '91 Conference on Software for Critical Systems (and ACM Software Engineering Notes), December 1991.

15. M. Pinedo, *On the Computational Complexity of Stochastic Scheduling Problems*, Deterministic and Stochastic Scheduling, M.A.H. Dempster et al. (eds), D. Reidel, 1982.

16. Weiss, Gideon, *Multiserver Stochastic Scheduling, Deterministic and Stochastic Scheduling*, M.A.H. Dempster et al. (eds.), D. Reidel, 1982.

17. T. Gifford, *Algorithms for Stochastic Scheduling Problems with Due Dates*.

18. R.M. Glorioso, F.C.C.Orsorio, *Stochastic Automata Models in Computer and Communication Networks*, Ch. 9 in Engineering Intelligent Systems, Digital Press, 1980.

19. C.D. Locke, *Best-Effort Decision Making for Real-Time Scheduling*, Ph.D. Thesis, CMU-CS-86-134, Department of Computer Science, Carnegie Mellon University, 1986.

20. R.K. Clark, *Scheduling Dependent Real-Time Activities*, Ph.D. Thesis, CMU-CS-90-155, School of Computer Science, Carnegie Mellon University, 1990.

21. B. Stewart, *Distributed Data Processing Technology*, Interim Report, Honeywell Systems and Research Center, March 1977.

22. E.D. Jensen, C.D. Locke H. Tokuda, *A Time-Value Driven Scheduling Model for Real-Time Operating Systems*, Proceedings of the Symposium on Real-Time Systems, IEEE, November 1985.

23. E.D. Jensen, *The Archons Project: An Overview*, Proceedings of the International Symposium on Synchronization, Control and Communication, Academic Press, 1983.

24. J.D. Northcutt, *Mechanisms for Reliable Distributed Real-Time Operating Systems* The Alpha Kernel, Academic Press, 1987.

25. D.P. Maynard, S.E. Shipman, R.K. Clark, J.D. Northcutt, R.B. Kegley, B.A. Zimmerman, P.J. Keleher, *An Example Real-Time Command, Control and Battle Management Application for Alpha*, Technical Report TR 88121, Archons Project, Computer Science Department, Carnegie-Mellon University, December 1988.

26. J.D. Northcutt, R.K. Clark, D.P. Maynard, J.E. Trull, *Decentralized Real-Time Scheduling*, Final Technical Report, Contract F33602-88-D-0027, School of Computer Science, Carnegie-Mellon University, February 1990.

27. H. Tokuda, J.W. Wendorf, H.Y. Wang, *Implementation of a Time-Driven Scheduler for Real-Time Operating Systems*, Proceedings of the Real-Time Systems Symposium, IEEE, December 1987.

28. F. Wang, D. Mao, *Worst Case Analysis for On-Line Scheduling in Real-Time Systems*, Dept. of Computer and Information Sciences, University of MA, June 1991.

29. S. Baruah, G. Koren, D. Mao, B. Mishra, A. Raghunathan, L. Rosier, D. Shasha, F. Wang, *On the Competitiveness of On-Line Real-Time Task Scheduling*, Proceedings of the Real-Time Systems Symposium, IEEE, December 1991.

30. G. Koren, D. Shasba, *Dover: An Optimal On-Line Scheduling Algorithm for Overloaded Real-Time Systems*, TR-594, Computer Science Department, New York University, February 1992.

31. J.M. Peha, F.A. Tobagi, *A Cost-Based Scheduling Algorithm to Support Integrated Services*, Proc. IEEE Infocom, April 1991.

32. K. Chen, *A Study on the Timeliness Property in Real-Time Systems*, Real-Time Systems, September 1991.

33. K. Chen, P. Muhlethaler, *Two Classes of Effective Heuristics for Time-Value Function Based Scheduling*, 12th Real-Time System Symposium, 1991.

Design of Real-Time Fault-Tolerant Computing Stations

K. H. (Kane) Kim

Department of Electrical & Computer Engineering
University of California
Irvine, California 92717
U.S.A.

1 Introduction

The steady increase observed during the past decade in distributed computer system (DCS) use in safety-critical real-time applications is expected to continue through the 1990's. For example, DCS's have been increasingly adopted in applications such as space navigation, air-traffic control, hospital automation, national defense, etc. [11, 16, 21, 43, 47]. To attain the desired level of reliability, such DCS's must be designed to possess effective fault tolerance capabilities.

A *fault-tolerant computer system* is a system that can continue to operate reliably by producing acceptable outputs in spite of occasional occurrences of component failures in both hardware and software components. In the late 1960's and 1970's, most research activities dealt with *circuit-level* or *register-transfer-level fault tolerance*, and in the mid-1970's research issues related to *processor-level fault tolerance* (i.e., treating as the *smallest replaceable unit*) started being addressed seriously. In the 1980's, tolerance of not only hardware component failures but also software component failures became a subject of serious discussion and so was born the notion and subfield of **system-level fault tolerance**.

Hardware fault tolerance has been maturing rapidly in recent years. Two major reasons are:

1. Hardware cost has become a relatively insignificant portion of the overall computer system cost. So, hardware redundancy is easily justified.

2. Major computer system vendors have succeeded in producing "cost-competitive" computer systems with substantial hardware fault tolerance capabilities. This has opened a market of substantial size.

However, these advances have been observed mostly in commercial transaction processing application fields. The technology for constructing real-time DCS's tolerant of hardware faults is much less mature than that for constructing commercial fault-tolerant transaction processing systems. Real-time computer systems must not only compute correct values but also deliver each value in time to its destination. In fact, missing deadlines on the part of a real-time computer system is often as dangerous as producing incorrect values. Therefore, if incorporation of fault tolerance mechanisms increases the chance of a computer system missing deadlines, it could decrease the overall system reliability rather than improve it.

In designing real-time DCS's, system designers must deal with faults in both computing nodes and inter-node connection/communication subsystems. Therefore, the problem of ensuring timely delivery of computation results to the environments has additional dimensions in the case of a DCS; reflection of concurrency and conflicts among distributed nodes as well as inter-node communication delays must be considered [40].

On the other hand, the problem of tolerating design faults, which is primarily of concern in the real-time software domain, has not been adequately dealt with by the research and development community. Therefore, system-level fault tolerance that combines hardware fault tolerance and software fault tolerance is the major remaining challenge in the area of fault-tolerant computing.

The factors mentioned above often make system-level fault tolerance in complex real-time DCS's a great challenge to computer system designers and researchers.

The purpose of this chapter is to summarize the fundamental principles governing the design of effective fault-tolerant real-time DCS's as well as some of the major design approaches established. The chapter starts with the presentation of an abstract model of fault-tolerant DCS structure in Section 2. The fundamental design principles are discussed in Section 3. A real-time DCS can be viewed as an interconnection of computing stations, where a **computing station** refers to a processing node (hardware and software) dedicated to the execution of one or a few application processes. In converting the abstract structure discussed in Section 2 into practical realizations, the core of the solution is to realize real-time fault-tolerant computing stations. Basic established approaches to designing such computing stations are reviewed in Section 4. Section 5 reviews network configuration management (NCM) techniques that can be combined with the techniques discussed in Section 4 to further reduce the worst-case **fault latency** (i.e., the time gap between a fault occurrence and its detection) of the real-time fault-tolerant DCS. The final section (6) summarizes some of the major issues that remain to be resolved.

2 An Abstract Model of Fault-Tolerant DCS Structure

Tolerance of component failures during system operation is generally realized through the four steps depicted in Figure 1 [30]. Once a system enters a faulty state, the fault must first be detected.

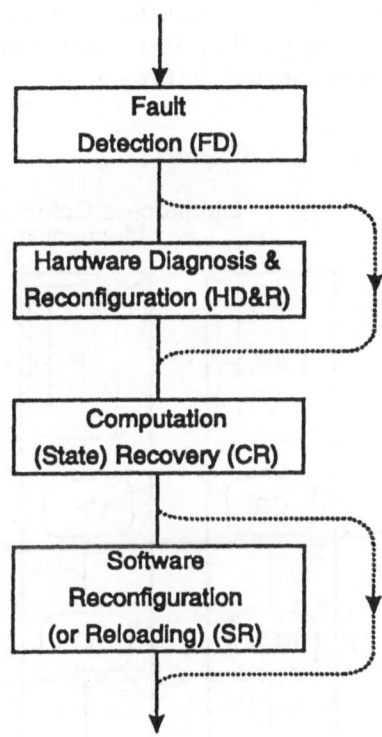

Fig. 1. Basic steps in fault tolerance (adapted from [30]).

Second, the source of the fault must be isolated at the level of replaceable/repairable components. The fault source may be hardware and/or imperfect software. Since software runs on hardware, it is natural to first test hardware to see if it is operational. If any malfunctioning hardware modules are detected, appropriate hardware reconfiguration (repair) actions (e.g., replacement of the detected malfunctioning modules with spare modules) are taken. The third step is to restore the system to a state where the system can resume the application-oriented computation that was interrupted due to the fault. Sometimes this involves reloading the memory with the previously saved state information of the computation (i.e., contents of variables). After this computation state recovery is completed, some suspected software modules may be replaced with alternate versions if available.

A model that extends the view in Figure 1 to reflect the nature of DCS's more closely is depicted in Figure 2. There are largely four layers of components in the system structure. The bottom layer is a hardware-software layer and the other three are software layers. Multiple hardware nodes together with an interconnection or communication network form the hardware part of the bottom layer. Each node contains a software kernel that supports coexistence of software components belonging to the upper three layers within the node and handles diagnosis and reconfiguration of the node hardware.

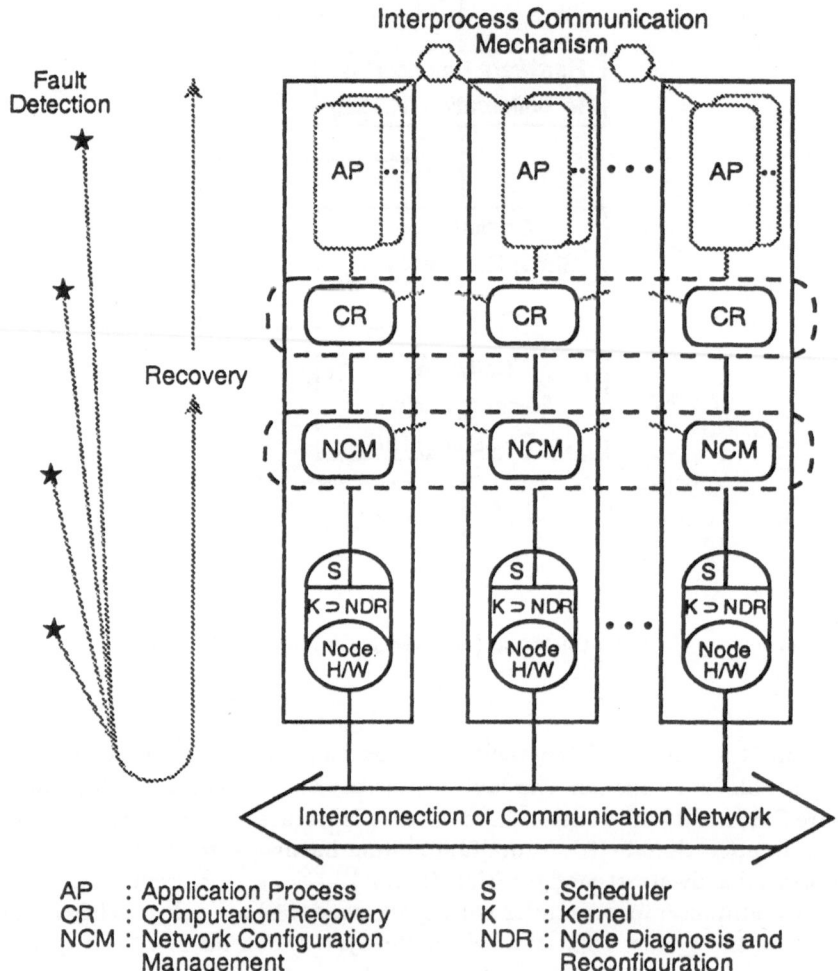

Fig. 2. An abstract model of fault-tolerant DCS structure.

The software components in the second layer, the *network configuration management (NCM) layer,* are responsible for diagnosing the health of the system hardware and, if necessary, reconfiguring it to establish an operational configuration. Suppose the software kernel in each node (to be exact, the node diagnosis and reconfiguration (NDR) component) either fails to establish an operational state of the node or makes an inaccurate report on the health of the node. The software components in the NCM layer can further diagnose the node status by using other nodes and, if necessary, arrange for functional or physical replacement of a bad node by other nodes. The interconnection networks are also checked out by the NCM layer.

The software components in the third layer, the *computation state recovery layer*, are responsible for establishing a computation state from which the execution of the application processes in the top layer can start or resume. These software components are also distributed among multiple nodes and may accomplish state establishment in a completely decentralized fashion or under some centralized control.

The software components in the top layer are distributed application processes cooperating among themselves. The software components that are actively running on nodes most of the time are the application processes, and the software components in the NCM and computation state recovery layers are invoked upon detection of faults and invoked for periodic diagnosis.

In the model, fault detectors are embedded in all four layers including the node hardware layer. Once a fault is detected, the follow-up action sequence starts from the bottom layer regardless of the location of the component that detected the fault. That is, the set of nodes to be involved in the follow-up actions is identified based on the information supplied by the fault detector, and the software kernel of each selected node diagnoses the node and attempts to establish an operational state of the node. The NCM layer is then called in to establish an operational system hardware configuration. This may involve diagnosing various nodes because the fault detector does not provide any clue on the damaged part of the system. This may also involve reincorporating the nodes that were amputated and have since been repaired. Next, the computation recovery layer establishes a consistent state of distributed application processes. This may involve reloading the memory with the previously saved state information of the processes (i.e., contents of variables). If neither the software kernel of each node nor the NCM software components have detected any hardware malfunction, then the detected fault could have been caused by a transient hardware fault or a residual design inadequacy in the application software. Therefore, after the computation state recovery is completed, some suspected modules in the application processes may be replaced with their alternate versions if available.

There is a trade-off between the cost of implanting fault detectors throughout the DCS structure and the cost of executing recovery actions. In general, the more fault detectors the system has, the shorter the fault latency is. The shorter fault latency in turn leads to a smaller recovery execution cost. Therefore, cost-effective incorporation of fault detectors requires clear understanding of the relationship among the fault detectors, the maximum fault latency, and the recovery execution cost.

If it is apparent from the information supplied by the fault detector that the damage has been confined within the fault-originating node, all non-trivial actions by the NCM and computation state recovery managers are not necessary. As a trivial example, an error-correcting code mechanism can catch a bit error in a word fetched from memory and fix it all by itself without necessitating any action from the NCM or computation state recovery managers and with practically no disruption of the application processes.

3 Fundamental Principles in Designing Real-Time Fault-Tolerant DCS's

(1) Fault tolerance in hard-real-time systems vs. Fault tolerance in soft-real-time systems

A DCS used in an application where the controlled objects cannot tolerate late arrival or omission of even a single control output of the controlling computer system, is called a hard- real-time (HRT) DCS. Therefore, it is of critical importance to achieve fault detection and recovery always within an acceptable time bound in HRT systems. **Recovery time for a fault** can be defined as the loss of computation time due to an occurrence of the fault, i.e., the difference between the task execution time in the absence of the fault and the task execution time in the presence of the fault. In HRT systems, what is important is the *worst-case recovery time* (or *recovery time bound*) rather than the average recovery time [38, 50]. Fault- tolerant HRT systems must be structured such that the recovery time can be predicted with a high degree of accuracy.

(2) Backward recovery vs. Forward recovery

A **backward recovery**, also called rollback-and-retry, involves validating and saving the computation state (e.g., saving the contents of registers within a processor and the contents of main memory into reliable backup storage) at various stages during system operation. Then if an error is detected, the backward recovery technique reestablishes the system to a previously recorded state and restarts the system from that point [13, 49]. A high time cost is the serious drawback of the backward recovery. Moreover, in real-time applications, any computation results sent to the environments or the passage of real time can not be recalled. Therefore, the backward recovery has severely limited applicability in real-time systems.

A **forward recovery** does not involve reestablishing the system to a previously recorded state. This is not to say that old state information is not needed in recovery. A design issue here is how and what part of the old state information recorded can be utilized in achieving forward recovery.

Desirable forward recovery techniques are those of generic type. Many exception handling approaches that have appeared in literature are examples of highly application-specific forward recovery. Such approaches assume localization of the damage (due to the fault) to a very small area within the system, e.g., one or two program variables. More generic forward recovery schemes which are capable of dealing with a broader range of fault conditions and more widely spread damages, are of *active replica* type, e.g., the triple modular redundancy (TMR) scheme [4, 24], active replication of computing stations [26, 38, 44], the distributed recovery block (DRB) scheme [32], the N-version scheme [6], etc. Drastic decreases in the hardware cost during the past decade enabled users of these schemes to become largely free of concern in employing twice or three times the amount of hardware used in non-fault-tolerant systems.

(3) Task-level fault tolerance vs. Instruction-level fault tolerance

Many fault tolerance techniques used in the past are **instruction-level fault tolerance** techniques in that in each case a computation segment protected with a forward recovery capability is an instruction execution [12, 56]. For example, if a parity error is detected as an operand is fetched into a register from a memory word, then an abandonment of the current instruction followed by a retry of the instruction may be attempted. Therefore, if a fault latency is greater than an instruction cycle, then a backward recovery involving rolling back over multiple instruction executions is incurred. This means a "task abortion" in the case of a HRT task. Ensuring the fault latency to be smaller than an instruction cycle is not an easy proposition; it is a prohibitively expensive goal to realize in quite a few applications.

Task-level fault tolerance techniques aim for timely delivery of an expected output of a real-time task in spite of component failures. Therefore, a computation segment protected with a forward recovery capability is a real-time task. Instruction-level fault tolerance techniques are inadequate in highly safety-critical real-time applications and instead task-level fault tolerance techniques must be mobilized.

(4) Redundancy unit

The **redundancy unit** defines not only the unit for replacement for repair but also the primary boundary for fault containment. As the system designers' interests have shifted from instruction-level fault tolerance to task-level fault tolerance, their choice of redundancy units has also shifted: from circuit modules or sub-instruction units as redundancy units in the 1960's and 1970's, to instruction processors in the late 1970's and 1980's, and further to computing stations in the 1980's and 1990's.

(5) Multi-task computing station vs. single-task computing station

Because of the dramatically reduced hardware costs, complex software schemes such as multiprogramming techniques for heavy utilization of hardware are losing their appeals rapidly in many safety-critical real-time applications. It is now often much more cost-effective to design *one-task-per-station systems*. Such approaches simplify the temporal behavior analysis and they encourage high-level optimizations such as those aimed for faster guaranteed response.

(6) Tolerance of strictly contained hardware faults vs. Tolerance of latent hardware faults and software faults

By a **strictly contained hardware fault** we refer to a hardware fault that is detected before the error caused by it can spread outside the containing redundancy unit. A redundancy unit subject to only such types of faults is often referred to as a **fail-silent unit** [46]. For example, if the latency for the faults occurring in a redundancy unit is always less than an instruction cycle, such a unit is an absolutely fail-silent unit. If all the units needed in building a fault-tolerant DCS are of fail-silent type, then the problem of designing a real-time fault- tolerant DCS is a relatively straightforward problem. However, in many real-time application environments, it is not feasible to ensure that every unit used is a fail-silent unit. Some **latent hardware faults** that cause errors propagating outside the originating redundancy units are unavoidable. In some challenging real-time application environments, software faults are known to be unavoidable, and a perfectly fail-silent unit subject to software faults is an illogical notion. Here, the problem of designing a real-time fault-tolerant DCS is much more complicated. For example, use of software/algorithm redundancy is essential in any solution approach of reasonable generality.

If a backward recovery scheme is to be mobilized, then the design of the scheme is affected again by whether the system designer determines to deal with strictly contained hardware faults only or other difficult types of faults as well. If only strictly contained hardware faults are to be dealt with, then *recovery points* (at which computation states are saved into reliable backup storage) can be established in a manner independent of the process context, e.g., clock-driven recovery point insertion [54]. On the other hand, if software faults and/or latent hardware faults are to be dealt with, then context- dependent recovery point insertion is needed in each process. This is because in order to design a meaningful recovery action that typically involves execution of an alternate algorithm, the program designer needs to know the state of computation from which the alternate try can start.

Considering software faults does not mean that a unit with potentially Byzantine behavior needs to be considered [41]. A Byzantine unit capable of displaying "malicious" behavior is rarely a justifiable model of a component of a fault-tolerant

DCS. This is because the probability of a redundancy unit produced by a non-malicious designer exhibiting malicious behavior is negligible. Therefore, while a Byzantine unit can be a proper subject for the security enforcement capability designer to deal with, it is largely irrelevant to the mission of the fault- tolerant system designer.

(7) Fault tolerance in LAN vs. Fault tolerance in WAN

With respect to achieving system-level fault tolerance, there are some fundamental differences in basic characteristics between the real-time local area network (LAN) applications and the real- time wide area network (WAN) applications [33]. For example, inter-node communication costs are very low in the case of real-time LAN's compared to that of real-time WAN's. Similarly, reliability of inter-node communication is much higher or can be made much higher at the same cost in LAN's compared to the case of WAN's. Therefore, location-independent reconfiguration of processes is an affordable and desirable capability in real-time LAN's whereas it is not a sensible approach to pursue in real-time WAN's such as WAN's covering multiple cities or those embedded in multiple cooperating satellites. Closely coordinated and highly interactive fault detection and recovery actions can also be designed into real-time LAN's at reasonable costs whereas such designs are not cost-effective for real-time WAN's. A certain degree of node autonomy in both application processing and fault handling is a desirable characteristic in real-time WAN's, but the node autonomy is much less important in real-time LAN's.

Fundamental differences also exist between real-time LAN's and real-time highly parallel multi-computer networks (HPM's). HPM's are used primarily for reasons of high throughput and fast turnaround whereas LAN's are used primarily for reasons of modular expansion, resistance to location-dependent faults, and employment of multiple distributed sensors. Therefore, implementations of task-level fault tolerance schemes that are effective in real-time HPM's are bound to be substantially different from those suitable for real-time LAN's.

(8) Indispensability of a state saving mechanism in applications subject to temporary blackouts

There are certain fault types that dictate recovery procedures more closely tailored to application details than other fault types. An example of such a fault is a system-wide simultaneous disturbance caused by lightning, unreliable power source, radiation, etc., which may be referred to by the generic term **temporary blackout** [34]. In the case of a LAN system, a temporary blackout means a global fault of the system. This is a unique characteristic since other types of faults usually create some localized damages to distributed computations. Efficiency and timing concerns lead to the selection of a procedure for detecting and recovering from temporary blackouts that is tailored to the detailed application logic. A typical forward recovery procedure involves first restoring critical state variables with the most recently saved values, next reading the current status of the application environment, and finally establishing the computation to an appropriate state compatible with the current environment.

Therefore, a state saving mechanism is almost indispensable in applications subject to temporary blackouts.

4 Basic Structures of Real-Time Fault-Tolerant Computing Stations

The most basic and important problem in constructing a real- time fault-tolerant DCS is to construct constituent computing stations of highly reliable and fault-tolerant type. Since a fault-tolerant computing station itself is typically a network of processors, constructing such a computing station already involves making an interconnection/communication network reliable and fault-tolerant. Therefore, with highly fault-tolerant computing stations obtained, there remains the problem of facilitating reliable and fault-tolerant communication among the computing stations, but whether the nature of that problem is totally new or similar to what has already been encountered (in the course of designing the computing stations) depends upon the communication network architecture adopted.

Computing stations tolerant of strictly contained hardware faults are considered first in Section 4.1, and those tolerant of latent hardware faults and software faults are dealt with in Section 4.2.

4.1 Active replication of hardware processors

Although a variety of techniques have been discussed in literature, only two of the most fundamental proven structures are discussed here.

4.1.1 The triple modular redundancy (TMR) scheme.

The essence of the **triple modular redundancy (TMR)** scheme is to use three copies of a computing component and take a vote with their execution results [4, 24, 28, 57, 58]. When there is discrepancy, the result with a majority vote is used. Figure 3 depicts an abstract model of a TMR- structured computing station.

An important issue is how to realize voting without degrading both the modularity of the system structure and the execution efficiency. For example, should a separate hardware processor be dedicated to the voting function? Or should the voting function be the responsibility of a software module in each of the three computing nodes? Here we can consider two drastically different types of TMR-structured computing stations:

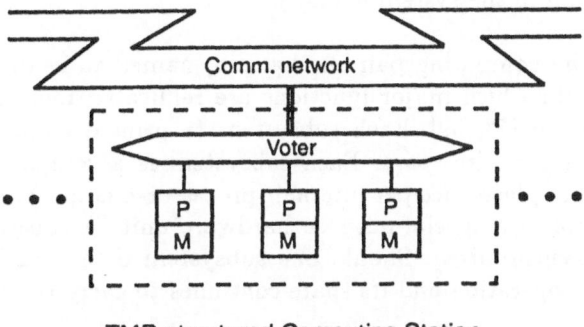

TMR-structured Computing Station

Fig. 3. A TMR-structured computing station.

Type-I performs voting once per instruction execution or per internal (processor-memory) bus cycle whereas
Type-II does the voting at points of communicating messages with other computing stations.

In type-II computing stations, voting takes place at the boundaries of atomic computation steps, i.e., non-interacting segments of processes. There is an obvious trade-off between the two types. In a type-I computing station, the voter is usually a special-purpose hardware unit and the fault latency is very short and bounded by an instruction cycle. In contrast, in a type-II computing station, the voter is typically implemented as a cooperating ensemble of software components, each housed in a separate member processing node of the computing station. The fault latency can be as large as the maximum execution time of an atomic computation step.

A related implementation issue is whether to place the voter in the output section of a TMR-structured computing station or in the input section; this is a design choice subject to a trade-off between the cost of voter replication plus the required communication bandwidth and the cost of hardening a single voter. If TMR-structured computing stations are subject to temporary blackouts, then additional mechanisms for temporary blackout handling must be incorporated into the computing stations.

4.1.2 Pair-of-comparing-pairs (PCP) scheme.

The **comparing processor-pair** scheme was adopted in No. 1A ESS and No. 3A systems [55]. In this approach, all critical components such as processor and memory are duplicated, and outputs from the components are compared for fault detection. If a mismatch occurs, an interrupt is generated, which causes the fault-recognition program to run. The basic function of this program is to determine which half of the system is faulty.

An extension of the comparing pair mechanism, named **pair of comparing pairs** (PCP) here, in which major functions are replicated four times, is used in the Stratus system [53, 59]. Each subsystem (a printed circuit board) has an identical counterpart, its spare. Each subsystem is a comparing pair, and the comparison takes place once per internal (processor-memory) bus cycle. The comparison executor is a special-purpose hardware unit. A subsystem and its spare are tightly synchronized. Should one subsystem detect an internal mismatch, it stops the operation and its spare continues to carry the load.

Figure 4 depicts an abstract model of a PCP-structured computing station. As in the case of the TMR scheme, no special recovery logic is needed. Yet, fast forward recovery is achieved. However, the comparison executor used in each half (i.e., subsystem) of a PCP-structured computing station takes less overhead than the voter used in a TMR-structured computing station. Also, the main subsystem and the spare subsystem can be physically separated further than the member processing nodes of a TMR-structured computing station in general. This reduces the probability of a fault damaging both subsystems. On the other hand, a PCP-structured computing station uses one more processing node.

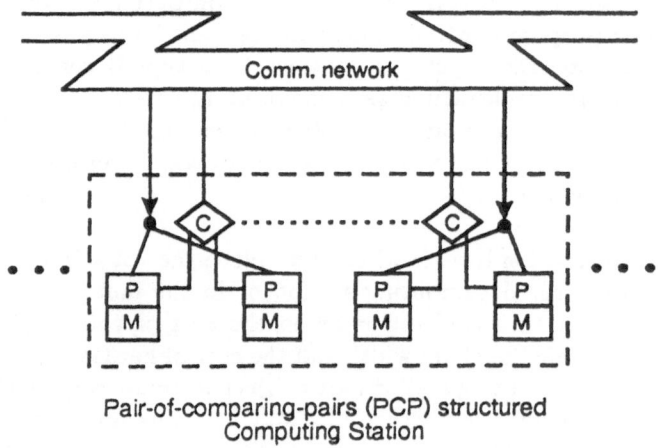

Pair-of-comparing-pairs (PCP) structured
Computing Station

Fig. 4. A PCP-structured computing station.

The above discussion dealt with the case where the comparison within a comparing processor-pair takes place once per internal bus cycle. Almost all existing implementations have adopted this approach. However, it is conceivable to adapt the PCP scheme so that the comparison takes place at points of communicating messages with other computing stations. In such a case, a comparison executor may be implemented as a cooperating pair of software components, each running on a separate processing node.

Again, this scheme does not deal with temporary blackouts.

4.2 Active replication of computing stations

Just two of the most fundamental structures demonstrated to some extent are discussed here.

4.2.1 The Voting N-Version Scheme

A straight extension of the TMR scheme in the direction toward tolerance of both hardware and software faults results in the **voting N-version** scheme [5, 6]. This scheme uses multiple functionally *equivalent* versions of each critical software component with the voting approach for fault detection and result selection. Due to the high cost of designing and maintaining multiple versions, the use of three versions is the standard practice in the case of the voting N-version scheme. Each version should run on a different node to facilitate hardware fault tolerance. For example, each of the three processing nodes in the TMR-structured computing station in Figure 3 can run a different version. However, the voting required here is not the responsibility of a single hardware voter. The voting routine must run on all three processing nodes in a cooperative manner. Some experimental studies have shown the plausibility of achieving software fault tolerance using this scheme [7, 29].

Moreover, the voting approach requires design of multiple versions expected to generate *truly identical computation results.* This could be a severe restriction in cases where complexity of a program component is high. The voting approach also requires close synchronization of the nodes executing multiple versions. On the other hand, the voting process itself does not require any help from the application developer while it requires at least three versions of the application software component.

The voting N-version scheme can be applied to atomic computation steps, i.e., non-interacting segments of processes. It requires development of N versions of a program module for each critical atomic computation step.

4.2.2 The Distributed Recovery Block (DRB) Scheme: A Generalized Hot Backup Scheme

4.2.2.1 Basic Principles

The **distributed recovery block** (DRB) scheme is an active redundancy scheme where multiple processors concurrently execute multiple versions of a software component and then the same reasonableness check routine [23, 32]. The reasonableness check routine in each processor, together with a watch-dog timer, checks reasonableness of the computational results of the version executed as well as the timeliness of the execution.

A **recovery block** consists of one or more routines, called **try blocks** here, designed to compute the same or similar results, and an **acceptance test** which is an expression of the criterion used for accepting the results of try blocks [25, 42, 48]. A *try* (i.e., execution of a try block) is thus always followed by an acceptance test execution. If an error is detected during a try or as a result of an acceptance test execution, then a rollback-and-retry with another try block follows.

While the original recovery block scheme incorporated the backward recovery approach, the DRB scheme incorporated a new forward recovery capability.

Under the DRB scheme, a recovery block is replicated into multiple nodes forming a *DRB computing station* for parallel redundant processing. In most cases a recovery block containing just two try blocks, i.e., the primary and the alternate, is designed and then assigned to two different nodes called the **primary** and **shadow nodes** as depicted in Figure 5. The roles of the two try blocks are assigned differently in the two nodes. Primary node X uses try block A as the first try block initially, whereas shadow node Y uses try block B as the initial first try block. Therefore, until a fault is detected, both nodes receive the same input data, process the data using two different try blocks (i.e., block A on node X and block B on node Y), and check the results using the acceptance test. Both nodes perform all these tasks concurrently. The **time acceptance test** (i.e., the time-out mechanism) is used to ensure timely behavior of both nodes.

In a fault-free situation, both nodes will pass the acceptance test with the results computed with their first try blocks. In such a case, the primary node notifies the shadow of its success in the acceptance test. Thereafter, only the primary node sends its output to the successor computing station(s). Both nodes then proceed to the next task cycle. However, if the primary node fails and the shadow node passes its own acceptance test, the shadow node assumes the role of the primary; i.e., the nodes exchange their roles. To be more specific, upon its failure in passing the acceptance test the primary node attempts to inform the shadow node. The shadow node will take over the role of the primary as soon as it receives the notice. If the primary node crashes completely, the sha-

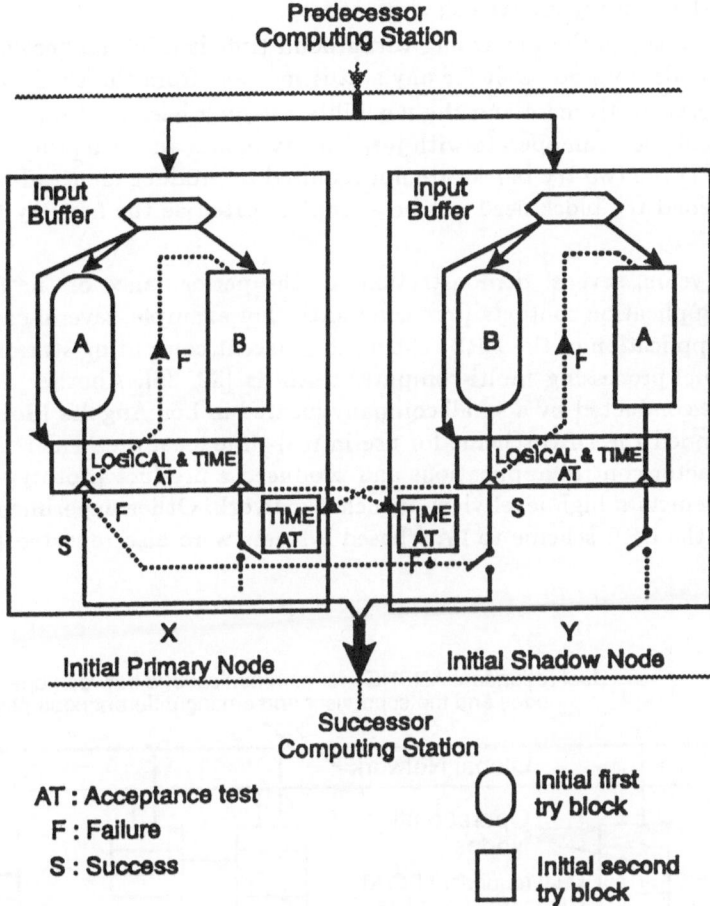

Fig. 5. The basic DRB computing station (adapted from [32]).

dow node will recognize the failure of the primary upon expiration of the preset time limit. It will then become the new primary. These interactions between two nodes are done asynchronously. On the other hand, if the shadow node fails first, the primary node need not be disturbed. In both cases, the failed node attempts to become an operational shadow node; it attempts to roll back and retry with its second try block to bring its application computation state including local database up-to-date. This attempt does not disturb the primary node.

This approach has the following useful characteristics:

a) Recovery can be accomplished in the same manner regardless of whether a node fails due to hardware faults or software faults;

b) The recovery time is minimal since maximum concurrency is exploited between the primary and the shadow nodes;

c) The increase in the processing turnaround time is minimal because the primary node does not wait for any status message from the shadow node;

d) The cost-effectiveness and the flexibility are high because (d1) a DRB computing station can operate with just two try blocks and two processing nodes and (d2) the two try blocks are not required to produce identical results and the second try block need not be as sophisticated as the first try block.

In recent years, several demonstrations of the performance of the scheme in practical application contexts were conducted. For example, several experiments involved application of the DRB scheme to adjacent computing stations in real-time parallel processing multi-computer testbeds [32, 35]. Another major validation was conducted by a small company located in Los Angeles (SoHaR, Inc). They extended the DRB scheme for use in real-time local area PC networks for nuclear reactor control applications and produced a product prototype [22, 23]. Figure 6 depicts a high level view of such a network. Other experimental applications of the DRB scheme to LAN based systems were also reported [3, 18].

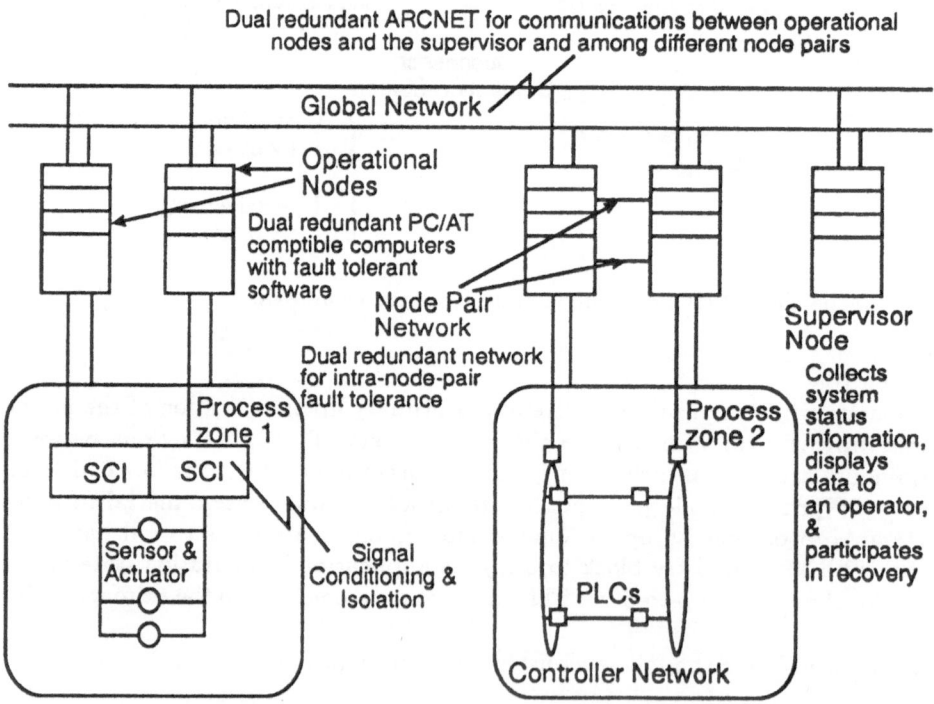

Fig. 6. The DRB-based fault-tolerant LAN architecture developed by SoHaR, Inc.

4.2.2.2 Single-Version DRB Computing Station: A Hot Backup Scheme

If the system designer is not concerned with the possible presence and activation of software faults, then the DRB scheme need not be utilized in its full generality. Alternate try blocks are not necessary. Only one algorithm needs to be designed for each task. Such a scheme can be viewed as a "hot backup" scheme, which is a software-implemented approach for achieving hardware fault tolerance without requiring special hardware mechanisms.

Moreover, it is not a requirement to design a task-specific acceptance test. A **common acceptance test** designed to perform spot checks on a few selected areas of the machine hardware or integrity checks for various data structures can be executed at the end of each task to decide whether to trust the task result as an acceptable one or not [52, 55, 60]. In such a case where a task-independent common acceptance test is used and no alternate try blocks are used, forming a DRB station dedicated to fault-tolerant execution of a task becomes a mechanical process that does not burden the application software designer in any way. This approach can thus be viewed as a concrete approach to mechanical replicated execution of real-time tasks. The cooperation between partner nodes follows the same protocol discussed above in Section 4.2.2.1.

In addition, to further increase the fault coverage of a single-version DRB computing station, a result comparison step can be inserted in each member processing node. Each node can then send its computation results to its partner after successful execution of the acceptance test and, upon receiving the computation results of the partner, compare it to its own result. This is essentially the comparing processor-pair scheme with the addition of the acceptance test step and with the comparison done at the boundaries of atomic computation steps. As such, the scheme needs to be either combined with a backward recovery mechanism that will be invoked when the comparison results in a mismatch or extended into the PCP scheme combined with the acceptance test step to facilitate forward recovery. In all these extension cases, the acceptance test step still plays the important role of significantly reducing the occurrences of comparison mismatch.

4.2.2.3 Implementation Techniques

(1) DRB computing station based on comparing processor-pairs

The basic DRB scheme relies on the logic acceptance test and the time acceptance test for fault detection. For faster detection of hardware faults, the DRB scheme can be extended to incorporate various established mechanisms. An extension of the DRB scheme under which each of the processing nodes (primary and shadow) in a DRB computing station is implemented in the form of a comparing processor-pair is highly appealing. In each comparing processor-pair, the comparison takes place once per instruction cycle or per internal bus cycle. Such a DRB computing station is different from both the PCP-structured computing station discussed in Section 4.1.2 and its extension incorporating the acceptance test step discussed in Section 4.2.2.2. A DRB computing station based on comparing processor-pairs should exhibit much shorter *latency* for most hardware faults than an ordinary DRB station does. Therefore, in such a DRB computing station, only some rare types of hardware faults and software faults will escape the guards set by the comparing processor-pair mechanism and will have to be detected by the acceptance test with concomitant larger fault latencies.

(2) Multiple recovery blocks in a DRB computing station

For reasons such as efficient node utilization or special characteristics of the applications, multiple tasks may often be designed to reside on the same node even though the single-task- per-node approach is becoming justified with increasing ease. This means that multiple recovery blocks may reside in a DRB computing station [35]. The following three cases are conceivable.

a) **Multi-procedure DRB computing station:** Each of multiple recovery blocks in the same DRB station is provided to process data items from a different source (predecessor computing station) or to process a different type of data items. The motivation for structuring this type of DRB stations is the node economy. The application software of a multi-procedure DRB station thus takes the form of a "case" statement enclosing multiple recovery blocks as depicted in Figure 7(a). A multi- procedure DRB station is depicted in Figure 7(b).

b) **Multi-phase DRB computing station:** This case arises where the mission life of a task running on a computing station consists of multiple phases and different phases require substantially different processing algorithms. The operations for each phase can be naturally designed into a separate recovery block. Although it is possible to form a separate DRB station around each recovery block, it is a wasteful approach since there is no parallelism among such DRB stations. Therefore, a multi- phase DRB station can be viewed as one running a single task structured in the form of a "case" statement enclosing multiple recovery blocks. Figure 7(a) and 7(b) are thus applicable to a multi-phase DRB station also.

c) **DRB computing station with serially bonded recovery blocks:** This DRB station contains multiple recovery blocks connected in series as shown in Figure 8. The figure shows only the software components in one processing node portion of the station. Such recovery blocks are called **serially bonded recovery blocks**. This case naturally arises where a task is required to deliver its processing results at several different stages, possibly to different destinations. This DRB station structuring can be motivated not only for node economy but also for improved data turnaround time. To be more specific, if two recovery blocks closely related in the form of a producer-consumer relation are assigned to two separate DRB stations, then data communication between recovery blocks involves inter-node communication. In LAN-based systems, such inter-node communication delay is significantly

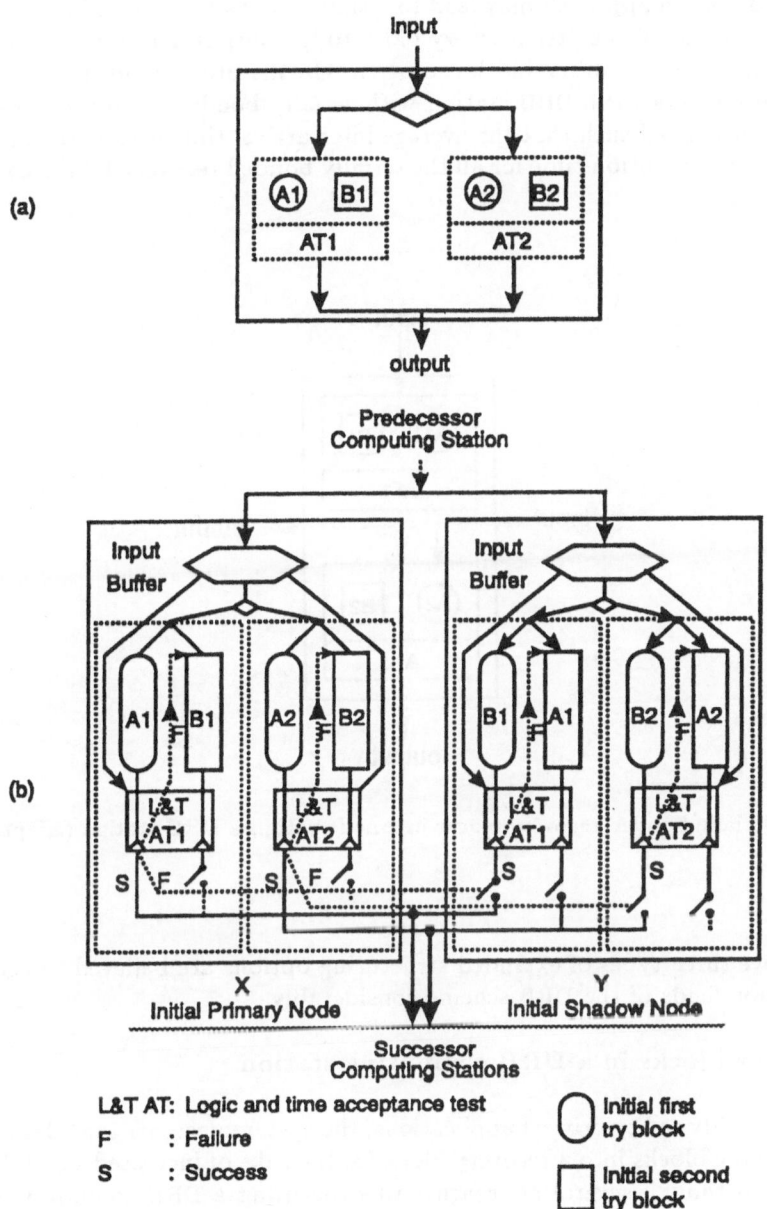

Fig. 7. A multi-procedure or multi-phase DRB station.

larger than the intra-node communication delay that would be incurred when both recovery blocks are assigned to one DRB station. Therefore, the single DRB station approach may lead to a shorter data turnaround time from the input action of the first recovery block to the output action marking the end of the second recovery block execution. On the other hand, the arrival rate of input data for a DRB station with serially bonded recovery blocks must be constrained such that the average inter-arrival time is substantially larger than the execution time for all the serially bonded recovery blocks combined.

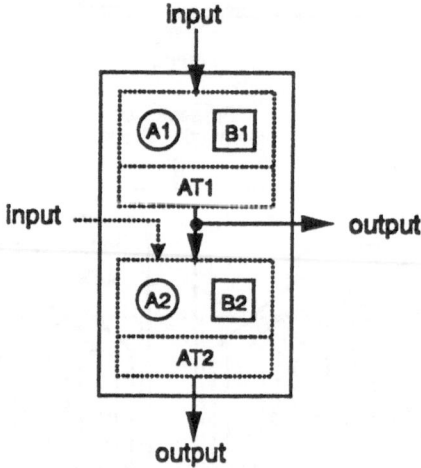

Fig. 8. Serially bonded recovery blocks in a node within a DRB station (adapted from [35]).

The above three types of extended structuring options are believed to widen the application fields of the DRB scheme considerably.

(3) N try blocks in a DRB computing station

In some highly safety-critical applications, the system designer may design more than two try blocks into a recovery block for the sake of increased reliability and comfort. Although several approaches to structuring a DRB computing station that uses three try blocks are conceivable, one of the most natural approaches is to treat the third node as a shadow node for the team of the first two nodes [35]. Such a computing station is depicted in Figure 9.

Node Z in the figure will normally use try block C as its primary try block and deliver its results only when both X and Y fail to produce acceptable results in

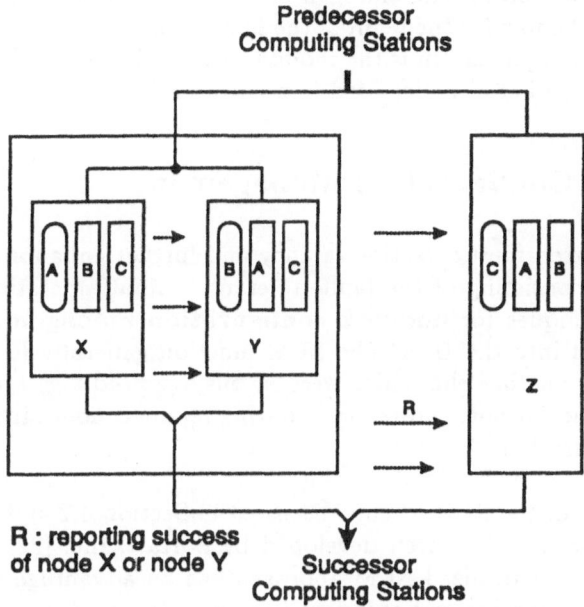

Fig. 9. A DRB computing station that uses 3 try blocks (adapted from [35]).

time. Nodes X and Y behave like a single functional node with respect to interfacing with their shadow node Z. They must share responsibilities for providing their status information to node Z at various points as well as responsibilities for understanding the status of node Z. For example, the type of the input data item picked, the acceptance test result (an indication enabling node Z to determine if any one of the two nodes X and Y has passed its acceptance test), the success of delivering the result by node X or Y to the successor stations, etc., are the information that needs to be provided to node Z.

If node X or Y crashes, then it can be replaced by node Z and thus the computing station can start functioning as an ordinary two-node DRB station. Similarly, crash of node Z will result in the computing station functioning as an ordinary two-node DRB station. If both X and Y fail at their acceptance tests but are alive, then node Z becomes the new primary node and one of the two failed nodes (X and Y) should become the new secondary node (a shadow for node Z) and the other should become the third node (a shadow for the team of Z and the secondary node). The time-out value used by the third node Z waiting for status information from the team of X and Y can be somewhat larger than that used by Y monitoring the primary node X.

An important advantage of the approach depicted in Figure 9 is the recursive nature of the approach. Therefore, in an n-node DRB station, the n-th node functions as a shadow for the team of the first n-1 nodes. A natural consequence of this recursive organization is the modest increase in the implementation complexity as the number of nodes used in a DRB station increases.

5 Network Configuration Management

In order to shorten fault detection latency and further enhance the survival period of a DCS consisting of the fault- tolerant computing stations discussed in Section 4, techniques for **network configuration management** (NCM) can be incorporated into the DCS. The NCM function generally involves detecting crashed nodes, whether the nodes were in busy (non-idling) application states before the crashes or not, and reincorporating repaired nodes into the operating network configuration.

The integration of the DRB scheme discussed in Section 4.2 and a practical centralized NCM scheme has been developed by SoHaR, Inc. [22, 23] as depicted in Figure 6. The centralized NCM approach has an advantage in its simplicity but can become a single point of failure. However, there are many known techniques for hardening the centralized network configuration manager or dynamically electing the manager [8, 10, 19].

Several decentralized approaches to NCM have also been studied in recent years [15, 17, 20, 27, 39, 36, 51]. One example is the "node-alive" protocol adopted in the Alpha operating system kernel [27]. Under the protocol, if a node has not seen any activity sign of another node over a certain period of time, the former node sends explicit queries to the latter. If the queries are not answered, the former assumes the latter to have failed. The other example is the **periodic reception history broadcast** (PRHB) scheme initially formulated in [39]. This scheme enables every active node to discover a change in the health status of any constituent nodes quickly and accurately.

The PRHB scheme was originally designed for use in the TDMA (time division multiplexed access) bus based LAN systems. Each node periodically *owns* the bus, i.e., holds exclusive right for broadcasting through the bus, for a fixed duration called a bus-slot. The key idea in the PRHB scheme is to have each node listen to the bus all the time and, during its bus-slot, broadcast a report on its listening experiences during the most recent TDMA cycle. Each broadcasted report on listening experiences is in the form of a *reception history vector* (RHV) [v1, v2, —, vn], where n denotes the number of bus-slots in a TDMA cycle and vi is 1 if the reporting node heard the most recent broadcast by the owner node of the i-th bus-slot and 0, otherwise. The RHV is broadcasted by every active node each time its bus-slot arrives, regardless of whether the node has any application message to broadcast. Each node keeps RHV's received from different nodes in its own data structure called the *reception history matrix* (RHM), and by analyzing this RHM it can discover recent changes in the health status of the constituent nodes of the LAN system quickly and accurately.

An RHM analysis procedure enabling every node to detect any single failure of either a processor or a link between a processor and the TDMA bus with a minimal delay which is less than 2 TDMA cycles, was developed in [36]. Here the failure may be of permanent or temporary nature. Also, once a repaired node is activated, its active status can be recognized by other healthy nodes within 2 TDMA cycles. In the case where multiple failures of processors or processor-bus links occur, every node can detect them through analysis of its RHM in time less than 3 TDMA cycles [37].

Therefore, in the case of a TDMA bus based LAN system incorporating the PRHB scheme, NCM is very efficient but it is achieved at the cost of the overhead processing power needed for RHM analysis and a small part of the bus bandwidth spent for RHV broadcast.

Techniques that combine the DRB scheme or the voting N-version scheme with decentralized NCM schemes are highly attractive approaches to use in constructing real-time fault- tolerant DCS's. However, further research is needed on trade-offs between centralized NCM and decentralized NCM.

Once a node in a DRB computing station or an N-version computing station is functionally or physically amputated for repair, the system resource manager attempts to find a replacement node. In general, such restructuring must be implemented in an architecture-dependent manner since efficient synchronization and efficient status exchanges between the constituent nodes of a fault-tolerant computing station are always desirable. Moreover, the issue of **non-disruptive rejoin** (i.e., incorporating a new node into a fault-tolerant computing station and conditioning it into an active member node without significantly disturbing the existing active nodes) is a non-trivial one. Therefore, implementation of a *repairable fault-tolerant computing station* is a subject awaiting much further study.

6 Remaining Issues

Some of the major issues remaining to be resolved in future research are briefly discussed below.

(1) Efficient integration of the task-level fault detection and recovery schemes with NCM schemes

As mentioned in Section 5, the task-level fault tolerance schemes discussed in Section 4 and NCM schemes complement each other. Efficient integration of these techniques (e.g., [22, 20]) is expected to be a subject of intensive research in the next few years.

(2) Techniques for hardening groups of computing stations

The techniques for structuring fault-tolerant computing stations discussed in Section 4 are designed to prevent errors from crossing computing station boundaries. In most real-time applications, those approaches are already considered to be quite expensive. However, in some challenging real-time applications, software faults are unavoidable and then the probability of faulty information crossing the computing station boundary cannot be ignored. Examples of such applications are frequently found in national defense areas. To realize highly reliable computer systems meeting such application requirements, schemes that make a group of computing stations cooperate in recovery, thereby forming a fault-tolerant computing station group, are needed. However, these schemes must be considered only as supplements to those techniques discussed in Section 4. Only if we can assume that computing stations can be designed with the capability for handling transient hardware faults and message communication between computing stations can be made to be always highly reliable and timely, then the problem of finding cost-effective schemes for handling faulty information crossing computing station boundaries becomes manageable. Some promising schemes such as the conversation scheme [48, 31, 2, 1], atomic action structuring schemes [9, ?] and the distributed conversation scheme [33], have been studied but their efficient implementation has been insufficiently studied. High costs associated with these schemes are another issue that needs to be resolved through future research.

(3) Software engineering environment (SEE) for real-time fault- tolerant DCS

Effective tools that support systematic design and validation of fault-tolerant DCS's are lacking. Two factors have caused the development in this area to lag behind. First, *software engineering environments* (SEE's) for real-time software in general have not yet been well established. This situation is expected to be corrected in the next few years. Second, not much effort has been invested to validate real-time fault tolerance techniques in convincing manners. Here testbed-based validation and evaluation are most desirable [14, 38, 43]. This is another manifestation of the fact that the real-time fault- tolerant DCS industry has been growing very slowly so far but there have been published forecasts that the growth of this industry will be significantly accelerated in the remainder of the 1990's.

Acknowledgement

The work reported here was supported in part by the University of California MICRO Program and Hitachi America under Grant No. 91–075. The author would also like to acknowledge the help received from the staff of the UCI DREAM Laboratory during the preparation of this chapter.

References

1. Ancona, M., Dodero, G., Gianuzzi, V., Clematis, A., and Fernandez, E.B., *A System Architecture for Fault Tolerance in Concurrent Software*, IEEE Computer, October 1990, 23–32.

2. Anderson, T. and Knight, J.C., *A Framework for Software Fault Tolerance in Real-Time System*, IEEE TSE, May 1983, 355–364.

3. Armstrong, L.T. and Lawrence, T.F., *Adaptive Fault Tolerance*, Proc. 1991 Systems Design Synthesis Technology Workshop, September 1991.

4. Avizienis, A., Gilley, G., Mathur G.C., Rennels F.P., Rohr, J.A. and Rubin, D.K., *The STAR (Self Testing and Repairing) Computer: An Investigation of the Theory and Practice of Fault-Tolerant Computer Design*, IEEE Trans. on Computers, Vol. C-20, No. 11, November 1971, 1312–1321.

5. Avizienis, A., *Fault tolerance and fault intolerance: Complementary approaches to reliable computing*, Proc. 1975 Int'l. Conf. Rel. Software, Los Angeles, CA, April 1975, 458–464.

6. Avizienis, A., *The N-Version Approach to Fault-Tolerant Software*, IEEE Trans. on Software Engineering, Vol. Se-11, No. 12, December 1985, 1491–1501.

7. Avizienis, A., Lyu, M.R., and Schutz, W., *In Search of Effective Diversity: A Six-Language Study of Fault-Tolerant Flight Control Software*, Proc. FTCS-18, 15–22.

8. Bagchi, A., and Hakimi, S. L., *An Optimal Algorithm for Distributed System Level Diagnosis*, Proc. IEEE Computer Society's 21st Int'l. Symp. on Fault-Tolerant Computing, June 1991, 214–221.

9. Best, E., and Randell, B., *A Formal Model of Atomicity in Asynchronous Systems*, Acta Informatica 16, 1981, 93–124.

10. Bianchini, R. and Buskens, R., *An Adaptive Distributed System-Level Diagnosis Algorithm and its implementation*, Proc. IEEE Computer Society's 21st Int'l. Symp. on Fault-Tolerant Computing, June 1991, 222–229.

11. Bhargava, B., editor., *Concurrency and Reliability in Distributed Systems*, Van Nostrand and Reinhold, 1987.

12. Carter, W.C., *Hardware Fault Tolerance*, Chapter 2 in Anderson, T., ed., Resilient Computing Systems, Vol. 1, Wiley-Interscience, 1985, 11–63.

13. Chandy, K.M., and Ramamoorthy, C.V., *Rollback and recovery strategies for computer programs*, IEEE Trans. on Computers, Vol. C-21, June 1972, 546–556.

14. Chu, W.W., Kim, K.H., and McDonald, W.C., *Testbed-based Evaluation of Design Techniques for Fault-Tolerant Real-Time Distributed Computer Systems*, Proceedings of the IEEE, Vol. 75, No. 5, Special Issue on Distributed Databases, May 1987, 649–667.

15. Cristian, F., *Agreeing on Who is Present and Who is Absent in a Synchronous Distributed System*, Proc. IEEE Computer Society's 18th Int. Symp. of Fault-Tolerant Computing, Tokyo, Japan, June 1988, 206–211.

16. Davis, C.G. and Couch, R.L., *Ballistic Missile Defense: A Supercomputer Challenge*, IEEE Computer, November 1980, 37–46.

17. Ezhilchelvan, P. D., and Lemas, R., *A Robust Group Membership Algorithm for Distributed Real-Time Systems*, Proc. IEEE Computer Society's Real-Time Systems Symp., December 1990, 173–179.

18. Fraga, J.S., Rodrigues, V., and Silva, E.S., *A Language Approach to Implementation of the Distributed Recovery Block Schemes*, Proc. 13th. CBC Conf. on Computer Sciences, Gramado, Brazil, August 1991.

19. Garcia-Molina, H., *Elections in a distributed computing system*, IEEE Trans. on Computers, January 1982, 48–59.

20. Gruensteidl, G., and Kopetz, H., *A Reliable Multicast Protocol for Distributed Real-Time Systems*, Proc. IEEE Computer Society's Workshop on Real-Time Operating Systems, May 1991.

21. Hecht, H., *Fault-Tolerant Software for Real-Time Applications*, Computing Surverys, December 1976, 391–407.

22. Hecht, M., Agron, J., and Hochhauser, S., *A Distributed Fault Tolerant Architecture for Nuclear Reactor Control and Safety Functions*, Proc. IEEE Computer Society's 1989 Real-Time Systems Symp., December 1989, 214–221.

23. Hecht, M., Agron, J., Hecht, H., and Kim, K.H., *A Distributed Fault Tolerant Architecture for Nuclear Reactor and Other Critical Process Control Applications*, Proc. IEEE Computer Society's 21st Int'l Symp. on Fault-Tolerant Computing, June 1991, Montreal, 462–469.

24. Hopkins, A.L., Smith, T.B., and Lala, J.H., *FTMP - A Highly Reliable Fault-Tolerant Multiprocessor For Aircraft*, Proceedings of The IEEE, Vol. 66, No. 10, October 1978, 1221–1240.

25. Horning, J.J., Lauer, H.C., Melliar-Smith, P.M., and Randell, B., *A Program Structure for Error Detection and Recovery*, Lecture Notes in Computer Science, Vol. 16, Springer-Verlag, New York, 1974, 171–187.

26. Ihara, H. and Mori, K., *Autonomous Decentralized Computer Control Systems*, Computer, Vol. 17, No. 8, August 1984, 57–66.

27. Jensen, D. and Northcutt, J.D., *Alpha: An Open Operating System for Mission-Critical Real-Time Distributed Systems - An Overview*, Proc. 1989 Workshop on Operating Systems for Mission-Critical Computing, ACM Press, 1991.

28. Katsuki, D., et al., *Pluribus - An Operational Fault-Tolerant Microprocessor*, Proc. of the IEEE, October 1978, 1146–1159.

29. Kelly, J.P.J. et al., *A Large Scale Second Generation Experiment in Multi-Version Software: Description and Early Results*, Proc. FTCS–18, 9–14.

30. Kim, K.H., *Error Detection, Reconfiguration and Recovery in Distributed Processing Systems*, Proc. IEEE Computer Society's 1st. Int'l. Conf. on Distributed Computing Systems, October 1979, 284–295.

31. Kim, K.H., *Approaches to Mechanization of the Conversation Scheme Based on Monitor*, IEEE Trans. on Software Eng., Vol. SE–8, No. 3, May 1982, 189–197.

32. Kim, K.H. and Welch, H.O., *Distributed Execution of Recovery Blocks: An Approach to Uniform Treatment of Hardware and Software Faults in Real-Time Applications*, IEEE Trans. on Computers, May 1989, 626–636.

33. Kim, K.H., *Approaches to System-Level Fault Tolerance in Distributed Real-Time Computer Systems*, Proc. 4th Int'l Conf. on Fault-Tolerant Computing Systems, Baden-Baden, W. Germany, September 1989, 268–281 (Invited paper), Informatik-Fachberichte 214, Springer-Verlag 1989.

34. Kim, K.H., Guan, W.J., Damm, A., and Rohr, J.A., *Approaches to Design of Temporary Blackout Handling Capabilities and an Evaluation with a Real-Time Tightly Coupled Network Testbed*, Proc. IEEE Computer Society's 21st Int'l Symp. on Fault-Tolerant Computing, June 1991, Montreal, 470–477.

35. Kim, K.H. and Min, B.J., *Approaches to Implementation of Multiple DRB Stations in Tightly Coupled Computer Networks and an Experimental Validation*, Proc. IEEE Computer Society's 15th Int'l Computer Software and Applications Conf. (COMPSAC '91), Tokyo, September 1991, 550–557.

36. Kim, K.H., Kopetz, H., Mori, K., Shokri, E.H., and Gruensteidl, G., *An Efficient Approach to Decentralized Network Diagnosis and Reconfiguration in Real-Time LAN Systems: The PRHB/ED scheme*, To appear in Proc. IEEE Computer Society's 11th Symp. on Reliable Distributed Systems, October 1992, Houston, TX.

37. Kim, K.H., and Shokri, E.H., *An Approach to Decentralized Maintenance of the Processor-Group Membership with Minimal Detection Latency Bounds in TDMA-Bus LAN Systems*, Tech. Rept. UCI-ECE-92-07, Dept. of Electrical & Computer Engineering, UCI, May, 1992.

38. Kopetz, H., Damm, A., Koza, C., Mulazzani, M., Wolfgang, S., Senft, C., and Zainlinger, R., *Distributed Fault-Tolerant Real-Time Systems: The Mars Approach*, IEEE Micro, February 1989, 25–39.

39. Kopetz, H., Grunsteidl, G, and Reisinger, J., *Fault-Tolerant Membership Service in a Synchronous Distributed Real-Time System*, Proc. IFIP WG 10.4 Int'l Working Conf. on Dependable Computing for Critical Applications, Santa Barbara, August 1989, 167–174.

40. Kopetz, H. and Kim, K.H., *Temporal Uncertainties in Interactions among Real-Time Objects*, Proc. IEEE Computer Society's 9th Symp. on Reliable Distributed Systems, Huntsville, AL, October 1990, 165–174.

41. Lamport, L., Shostak, R., and Pease, M., *The Byzantine Generals problem*, ACM Trans. Prog. Lang. Syst., Vol. 3, No. 4, July 1982, 382–401.

42. Lee P.A., *A Reconsideration of the Recovery Block Scheme*, Computer Journal, Vol. 21, No. 4, November 1978, 306–310.

43. McDonald, W.C. and Smith, R.W., *A flexible distributed testbed for real time applications*, Computer, Vol. 15, No. 10, October 1982, 25–39.

44. Mori, K., et. al., *Autonomous Decentralized Software Structure and Its Application*, Proc. Fall Joint Computer Conference, Dallas, TX, November 1986, 1056–1063.

45. Nett, E., *Supporting Fault Tolerant Computations in Distributed Systems*, Habilitation Thesis, Univ. of Bonn, Germany, 1991.

46. Powell, D. et al., *The Delta-4 Approach to Dependability in Open Distributed Computing Systems*, Proc. IEEE Computer Society's 18th Int'l. Symp. on Fault-Tolerant Computing, June 1988, 246–251.

47. Ramamoorthy, C.V. et al., *Application of a Methodology for the Development and Validation of Reliable Process Control Software*, IEEE Trans. on Software Engr., Vol. SE-7, No. 6, November 1981, 537–555.

48. Randell, B., *System Structure for Software Fault Tolerance*, IEEE Transactions on Software Engineering, June 1975, 220–232.

49. Rohr, J.A., *STAREX Self-Repair Routines: Software Recovery in the JPL-STAR Computer*, Digest of Papers FTCS-3, International Symposium on Fault-Tolerant Computing, Palo Alto, CA, June 1973, 11–16.

50. Stankovic, J.A., *Misconceptions About Real-time computing: A Serious Problem for Next-Generation Systems*, Computer, Vol. 21, No. 10, October 1988, 10–19.

51. Strong, R., *Problems in Maintaining Agreement*, Proc. IEEE Computer Society's 5th Symp. on Reliability in Distributed Software and Database Systems, Washington, DC, 1986, 20–27.

52. Taylor, D.J., Morgan, D.E., and Black, J.P., *Redundancy in Data Structures: Improving Software Fault Tolerance*, IEEE Trans. on Software Engineering, Vol. SE-6, No. 6, November 1980, 585–594.

53. Taylor D., and Wilson, G., *Stratus*, in Dependability of Resilient Computers, ed. T. Anderson, BSP Professional Books, Oxford, 1989, 222–236.

54. Tong, Z., Kain, R.Y., and Tsai, W.T., *A Lower Overhead Checkpointing and Rollback Recovery Scheme for Distributed Systems*, Proc. IEEE Computer Society's 8th Symp. on Reliable Distributed Systems, October 1988, 12–20.

55. Toy, W.N., *Fault-Tolerant Design of Local ESS Processors*, Proceedings of the IEEE, Vol. 66, No. 10, October 1978, 1126–1145.

56. Toy, W.N., *Fault-Tolerant Computing*, in Advances in Computers, Vol. 26, Academic Press, 1987, 201–279.

57. Wensley, J.H., et al., SIFT: *Design and Analysis of a Fault-Tolerant Computer for Aircraft Control*, Proc. of the IEEE, October 1978, 1240–1255.

58. Wensley, J.H., *An Operating System for a TMR Fault-Tolerant System*, Digest of Papers FTCS-13, Thirteenth Annual International Symposium on Fault-Tolerant Computing, Milano, June 1983, 452–455.

59. Wilson, D., *The STRATUS computer system*, Chapter 12 in T. Anderson ed., Resilient Computing Systems Volume I, John Wiley & Sons, 1985, 45–67.

60. Yau, S.S. and Cheung, R.C., *Design of Self-checking Software*, Proc. Int'l Conf. on Reliable Software, 1975, 450–457.

Graphical Design of Real Time Applications

Jacques J. Skubich, Jean Jacques Schwarz

LISPI — Institut National des Sciences Appliques
69621 Villeurbanne Cedex
France

Abstract

The major difficulties encountered by those who have to solve Industrial Real Time Applications, in a multitask computing environment, are:

- the expression of the dynamic aspect of this type of applications,
- the number and the variety of these Real Time Executives.

An answer is given to the second problem by the Standardisation efforts, now performed by Real Time Executive constructors in order to promote Real Time Executive standards.

In order to take both problems into account and to bring up global answers, we define the LACATRE language (LAngage de Conception d'Applications Temps REel) which allows the modelling of an application using graphical representations of the main entities handled in commonly used Real Time Executives.

LACATRE is a language, with a graphical and a textual mode, devoted to facilitate both the Preliminary and Detailed Design of applications involving real time multitask executives. LACATRE uses intensively a graphical symbolism allowing a synthetic and precise vision of multitask applications. It allows the expression of the dynamic decomposition and task relationships, in order to obtain the skeleton of the multitask program but not a precise description of the computation.

Keywords

Real Time, Industrial Application Design, Graphical Language, Real Time Software Engineering.

1 Introduction

The development of Real Time Applications raises a number of problems which add themselves to those, already non-trivial, generated by the development of all Information Systems, either during their design or their implementation. Nevertheless it is worthy of note that industrial Real Time Applications design ("Hard Real Time") always introduces a certain number of specific difficulties because such applications are closely coupled to the physical world with which the application interacts.

If relevant improvements have been made in the field of Specification (SART) and Preliminary Design (SD) [3], [5], [7], [9], the passage to Detailed Design still remains an actual problem. These remarks are true for both industrial application design and teaching related techniques and methodologies.

Programming of such applications relies essentially on a multitask (mono or multiprocessor) computing basis. The available tools are those introduced for the design and description of parallel computing, in opposition of those dedicated to the sequential processing. These tools are modelling tools on one hand and on the other, operating systems, languages.

Today, it seems of prime necessity to bring up complementary tools to ease the design, realisation and maintenance (i.e. documentation) of multitask applications based on Real Time Executives [4], [7], [8].

That is why, in the same effort of standardisation which has come about among Real Time Executive constructors and which, thanks to the Real Time Consortium, tries to promote standards preserving the sometimes opposing specificities of every Real Time product and leading to Interoperability between hardware and software, we apply ourselves to determine a set of basic objects necessary to Real Time Application Design, to take into account the Real Time standards of the market, in order to express graphically every Real Time Application from this set of objects independently of the target machine or target system.

The graphical language we define [10], [11], LACATRE (LAngage de Conception d'Applications Temps REel) acts as an extra layer above commonly used Real Time Executives (i.e. VRTX, RTC, RMX, ...). It covers the end of Preliminary Design and the beginning of Detailed Design. The LACATRE graphical language has a dual textual form which allows the production of a textual program associated with the drawing. By means of an ad hoc compiler, one may automatically generate skeletons of application programs in a target language (for example: the C language) with the appropriate system calls and all the required declarations.

It may be used in two different ways:

- a free-hand use for the design and/or graphical documentation of programs in which case it may be considered as a method of design,
- an interactive tool as a generator of multitask Real Time Application program skeletons. In this aspect, it may form the basis of a Real Time Software Engineering Workshop (RTSEW).

It simplifies the use of Real Time Executives keeping the application designer in a familiar situation for design.

In the following section, we give a description of the LACATRE language and the definitions of the objects and actions (communication, synchronisation). Section 3 will be devoted to the use of the language as a method to help in the design of Real Time Applications. Then, in Section 4, the main features of the RTSEW based upon this language will be developed.

2 The Lacatre Language

The LACATRE language (La4 in abbreviation: La4 is a short form of the French phonetic equivalent of LACATRE) appears as a layer above many multitasking real time executives. It acts upon entities which are images of the objects handled by these executives. These entities, called LACATRE objects, are the task, the semaphore, the message, the mailbox, the event, the resource and the interrupt.

Relationships between objects: LACATRE actions or System calls, which describe Real Time Applications' dynamic behaviour, follow precise rules complying with a grammar of connection rules and are symbolised by various shapes according to their functionality [10].

LACATRE allows:

- the expression of dynamic decomposition and task relationships,
- the attainment of a synthetic view of the Real Time Application,
- the structuring of the application technically free from the target machine, system or language.

Note: The sense "technically free" in LACATRE means that it allows the designer to focus on the essential aspects of application design whilst being freed of technical details dependent on the target machine, Real Time Executive or language. That does not necessarily imply Portability; LACATRE objects do not have an equivalent in all the target Real Time Executives, but perhaps they may be emulated.

2.1 The Lacatre Graphical Language

An application designed with the LACATRE graphical language (La4_g) is a diagram made up of La4 graphical objects linked together by means of the symbols of the La4 actions.
There are 2 types of object:

Configurable objects:
Those whose behaviour is completely defined by parameter values (queuing management, limits, ...) set up during creation. They are the semaphore, the mailbox, the message, the event and the resource. The application programmer can only act on the attributes of these objects and their behaviour is that of the

corresponding real time executive equivalent object.

Programmable objects:
Their behaviour is defined by the application programmer, using La4 actions. The two programmable objects are the task and the interrupt. These objects present a body which is to be filled in the form of a sequence of real time actions (essentially synchronisation).

2.1.1 Object Composition

The graphical symbol of a La4 object (configurable or programmable) is made up of basic elements (lines) called Bars from which the linking symbols associated with La4 actions start and finish. Bars are made with lines and are classified into 3 types:

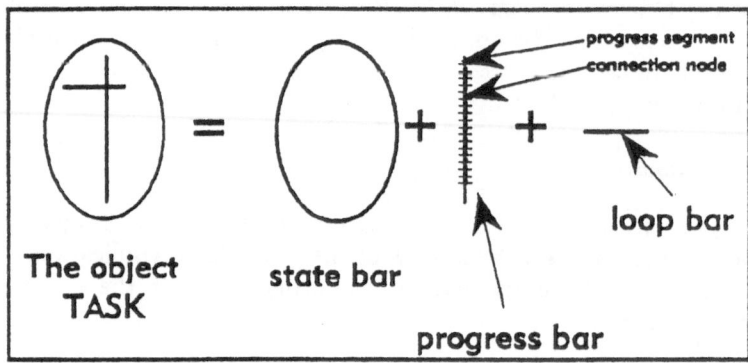

Fig. 1.

State Bar:
This is a bar where creation/deletion calls (which may be applied to all La4 objects) finish; the same applies to some specific programmable object's state setting calls. These calls are La4 State System Calls. All points belonging to a state bar are equivalent: they are not ordered. In general, the state bars are located on the right and left side of the general shape of an object.

Progress Bar:
This bar is specific to programmable objects. It is an oriented bar and it describes the sequence of the La4 system calls. The sequence may be altered by means of the La4 Algorithmic Forms (if ... then ... else ..., while ..., ...). The progress bar gives a graphical representation of the "program" of a programmable object and is located inside the programmable object's shape.

Action Bar:
These bars exist only for configurable objects and have specific names (for instance a deposit bar and a withdrawal bar). All points of an action bar are equivalent. The action bars are usually located on the upper and lower side of the shape of a configurable object.

2.1.2 Relationship between Objects: The La4 System Calls

The La4 actions provided by the LACATRE language allow the designer the expression and the modelling of the dynamic interactions or links between the various objects composing a Real Time Application.
To be used, objects must first be created; when the application ends they must be deleted.
The symbolism associated with an action is basically an oriented line with a graphical "decor".

LACATRE ACTIONS are composed of:

- a general (basic) shape — an oriented line which reflects the unidirectional nature of the dynamic relationship,
- a specific decor — which denotes the environment of the interaction: information types, communication conditions, ...
- connectors — origin and target connectors,
- connection rules — defining the starting and the ending points as well as the objects concerned with the relationships.

There are three types of system calls:

State System Calls:
They allow the modification of the state of an object: e.g. creation/deletion of all La4 objects (see Figure 2). Specific state system calls modify the activity (active/inactive) of programmable objects (sleeping, suspension, interrupt disabling/enabling, ...).

Action System Calls:
They introduce a communication/synchronisation relation between programmable objects (mainly tasks) with the help of configurable objects. A task uses configurable object such as mailboxes, semaphores or events with the help of these action system calls. These calls are strongly tied to the required configurable object.

Progress System Calls:
They provide a direct synchronisation mechanism between programmable objects (without any use of explicit configurable objects).

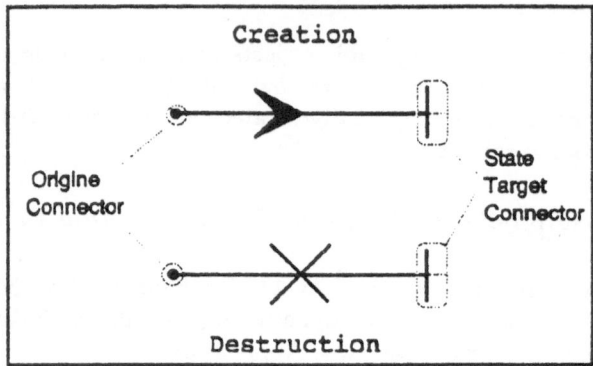

Fig. 2.

2.2 The Lacatre Textual Mode

The aim of the LACATRE textual mode (La4_t) [11] is to make possible (from a real time software engineering workshop point of view) the automatic generation of the skeleton of the application program in the chosen target language (including the actual system calls of the required real time executive).

The definition of the LACATRE objects and their mutual interactions are defined by a grammar. This allows us, from the beginning, to associate with the graphical formalism of the La4_g language a textual equivalence expressed in the La4_t language.

Therefore:

- every symbol is coupled to a textual equivalent.
- every La4_g action is linked to a La4_t "statement". The graphical attributes of a La4_g action are parameters of the equivalent La4_t statement.

The main characteristic of the textual mode is the absence of variables. LACATRE does not handle variables. There is no particular primitive for the creation of an object: the creation is made by giving the keyword of the object.

The grammar of the La4_t language is given, in standard BNF, appendix B.

2.3 Lacatre Objects and System Calls

2.3.1 Programmable Objects

The progress bar is the main characteristic of programmable objects as tasks and interrupts.

The TASK Object

In a real time application, the task often consists of an initialisation sequence followed by an infinite loop involving at least one waiting event. In such a case,

Tasks

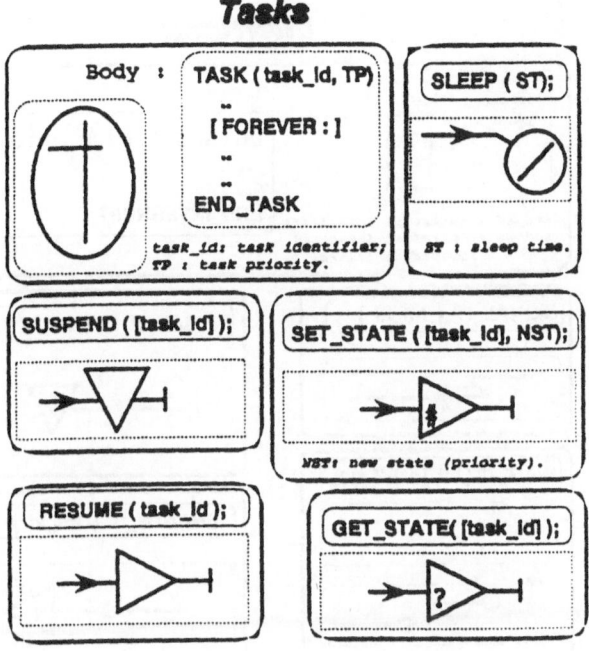

Fig. 3.

the progress bar of a task is usually a vertical straight line split in two parts by the symbol (the loop bar) of the Forever La4 Algorithmic Form.

The state bar of a task is composed of a closed elliptic line to which the task identifier and the task priority are tied. The task object has specific system calls which can act upon its current state or the state of an other task: SLEEP, SUSPEND and RESUME.

Other primitives (GET_STATE, SET_STATE) are closely dependent on the target executive, and allow the reading and possibly the modification of some of the task state parameters. The parameter task_id mentioned in Figure 3 is the identifier of a target task (for the system call). If it is absent, the target task is then the calling task itself.

The INTERRUPT Object

The La4 interrupt is a programmable object provided with facilities for creation, deletion and handling system calls. Usually, the interrupt is not considered as an object in Real Time kernels. In LACATRE the creation of an Interrupt object consists of the implementation of all the mechanisms needed for the consistent management of physical interrupt signals (interrupt vector, interrupt handler, ...). As the interrupt is a programmable object, it is up to the programmer to define which process to implement within the interrupt handler. The "programmable" part of the interrupt object is, in fact, the interrupt servicing routine.

Interrupts

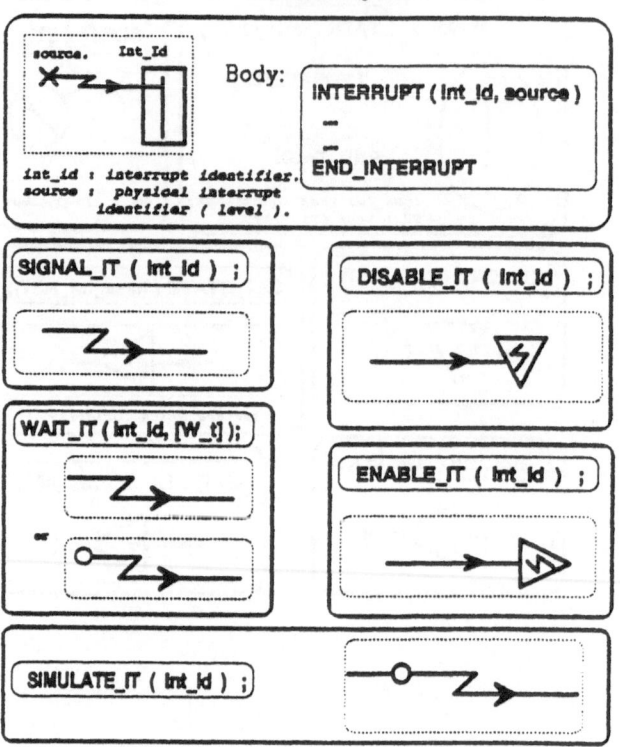

Fig. 4.

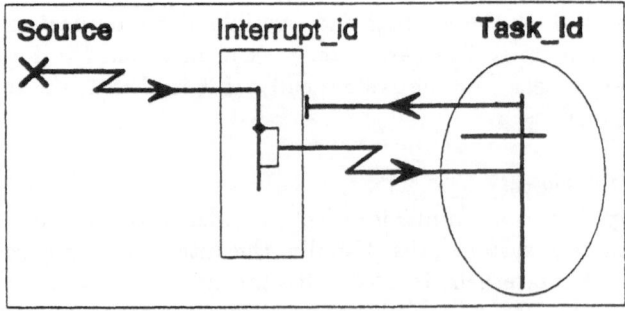

Fig. 5.

In addition to the creation and deletion calls, the interrupt object has two other specific state system calls which are used for enabling and disabling interrupts. The main progress system call, associated with the interrupt object, is an interrupt signalling system call which resumes the corresponding waiting interrupt task. The last interrupt system call shown in Figure 4 allows the generation of software interrupts. The SIMULATE_IT primitive is another progress system call: the interrupt mechanism can thereby be initiated from any task of the application.

Figure 5 gives an example of classical coupling between an interrupt and an interrupt task: in the initialisation sequence, the task creates the interrupt object, then in the infinite loop waits for the interrupt to be signalled.

2.3.2 Configurable Objects

The Semaphore, the Mailbox, the Message
Semaphores, mailboxes and messages are common objects for communication and synchronisation between tasks. Semaphores and mailboxes are used for the deposit and withdrawal of data elements (abstract units and messages respectively). Therefore their handling of system calls exhibit a strong resemblance to their textual or graphical appearances. Configurable objects own state bars and action bars. The action bars of semaphores and mailboxes are deposit bars or withdrawal bars. The deposit bar is located at the top of the graphical symbol and the withdrawal one at the bottom. These are shown in Figure 6.

Both objects allow flow control (in this case, the graphical parameter is a small circle on the symbol of the sending or waiting primitive) by means of a watchdog associated with deposit disabling when sending, and withdrawing task waiting time when receiving respectively. The La4 semaphore is a container of abstract units: it is made up of an up/down counter with initial and maximum values. Withdrawal is managed using a queuing scheme. Depending on the type of the scheme (FIFO or priority), the semaphore has two graphical variants.
The mailbox is used for message object passing. Messages are tagged by message identifiers (Mes_id) which can be generic names for data structures in the target language (array, record, structure).

Figure 7 shows the simplified and typical message communication, with the help of a mailbox, between two tasks. In the infinite loop, Task_a creates a message named Req1.
The task waits for some hypothetical event and then sends the message to Task_b by way of the mbx_ab mailbox. Task_a loops: it creates a new message and waits again for the event. Task_b waits for a message in the mbx_ab mailbox, deals with the message (not shown on the diagram), signals something to another task and finally kills the received message. It can be seen that each task works, at any one time, with only one message which always has the same identifier. However, if Task_a works temporarily more rapidly than Task_b, then mailbox mbx_ab

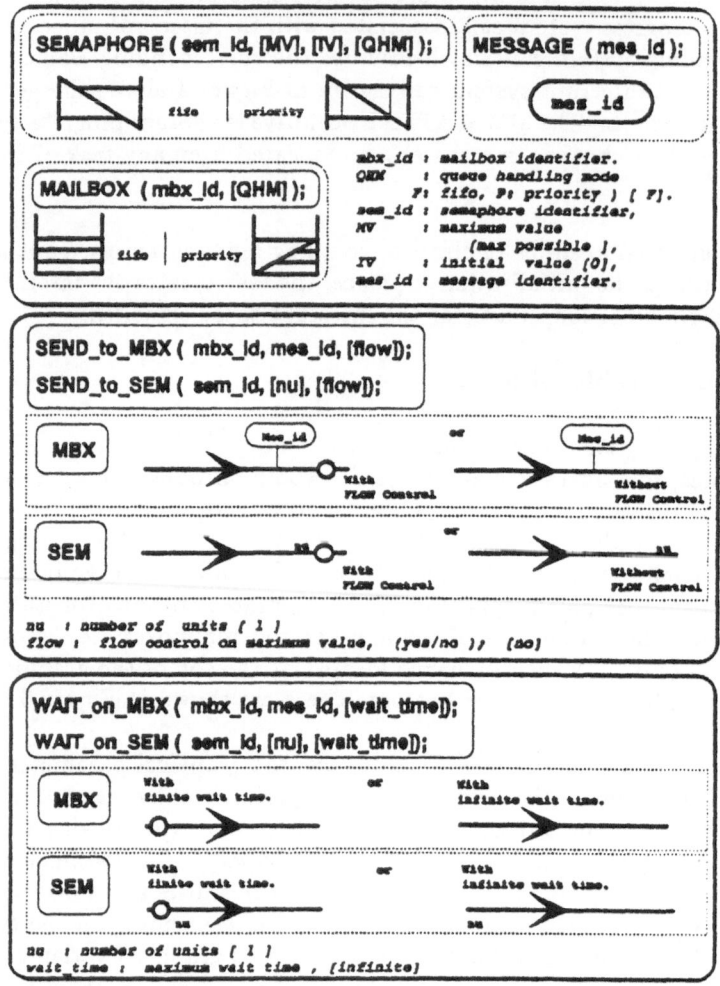

Fig. 6.

will store the excess of messages sent. Some primary verifications can be made using such a diagram: as the creation of the message Req1 is made in a "Forever" loop, the deletion of the message must also be made in the same kind of loop.

Figure 8 gives a complete example that uses a semaphore as a mechanism to stop the application.

A task named display has to write five lines to the screen, one after the other, each time unit. The application begins with the task Main, which creates a semaphore with default parameter values (initial value of 0 and maximum value

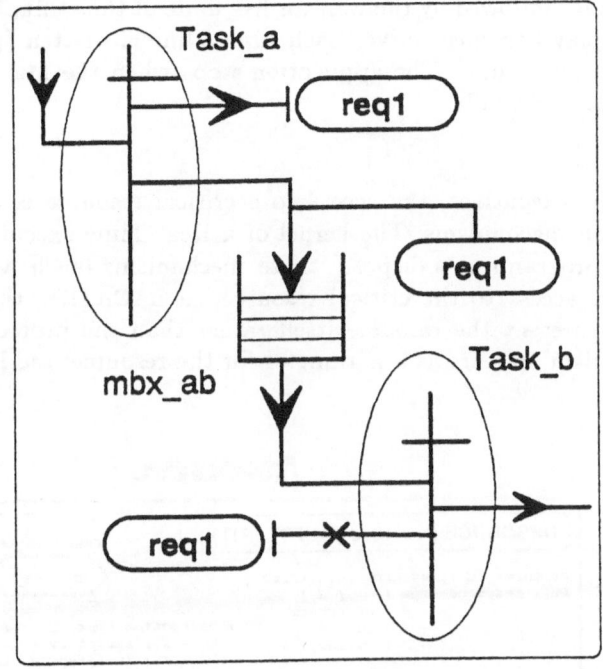

Fig. 7.

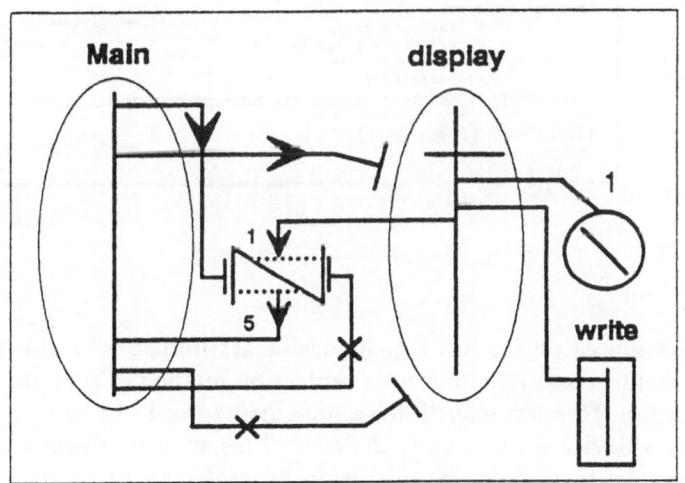

Fig. 8.

infinite). The next instructions starting from the progress bar are the creation of
the display task followed by the wait for five units at the semaphore. At this time
the task display becomes active. Each time a line is written (procedure write),
the task deposits a unit. The application stops when the Main task withdraws
the five units as a whole.

The resource

In Real Time executives, the access to a critical resource is managed by mutual exclusion mechanisms. The kernel of a Real Time executive places at the
application programmer's disposal those mechanisms (such as semaphores) to
allow correct access to the critical resource. In LACATRE, the programmer is
allowed to represent the resource itself rather than the protection mechanism.
This mechanism appears as a parameter for the resource: see Figure 9.

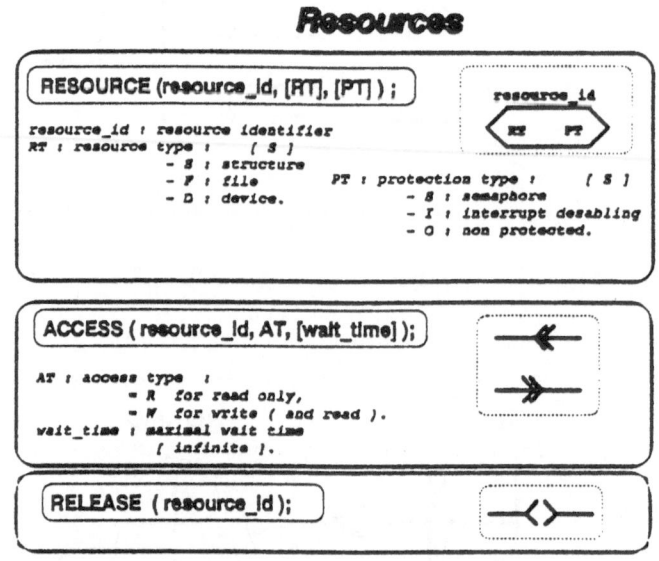

Fig. 9.

The La4 resource object has 2 configurable attributes: RT, which indicates the
type of resource; and PT, the access protection method. There are three different
values for the RT parameter: S for a data structure; F for file (local or remote),
and D for a device (in this case, the critical resource represents code).
The access protection mechanism is in general dependent on the target real
time executive. The usual cases include the semaphore (PT=S), interrupt ena-
ble/disable (PT=I) or non protected (PT=O). The resource creation primitive
represents the creation of all the elements required for resource management
(semaphore creation, file opening, ...). It should be noted that, if the protec-

tion key used for accessing the resource is a semaphore, then this semaphore is not the LACATRE semaphore object and is therefore not graphically represented.

Two action system calls are associated with the resource: they give access (read-read/write) to the resource and release it.

The Event
The event object is a communication and synchronisation object based upon implicit information: only the occurrence of the event is seen as significant: see Figure 10.

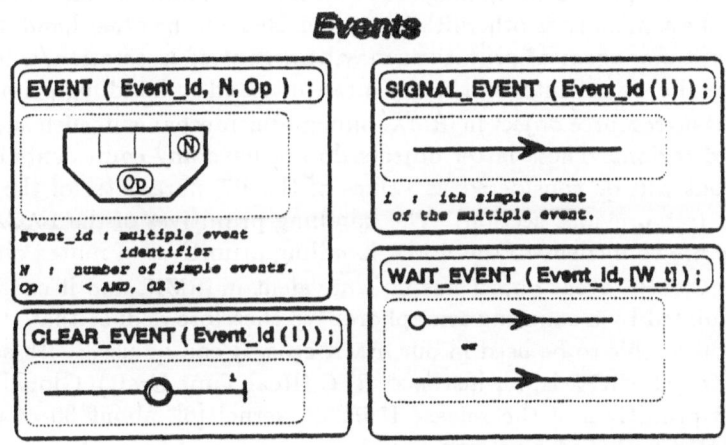

Fig. 10.

The La4 event object is a composed event when it requires, and a single one when signalled. The composition operator consists of a Multiple conjunction (AND) or Multiple disjunction (OR) of single events, but no mixing between these operators is allowed. The action system calls have graphical symbols which look like the primitives of semaphores and mailboxes. However their behaviour is different: when a task which is waiting on an event, the event is not withdrawn. When the event is out of date it must be cleared.

There are 3 action system calls associated with the event. They allow single event signalling, composed event awaiting and event clearing. The event object introduces a broadcast communication mechanism.

3 Design with Lacatre

When starting with LACATRE, the first task is to model the target Multitasking Real Time eXecutive (MRTX) with the help of LACATRE objects and system calls. In our case (Real Time Engineering Courses), this target MRTX is iRMX. For this modelling, the main primitives and real time objects of the MRTX are described in order to be "translated" into La4 primitives and objects which are the most closely equivalent. We did such a task with the iRMX operating system [11], and several points can be emphasised:

-   tasks, mailboxes, messages and semaphores have been translated in a reasonably straightforward way,
-   iRMX interrupts are not managed as objects which may be created and handled in the same way as other iRMX objects. But, on the other hand, the iRMX interrupt management primitives may be organised in creation/deletion primitives (i.e. rq set interrupt, reset interrupt) and in handling primitives,
-   there is no resource object in iRMX, only mutex mechanisms such as semaphores and regions. These latter objects do not have any equivalents in LACATRE but will be considered as values of the PT parameter of the resource object (see previous section). The handling primitives of the LACATRE resource are equivalent to the iRMX handling primitives of mutex objects,
-   the LACATRE event object has no equivalent in iRMX, and it cannot easily be emulated by a counting semaphore. We therefore deduce that this object will not be able to be used in our iRMX case. It can be used with advantage if the target MRTX is, for instance, RTC (Real Time Craft). Globally among the 93 primitives of the release II iRMX kernel [6], about 30 of them are associated with La4_g actions.

As with all graphical methods, representations may quickly grow too intricate and thus the legibility of the diagram may decrease. It is then necessary to introduce a structure which may be obtained by a hierarchical analysis of the application as well as by the use of tracing notions. The graphical representation of an application is clearer if one splits, into different tracings, the starting phase of the application, the normal running mode, the exception management, and the stop phases of the application associated with objects' deletion.

When approaching the problem, the designer has to start the design by considering the application kernel, extracting this phase from the creation/deletion and the exception handling phases. We settled on 3 main steps: the kernel phase, the exception phase and the environment phase.

The kernel phase corresponds to the normal running of the application: actions are sequenced normally without taking any account of side effects or exception misfunction.

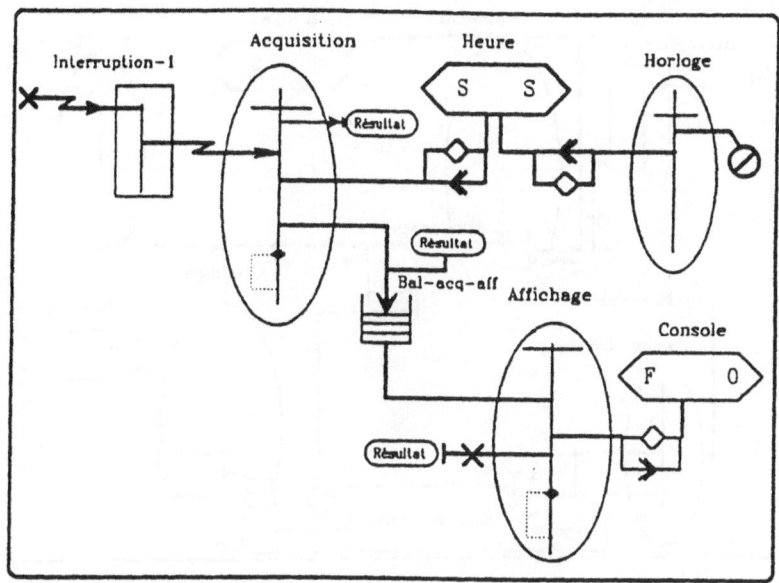

Fig. 11.

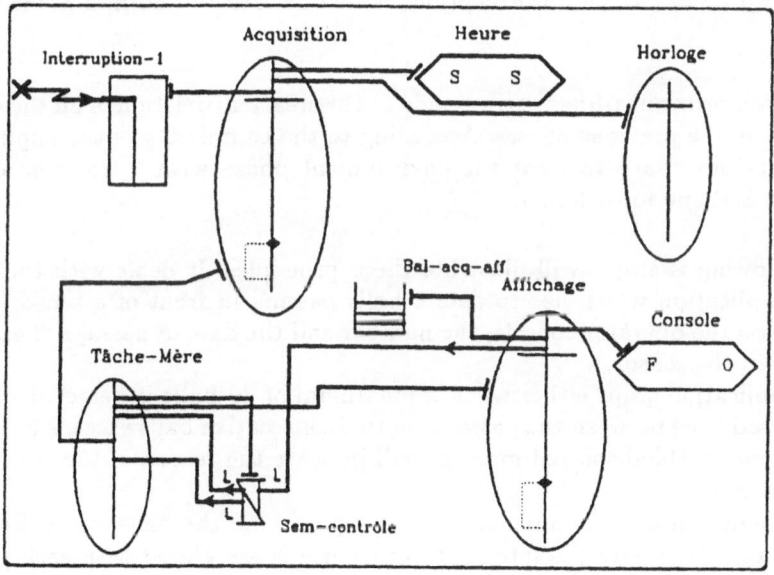

Fig. 12.

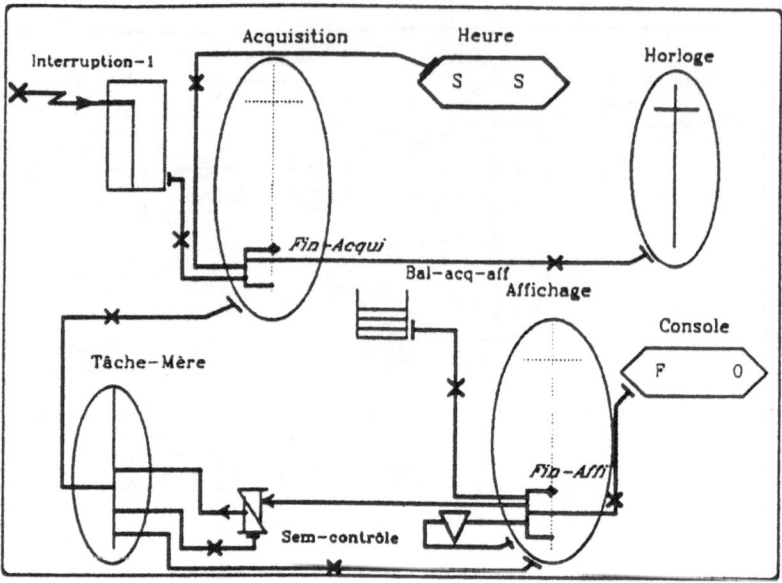

Fig. 13.

The exception phase corresponds to transient running, i.e. it includes the start/stop phase, as well as exceptions which disturb the normal mode of running.

The environment phase corresponds to the creation/deletion of all the objects involved in the previous phases. According to the complexity of the application, it may be necessary to treat the environment phase with 2 tracings: one for creation and one for deletion.

The following example will illustrate these principles. It deals with the design of an application which has to detect balls passing in front of a sensor and to display, on the operator console, the number and the date of passage of each ball in front of the sensor.

This application stops either when a maximum of 20 balls is detected or when the elapsed time between the passages of two consecutive balls exceeds 3 seconds. In both cases, the displayed message will indicate the reason of the stopping of the application.

One may decompose the application into 2 processes: the first one dealing with acquisition of the data (an interrupt occurrence is associated with each passage of a ball in front of the sensor), the second one dealing with the display of the messages associated with each ball. These 2 processes must run asynchronously according to the fact that the displaying process execution must not slow down the acquisition of the data. They will communicate thanks to one mailbox and messages.

Figures 11, 12, 13 show the diagrams of the kernel phase, the environment phase and the exception phase respectively.

4 Real Time Software Engineering

As discussed in the previous section, the expression of the design of a Real Time Application using a LACATRE graphical diagram allows not only the obtainment of a synthetic view and the expression of the dynamic decomposition and inter-task relationship, but also to make the structure of the application technically free from the target system and target machine.

4.1 Introduction and Principles

The definition of the LACATRE objects and their mutual interactions are defined by a grammar. This allows us, from the beginning, to associate with the graphical formalism of the La4_g language a textual equivalence expressed in the La4_t language.

Therefore:

- every symbol is coupled to a textual equivalent. The body of the programmable objects is user-defined and initially empty while the configurable object one is always empty.
- every La4_g action is linked to a La4_t "statement". The graphical attributes of a La4_g action are parameters of the equivalent La4_t statement. It is worthy of note that it is obviously of interest to start with the La4_g graphical mode and to produce a La4_t text technically free of any Real Time Executive and target machines. This text is then the skeleton of the graphically designed Real Time Application.

The La4_g graphical mode essentially allows a first step of control and verification according to the semantics associated with the objects, actions and connection rules. Following this, in La4_t textual mode, the existence of the grammar associated with the language will permit:

- syntactic and semantic analysis,
- coherence analysis of the application and its architecture,
- cross reference analysis,
- complexity analysis,
- response time delay evaluation,
- ...

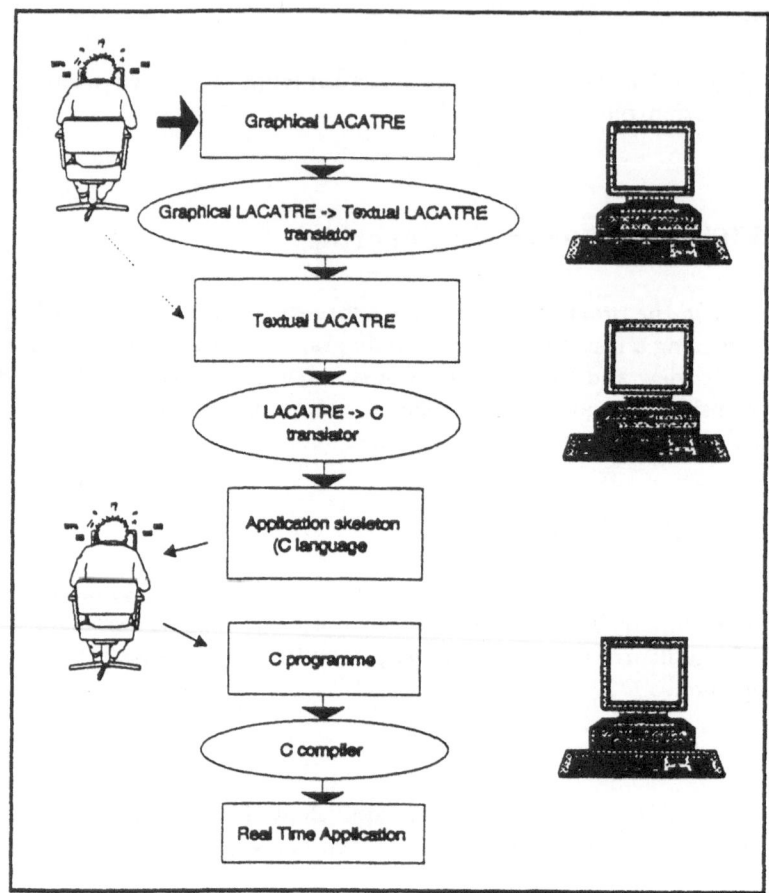

Fig. 14.

It also allows returns to the graphical design mode to modify the application
diagram in order to make it coherent, or directly to correct the text generated
by the textual mode.

Once the textual equivalence has been obtained from the graphical diagram, the
use of La4_t target language translators will allow the generation of skeletons of
programs composing the Real Time Application for a given machine and a given
Real Time Executive. The design and production process is as shown in Figure
14.

The tool discussed hereafter may be considered as a basis of a RTSEW, its ambi-
tion is to be helpful to engineers in charge of modern commonly used Real Time
Executives.

It deals partly with Preliminary and Detailed Design within the Software Life
Cycle. At the specification and module identification stages, the designer may

use various methods and using the graphical mode describe his Real Time Application.

The prototype must have some necessary media and needs. It has to rely on a graphical system providing textual description facilities which allows the user to work with the equivalent textual description and then using an appropriate compiler to generate the target language code for the chosen target system.

In conclusion, the tool has to provide the designer with on-line help during the object creation or the creation of relationships between objects.

4.2 The Lacatre Prototype

We implemented a first prototype [12] using the graphical system Sylva Foundry of Cadware [2] and its generator of graphical methods. It runs on AT compatible machines under MS-DOS.

This prototype consisted of 3 parts:

- the graphical interpreter built up by means of the Sylva Foundry software which allows the creation of application graphical diagrams,
- the La4_g-> La4_t translator developed using the Compiler Design System STARLET [1],
- the La4_t-> PLM286 compiler (chosen target language) developed with the help of STARLET.

This implemented prototype showed the feasibility of our study, without full integration of the 3 parts composing the tools. Improvements are being brought to both LACATRE symbolism level and symbol design, in order to get a well-specified language using a minimum set of powerful concepts.

The new prototype we have been developing now is based on the Windows environment on one hand, and on the STARLET Compiler Design System, on the other hand.

It consists of 2 parts :

- the graphical generator built up in the Windows environment and written in C language. It allows the creation of application graphical diagrams and the simultaneous generation of the La4_t equivalent program,
- the La4_t/C(iRMX) compiler (chosen target language and system) developed with the help of STARLET.

4.2.1 The Graphical Generator

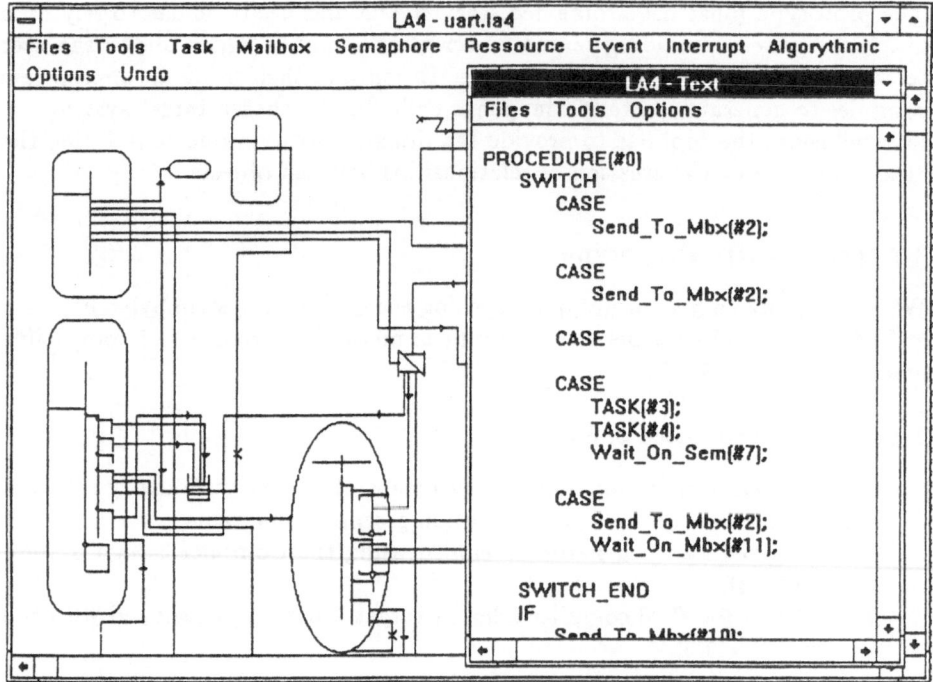

Fig. 15.

4.2.2 The LA4_T/C Translator

It has been developed in respect with Software Quality constraints. The translation of the La4_t source file is performed in 2 steps :

- the source file is first read and analysed by the LA4 parser,
- if no error occurs the C file is generated.

The La4 Parser
It is made up of 2 parts: the syntax parser and the semantic analyser which both eventually produce error messages in an error file.

- The parser — based upon a top down parser with automatic backtracking provided by STARLET, it checks the sequence of instructions, the parameters and builds a first version of the internal representation.
- The semantic analyser — using the internal representation generated by the parser, it checks:
  - whether instructions are used properly or not, for example: slow instructions (loops, wait instructions) used within an interrupt handler must be forbidden.

- the creation/deletion/use of objects of the La4_t source file and solves the ambiguities left by the parser, then it consequently modifies the internal representation of the La4_t source file.

The Code Generator

It operates upon the internal representation produced by the La4_t parser. The C program it generates is only the skeleton of a Real Time Application under iRMX.

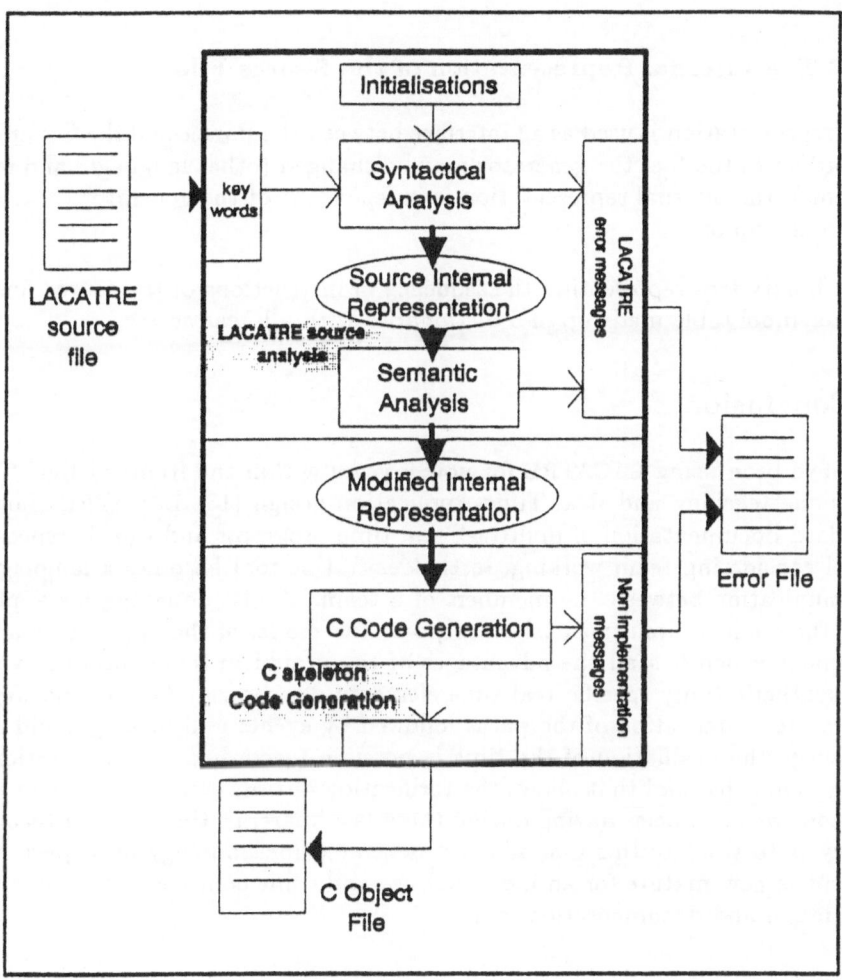

Fig. 16.

The target file includes:

- include files,
- declaration of task tokens and global objects ones used for communication and synchronisation between tasks,
- the list of the C procedures associated with the programmable objects described in the source file and the declaration of local variables used during iRMX system calls.

It also generates messages of non implementation of objects and file error messages.

4.2.3 The Internal Representation of the Source File

This representation is used as an interface between the Parser and the Generator. According to the fact the generator may be changed (other languages and other systems), the internal representation is independent of the generator.
It is made up of:

- a binary tree representing the sequence of instructions of the source file,
- a symbol table made up of 6 dictionaries with a linear access.

5 Conclusion

We have been using LACATRE for now 5 years within the frame of Real Time technique teaching and Real Time Application design [13]. LACATRE allows a standard documentation of multitask real time programs and that is especially useful considering team working. In that case, this tool becomes a language of communication between the members of a team. Whilst designing his application, the student simultaneously transposes the model of the application and a document which has all the advantages of the graphical representation: visual and synthetic (only specific real time elements are shown off). This document allows the visualisation of the paths followed by events and messages and consequently, the evaluation of the time is possible (according to the duration of the system calls) and that allows the verification of time constraints. The use of this tool we have been having during these last years, in the frame of teaching allows us to validate this tool and the associated methodology principles. This concept is now mature for an industrial use and some companies already use it as a design and documentation tool.

References

1. J. Beney, J.F. Boulicault, *STARLET: An Affix-Based Compiler-Compiler designed as a logic programming system*, Proc. of the third International Workshop on Compiler Compilers CC'90, Schwerin (RFA), October 1990, LNCS 1990, Springer Verlag.
2. Cadware, *Sylva Foundry User's Manual V1-2*, Cadware 1988.
3. A. Dorseuil and P. Pillot, *Le temps rél en milieu industriel*, Masson, Paris, 1990.
4. H. Gomaa, *A software design method for real time systems*. Communication of the ACM, Vol. 27-9, September 1984.
5. D.J. Hatley, I.A. Pirbhai, *Stratégie de spécification des systèmes temps réel*, (SART), Masson, Paris, 1990.
6. INTEL, *iRMX II.4*, Operating System V1-V7, 1989.
7. J. Ludewig, *Practical methods and tools for specification*, Embedded systems, Springer Verlag, March 1986.
8. H.G.Mendelbaum, D. Finkelman, *CASDA: Synthesized Graphic design of real time systems*, IEEE Computer Graphics & Applications, January 1989.
9. J.P. Perez, *Systèmes temps réel, Méthodes de spécification et de conception*, Dunod, Paris, 1990.
10. J.J. Schwarz, LACATRE, *Notice résumé V2.01. Polycopi*, Département Informatique INSA Lyon, November 1990.
11. J.J Schwarz, J.J. Skubich, M. Miquel, *A graphical language for multitasking real time application design*, An application to iRMX programming, 8th IRUG International Conference, Proceedings, Baltimore, USA, October 1991.
12. J.J. Schwarz, J.J. Skubich, R. Aubry, LACATRE, *The basis for a real time software engineering workshop*, PEARL'91 Workshop über Realzeitsysteme, Boppart, RFA, November 1991, Informatik Fachberichte 295, Springer-Verlag.
13. J.J. Schwarz, M. Miquel, J.J. Skubich, *Graphical Programming for real time systems*, An Experience from the world of education, WRTP'92 International Workshop Real Time Programming, Bruges, Belgium, June 1992.

Appendix A: A Graphical Language for Real Time Applications Design

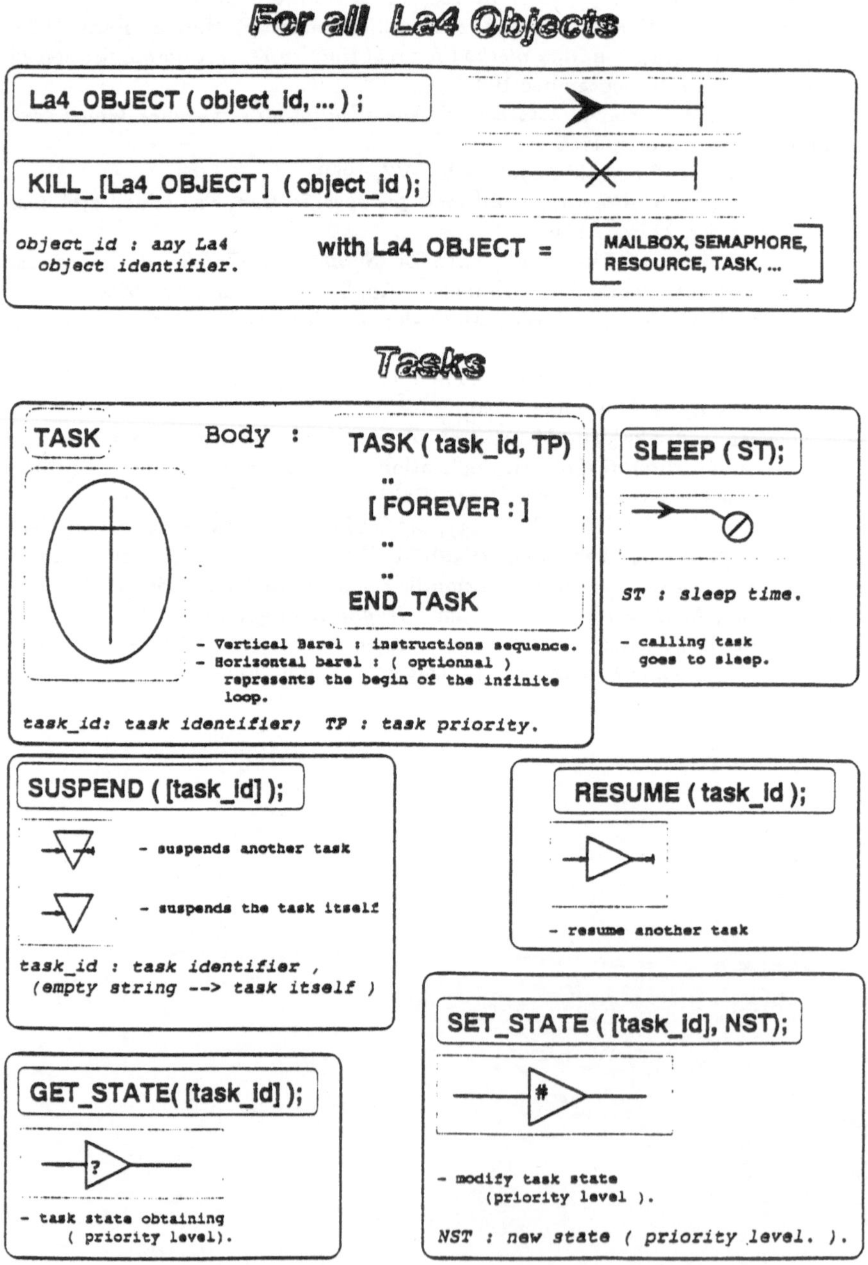

For all La4 Objects

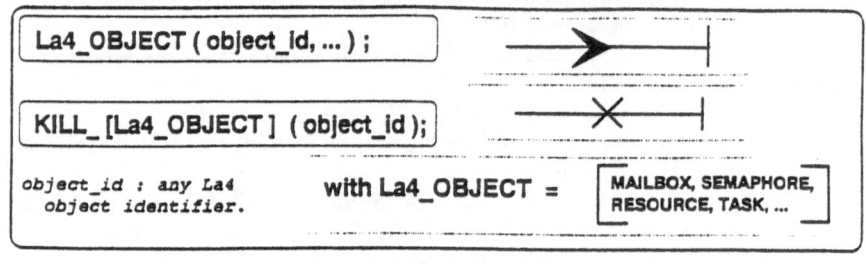

La4_OBJECT (object_id, ...) ;

KILL_ [La4_OBJECT] (object_id);

object_id : any La4 object identifier.

with La4_OBJECT =

MAILBOX, SEMAPHORE, RESOURCE, TASK, ...

Tasks

TASK   Body :   TASK (task_id, TP)

..

[FOREVER :]

..
..

END_TASK

- Vertical Barel : instructions sequence.
- Horizontal barel : (optionnal) represents the begin of the infinite loop.

task_id: task identifier; TP : task priority.

SLEEP (ST);

ST : sleep time.

- calling task goes to sleep.

SUSPEND ([task_id]);

- suspends another task

- suspends the task itself

task_id : task identifier , (empty string --> task itself)

RESUME (task_id);

- resume another task

SET_STATE ([task_id], NST);

- modify task state (priority level).

NST : new state (priority level.).

GET_STATE([task_id]);

- task state obtaining (priority level).

Semaphores, Mailboxes and Messages

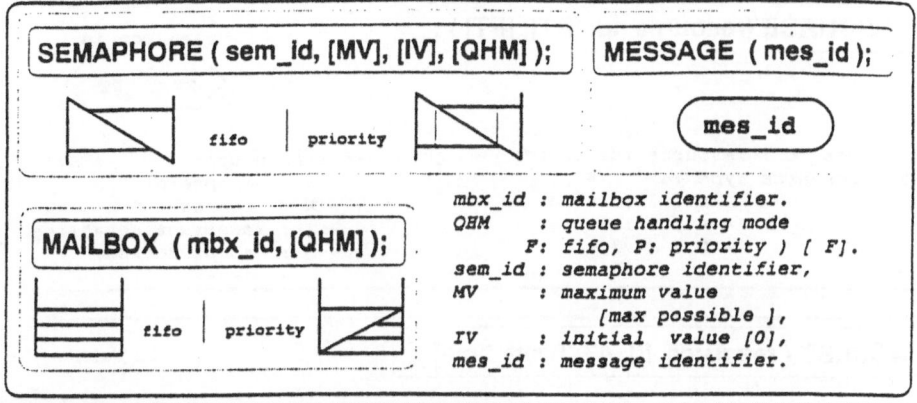

SEMAPHORE (sem_id, [MV], [IV], [QHM]);

fifo | priority

MESSAGE (mes_id);

mes_id

MAILBOX (mbx_id, [QHM]);

fifo | priority

```
mbx_id  : mailbox identifier.
QHM     : queue handling mode
         F: fifo, P: priority ) [ F].
sem_id  : semaphore identifier,
MV      : maximum value
         [max possible ],
IV      : initial  value [0],
mes_id  : message identifier.
```

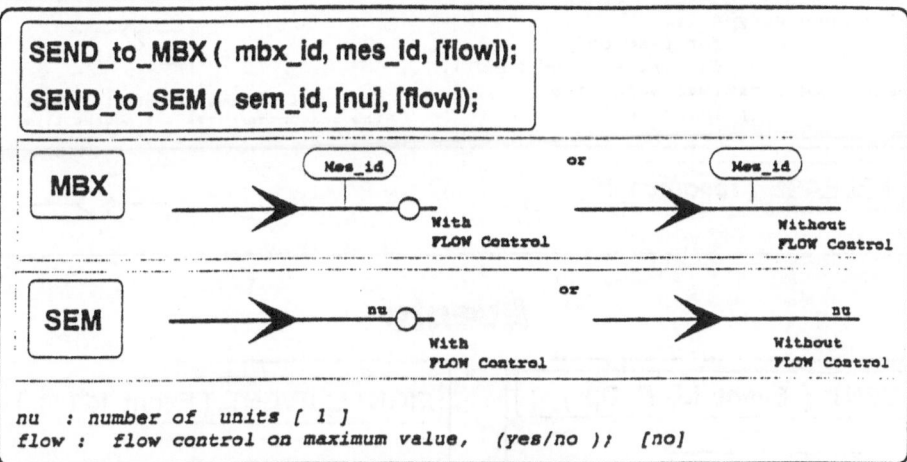

SEND_to_MBX (mbx_id, mes_id, [flow]);

SEND_to_SEM (sem_id, [nu], [flow]);

MBX   Mes_id   or   Mes_id

With FLOW Control   Without FLOW Control

SEM   nu   or   nu

With FLOW Control   Without FLOW Control

```
nu   : number of  units [ 1 ]
flow : flow control on maximum value,  (yes/no );  [no]
```

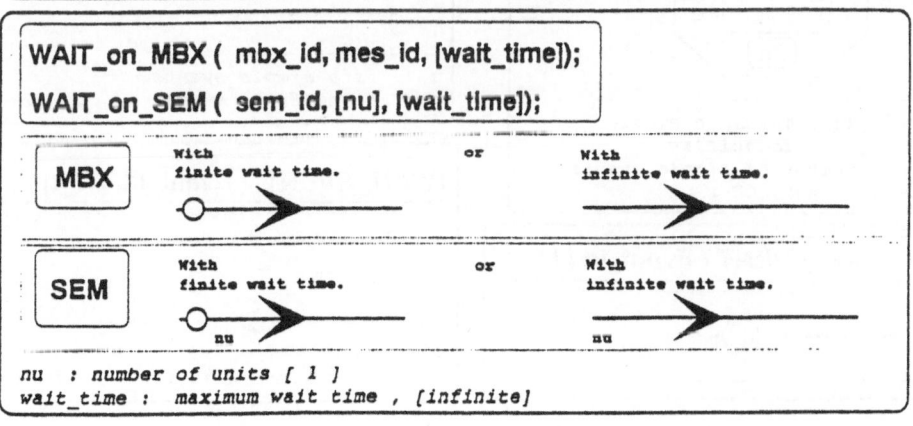

WAIT_on_MBX (mbx_id, mes_id, [wait_time]);

WAIT_on_SEM (sem_id, [nu], [wait_time]);

MBX   With finite wait time.   or   With infinite wait time.

SEM   With finite wait time.   or   With infinite wait time.

nu   nu

```
nu   : number of units [ 1 ]
wait_time :  maximum wait time , [infinite]
```

Resources

RESOURCE (resource_id, [RT], [PT]) ;

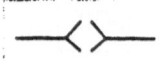

resource_id : resource identifier
RT : resource type :   [S]
              - S : structure
              - F : file
              - D : device.

PT : protection type :   [S]
              - S : semaphore
              - R : region
              - I : interrupt desabling
              - O : non protected.

ACCESS (resource_id, AT, [wait_time]);

AT : access type :
              ■ R for read only,
              ■ W for write (and read).
wait_time : maximal wait time
                  [infinite].

The double arrows orientation versus
the ressource gives the access type.

RELEASE (resource_id);

Events

EVENT (Event_id, N, Op) ;

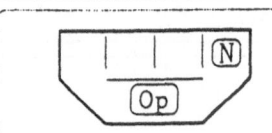

Event_id : multiple event
                  identifier
N : number of simple events.
Op : < AND, OR > .

CLEAR_EVENT (Event_id (i));

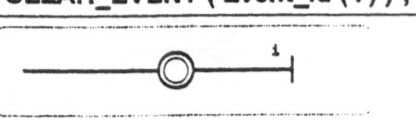

SIGNAL_EVENT (Event_id (i));

i : ith simple event
 of the multiple event.

WAIT_EVENT (Event_id, [W_t]);

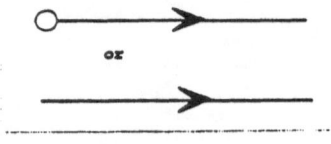

                  or

W_t : maximum wait time.

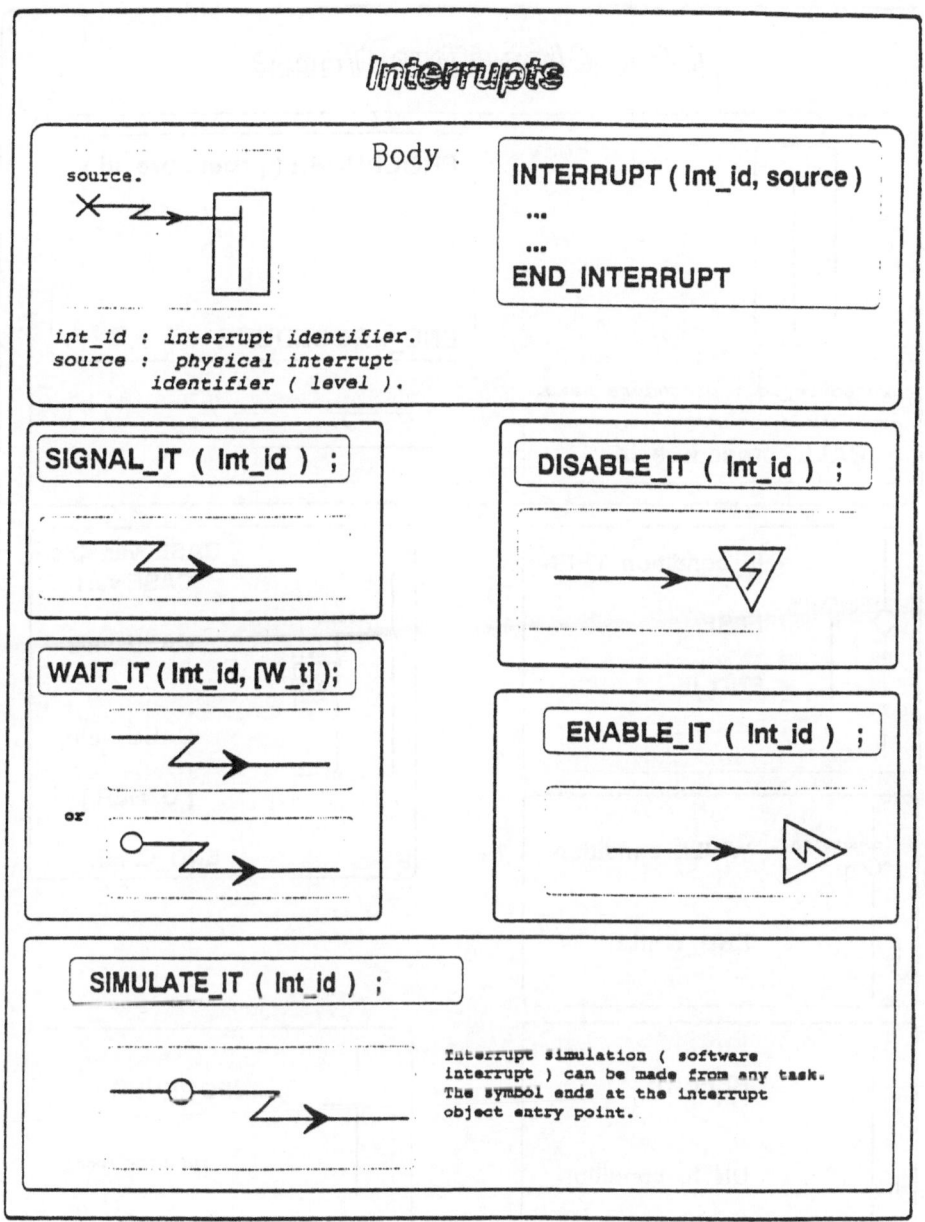

Interrupts

Body :

INTERRUPT (Int_id, source)
...
...
END_INTERRUPT

source.

int_id : interrupt identifier.
source : physical interrupt
identifier (level).

SIGNAL_IT (Int_id) ;

DISABLE_IT (Int_id) ;

WAIT_IT (Int_id, [W_t]);

or

ENABLE_IT (Int_id) ;

SIMULATE_IT (Int_id) ;

Interrupt simulation (software
interrupt) can be made from any task.
The symbol ends at the interrupt
object entry point.

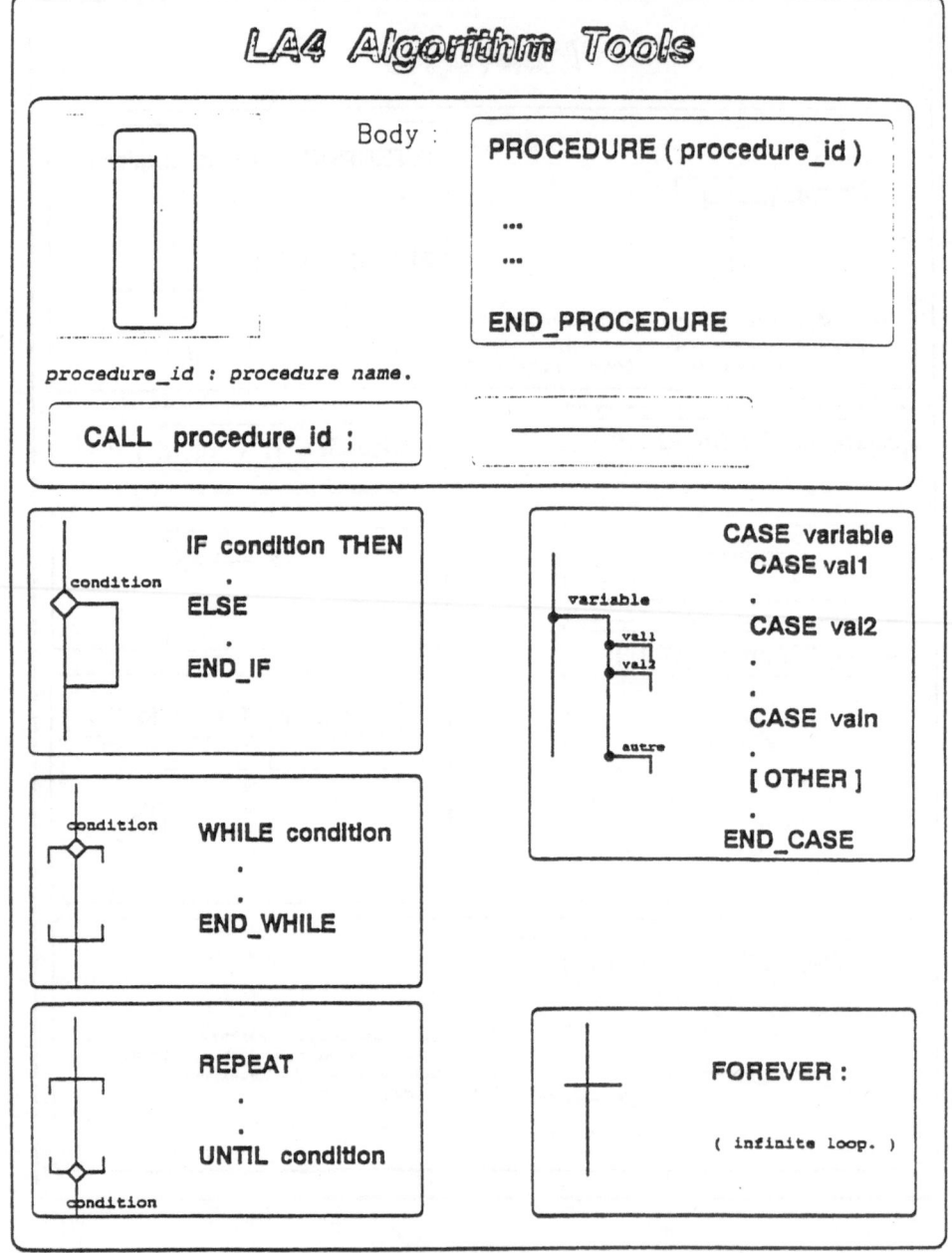

Appendix B: Grammar of La4_t

```
< La4_t Application >  :: = < declaration >
< declaration >          :: = < basic_declaration >  |  < basic_declaration >  < declaration >
< basic_declaration >  :: = < prog_obj_dec >  |  < conf_obj_dec >  |  < procedure_dec >
< procedure_dec >      :: = PROCEDURE ( < identifier > ) CR < body > END_PROCEDURE  CR
< prog_obj_dec >       :: = < definition_header > CR < body > < definition_end >
< conf_obj_dec >       :: = [ < definition_header > ]
< definition_header > :: = < obj_keyword > ( < La4_obj_Id > [ < parameter_list > ] ) CR
< definition_end >     :: = END < _obj_keyword > CR
< La4_obj_Id >         :: = < identifier >
< obj_keyword >        :: = TASK | INTERRUPT | MAILBOX | MESSAGE |
                              SEMAPHORE | EVENT | RESOURCE
< body >                 :: = < instruction >  |  < instruction > < body >
< instruction >         :: = < La4_t_instruction >  |  < branch_instruction >
< La4_t_instruction > :: = < creation_deletion_inst >  |  < other_La4_t_inst >
< creation_deletion_inst > :: = < La4_t_creation_inst >  |  < La4_t_deletion_inst >
< La4_t_creation_ins >    :: = < definition_header > ; CR
< La4_t_deletion_inst >   :: = DELETE [ < obj_keyword > ] ( < La4_obj_Id > ) ; CR
< other_La4_t_inst >      :: = < primitive_name > ( < parameter_list > ) ; CR

< primitive_name > :: = SLEEP | SUSPEND | RESUME | GET_STATE | SET_STATE|
           ENABLE_IT | DISABLE _IT | SIGNAL_IT | SIMULATE_IT  |
           SEND_to_MBX | SEND_to_SEM | WAIT_on_MBX | WAIT_on_SEM |
           SIGNAL_EVENT|WAIT_EVENT | CLEAR_EVENT | ACCESS |
           RELEASE

< branch_instruction > :: =
              IF < condition > THEN CR  < body > [ELSE CR < body >] END_IF CR |
              WHILE < condition > DO CR < body > END_WHILE  |
              REPEAT CR < body > UNTIL < condition > CR |
              LOOP: CR < body >  |
              CASE < variable > DO CR  < case_bloc > END_CASE CR |
              CALL ( < identifier > ) ; CR

< case_bloc >       :: =   < case_inst >  |  < case_inst >  < case_bloc >
< case_inst >       :: =   CASE < value > : < body >
< parameter_list >  :: = < param >  |  < param > , < parameter_list >
< condition >  :: = < string >        < variable >  :: = < string >       < identifier > :: = < string >
< param >      :: = < string >        < value >     :: = < string >
```

HARTS: A Distributed Real-Time Architecture

Kang G. Shin

Real-Time Computing Laboratory
Department of Electrical Engineering and Computer Science
University of Michigan
Ann Arbor, Michigan 48109-2122
U.S.A.

Abstract

This paper describes the design and implementation of a distributed real-time architecture, called HARTS (Hexagonal Architecture for Real-Time Systems), which is currently under development at the Real-Time Computing Laboratory (RTCL), University of Michigan.

HARTS consists of shared-memory multiprocessor nodes which are interconnected via a wrapped hexagonal mesh. This architecture is intended to meet three main requirements of real-time computing: high-performance, high-reliability, and extensive I/O.

1 Introduction

The growing importance of real-time computing in a large number of applications, such as aerospace and defense systems, industrial automation and control, has given impetus to the development of concepts and solutions to the various issues related to architectures, operating systems, fault-tolerance and evaluation tools.

There are three major components and their interplay that characterize real-time systems. First, "time" is the most precious resource to manage in real-time systems. Tasks must be assigned and scheduled to be completed before their deadlines. Messages are required to be sent and received in a timely manner between the interacting real-time tasks. Second, reliability is crucial, since failure of a real-time system could cause an economical disaster or loss of human lives. Third, the environment under which a computer operates is an active component of any real-time system. For example, for a drive-by-wire system it is meaningless to consider on-board computers alone without the automobile itself.

Due mainly to their potential for high-performance and high-reliability with the multiplicity of processors and inter-node routes, distributed systems with point-to-point interconnection networks are natural candidate architectures for time-critical applications. The main focus of this paper is thus to address some

of the key issues and solutions related to distributed real-time architectures with
point-to-point interconnection networks. Specifically, we focus on the design, implementation, and evaluation of the architectural features of HARTS to support
time-constrained, fault-tolerant communication and I/O requirements.

Although "predictability" of task execution behavior is essential for any real-
time system design to guarantee the completion of tasks in time, it is not an
architectural issue but an operating system's issue. Real-time systems architects
must provide hardware facilities on which one can readily build an operating
system so as to guarantee deadlines.

The paper is organized as follows. The high-level architecture of HARTS is
described in Section 2 while the low-level architecture is detailed in Section 3.
Section 4 deals with the performance evaluation of the fast switching methods
used in HARTS. Section 5 is concerned with fault-tolerant routing. Since time-
constrained communication and distributed task scheduling require a global time
base, the problem of clock synchronization is addressed in Section 6. I/O device
placement and management is treated in Section 7, and the current status of
HARTS is given in Section 8.

2 High-Level-Architecture

The primary goal of HARTS is to allow low-level architectural issues such as
message buffering, instruction set design, scheduling, and routing to be studied
in a setting that allows the designers internal access to many of the system parameters. To meet this goal, a hybrid system of commercially available processors
and custom-designed interfaces is being used. Several processor cards are grouped together to form a cluster of *Application Processors* (APs). Each cluster then
serves as a **multiprocessor node** and is interconnected using custom interfaces
to form a distributed system. Due to the presence of both multiprocessor and
distributed aspects in the system, the behavior of real-time tasks under either
of these architectures can be easily investigated. In parallel with the hardware
development, the work on real-time operating systems [5] influences the specification, architecture, and implementation of the custom-designed components.

2.1 Node Architecture

Each node in the testbed consists of up to three APs, a system controller, a
shared memory segment, an Ethernet processor, and a custom-designed interface, called the *Network Processor* (NP), to the interconnection network.

The APs are commercially available VMEbus multiprocessing engines based on
Motorola's MC68020. Each processor card has four major sections:

(i) a CPU core,

(ii) a VMEbus Interface,

(iii) a Memory System, and

(iv) a VMXbus Interface.

The CPU core consists of a 32-bit 16-MHz MC68020 CPU, an MC68881 Floating
Point Processor, and an MC68851 Paged Memory Management Unit. The memory subsystem provides 4 MB of high-performance dual-ported dynamic RAM
with special mailbox hardware on 256 bytes. This mailbox feature facilitates efficient interprocessor communication by allowing a remote processor to write a
semaphore which automatically interrupts the local processor.

The Ethernet processor card supports several functions for the nodes, though it
is not a permanent component of HARTS. First, it provides a secondary means
of distributing code and data. This is especially important during the early
stages of development of the network interfaces. Second, the high-level protocols
that manage reliable packet handling and provide inter-node communication
can be tested on the Ethernet processor on an experimental basis. Third, the
Ethernet processor is used to collect experimental data by monitoring the APs
and network interfaces with minimal interference.

2.2 Interconnection Network

The interconnection network of a distributed system is often required to connect
thousands of homogeneously replicated processor-memory pairs, each of which
is called a *processing node* (PN). All synchronization and communication between PNs for program execution is done via message passing. The homogeneity
of PNs and the interconnection network are very important because they allow
for cost/performance benefits from the inexpensive replication of multiprocessor components [12]. Each PN in the multiprocessor is preferred to have fixed
connectivity, so that standard VLSI chips and communication software can be
used. Also, the interconnection network needs to contain a reasonably high degree of connectivity, so that alternative routes can be made available to detour
faulty nodes/links. More importantly, the interconnection network must facilitate efficient routing and broadcasting so as to achieve high performance in task
executions. For structural flexibility a system must also possess fine scalability,
where scalability is measured in terms of the number of PNs necessary to increase the network's dimension by one.

To meet all of these requirements, several topologies are considered including
hypercubes, square meshes, 3-D torus, hexagonal and octal meshes. The requirements of fixed connectivity and planar architecture for easy VLSI and communication implementation, finer scalability, reasonably high-degree fault-tolerance,
and ease of construction can best be met by the hexagonal (H-)mesh among
the various topologies considered. Detailed comparisons between an H-mesh and
others can be found in [12, 2] and the robustness of an H-mesh to link and node

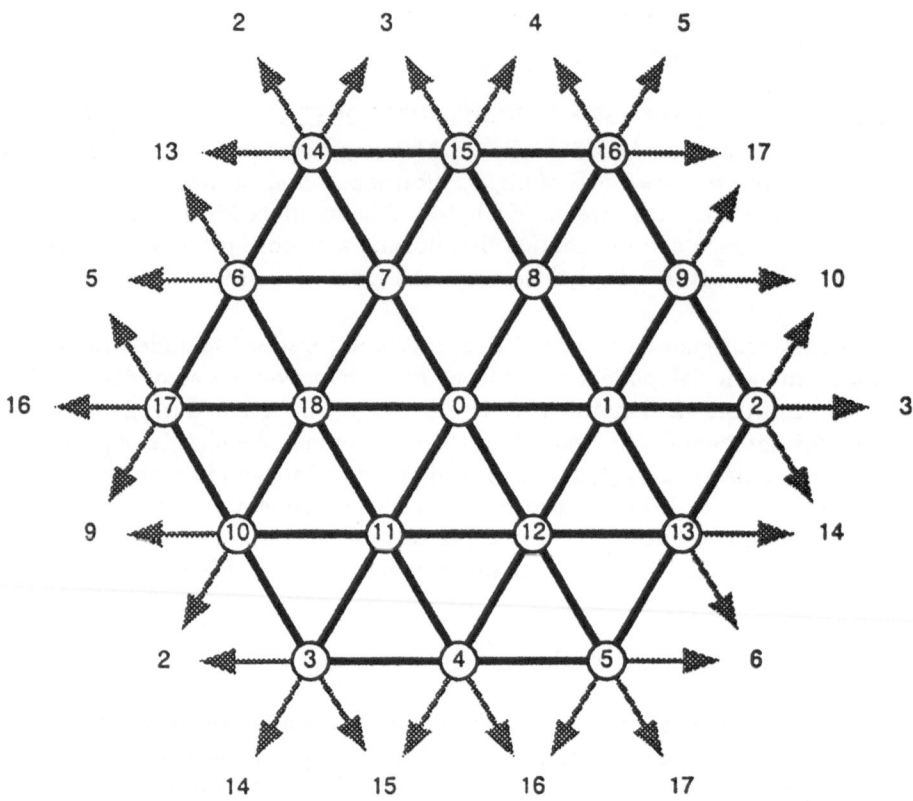

Fig. 1. A hexagonal mesh of size 3.

failures is shown in [9]. Hence, a *C-wrapped*[1] H-mesh topology is chosen to interconnect the nodes of HARTS. The size[2] of an H-mesh is defined as the number
of nodes on a peripheral edge of the H-mesh. One can better visualize what is
happening in the C-wrapping by first partitioning the nodes of a non-wrapped
H-mesh of size e, denoted by H_e, into rows in three different directions. The
mesh can be viewed as composed of $2e - 1$ horizontal rows (called the d_0 direction), $2e - 1$ rows in the 60-degree clockwise direction (called the d_1 direction),
or $2e - 1$ rows in the 120-degree clockwise direction (called the d_2 direction).
In each of these partitions we label from the top the rows R_0 through R_{2e-2}.
The C-wrapping is then performed by connecting the last node in R_i to the first
node in $R_{[i+e+1]_{2e-1}}$ for each i in each of the three partitions, where $[a]_b$ denotes
$a \bmod b$. Fig. 1 illustrates an example of a C-wrapped H_3 in which the gray links

---

[1] The letter 'C' stands for 'continuous'.

[2] This was termed *dimension* in [2].

on the periphery are connected to the nodes as indicated by their labels.

The C-wrapped H-mesh is isomorphic to the interconnection topology presented in [12]. However, the above formalism allows routing of messages between all pairs of nodes to be treated uniformly and does not require any special treatment of the "wrap lines" as was necessary in [12] when the "axial offset" was between e and $2(e-1)$.

A C-type wrapping has several salient properties as shown in [2]. First, this wrapping results in a homogeneous network. Consequently, any node can view itself as the center (labeled as node 0 in Fig. 1) of the mesh. Second, the diameter of an H_e is $e-1$. Third, there is a simple, transparent addressing scheme that uses only one — instead of three as in [12] — coordinate to uniquely identify any node in an H-mesh. An example of this addressing for an H_4 is given in Fig. 2a, where all edges are omitted for clarity. Based on this addressing scheme, one can determine all shortest paths between any two nodes with a $\Theta(1)$ algorithm, i.e., the complexity is constant and independent of system size. Note that at each node on a shortest path there are at most two different neighbors of the node to which the shortest path runs. Fourth, based on this addressing scheme it is possible to devisea simple routing algorithm that can be efficiently implemented in hardware as shown in [4].

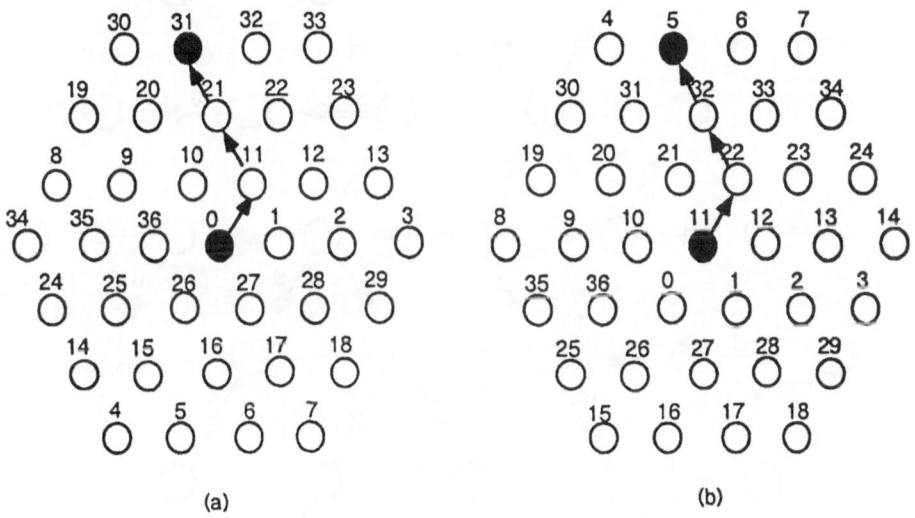

Fig. 2. Illustrative example for routing in an H_4.

To send a message, the source calculates the shortest paths to the destination and encodes this routing information into three integers denoted by m_0, m_1 and m_2, which represent the number of hops from the source to the destination along the d_0, d_1 and d_2 directions, respectively. Before sending the packet to an appropriate neighbor, intermediate nodes update these values to indicate the remaining hops in each direction to the destination. Hence, $m_0 = m_1 = m_2 = 0$ indicates that the packet has reached its destination.

Suppose node 11 sends a message to node 5 in the H_4 of Fig. 2. The original H_4 is given in Fig. 2a and $H_4(11)$ — node 11 is placed at the center of the H_4 — is in Fig. 2b. From the routing algorithm in [2], we get $m_0 = 0$, $m_1 = -2$ and $m_2 = -1$. Note that the route from node 11 to node 5 in Fig. 2b is isomorphic to that from node 0 to node 31 in Fig. 2a. This is not a coincidence, but rather a consequence of the homogeneity of H_4.

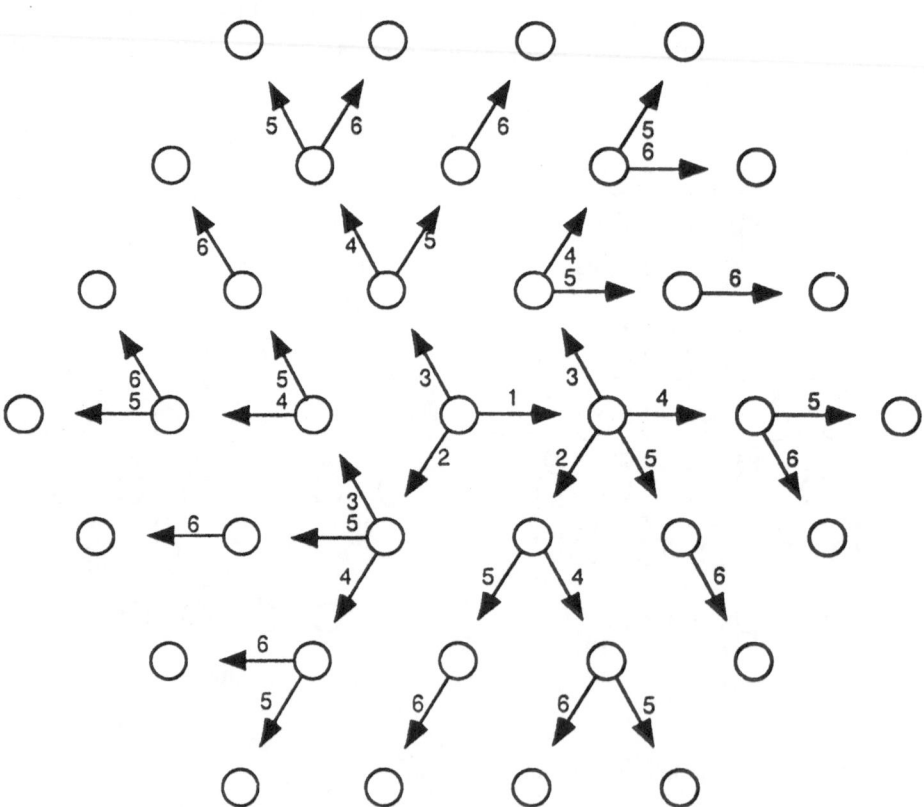

Fig. 3. Broadcasting in an H_4.

Applications in various domains require an efficient method for a node to broadcast a message to all the other nodes in an H-mesh. Due to interconnection costs, it is very common to use point-to-point communications for broadcasting. Without loss of generality, one can assume the center node to be the source of the broadcast. The set of nodes which have the same distance from the source node is called a *ring*. The main idea of this algorithm is to broadcast a message, ring by ring, toward the periphery of an H-mesh. The algorithm consists of two phases. In the first phase which takes 3 steps, the message is transmitted to the 6 nearest neighbors of the origin. Note that there are six corner nodes in each ring. In the second phase which takes $e - 1$ steps, the six corner nodes of each ring send the message to two neighboring nodes respectively while all the other nodes propagate the message to the next node along the direction in which the message was previously sent. An illustrative example of broadcasting in an H_4 is given in Fig. 3, where the labeled numbers denote the communication step numbers.

3 Low-Level Architecture

Based on the above addressing, routing and broadcasting methods, we describe in this section special hardware support for time-constrained, fault-tolerant communications in HARTS. We first briefly discuss why extra hardware is necessary for communication processing, and then list the main functional requirements of the NP. Finally, we present a system-level description of an architecture which realizes these functions.

3.1 Why Communication Hardware?

Each node in a distributed system must be responsible for packet processing, routing, and error and flow control. Real-time applications impose additional functions related to meeting deadlines, time management and housekeeping.

Packet processing can consume a substantial number of processor cycles and, in the absence of communications hardware, can deprive the (node) host of much needed computation power. In particular, the host is saddled with breaking a message in packets for transmission, constructing packet headers and trailers, framing packets, and calculating checksums. On reception of packets, the receiving host has to de-packetize the message, strip headers and trailers, and compute the checksum for error checking. Each time a packet is transmitted or received, the host must be interrupted and context-switched to routines which perform these chores. This introduces substantial overhead in contemporary off-the-shelf processors as they are optimized for computation to be performed with register and cache data, which is lost in a context-switch. For time-constrained, fault-tolerant communications, the host processor (AP) also has to handle several other functions which introduce significant computational overhead. These include message scheduling, route selection for reliable and timely delivery of messages, and clock synchronization.

All the above functions divert significant computing power from time-critical applications. It is therefore necessary to offload such processing from the AP to special communication processing hardware, i.e., the NP.

3.2 Requirements of the Network Processor

Before designing and building the NP, one has to identify its required functions. These functions must include efficient support for message processing, low-latency message transmission, and support for time-constrained, fault-tolerant communications. Deadline guarantees must be established by the operating system based on these functions.

Communication Protocol Processing:
The NP's main function is to offload communication processing from the APs. When an AP needs to transmit a message, it provides the NP with information about the intended message recipient and the location of the message data. The NP's function is then to execute the operations necessary to pass the message data through the various layers of protocol down to the physical layer where it can be transmitted. In terms of the OSI reference model, the NP is responsible for the functions from the transport layer down to the physical layer.

At the transport level, the NP establishes connections dependent only on the source and destination nodes, without concern for the route to be used. It also handles end-to-end error detection and message retransmission.

At the network level, the NP selects primary and alternate routes for establishing virtual circuits, forms data blocks and segments, and reassembles packets at the destination node. There are various switching methods such as virtual cut-through switching, wormhole routing, store-and-forward packet switching, and circuit switching. Depending on traffic conditions in the network and the message type, the NP chooses an appropriate switching method for the message. Detection and correction of errors are also done at this level.

At the data link level, the NP provides access to the network for the messages. It performs framing and synchronization, and packet sequencing. In addition to error checking at the network level, checksum error detection and error correction are done at this level.

Low-Latency Message Transmission:
Low communication latency is a key goal for the design of the NP and impacts considerations such as task migration and distribution, and load sharing. Latency considerations extend from the application tasks on the system down to the hardware components. Since a significant portion of latency occurs in communication processing, achieving low latency communication is intimately

related to implementation of communication protocols.

Support for Time-Constrained Communications:
Timely delivery of messages requires a global time-base across the different nodes in HARTS. The NP is equipped with special hardware for clock synchronization and time-stamping of messages that provides the basis for the implementation of various real-time communication algorithms.

The NP also has to support multiple levels of interrupts to manage messages with different priority levels. The hardware must provide the requisite number of levels of interrupts, so that urgent messages can be given higher priority over less urgent ones. For scarce resources such as message buffers and bandwidths, urgent messages will also be given priority for usage. The NP has to implement buffer management policies that maximize utilization of buffer space, but guarantee the availability of buffers to the highest priority messages. Similarly, if non-critical messages hold other resources that are needed by more critical ones, it is necessary to provide a means for preemption of such resources for use by the critical messages.

Another important function of the NP is to monitor the state of the network in terms of traffic load and link failures. The traffic load affects the ability of the NP to send real-time messages to other processors, while link failures affect the system reliability. It is also possible for the NP to keep track of the processing load of its host (or hosts), and use the information for load balancing/sharing and task migration operations.

3.3 NP Architecture

The NP architecture must support the functions discussed above. Although our architecture is similar to other communication architectures [1], it adds new features to facilitate real-time communication. At the same time, it attempts to cost-effectively minimize message latency by intelligent management of messages and buffer memory.

There are six major components of the NP: the interface manager unit (IMU), the packet controller (PC), the routing controller (RC), the buffer memory, and the Application Processors interface (API), interconnected as shown in Fig. 4. The API moves data between the NP and the host-node APs, while the RC moves data between the NP and the network. Within the NP, the IMU is the main processor which controls the movement and processing of message data. The buffer memory acts as a staging area for data that is to be transmitted to, or received from, the network, and for message data that needs to be temporarily stored at the node due to unavailability of outgoing links to the next node on its route to the destination. The RC implements the physical layer protocols for accessing the network and routing data to the node's neighbors. It also supports

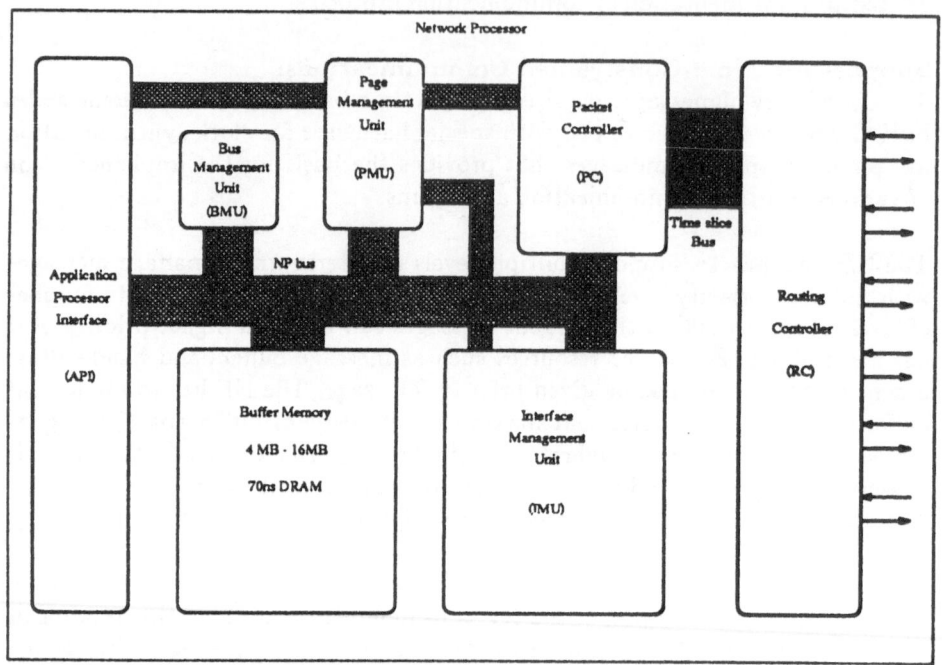

Fig. 4. A block diagram of NP.

virtual cut-through and wormhole routing by moving a message from an incoming to an outgoing link without buffering the message at the NP. Finally, the PC performs transport layer processing on the packets such as checksumming, packet framing and de-framing.

Interface Manager Unit:
The IMU packetizes and de-packetizes messages, schedules messages with different levels of priority, decides on switching methods based on message priority levels and network state, monitors the network state, performs error correction and message acknowledgment, and implements various real-time communication algorithms. A general-purpose RISC processor is a reasonable choice for the IMU due to the ease of software and hardware development and support, and its availability.

An important requirement of the IMU is to provide multiple levels of interrupts, and a small context switching time. In order to minimize message latency, the IMU must be able to respond fast to requests from the host for message transmission/reception services. Register window schemes provided in a typical RISC processor allow fast context switches, and meet this requirement.

The IMU has memory that can be used to store code and data. It also has access to the buffer memory, which is the staging area for messages being moved between the host and the network. To avoid excessive copying, the buffer memory will in most instances serve as the data memory of the IMU. Hence, the buffer memory is part of the address space of the IMU.

Buffer Memory:
The buffer memory consists of the RAM required for the buffers, and a buffer management unit. It stores messages that are waiting to be transmitted to or from the current node, and act as a temporary storage area for messages being routed through the current node. The amount of memory needed is determined by the usage patterns of the application tasks and is usually not greater than a few megabytes.

The word size used for the buffer memory is 32 bits. With the current access speeds of DRAMs at 70 ns, this gives a memory bandwidth as high as 457 megabits/s. This bandwidth is sufficient for access by the RC, the API, and the IMU, and for refresh cycles. It is therefore unnecessary to use expensive static RAM or multiport memories for the buffers.

The buffer manager arbitrates between access to the buffer from the IMU, the API, and the PC. It also handles the refresh of the buffer memory by periodically accessing rows in the DRAM. The access priorities given to these different sources can be static, dynamic or random, depending on the buffer management policy being adopted.

Another function of the buffer manager is to provide addresses of free buffers to store incoming packet data, and determine the location of packets that are ready to be forwarded to an outgoing link. In other words, the buffer manager keeps the free list of buffer pages, and keeps track of the locations of various messages stored in the buffer. In instances where a message/packet spans more than a single page, the buffer manager keeps track of the linked list of pages of the message. The buffer management policy for the free list and the buffer allocation policy can be implemented with a separate microcontroller or the IMU.

Packet Controller:
The PC functions as a DMA interface between the RC and the buffer memory, providing the IMU with inbound and outbound channels with which to transmit messages from, or receive messages into, the buffer. It accesses the buffer memory through the arbitration block of the buffer manager, and transmits and receives messages without the IMU's intervention.

In transmitting and receiving packets, it implements transport layer protocols by transparently framing and de-framing packets. This is done by adding start-of-packet (SOP) and end-of-packet (EOP) bytes to the data bytes, and computing the checksum as a packet is being sent. On reception of packets at the destination

NP, the PC removes the packet header and trailer, and computes the checksum to detect transmission errors. The detection of errors will be signaled to the IMU via an interrupt to trigger an appropriate recovery procedure.

Another function of the PC is to time-stamp messages as they are received and transmitted. As will be discussed later, hardware time-stamping support is crucial to clock synchronization. The time-stamp will be appended to the message before the checksum bytes.

Routing Controller:

The RC is the interface between the NP and the network; it implements the physical and part of the datalink layers, and has already been designed and implemented [4]. As shown in Fig. 5, the RC consists of 6 receiver-transmitter parts that are connected to the buffer manager and IMU through a time-sliced bus. The function of a transmitter is to convert outgoing data into serial form for transmission on the outgoing serial line. Correspondingly, the function of a receiver is to convert incoming serial data into parallel form, and to forward the data to either a transmitter for onward transmission in the case of virtual cut-through/wormhole routing, or to the buffer manager if the data is to be stored in the current node. Each receiver is connected via a single half-duplex serial line to a transmitter in a neighboring node.

A distinct feature of the RC is the fact that the receiver can be microprogrammed to implement different routing algorithms used in HARTS. Different switching methods can simultaneously be programmed into the RC and used selectively based on the type of messages being sent through the node, and also on the traffic on the network at any particular time. This will allow critical messages to be given highest switching and routing priority, while optimizing the overall latency of other types of messages.

AP Interface:

The interface between the NP and the host APs is through a VME bus. Data copying between a host AP and the NP is done by the API, which is a DMA interface to the VME bus. There are two ways of designing this interface for data transfer: mapping the NP's data memory into the host address space, or copying data from the host data memory to the NP data memory. It may appear that mapping the NP into the address space of the host is efficient as it avoids the overhead of a system call. However, this mapping requires dedicated memory management hardware and kernel support for mapped address spaces, and also incurs the overhead of data access over the VME bus. Depending on the typical size of the messages, it may be more efficient to use burst-mode DMA transfer from the host memory to the NP memory.

The host will initiate data transfer to the NP by writing to a control register in the API a pointer to the data in the host, as in a typical DMA sequence. The API will then contend for the host VME bus and the NP buffer memory. When both resources are acquired, it will proceed to copy the message data in burst

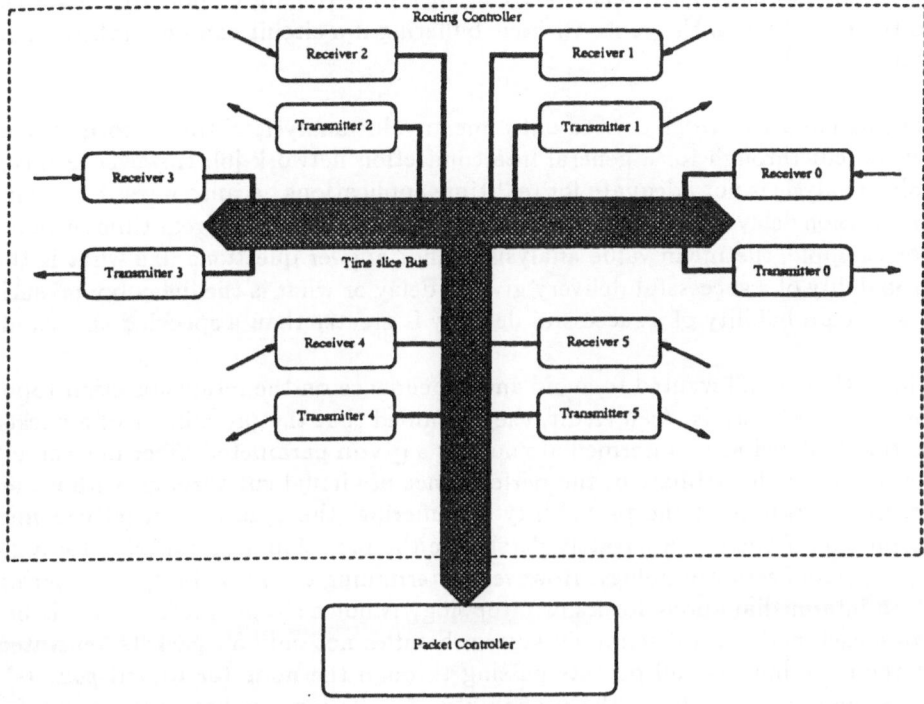

Fig. 5. A block diagram of the routing controller.

mode directly from the host to the NP buffers. Upon completion of the transfer, the IMU will be notified, and the communication processing can begin. A similar sequence of operations will be performed in the reverse order, for the reception of messages.

4 System Evaluation

The performance of HARTS is comparatively evaluated using both modeling and simulation with the actual parameters derived from our implementation. Specifically, we analyze how different switching methods can be combined to yield low latency. First, we evaluate the performance of virtual cut-through switching by developing analytic models and a low-level event-driven simulator. Then, virtual cut-through switching and wormhole routing are comparatively evaluated.

Modeling and Simulation of Virtual Cut-Through:
Since real-time applications normally require small response times, simple store-and-forward switching schemes are not suitable for HARTS. Hence, it supports fast switching methods such as virtual cut-through [6] and wormhole routing [3].

In virtual cut-through, packets arriving at an intermediate node are forwarded to the next node in the route without buffering if a circuit can be established to the next node.

Kermani and Kleinrock carried out a mean value analysis of the performance of virtual cut-through for a general interconnection network [6]. However, a mean value analysis is not adequate for real-time applications because worst-case communication delays often play an important role in the design of real-time systems. For example, the mean value analysis cannot answer questions like what is the probability of a successful delivery given a delay or what is the delay bound such that the probability of a successful delivery is greater than a specified threshold.

The authors of [6] wanted to avoid any dependence on the interconnection topology in their analysis. As a result, they assumed that the probability of a packet getting buffered at an intermediate node is a given parameter. Since one cannot get a reasonable estimate of the performance of virtual cut-through without an accurate estimate of the probability of buffering, the approach in [6] becomes useful only if one can accurately determine the probability of buffering for a given interconnection topology. However, determining the probability of buffering at an intermediate node for a given topology is not a simple matter. This is because each node in a distributed system handles not only all packets generated at the node but also all packets passing through the node (or *transit packets*). Consequently, to evaluate the probability of buffering, we have to account for the fraction of packets generated at other nodes that pass through each given node.

In contrast to [6], we first derive the probability that a packet is destined for a particular node by characterizing the H-mesh topology. This *probability of branching* is then used as a parameter in a queueing network to determine the throughput rates at each node in the mesh. After the throughput rates are found, the probability that a packet can establish a cut-through at an intermediate node is derived. From these parameters we finally derived the probability distribution function of delivery times for a packet traversing a specified number of hops.

Fig. 6 shows a plot of the inverse of the probability distribution function for a message traveling 5 hops. The three curves in the figure show the variation in the inverse of the probability distribution function for different message generation rates or network traffic. These curves are useful to determine design parameters like delay bounds. For example, one can select a delay bound such that the probability of a message being delivered within that bound is greater than a specified threshold. This would provide a probabilistic measure on the guarantees that can be provided in a real-time system during its operation.

In contrast to the analytic model, a simulator makes very few simplifying assumptions in modeling the behavior of virtual cut-through in HARTS. The simulator accurately models the delivery of each message by emulating the timing of the routing hardware [4] along the route of a packet at the microcode level.

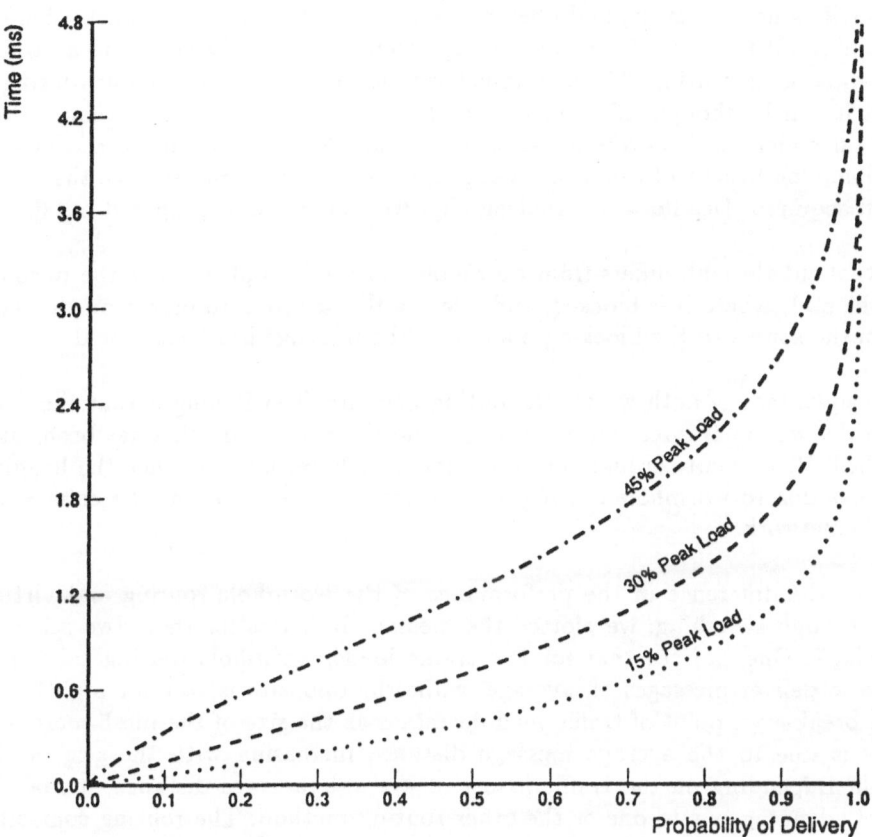

Fig. 6. Delivery time vs. probability of successful delivery.

Also captured are the internal bus access overheads that the packets experience if they are unable to cut-through an intermediate node. The simulator's detailed timing and tracking of messages allows different message scheduling, access protocols, and memory management strategies to be investigated. The simulator can also use any discrete distribution of packet lengths where the user specifies the number of different types of messages, their lengths, and the probability of each type of message. This simulator has been used to check the validity of analytic models by evaluating the communication subsystem of HARTS under various realistic settings.

Evaluation of Hybrid Routing Schemes:
The basic idea of wormhole routing [3] is that a message waits for a channel whenever it is not available, and does not get removed from the network, thereby retaining all resources from the message source to the current node at which the message is waiting. The distinguishing characteristic of wormhole routing is that it can be thought of as incrementally establishing a route in that it does not surrender the resources it has acquired along the path from source to destination. One benefit of this is not needing to reacquire resources once they have been acquired. Deadlock-free routing algorithms have been proposed in [3].

Virtual cut-through differs from wormhole routing in that it stores the message at the node where it is blocked, and releases the acquired resources on the path from the source to the blocking node once the message has been stored.

The advantage of both wormhole routing and circuit switching is that they can offer delivery guarantees once a source-to-destination connection has been established. Virtual cut-through, however, can offer lower latency when the hogging of links due to wormhole routing and circuit switching worsens the congestion in the network.

To see the difference in the performance of the wormhole routing and virtual cut-through switching, we plotted the message latencies for these two schemes in Fig. 7. One can see that for low traffic loads, wormhole routing takes less time to deliver messages on average, while the opposite is true for high loads. The break-even point of traffic load decreases as the size of the mesh increases. This is due to the average message distance increasing with the size of the mesh. Depending on the traffic load and average message distance, it may be more advantageous to one or the other routing method. The routing controller described in Section 3.3 has the flexibility in dynamically selecting the better of the two switching methods.

5 Fault-Tolerant Routing

One of the attractive features of point-to-point networks is their ability to withstand link and node failures. To exploit this feature, it is necessary to develop algorithms and provide mechanisms which preserve network communication in the presence of component failures. In this context, one has to address the issue of correctly routing messages when one or more of the mesh components has failed. This becomes of particular importance when the mesh is large, and thus component failures become more likely, or when the system is expected to operate for long periods between maintenance. The ideal fault-tolerant routing algorithm would route messages by the shortest fault-free path, would require no extra hardware, would not cause unnecessary delays at intermediate nodes, and would quickly determine if a destination was unreachable. The algorithm in

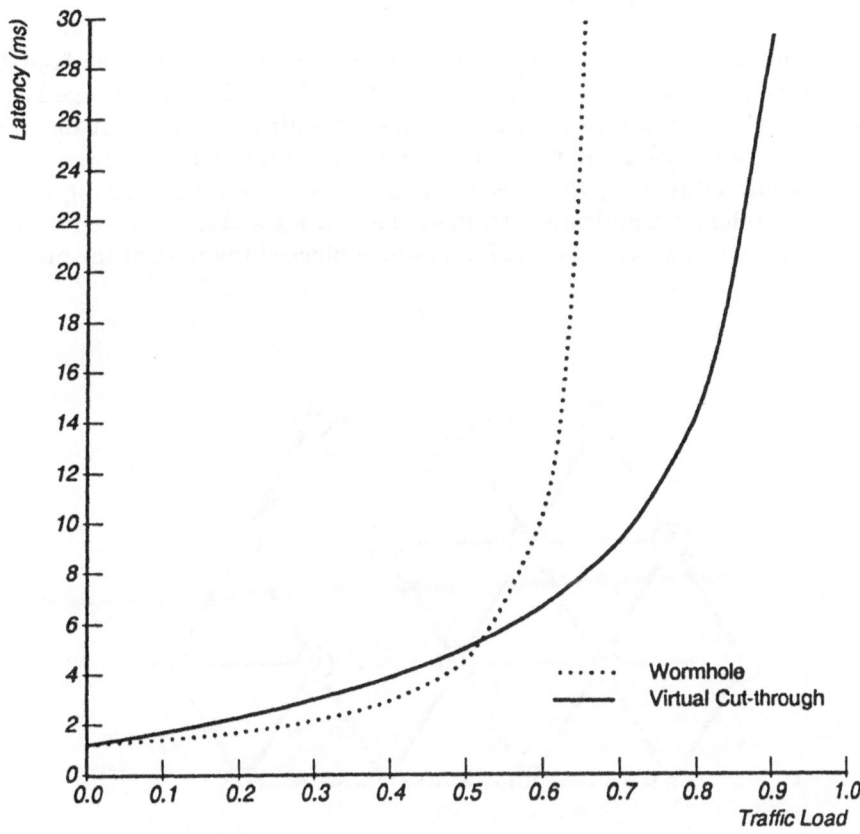

Fig. 7. Latencies of wormhole routing and virtual cut-through switching for an H_5.

[9] comes close to meeting these criteria, and requires each node to know only the condition (faulty or non-faulty) of its own links.

Each node of an H-mesh can be seen as the convergence point of three axes, and the shortest path between two nodes can be expressed as offsets along no more than two of the three axes. Since each of the six links represents movement along one of these three axes, either in the positive or negative direction, fault-free routing can be accomplished by forwarding messages along links which will bring them towards zero. Our idea is to not interfere with this process until the message finds its path blocked. A message is routed by the fault-free algorithm until it reaches a node where all the links through which the message would ordinarily be forwarded (called the *optimal links*) are faulty. At that point the fault-tolerant algorithm intervenes.

At the point of message *detouring*, routing control is split between the fault-free algorithm and the fault-tolerant algorithm. A single bit in the message header determines which algorithm is currently making routing decisions. If this bit is clear then the message is said to be in *free* mode and routing is done by the fault-free algorithm. Otherwise, the message is in *detour* mode and routing is done by the fault-tolerant algorithm. The fault-tolerant algorithm remains in control until it believes it has bypassed the faults which blocked the path of the message.

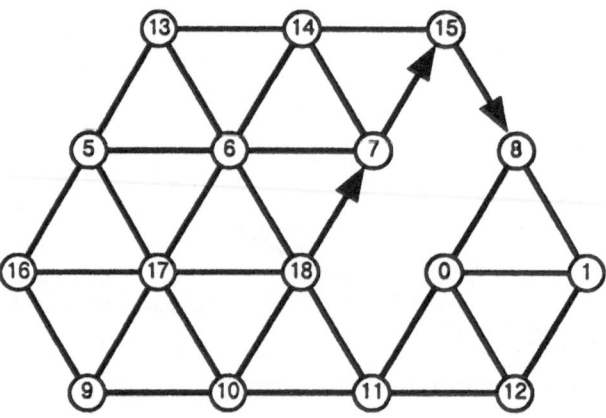

Fig. 8. Example of fault-tolerant routing.

The fault-tolerant algorithm can be seen as a simple wall-following algorithm. The message travels around the edge of a cluster of faults until it reaches the other side. Implementation is simple. When the optimal links are found to be faulty, the message is placed in detour mode and the NP looks for non-faulty links starting with the link immediately counter-clockwise of the optimal links, and proceeding counter-clockwise. The message is sent out on the first non-faulty link found. If a message arrives at a node already in detour mode, it is sent out on the first non-faulty link counter-clockwise of the link by which it arrived. While in detour mode the offsets to the destination are continually recalculated, and the message leaves detour mode when the distance to the destination is less than what it was when the message entered detour mode.

As an example, consider the situation in Fig. 8. In this case a message has arrived at node 18, with node 1 as its eventual destination. At 18 the only optimal link is the one to node 0, which has failed, the message is placed in detour mode and sent to node 7. At 7, the fault-tolerant algorithm first tries to send the message to node 0, then node 8, but finally must send it to node 15. At 15, the message is immediately forwarded to node 8. At 8, the message returns to free mode as node 8 is closer to node 1 than node 18 is. The message then completes routing normally.

An unreachable destination is detected by the presence of a cycle. If the fault-tolerant algorithm cannot get the message to the destination, the message will cycle. Unfortunately, for certain classes of fault configurations, called *incisions*, the message will cycle even though the destination is reachable. Simulation results show that this type of fault is rare, occurring only with large numbers of faults. It can be dealt with at a cost of increased complexity in the routing algorithm, and strategies for detecting and routing in the presence of incisions are outlined in [9]. The H-mesh is also shown to be extremely robust to component failures; in case 50% of the links in an H_3 are faulty, a randomly chosen destination is reachable with probability greater than 0.95 [9].

6 Clock Synchronization

The need of a global time-base has been widely recognized as one of the important requirements for distributed real-time systems to simplify the solutions to several design problems like checkpointing, inter-process communication, and resource allocation [7].

Central to the establishment of a global time-base is the problem of synchronizing the local clocks on different nodes in the system. Both hardware and software solutions to this problem have been proposed. The software solutions are flexible and economical, but require the exchange of additional messages solely for synchronization [8]. The overhead imposed by these additional messages could be substantial, especially if a tight synchronization between the processes is desired. Hardware solutions, on the other hand, require additional hardware at each node of the distributed system. They can achieve very tight synchronization between the processes in the system with very little time overhead, but they require a separate network of clocks that is usually different from the interconnection network between the nodes.

For the clock synchronization of HARTS, we use a software solution which requires minimal hardware support at each node [10]. It is based on the interactive convergence algorithm in [8].[3] The algorithm assumes that the clocks drift apart only by a bounded amount during each resynchronization interval, R, during which each process reads the value of every process's clock. If the value of a clock read differs from its own clock by an amount greater than a threshold, the process replaces that value by its own clock value. The process then computes the average of all such values and sets its own clock to this average. In [8] it

---

[3] Note, however, that any other software clock synchronization algorithm can be used equally for our scheme.

is shown that this algorithm can achieve synchronization, and requires $3m + 1$ processors to tolerate m faults.

Three major problems arise when this algorithm is used in a distributed system with a point-to-point interconnection network. First, it is difficult for a process to read the clock of a process to which it is not directly connected. Second, the message received by a process may be corrupted by a faulty intermediate process through which the message was relayed. Third, due to queueing delay for the clock messages, there may be a substantial difference between the real time at which a process sends its clock value and the real time at which a process receives that message. Therefore, subtracting the clock value in the received message from the current clock value will not reflect the actual skew that exists between the clocks of the two processes. This problem gets aggravated when the clock message has to pass through multiple intermediate nodes.

In [10], the first problem is solved by letting each process broadcast its clock to all processes at a specified time, with respect to its own local clock, in the resynchronization interval. The second problem is eliminated by using a broadcast algorithm that delivers multiple copies of the message to all processes through node-disjoint paths. For the third problem, it is recognized that it is not the size of the delay, but the fact that it is not known, that affects the clock skew. The message delivery time for clock messages is obtained by requiring each intermediate process to append to the message the delay incurred by the message at that process.

The accurate computation of this delay needs some hardware support. There is some uncertainty in determining the time at which a message was received, because there is a variable delay between the time when the processor is notified about the message arrival and when it actually "sees" the message. Also, to compute the time delay within the node the processor needs to have control on the exact time at which a message is transmitted on a link. These potential errors in estimating the time delay limit the accuracy with which we can compute the clock skew. This in turn affects the clock skew achievable with the synchronization.

To alleviate this problem, we use a hardware time-stamping mechanism at the link level for clock messages (see Section 3.3). When a clock message is detected by the link receiver, a *receive time-stamp* is appended to the end of the message. Similarly, when a clock message is transmitted, the link transmitter appends a *transmit time-stamp* to it. At an intermediate node, the receive and transmit time-stamps use the same local clock and so their difference gives a very accurate estimate of the time spent by the message in that node. By computing the difference at intermediate nodes, we can make sure that the total number of time-stamps that are appended to a message does not exceed five and thus, the message length does not grow as the size of the network increases.

For any synchronization algorithm, R is a function of the maximum clock skew that is desired. R decreases with the desired maximum skew and it becomes *negative* for small values of the skew. From a practical viewpoint, the overheads for the synchronization algorithm increase as R decreases, so it is desirable to have R as large as possible. This function effectively determines the type of skew that can be achieved for the system, with a particular synchronization algorithm. The derivation of this function for the synchronization algorithm described here can be found in [10]. The clock synchronization algorithm described above can achieve moderately tight synchronization. For example, in an H_3 a maximum clock skew of 100 microseconds can be achieved using $R = 6.23$ seconds.

7 I/O Architecture

Most work on distributed computing systems has centered on interconnection networks, programming and communications paradigms, and algorithms. However, little has been done specifically about the I/O subsystem in a real-time environment, despite its obvious importance. Clearly, a real-time computer can process data no faster than it can acquire the data from sensors and operators. Note that I/O devices in a real-time environment are sensors, actuators and displays, whereas they are magnetic disks and tapes for general-purpose systems. Due to the distinct timing and reliability requirements of the former, solutions to the latter are not usually applicable to the real-time environment.

To avoid the accessibility problems of non-distributed I/O, I/O devices need to be distributed and managed by relatively simple, and reliable, controllers. Moreover, to improve both accessibility (reliability) and performance, there must be multiple access paths (called *multi-accessibility* or *multi-ownership*) to these I/O devices.

The desire for simple I/O controllers presents a problem in HARTS, because the natural tendency would be to have sensors and actuators belong to individual nodes or NPs, both relatively complex and expensive devices, and use the given inter-process communication (IPC) channels in HARTS to handle the I/O traffic. We can still use the given IPC channels, but instead of permanently tying down a given I/O device to one node, we allow several nodes to communicate with each I/O device. There are two fundamentally different protocols for managing this communication, but we will introduce the architectural considerations first and then discuss the protocols.

7.1 I/O Interconnection Architecture

I/O devices are clustered together and a controller is assigned to manage access to the devices of each cluster. However, the controller can be made simple since simple data links to the computation nodes are used in HARTS. The I/O controller need only be able to handle sending and receiving simple messages via a set of full-duplex links, not providing virtual cut-through capabilities and other features of a full-blown NP. To keep the number of I/O controllers and the number of I/O links down to a reasonable number, the number of I/O controllers (IOCs) is restricted to be no greater than the total number (p) of computation nodes in the mesh. This will have certain benefits for one of the management protocols explained later.

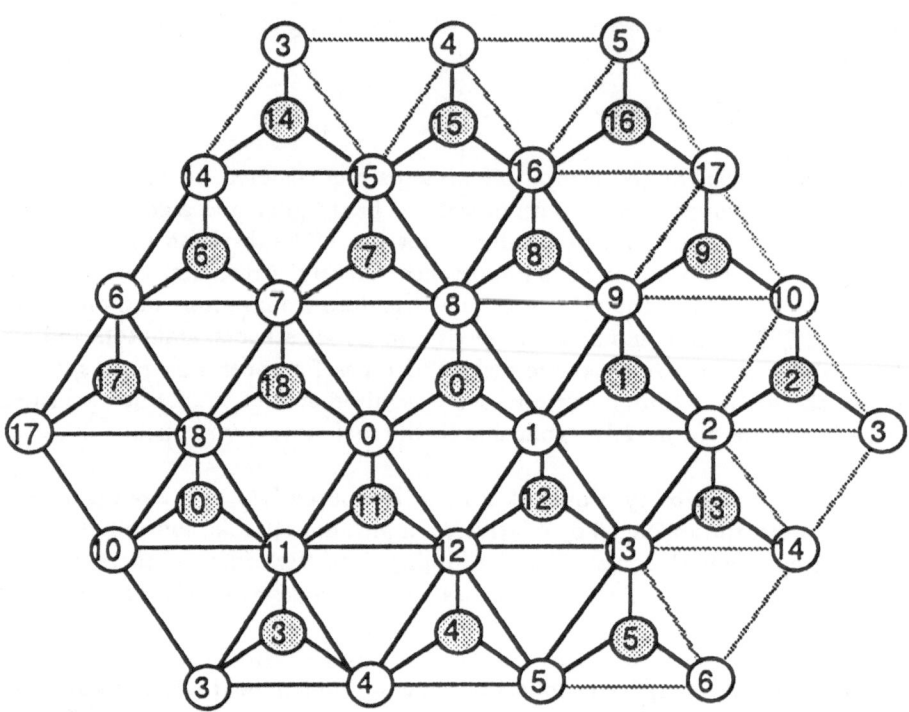

Fig. 9. I/O controller placement.

Having established the potential number of I/O nodes, we need to decide how many nodes each IOC will be connected to. If the maximum number (p) of IOCs are assumed to exist in an H_3, for example, then Fig. 9 shows a logical connection scheme [11]. Each IOC can be thought of as being in the center of one of the upward-pointing triangles in this figure and the IOC is then connected to each of the nodes which make up this triangle and are called its left, right, and upper "partners". This gives three possible avenues of access to each IOC. Note that if the maximum number of IOCs are used, the number of I/O links required is equal to the number of standard communication links, or $9e^2 - 9e + 3$ for an H_e. There is no particular reason that one could not similarly place IOCs at the (logical) center of the downward-pointing triangles as well, allowing for up to $2p$ IOCs, but this will double the maximum possible number of I/O links required and will disturb certain homogeneous effects of limiting the number of IOCs to the number of nodes.

7.2 Management Protocols

The first management (static) protocol assigns one node to each IOC as its owner, but with the important provision that the owner can be changed if the original owner becomes faulty. In this protocol one of the IOC links is defined to be the active link and the rest remain inactive as spares. The second (dynamic) protocol allows the IOC owner to be defined dynamically, allowing for greater accessibility and fewer average hops required to reach the IOC owner. In this protocol the IOC decides which link will be active at any given time.

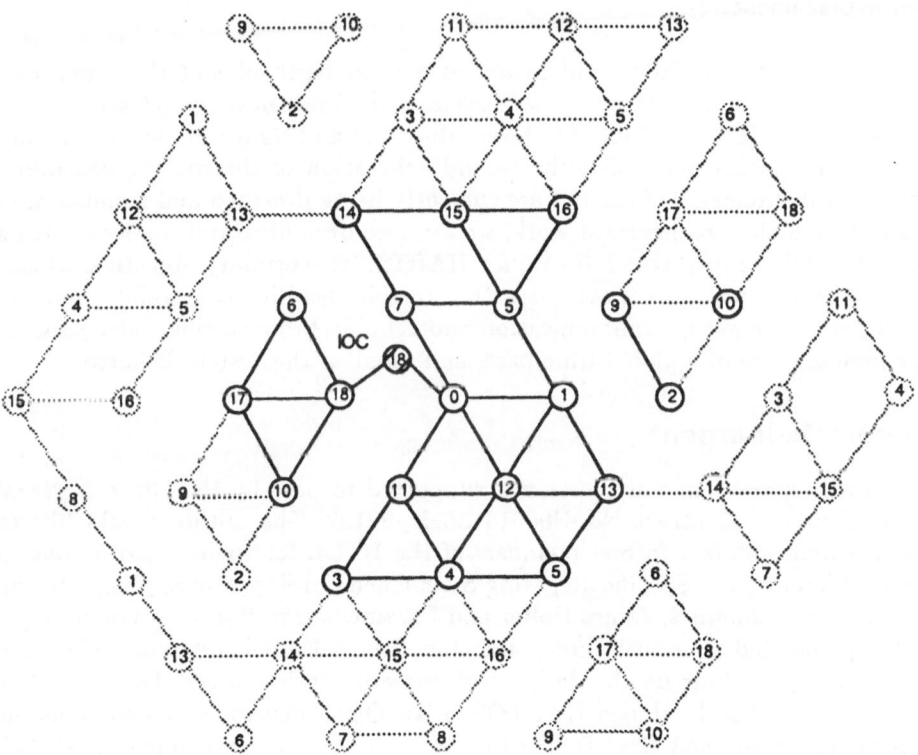

Fig. 10. Unreachable static owner.

In Fig. 10 we have an example where a process in node 13 wants service from IOC 18, but since node 18 is the owner under the static protocol and is not reachable from 13, it cannot obtain service. If node 0 were the owner instead of 18 — which is possible under the dynamic protocol — it could be serviced.

In addition to making IOCs accessible where static ownership would make them inaccessible, the dynamic protocol also takes into account the fact that one partner may be closer to a node requesting service than the other partner. Since this protocol chooses the closest of the partners that respond, the I/O traffic may have fewer hops to travel. However, its disadvantages are that it is more difficult to implement, it involves arbitration overhead after each I/O request has been serviced, and it may be undesirable because there is no single node through which all I/O requests will travel and which could perform some I/O management tasks. See [11] for a comparative analysis of these two protocols.

8 Current Status

This article describes the architectural aspects of HARTS, an experimental distributed real-time system currently under development at the RTCL, with emphasis on time-constrained, fault-tolerant communications and I/O placement and management.

All the high-level architectural issues have been resolved and the lower-level components are being designed or implemented. The routing controller, a key component for fast switching, has been fabricated and its testing is almost completed. The packet controller, the second generation of the routing controller, and other components of the NP are currently being designed and simulated. In parallel with the architectural work, we are also designing and implementing a communication subsystem software for HARTS. The primary objectives of this subsystem are to deliver messages within certain deadline constraints, support mechanisms for group communication and reliable broadcasting, offer services like maintenance of a global time-base, and monitor the system behavior.

Acknowledgement

The work reported in this paper was supported in part by the Office of Naval Research under Contract No. N00014-85-K-00122. The author would like to thank all current and former members of the RTCL for their contributions to the HARTS project. Specifically, Ming-Syan Chen developed wrapping, labeling and routing techniques, James Dolter and Parameswaran Ramanathan designed and implemented the routing controller chip, Stuart Daniel and Teng-Kean Siew are currently working on the design and implementation of NP, Dilip Kandlur and Daniel Kiskis developed HARTOS, Alan Olson developed a fault-tolerant routing algorithm, and Greg Dykema played a key role in developing the HART I/O architecture. The author is also indebted to Andre van Tilborg, Gary Koob, and James Smith at the Office of Naval Research for their encouragement and financial support.

References

1. E. A. Arnould, F. J. Bitz, E. C. Cooper, et al., *The design of Nectar: A network backplane for heterogeneous multicomputers*, in: ASPLOS-III, ACM, April 1989, 205–216.
2. M.-S. Chen, K. G. Shin, and D. D. Kandlur, *Addressing, routing and broadcasting in hexagonal mesh multiprocessors*, IEEE Transactions on Computers, Vol. 39, No. 1, January 1990, 10–18.
3. W. J. Dally and C. L. Seitz, *Deadlock-free message routing in multiprocessor interconnection networks*, IEEE Trans. Comput., Vol. C-36, No. 5, May 1987, 547–553.
4. J. W. Dolter, P. Ramanathan, and K. G. Shin, *A microprogrammable VLSI routing controller for HARTS*, in: Int. Conf. on Computer Design: VLSI in Computers, October 1989, 160–163.
5. D. D. Kandlur, D. L. Kiskis, and K. G. Shin, *HARTS: A distributed real-time operating system*, ACM SIGOPS Operating Systems Review, Vol. 23, No. 3, July 1989, 72–89.
6. P. Kermani and L. Kleinrock, *Virtual cut-through: A new computer communication switching technique*, Computer Networks, Vol. 3, 1979, 267–286.
7. L. Lamport, *Using time instead of timeout for fault-tolerant distributed systems*, ACM Trans. on Programming Languages and Systems, Vol. 6, No. 2, April 1984, 254–280.
8. L. Lamport and P. M. Melliar-Smith, *Synchronizing clocks in the presence of faults*, Journal of ACM, Vol. 32, No. 1, January 1985, 52–78.
9. A. Olson and K. G. Shin, *Message routing in HARTS with faulty components*, in: FTCS-19, Digest of Papers, June 1989, 331–338.
10. P. Ramanathan, D. D. Kandlur, and K. G. Shin, *Hardware–assisted software clock synchronization for homogeneous distributed systems*, IEEE Transactions on Computers, Vol. 39, No. 4, April 1990, 514–524.
11. K. G. Shin and G. L. Dykema, *Distributed I/O architecture for HARTS*, in: Proc. 17-th Int. Symp. on Comput. Arch., June 1990, 332–342.
12. K. S. Stevens, *The communication framework for a distributed ensemble architecture*, AI Technical Report 47, Schlumberger Research Laboratory, February 1986.

Knowledge-Based Techniques with Special Emphasis on Real-Time Expert Systems

R. J. Lauber

Institute for Control Engineering and Industrial Automation
University of Stuttgart
Pfaffenwaldring 47
70569 Stuttgart
Germany

Abstract

The use of knowledge-based techniques in real-time applications is still a challenge. Problems to overcome are, for example:

- Representation of time and reasoning about events in time
- Handling of asynchronous events
- Inferencing within a given interval of time
- Integrating knowledge-based components into conventional real-time software with a real-time operating system

The paper adresses these fundamental concerns and presents the state of the art in providing solutions, as well as the results of current research. Additional unsolved problems, such as validating knowledge-based systems and proving their reliability and safety, are briefly discussed.

1 Introduction

Both the challenging potential of knowledge-based techniques for the real-time domain as well as the problems which have to be overcome result from the very nature of real-time systems: They are always coupled systems, consisting of a physical system part (like, for example, a subway train, a chemical plant, or a telephone switching network) and a control computer system part. As shown in Fig.1, these two parts are closely coupled to each other. While the physical system part reacts to the control signals from the computer, the control computer part and its software including knowledge-based components must interact with the dynamic properties of the physical system part [12].

Therefore, by definition, real-time systems are reactive systems. Using an analogy, a real-time system may be compared to a dancing couple (Fig.1), where the two partners have to react to each others movements [10].
When using their "knowledge-base" about the type and style of dancing movements, they have to take into account a time schedule (the music rythm) as

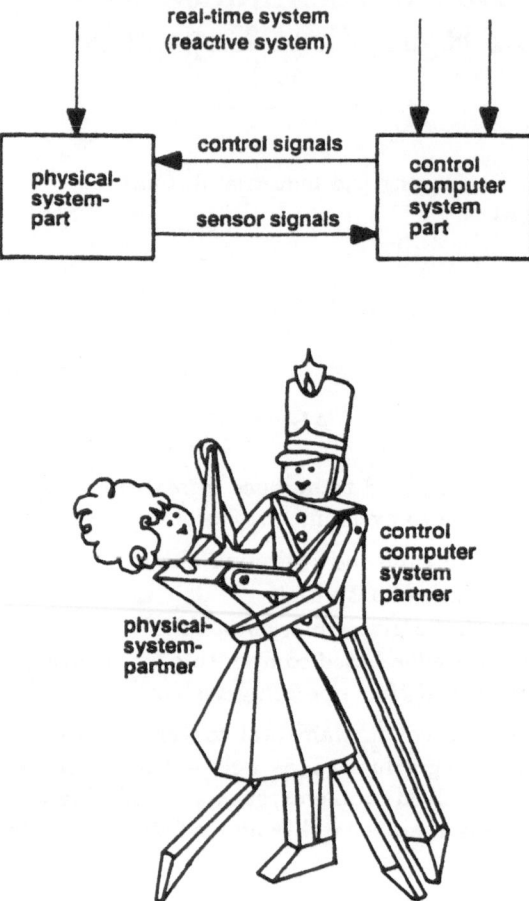

Fig. 1. Analogy to illustrate the very nature of a real-time system as a reactive system consisting of a physical system and a control computer system. It is the interaction between these two that drives real-time and reliability requirements when knowledge-based techniques are considered.

well as external events at certain times (such as movements of other dancing couples).

What is true for the example of the dancing couple is true for the real-time computer system: It is the interaction between the physical system part and the control computer part that drives the software requirements including its knowledge-based components. These requirements are of two different categories [12]:

— Requirements to react simultaneously (in parallel) according to the physical

systems and its subsystems behaviour
- Requirements to react within certain time constraints imposed by dynamic properties of the physical system involved (i.e., time constants, occuring events etc.).

As described in [13], there are several problems occuring if knowledge-based techniques are considered to be applied for real-time systems:

- Tempus fugit. The time never stands still. There are problems such as time representation and reasoning about time.
- New knowledge may be inconsistent with knowledge in the knowledge-base. It must be possible to handle a non-monotonic knowledge-base.
- There is only a fixed amount of time available for infering a solution. An expert system should, therefore, provide the best possible response within a given deadline.
- There may be the need to interrupt an inference process by asynchronous events within the physical system part or from the environment.
- There may be a need to perform inferences in parallel in order to cope with several events occuring in parallel.

In addition, there may be other problems concerning the interface of knowledge-based system:

- According to Fig.1, an interface between the computer control system and the physical system involved has to be provided.
- The physical variables transmitted by the sensor signals have to be translated to the symbolic level of the knowledge-based system.

The organization of this paper is as follows: In section 2, the actual state of the art of coping with the problems stated above and of using knowledge-based techniques for real-time system applications is discussed and areas of unsolved problems are defined. In the following sections 3 to 7 recent research aimed at coping with these problems is reported on (without giving details; these may be found in the references). Section 3 is devoted to time representation methods in real-time expert systems. In section 4, methods to treat asynchronous events and parallel inferences are discussed. In section 5, the problem of guaranteeing a specified response time is covered. In section 6, the problem of integration of knowledge-based components into a conventional real-time software system are treated and methods are presented to use knowledge compilation in order to solve these integration problems. Section 7 explains these methods by using an example. The conclusion in section 8 summarizes the results and mentions topics for further research.

2 Real-time knowledge-based systems — state of the art and main problem areas

As was discussed by [24], [15] the principal reason for using real-time knowledge-based systems is to reduce the cognitive load on users or to enable them to increase their productivity without the cognitive load on them increasing.

An extensive survey of applications of real-time knowledge-based systems was performed by Laffey et al. [13]. They found that real-time expert systems are being applied especially when conventional techniques have failed or are not sufficiently effective. The results of their survey indicates that real-time knowledge-based techniques might be appropriate for problem solving where humans suffer from cognitive overload, fail to effectively monitor all available information, are unable to resolve conflicting constraints, are expensive or scarce, make high-cost mistakes, miss high-revenue opportunities, cannot simultaneously manipulate all the relevant information to obtain optimal solutions, or cannot provide a solution quickly enough.

Of the over 100 different commercially available expert system shells which were investigated, only two (PICON [16] and G2 [17]) had been built explicitly for real-time monitoring and control applications. This resulted in a list of disappointing deficiencies of the expert system shells which were evaluated in the survey:

- Little or no capabilities for temporal reasoning
- No guaranteed response times
- Little or no facilities for focussing attention on significant events
- No facilities for handling asynchronous inputs
- Difficult to integrate in an efficient manner with conventional software
- No methods or tools for verifying and validating the knowledge basis

From this list of deficiencies, the following main problem areas have been attacked in a recently finished research project [3]:

- Temporal reasoning: Typically, a real-time system needs the ability to reason about time as an important variable, for example in connection with past, present, or future events, as well as the sequence in which these events happen.
- Asynchronous events: A real-time system must be capable of being interrupted to accept inputs from an asynchronous event. Additionally, those inputs should be processed according to importance, even if the processing of less important inputs must be stopped or rescheduled.
- Guaranteed response times: The computer system must be able to respond by the time the response is needed. Within a given deadline, the best possible response should be produced.
- Integration with conventional real-time software: While traditionally, knowledge-based systems (i.e., expert systems) have been self contained and independent of other software systems, a real-time knowledge-based system must typically be integrated with conventional real-time software. Conventional code being processed under a real-time operating system will be used to perform tasks such as signal processing, simultaneous processing of control algorithms for parallel operations of the physical system involved [21].

The tasks performed by the knowledge-based software components must co-operate with these "conventional" system parts.

In the following sections, techniques which have been developed to solve these problems will be examined.

3 Temporal reasoning

In the physical system which is coupled to the computer system in Fig.1, variables such as temperature, pressure etc, may vary over time. Therefore, a time representation and the possibility of reasoning about time is essential for a knowledge-based part of the software system.

Much temporal reasoning research has been focused on theoretical modelling and representations of time-varying aspects [1], [4]. A time line is the linear model of a circular clock (see Fig.2). The line is divided into equal sections called basic time intervals (marked with T in Fig.2). The duration of the basic time interval may be defined by the knowledge engineer according to the time constants of the technical system involved (for example, 1 millisecond for a motor control system, 10 minutes for a temperatur control system).

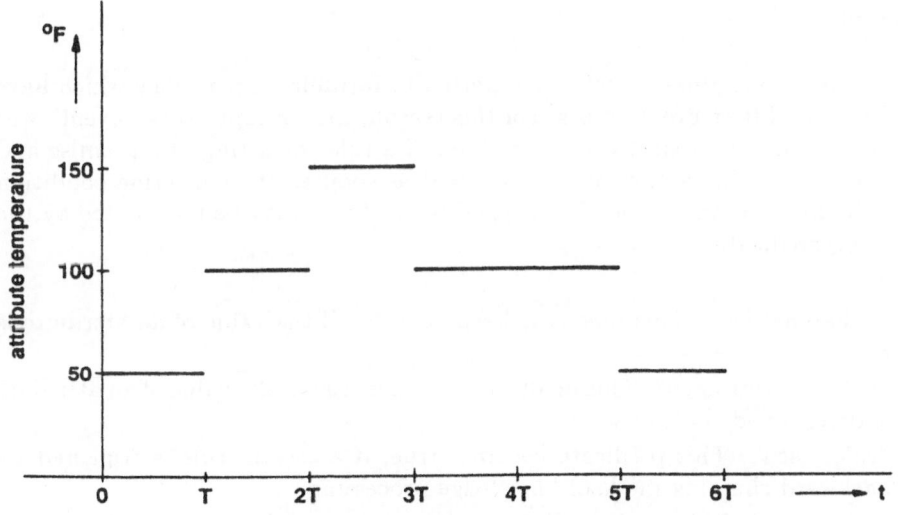

Fig. 2. Time representation by using a time line with varying attribute values.

The elementary entity of the knowledge base (a triple <fact, attribute, value>) is attached with additional time information describing the beginning and the ending of the validity of an attribute value.

Based on this model, the premises of the rules of an expert system [8] may be extended by temporal statements of the following types:

- General statements. The general operators "henceforth" and "always" can be used to formulate the premise of a rule.
- Qualitative statements. Qualitative temporal statements refer to the relation of time points or time intervals without an exact time specification. "Earlier", "after", "beginning", "ending" and "overlapping" are examples of qualitative relations between time intervals.
- Quantitative statements. They allow to express conditions referring to an exact point in time (for example, at 12:00:00 p.m.) or a duration of a time interval.

4 Representing and handling of asynchronous events

Reacting to asynchronous events is a basic requirement for a real-time expert system. For example, if the pressure in a chemical plant reaches a critical value, the current processing of the expert system has to be interrupted or even be suspended to continue with a new task which is dealing with the dangerous situation.

The knowledge engineer must be supported to formulate operations which have to be executed if an event occurs. For this reason, the concept called "event" was developed [2]. It is basically a special kind of a rule consisting of a premise and an action part. The action part is executed as soon as the triggering condition of the premise becomes true. The triggering condition may be formulated by the following predicates:

- "value_needed". This predicate becomes true, if the value of an attribute is read.
- "value_determined". This predicate becomes true, if the value of an attribute is determined.
- "rule_used". This predicate becomes true, if a certain rule is triggered by backward chaining mode of knowledge processing.
- "rule_fired". This predicate becomes true, if a certain rule is fired.
- "external". This predicate becomes true, if an external interrupt, for example a signal from the physical system, occurs.

All events are asynchronous, and two or more events may occur at the same time, each of them requesting its own action.

5 Responding within a given response time

A basic prerequisite for guaranteeing a certain response time of a software system with hard real-time requirements is determinism of the algorithms [7]. But knowledge-based systems are by their very nature non-deterministic: The time of inferencing conclusions is dependent on the given situation, e.g. the values of the facts which are in the knowledge-base [18].

Considering the searching time needed for a certain inference, three alternatives may be distinguished (Fig.3):

- A guarantee to respond within a given response time limit $t_{responselimit}$ is only possible, if the maximum searching time $t_{searchmax}$ is less than $t_{responselimit}$: $t_{searchmax} < t_{responselimit}$
- If $t_{searchmin} < t_{responselimit} < t_{searchmax}$ the response time, may be sufficient, depending on the minimum searching time $t_{searchmin}$. But no guarantee is possible.
- If $t_{responselimit} < t_{searchmin}$, the response time requirements cannot be met.

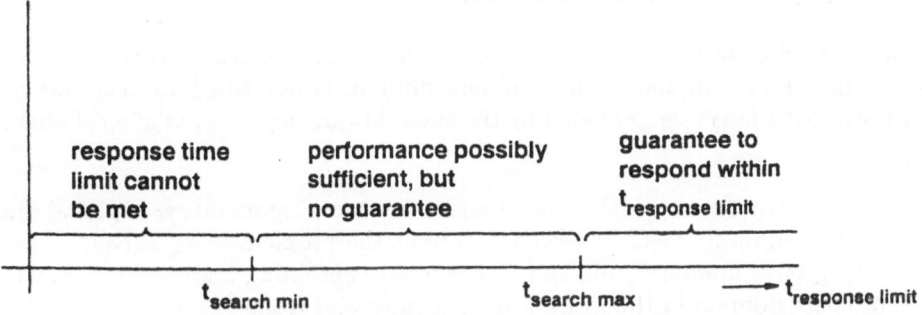

Fig. 3. The three different situations concerning meeting a response time limit in knowledge-based systems
$t_{searchmax}$: maximum searching time needed for inference
$t_{searchmin}$: minimum searching time
$t_{responselimit}$: response time limit (maximum allowed response time)

In order to meet the requirements concerning response time in real-time expert systems, two strategies may be applied:

- Reducing the searching time $t_{searchmax}$ by transferring searching subtasks from runtime to compile-time.
- Implementing algorithms to quantitatively estimate the maximum searching time, and thus to support the knowledge engineering.

6 Integrating knowledge-based software with procedural real-time software

Conventional real-time software systems are realized by using the concept of parallel processes (tasks), which are running under the control of a real-time operating system. It may use dynamic priority or deadline scheduling strategies, as well as synchronization mechanisms in order to fulfill real-time requirements [11]. The tasks may be implemented either by using special high-order programming languages with real-time language features (such as, for example, Ada, PEARL, OCCAM or Edison) or by a combination of non-real-time programming languages (for example C) with assembly language inserts.

When using a high-order real-time programming language, time conditions as well as events may easily be programmed, using the capabilities of the operating system involved. For instance, in PEARL the cyclic activation of a task named "diagnosis" with a cycle time of 2 seconds is written:

> every 2 sec activate diagnosis;

An external event producing an interrupt signal "alarm" may be programmed to execute a task $fault_{diagnosis}$ by the statement:

> when alarm activate fault_diagnosis;

Conventional expert systems, on the other hand, are realized mostly by means of an expert system shell. The problem domain is described by a knowledge representation language provided by the shell. Major components af a rule-based shell are:

- a short term memory (also called a fact list, working memory, or global data base) containing facts or assertions about the problem being solved
- a long term memory (rule and frame base) containing knowledge about the problem domain in the form of if-then-rules and frames
- an inference engine (or rule interpreter) that carries out the problem solving. Facts in short term memory are matched with conditions on the left-hand side of rules. Only those rules with all conditions matched are activated. The inference engine selects one of the activated rules for execution using a conflict resolution strategy (for example priorities).

Thus, procedural software and rule-based software differ in their underlying execution models. Procedural software uses an imperative model in which the software engineer explicitly determines the sequence of actions. Rule-based systems, on the other hand, offer a generalized control scheme for matching, selecting, and executing rules.

In order to integrate these completely different models, we propose a solution concept where the expert system is transformed from the knowledge level to the procedural level by using a *knowledge compiler* [22]. As shown in Fig.4, the result of the transformation process is a generated program in a conventional

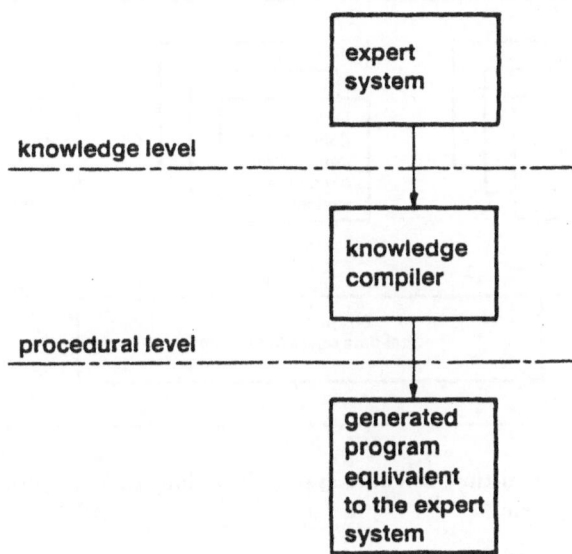

Fig. 4. Transformation of an expert system from the knowledge level to the procedural level by use of a knowledge compiler

programming language (e.g., in C), which may then run as an asynchronous task under control of a real-time operating system.

The objects of a real-time software system resulting from integration of expert system components according to this concept are shown in Fig.5.

The expert system is represented by a set of tasks. Rules are transformed to asynchronous tasks, which can run in parallel. They are activating each other according to their goal driven way of processing. Frames are transformed to data types and facts become data which are located in a global memory section. Events are transformed to tasks as well. For the real-time operating system, there is no difference between a conventional task and a generated *expert system task*. Therefore, all services of the real-time operating system can be used to efficiently execute the transformed expert system. For example, the scheduling of tasks which are generated from events can be done by the event handling of the operating system.

7 Example

In order to demonstrate the capabilities of the methods mentioned above, the example of supervision of a technical system is given, using a semi formal language which is very similar to the syntax of our knowledge representation language. The problem at hand may consist of a control part and a diagnosis part. In order to control a continuous technical process, a control algorithm may be used which is implemented in a conventional programming language (e.g. C):

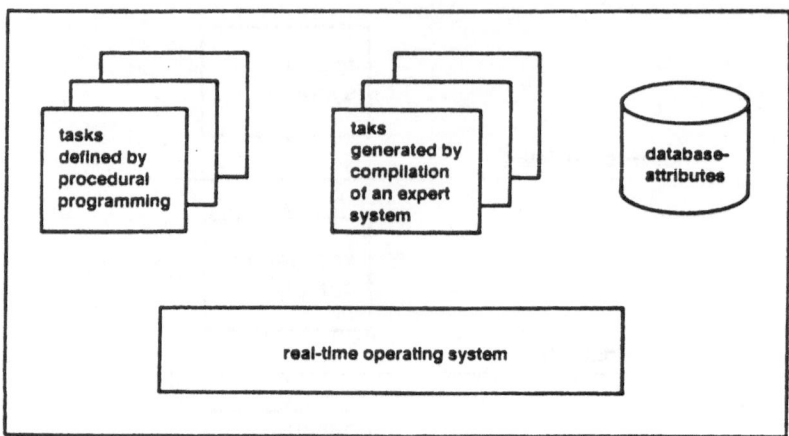

Fig. 5. Objects of a real-time software system including tasks resulting from compilation of an expert system

```
void control_task() {
    /* reading some data form sensor */
    take_sensor_values();
    /* calculate the control algorithm */
    calculate_PID_algorithm();
    /* send the new values to the physical system */
    send_data();
}
```

The diagnosis part — detecting faults in the technical process and localizing their causes — may be formulated using our knowledge representation language. After compiling it to the procedural level, it may be integrated with the control part. The new language feature *event* (see the above section 4) is applied describing what to do if a dangerous situation suddenly occurs.

The triggering condition of the event 'dangerous_situation' becomes true if the temperature and the pressure reach critical values. In the action part of the event the activation of the task 'DIAGNOSIS' is specified.

```
EVENT dangerous_situation
IF temperature > 150
AND pressure > 5
THEN activate DIAGNOSIS
```

Other events may handle further dangerous situations e.g. an external interrupt (SIGNAL 1):

```
EVENT halt_the_system
IF external (SIGNAL 1)
THEN activate STOP_PROCESS
```

The task 'DIAGNOSIS' is triggered by the event 'dangerous_situation'.

```
void DIAGNOSIS() {
    /* some actions which are always done when a fault is occuring */
    /* use of knowledge based techniques to determine the fault */
    infer (fault);
    /* actions which must be done to restore the process */
    message();
    restore();
}
```

Rules must be formulated to conclude the cause e.g. the cause for the rising of the temperature and the pressure. One reason for that may be a failure in the cooling system. The following rule 'water_pump' infers a possible reason for the incorrect work of the cooling system.

```
RULE water_pump
IF power = on
AND water_flow = 0 for more than 30 sec
THEN fault = water_pump
```

A simple condition (for more than 30 sec) is included in the premise of the rule to hint at the possibilities of representing temporal knowledge. The objects 'power', 'water_flow' and 'fault' which are referenced in the rule are defined as attributes of a frame 'cooling_system':

```
int water_flow infer;
FRAME cooling_system {
enum { on, off } power ask "power supply"?
enum { water_pump, ...} infer; }
```

The example shows in which way the different means of knowledge representation support the design of knowledge based systems for real-time application.

8 Conclusion

There is a need to apply knowledge-based techniques, e.g. expert systems in real-time environments [23]. For example, an operator in a nuclear power station can be confronted with 4000 analog and 5000 digital signals, resulting in a cognitive load in the event of a system problem. For the future, in many similar application areas, a few operators are required to evaluate complex situations and recommend actions. For knowledge-based systems to be effective in reducing this cognitive load in a real-time environment, they must have capabilities

- to reason about events occurring at certain times in the past, present or future
- to interrupt or change a reasoning process upon upcoming new inputs

- to respond predictively to important events within a given time interval, thus coping with hard or soft real-time deadlines
- to form an integral part of a real-time software system and to run under a real-time operating system.

In the preceding sections, methods have been presented which may provide some of these capabilities. The suggested method for integrating conventional real-time and knowledge-based programming brings along advantages and disadvantages:

- definite advantages are the ease of mixing conventional and knowledge-based techniques, as well as the fact that processing of compiled knowledge is faster than by using an inference engine of a shell
- disadvantages result from the strategy of using a host computer to develop the expert system, and to load the compiled *expert programs* into a target computer. Thus, debugging, modifying and maintaining of the expert system parts has to be performed off-line on the knowledge level. The consequences of changes can only be tested on-line after compiling to the procedural level.

The new concepts explained in this paper have been implemented, and they will be applied to additional examples in order to be evaluated further.

There are additional important concerns which have not been discussed in this article:

- The need of validating an expert system's knowledge. Methods have to be developed which allow to determine that an expert system accurately represents an expert's knowledge in a particular problem domain [14], [5].
- The requirement to prove the reliability or even the safety of an expert system, especially in life-critical applications such as nuclear power stations, oil platforms, or medical diagnosis. Unfortunately, there is not even a definition of reliability of knowledge-based systems, and we are far from being able to answer reliability questions [20]

In a recent editorial [6], the headline was: *Expert systems — ready for real-time?* Much research will still be needed to give a positive answer to this question, and current knowledge-based techniques will have a long way to go before they satisfactorily address all the concerns of real-time processing.

Acknowledgement

In his recent dissertation for Ph.D., Thomas Beck has developed and implemented methods to cope with real-time problems in expert systems [3]. The research results reported in this article are mainly based on this work.

References

1. J.F. Allen, *Maintaining Knowledge about Temporal Intervals*, Comm. of the ACM Vol. 26, No.11, 1983, 832–843.

2. Th. Beck, *A tool system for knowledge-based on-line diagnosis in Industrial Automation*, Proc. 2nd IEEE Int. Conf. on Tools for Artificial Intelligence, Herndon, VA 1990 (TAI'90) (W.T. Tsai, ed.), 424–429.

3. Th. Beck, *Verfahren zur Behandlung zeitlicher Beziehungen in Echtzeitexpertensystemen und zur Integration wissensbasierter Komponenten in Automatisierungssysteme* (Methods to consider time relations in real-time expert systems and to integrate knowledge-based components in automation software systems), Dissertation (in Germany), University of Stuttgart, Germany, 1992.

4. Th. Beck and R. Lauber, *Integration of an Expert System into a Real-Time Software System*, Preprints, 11th IFAC World Congress, Tallin, Estonia, August 13–17, 1990, Vol. 7, 158–161.

5. Childress, R., *Knowledge-based systems: Verification, Validation, and Testing*, IEEE Expert Vol. 7, No. 1, 1992, 73–75.

6. F. Coyle, *Expert Systems: Ready for Real-Time?*, IEEE Expert Vol. 5, No. 5, 1990, 12.

7. W. Halang and A.D. Stoyenko, *A comparitive evaluation of high-level real-time programming languages*, The Journal of Real-Time Systems, Vol. 2, 1990, 365–382.

8. R. Lauber and G.A. Permantier, *A Knowledge Representation Language for Process Automation Systems*, Preprints, 10th World Congress of IFAC, Munich, Vol. 6, July 1987, 330–333.

9. R. Lauber and U. Sens, *Tutor — ein wissensbasiertes System für die Ausbildung von Automatisierungsingenieuren* (TUTOR — a knowledge-based training system for automation engineers), Proceedings, Interkama-Kongress 1989 (G. Schmidt and H. Steusloff, editors), Munich: Oldenbourg 1989, 681–690.

10. R. Lauber, *Guest Editor's Introduction: Software for Industrial Process Control*, IEEE Computer, Vol. 17, No. 2, 1982, 6–8.

11. R. Lauber, *Automated Software Production*, AIAA/NASA Int. Symposium on Space Inf. Systems in the Space Station Era, June 22–23, 1987, Washington, D.C. Paper No. AIAA 87–2219.

12. R. Lauber, *Forecasting Real-Time Behaviour During Software Design Using a CASE Environment*, The Journal of Real-Time Systems, Vol. 1, 1989, 61–76.

13. T. Laffey, P.A. Cox, J.L. Schmidt, S.M. Kao and J.Y. Read, *Real-Time Knowledge-Based Systems*, AI Magazine Spring 1988, 27–45.

14. T. O'Leary, M. Goul, E. Moffitt and E. Radwan, *Validating Expert Systems*, IEEE Expert, Vol. 5, No. 3, 1990, 51–58.

15. W. Mettrey, *Expert Systems and Tools: Myths and Realities*, IEEE Expert, Vol. 7, No. 1, 1992, 4–12.

16. R.L. Moore, L.B. Hawkinson, C.G. Knickerbocker and L.M. Churchman, *A Real-Time Expert System for Process Control*, Proc. 1st Conf. on Artificial Intelligence Applications, IEEE Computer Soc., Washington, D.C., 1984, 569–576.

17. R. Moore, H. Rosenhof and G. Stanley, *Process Control using a Real-Time Expert System*, Proc. 11th IFAC World Congress, Tallinn, 1990, Vol. 7, 234–239.

18. C.J. Paul, A. Acharya, B. Black and J.K. Strosnider, *Reducing Problem-solving Variance to improve predictability*, Comm. of the ACM, Vol. 34, No. 8, 1991, 81–93.

19. W.A. Perkins and A. Austin, *Adding Temporal Reasoning to Expert-System-Building Environments*, IEEE Expert, Vol. 5, No. 1, 1990, 23–30.

20. T.L.D. Regulinski, *On Reliability of Expert Systems*, IEEE Trans. on Reliability, Vol. 40, No. 4, 1991, 401.

21. R.S. Shirley, *Some Lessons Learned using Expert Systems for Process Control*, IEEE Control Systems Magazine, Vol. 7, No. 6, 1987, 11–15.

22. Ch. Tong, *The Nature and Significance of Knowledge Compilation*, IEEE Expert, Vol. 6, No. 2, 1991, 88–91.

23. J.J.J.-P Tsai and H.-C Jang, *A Knowledge-based Approach for the Specification and Analysis of Real-Time Software Systems*, Int. Journal on Artificial Intelligence Tools, Vol. 1, No. 1, 1992, 1–35.

24. M. Truner, *Real-Time Expert Systems*, Systems International, Vol. 14, No. 1, 1986, 55–57.

Requirements Engineering and Design Tools for Real-Time Systems: the Protob Approach

Giorgio Bruno, Andrea Castella

Dipartimento di Automatica e Informatica
Politecnico di Torino
Corso Duca degli Abruzzi 24
10129 Torino
Italy

Abstract

The Protob methodology integrates several innovative features which have a strong impact on the software life cycle.

It can be applied to discrete event dynamic systems in general, such as real-time embedded systems, distributed systems, communication protocols and manufacturing control systems.

Protob exploits the object oriented paradigm throughout the software life cycle, including the feasibility study and the specification phase, while current specification techniques are based on functional decomposition. The internal dynamic behavior of objects is graphically defined by Prot nets, a formalism which integrates extended dataflows and Petri nets. Prot nets are executable: they enable the model dynamical analysis by means of simulation and rapid prototyping. They visually capture concurrency and synchronization in graphical if-then rules.

Operational, object oriented specifications are easy to understand and reuse. The specification model may be decomposed in components which may be studied and defined by several teams working in parallel. Problem knowledge may be formalized in models and passed on to others to form a library of building blocks.

The Protob methodology also covers the design, implementation and maintenance phases. Its formalism integrates high-level programming languages to form a model of the implementation software. The entire implementation code can be generated automatically.

Keywords

Automatic Code Generation, Dataflows, Distributed systems, Executable Specification, Object Oriented Design, Operational Software Life Cycle, Petri nets, Prot nets, Rapid prototyping, Real time systems, Simulation.

Acknowledgement

This work has been partly funded by the Italian C.N.R. project, *Progetto Finalizzato Sistemi Informatici e Calcolo Parallelo, obiettivo SPECTER*.

1 Introduction

It is well known that developing software for real-time systems is a challenging task. We point out two major problems:

1. *behavioral specification*; the system is conceived as made of concurrent activities interacting with each other and with external devices with well defined timing constraints; state-based evolution, concurrency, synchronization, communication, timing constraints are to be expressed in a rigorous way; we call *conceptual model* the rigorous description of such a behavior. The use of models is common in all disciplines in order to better understand and investigate the properties of complex systems. The same is true in software development where models help specify the functionalities of the software system and also define the architecture of the implementation: the latter models are called architectural models.
2. *validation and performance evaluation*; once defined, the model must be analysed in order to assess its quality (correctness, completeness) and its performance; this is a very difficult activity which is only partially assisted by tools; model inspection, discrete event simulation, analytical techniques must be combined in order to obtain the greatest benefits.

The use of models in accordance with operational [1] and evolutionary [2] principles can give raise to a powerful software development paradigm, which is characterized by the following aspects:

1. The model can be directly executable (operational) to allow a behavioral analysis of the model to take place at all stages of its development. Because of its complexity, a static description of the system does not provide sufficient insight into its real behavior. Model simulation is necessary to introduce a dynamic dimension, allowing both the validation of functional aspects and the performance evaluation of quantitative aspects to be carried out. Such analysis of the model, quite similar to a discrete event simulation [3], is to be performed on the requirements model itself instead of requiring an ad hoc simulation model to be built.
2. The model can be refined by adding new details so as to obtain a progression of more and more accurate prototypes the last of which leads to the actual implementation of the system.
3. A strong link as much automated as possible exists between the model and the actual code; we call automatic code generation the activity of obtaining from a model the actual implementation of the real-time system, which, in

general, consists of several execution processes distributed over a network of processors.

4. Maintenance is performed on the software model rather than on code. Automatic code generation guarantees code and its model to be consistent.

This paper presents the Protob methodology, comparing it to existing specification approaches and design techniques, and the operational life cycle it enables. Section 2 is a rapid overview of current specification and design methodologies. Section 3 introduces the Protob methodology with the feature it provides and the experiences of its application, while section 4 and section 5 give a detailed description of the Protob formalism and the Artifex support environment respectively. Section 6 describes the operational life cycle for the development of real-time systems.

2 Specification Methodologies

Structured analysis, based on *dataflows* [4], [5] or SADT diagrams [6], is one of the most popular specification techniques, but it is inadequate to describe a real-time system. The behavior of such systems, that is, their response to external stimuli, depends on their internal state.

The state is a mode of operation determining which activities are appropriate and which are not. The mechanism that triggers a certain activity or a change of state is referred to as an event. An event may indicate that a specific condition occurred, a certain time interval has elapsed or some message has been received. A state based behavior cannot be expressed using the traditional dataflow technique which accounts for data driven computations. For these reasons several extensions to dataflows were proposed, such as Hatley-Pirbhai's [7] and Ward-Mellor's [8] which have been termed *Structured Analysis/Real Time* (SA/RT). The two formalisms are equivalent and based on the same concepts: ESML, Extended System Modelling Language [9], is a proposal of integration of the two notations into a standard.

The basic idea of such extensions is to add to the usual dataflow specification a control specification based on a state transition diagram which describes the evolution of a subsystem's behavior through states and event-driven state transitions. At each state transition the proper dataflow transformations are enabled while the others are disabled. On a similar basis *statecharts* have been introduced by Harel [10] as extensions to finite state machines to control the activities of the modelled system and Stockenberg [11] extended SADT to deal with events. However, such extensions are limited in several aspects:

1. It is hard to understand statically a complex model described with extended dataflows. Its functional decomposition of data and control transformations results in a hierarchy of diagrams with a tangle of control flows going up and down the diagrams.
2. The model is not executable because data and activities are informally described. Some execution mechanisms have been illustrated in [12], [10], but

they require a continuous interaction with the user or a simulation control program to be written. The model has no information on time so the behavior of the system with respect to timing constraints may not be simulated.

3. As proposed by Ward in [8] and by Harel in [13] the specification model has to be substantially reworked to show the introduction of implementation details and to obtain the software architectural design consisting of processors, tasks and communication mechanisms.

If we focus on the specification of activity control we must consider Petri nets, well described by Peterson [14] and Murata [15], which are a powerful formalism for representing concurrency and synchronization issues. A mathematical theory that has developed around them to analyse their properties unfortunately requires a big effort to be understood and used. The complexity of unstructured Petri nets grows rapidly with the size of the modelled system and this limits their effective use to the description of parts of the system behavior. Several extensions to Petri nets have been proposed and studied to introduce structuring and timing: colored [16], timed and high-level Petri nets suitable for system specification [17]. The problem of casting Petri nets into programs and their usage as operational specifications has also been tackled by several authors [18], [19]. Petri nets are relatively simple to understand if their graphical meaning is used to describe activity synchronization. In fact they are more expressive and powerful than state transition diagrams to define the control of activities.

In the architectural design phase, the object oriented paradigm has gained a large consensus. The object oriented design was first proposed by Booch [20], [21] and subsequently enhanced by Buhr [22] for the design of Ada programs. On this experience several object oriented design methods have grown, one of which is a rigorous formalism and methodology called HOOD [23], [24] that has been adopted as a standard by the European Space Agency.

Buhr also proposed CAEDE [25], an enhancement of his previous work, for use with a data flow driven design methodology to design Ada embedded systems, automatically producing Ada skeletons, performing temporal and performance analysis of operational specifications. Wasserman [26] introduced object oriented structured design (OOSD) as an attempt of integrating structured design with object orientation not committed to the use of Ada. These visual design languages, however, tend to become rather intricate and dense when dealing with complex systems.

The application of the object oriented paradigm to the requirements specification phase would certainly contribute to fill in the gap between requirements and design. Moreover specifications would benefit of the well recognized qualities of object orientation. Object oriented analysis is a relatively young research topic and mainly addresses business applications [27], [28], [29].

A very promising research area concerns formal methods [30]: they are based on a sound mathematical background and intend to provide proofs about the properties of the modelled system. Despite of their theoretical interest those methods are not mature for actual applications except in very limited situations.

For a broad comparison of current specification techniques the reader is referred to the article by Davis [31].

3 Protob Major Features

The Protob methodology is the result of a research activity that started at the end of 1984. Milestones of this activity have been the definition of Prot nets [32] and their usage [19] in 1986, their organization and integration in the Protob object oriented formalism [33] in 1987, and the completion of the supporting CASE environment that performs the automatic generation of executable programs implemented using C or Ada [34] in 1989.

The scientific foundations consist of several concepts and techniques: operational software life cycle, executable specifications, object oriented paradigm, visual programming [35] and design [25], rapid prototyping. These ideas needed to be integrated in a common methodology and supporting environment to be used effectively.

Protob integrates these concepts in a unique methodology that can be applied to all the development and maintenance phases of a discrete event system. It allows a model of the whole system to be built. Each physical, hardware and software component can be modelled with a different object. The behavior of the modelled system and of each system component can be simulated, analysed and fed back to the specification, design and implementation phases. The software components can be generated automatically from the software model to be composed of several processes and distributed over a network. Interprocess and internode communications are handled in a transparent way by the software that the environment generated automatically. The environment allows the interactive monitoring of the generated code execution.

In brief, Protob provides four main, innovative features:

1. Object oriented paradigm. It is applied throughout the model at all stages of its development. The greatest benefits come from the application of the object oriented paradigm to the analysis phase rather than to the design and implementation ones. Concepts and solutions may be reused: company knowledge may be formalized in reusable building blocks. Protob emphasizes the effective object oriented analysis and specification of systems.

2. Graphical description of objects. A formal visual language describes each object clearly. Message passing and hierarchy mechanisms are defined in a formal and simple way. The dynamic behavior of an object is defined operationally in terms of graphical if-then rules that describe concurrency and synchronization aspects rigorously. The visual language is executable and enables the operational software life cycle: it may be automatically translated into code and executed.

3. Integration of standard, high-level programming languages. Each element of the graphical description may be associated with a fragment of code in a standard programming language like C or Ada. While the graphical language defines the control structure, data and sequential operations on data are

defined rigorously by code fragments. External functions in other modules and written in other languages may be called. This makes the model open to system integration and permits the reuse of existing software.

4. Automatic code generation. Each Protob model is automatically translated by the supporting environment into code and executed. This feature is used at all stages of the model development for different purposes: specification simulation for behavioral analysis and validation; prototype simulation for architectural design and implementation validation; device emulation for off-line system testing; system implementation and integration in the operating environment.

4 The Protob Formalism

Protob is based on high level Petri nets, called Prot nets, which are structured according to the object-oriented paradigm.

The object oriented paradigm focuses on objects, each object encapsulating a set of attributes and a set of operations which are the only means to manipulate such attributes. Classification, composition and inheritance are the structuring mechanisms provided by the object oriented approach.

The object oriented paradigm primarily is an architectural method stressing the interface and the structure of the building blocks constituting the overall software system. This is not sufficient to meet the needs of real time systems, because the major issues of concurrency and synchronization are not dealt with. To overcome this limitation several proposals have been presented: various alternatives are discussed in the reference [36]. For example, a server process may be associated with each object: the server is able either to carry out operations serially or to fork a different thread for each operation (in this case synchronization mechanisms are needed to manipulate the local variables of the object). However, this approach does not allow the actual dynamics of the object to be conceptually represented.

In Protob we emphasize a different point of view:

− each object is characterized by a behavior which is expressed by a high level net; its interface consists of input places and output places where tokens (i.e. messages) may be received or sent respectively;
− the overall model consist of communicating objects, communication being performed conceptually by message passing;
− objects may be mapped onto implementation processes (or threads) in a flexible way: one object into one process or several processes, several objects into one process; this mapping depends on the application and may be directed by the designer.

The remainder of this section describes the technical aspects of Protob. More details can be found in reference [37].

Classes in Protob convey most information visually by means of a formal graphical representation called net. Complementary textual information is provided in a script file. The graphical description of a class consists of several interconnected symbols which are illustrated in figure 1.

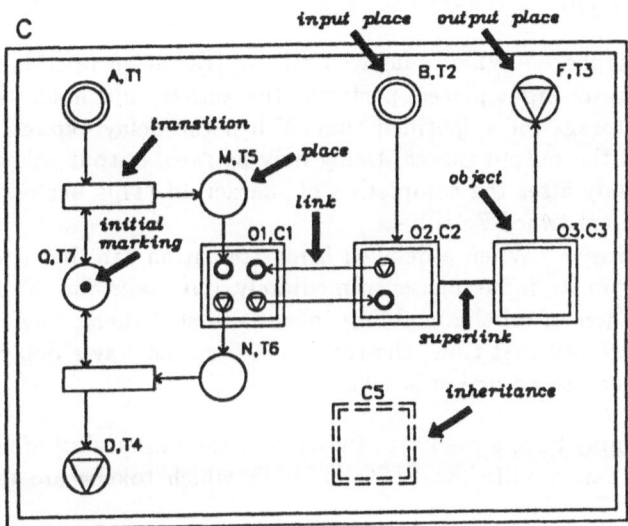

Fig. 1. Example of a Protob class.

Places, such as A, D, M contain units of information called tokens. Tokens are *mobile information packets.* They are structured data: essentially records. Each place can contain several tokens at a time, all of the same type. Places are basically queues of tokens; when a token is put into a place, it is added at the end of the queue. Tokens are usually taken from places in FIFO order. The type of tokens to be contained in a place is written, separated by a comma, after the place name. The type definition is given in the script using a standard programming language, such as C or Ada. The initial distribution of tokens, called *initial marking,* may be determined by associating with each place containing initial tokens a natural number (the number of initial tokens). Pictorially, places containing initial tokens are shown with a dot inside.

Transitions are the *processing units* of the model: when they are activated, they are said to fire. A transition carries out a token-driven computation, where the activation of the computation and the propagation of the information is established unambiguously by the input places and the output places of the transition. In fact, the necessary condition for a transition to fire is that each of its input places is not empty. When a transition fires, it removes one token from each of its input places and adds one token to each of its output places. When a transition fires, an action, specified in the script, can be executed: it is a piece of code, written in a conventional programming language, such as C or Ada, having the visibility of the tokens acted on by the transition. The action can modify the contents of propagated tokens, initialize the contents of created tokens and also perform external operations.

Transitions may also be given predicates, priorities and timing constraints. With respect to the timing constraints, the firing of a transition can be given two different behaviors:

Delayed release — When a delayed release transition fires, it fetches the tokens from its input places, performs the action, and holds the tokens in a private storage for a specified time. When the delay expires it delivers the tokens to the output places. Delay may be zero: output tokens are released immediately after the completion of the action. This behavior corresponds to the one of timed Petri nets.

Delayed firing — When a delayed firing transition can fire, it does not fetch tokens from its input places immediately, but waits for the firing delay to elapse. Then, if all the enabling tokens are still there, having been in the input places all that time, the transition fires the way a delayed release one does; otherwise no action is taken.

A transition may have a predicate (written in the underlying programming language), that can modify the FIFO order in which tokens are taken from the input places.

Finally, transitions may be given priorities (a positive integer following the name of the transition). When two transitions can fire at the same time, the one with the highest priority is chosen.

A Protob model is structured hierarchically into objects. An object, such as O1, has two identifiers, the first is its name, the second is the name of the class it belongs to.

Each class has an interface composed of special places, called input places or output places. An input place (A,B) allows the owner object to receive tokens from the outside, while an output place (D,F) allows it to send tokens to the outside. Two objects may communicate by sending tokens each other: the communication is defined graphically by drawing a link (i.e. an oriented arc) from an output place of the sender object to an input place of the receiver object: connected places must have the same type. A set of links between objects can be grouped into a single connection line, called superlink.

A class may contain objects (principle of composition) or may inherit other classes; the latter case is depicted by drawing the inherited class with dashed borders (C5).

4.1 An Example

As an example in figure 2 a portion of a real time system is shown. It is a part of an embedded automotive system for the measurement and display of the car speed. The system receives a pulse from a sensor every time the wheel completes a revolution. It must measure the periods of the input pulses, filter them with a simple low-pass digital filter and drive a hardware display. A hardware timer is to be used to measure the flow of time and to request an interrupt to be generated after a settable amount of time. The system must be able to drive the display and estimate the car speed independently. Initially, the estimated output period is set equal to a given starting value. The calls to the display driver must be made always, even if the measure of the last estimate is not over yet.

Transition	Delay
COMPUTE_FIRST_IN_P	1
COMPUTE_IN_P	1
SET_IN_P	1
UPDATE_IN_P	1
COMPUTE_OUT_P	2
UPDATE_OUT_P	1
EMIT_LOW	0.5
EMIT_HIGH	0.5

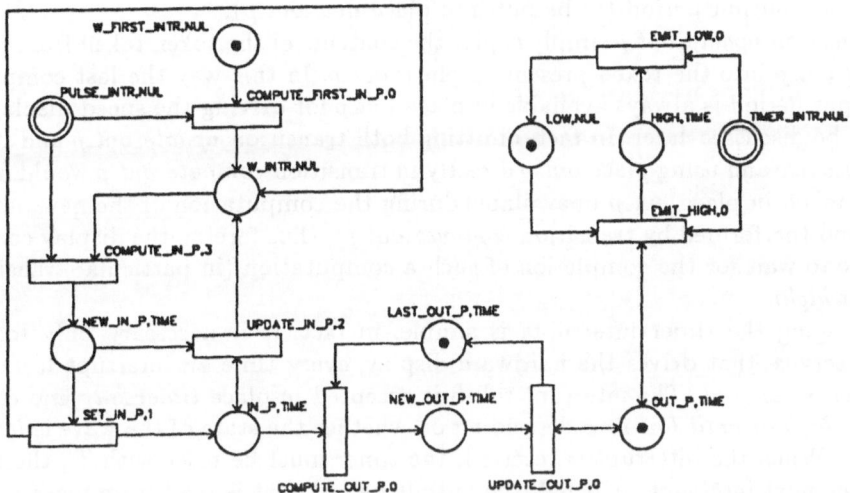

Fig. 2. Model of the automotive real time system

In the model shown in figure 2 three activities are to be performed concurrently:

1. to receive pulses at each wheel revolution and to calculate the input period (the time between two pulses);
2. to calculate the new period estimate as an average of the new measure and the old estimate;
3. to emit a signal (square wave) at a frequency proportional to the estimated speed.

Pulses are received in input place *pulse_intr*. The initial token in place *w_first_intr* enables transition *compute_first_in_p* that, when a pulse is received, gets the

first period from the timer. This value is discarded because it refers to the
interval from the instant at which the timer was started to the instant of the first
pulse. The second pulse and next ones are managed by transition *compute_in_p*
which gets from the timer the current period (from the previous pulse to the
current one): this period is written into the token to be released into place
new_in_p. Then, one of two transitions, *set_in_p* or *update_in_p*, fires: the former,
only if place *in_p* is empty, the latter otherwise; such a behavior is obtained by
giving priority to transition *update_in_p*. The reason for this is the following:
in some cases the period of pulses is less than the time needed to compute the
output period and tokens would queue in place *in_p* if transition *update_in_p*
were missing. To avoid such queueing of tokens, transition *update_in_p* replaces
the token present in place *in_p* (the old period) with the token taken from place
new_in_p (the new period).

Compute_out_p uses the most recent values of the input period and of the output
period, which are stored in places *in_p* and *last_out_p* respectively, to compute
the new output period (to be put into place *new_out_p*).

Transition *update_out_p* simply copies the contents of the token taken from place
new_out_p into the token present in place *out_p*. In this way the last computed
output period is always available in place *out_p* for driving the speed display, as
will be discussed later. In fact, omitting both transition *update_out_p* and place
new_out_p and using place *out_p* directly in transition *compute_out_p* would make
the token in place *out_p* unavailable during the computation of the new output
period (performed by transition *compute_out_p*), thus forcing the display control
logic to wait for the completion of such a computation (in particular transition
emit_high).

Managing the timer interrupts is simple: in fact, it is necessary only to call
the service that drives the hardware display, every time an interrupt from the
timer is received. The interrupt token is accepted in place *timer_intr* and either
emit_high or *emit_low* fires depending on whether the state of the wave is *low* or
high. When the interrupt is received, the timer must be reset with T_i, the time
to the next interrupt. It is half the output period that is read from place *out_p*.
T_i is then copied into the token put into place *high*, so that *emit_low* may set
the timer to the same value even if *out_p* has changed in the meanwhile.

For simplicity the contents of the script are omitted. More details on the example
can be found in reference [38].

5 Overview of Artifex

The Artifex toolset carries out the evolutionary model-based software development enabled by the Protob formalism. Its major tools are now illustrated.

The Editor/Animator allows the graphical representation of models to be built
and modified while performing immediate consistency checks; moreover, as an
animator, it is able to animate the model during simulation and actual execution
to facilitate system monitoring and debugging.

The Translators generate the executable programs in C or Ada (single process
or distributed) from Protob models into a variety of operating systems (UNIX,

VMS, DOS), communication networks (TCP/IP, DECNET), real-time kernels and customized platforms.

The Simulator Kernel implements a discrete event simulation engine which enables step-by-step execution, breakpoints, animation.

The Distributed Code Generator includes a translator for distributed systems, a configuration language and a set of servers for managing inter-process communication, a monitoring process.

The example given in figure 3 shows a model made of four objects, A,B,C and D, which are mapped onto distinct processes, A and B on node X, C and D on node Y; X and Y, for example, are heterogeneous workstations connected in LAN. For each node Artifex provides two servers: a local server (LS) which manages process activation/deactivation and responds to monitoring requests, a network server (NS) which carries out inter-node communications and detect node failures.

The third node shown in figure 3 may be optionally used to observe in real-time the state of the system through its model.

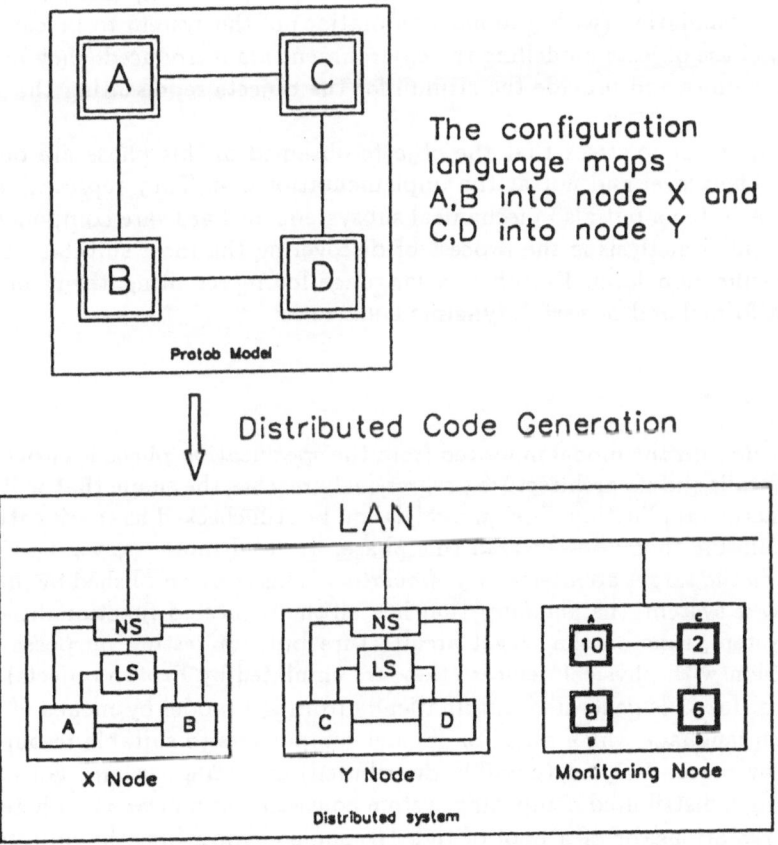

Fig. 3. Example of Distributed Code Generation.

6 The Operational Life Cycle Exploiting Protob and Artifex

Software development proceeds through the construction and refinement of models. It is an incremental process along which three major milestones can be identified: the specification model, the design one and the actual application. Such models are homogeneous, because they are based on the same formalism. Models are *conceptual* since they are based on a formalism providing a problem-oriented language rather than a high-level solution (programming) language. However, models are *operational* or *executable*: they can be automatically translated into *implementation code*, which are, in general, distributed software systems.

6.1 Specification

The **specification** model captures the high level behavior of the system (major functionalities and performance issues). Its executability results in a discrete event simulation program which is automatically produced; this allows the interactive validation (with graphical animation) of the system to be carried out. In this phase objects modelling the environment are introduced: they have their own dynamics and provide the stimuli for the objects representing the software system.

It is important to stress that the objects obtained in this phase are objects at the problem level and not at the implementation one. They represent abstract software systems but also mechanical subsystems or hardware components. Object oriented analysis is the process of discovering the most suitable objects at the specification level: Protob is a language for representing them and giving them a formal and powerful dynamic behavior.

6.2 Design

During **design** the model inherited from the specification phase is enriched with more details and its architecture progressively reaches the shape that will be kept in the actual application. Design models can be still checked as specification ones by simulating them; however, in this phase, we need more: we want to test the model on the target architecture in *emulation*. This is accomplished by producing a software system, the *emulator* that has all the requested functionalities of the final system, runs on the target architecture but, for testing purposes, has no connection with physical devices (they are emulated by Protob objects).

The **emulator** is generated automatically from the model by means of a configuration language which maps the model components to suitable resources managed by the underlying (possibly distributed) operating system. For example, assuming a distributed computing system consisting of a network of heterogeneous workstations, or of a pool of tightly coupled processors, the objects of the model can be automatically mapped to processes running on the target architecture; if two objects communicate in the model and they are mapped to different processes in the target architecture, their communication actually involves the use of the appropriate interprocess communication mechanisms.

Artifex generates a distributed program from a design model, provides management and communication services for the processes in the network and also allows real-time animation and monitoring of the distributed program to be carried out.

6.3 Application

The application model is generally obtained from the design one by replacing the objects emulating physical devices with suitable interfaces. At this point the conceptual model turns out to be the representation of the final system: it can be translated automatically into the final (possibly distributed) application.

It is clear that the model is the unique entry point to the software system: the maintenance will be performed on models.

7 Results

Artifex has been used in industrial applications since 1989:

- industrial users love it (and of course the underlying method) and in many companies it has become a standard. The major advantages they stress are the following:
  - understanding is improved. Artifex is an effective common language which facilitates communication among different people (with different skills) involved in a complex project: technologists, end-users, software implementors, system-integrators. Reusability is also greatly improved because the model is the only entry point to the actual software.
  - immediate feedback is provided. By executing the model, the analyst can get insight into the behavior of the intended system and perform accurate testing on the model; this reduces dramatically the time spent in tests carried out on the actual target.
  - productivity is enhanced. Automatic code generation allows efforts to be focused on the conceptual phases while implementation details, such as inter-process communication, are managed by Artifex. The statistics on the use of Artifex indicate, in the average, 30% saving on development costs.
- several software products designed and built with Artifex (this means that the code automatically produced by the model *is* the actual application) have been delivered and are in operation. Examples of applications are: numerical/robot controllers, supervisors of distributed systems in manufacturing and telecommunication.

8 Conclusion

The Protob methodology allows the same language to be used throughout the life cycle, thus eliminating risks of information losses, inconsistencies and time consuming translations. Attention may be focused on the conceptual aspects of the problem. The project history is documented by a series of models that are easy to understand, may be reused and can be passed on to others. By means of automatic code generation the software model is the software itself in a conceptual software language that is also the software documentation. The software model has all the information that was the product of the specification and design phases. The system's enhancement and maintenance will be performed on the model itself, not on code.

Protob therefore provides a common language to the teams in charge of system simulation, software and system specification, software development, software quality control and maintenance.

The development and maintenance efforts are reduced drastically.

Code is generated directly from Protob models during the whole life cycle. As the model is refined and shifted from the specification to the design and system integration phases, the generated code is used for specification animation, rapid prototyping and system implementation. Software maintenance can then be performed on the model itself rather than on code. When systems are very large and their behavior is complex, coding is not the problem. It is by far more important to build a correct and accurate model of the total system. Code optimization is a local aspect. It is of little use if the system specification and design are incorrect or have not been optimized themselves.

When developing large systems, each subsystem may work well on its own but fail to respond to all the prescribed events when connected to others. This is often the case when subsystem composition is tested only at the end of the development process. Prototypes should be generated automatically from models in order to test the software architecture, even on distributed hardware. Automatic code generation virtualizes task to task and node to node communications. Refining the model and adding suitable interfaces to the environment objects should have automatic code generation produce the deliverable system as final result.

References

1. P. Zave, *The operational versus the conventional approach to software development*, Communications of the ACM, February 1984, 104–118.
2. R. Balzer, T. E. Cheatham, and C. Green, *Software technology in the 1990's: using a new paradigm*, IEEE Computer, November 1983, 39–45.
3. G.S. Fishman, *Concepts and Methods in Discrete Event Digital Simulation*, John Wiley and Sons, 1973.
4. T. De Marco, *Structured analysis and system specification*, Prentice-Hall, 1979.
5. C. Gane and T. Sarson, *Structured systems analysis: tools and techniques*, Improved System Technology, 1979.

6. D. T. Ross, *Structured analysis (SA): a language for communicating ideas,* IEEE Transactions on Software Engineering, January 1977, 16–34.

7. D. Hatley and I. Pirbhai, *Strategies for Real-Time System Specification.* Dorset House Publishing, 1987.

8. P.T. Ward and S.J. Mellor, *Structured Development of Real-Time Systems,* Yourdon Press, 1985.

9. W. Bruyn, R. Jensen, D. Keskar, and P. Ward, *ESML: an extended systems modelling language based on the data flow diagram,* ACM SIGSOFT Software Engineering Notes, Vol. 13, 58–67.

10. D. Harel, *Statecharts: A visual formalism for complex systems,* Sci. Comput. Prog., Vol. 8, 1987.

11. R.H. Wallace, J.E. Stockemberg, and R.N. Charette, *A Unified Methodology for Developing Systems,* Intertext Publications Inc., 1987.

12. R. Blumofe and A. Hecht, *Executing real-time structured analysis specifications,* ACM SIGSOFT Software Engineering Notes, Vol. 13, 1988, 32–40.

13. D. Harel et al, *Statemate1: a working environment for the development of complex reactive systems,* Proceedings of the Tenth International Conference on Software Engineering, IEEE Press, 1988.

14. J. Peterson, *Petri nets,* ACM Computing Surveys, Vol. 9, September 1977, 223–253.

15. T. Murata, *Petri nets: Properties, analysis and applications,* Proceedings of IEEE, Vol. 77, April 1989.

16. K. Jensen, *Coloured Petri nets and the invariant method,* Theoretical Comput. Sci., Vol. 114, 1981, 317–336.

17. W. Reisig, *Petri nets for software engineering,* Petri Nets: Applications and Relations to Other Models of Concurrency, 1986, 63–96.

18. R.A. Nelson, L.M. Haibt, and P.B. Sheridan, *Casting petri nets into programs,* IEEE Transactions on Software Engineering, September 1983, 590–602.

19. G. Bruno and A. Balsamo, *Petri net-based object-oriented modeling of distributed systems,* ACM Conference on Object-oriented Programming, October 1986, 284–293.

20. G. Booch, *Object oriented development,* IEEE Transactions on Software Engineering, Vol. 12, February 1986.

21. G. Booch, *Software Engineering with Ada,* Benjamin/Cummings, California, 1987.

22. R. J. A. Buhr, *System Design with Ada,* Prentice Hall, Englewood Cliffs, 1984.

23. M. Heitz, *HOOD: Hierarchical Object Oriented Design for development of large technical and realtime software,* Technical report, CISI Ingenierie, Direction Midi Pyrenees, 1987.

24. HOOD Working Group, *Hood reference manual, issue 3.0,* Technical report, September 1989.

25. R.J.A. Buhr, G.M. Karam, C.J. Hayes, and C.M. Woodside, *Software CAD: a revolutionary approach,* IEEE Transactions on Software Engineering, Vol. 15, March 1989.

26. A. Wasserman, *An object oriented structured design method for code generation,* ACM SIGSOFT Software Engineering Notes, Vol. 14, January 1989.

27. P. Coad and E. Yourdan, *Object-Oriented Analysis,* Prentice Hall, Englewood Cliffs, 1990.

28. S. Shlaer and S. J. Mellor, *Object oriented systems analysis: modelling the world in data,* Prentice-Hall, 1988.

29. J. Rumbaugh, *Relations as semantic constructs in an object-oriented language*, OOPSLA '87 Proceedings, 1987, 466–481.
30. B. Cohen, W.T. Harwood, and M.I. Jackson, *The Specification of Complex Systems*, Addison-Wesley, 1986.
31. A. M. Davis, *A comparison of techniques for the specification of external system behavior*, Communications of the ACM, Vol 31, No. 9, September 1988, 1098–1115.
32. G. Bruno and G. Marchetto, *Process-translatable Petri nets for the rapid prototyping of process control systems*, IEEE Transactions on Software Engineering, February 1986, 346–357.
33. M. Baldassari and G. Bruno, *An environment for object-oriented conceptual programming based on prot nets*, Advances in Petri Nets, Lecture Notes in Computer Science Vol. 340, Springer-Verlag, 1988, 1–19.
34. M. Baldassari and G. Bruno, *An environment for operational software engineering in Ada*, Proceedings of the TRI-ADA'89 Conference, October 1989, 126–146.
35. *IEEE Computer special issue on visual programming*, August 1985.
36. R.S. Chin and S.T. Chanson, *Distributed object-based programming systems*, ACM Computing Surveys, Vol. 23, March 1991.
37. M. Baldassari and G. Bruno, *PROTOB: an object oriented methodology for developing discrete event dynamic systems*, Comp. Lang., Vol. 16, January 1991, 39–63.
38. M. Baldassari and G. Bruno, *A methodology and environment for the object oriented analysis and design of real time systems*, EUROMICRO'90 workshop on real time, 1990, 72–78.

The Role of Standards in Real-Time Systems

Hartwig U. Steusloff

Fraunhofer-Gesellschaft IITB
Fraunhoferstraße 1
76131 Karlsruhe
Germany

Standards and standardization are frequently regarded as matters of interest for trade and commerce. This is certainly true; however, recent standardization in the field of real-time systems for industrial automation shows clearly that standardization is increasingly influencing the technical development of areas under standardization. Therefore it is important for scientists and developers of such systems to know about the impact of standards and about the procedures towards the establishment of standards.

1 Why Standards? Which Standards?

Real-time systems for industrial automation need to be designed as Open Systems for achieving functional and economic optimization of complete production systems. Following a principle of duality between the flow of production and the flow of the related information, the openness of systems is a systematic way of matching the flexibility of production systems and the required adaptation of the information processing system. Open systems have to exhibit three properties:

OPEN = Extending existing information processing systems by new and possibly heterogenous components (i.e. different design or manufacturing of systems components on the basis of one set of well defined specifications) will not influence the cooperation of already existing components. If the specifications of the **communication functions** of such components are correct and complete, and if the new components are implemented in conformance to these specifications, the existing and the new compontents will be immediately able to communicate with each other.

SAFE = New components will not affect the safe operation of the existing components. This means that the underlying specifications of **system behaviour** are met and properly implemented.

TRUSTED = New components will not affect the **security sensitive aspects** of the already existing system. This is again achieved by properly and completely defined security specifications which are mandatory for the entire system.

Such definitions of properties of Open Systems indicate the requirements for standards at least for the communication functions ("open"), the safety functions ("safe") and the security properties ("secure"). These requirements are highly independent of the general application area of open systems and, therefore, hold for real-time systems as well.

2 Classes of Standards; Importance and Effect of Standards

When discussing standards for information processing systems, we have to be aware of dramatic changes in the duration of technology life cycles. In information processing we observe life cycles of only some years now, ranging from ca. 5 years for operating system software to one or two years of processing component innovation. Considering the ever increasing complexity of information processing systems, it is clear that the development of standards cannot wait for mature technologies as a basis for long term standardization.

Considering standardization in general, we will find two kinds of standards:

(a) *Standards fixing the state of the art:*
    the complexity of items for standardization is not too high; the number of variations is limited; applications are clear and application experience is available.
(b) *Standards capturing the state of development:*
    High complexity of items is handled by so-called PROFILES (application-area-oriented sets of functions and parameters out of the broader standard); application areas are broad and application experience is only available from prototypic implementations; this means that the elaboration of standards is part of the system or product development.

Frequent modifications of such standards are the result of experience from development and prototypes.

It should be pointed out that standards for information processing systems belong to class (b). In addition, standards for general information processing systems as well as for real-time systems (which will be applied to automation functions in production or products) have strong influences on positions and market shares of companies in national and in international markets. Standards have never played the role of just defining technical issues. But in to-days international markets, in Europe as well as world-wide, harmonized international standards are of outstanding importance for the economic efficiency of a company's production; development, production and maintenance of many product variations according to various national standards are no longer affordable.

3 Establishment and Acceptance of Standards

The establishment of standards for Open Systems today is taking place in very early phases of the underlying technology and the development of systems. This results in a strong influence of those scarce experts who are involved in the definition of standards as well as in the industrial development process of technologies; the influence of specific industrial interests, driven by market considerations, is hardly avoidable!

Standards of class (a) are developed on well established technologies meeting the requirements of an already existing market and therefore are based on a CONSENSUS at least of the key market players; this results in a broad acceptance and long-term stability of such standards.

Class (b) standards tend to represent a COMPROMISE achieved within a limited world of interested experts. The acceptance of those standards is market-oriented and their stability is therefore depending on changing market requirements.

From this market point of view, a third class of de-facto-standards must be considered. These class (c) standards describe commonly accepted technology platforms expressed and defined through "REPORTS" or "RULES". They are also subject to standardization procedures resulting in non-binding standard proposals. Depending on the degree of acceptance, these rules or reports can be as important as official standards (a) and (b); they may even turn the perhaps inefficient compromise of a class (b) standard into the precision of a class (a) standard. The effect of such class (c) "standards" and their stability may be much higher than the effect and stability of class (b) and even of class (a) standards; a well known example is the INTEL/IBM/DOS/AT-Bus–PC-standard.

The acceptance of standards is highly dependent on their quality. The quality of standards is determined by several aspects like

- the quality and availability of documents,
- the international harmonization,
- the support of market penetration through organisations,
- available pilot experience with the use and implementation of a standard,
- quality assurance provisions for the implementation of a standard.

The latter aspect has become particularly important during the last 10 years resulting in standards for quality assurance in general as well as in specific testing standards which will be discussed later.

4 Standards in the Field of Real-Time Systems

Standards are indispensible for the economic development and application of real-time systems and for industrial production and products. They provide information and clarity about properties of products and production processes.

Real-time systems need standards in various areas. In the following we will discuss some of these areas which attract particular interest at present.

4.1 Engineering of Real-Time Systems

Engineering is of ever increasing importance for the correct and economic planning, implementation and operation of real-time systems. Areas of concern are:

- Methods for system engineering
- Languages for describing system properties and configurations
- Methods and tools for the support of the life cycle of a system
- Specification languages and their (automatic) transformation into programming languages for system implementation
- Symbols for expressing system properties and configurations in an internationally understood uniform and unique way.

This all has to be considered under a basic engineering model for industrial real-time systems underlying most of the standards mentioned later. First we have to distinguish betweeen the technical process and the equipment for its operation where equipment comprises the genuine production equipment as well as auxiliary equipment like the automation system. The engineering model then includes the aspects of planning, operation, maintenance and documentation of the system under consideration.

Even if in some areas process technology is a matter of standardization, we will discuss the engineering of the real-time information processing part of such systems. Apart from the engineering of basic processing equipment like computers which is not specific to real-time or automation systems, there is an increasing number of engineering-oriented language standards for application engineering. Examples of such standards include:

- STEP: a programming language for industrial controllers
- IEC 1131-3: a family of programming languages for manufacturing control
- IEC 848: specification of production operations
- EDIF: interchange format for engineering data
- ISA SP88: batch control systems

4.2 Real-Time System Architectures and Components

Components of general real-time computer systems as

- processing and storage hardware,
- operating systems,
- programming languages,
- database systems,

– communication networks,

are under standardization as well. Industrial real-time computer systems are subject to electrical and functional safety and EMI (ElectroMagnetic Inference) standards. Some of the a.m. components are summarized under the new term "information logistics" where

– Communication,
– Storage (DBS),
– Presentation and
– Modelling

are discussed under the aspects of interdependencies with the goal of achieving an optimized infrastructure for complete real-time systems in industrial automation. The German standardization body of DKE (Deutsche Elektrotechnische Kommission) has just started considerations on system aspects as a basic structuring means for establishing required standards in the field of industrial automation.

System aspects introduce the notion of system architectures as a work item for standardization. In real-time systems standardization currently highly efficient communication architectures are under special consideration: Time Critical Communication Architectures (TCCA) and the Fieldbus.

TCCA constitute a reduced layer communication architecture for special purpose applications where full networking capabilities are not required and fast reaction is of outstanding importance. Such architectures usually consist of three layers with respect to the seven ISO-OSI-layers defined for safe and dependable communication facilities between two partners in an arbitrarily structured communication network (WAN = wide area network). These three layers are the Physical Layer (OSI-layer 1; the physical data transportation medium, like twisted pair wires, coaxial lines etc. plus the required definition of electrical or optical signals), the Link layer (OSI-layer 2; medium access and logical link control plus interface to the application layer) and the Application layer (OSI-layer 7; application supporting functions).

The absence of the OSI-layers 3 through 6 dealing with arbitrary networks speeds up the operation of such protocol architectures, but restricts them to Local Area Networks (LAN) and to messages of link unit length. Some fieldbus standards have recently been proposed for TCCA.

TCCA is an activity of ISO/TC 184/SC 5. Among the goals of this committee are the definition of user requirements for systems supporting time-critical communications, performance testing for time-critical application protocols, network management for time-critical communication systems and the use of the MMS standard (manufacturing message specification, part of most industrial LAN protocol standards, like MAP and fieldbus standards) in time-critical communication systems.

Special problems under consideration are the size of messages (alarm messages!), delivery times to be guaranteed, message priority at MAC layer (part of OSI layer 2: medium access control), assessment of the probability of meeting timing constraints, performance metrics and the Quality of Service framework comprising QoS–categories (requirements) and QoS–characteristics (models).

4.3 Fieldbus Standards

After experiences with the standardized LAN protocols for manufacturing and technical office applications (MAP = Manufacturing Application Protocols; TOP = Technical and Office Protocols [1]) the communication in the field level of industrial real-time became the next area of interest. In the field level we have to consider the communication between field devices (sensors, actuators, intelligent devices of various kinds) and the plant computers. While this communication so far is performed by a star-shaped cabling structure with analog communication of measurement and actuator data (digital control information for intelligent field devices being transferred separately via dedicated additional cabling), the increasing complexity of production processes and consequently the rising costs for traditional cabling generated the digital field bus. The fieldbus, a LAN, connects a number of field devices to a number of plant computers.

This connection provides digital information transfer by use of a LAN protocol which is subject to TCCA criteria. A number of protocols for this purpose are already existing at present and it is very important for the international automation and measurement industry to arrive at one international standard as soon as possible.

The current situation of fieldbus standards may be characterized by at least two problems:

- The definition of "field" is still unclear! A field device could be a "near-line" device for monitoring or analyzing process data, but also an "on-line" device within a control loop of high sampling rates.
- Several national fieldbus proposals are already existing! Some of these proposals have even been implemented in silicon chips and much effort and money has already been invested to evaluate the porperties and the applicability of these national standards.

National or market driven fieldbus standards as presently available are

- in France : FIP (AFNOR-standard)
- in Germany: PROFIBUS (DIN-standard)
- in USA: Honeywell, Rosemount et.al.
- in Japan: FAIS

Other bus system proposals for field applications are the so-called "sensor/actuator bus" protocols. The idea behind these developments is a complementation of the fieldbus standards for high performance applications within the closed loop; some industrial groups feel that the special requirements of such applications (very high data rates, strict observance of real-time conditions, short telegram length, environment with severe EMI) would overstress the a.m. fieldbus protocols. Examples of such proposed standards are

- in Germany: InterBus-S et.al.
- international: SERCOS = "Electric Drive Cell Bus" (IEC, under standardization).

Current international activities in the fieldbus areas are carried out by

- IEC SC 65C WG6: International fieldbus committee
- ISA SP50: Definition of the international fieldbus co-operating with IEC SC 65C
- Industrial group (Fisher/USA, Siemens/FRG, Rosemount/USA, Yokogawa/JAP): "Interoperable Systems Project" (ISP). This group tries to establish an industry driven standard as soon as possible; ISP wants to combine features of existing fieldbus standards in an economically optimized manner.

The acceptance of specific standards can be supported by user groups. Some of the standards with already available products in the market have built up user groups like

- FIP-Club → FIP bus (France)
- PROFIBUS Nutzer Organisation (PNO) → PROFIBUS (Germany)
- DriveCom-Group: InterBus-S (Germany).

Membership of these groups is not restricted to those nations where the bus development has taken place. The fieldbus movement is an international matter and is certainly considering the world-wide market of real-time systems in measurement and automation.

The question may arise whether it is already too late for *one* international fieldbus standard. Certainly it is a fact that much effort has been put into the development of the currently available national standards. It is, however, rather clear that from an application point of view there may well be several standards for the communication in the field level of industrial production. Therefore it is of outstanding importance to define fieldbus standards in a consistent way in order to support the interoperability of different standards. Presently two test methods are favoured for this purpose: the conformance test and the interoperability test. For the acceptance of even various standards in the same area of technology it is necessary to define and standardize such tests in a consistent and reproducible way.

4.4 Quality Assurance and Standards

Considering quality assurance in real-time systems for industrial production we have to mention two different kinds of quality standards.

First real-time systems must meet quality standards for coping with product liability aspects and safety aspects. Such obligations are supported by a family of international quality standards: ISO 900x. ISO 900x supports a quality management system:

- ISO 9004: Organisation, responsibilities, procedures and resources for quality management;
- ISO 9001: Development, supply and maintenance of software.

The requirements of ISO 900x so far do not seem to be complete and sufficient since there are several other activities towards a complete quality management [2]:

- Europe: "Total quality management"
- World-wide: "Zero-fault-strategy"
- Japan: "Poka-yoke".

However, the increasing importance and consideration of ISO 900x shows that this is a promising way of tackling the problems of quality in complex industrial production processes.

Another issue is the quality assurance of standards themselves. Standards for open systems need verification of their implementations as a support of their acceptance. In particlar, open systems must provide interoperability between components developed and manufactured according to standardized specifications.

A recommendable way of achieving and maintaining interoperability would enforce strictly formal specifications of standards which then would allow the formal verification of system components developed according to such specifications. So far, the state of the art in formal specification and verification of complex system components is still insufficient. Specifications usually contain natural language parts and, due to the ambiguities of natural languages, formal verification of such specifications is not possible. The only realistic way of predicting interoperability is *testing* the compliance of products with their (standardized) specifications ("conformance test") or testing the behaviour of several interoperating products under real-life conditions ("interoperability test").

The basic idea of conformance testing is transitivity; if two or more implementations of the same specification respond to the same test cases in an identical way then these implementations should be able to interoperate correctly and according to the underlying specification. If such conformance tests are complete and themselves correct then this assumption is correct as well.

Fig. 1 shows the basic structure of a conformance test system. The IUT, the implementation under test, is embraced by the lower tester and the upper tester. The IUT may be an OSI layer implementation as part of a LAN. The lower tester must behave like the underlying OSI layers, and the upper tester replaces the OSI layers on top of the layer under test. The lower tester executes the test cases by sending protocol data units ("PDU"s) to the IUT which then responds to the lower tester, and the upper tester by sending back appropriate PDUs. The result of such a test case is either the expected and correct PDU or an unexpected PDU indicating an implementation error of the IUT.

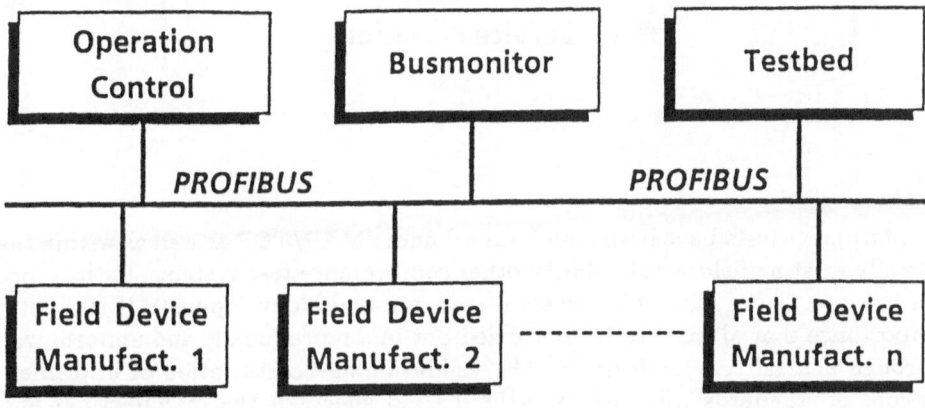

Fig. 1. Conformance Testing.

Unfortunately, tests will never have a coverage of 100% of all possible test cases and cannot, like verification, ensure the absence of errors. Even a successful conformance test of several protocol implementations therefore will not assure interoperability of these components. The only way of achieving a high probability of real life interoperability is another test, the already mentioned interoperability test. Fig. 2 shows a possible configuration for testing the interoperability of system components. Presently a number of research institutions is developing interoperability test systems even if a way of arriving at standards for interoperability testing is still not visible.

Even interoperability tests will not necessarily cover all the parameter variations which are included in some standards. Additional testing methods are therefore under definition or at least under consideration like performance tests or security tests. On the long term, all these tests will be included in standards for open systems, providing means for assuring the quality of standardized functions within system components [3].

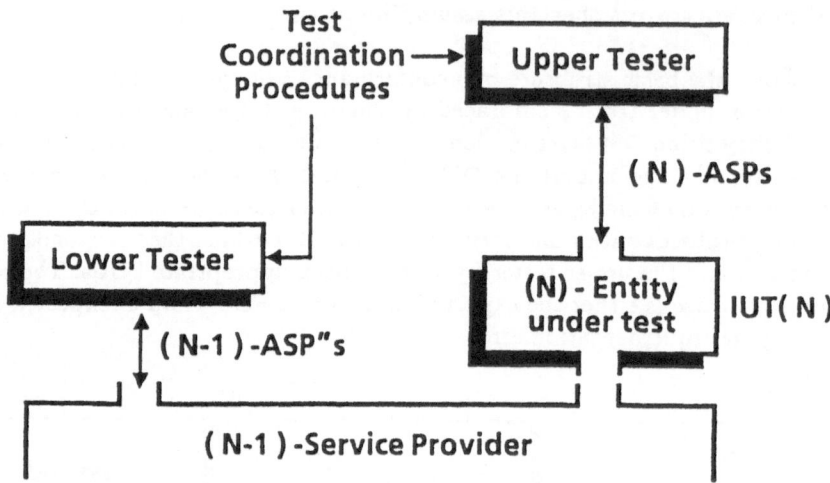

Fig. 2. Interoperability Testing.

Conformance tests have been standardized under MAP/TOP as well as within the already existing fieldbus standards; other conformance test systems, for instance for the a.m. sensor/actuator bus standards, are under development. It is of vital importance that all such tests are carried-out in a reproducible and uniform way through neutral test institutions. The validation and certification of implementations of standards will only have the desired effect for the manufacturer and end user of open systems if the results of conformance or interoperability tests are reproducible throughout the system life cycle and are free of any suspicion of manipulation. The European approach for the establishment of test facilites consists of two layers:

- ETCOM defines standards for the approval of test labs; these standards comprise procedures for the organization of such labs, for the documentation of test systems and test results and for audits.
- National accredited test labs will be accredited by national authorities assuring and auditing the correct implementation of ETCOM standards.

Currently, accredited test labs will issue validation documents presenting the results of standardized tests under the ETCOM rules. Certifications of tested system components will be the next step and are under preparation by the international and national standards organizations.

5 Failure and Success in Standardization

Standardization projects sometimes fail! There are several reasons for such failures:

- No strong demand for the standardization item from the market! A well known example is the PROWAY standard (IEC Public. 954)) aiming at similar goals as to-day's fieldbus standards.
- Standardization item too complex! The item may be too far ahead of the market demands or related scientific work is still incomplete.
- No sufficient availability or support of experts! Key market players may not be interested in the standard.
- Completion time for the standard was too long! Technology development was faster than the development of a related standard.
- Pilot implementations were not succesful or not considered! The development of standards in parallel with the development of technologies needs early prototyping.
- Competition of several standardization projects! Situation with relation to the introduction of standards may be confusing, standards may be ill defined.

Reasons for successful standards can be:

- All market players involved benefit from the standard!
- Standards are built on experience! This experience should be based on the use of standards in the market or at least on pilot implementations.
- Clear application demands! This is of outstanding importance for a successful standard.
- Sufficient support of experts! This support should include expert work from industry as well as scientific side activities for complex and highly advanced standardization items.
- Pilot implementations! Early prototyping in the course of defining standards is essential for the quality of standards.

The international standardization community is increasingly accepting these basic requirements. Nevertheless, market considerations will be the driving force towards or against standards; not all future standardization projects will be successful.

6 National and International Standards

The market of industrial products and systems nowadays is clearly an international and world-wide market. This holds as well for the market of real-time systems in industrial measurement, control and automation. Certainly there are numerous aspects to be considered like market protection and different legal and economic environments (e.g. safety regulations). On the other hand, users as well as manufacturers of real-time systems need large and world-wide markets for exploiting technologies and providing attractive pricing conditions through the production of large quantities of uniform products. Another aspect is international maintenance of systems and the education of an international user community. All these aspects ask for world-wide standards for real-time systems.

Standardization of real-time systems in automation and general information processing systems is performed by national standardization bodies under international rules. Examples for national standardization authorities are in

- Germay: DIN with its suborganisations for different fields of technologies (DKE → electric/electronic; NAM → manufacturing; NI → information processing; etc.)
- France: AFNOR
- UK: BSI
- USA: ANSI.

It is certainly not possible to mention all national standardizations authorities here. The different ways of financing those national activities is an important and sometimes crucial issue.

In international standardization we find some very well-known organizations:

- ISO (USA, world-wide)
- IEC (USA, world-wide)
- CEN / CENELEC (Europe)
- CCITT (Europe, world-wide).

In ISO and IEC some specific committees are of importance for real-time systems:

- ISO TC 184 "Industrial automation systems & integration"
- ISO/IEC JTC 1 → ISO 7498 (7-layer communication model)
- IEC TC 44 "Electrical equipment of industrial machines"
- IEC TC 65 "Industrial process measurement & control".

There is a world-wide correspondence between national standardization bodies and those a.m. international organizations. Institutes and institutions like ISA in the USA or VDI/VDE in Germany are co-operating with the official standardization organizations.

Standardization is an important field for industrial and, not at all to be missed, the military markets and systems. In the area of real-time systems, standardization is a highly challenging and interesting matter which needs the best experts and scientists available for a fruitful international co-operation towards useful and high quality standards.

References

1. Birtel, P., *Conformance Testing for MAP/TOP*, ENTERPRISE Conference Proc. 88, Baltimore, Maryland, 4-117–4-128.
2. Schmitt, K.H., Wünnenberg, J., *Quality Management in Process Control Engineering and Control*, Proceedings of the INTERKAMA Congress 92, Oldenbourg, München (in English), 516–524.

3. *Integration of Design, Implementation and Application in Measurement, Automation and Control*, H. Steusloff, M. Polke (eds.), Proceedings of the INTER-KAMA Congress 92, Oldenbourg, München (in English), 473–480.

Design of the Local Network Administrator in the Maritime Information Technology Standard (MITS) Real-Time Network

Petter Haave

SINTEF
7034 Trondheim
Norway

The purpose of the MITS project has been to design and build a network system which can be used on-board ships to interface sensors and control systems using conventional communication standards. The backbone system will be based on ethernet and the TCP/IP protocol, but also components using other serial communication standards like RS-232 or fieldbus can be a part of the network.

The network has been designed with number of Local Network Administrators (LNAs) connected to an ethernet LAN, acting as hubs in the network. Each sensor or control system has a MITS Application Interface (MAPI) which together with the application forms a MITS Application Unit (MAU). Each MAU can connect to a LNA through the ethernet or through a serial line. This connection enables it to communicate with all other MAUs in the system using a symbolic names for the MAUs and their data. The LNA will handle the routing of the messages. In addition to these units, is there also a set of Communication Nodes for Administrative Messages (CNAs) which handles the database of the names and locations of connected MAUs.

The LNA will be an event driven system. It has to respond to input events from four different types of sources: MAUs that are local to this LNA, other LNAs, the local CNA and the console interface. In addition to this, it must also be able to handle timeout events.

Our solution to this problem has been to implement a generic event scheduler multiplexing between the different I/O and timeout events. This scheduler is based on BSD sockets and the UNIX select system call.

Obvious advantages of this solution are:

- Simple design that is easily ported to other platforms.
- Allows several concurrent "state machines".
- No need for protection of the data structures since there are no race conditions.
- All event "processes" can use the same context.
- Compatible with the X windows system.

On the other hand has this solution also its disadvantages.

- No possibility for per message priority.
- No preemption for higher priority events.

The scheduler has worked very well in our demonstration versions of the network, but being a system that can be used for transport of vital messages within a ship's control systems, we are concerned about the lack of priority in this scheduling scheme.
We see some possible solutions to these problems:

- Using the TPC/IP urgent mechanism to get message priority
- Adding priority to the message channels.
- Using threads / lightweight threads.
- Using a multi process solution.

I will discuss the pros and cons of these solutions in my talk.
Albeit its lack of priority mechanisms, the current design is in any case useful for transporting non-vital information from different sensors to monitor systems and for administrative purposes. The main benefits as seen from the maritime industry are reduced cabling cost and the ability to interface equipment from different vendors.

The Reality of a Real-Time UNIX Operating System

Borko Furht

Department of Computer Science & Engineering
Florida Atlantic University
Boca Raton, Florida 33431
U.S.A.

1 Introduction

Industry standards will be the basis for the next generation of real-time systems. These industry standard systems, termed Open Systems, provide a number of advantages for users. Open systems reduce system cost and time to market, increase availability of software packages, increase ease-of-use, facilitate system integration, and can provide complete software portability.

The UNIX operating system has become a de facto standard operating system gaining rapid acceptance because of its superior flexibility, portability, and the large number of available support tools for increased programmer productivity. However, since the UNIX operating system was originally designed for multitasking and time-sharing, it does not provide the necessary response time nor the data throughput capacity to support most time-critical applications. This presentation discusses techniques to transform the UNIX operating system into a high performance real-time operating system and presents a case study of the REAL/IX operating system.

Numerous attempts have been made to adapt the UNIX kernel to provide a real-time environment. Because each implementation is dependent on the type of processor and the specific application code used, it is very difficult to compare performance among all of the real-time versions of the UNIX systems.

One classification method, that we propose, divides real-time UNIX implementations into six categories. These six categories, along with the companies taking these approaches, are summarized in Table 1. These six approaches are discussed below.

2 Adding Extensions to the Standard UNIX Operating System

In this implementation approach to a real-time UNIX operating system extensions are added to the core UNIX operating system. The real-time extensions can be implemented in the kernel or outside of the kernel. This is the approach taken by system-level vendors, such AT&T in its System V.4 UNIX release. Some

TECHNIQUES	OPERATING SYSTEM & COMPANY	
1. Adding extension to the standard UNIX operating system	• AT&T System V.4	
2. Host-target approach	• VxWorks	(Wind River Systems)
	• OS/9	(Microware)
	• VRTX	(Ready Systems)
3. Integrated UNIX and real-time executives (or real-time OS)	• MTOS-UX	(IPI)
	• RTUX	(Emerge Systems)
	• CSOX	(Computer X/Motorola)
	• D-NIX	(Diab Systems)
4. Proprietary UNIX operating system	• LynxOS	(Lynx Real Time Systems)
	• Regulus	(Alcyon)
5. Preemption points	• RTU	(Concurrent/Masscomp)
	• HP-UX	(Hewlett Packard)
	• VENIX	(VenturCom)
6. Fully preemptive kernel	• REAL/IX	(MODCOMP)
	• CX/RT	(Harris)
	• HP-RT	(Hewlett-Packard)
	• Solaris 2.0	(SUN)
	• AIX	(IBM)
	• DEC OSF/1	(DEC)
	• IRIX	(Silicon Graphics)

Table 1. Classification of Real-Time UNIX Implementations.

examples of adding extensions to the UNIX operating system include priority-based scheduling, real-time timers, and priority disk scheduling. Although this approach provides real-time functionality, it has its drawbacks. The main drawback is that this approach does not allow full preemption in the kernel mode. When an application task makes a system service call, and the task goes into kernel mode, the system has to complete that service call before a higher priority task can get the CPU.

3 Host/Target Approach

The host/target approach to using the UNIX operating system in a real-time environment is to develop an application on a UNIX host and then download it to a proprietary real-time kernel or to another operating system running on a target system. For example, in the case of VxWorks operating system, developers use the UNIX host for development, which includes editing, compiling, linking, and storing real-time applications. Then the program is tested, debugged and executed on the target machine running VxWorks. The host and target communicate via sockets and TCP/IP protocol.

The host/target approach combines the advantages of the UNIX operating system with those of a proprietary real-time kernel. The response time of a reduced functionality proprietary kernel (under 10 microseconds) is still faster than the response times of real-time UNIX implementations (from 70 microseconds to a few milliseconds). However, this approach requires two operating systems and the porting of application software to other platforms is more difficult.

4 Integrated UNIX Environment and Real-Time Executive/OS

This technique provides a UNIX interface to a proprietary real-time kernel or a proprietary real-time operating system. Both a UNIX system and the proprietary kernel/OS run on the same machine. The MTOS real-time kernel has been developed, for example, which can log onto a UNIX system. The user can utilize the development tools in the UNIX environment to develop the real-time application, and then run that application in the proprietary operating system environment. This implementation provides the fast real-time response of the proprietary real-time systems, however it requires two operating systems, and the porting of applications is more complicated.

5 Proprietary UNIX Operating System

This approach to a real-time UNIX operating system consists of developing a proprietary real-time kernel from the ground up while maintaining the standard UNIX interfaces. For example, Lynx and Regulus operating systems use this approach. Their internal implementations are proprietary, however the interfaces are fully compatible with a traditional UNIX operating system such as the AT&T System V operating system. These interfaces are specified with standards such as SVID and IEEE POSIX.

A proprietary (custom) real-time UNIX operating system provides relatively high-performance, however porting real-time applications to or from another real-time UNIX implementation requires rewriting code. Standard UNIX applications will run under these operating systems, but code that uses the real-time extensions will need to be rewritten.

6 Preemption Points

Another real-time UNIX implementation approach is to insert preemption points, or windows into the operating system kernel. Preemption points are built into the kernel, so that system calls do not have to block or run to completion before giving up control. This can reduce the delay before the higher-priority process can begin or resume execution. However, as an impact of preemption points, there is still a preemption delay which may be as high as several milliseconds.

7 Fully Preemptive Kernel

A fully preemptive real-time UNIX operating system allows full preemption anywhere in either the user or the kernel mode. The preemptable kernel can be built by incorporating synchronization mechanisms, such as semaphores and pin locks, to protect all global data structures. By implementing a fine granularity of semaphores, the preemption delay can be reduced to no more than approximately 100 microseconds. A fully preemptive kernel provides the system with the ability to respond immediately to asynchronous events, to break out of the kernel mode, and to execute a high-priority real-time process. Most real-time UNIX operation systems of the new generation, listed in Table 1, implement a fully preemptive kernel.

The REAL/IX operating system is MODCOMP's real-time implementation of the UNIX System V.3 operating system. By providing a full kernel preemption, enhanced task scheduling, extended interprocess communication, as well as a fast file system and enhanced I/O subsystem capabilities, the REAL/IX operating system delivers the predictable performance required by real-time applications.

A major design feature that provides deterministic behavior and high performance interrupt handling is the fully preemptive nature of the kernel. In conventional implementations of the UNIX operating system, a process executing a system call (i.e., operating within the kernel system space) cannot be preempted. Regardless of the priority of the calling process, system calls execute until they block or run to completion. In contrast, within the REAL/IX operation environment, lower priority processes can be interrupted at any time and a higher priority process can begin executing.

The fully preemptive kernel has been implemented through the use of semaphores that protect global data structures in the REAL/IX kernel and assure their integrity. Through the fine granularity of the semaphore implementations the process dispatch latency time has been reduced to about 6 microseconds on the MODCOMP Real/Star 1000 system. The Real/Star 1000 is based upon a 25 MHz Motorola 88100 CPU running the REAL/IX operating system. The REAL/IX operating system uses spin locks and suspend locks (or kernel samphores) to ensure data structure integrity in the preemptive kernel. If two processes access the same global data structure, it is important that the first process completes any update of that structure before the second process accesses it. In a traditional UNIX kernel, this is handled by disabling interrupts to prevent an interrupt handler from accessing a data structure that was being manipulated by process-level kernel code. If the preemptive kernel were implemented without locks, a higher priority process could cause a context switch from a lower-priority process even though it is in the process of updating a data structure, and thus corrupt the structure.

Other real-time functions, implemented in the REAL/IX operating systems and discussed during the presentation include: fixed priority scheduling, fast interrupt handling, fast and reliable interprocess communication and synchronization facilities, fast file system, improved I/O system, and user control of system resources.

Real Time Aspects of Manned Space Flight Avionics Computing

Alfred Anderman

Rockwell Space Systems Division, MS/FB96
12214 Lakewood Blvd
Downey, CA 90241
U.S.A.

1 Summary

A Category III Precision instrument landing system (ILS) approach requires 18 ft horizontal and 2.2 ft vertical accuracy at 50 ft above the ground, and is probably the most severe real-time flight control task. If the Global Positioning System in differential mode (DGPS), integrated with inertial, barometric and/or radar altitude sensors, and supported by real-time fault tolerant computing, is to be approved by the ICAO and FAA for automatic landings, additional requirements of availability and integrity at the $(1 - 10^{-9})$ level must be met for civil aviation. Onboard real-time health management requires advances in on-board processing, memory, and communications. Technical feasibility was established as part of the DARPA Pilot's Associate project, but it did not function in real-time. To minimize cost and risk of migrating GSE diagnostic systems to the onboard environment, use of the Rockwell Science Center developed "Simulation Analysis of Distributed Systems (SADS)" is being recommended to ensure adequate real-time performance.

2 Discussion

As an example of the real time constraints applicable to future reusable launch vehicles, some recent results of RTCA data collection and analysis for GPS Receiver Autonomous Integrity Monitoring (RAIM) may be cited. The RAIM criterion is to detect within x seconds when the navigation error exceeds y meters, where x and y depend on the flight phase. RAIM requires redundant measurements with consistency checks.

If all users can generate a cluster of acceptable size with a failed satellite, then a "sole user" system can be defined. The RAIM search is for a consistent set of measurements, not for a failed satellite. The required integrity level (error bound) of a position estimate is defined as: **Prob** $\{p > 10^{-5}\} > 0.99995$, where p = Prob{nav error > r/measurements on visible satellites, one of which may be in error}.

Baseline Fault Detection and Isolation (FDI) algorithms designed to be certified as flight critical will also be tested at the 10^{-9} level. Minimum FDI detection probability, expressed as a system requirement, will be on the order of $(1-10^{-9})$. Equally severe timing, algorithmic precision and reliability requirements apply to other guidance, navigation, and control (GN&C) phases, to telemetry and communications processing, as well as to main engine and auxiliary power unit monitoring.

The adaptation of a Simulation Analysis of Distributed Systems (SADS) methodology, originally applied to optimal selection of robotics processors, is being planned for autonomous systems architecture, including artificial intelligence applications, such as expert systems, describing software modules at high level. An in-house GSE Power Systems Diagnostic Expert System, as well as results from the USAF/DARPA funded Pilot Associate and follow-on studies were intended as "proof-of-concept" feasibility studies and were not expected to operate in real time. Outputs from these prior efforts are to be analysed and simulated from the point of view of identifying architectural parameters needed to ensure onboard real time performance with growth capabilities.

3 Acknowledgement

SADS-related ideas/comments received from Dr. J.R. Agre, Software Systems Department, Rockwell Science Center, are hereby acknowledged.

Issues in Object-Oriented Real-Time Language Design

Mehmet Akşit and Jan Bosch

Department of Computer Science
University of Twente
P.O. Box 217
7500 AE Enschede
The Netherlands

To express real-time applications, most real-time languages introduce specific constructs to specify features like *deadlines, periodic behavior* and *time intervals*. These constructs, in general, can be seen as annotations to conventional language structures. Object-oriented programming languages have gained popularity in non real-time applications. These languages are highly modular and provide protection through strictly encapsulated abstract data types called *objects*. In addition, *classes* and *inheritance* mechanisms enable programmers to reuse existing software. Recently, there have been some attempts to define real-time object-oriented languages . One motivation for introducing these languages is to reduce the complexity of applications through modularization so that *predictability* and *reliability* of applications can be increased. Secondly, inheritance mechanisms allow reuse of software modules that have well-defined behavior. This may simplify analysis for a particular real-time application. Thirdly, since object-oriented languages are now more frequently applied to software implementations, it would not be practical to adopt different languages for real-time and general parts of an application. However, there are several issues to be addressed in order to fully utilize object-orientation in real-time applications. Firstly, real-time specifications must be reused separately from the 'application code'. This allows the reuse of classes in applications with different real-time behavior. Otherwise, changes made to the application requirements or real-time specifications in the sub-classes may result in excessive redefinitions of super-classes although this seems to be intuitively unnecessary. This we refer to as the *real-time specification anomaly*. Secondly, since a subclass may extend, exclude or replace the real-time specifications of its super-classes, semantics of inheritance must be clearly defined. Thirdly, there must be language mechanisms to modularly specify and reuse alternative implementations. For example, inter-object interactions often result in blocking execution threads. Blocking time can be minimized using dedicated strategies. This requires abstraction of inter-object communications and large scale synchronization among objects as first class objects. In addition, an object may adopt different implementations for its public interface. Lastly, all these language mechanisms must be uniformly integrated in a single consistent framework. We believe that the conventional object-oriented model is far too restricted to fulfil these real-time requirements. Language annotations made to conventional languages may result in real-time specification anomalies and non-uniform language constructs. At the University of Twente, we have been working on new object-oriented language mechanisms using the *composition-filters* approach [1]. Composition filters affect the received and sent messages to or from an object. By proper configuration of filters, one can specify inheritance, delegation, inter-object communications and "real-time constraints" in a single framework.

References

1. M. Akşit, L. Bergmans, S. Vural, *An object-oriented language-database integration model: The composition filters approach*, ECOOP'92 Conference Proceedings, Springer-Verlag, Vol. LNCS–615, June 1992, 372–395.

Combat System Prerequisites on Supercomputer Performance Analysis

Robert D. Harrison, Jr.

Systems Research and Technology Department
Naval Surface Warfare Center, Dahlgren Division
Dahlgren, Virginia 22448
U.S.A.

Modern naval combatants host many highly complex systems. Each system performs one or more tactical capabilities. The single large-scale system formed via integration of these complex systems is a Combat System. This system is required to exhibit behavior described by the following attributes: deterministic, responsive, fault tolerant, automated and controlled.

The combat system processing demand per time unit is defined as follows. Each tactical capability, e.g. track management, has its own processing demand. This demand is dependent on the number of objects, e.g. tracks, that will utilize this capability. The total number of capabilities active concurrently varies with time. The total number of objects driving each capability varies with time. Thus, the combat system processing demand per time unit is dependent on the number of objects per capability in the time unit and the number of capabilities active during the time unit.

Supercomputer technology has been proposed as a combat system processing supply mechanism. The supply is defined in terms of number of processing nodes, the processing power per node, the communication cost per transfer between nodes, and the number of transfers per time unit that may be supplied.

Support of supercomputer performance analysis for combat system application consists of the following three aspects:

1. A definition of demand space features and supply space features is needed. The mapping of demand space features onto the supply space features is needed. Indices that support clustering or partitioning of demand features on or across supply features also is needed. The resulting mapping must be balanced across the supply features under stressful demands.
2. Instrumentation must support the determination of system attributes, distinguishing specific tactical capability demands and parametric studies of the utilization patterns of tactical capabilities in the actual execution context. The typical software development tools which allow for debug level support and timing in an emulation mode have insufficient breadth for this task.

3. New techniques are needed to support statistical trend analysis of utilization patterns, interdependencies of resources, visualization of extremely large data sets and manipulation of large data sets. These techniques must provide as outputs: guidance for mapping demand features to supply features, balancing the mapping, partitioning and clustering guidance for demand features and attribute indices.

Concurrent Engineering of Real-Time Systems Through Heterogeneous Prototypes

Petri J. Pulli

Technical Reserch Centre of Finland (VTT)
Computer Technology Laboratory
P.O. Box 201
90571 Oulu
Finland

A heterogeneous prototype is an executable system model whose different parts may present different levels of abstraction (maturity), and yet they can be executed together as a total system. Abstract models may be presented by means of a graphical specification language whereas more mature physical models may be presented by programming language code.

Heterogeneous prototypes can be used to support concurrent engineering. There may be several teams working simultaneously with different heterogeneous prototypes. Each of the teams may use relatively abstract models of the other parts of the systems as a testbed (environment model) for their own part, yet they can proceed developing their own part full speed by means of advancing the maturity of their part to the next abstraction level(s).

Our approach addresses the future requirements of the software engineering process: overcoming increasing complexity and development risks and supporting flexible just-on-time product development:

- It improves communication by improving the visibility of the software engineering work, allowing user needs to be accommodated earlier and more accurately.
- It allows efficient development work structuring and allocation to concurrent development teams and individuals. It allows teams to use intermediate results from other teams for validating their own progress.
- It strengthens the organisational infrastructure by providing better control over development time, subcontracting, and product quality elements.

The approach presented in this paper is being developed in the IPTES project, funded by the European Communities under the ESPRIT programme, project no. EP5570 and the Technical Development Centre of Finland (TEKES). The IPTES consortium is formed by IFAD (DK), VTT (SF), MARI (UK), CEA/LETI (F), ENEA (I), Synergie (F), Universidad Politécnica de Madrid (E), Telefónica I+D (E), Politecnico di Milano (I), and Rautaruukki (SF).

On-Line Surveillance and Diagnostic System for Nuclear Power Plant Monitoring

*Özer Ciftcioglu * and Erdinc Turkcan*

Dutch Energy Research Foundation
P.O. Box 1
1755 ZG Petten
The Netherlands

The on-line surveillance and diagnostic system for the Borssele nuclear power plant (NPP), designed and established by the Energy Research Foundation of the Netherlands, has been operating continuously since a decade. The system is structured in the form of multi-processing, multi-tasking performing real-time executions for monitoring, reactor parameters' calculation, data-base formation for expert systems and providing early information on possible malfunctions by means of plant-wide monitoring possibilities [1-5]. Along a decade of operation, the system is updated in parallel with the technological developments, in particular in the computer and real-time computing technology.

The system has rather sophisticated software as well as hardware structure analyzing the implementation of the advanced techniques for the intended tasks in real-time, on-line. In this respect the basic tasks can be divided into four major groups as follows.

a) Computer based instrumentation for instrument setting, signal conditioning and data transmission.

b) Pre-processing of the data following acquisition and storing them in a data base and circular file for later use for long-term and for short-term reference purposes, respectively.

c) Multi-channel signal processing in both time and frequency domains in real-time. Outputs resulting from the computations are transferred to a large block of shared memory which is accessible commonly to several users and real-time applications.

d) Performing multi-purpose analyses in real-time using the processed data made available in the common block.

The instrumental settings in the NPP for sensors are done by remote control through the processor (CPU) supervision in the main computer environment. The main computer is a VAX 4000/200 equipped with an array processor (floating point system FPS 5105). Additional workstations are integrated to the main processor through a universal communication net (Ethernet) so that the configuration forms a distributed system operating in real-time.

---

* Visiting Professor from Istanbul Technical University

The plant-wide monitoring possesses the following essential characteristics during the operation, provided by the existing hardware and real-time software.

1. Timely, precise and mission-oriented information
2. Retrospective process characteristics and parameters
3. Multi-level execution

The first feature implies that the system complies with the real-time data processing requirements of various tasks being executed. The second feature implies that data acquisition is performed on a continuous basis, and the previous information obtained as a result of the data acquisition and processing is stored both on a short and a long-term basis. Such retrospective information is vitally helpful, in particular in detecting and diagnostic identification of system malfunctions and fault-prone trends in the incipient stage.

The third feature implies different objectives in the plant monitoring. These may start from condition monitoring of system components, such as reactor internals, and extend up to total system (plant-wide) monitoring. Considering the multi-level distributed structure in hardware and software, the system has ample flexibility to perform any real-time signal processing task in the most efficient and effective way that it provides at the same time outstanding goal-oriented research and development possibilities such as estimation, filtering, verification and validation, neural networks and others, in parallel with the technological advancements.

References

1. E. Turkcan et al., *Operational Experiences on the Borssele Nuclear Power Plant Using Computer Based Surveillance and Diagnostic System On-Line*, Symposium on Nuclear Reactor Surveillance and Diagnostics (SMORN-V), Gatlinburg, Tennessee, U.S.A., May 19–24, 1991.
2. M. Kitamura and E. Turkcan, *Empirical Modelling Approach to Fault Detection and Identification in Nuclear Power Plant*, IFAC, Identification and System Parameter Estimation, York, U.K., 1985.
3. B.R. Upadhyaya and E. Turkcan, *Analysis of Neutron Detector and Core-Exit Thermocouple Signals in the Borssele PWR*, The Netherlands, Report, ECN-84-193, 1985.
4. 0. Ciftcioglu and E. Turkcan, *Sequential Decision Reliability Concept and Failure Rate Assessment: Application to NPP instrumentation*, IAEA On Nuclear Power Plant Control and Instrumentation (IWG-NPPCI), Arnhem, The Netherlands, October 16–19, 1990.
5. E. Turkcan and 0. Ciftcioglu, *On-Line Plant Wide Monitoring Using Neural Networks*, 8th Power Plant Dynamics, Control and Testing Symposium, University of Tennessee, Knoxville, Tennessee, May 27–29, 1992.

A Toolset for Developing Real-Time Systems

Constance Heitmeyer

Center for High-Assurance Computer Systems
Naval Research Laboratory
Washington, D.C. 20375
U.S.A.

We describe a prototype toolset [1],[2] whose goal is to provide comprehensive support for constructing verifiably correct real-time systems. The toolset, a product of joint research by the Naval Research Laboratory (NRL) and the University of Texas (UT), has two purposes:

1. to demonstrate and evaluate the utility of formal methods for developing real-time systems and
2. to obtain information needed to build production-quality CASE tools supporting the methods (e.g., how to design the user interface, how to integrate the tools, etc.).

Two formal methods that underlie the toolset are the Modechart language and a mechanical verifier, both developed at UT. Modechart is a graphical language for expressing a system's timing behavior that is derived from Statechart and NRL's concept of modes. In Modechart, the time that a system can remain in a selected mode is defined by *delays* and *deadlines*.

The Modechart verifier determines whether a timing assertion can be derived from a set of Modechart specifications. Each timing assertion, expressed in a form of first-order logic called Real-Time Logic (RTL), is a logical statement of the properties that must hold for the specifications to be considered correct. The verifier classifies each assertion as valid or invalid.

The software for the prototype toolset consists of user interface software and application software. The user interface software supports the creation and modification of a Modechart specification. The application software contains the Modechart data base, which stores the modes, mode transitions, and other components of a Modechart specification, and tools for analyzing a Modechart specification. Current tools include a semiautomatic layout program that generates graphical representations of Modecharts expressed in textual form, a simulator that allows the user to view and guide executions of a system specified in Modechart, a consistency and completeness checker, and the Modechart verifier described above.

The current version of the toolset supports the entering of a new Modechart specification; the loading, modification, and saving of an existing specification; the automatic (graphical) layout of a specification entered in textual form; and user "analysis" of a specification. Entering and modifying a large, complex specification is facilitated by the availability of zooming and scrolling operations, flexible ways to move parts of a specification, and undo and redo operations. The user may analyze a specification by executing either the verifier or the Modechart simulator.

The toolset software is coded in C and C++ and runs on Sun workstations. The toolset's user interface software was developed using OpenWindows and the DevGuide toolkit. The toolkit provides C programs for the windows, menus, scrollbars, and other standard widgets required by the toolset's user interface software.

References

1. A. Rose, M. Pérez, P. Clements, *Modechart User Interface Tool User's Guide*, NRL report, Naval Research Lab, Wash., DC, 1992 (forthcoming).
2. C.L. Heitmeyer, P.C. Clements, B.G. Labaw, A.K. Mok, *Engineering CASE Tools to Support Formal Methods for Real-Time Software Development*, Proc., Fifth Intern. Workshop on Computer-Aided Software Engineering, Montreal, Quebec, CAN, 6–10 July 1992.

Integration of Large Scale Systems

Wilhelm Rossak

Systems Integration and Real-Time Computing Laboratory
Department of Computer and Information Science
New Jersey Institute of Technology
Newark, NJ 07102
U.S.A.

To be able to handle the complexity of large scale systems development in a specific application domain, a product can be partitioned into systems which are independently developed in distributed projects. These systems are designed to work autonomously and to interoperate with the other systems in the domain as a "mega-system" to provide the necessary functionality. Systems integration addresses the challenge to provide a pre-planned and integrated development process in this kind of environment which combines a maximum of independence and flexibility with the necessary standardization and tool support[1].

To support this task, we propose the use of a Generic Systems Integration Framework — GenSIF — as an additional level of control and management, which coordinates the otherwise independent projects [1], [2]. A domain model and an integration architecture are the two main components of the proposed framework. The domain model allows the project team to handle requirements and to communicate knowledge about the domain on the basis of a standardized common model. It describes all phenomena regarding a specific application domain on a conceptual level from different points of view, as given by the roles established in the user population, and is organized according to various aspects of modeling, e.g., static, dynamic, logical, legal, etc [3]. This type of domain modeling strives to structure the domain along a set of user-definable criteria. It is restricted to the conceptual level.

The constructive element of the GenSIF framework is the integration architecture [2]. A conceptual integration architecture provides a design reference model used to guide projects during their internal design activities.
A technical infrastructure supports the implementation phase of the project by providing a standardized set of tools and technologies which are shared by all projects.

The philosophy of systems integration is to strive for coordination on a domain wide basis instead of relying on patching up existing, incompatible systems later on. A mega-system level in the process model coordinates otherwise independent projects. It provides the domain model which drives the integration effort and supports synthesis of mega-systems from single systems on the basis of a domain wide integration architecture.

References

1. W. Rossak and P.A. Ng, *Some Thoughts on Systems Integration — A Conceptual Framework*, Journal of Systems Integration, Kluwer, Vol. 1, No. 1, 1991, 97–114.
2. W. Rossak and P.A. Ng, *Systems Development with Integration Architectures*, Proc. of IEEE Second International Conference on Systems Integration, Morristown NJ, USA, June 1992, 96–103.
3. T. Zemel, W. Rossak and H. Thimm, *Domain Analysis as a Major Component of Integrated Systems Development*, Proc. of SERF 92, 1992 Software Engineering Research Forum, Indialantic FL, USA, November 1992, to appear.

Architectural Design Considerations for Critical Real-Time Systems

A. Pedar

Resident Research Associate
NASA Ames Research Center MS:269–3
Moffett Field, CA 94035
U.S.A.

In the past decade, there has been a considerable amount of effort in the design, analysis, implementation of highly reliable computing systems for critical real-time applications. The computing power per unit cost is increasing continuously due to rapid advances in semiconductor technology. The amount of functions to be automated in any complex real-time system is also increasing. These two factors coerce the designer to think of highly sophisticated complex computing systems for such applications.

In spite of the availability of advanced hardware and software modeling techniques, the difficulty and effort required for validating such complex systems are very large. There is enough reason to optimize the system for the required performance, reliability, and cost. Also, there is a need for the current modeling techniques to take into account some factors that are very specific to critical real-time systems.

The important practical factors that should be considered in the design, modeling, and analysis of critical real-time systems are discussed. A modeling framework is described which enables a designer to optimize the hardware in a given real-time environment under constraints such as hardware reliability, performance, and cost. When a gracefully degradable multiprocessor system is used for critical real-time applications, the system reconfigures itself to a degraded working state on encountering a failure. As the amount of computation remains the same, the workload increases in degraded states. This results in increased resource conflicts which results in more timing failures. It is important to take timing failure in the modeling framework for critical real-time systems. Instead of using the job completion time as an indirect measure to interpret the probability of missing deadline, a direct measure is evaluated using the Generalised Stochastic Petri Net of the task model for each working configuration of the system. Using this as a reward function, the performability of the system is computed as the cumulative reward over the entire system configuration.

Head Up Display. Requirements on an Avionic System

Kim Bengtsson

Defence Material Administration
Avionics Division
115 88 Stockholm
Sweden

In our aircraft we have the need to display various data on a Head Up Display (HUD) in order to provide the pilot with necessary information about flight data (attitude, speed etc.) together with tactical data, at the same time as he is looking at the world outside the aircraft. We have been using HUDs in our aircraft since the sixties, and have developed three versions. All the versions use the same basic principle, which means that the primary information displayed is the velocity vector of the aircraft and the horizon. Round this mode dependant symbols for e.g. steering commands, warnings and tactical information are displayed.

Early simulations showed that the attitude information is very time critical, as the pilot often has the possibility to compare the displayed horizon with the real one, and only will allow for very minor errors caused by the computations. At the same time the velocity vector changes rather slowly, due to the inertia of the aircraft, and it must during fast manoeuvres be speeded up with information about changes in attitude etc. Otherwise the pilot is unable to use it to control the aircraft, as he always will apply too powerful commands while waiting for the velocity vector to react.

In the first version we had just one digital computer, while all sensors and the HUD itself were analog. This meant, that all information had to be transferred to the computer where all computations were made and from which the desired information was transferred to the display-unit. Most data was transferred in analog form but some, e.g. the attitude angles, were transferred as a multiplexed digital word.

We soon found out, that a straightforward solution caused such delays that the system was totally unacceptable. In order to give the pilot good possibility to control the aircraft using the HUD the age of displayed data must not exceed 20-50 ms for data with fast variations. In order to solve the task we had to concentrate on the timing and reduce or compensate for all delays. It was not enough just to increase the speed of computation, as the possibilities in that area were limited, and much of the delay was caused by equipment outside the computer, so we had to reduce all delays.

We succeeded by putting firm requirements on the sensors so that none of the time critical data would be older than a certain limit, when read from the computer. We could then start the computations with data of a known age and by synchronizing the start of the display cycle we also knew when a critical group of symbols would be displayed. Thus we had the possibility to predict true values by using rate-information for the most time-sensitive symbols.

In the computer we could choose betweeen different iteration rates and use the higher only for sensitive data in order to reduce the load of the computer. Since much of the time critcal data also is used in functions where time is not as essential and a number of "slow" data must be used for display purposes there is a large amount of data used in the different rate groups. We found, that this forced us to implement strict rules for such data in order to retain consistency of data between different rate groups.

We ended up with a system that is absolutely dependant on the timing of the system computer, and where the sensors and the HUD was in some way synchronized to the computations.

This first system has now been flying for 25 years with very good results.

Our next version was developed during the seventies. Now the use of computers had increased, and we had computers both in sensors and in the display unit. As we had good experiences from the first system we wanted to keep the same structure of the system. We developed a new digital interface, with serial point-to-point communication between the system computer and most other equipment even if we had to retain some analog interfaces.

The additional computers caused some problems, as we had not foreseen the need to synchronize all computers with the system computer. Only the display computer has a real synch-signal from the system computer. In the beginning the ordinary iteration rates used in the sensors were not high enough to ensure that the data always was fresh when transferred to the system computer. We had therefore to modify some sensor computations in order to get the needed freshness of data when the I/O-system was asked to transmit data. However, the use of computers in the sensor equipment was rather restricted so we could quite easily use the same concept as in the earlier version. This version has been used successfully for about 15 years.

For our new aircraft a new system is being developed. The development started about 10 years ago. Now the system has much more computer power and all avionic systems rely heavily on computers. The system still has a system computer as the heart of the system and three buses (Mil Std 1553B) are used for all communication. The buses also are used to synchronize the different computers. All buses are controlled by the system computer, and the computation cycles are firmly fixed in time to the cycles of the bus. The goal has been to have a system where the system computer can fetch time critical data from the sensors, compute the critical outputs, and transmit them in 60 Hz such that the display system can start to display the critical data with a minimum delay.

The sensor equipment should always have freshly computed data to transmit over the bus when ordered by the system computer. This requirement has not been fulfilled, as we use some "off the shelf" equipment, where iteration rates cannot be changed. We have instead had to use "time-tags" to be able to correct the data delays. This system has been flying for a couple of years in test aircraft, and will be delivered to the Swedish Air Force next year.

As can be seen, we have developed three time-driven systems. When the third system was to be developed there were many discussions about using an event-driven system instead. The decision to stay with a time-driven system was based on two main factors. In a time-based system it is easier to monitor time and take corrective actions if more than 100% of the computer is needed. It is also easier to ensure that all data are consistent. We have had some experience with event-driven displaysystems where suddenly some symbols are displayed using old or even faulty data. This cannot be allowed in an aircraft where pilot safety is dependent upon correct information on the display.

In our latest system, we rely much more on computed information than in the older systems and have just a basic fall-back system for flight information. This stresses the safety aspects of displayed information to a higher degree than before and forces us to monitor information, data communication and computations very strictly. The testing of software in the different subsystems and their integration are also much more formalized than before. These activities have also been seen to be easier in a time driven system.

On Design and Practice of Fault-Tolerant Real-Time Computer Systems

Michael Y. Chang

Systems Research and Technology Department
Naval Surface Warfare Center
Dahlgren Division
Dahlgren, Virgina 22448-5000
U.S.A.

One major group of real-time computer systems are those specialized in supervisory control of several highly complex systems. Computer systems used in such a supervisory control role tend to be tightly coupled with respect to time to the other complex systems and need to operate under very strict response times imposed by the problem domain. The main task for the designer of such a computer system is the proper mapping of currently available technologies to the computer system design under pre-established financial, performance and reliability constraints. Clearly, this task can only be accomplished by acknowledging the limitations, resource requirements, and characteristics of the available technology relative to the dynamics of the supervisory control time lines. Furthermore, most supervisory control systems are developed under an evolutionary approach of separate independent developments of the controlled components. The compatibility of the supervisory system with new components as well as the backward compatibility with previous versions of the supervisory system are major design issues. Typically, the life cycle for the controlled components as well as the supervisory control system itself are measured in decades.

In this presentation we focus on the problems and issues which many practitioners and designers of the modern fault-tolerant real-time computer systems have. First, interpretation of the real implication of the specified response times, on the fault-tolerance, resource utilization, and degree of compatibility of a specific design scheme. Identifying underlying assumptions and their impacts on the particular design would be one major hurdle which many computer practitioners and designers need to overcome. Second, identification of the inherent range of capabilities and limitations and implementation variations of each technique used in fault-tolerant computer system design. For example, on-the-fly reconfiguration of components when the supervisory system detects and identifies a failure could take many different forms. Depending on the granularity of the reconfigurable units and the reconfiguration scheme, the overall utilization of system resources and their required execution time will, in general, be quite different. Third, finding the proper mapping between the specific design scheme and the control requirements imposed by the supervisory control problem. Even though it might be possible to determine all the timing and performance measures of the specific real-time computer system under study, without a fundamental understanding by the designer of the interactions between the real-time computer system and the supervisory control problem which have evolved over the years, the values obtained would not have much relevance to the overall designer of the control system.

The basic understanding of the dynamics of the supervisory control problem implemented by the real-time computer system under design as well as understanding of essential characteristics of available computer system design methods are two fundamental keys to which the real-time computer system designer must pay attention. This presentation will focus on how one can determine these fundamental keys by the examination of design examples of fault-tolerant real-time computer system design.

The Design of Distributed, Dependable Real-Time Systems Using a Functional Paradigm

A. Bondavalli[1], L. Simoncini[2] and C. Bernardeschi[2]

[1] CNUCE-CNR
Via S.Maria 36
Pisa
Italy

[2] Department of Information Engineering
University of Pisa
Via Diotisalvi 2
Pisa
Italy

Abstract

Distributed real-time computer systems are replacing conventional control systems in many applications. Most of these systems are higly critical ones, e.g. design of a traffic flight control or an industrial process control system. In addition to the specified functional capabilities, these applications demand predictable timeliness and a high level of dependability which includes non functional attributes such as availability, reliability, safety and maintainability [4]. The systematic development of *fault-tolerant real-time systems* with guaranteed *timeliness* and *dependability* requires an appropriate system architecture and a rigorous design methodology.

1 Design Methodology

To achieve a high level of dependability, the classical techniques of *fault avoidance, fault tolerance, fault removal* and *fault forecasting* must be combined with the use of *formal methods*. In this way faults in the design and development of the system can be eliminated or reduced. *Dependability* must be designed in a system and cannot be considered as an add-on after the system has been developed. The key notion in dependability is that reliance must be justifiably placed on system service [3]. This means that we need explicit and testable requirements and specifications to be used in a top down refinement design of the system. Therefore, a design methodology, in addition to the structural description of the system, should include more information to allow proving typical design properties such as timing and dependability. The use of a *functional language*, together with a *dataflow* computing model for the design of dependable large-scale parallel computing systems, have been shown to be a basis of a design description language satisfying many of the challenging requirements of predictable distributed systems [1]. In [2] a *design methodology* has been defined which provides:

- a *design description language* and some extension for dealing with dependability issues, with the creation of a library of fault tolerance schemes which can be used for modular insertion of redundancy;
- a set of *tools* as part of a design development environment allowing the designer to proceed in successive interactive steps, each of which can be validated;
- a set of *design constraints* on the supported architecture.

The design description language is based on *coarse-grained* dataflow notation which, quite apart from its natural ability to describe highly parallel applications, has other very interesting advantages:

- modules composing a system have *functional behaviour* and *locality* of effects; these imply *composability* which puts in direct relation the general behaviour of a system from its constituent parts;
- modules are *atomic* and satisfy *referential transparency;* they work in local environments and two executions of the same module with the same input data produce equal results, simplifying re-execution or recovery of a module;
- systems structured in this way are inherently *fault-tolerant* in the sense that simple failures may be tolerated by simply resubmitting the same inputs to a module describing the same function;
- *structural models* for *software reliability assessment* can be applied since all data necessary to their use can be obtained by a simple instrumentation of software code;
- the data-flow graph representing the system can easily be translated, with proper techniques, into some sort of timed Petri-net for *timeliness analysis* purposes.

The construction of an *interactive design environment*, populated by a set of tools for the automatic insertion of fault-tolerance in the system, for the automatic translation into analysable timed Petri-nets and into analysable stochastic Markov systems for reliability analysis, and for the evaluation of structural models for software reliability, is feasible. The interactive approach is used for calibrating the design so that dependability and timeliness requirements can be attained with a high level of predictability.

References

1. A. Bondavalli, L. Strigini, L. Simoncini, *Dataflow-Like Languages for Real-Time Systems: Issues of Computational Models and Notation*, International Symposium on Reliable Distributed Systems, SRDS–11, Houston, Texas, 1992, 214–221.

2. A. Bondavalli, L. Simoncini, *Functional Paradigm for Designing Dependable Large-Scale Parallel Computing Systems*, International Symposium on Autonomous Decentralized Systems, ISADS'93, Kawasaki, Japan, 1993 (to appear).
3. J.C. Laprie (ed.), *Dependability:Basic Concepts and Terminology*, Dependable Computing and Fault-Tolerant Systems 5, Springer-Verlag, 1991.
4. G. Le Lann, *Designing real-time dependable distributed systems*, Rapports de Recherche 1425, INRIA, Rocquencourt, 1991.

Goal Oriented Resource Management

Christos Nikolaou

Department of Computer Science
University of Crete
Greece
Institute of Computer Science
FORTH Heraklion, Crete
Greece*

Managing the performance of distributed computing environments is today a serious challenge, because of their complexity and the diversity of new applications. Digital audio and video data, with strict delay and jitter constraints, are moved and manipulated in a computing, storage and communication medium where more traditional batch, transaction and query processing applications are already in operation and expected to achieve preset levels of throughput or average response time. Enterprise wide systems will soon surface where, for example, resources are shared among applications running high volume, low response time inventory control transactions with strong CPU time demands, applications managing videoconferences with tight delay and massive bandwidth requirements, engineering visualization tools with similar requirements, background decision support queries with soft completion deadlines and large memory needs, or process control tasks with hard real time constraints and demands for immediate use of CPU, memory or bandwidth.

Managing the performance of these systems through direct operator adjustment of system parameters (e.g. buffer pool sizes, dispatching priorities, multiprogramming level, routing policies, data and bandwidth allocation policies, etc.) is impractical. It is customary today for user groups to require computer hardware, software or service vendors to sign a "service-level agreement", that binds the vendor to deliver a system that satisfies distinct performance goals for various kinds of work. Users of integrated video, voice and data networks require explicit guarantees of "quality of service", see [1].

A distributed system should allow its users or administrators to specify *what* the performance expectation for their work is, *not how* to achieve this expectation. The users should also be allowed to specify how *critical* each class of work is relative to the other classes. The work characteristics (e.g. arrival rate, resources consumed) may be different at different times and as a result the system may become overloaded for a certain period. In this case, the specified performance goals may not be satisfiable and the system is considered as being in *degra-*

---

* The research reported here was conducted while the author was with the IBM T.J. Watson Research Center, P.O. Box 704, Yorktown Heights NY 10598, USA.

ded mode. In degraded mode, attention should be shifted to the more critical groups of work. In the past few years we developed at IBM Research in Hawthorne, New York, a number of practical low overhead goal oriented algorithms for specific resources and resource managers and tested their performance with prototypes and detailed simulation models. We started with goal oriented CPU scheduling. Heuristics were then proposed to manage memory adaptively relative to class goals. In addition, we designed dynamic transaction routing and scheduling algorithms for achieving response time goals in a closely coupled system of transaction processing nodes. If a transaction processing installation has a Service Level Agreement that specifies response time goals, then this approach enables the installation to sustain higher arrival rates before the agreement is violated. The algorithms consider transaction affinity to data, current system loads and goal satisfaction in transaction priority assignments and transaction routing decisions. Simulation shows that these algorithms achieve substantially better goal satisfaction and higher maximum throughput compared to a wide variety of other algorithms and have low overhead [2].

There is a very rich set of problems which is left open or on which we have only recently started working. We recently started work on adaptive control of database buffer sizes, given access times objectives specified per buffer pool. But we have not looked at problems of interaction between various adaptive resource managers, for example, how would an adaptive transaction router interact with an adaptive CPU scheduler? Are there stability problems to be taken care of? How would an adaptive buffer manager interact with an adaptive memory hierarchy manager operating at the operating system level? How do we handle units of work that spawn multiple threads of control — possibly on different processors — when they start executing, as is the case with parallelized complex queries? What communication is necessary between the goal-oriented algorithms and the parallelizing query optimizer? Similarly, what communication should exist between the goal oriented algorithms and a parallelizing compiler, producing code for a scientific or engineering application?

Distributed systems present the problem of unavailability of global state information, necessary to understand how each service class is doing relative to its goals. Goal oriented algorithms could benefit from previous work on state information propagation algorithms in distributed systems. Goal oriented resource management should coexist with deadline scheduling, where emphasis is on meeting hard or soft deadlines of individual units of work, as opposed to satisfying statistical performance goals defined for service classes. Adaptive resource management should interact with recovery management and problem determination management for failure avoidance and load redistribution.

References

1. D. Ferguson, C. Nikolaou, L. Georgiadis, K. Davies, *Satisfying Response Time Goals in Transaction Processing Systems*, Technical Report RC18139, IBM Research, 1992.

2. C. Nikolaou, D. Ferguson, P. Constantopoulos, *Towards Goal Oriented Resource Management*, Technical Report RC17919, IBM Research, 1992.

Experiences with Distributed Data Management in Real-Time C^3 Systems

Paul J. Fortier[1], David V. Pitts and John C. Sieg, Jr.[2]

[1] Naval Undersea Warfare Center Div.
NUWC, Newport, RI 02841-5047
U.S.A.
[2] University of Massachusetts - Lowell
Dept. of Computer Science
UMass - Lowell, One University Ave.
Lowell, MA 01854
U.S.A.

Abstract

Distributed real-time command, control, and communications (C^3) systems are being used in many industrial and military applications. Real-time systems differ from conventional systems in that the consistency and correctness of the controlling process depends on the timeliness and predictability of the actions of the controlling system on the controlled process. Real-time C^3 systems usually have not adequately addressed these requirements in a methodical fashion; systems have been hand-crafted and fine-tuned until they met testing requirements. In this paper, we review the evolution over the past three decades of the U.S. Navy's real-time C^3 database systems for its submarines. We note the lessons learned in the development of these systems and describe briefly a coming generation.

1 Evolution of C^3 Information-Management System

In this section, we outline the evolution of the hardware architecture upon which naval submarine C^3 systems were built. We also describe the parallel evolution of the software designs for the C^3 information-management system, focusing on the way the system uses, stores, and manages information in providing real-time support to the users of the system.

In 1964, the U.S. Navy determined that the existing analog systems could not meet future needs, due to changing missions and threats. To address this need, the Navy began investigating digital computing systems. The initial resulting system was a hybrid that possessed numerous elements from the analog system, along with a central digital computer complex. The central computer complex replaced many of the tracking and navigation functions previously performed with the analog equipment. The hybrid system proved the usefulness of digital computers for managing command, control, and communications information within a real-time system. It led to a wide range of functional improvements and innovations not possible without the added flexibility, computational power, and database management services available with a digital system.

The earliest fully digital system used a shared memory-resident central repository of encoded data, called the *resident regional*. The data was encoded with a number of information fields. The fields could be as small as one bit, or as large as an entire word or multiple words. This hardware and database architecture provided a research platform upon which to investigate and test concepts for digital real-time systems information management.

The next generation real-time system was federated. The database architecture was based on centralized master copies of database objects, with shadow copies distributed to peripheral sites.

The peripheral sites operated on their stored copies sending updates to the centralized sites periodically to maintain consistency of the centralized database. The major lessons learned at this stage were that database management had a place in real-time C^3 systems, and that future systems would require new techniques if features within conventional database management systems could be used. In addition, distribution of data was an essential ingredient, as was the need to have database requests serviced according to criteria not considered by the builders of database systems.

The two were fully distributed. The first, called BSY-1, used a suite of global shared busses interconnected by bridges. Processors were distributed over the separate sub-busses according to function. For example, one subbus possessed processors and processes to perform signal processing, another performed background functions, and yet another performed display processing functions.

The second distributed system, called BSY-2, introduced subdomains connected in a ring topology. This approach limits the volume of processors and processes on a domain, and clusters processes in a domain based on the similarity of processing and data requirements of the processes.

With both BSY-1 and BSY-2, the approach has been to use conventional database management facilities and directly access information during critical time periods. In BSY-1, the database management system was essentially a global file system, with a user interface glued on to give it the appearance of a full fledged database system. This design allowed programmers to develop software around a common interface, and provided for the future inclusion of a real distributed database management system when one became available. Experience with BSY-2 showed the need for a system-wide, integrated, real-time database management system. BSY-2 uses a company proprietary CODASYL like database interface with no system-wide controls. Database access is performed in fixed code partitions called messages which are called by embedded processes to manipulate needed information.

2 Future Efforts

The authors are investigating [1] unconventional DBMS concepts to better support the needs of tactical systems. A real-time database management system requires frequent deadline driven interactions with sensors to extract physical environmental data, cannot use conventional rollback for recovery since the past history does not reflect reality of the sensored environment, requires that critical/time driven updates and queries take precedence over others, requires that operations respond and adjust to dynamically changing conditions, and applications should pay only for a level of recovery, consistency and integrity needed. Our research examines database partitioning into sets that can have their consistency maintained separately from each other, transaction decomposition over the disjoint data sets, nonserializable concurrency control protocols, forward fault recovery protocols, integration of DBMS services with real-time scheduling protocols, and formal development of consistency and correctness criteria for these protocols.

3 Summary

We have described the evolution of the naval real-time C^3 system used in submarines, from the use of specialized analog components to the present use of specialized digital components. For each of the major stages in this evolution, we have discussed the benefits and limitations of the approaches used at that stage, and presented the lessons that were learned. Finally, we outline current work being done in the development of the next-generation C^3 DBMS-supported system. Our approach promotes distributed management of data and real-time processes.

References

1. P.J. Fortier *Decomposition of Consistency Constraint Enforcement in Databases*, D.Sc. Dissertation, Computer Science Department, University of Massachusetts – Lowell, Lowell, Massachusetts, 1992. In progress.

The Impact of Real-Time on the Fault-Tolerant Distributed RDC-System

Gottfried Bonn

Fraunhofer-Institute for
Information- and Data-Processing (IITB)
Fraunhoferstraße 1
76131 Karlsruhe
Germany

The RDC-System (Really Distributed Computer Control System) developed by IITB has been successfully applied in many industrial automation projects. It provides distributed fault-tolerance and is based on a redundant fibre optical network. The application programs are highly real-time sensitive and are written in PEARL with extensions for distribution and fault-tolerance support. This paper gives a short outline of the main characteristics of RDC with respect to real-time, fault-tolerance and distribution and summarizes some lessons learnt from the multiple industrial applications in steel production and car manufacturing.

The Architecture

The RDC system is built on a set of automation devices interconnected by a local area network. The automation devices are running the distributed computational processes performing the automation application, in particular the open-loop and fast feedback control algorithms. Specific network stations with graphical human interfaces (SCADA) allow for monitoring and controlling the behaviour of the automation system and the technical process. The local area network is built upon a fibre optical ringbus using buffer insertion as medium access control mechanism. This MAC protocol is currently of increasing interest also within standardisation related activities.

For providing fault-tolerance, all components of the RDC system may be configured redundantly, i.e. doubled process-I/O devices and interconnections, doubled network transmission medium and redundant SCADA and automation devices. The computational application processes provide distributed fault-tolerance by beeing passively replicated on different automation devices using appropriate checkpointing techniques. The passive replicates approach makes the fail-stop assumption and requires a self-checking mechanism with high error detection coverage which is achieved by using a small core of specific hardware supplemented by a variety of built-in tests.

The Distributed Automation Computing Environment

RDC automation devices are programmed in Multicomputer-PEARL, a German DIN standard. This language provides specific constructs for multitasking, time- and event-scheduling and a couple of intertasking mechanisms such as semaphores and client/server relationships. It supports location transparency, allows for configuration descriptions and provides expressive means for fault-treatment, e.g. the definition of reconfiguration strategies in the case of station failures. Multicomputer-Pearl and its runtime support has been shown as an excellent distributed computing environment for industrial automation with fault-tolerance requirements.

The Local Real-Time Operating System

Each automation device runs a local operating system, which in particular serves as runtime support environment for the rich real-time features of PEARL. It uses priority based scheduling with preemption and achieves fast context switch (30–100 machine instructions). It supervises on missed soft deadlines (given by PEARL-schedules) and allows for invocation of application specific reactions, such as the adaption of sampling rates and PID parameters of fast feedback control algorithms. Hard deadlines are set by means of parametrizing time-based self checking tests. If they are missed, the corresponding station is treated as being faulty.

For specific fault-tolerance support, the local operating system must allow for the dynamic instantiation of passively replicated task groups, which form the smallest configurable units within RDC.

The Network Support

The main features of the RDC network to support the distributed fault-tolerance approach are the built-in medium redundancy management and the specific protocols for fast station status change reporting which allow for reconfiguration times of less than 50 ms.

As in MMS, RDC provides services and protocols such as remote I/O, remote tasking and event scheduling. From the application programmer's viewpoint this is performed in a fully transparent manner.

The Management Tools

A couple of network, system and application management tools to support commissioning, daily operation and maintenance have been shown to be very useful. Among these are tracing for real-time operations, measurements of task execution times, remote testing of distributed PEARL applications on source code level, state dependent automatic downline loading, upload for post mortem analysis, fault diagnosis support and other configuration and performance monitoring tools.

Some Lessons Learnt and Conclusions

The RDC fault-tolerance approach using passive replication techniques is well applicable. The application specific explicit checkpointing requires experience with respect to the selection of checkpoint contents and setting-up rates.

Achieving high coverage of self-checking to satisfy the fail-stop assumption is a longer term activity. The design of tests requires the knowledge of faults which may occur and the errors they may cause in advance.

Priority-based scheduling with (!) preemption has been schown as an appropriate means, the costs-versus-benefit question for deadline-based scheduling remains open.

The decoupling of cooperating computational processes, i.e. the layout of synchronisation and in particular communication relationships (timeout-retransmission!) must be done very carefully.

Process control engineers — at least for feedback control — always need more processing power than providable, i.e. the increase of sampling rates (soft deadline) increases the quality of service. Therefore the measurement of execution times is mandatory to select appropriate task priorities and to configure the time-schedule layout.

Many built-in features of the RDC network, such as redundancy management, status reporting and multicasting are strongly missed in standardized LANs and are inefficiently rebuilt on upper layers.

The approach of the Multicomputer-PEARL environment could be seen as a prototype model for current activities on building distributed computing environments for specific application areas such as CIM.

The provision of management tools is mandatory to achieve system acceptance. The restriction to network management (OSI approach) is not acceptable to the users. The integration of managed objects other than those related to communication (e.g. power supply, temperature, process-configuration) should comprise all system components and the application itself.

Though these conclusions derived from the RDC experiences may be regarded as not general applicable, we think that the industrial application scenarios and the functional approach of RDC typically cover a wide area in the field of distribution, real-time and fault-tolerance for industrial automation.

Annotation for System Engineering of Large, Complex, Real-Time Systems

Steven L. Howell

Naval Surface Warfare Center, Code U33
10901 New Hamsphire Avenue
Silver Spring, Maryland 20903
U.S.A.

The system engineering of large complex real-time systems is critical since it provides an integrated view and analysis of the system under design. However, to date, most methods and techniques have focused on the implementation aspects of real-time systems (hardware engineering, software engineering, human computer interaction). A number of methods exist at the system engineering level; however, they concentrate on the structure versus the attributes of the system. Computer aided software engineering (CASE) and system engineering tools tend to focus only on the structural aspects of the system as related to performance. Efforts, such as the IEEE Computer Base System Engineering (CBSE) Task Force are also currently concentrating on system design structure. However, in real-time systems, the design is also dependent on many other attributes. Current methods lack the ability to formal annotate and analyze factors which have non-structural components.

Research has begun to address this problem. The methods and techniques under development allow the system designer to specify non-functional as well as functional attributes integrated with the structural descriptions in a manner that lends itself to analysis. In addition, meta-rules are in development which allow the system engineer to define and tailor attributes and relationships for specific projects.

The goal of this effort is to provide multiple benefits to systems developers. It provides a closer linkage between the specification of the system design and the simulation/modeling/prototyping/analysis of the design. It provides a closer linkage between the alternative models of the design such as the conceptual and implementation models. It provides closer linkage between the design and the original system requirements. Finally, It allows enhanced trade-off between design alternatives to be better understood and analyzed.

The annotation is performed with System Design Factors (SDF) which are attributes that are used to characterize strengths and weaknesses of the system or system components. An initial taxonomy of the SDF has been defined. The framework for meta-rules has also been defined. The initial prototype that illustrates the concepts is integrated to a commercial CASE tool. The prototype, called DESTINATION, allows both the conceptual (logical) design and the implementation design to be annotated. DESTINATION allows allocations to be made between the conceptual and implementation design based on tailored objective functions, mapped through brute force or randomized (genetic or simulated annealing algorithms). This provides the designer with the capability to make the allocations not based only on single criteria-based algorithms, but on complex relationships between the various criteria through the SDF.

SDF is defined in a hierarchial manner with a class structure. The taxonomy developed is not expected to be exhaustive. The approach is to identify and fully define the most relevant factors, and provide mechanisms for designer to define additional factors, as needed. The meta-rules will allow system designers with this flexibility.

Performance aspects of real-time systems are extremely complex. Real-time performance requirements can be in terms such as function latency, function throughput, message latency, and message throughput. Issues of utilization, load balancing, deadline hardness, and predictability are also performance concerns. SDF and the meta-rules allow mechanisms by which these performance aspects of real-time systems can be analyzed while also considering other important aspects such as system dependability, security, physical constraints, cost issues, logistics, etc. These methods have the potential to provide a framework which facilitates more systematic analysis of performance as well as non-performance related concerns.

Real-Time CAN Control Systems in Weaving Machines

Current Experience and Future Trends

Lars-Berno Fredriksson

Kvaser AB
Box 4076
511 04 Kinnahult
Sweden

During recent years control systems of weaving machines have developed rapidly. A weaving machine is constructed of some advanced components, each having a micro controller of its own. The interface between these components and the main control system is complicated since they must interact in a fraction of a millisecond. A true real-time controller area network is then a feasible basis for the control system of a weaving machine. When the fast serial CAN protocol, developed by Bosch and Intel for the automotive industry, was presented in 1988, it immediately gained a high degree of interest for the leading textile machine producers. In 1990 the Dornier company launched the first CAN controlled weaving machine on the market and has to date installed some 20000 CAN nodes working successfully all over the world. This field experience together with excellent test site results from other textile machinery producers have convinced the main European producers to chose a real-time controller area network architecture based upon CAN for their next generation control systems.

The CAN protocol is fast enough for many advanced real-time systems. The first CAN Controllers however lacked some essential functions that can be provided without violating the ISO draft standard. In 1990 the CAN Textile Users Group was founded by textile machinery producers developing CAN products. Within this group, extensive work has been done in order to find the optimum way to use CAN in real-time control systems. This cooperation has resulted in the development of a new philosophy; "A CAN Kingdom", and a related product; the "T-CANnector." The work has been well received by the chip manufacturers and already this year we will see CAN Controllers suited also for time triggered real-time systems.

"A CAN Kingdom" is a set of design rules and frame work of a few predefined messages enabling the system designer to customize standard modules to the needs of the system. The requirement of software and memory for this can be kept to a minimum. "A CAN Kingdom" also makes it possible to create a global clock and to make the maximum latency time of any message predictable.

The "T-CANnector" is a connector with the standard CAN Controller interface towards the module side. The bus side can be adopted to a multitude of physical layers. The "T-CANnector" also contains a small serial memory with information about the network identification number of the module, CAN controller settings etc. needed to establish the communication. The module micro-controller reads this information when connected to the network. "A CAN Kingdom" together with the "T-CANnector" makes it possible for a module designer to make standard modules that adopt themselves to any "CAN Kingdom" controller area network.

"A CAN Kingdom" and the "T-CANnector" put the missing pieces of the CAN protocol in place. Advanced real-time control systems can be built of standard modules and the non-automotive industry can then benefit from CAN chips made cheap by the vast automotive market.

The CAN Textile Users Group is also a member of the organization CAN in Automation (CiA) which is working towards a further set of standards enabling the efficient use of CAN outside the automotive industry. Through CiA the experience from the textile machines will be available for other lines of business.

Portability and Reusability in Real Time Systems

The Promise of Open Systems in Real-Time Environments

Carl H. Burmeister

Digital Equipment Corp.
8085 South Chester Street
Englewood, CO 80112
U.S.A.

Open systems technology has enabled developers in general to take advantage of the latest advances in computational technology by providing the mechanism for easily moving software from one hardware and operating system platform to another. Those who deal in real-time environments, however, have remained mostly unable to benefit from advances in technology through the use of so-called Open Systems. Open systems technology has yet to address issues beyond portable programming languages and standard system call interfaces. In this paper we investigate what additional elements are necessary to enable truly portable real-time systems development.

Real-Time Computing Systems are slow to change. These systems almost always involve the use of older software and hardware technologies. This is the result of the painstaking trial and error approach to system design which, once resulting in a working system, is difficult to change. This conservatism is imposed a) by the very consequences of system failures in so-called mission-critical environments and b) by the nature of current programming language and operating system support for Real-Time.

Five years ago the title of this paper might have read, "Real Time UNIX". For these past several years, much has been made of products which made this claim, all with varying degrees of technical merit. The debate has even been waged as to whether or not real time UNIX was feasible or desirable, but to my knowledge no one has addressed the issue of why someone would want real time UNIX or what its anticipated advantages might be. For some of us involved in developing software in a UNIX environment, the answer may have been obvious; for others, UNIX may have been regarded as the answer to every problem.

Some clarification was necessary of what our requirements for such an environment (portable Real-Time or Real-Time UNIX) might be because we felt the system perspective had yet to be applied to the subject and we felt that current standards for real-time system interfaces and programming language constructs were not covering important aspects of this problem.

Real time systems development in a UNIX environment has been thought to be desirable because industry decision makers feel that UNIX represents the best environment for developing vendor independent software and systems.

There are two basic perceptions behind this reasoning:

1. one can use the same people expertise when changing systems vendors and
2. one can use the same software source code when changing systems vendors.

And to remain competitive today, providers of any computer based solution must be able to respond to technology advances quickly. That frequently means changing systems vendors.

The central consideration in Real-Time is its system perspective. One does not consider Real-Time tasks in isolation, but as parts of an inter-related whole. The portability of such a system must take into account the timing requirements of the individual components and the necessary interactions between them.

In order to make these systems portable, operating systems and programming language constructs must be developed capable of the most critical and difficult time constraints on one hand and having standard interfaces including the ability to easily model timing behavior of the system components.

It is our goal to show how truly portable Real-Time systems can be developed now and the potential for Real-Time applications once open and interoperable systems are made easy to develop.

US Navy Next Generation Computer Resources Operating System Performance Measurement Guidelines

Daniel Juttelstad

Naval Undersea Warfare Center Division
Code 2221
Building 1171-3
Newport, RI 02841-5047
U.S.A.

Abstract

This effort was originated to provide guidance to application developers for evaluating implementations of the Next Generation Computer Resources (NGCR) Operating System Interface Standard (POSIX) and to define a common terminology. The results were developed by a joint effort between the following Navy Laboratories: NSWCDD, NAWC AD, NAWC AD Indianapolis, NRaD, NAWCWPNS, and NUWC DIV NPT.

Approach

The approach that the effort took was to define views of the system to establish a common perspective with respect to performance measurements. The classic black box/white box perspective is also utilized in all views. The views of the system were defined as 1) Total System, and 2) Application/Operating System (OS). The Total System view considers the system as a whole with no distinction between the OS and the other parts of the system. The Application/OS View identifies the OS interface and the Application as any other portion of the system that makes a request on the OS via the OS interface.

The Metrics are defined as timelines. These timelines are not to be considered as all inclusive, but rather to provide guidance in how to define a metric that a test will measure. They take into consideration black box and white box views of the system along with events of interest to be measured.

The Conditions provided identify examples of conditions that may affect performance. Not all conditions identified are applicable in all situations. Nor are all conditions for all situations identified. The intent is to provide the performance test designer with guidance in defining conditions that affect his specific performance metric that he is measuring.

The final portion of the approach provides recommended guidance for performance measurements. This provides guidance in the merging of the Views, Metrics, and Conditions. Areas addressed include the guidance in the definition of the architecture, the OS services provided, description of implementation of services, test design, and results of test. The test design includes issues with respect to the system view, metrics conditions, test implementation, and test procedure. This provides guidance in the content analysis presentation of the results. Special emphasis is put on the definition of the anomalies which occur in a given performance metric.

A Generic Systems Integration Framework for Large and Time-Critical Systems

Wilhelm Rossak[1], *Lonnie Welch*[1], *Tamar Zemel*[1], *Johan Eder*[2]

[1] New Jersey Institute of Technology Systems Integration
Laboratory and Real-Time Computing Laboratory,
Dept. of Computer and Information Science,
University Heights, Newark NJ 07102
U.S.A.

[2] Universität Klagenfurt — Institut für Informatik,
Universitätsstr. 65–67
9022 Klagenfurt
Austria

Abstract

The concepts presented in this paper propose a pre-planned and integrated development process for large and complex systems which include time-critical components. A system is partitioned into subsystems which are developed relatively independently within an integration framework, but work in an integrated manner — as a "system of systems" — to provide the necessary functionality within an application domain. To do this, we propose a generic systems integration framework (GenSIF) which includes a meta-level of control and management, coordinating the independent development projects. Domain modeling, integration architecture design and infrastructures design are identified as the main elements of the proposed framework. Based on these basic concepts, a generic process model for system development and integration is presented. A possible way to handle time-critical requirements in this environment is discussed.

1 Introduction

Over the past years, systems development has become increasingly demanding. We have to recognize the fact that current methodologies and development strategies are unable to deal with new challenges such as very large, distributed systems which should finally work in an integrated manner but are built by different contractors at different times in relatively independent projects. Mittermeir [13] and Eisner [5] characterize this problem by naming a set of critical factors which are not supported by traditional technology and the state-of-the-art of available process models. These critical factors can be summarized as follows:

– More than a single client is involved.

- More than a single producer is involved.
- More than a single project is involved.

What this paper addresses is the engineering methodology for such very large, long living, hybrid systems. Each of these systems handles a single application as a part of a larger, strategic system architecture. The basic idea is that looking at the set of all these applications as individual entities is not good enough. In an environment which has to deal with long term decisions, reasoning on a level above single applications is imperative [20], [28].

To guarantee the integration, optimization, timing behavior, and consistent user semantics of the final product, control over the autonomously running projects is mandatory [5], [13], [17]. Going beyond software engineering, we want to reach this meta-level of systems engineering by pre-planning and organizing the integration process. This includes the task to develop applications using a larger process framework like GenSIF (Generic Systems Integration Framework) [18] and to use a pre-specified integration architecture, e.g., an architecture of a loosely coupled system of systems or an industrially available architecture like the OSCATM architecture by Bellcore [14].

A fitting integration architecture is selected on the basis of a domain model [16], derived during a preceding step which analyzes the objects and requirements of the system's application environment [17]. The integration of all the individual projects (and their resulting systems) is then handled on the basis of such an architecture which also supports long term strategies and standards.

The Generic Systems Integration Framework (GenSIF) serves as a generalized blueprint for the description and handling of a development process [20]. It is based on domain modeling, integration architecture design, and utilization of enabling technologies. From the point of view of GenSIF, the integration architecture closes the gap between domain knowledge and off-the-shelf technologies. It works as a mediator between domain requirements and general purpose technologies. It also provides the basis for a framework that coordinates system development in independent projects.

Our research in systems integration includes the investigation of domain analysis methods and the evaluation of enabling technologies. However, our main concern is the study and development of integration architectures and the specification of a complete process model for (mega-)system development in the proposed integration framework [28], [29].

The rest of this paper is organized as follows: Section 2 describes the basic components of GenSIF and their relationships. In section 3 we discuss the conceptual model and the technical infrastructure which are the two major elements of an integrated development approach. Section 4 utilizes the "system of systems" integration architecture to outline a process model for the integrated development of (mega-)systems. Finally, section 5 investigates the applicability of schedulability analysis to decide on timing properties of applications developed as systems of systems.

2 GenSIF — A Generic Systems Integration Framework

The three major components of GenSIF are [18], [29]: a global domain model, an integration architecture, and assessment and usage of enabling technologies/infrastructures. These three components address different goals and needs at different levels of abstraction during the integrated development process.

The global domain model is derived during a domain analysis phase [16]. It specifies the application environment for all projects in the domain and is the basis for a conceptual integration architecture. One aspect of domain analysis is to deal with the elements and dynamics of an application domain. These domain phenomena are then mapped into the various systems and used as inputs for the projects which develop computer based systems. This involves the integration of information into a meta-data system, such as proposed by Hsu et al. [6] and Eder [19], and an analysis of the application domain to specify a common model of the environment the system is going to serve. In GenSIF domain analysis does not only provide a basis for semantic integration, but it is also the main input for the decision on the design of the integration architecture.

The integration architecture is the core of GenSIF. An integration architecture is a conceptual (design) model that bridges the gap between the domain model and enabling technologies by specifying and supporting system interoperability. It specifies also the requirements for an underlying infrastructure which provides the necessary utilities and components to implement an application system. An integration architecture must fit the needs of the application domain like a given hardware-architecture must fit the needs of the typical working environment it is serving.

Enabling technologies comprise all the tools and products that are required by the infrastructure for the development and execution of applications which will fill the abstract architecture with functionality and data. The goal here is to provide an execution platform which offers a standardized interface for all projects/systems in the domain. This infrastructure is not only concerned with the state-of-the-art but should also shield systems and architecture from the steady changes of underlying technologies.

Domain model, integration architecture and infrastructure provide the necessary models to handle strategic decisions and technical integration issues. As the major system engineering elements of GenSIF they guide the realization of all systems in the application domain by establishing a meta-level of planning and management above the project level [20] (Fig. 1).

GLOBAL DOMAIN MODEL

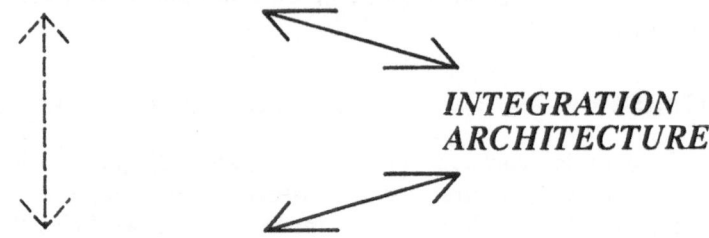

*INTEGRATION
ARCHITECTURE*

ENABLING TECHNOLOGIES

Fig. 1.

Projects on the system level are initialized and executed whenever a new system is added or updated within the related system of systems framework. If necessary, many projects can be active at the same point in time. Projects can also be started once other projects have already been finished to take care of maintenance, adaptation, or simply further development in the domain. Each project, if seen by itself, can run as usual. The only difference is that every project accepts the same models and standards, provided by the meta-level of the framework, as inputs and guidelines to implement a system that is compatible with the specified development philosophy and can thus be integrated into a comprehensive domain wide solution, a so-called mega-system [28], [29].
Systems of systems are an example for the mega-system type of applications.

Such a framework allows one to keep projects relatively small and manageable and to avoid the problem of huge monolithic systems. The challenge is to make sure that each project, even though working rather independently, does not develop an island mentality and produces isolated and incompatible solutions.

This concept of a layered approach to systems integration coordinates the influences of domain analysis, project management, and supporting technologies, and filters them through the integration architecture, thus providing a controlled process of reasoning, evaluation and adaptation.

3 The Main Elements of Coordination in GenSIF

3.1 The Integration Architecture

An integration architecture is a domain specific reference architecture which describes the meta-level of control and guidance, the basic rules and design constraints, and the support for all development projects in a given application domain [20].

A conceptual model of the integration architecture is specified on the meta-level of system development. It sets the standards and rules for system design in a given domain. However, it is not concerned with the design details of one specific system/project. It is a global reference architecture which sets the rules for inter-system communication, etc. Thus, it is concerned with the external interface and behavior of systems, making sure that these systems can be seen as part of an integrated mega-system [28], [29], and leaves the internal design of every system/building block to the various projects.

The conceptual integration architecture is the result of a "domain design" step — which is part of the mega-system tasks discussed in section 4 — that guarantees the coordination of otherwise independent design solutions. As it is a conceptual model, it is kept as implementation independent as possible, leaving coordination and integration of the tool level to the technical infrastructure.

The conceptual architecture model usually includes:

- Standards and guidelines for building blocks,
- a general strategy for system decomposition,
- standards for interfaces (internal and user),
- a communication model, and
- a model for handling of data storage and access.

A building block is the elementary concept of integration architectures. Building blocks are the components which provide the different functionalities in an application domain. The sum of all installed building blocks and the relationships between these building blocks form the systems of the domain and are finally integrated into a mega-system [14], [20], [28].

A building block acts like a black-box which offers services via a predefined interface but hides implementation details. It can be realized as a subroutine, a main program, a system of programs, a data-capsule, an object, etc.; i.e. every executable unit or set of executable units you can have in your environment. The used implementation language and the applied development method are of no concern to the integration architecture, as long as no rule of the conceptual model is violated. Every project is allowed to pursue its own locally optimized software engineering effort, e.g. in a format like COSMOS [27]. The important point is that every building block emulates the same type of interface, regardless of its internal structure, and uses the same method of communication and data access, as defined in the guidelines of the integration architecture. Services and functionality offered by building blocks are usually guaranteed to be available and compatible to other services over the lifetime of different versions and releases (See also the discussion on so-called "contracts" in the OSCA architecture [14]).

To connect building blocks to form fully functional systems, a communication model must be defined. This model specifies the standardized way by which one building block sends (and receives) data or control to (and from) another building block. This communication standard is only of concern on the system level of the application domain, but does not interfere with the internal characteristics of building blocks. So far we see two main strategies on this level: The free communication of standardized messages between building blocks [14], [2], or a centralized approach based on a structure similar to bulletin boards and traditional databases [3]. Whatever approach is chosen, one of the most important characteristic is usually to guarantee access and location transparency for building blocks.

By standardizing the way data is modeled, accessed and stored, or by providing mapping algorithms between different models, an integration architecture can open up the set of global data items to all building blocks. In a traditional environment these data items would have been guarded and hidden by a given application system. In an integrated system, built according to a global integration architecture, data is not "possessed" by a specific, limited application, but is seen as a global resource which has to be managed and organized. This support for data handling goes beyond data base systems as we know them today. The aim is to combine multiple data storage systems into an integrated data handling environment which is internally organized and publicly accessible by applying the communication and structuring elements of the open integration architecture (and not by introducing a parallel universe of communication and access rules).

Federated databases [7], [8], [11], [22] provide a very flexible means to model and implement this type of system. They overcome the traditional dichotomy of centralized databases vs. decentralized communication architectures and permit various degrees of local autonomy of a building block participating in a federation (system of systems) while providing partial and controlled sharing of their data. According to [22], autonomy can be discussed in four dimensions:

Design autonomy refers to the possibility not to include the design of a building block in a global design but design the building blocks independent from each other. *Communication autonomy* lets a building block decide whether or not to communicate with other building blocks. *Execution autonomy* permits a building block to execute local operations independent from other building blocks. Finally, *association autonomy* relates to the decision whether and which resources a building block shares with others.

Combining the concepts of decomposition rules, building blocks, standardized communication, and data handling, reuse becomes a natural part of every development process [2], [4]. Reuse on this level addresses not only tool-reuse on a relatively low level but encourages and supports also standardization and reuse on the level of designs, specifications and architectures.

A good example for a conceptual integration architecture are systems of systems, as we know them from the OSCA architecture [14] and Eisner [5], and discuss them in [28]. Eisner characterizes a system of systems as a multi-functional system, with several independently acquired and interdependent building blocks. Each building block in itself is a full system. The combined functionality of the systems constitutes and represents the satisfaction of an overall coherent mission. Each system that is part of the system of systems is developed in a separate project within the integration framework. The FAA's advanced automation system for air traffic control, as described in [9] and used in [5], is a typical example for a type of application that is naturally close to a system of systems design.

From an engineering point of view, a system of systems is a conceptual integration architecture which supports the development of a network of loosely coupled building blocks. Every building block relies on the free and implementation-independent communication of messages in a distributed environment via a predefined "channel". Data of global (domain wide) interest is stored in building blocks acting as data capsules. By specifying means to ensure upwards compatibility, data integrity, and other attributes, this system of systems architecture guarantees functionality and data handling on a very high level of abstraction. The development process is usually supported by decomposition rules that help define "good" building blocks. By studying the characteristics of systems of systems and by imposing further standards and restrictions, this architecture might also provide a basis for the handling of timing requirements of large and distributed systems, as discussed in section 5.

3.2 The Technical Infrastructure

The technical infrastructure is the basis for the implementation of systems which follow the rules of the conceptual model. The infrastructure, as the name suggests, provides the necessary standardized services which are an essential ingredient of the architecture. By providing basic system support in a structure which is an integrated development, execution, and maintenance environment, the infrastructure makes sure that all projects in the application domain can rely on a standardized implementation platform. The development of the elements of this platform is part of the efforts to specify and realize the integration architecture and is not a part of individual projects in which the architecture is used.

What finally is included in the infrastructure depends to a large extent on the type of architecture described by the conceptual model. Typical elements, useful for most types of architecture are [2], [3], [5]:
A software bus (channel) for communication, data storage facilities with standardized interface, and tools to build a user interface.

A software bus facilitates the communication between building blocks. It works like a bus or channel in a hardware architecture, providing an open standard to interconnect the building blocks which act like "boards" and are simply "plugged in". A software bus also gives the system engineer a chance to hide a set of distributed hardware/software platforms underneath the interface of the bus. By using logical addresses, a building block can communicate with another block via the bus without having to know where the other building block is installed. Changes in networking technology can be masked by this information hiding concept which is a factor in helping to maintain the upwards compatibility of successive versions of the integrated system. This concept of a software bus, providing at least location and access transparency, is found as an explicitly specified element in many existing architectures, e.g. in [2], [21], and is also offered as a separate tool you can buy off-the-shelf [1].

For most applications in a business oriented environment, the structured storage of permanent data is as important as the communication between building blocks. To facilitate an integrated approach, data storage must be provided according to the guidelines of the conceptual architecture model. If the architecture is oriented towards a centralized database system, e.g. [3], this component not only provides the handling of data, but also a main element of communication in the system. To realize such a data storing infrastructure component means to find a good database system and to fine-tune it for the use with the other components of the infrastructure. A solution of relatively independent data storage building blocks which are accessible over the software bus would offer a distributed, but still integrated data environment [12].

To include tools for user interface handling in the infrastructure of an integration architecture allows for unification and integration of the external appearance and the functional structure of different applications. Standardized interface solutions for the PC market have proven this concept. For the system designer who works on a project, a predefined set of interface tools, provided by the infrastructure, gives him a chance to separate his functional design from concerns about the interface. Issues regarding upwards compatibility and unification, as far as guidelines and standards are concerned, are part of the conceptual integration architecture. If tools and implementation issues are concerned, they are part of the infrastructure.

In our example, with a conceptual architecture of systems of systems, we would need at least the channel (or software bus) as a minimum requirement for the infrastructure. An example for an existing channel as described above would be the ANSA approach [1]. RAPID/NM [2], a reuse-oriented software platform, is an example for a more comprehensive approach. This infrastructure system includes not only a software bus, but also components to support user-interfaces, data storage, scheduling, etc.

4 A Process Model for the Integrated Development of Systems

The basic principle of systems integration as discussed in this paper is to upgrade the typical software engineering life cycle to overcome the problems encountered during development of mega-systems [28], [20], e.g. a system of systems. The major point is not to revolutionize the way systems are developed, but rather to lead to a gentle evolution of concepts, preserving knowledge and tools which exist for traditional development processes and environments, while introducing at the same time an additional level of reasoning and control above the single project. The goal is to make another step towards a more comprehensive and complete systems engineering process, and to support that process with methodologies and tools.

Figure 2 describes a simplified process model for such an integrated development effort [29]. It uses an extended version of SADT [29] to describe involved activities (shown as boxes) and data/control flows (shown as arrows). Flows entering an activity from the left are inputs and flows leaving from the right hand side are outputs. Flows used to guide activities (as a "reference model") are shown as entering from the top. So-called processors, supporting components for an activity, are flows going to the bottom of the corresponding box.

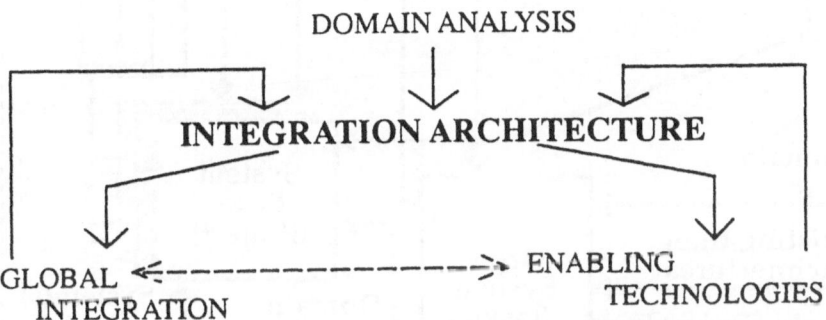

DOMAIN ANALYSIS

INTEGRATION ARCHITECTURE

GLOBAL
INTEGRATION

ENABLING
TECHNOLOGIES

Fig. 2.

In a development process for a system of systems, multiple system tasks (projects) can be active at the same point in time. System tasks represent the traditional system development process, transforming requirements into user-specific systems. To support the various projects and to guarantee an integrated result (e.g. a system of systems and not a set of unrelated systems), the domain model, the conceptual integration architecture, and the infrastructure are used, and all projects are scheduled and controlled by a meta-management task. A synthesis-task finally links all delivered systems into a comprehensive system of systems.

System tasks (Fig. 3) represent a rather traditional system development process (a project) that transforms problem specific user requirements into a self-contained, user specific system. In GenSIF projects form the lower level of system development activities in the process model (see Fig. 1). Taking into account the nearly endless list of existing solutions in the area of software development methodologies and life cycles, we limit ourselves to the rather abstract and general point of view that requirements analysis, system design, and implementation are the essential ingredients for a development model on this level. In whatever variation these elements are specialized to finally provide a complete project model is not our major concern in this presentation, as long as the minimal process elements, as identified above, are present.

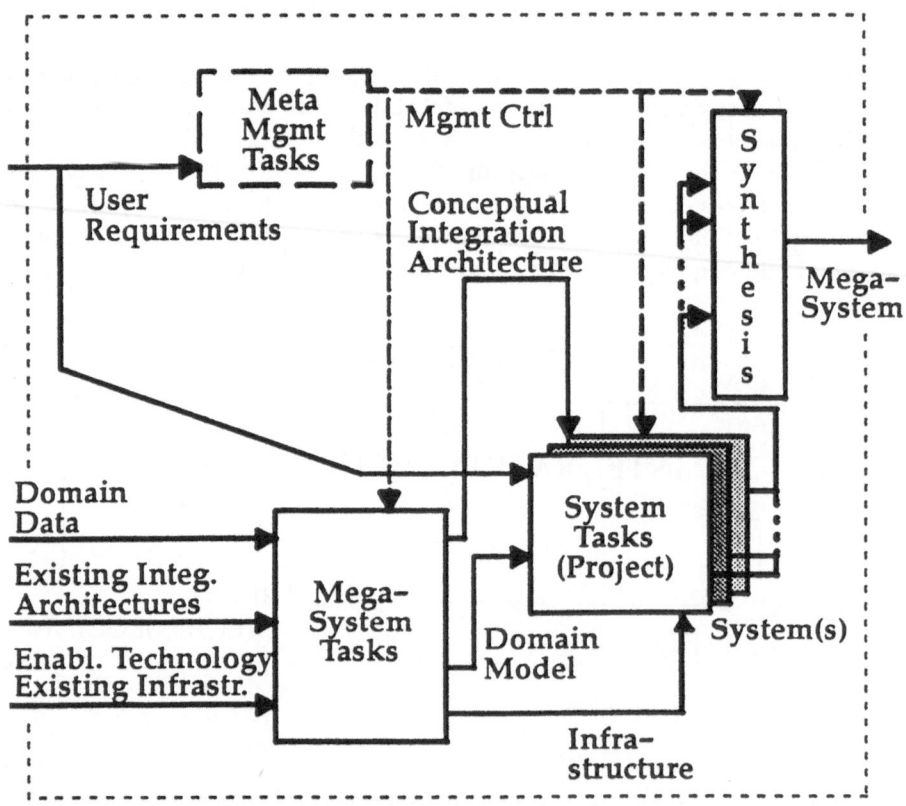

Fig. 3.

The main point is that a project does not run isolated and solemnly focused on local optimization but is an integrated part of a larger mega-system development effort: The domain model allows the project team to handle their local user requirements in the framework of a more comprehensive model and to communicate knowledge about the domain on the basis of a standardized common model. The conceptual integration architecture guides the traditional system development process by providing design concepts and by limiting possible alternatives — making sure that all results comply to the architecture. The technical infrastructure supports the implementation phase of the project by providing a standardized set of tools and techniques which are shared by all projects.

Integration architecture, domain model, and infrastructure are specified and maintained by the mega-system tasks activity. Mega-system tasks form the meta-level of system development activities in GenSIF (see Fig. 1). They complement the system tasks by providing the "links", the engineering models, that allow one to control and to coordinate the projects in the application domain. The goal of this set of tasks is to keep the projects as independent as possible while specifying the minimal necessary design framework to enable an integrated approach.

There is one task for each desired result: domain analysis to derive the domain model, integration architecture design to select and specialize an architecture for the given application domain, and infrastructure design to derive a fitting implementation platform for the given integration architecture.

The basic idea is that of a top-down, model driven approach, as opposed to current practice which is usually tool-driven and lacks any higher level of concepts. During the start-up phase, the tasks of the mega-system activity strive to reuse and to adapt existing and maybe standardized solutions, e.g. existing architectures, rather than to reinvent from scratch. However, it is important to understand that mega-system tasks, even though initialized with a top-down philosophy in mind, form an ongoing process and are not finished after a first design cycle. Domain analysis, integration architecture design, and infrastructure design remain active over the lifetime of the related application domain. External feedback from projects and synthesis tasks (not shown in Figures 2 to 3 to keep them simple) and internal feedback about the currently valid architecture and infrastructure are used to keep the resulting models up-to-date. Thus, mega-system tasks form a network of steadily active coordination and engineering activities but preserve the basic concept of a model driven approach.

Even though the systems which are the outputs of the various projects have been developed with systems integration in mind, a synthesis activity is shown (Fig. 2). This activity derives a new version of the mega-system from the set of systems produced by the projects every time a new element (system) is added or a change is made. This basic linking task is complemented by other mega-system related activities, e.g., the analysis of timing behavior for the system of systems if a new system is linked to the global mega-system structure.

5 Schedulability Analysis for Systems of Systems

A system of systems [5] is one way to design very large and complex applications on the basis of integration architectures. It is very likely that in such an application timing requirements will be of importance for at least some parts of the resulting "network" of components. To be able to handle these timing requirements, especially during the introduction of new systems to the existing system of systems over its possibly very long life cycle, predictability of (real-)time behavior is of high importance.

For the purpose of an analysis of timing behavior, a system of systems can be seen as a highly modular (mega-)program where every subsystem acts as an aggregation of components which introduce indirect timing effects on the rest of the application. The following paragraphs discuss a way to take advantage of this viewpoint to introduce schedulability analysis to application development with an underlying system of systems integration architecture.

Schedulability analysis is concerned with predicting real-time performance before the application is actually running [23], [24]. Even when done for programs written in languages that conform to time-constrained real-time languages, exact schedulability analysis is NP-complete. Essentially, existing accurate algorithms are exponential in the number of alternate conditional branches found in real-time programs and, in the case of parallel real-time systems, in the number of processors and software components in consideration. Furthermore, even polynomial-time algorithms may still be computationally-prohibitive, when the number of processors and components is very large, which is often the case with the class of applications designed as systems of systems.

We make the assumption that the code of components is amenable to static analysis, as in Real-Time Euclid [10]. We assume that loops have been unrolled, that no recursion is used, and that conditionals have been balanced and transformed [25], [26] to eliminate the number of alternate paths schedulability analysis [23], [24] has to consider. We also make the assumption that the call-DAG of components is statically-known. We require that the sizes of all variables and object states be statically determinable. In particular, we employ standard techniques used in RPC and distributed system implementations to compute the size of each operation parameter. The direction of each parameter (IN, OUT or IN/OUT) is either available from the language definition or is provided as a remote call annotation.

Consequently, each component specification contains sufficient information that describes how much time each operation of the component takes to execute, what other operations of what components each operation of the component calls and how many times, and how much data needs to be transmitted in each direction on each call. Given the interface description for the component (system) being integrated into an existing or new system of systems, a performance estimate of the entire application is undertaken in three steps.

First, the demand for each resource (PE or element of the infrastructure) is projected. For every resource at the node where the component will reside, this demand is computed according to polynomial-time heuristics, which project accurate accumulated execution or communication demand due to every assigned component within a certain interval of time (such as the least-common-multiple of the periods of all real-time processes using the component) and estimate such demand due to the components that have not yet been assigned. (Note that even these are heuristics in the sense that the demands are accurate in the accumulated sense only and not necessarily at any particular instance of time.) Should there be sufficient time, the same heuristics are applied to nodes and links neighboring this node.

In systems with a large number of nodes, as to be expected in a systems of systems, the corresponding demands (with the contribution of the component in consideration) are only estimated in the sense that individual nodes are not considered but groups of nodes are, as "mega-nodes" (one such mega-node includes the node of the component and its immediate neighbors). Should there be a very large number of nodes, then the mega-nodes are combined into "mega-mega-nodes" and so forth. Thus, systems in a system of systems architecture will be modeled on the basis of that mega-node concept, which makes it possible to see such a system just as another "mega-program", as claimed above.

Once accumulated demands for every resource have been estimated, they are easily converted into utilizations (by dividing over the size of the same time interval over which they have been accumulated). Should any utilization exceed 100%, the component is rejected as too time-consuming for the system.

Otherwise, the utilizations are in turn used to compute progress rates incurred by individual or groups of processes when attempting to use a particular resource. Each rate is estimated as an expected value, where the expected probabilities are the probabilities that

1. no request is made for the resource,
2. this process is the only one making a request, and
3. other processes made their requests when this component's request has come.

The expected values for each probability are, respectively, 100% (rate of progress), 100% and the fraction of this process's contribution to the total demand for the resource. Finally, response times of each process or a group of processes are computed as sums of ratios of each process's contribution to the total demand for a resource over the rate of progress of the process for this resource, for every resource.

The response times are contrasted with the corresponding process periods. Should a response time exceed a period, the performance prediction has identified a potential missed deadline, and the component (or system) is marked as too time-consuming. Should there be multiple choices for the same component or subsystem, the one which maximizes the laxities (computed as sums of differences between periods and projected response times) in the system can be singled out.

To further speed up the performance estimation, demands, utilizations, rates of progress and response times are computed incrementally. Typically, while relatively more work is needed to update the values of these metrics at the PE where the component is to reside, little extra work is needed for the mega- or the mega-mega- etcetera nodes necessary to handle integrated systems of systems. Furthermore, in systems where reusable component selection is provided and combined with the selection of the node to assign the component to, the performance estimate incorporates a fast assignment algorithm that considers a fixed number of nodes from among the least utilized ones.

The overall performance estimating procedure runs in fast polynomial-time, and is expected to provide good predictions of run-time real-time performance. A quantitative evaluation of the procedure is in progress.

6 Summary

The concepts presented in this paper go beyond an integration approach that glues together existing application systems to form a global system in a kind of "post-facto" approach [15]. Even though we accept the necessity of such an approach, our main goal is to provide a comprehensive model for systems integration based on a generic systems integration framework like GenSIF.

This framework is based on the idea to integrate the activities of the development process within a specified application domain by modeling the domain and deriving an integration architecture. This integration architecture is formulated as a conceptual architecture model, providing design guidelines and standards for all systems in the domain. An infrastructure, providing the environment for development and usage of such an integrated system, complements the abstract architecture on the tool level.

Using domain analysis and integration architecture design as the main elements of a process model for integrated systems development, we can improve (scale up) current technology in software engineering and real-time system development. As an example, we have discussed the possible usage of schedulability analysis as an element of the mega-system design and synthesis activities in the integrated process model.

Acknowledgement

We want to thank Alex Stoyenko for his work on earlier versions of this paper, especially for his contributions to the section on schedulability analysis. We also would like to thank all the members of the Systems Integration and Real-Time Computing Laboratories at NJIT for their continuous interest and support during the long hours of discussion.

References

1. ANSA, *An Engineer's Introduction to the Architecture*, Architecture Projects Management Limited, UK, Release TR.03.02, November 1989.

2. R.P. Beck, S.R. Desai, R.P. Radigan and D.Q. Vroom, *Software Reuse: A Competitive Advantage*, report, AT & T Bell Laboratories, Columbus Ohio, 1991.

3. L.J. Best, *Application Architecture — Modern Large Scale Information Processing*, Wiley, New York, 1990.

4. T.J. Biggerstaff and A.J. Perlis (eds.), *Software Reusability*, Vol. I & II, ACM Press, Addison Wesley, New York, NY, 1989.

5. H. Eisner, J. Marciniak, and R. McMillan, *Computer-Aided System of Systems (S2) Engineering*, Proceedings of the 1991 IEEE/SMC International Conference on Systems, Man, and Cybernetics, Charlottesville, VA, IEEE Computer Society Press, October 1991, 531–537.

6. C. Hsu, M. Bouziane, W. Cheung, J. Nogues, L. Rattner and L. Yee, *A Metadata System for Information Modeling and Integration*, Proceedings of the First International Conference on Systems Integration, Morristown, NJ, IEEE Computer Society Press, April 1990, 616–624.

7. D. Hsiao, *Tutorial on Federated Databases and Systems*, Part I, The VLDB Journal, Vol. 1, No. 1, 1992, 127–179.

8. D. Hsiao, *Tutorial on Federated Databases and Systems*, Part I and II, The VLDB Journal, Vol. 1, No. 2, 1992, 285–310.

9. V. Hunt and A. Zellweger, *The FAA's Advanced Automation System: Strategies for Future Air Traffic Control*, IEEE Computer, Vol. 20, No. 2, February 1987, 19–23.

10. E. Kligerman and A.D. Stoyenko, *Real-Time Euclid: A Language for Reliable Real-Time Systems*, IEEE Transactions on Software Engineering, Vol. 12, No. 9, September 1986, 940–949.

11. W. Litwin, L. Mark and N. Roussopoulos, *Interoperability of Multiple Autonomous Databases*, ACM Computing Surveys, Vol. 22, No. 3, 1990, 267–293.

12. J.A. Mills, *The Operations Systems Computing Architecture*, Proceedings of the First International Conference on Systems Integration, Morristown, NJ, IEEE Computer Society Press, April 1990, 482–491.

13. R.M. Mittermeir, POWDER — *A Recursive Methodology for Prototyping of Wicked Development Efforts with Reuse*, Institut für Informatik, Universität Klagenfurt, Austria, report for International Software Systems Inc., Austin, TX, USA, April 1991.

14. *The Bellcore OSCATM Architecture*, Bellcore — Bell Communications Research, Technical Advisory, TA-STS-000915, Issue 3, March 1992.

15. L.R. Power, *Post-Facto Integration Technology: New Discipline for an Old Practice*, Proceedings of the First International Conference on Systems Integration, Morristown, NJ, IEEE Computer Society Press, April 1990, 4–13.

16. R. Prieto-Diaz and G. Arango (eds.), *Domain Analysis and Software Systems Modeling*, IEEE Computer Society Press, Los Alamitos ,CA, 1991.

17. W. Rossak and S. Prasad, *Integration Architectures — A Framework for System Integration Decisions*, Proc. of the IEEE Internat. Conference on Systems, Man, and Cybernetics, Charlottesville, VA, October 1991, 545–550.

18. W. Rossak and P.A. Ng, *Some Thoughts on Systems Integration — A Conceptual Framework*, Journal of Systems Integration, Kluwer, Vol. 1, No. 1, 1991, 97–114.

19. J. Eder and W. Rossak, *Using a Data-Oriented Approach to Decide on Similarity of Objects during Domain Analysis*, 11th European Meeting on Cybernetics and Systems Research — Vienna, in R. Trappl (ed.): Cybernetics and Systems Research '92, Vol. 1, World Scientific Publisher, Singapore, April 1992, 81–88.

20. W. Rossak and P.A. Ng, *Systems Development with Integration Architectures*, Proc. of the IEEE Second International Conference on Systems Integration, Morristown NJ, June 1992, 96–103.

21. W. Schaefer and H. Weber, *European Software Factory Plan — The ESF Profile*, in P.A. Ng and R.T. Yeh (eds.), Modern Software Engineering, Van Nostrand Reinhold, New York, 1989, 613–638.

22. A.P. Seth and J.A. Larson, *Federated Databases for Managing Distributed, Heterogeneous and Autonomous Databases*, ACM Computing Surveys, Vol. 22, No. 3, 1990, 183–236.

23. A.D. Stoyenko, *A Schedulability Analyzer for Real-Time Euclid*, Proc. of the IEEE Real-Time Systems Symposium, San Jose, CA, December 1987.

24. A.D. Stoyenko, V.C. Hamacher and R.C. Holt, *Analyzing Hard-Real-Time Programs for Guaranteed Schedulability*, IEEE Transactions on Software Engineering, Vol. 17, No. 8, August 1991.

25. A.D. Stoyenko and T.J. Marlowe, *Schedulability, Program Transformations and Real-Time Programming*, in Proc. of the IEEE/IFAC Real-Time Operating Systems Workshop, Atlanta, Georgia, May 1991.

26. A.D. Stoyenko and T.J. Marlowe, *Polynomial-Time Transformations and Schedulability Analysis of Parallel Real-Time Programs with Restricted Resource Contention*, Real Time Systems, 1992, to appear.

27. R.T. Yeh, D.A. Naumann, R.T. Mittermeir, R.A. Schlemmer, G.E. Sumrall and J.T. LeBaron, COSMOS: *A Common Sense Management Model for Systems*, Internal report, ISSI International Software Systems Inc., Austin TX, 1991.

28. T. Zemel and W. Rossak, *Mega-Systems — The Issue of Advanced Systems Development*, Proc. of the IEEE Second International Conference on Systems Integration, Morristown NJ, June 1992, 548–555.

29. T. Zemel, *A Mega-System Development Framework*, Ph.D. Thesis, Department of Computer and Information Science, NJIT, in work.

A Dependable Distributed Software Architecture

Lambert J.M. Nieuwenhuis

Royal PTT Nederland NV
PTT Research
2260 AK Leidschendam
The Netherlands

Summary of Presentation

In this session we propose an architecture for dependable real-time software systems, which is based on fault tolerance through transformations of distributed programs. A transformed program consists of *replicas*, i.e., copies of the original program. The replicas of the original program must be executed by distinct units of a processor network after which the final result is obtained by means of majority voting on the replica results.

It is assumed that a majority of the program replicas is executed correctly and provide identical results. Deviations due to failures of a minority of the processor units can be detected and masked. The proposed program transformation reduces the risk of faults during the design process because decisions related to the reliability of the system are performed automatically. Furthermore, the reliability of the system is flexible because it depends on the number of separately executed replicas of the program only. The transformed programs can be executed by any parallel or distributed system using general purpose processor units. The drawback of the proposed program transformations is the additional overhead caused by the exchange of replica results through rather complex protocols.

Generally, real-time, high performance computing systems execute distributed programs by multiple processors in order to meet the requirements of the application. The application programs for such systems are divided into communicating processes, which are executed in parallel by multiple processors. Basically, the *performance* depends on the number of distinct processors executing the program. A similar approach is proposed with respect to reliability. The *reliability* depends on the number of process replicas that are executed by distinct processors.

The distributed programs and processor network can be modeled by means of directed graphs. The allocation of processes to processors is a function mapping nodes of the process graph onto the nodes of the processor graph. The proposed program transformation is defined elegantly by means of the graph product of the original process graph and a so-called replication graph.

A transformed program consists of replicas of the processes of the original program. Each process replica is composed of a copy of the original process and a small number of additional processes for comparison of input and output messages. Obviously, the comparison based on majority voting is useful only if the correct process replicas send *equal* messages. Correct process replicas may diverge due to small differences between input messages from the environment of the system or due to nondeterminism inside the replicas of a process. Replica divergence is a well-known complication of fault tolerant systems based on replication. Replica divergence in the transformed programs is prevented by means of an exchange of information between replicas of the same original process through a specific (Byzantine) protocol.

Technology Transition: Rate Monotonic Analysis in Real-System Developments

C. Douglas Locke

IBM Federal Systems Company
6600 Rockledge Drive
Bethesda, MD 20817
U.S.A.

1 Introduction

An important part of any successful research program is the transition of its results to the organizations and people who are architecting systems in its domain. In this paper, we describe the transition of the Rate Monotonic Analysis (RMA) technology into regular use within IBM's Federal Systems Company.

Sha, Goodenough [1] describe the use of Rate Monotonic Analysis technology for Ada software design, consisting of major conceptual expansions of the initial analysis of Rate Monotonic Scheduling described by Liu and Layland [2]. Because of its basic simplicity, stability, and its ability to be used without requiring major infrastructure modifications (i.e., languages, operating systems), RMA provided a natural technology to improve the ability to analyze and predict the ability of a system to meet its time constraints.

The question was how to insert this technology into existing and new system developments. IBM has a long history of successful system developments with critical time constraints; why was a new technology needed for such systems? Applications such as SAGE, A–7, LAMPS, Gemini, Apollo, Space Shuttle, B–52, and the FAA's Air Traffic Control systems had met their system requirements without RMA.

In this context, we must note the significant changes that have occurred in computer technology since IBM built systems such as SAGE and A–7. Memories of real-time processors have grown from about 16K to 32M and more. Processor speed has jumped from 0.2 MIPS to over 30 MIPS. While these changes have opened exciting vistas of opportunity, the software to run these system has jumped two orders of magnitude from about 15K Source Lines of Code (SLOC) to over 1.5M SLOC. It is this dramatic increase in complexity, resulting in a major challenge to maintain intellectual control over the developing system that necessitates improvements in our ability to produce systems that will be predictably successful meeting time constraints.

2 Prior Architectures for Real-Time Systems

Since the late 1950's, IBM and other real-time systems practitioners have generally used one of two basic software architectures:

1) Priority-Driven, in which semantically important tasks have priority over less important tasks when external or timer events occur, and
2) Timer-Driven, in which a sequence of procedures are called by a Cyclic Executive according to a list created off-line on a precisely defined schedule of timed intervals called frames.

Neither of these are satisfactory for creating predictable systems because they do not provide any way to predict their ability to remain within their design limits. A priority approach based on semantic importance can assure the ability of the highest priority tasks to meet time constraints, but little assurance can be given about low priority tasks. The Cyclic Executive approach means that the schedulability of the entire program is tightly coupled with the ability of each individual task to fit within its frame. As the programs become larger and more complex, these problems are greatly exacerbated.

What has been increasingly needed is an analyzable approach that would increase the separation of concerns between logical and timing correctness, but which would not require significant changes in the infrastructure, avoiding greatly increased life-cycle costs. While sub-optimal (with respect to resource utilization), the Rate Monotonic approach allows for exactly this analyzability within a generally familiar paradigm, resulting in a reasonable expectation that the transition would not be extraordinarily difficult.

3 Steps to Technology Transition

Basically, four steps were undertaken to perform this transition; these steps, undertaken concurrently, were:

1. In conjunction with CMU's Software Engineering Institute and the Naval Weapons Laboratory, a Generic Avionics Platform [3] was defined which captured the structure of an aircraft mission computer. The system's structure was implemented and analyzed using RMA, and was shown to perform as expected, including under overload conditions.
2. A regular series of 1–2 day seminars was created, both for software engineers and for systems engineers covering both the underlying theoretical basis of RMA and its application to existing systems and new developments.
3. Several ongoing projects used the RMA technology to assist them in resolving their time constraint problems. The results of these experiences were made widely available using the seminars as a communication medium.
4. Although the seminars emphasized the use of RMA in the context of the existing infrastructure, including the 1983 Ada standard and existing commercial operating systems, efforts were also undertaken to remove weaknesses in

the infrastructure. This has taken the form of activity in the Ada-9X update, the POSIX 1003.4 Realtime Extensions standardization process, coordinated activities with Ada compiler vendors, and efforts on other related hardware and software standards.

4 Conclusions

There have been a number of important benefits of this transition so far. The first, and probably the most important benefit is the ability to analyze a large and important class of real-time systems either before or after development, and correct timing problems as early as possible in the development cycle. Beyond this, the general awareness of the causes of timing problems has greatly increased, producing significant qualitative improvements in real-time designs even where quantitative analysis has not been performed.

As a result, engineering and programming personnel are increasingly able to concentrate on the logical correctness of a system, assured that the timing correctness can be kept under control. Management is increasingly aware of the necessity to create and maintain resource budgets, such as CPU and I/O bandwidth, and RMA has identified techniques for doing this.

Finally, this new awareness of the importance of an analytical approach to real-time system design is preparing engineers for more advanced and powerful real-time technology, including dynamic scheduling techniques, imprecise computations, etc.

References

1. L. Sha, J. Goodenough, *Real-Time Scheduling Theory and Ada*, IEEE Computer, Vol. 23, No. 4, April 1990, 53–62.
2. C.L. Liu, J.W. Layland, *Scheduling Algorithms for Multiprocessing in a Hard Real-Time Environment*, Journal of the ACM, Vol. 20, No. 1, January 1973, 46–61.
3. C.D. Locke, D.R. Vogel, T.J. Mesler, *Predictable Real-Time Avionics Design Using Ada Tasks and Rendezvous: A Case Study*, Ada Letters, ACM Press, Vol. 10, No. 9, Fall 1990, 118–125.

Scheduling in Fieldbus Based Real-Time Systems

Carlos Cardeira[*1,2], *Zoubir Mammeri*[3,4] *and Jean-Pierre Thomesse*[4]

[1] Sistemas - DEM - Instituto Superior Técnico
   Avenida Rovisco Pais, 1096 Lisboa Codex, Portugal

[2] CRAN (Centre de Recherche en Automatique de Nancy)
   Ensem, 2 av de la Forêt de Haye, 54516 Vandœuvre Cedex, France

[3] ENSAM (Ecole Natinale Supérieure des Arts et Métiers)
   BP 508, 51006 Chalons-sur-Marne Cedex, France

[4] CRIN (Centre de Recherche en Informatique de Nancy)
   Ensem, 2 av de la Forêt de Haye, 54516 Vandœuvre Cedex, France

Abstract

In this paper we discuss the characteristics that hard real-time networks (in particular fieldbuses) should satisfy to meet real-time requirements. Fieldbuses are networks that interconnect sensors, actuators and machines at the lowest level of a Computer Integrated Manufacturing (CIM) architecture. We propose that they should provide the services of a distributed real-time database. We found scheduling as the essential support to ensure the maintenance of this distributed real-time database in a consistent state, and we propose the analysis of pre-run-time schedulability of both tasks and network traffic to ensure predictability.

Keywords: Task-Scheduling, Real-Time Networks, Communication Systems, Network Configuration, Fieldbus.

1 Introduction

Real-Time Systems are those systems in which the correctness of the system depends not only on the logical result of computation but also on the time at which results are produced [19]. Many other definitions exist and it is current to distinguish them from Hard Real-Time Systems, when the error function of a result becomes more a step function than a continuously rising function [10]. Real-Time Systems interact with the environment. Real-Time Systems usually consist of tasks to read inputs, to process them, and to produce results affecting the evolution of the environment.

Needs for inter-networking Real-Time Systems may be seen at different hierarchical levels:

---

* Supported by Program Ciência-JNICT-Portugal (BD-1052)

- A high hierarchical level considering reconfiguration, supervision, historic journals. Networks like MAP are well suited to deal with these problems.
- A low hierarchical level where variables concerning the state of the real-time process are exchanged. In particular, fieldbus networks belong to this domain.

Fieldbuses are networks used at the lowest level of a CIM architecture [22], [21]. They interconnect sensors, actuators and processing machines replacing traditional 4-20 mA point-to-point connections.
Motivations for fieldbuses are:

- Wiring costs are ofen more than 75% of the whole distributed control system cost.
- They provide a more reliable communication (digital communications are more error free than analog ones).
- Hardware costs are becoming lower and lower, permitting the integration of a standard fieldbus interface in sensors and actuators.
- They suggest the development of Smart Instruments.
- They may assure the services of a distributed real-time data base.

Nevertheless, new problems arise. Among all these problems, we may cite:

- The fieldbus, even if it may be an excellent physical support, is a shared support (a communication bottleneck), so medium access protocols ensuring medium access at precise time must be provided.
- Usual problems of distributed systems also arise: No central memory, no central clock, no global view of the system, so mechanisms to ensure the spatial coherence of variables and clock synchronization must be provided.

In our opinion a fieldbus should provide the services of a real-time distributed data base. This real-time data base should have the following characteristics:

- Abstraction of data origin. Every object should be identified by its name, not its producer.
- Real-Time Consistency in the sense of Kopetz. To maintain this data base in a consistent state, Kopetz [12] defined that all its values should not be different from its real image for more than a well known Δt.

To ensure that all the variables represent a copy of its real value in the environment, acquisition tasks, processing tasks, and network traffic must be started, executed and concluded at the right instances of time. *That's why scheduling of tasks and network traffic are extremely important in real-time systems.*
The impact of this discussion on fieldbus architecture is that we think that for a fieldbus, some of the traffic must be configured off-line as it happens for some tasks in real-time systems. Static traffic and tasks must be pre-run-time scheduled [17], [29] to ensure that hard real-time constraints will be met [13], in case that no undefined faults occur.

In a real-time system, both a variable and the time it was produced, should be considered an atomic entity and so, should always be broadcast together. This timing information is analyzed by consuming tasks to verify their temporal validity.

FIP protocols [25], [23], [26], [24], [14], support some of the above detailed characteristics. In particular they provide:

- Pre-run-time configuration of traffic.
- Flags associated to transmitted variables indicating their temporal validity.

Our aim is to establish models for the activation, execution and termination of real-time tasks and fieldbus network traffic, to schedule them statically with the objective of guaranteeing that a given configuration will respect its timing constraints.

2 The Approach

To achieve our objectives of a pre-run-time scheduling of both tasks and network traffic, our approach has been to divide the problem in five phases:

1. We should look for the current practices used to model tasks, machines and networks, from the viewpoint of scheduling. Much earlier work exists concerning scheduling algorithms. The idea is to analyze those algorithms specially by how they consider a task. For instance, one of the classical references for scheduling algorithms, the article from Liu and Leyland in 1973 [15], considered all the tasks with deadlines as periodic and independent ones. From then to nowadays, further work has been done to remove some of these constraints, and now we can find algorithms exist supporting aperiodic tasks, precedence constraints, resource constraints, imprecise computations, etc.
2. See if these existing models are enough. This phase should end with a chosen model or a new model proposal to handle some more necessary constraints.
3. As for network traffic modelling, as we said in the beginning, we are specially concerned with fieldbuses, in particular FIP. In this fieldbus, the network scheduler supports pre-run-time configuration of the traffic. Our idea is to apply the algorithms studied above to the network scheduler comparing performances of same class algorithms.
4. Propose algorithms to the overall scheduling analysis of both tasks in each node and messages in the network.

As we may see this is a very large plan. We'll present the work done and the results obtained.

3 Results

Phase 1 consists of a bibliographic research [4] making a state-of-art survey of existing scheduling algorithms. The analysis began by considering Liu and Leyland's work [15] and continued with the other works.

Through our analysis we've found algorithms considering this kind of tasks:

- Periodic and independant Tasks [15].
- Aperiodic Tasks [18].
- Tasks with precedence constraints [7], [28].
- Tasks with resource constraints [16], [30].
- Tasks with imprecise computations [8], [9].
- Tasks with allocation contraints [27], [2].

Some of the references shown above, support more than one kind of constraints. References aren't exhaustive (see [4] for more). Some other papers provide good synthesis such as [6], [29], [1], [3].

By Phase 2, we were specially interested in seeing how these algorithms handle tasks. Our aim was to get a good and complete task model to support most of the above constraints, and a discussion of this has been presented by [5] . In [5] we've made several improvements on a simple model, but our conclusion was that, as more and more constraints must be handled, more formalisms approaching the formal representation of natural language are well suited to represent those tasks' constraints.

In particular we think that Jahanian and Mok's work [11], who proposed a real-time logic to analyze systems specifications, represent good tools to handle most of these real-time constraints.

4 Conclusions

As for the objectives initially presented, we've elaborated state-of-art scheduling algorithms in real-time systems. Each algorithm is always connected to a certain way of viewing the reality. One of the problems is that reality is not so easy to model, and real-time tasks are more complex than usual models propose it. As more and more constraints are supported more and more the algorithms increase their complexity even if this isn't a problem for off-line configuration.

Another solution is the analysis of real-time programs, to extract their constraints, making the necessary transformations to determine worst-case execution conditions [20] like critical paths to enable a schedulability analysis. This approach suffers from the usual inconvenient resource waste, but nowadays one may ask for some redefinition of the concept "resource waste", because of the always decreasing hardware costs.

References

1. M. Alabau and T. Dechaize, *Ordonnancement temps réel par échéance*, Technique et Science Informatiques, Vol. 11, No. 3, 1992, 59–123.
2. J. Bannister and K. Trivedi, *Task allocation in fault-tolerant distributed systems*, Acta Informatica, Vol. 20, 1983, 261–81.
3. J. Blazewicz, K. Ecker, G. Schmidt, and J. Weglarz, *Scheduling in Computer and Manufacturing Systems*, Springer-Verlag, 1993.

4. C. Cardeira, *Algorithmes d'ordonnancement temps réel – Étude et classification*, Rapport interne, CRAN, Nancy, November 1991.

5. C. Cardeira, Z. Mammeri, and J.-P. Thomesse, *Task specification for scheduling in distributed real-time systems*, Technical report, Centre de Recherche on Informatique de Nancy, 1992.

6. T. Casavant and J. Kuhl, *A Taxonomy of Scheduling in General-Purpose Distributed Computing Systems*, IEEE Transactions on Software Engeneering, Vol. 14, No. 2, February 1988, 141–54.

7. H. Chetto, M. Silly, and T. Bouchentouf, *ynamic scheduling of real-time tasks under precedence constraints*, Journal of Real-Time Systems, Vol. 2, No. 3, March 1990, 181–94.

8. J. Chung, J. Liu, and K. Lin, *Scheduling periodic jobs using imprecise results*, Technical Report UIUCDCS-R-87-1307, Department of Computer Science, University of Illinois, Urbana, IL, November 1987.

9. T. Dean and M. Boddy, *An Analysis of Time-Dependent Planning*, Proceedings of the 7th National (USA) Conference on Artificial Inteligence, 1988, 49–54.

10. Hoogeboon and Halang, *The Concept of Time in Software Engineering for Real Time Systems*, 3rd International Conference on Software Engineering for Real Time Systems, IEEE, 1991, Vol. 344, pages 156–163.

11. F. Jahanian and A. Mok, *Safety Analysis of Timing Properties in Real-Time Systems*, IEEE Transactions on Software Engeneering, Vol. 12, No. 9, September 1986, 890–904.

12. H. Kopetz, *Scheduling in Distributed Real Time Systems*, Technical report, Technical University of Vienna, Austria, January 1986.

13. T. Laine, *Modélisation d'applications réparties pour la configuration automatique d'un bus de terrain*, Thèse de Doctorat de l'Institut National Polytechnique de Lorraine, Mai 1991.

14. P. Leterrier and J.-P. Thomesse, *Fonctions d'un bus de terrain. Application et bases de données industrielles réparties. Services du système de communication FIP*, Mini Micro, Vol. 328, October 1989, 34–36.

15. C. Liu and J. Layland, *Scheduling algorithms for multiprogramming in a hard real-time environment*, Journal of the ACM, Vol. 20, No. 1, January 1973, 46–61.

16. K. Ramamrithan and J. Stankovic, *Distributing Scheduling of Tasks with Deadlines and Ressource Requirements*, IEEE Transactions on Computers, Vol. 38, No. 8, August 1989, 1110–1123.

17. T. Shepard and J. Gagné, *A Model of the F18 Mission Computer Software for Pre-Run-Time Scheduling*, 10th International Conference on Distributed Computing Systems, IEEE/INRIA, May 1990, 62–69.

18. B. Sprunt, L. Sha, and J. Lehocsky, *A periodic Task Scheduling for Hard Real-Time Systems*, Real-Time Systems, Vol. 1, No. 60, 1989, 27–60.

19. J. Stankovic and K. Ramamritham, *The Spring kernel: a new paradigm for real-time systems*, IEEE Software, Vol. 8, No. 3, May 1991, 62–72.

20. A. Stoyenko, T. Marlowe, and W. Halang, *Enabling efficient schedulability analysis through program transformations and restricted resorce contention*, IFAC/IFIP International Workshop on Real-Time Programming, Bruges (Belgium), June 1992, 269–274.

21. J.-P. Thomesse, *Les réseaux de capteurs actionneurs*, Actes Colloque Automatique et Informatique avancées dans la Sidérurgie, Nancy, September 1989.

22. J.-P. Thomesse, *Les réseaux locaux industriels dans les architectures des systèmes automatisés*, Actes 2ème Colloque de Transitique, Paris, September 1989.

23. J.-P. Thomesse and J.-L. Delcuvellerie, *FIP - a standard proposal for fieldbuses*, Proceedings IEEE-NBS Workshop on Factory Communications, Washington (USA), March 17-18, 1987.

24. J.-P. Thomesse and T. Laine, *The Field Bus Application Services*, Proceedings IECON'89 (15th Conference IEEE-IES Factory Automation), Vol. 3, Philadelphia (USA), November 1989, 526–530.

25. J.-P. Thomesse, P. Lorenz, J.-P. Bardinet, P. Leterrier, and T. Valentin, *Factory Instrumentation Protocol: Model, Products, and Tools*, Control Engineering, Vol. 38, No. 12, September 1991, 65–67.

26. J.-P. Thomesse and P. Noury, *Le réseau de terrain ouvert: FIP*, Revue d'Automatique et Productique Appliquées, Vol. 2, No. 2, 1989, 23–32.

27. K. Tindell, A. Burns, and A. Wellings, *Allocating hard real-time tasks: An np-hard problem made easy*, The Journal of Real-Time Systems, Vol. 4, 1992, 145–65.

28. J. Xu and D. Parnas, *Scheduling Processes with Release Times, Deadlines, Precedence and Exclusion Relations*, IEEE Transactions on Software Engineering, Vol. 16, No 3, March 1990.

29. J. Xu and D. Parnas, *On Satisfying Timing Constraints in Hard-Real-Time Systems*, Proceedings of the ACM SIGSOFT'91 Conference on Software for Critical Systems, ACM, ACM Press, Vol. 16, December 1991, 132–146.

30. W. Zhao, K. Ramamrithan, and J. Stankovic, *Scheduling Tasks with Ressource Requirements in Hard Real-Time Systems*, IEEE Transactions on Computers, Vol. 13, No. 5, May 1987, 1186–1203.

Ship System 2000

Ulf Olsson

Naval Systems
NobelTech
175 88 Järfälla
Sweden

Real-time computing is a term that seems easy enough to understand, but that eludes most attempts at strict definition. The Ship System 2000 family of naval Command, Control, Communications and Weapon Control systems does, however, encompass most variants of computer programming that fall under the real-time heading. Towards the soft end, the systems are expected to handle large amounts of data and provide decision support tools that are used to analyze tactical scenarios a number of hours into the future. There, response time is not extremely critical, but size and algorithmic performance issues can nevertheless be crucial. In the middle of the spectrum, data fusion and display functions (for instance), should have response times compatible with human reaction times. Approaching the area of hard real-time programming, we have servo loops in, e.g., the fire control system running at more than 50 Hz. The extreme cases are also present: signal processing in the radars themselves, running at several kHz.

The SS2000 architecture is built to provide a platform for most of these applications. Current state of the practice does not allow us to build anything but tailor-made solutions in the signal processing end, but apart from those areas, we have found a common ground for the implementation of a very large set of different applications. The story of SS2000 is not so much one of technical achievement: the architecture is based on well-known principles and sound engineering practices. The real challenge has instead been how to make the large number of people involved (>200 SW engineers) work in concert to build a comparatively large system (>1.5M DSI Ada currently in use aboard ships, in 4 different configurations for 3 navies). The real issues then become centered around the architecture itself: finding a core set of components that provide the necessary and sufficient application support, finding the appropriate abstractions to provide interchangeability of components, creating the necessary stability in those basic assumptions to make it possible to actually let the bulk of the work proceed in parallel.

Above all, however, it becomes quite clear that the path towards better, more reliable systems goes neither through tons of specifications nor via clever new ways of drawing little bubbles with arrows. They help (sometimes), but the only decisive factor is the motivation, competence and application awareness of the people involved. Therefore: if you want to build good systems, find good systems designers.

Reuse in Ship System 2000

The SS2000 family of naval systems was designed from the outset to be reusable, in the sense that it had to be easy to select and reconfigure the software components necessary to match a new configuration of ship's weapons and sensors. It is important to understand that reuse in this sense is not taking things out of a library as raw material for a new component, but rather the reuse of unmodified, tested and therefore reliable components. The reasons are obvious: apart from the economy involved in using ready-made parts instead of building them (*the advantages of theft over toil*, as Grady Booch puts it), it is also important to realize that if a system can be made to a large extent from pieces that have already had thousands of hours of accumulated usage time, the effects on software reliability are substantial.

Reuse is easily said, but sometimes harder to do. In this case, we had substantial experience from previous generations of systems, as well as two parallel launching projects (the Danish Standard Flex 300 multi-role ship, and the Swedish Göteborg-class Coastal Corvette). This meant that we were forced to do what we now would call a domain analysis, to determine which parts of the architecture that could be trusted to be stable and common, and which parts that were likely to change from customer to customer. The result was a design that was inspired heavily by Object-Oriented Design, but where many design decisions were directly motivated by the wish to promote reusability where necessary.

At this time, six years into the program, it seems that the architecture lives up to our intentions. We regularly see reuse rates for new projects in the 60 to 80% bracket. Also, we have conducted a very successful experiment with another kind of reuse: porting the architecture to a drastically different hardware and software platform. This experiment has proven to us that we will actually be able to do what reuse really is meant to provide: to amortize our investment in application components over a long time. This may well turn out to be the most useful kind of reuse there is, since it allows us to cash in on the enormous improvements in price/performance that computer hardware exhibits, while still protecting our main asset: *the applications that solve the real end-user problems.*

Adaptive Fault Management

Thomas F. Lawrence

Rome Laboratory
C3AB, Griffiss AFB
525 Brooks Road
Rome, NY 13441-4505
U.S.A.

Adaptive systems are not unusual at all. Adaptivity defines natural processes from evolution to the behavior of the individual human on a moment to moment basis. We should not confuse the sparsity of artificial adaptive systems created by man with the abundance of such systems produced by nature. Since nature has validated the concept, the technologists should have no fear in pursuing adaptive systems of the artificial kind, including adaptive fault management. Adaptive fault management is the process of changing in run time, the fault management techniques and strategies of the system to adjust to the external and internal system state. For instance change in the fault type or fault/error rate would cause an automatic adjustment in fault management. A change in mode of operation of a command control system (e.g. peace time, alert, war) can also cause adaptivity to occur. Every system can be characterized by a set of specifications called object function. Each objective function includes a specification for: function (processing, communications or data storage), performance, availability, precision, mutual consistency, security, safety, etc.

Anomalies in the system can prevent the system from achieving any or all specifications in the objective function. However, fault management mechanism and strategies cause the system to meet the specification in the presence of these anomalies. Sources of anomalies includes (1) design faults, (2) failure of a once properly operating component, and (3) shared resource conflicts.

In an adaptive system the objective function set is dynamic and can change as the external environment changes. Further each of the terms in the objective function is specified not rigidly by one number but by a range of numbers, for each of which there is an associated "Value" determined by the application. These specification/value functions provide the basis for extreme adaptivity where the system can tradeoff one specification for another at run time and release resources for the most important tasks.

From our research at Rome Laboratory we have found that adaptive fault management is quite feasible and not as complex as one might at first think. Techniques for fault management have been classified as optimistic, pessimistic or ultra-pessimistic. Ultra-pessimistic strategies rely on techniques of approximation, that is approximate processing, approximate communication and approximate data and use application level information. Adaptivity is accomplished by switching from one class of technique to another.

Important ideas in adaptive real-time systems includes (1) using the maximum amount of information available especially application level semantics, and (2) using metrics that are consistent with the level of abstractions. The complex adaptivity posed above and its impact on real-time control is still a research topic.

Programming Language Standardization. A Case Study for Forth

V. Vande Keere, J. Vandewege

Laboratory for Electromagnetism and Acoustics
University of Gent
Sint-Pietersnieuwstraat 41
9000 Gent
Belgium

Abstract

Programming language standardization is presented as a major aid in making the right language choice to solve a software problem. This is illustrated using the historical and conceptual background of the language Forth. Subsequently we summarize general aspects of a good language standard. The relation between abstraction level and standardization suitability is analyzed. The impact of standardization on software quality is determined in connection to the McCall quality model and its contribution to general language acceptance is illustrated.

1 Introduction

The selection of an appropriate programming language is a matter of considerable importance in the design of software for real-time systems. At this stage of the design, the availability of a good language standard contributes to the elimination of misconceptions and obscure argumentation leading to a wrong choice. This is particularly well illustrated in the case of Forth, which is currently under ANSI standardization[1]. Forth was developed by C. Moore in the late 60s[2], its main application area being real-time interaction with hardware. Despite the previous Forth 79 and 83 standardization efforts, the language didn't experience a well-coordinated evolution. Consequently it became subject to a number of misconceptions, such as the common misinterpretation of Forth as the ultimate, universal programming language, its breath of non-professionalism and the impression of limited code portability. They are all explained by shortcomings in standardization.

2 Standardization Characteristics

Five requirements of a good standard are presented next. The degree to which they are met, determines the intrinsic quality of the standard.

1. A good standard contains unambiguous and consistent defining elements on terminology and language.
2. It is unique in the sense that statements are universal and interpreted in an identical way by any eventual user.
3. It is complete, i.e. it addresses all aspects that are suited for standardization, thus preventing individual modifications.
4. The standardization approach is general, and therefore implementation independent.
5. The standard is the result of profound investigation and consideration by a representative part of the programmers community.

Final standardization success however is not only determined by its intrinsic quality, but also by the important factor of overall acceptance and discipline in use.

3 Standardization Suitability

A common classification of programming languages is one according to their level of abstraction, i.e. the width of the semantic gap they span between hardware and formal application description. We make a four level classification consisting of

1. machine languages,
2. system programming languages,
3. general programming languages, and
4. application specific languages.

Not all presented levels are equally suited for standardization. The machine language level is hardware dependent and hence unsuited for standardization. On the high level end, languages are highly specific so that standardization is somewhat irrelevant because there is no proliferation of different versions. Main standardization interest is found on the two intermediate levels. A two- dimensional representation of this relation between abstraction level and standardization suitability results in a sort of "boomerang" plot.

4 Shortcomings in Forth Standardization

Reconsidering the five requirements of a good standard, we see that three of them are offended by the Forth 79 and 83 standardization efforts:

1. standardization was not unique because of differences between both,
2. it was not complete since a number of features presented as a matter of evidence in other languages (e.g. floating point, string and file support, interfacing to other OS) were not covered, and

3. the standardization effort was not sufficiently general because both Forth 79 and 83 were based on a particular machine architecture and imposed an implementation model known as the *Forth virtual machine*, prohibiting direct hardware implementations [3].

Another particularity of Forth standardization appears when the relation between language abstraction level and standardization suitability is taken into account. Forth applies a programming concept that allows to span all levels of abstraction within the same environment. Standardization however is only useful for some levels, so it is important to make a careful distinction between what to include and not to include in the standard. Previous standards have failed in doing this. Therefore and for reasons of competitivity, many Forth vendors and users chose to develop their own modifications instead of complying with an existing standard. This evolution brought in a number of misconceptions, some of which are mentioned before.

5 Impact of Standardization

Two main areas of impact are explored next, viz. software quality and general language acceptance. Software quality as described in[4] includes product quality, for which the McCall quality model is applied. Most standardization aspects discussed earlier are related to a number of attributes in this model. A standard provides completeness and consistency of language elements and contributes to software correctness. Clear definitions of word names improve readability, thus contributing to software maintenance. Standard generality means hardware independence, which improves software reusability and portability. A standard provides transparency for system dependent aspects, making the language easier to use. Particularly for Forth, a good standard should support compatibility with other OS, increasing software adaptability. In addition, a standard provides means for product leverage. It can function as a starting point for teaching and makes it easier to bring in other programmers who may be familiar with the standard[5]. It provides a common language for communication among users, programmers and vendors. It contributes to unification by presenting a uniform programming platform, facilitating the design of general tools and environments similar to the ones available for the mainstream programming languages.

6 Conclusion

Five factors determining the intrinsic quality of a programming language standard have been summarized. A relation has been found between language abstraction level and standardization suitability in the form of a "boomerang" plot. Shortcomings in Forth standardization have been explained. The impact of standardization on software quality and its contribution to general language acceptance have been illustrated.

References

1. X3J14 - FORTH Technical Committee, dpANS-3, *Programming Language FORTH*, June 1992, X3 Secretariat CBEMA.
2. Moore, C. H., *The Evolution of* FORTH, *an Unusual Language*, BYTE, Vol. 5, No. 8, August 1980, 76–92.
3. Koopman, P.J. jr., *Stack Computers, The New Wave*, Ellis Horwood, Chichester, UK, 1989.
4. Hindel, B., *How to ensure software quality for Real-Time Systems*, Proc. Internat. Workshop on Real-Time Programming, Bruges, June 1992, IFAC, Pergamon Press, 1992, 231–236.
5. Peterson, J.V., *The Forth "Standards"*, FORML Conference Proceedings, November 1986, FIG Inc., San Jose, 1986, 170–175.

Monitoring of Distributed Real-Time Systems

Ulrich Schmid

Technical University of Vienna
Department of Automation
Treitlstraße 3
1040 Vienna
Austria

An important part of a major research activity on *real-time-performance analysis of event driven systems* pursued at our department is devoted to monitoring of distributed real-time systems: The project VTA[1] aims at the development of the research prototype of a flexible monitoring system (the *Versatile Timing Analyzer VTA*), which is required for observing the external and internal (timing-) behaviour of a distributed real-time system; see [1] for an overview.

The scope of applicability of such a monitoring system comprises

1. **Theoretical research**

   Another project within our major research activity is devoted to the (mathematical) analysis of deadline meeting properties of event driven real-time systems subjected to general dynamic event arrivals: Hard real-time systems usually rely on the assumption of (essentially) cyclic events, where deadline meeting guarantees may be given. On the other hand, dynamic models suitable for general aperiodic arrivals and associated (soft) real-time computations have not been known yet — despite of the large number of event driven real-time applications demonstrating that such systems are common in practice. Therefore, we tried to find dynamic event arrival models which

   (a) apply reasonably well in practice,
   (b) permit the definition of significant real-time performance metrics,
   (c) render a rigorous analysis of such metrics feasible.

   We found that the above requirements are — to a certain extent — satisfied by a simple model based on independent, generally distributed event arrivals during a constant (application-dependent) cycle time in conjunction with independent task sets. In a number of papers (e.g.[2], [3]), we analyzed the appropriate deadline missing probabilities for a few simple scheduling disciplines. The results, as limited as they are, convinced us that our (non-queuing theory) analysis approach works and provides a suitable basis for further research.

---

[1] Supported by the Austrian Science Foundation (FWF), Grant P8390-PHY.

However, we recognized soon that we — and it seems, scientific work on real-time systems as a whole — lack realistic information concerning event arrivals in existing real-time systems. Without it, however, an answer to the question wether our models are appropriate in practice or not is impossible. Consequently, a flexible and powerful monitoring system is needed to facilitate the process of gathering the required information. Note that an observation of the "raw data stream" accessible via the environmental interface of a real-time system is usually not sufficient, since the most important events appear in "higher-level data streams" generated by various preprocessing stages.

2. System checking

A certain class of applications of a monitoring system support — in a certain sense — the requirements engineering phase within real-time systems development: Since there is a certain danger to build a real-time system upon wrong assumptions concerning the controlled environment, a continuous monitoring of its behaviour is invaluable to decrease the risk of a failure due to a specification error. Note that this is especially true for static systems.

Another very important application of a monitoring system is to use it as a testing tool. Due to the usually poor conceptual basis of today's real-time systems, many of them are designed rather ad hoc. Consequently, one should at least check their timing properties by an actual measurement, e.g. by checking

(a) deadline meeting properties,

(b) internal (timing) behaviour,

(c) resource (under-)utilization,

instead of believing in their correctness/appropriatness only.

Given such requirements, it is clear that flexibility and extendability are two essential features of a monitoring system suitable for our purposes. Consequently, we designed our VTA according to the so-called *event-action model* relying on user-programmable monitoring actions triggered by the occurrence of user-definable events within the observed real-time system's hardware and software. Despite of some valuable research experience from traditional event-based debugging, however, the development of our VTA involves a lot of interesting research in many fields and — last but not least — laborous design and implementation work to be done.

References

1. U. Schmid and S. Stöckler, *A Versatile Monitoring System for Distributed Real-Time Systems*, Proc. SAFECOMP '92, Zürich (to appear).
2. U. Schmid and J. Blieberger, *Some Investigations on FCFS Scheduling in Hard Real Time Applications*, J. Comput. Syst. Sci. (to appear).
3. M. Drmota and U. Schmid, *Exponential Limiting Distributions in Queueing Systems with Deadlines*, SIAM J. Appl. Math. (to appear).

State-of-the-Art in Real-Time Computing Research, Development and Technology

John Cullyer

Dept. of Engineering
University of Warwick
Coventry CV4 7AL
U.K.

Despite the large sums of money expended on research and development in the area of real-time computing, the subject remains immature and poorly understood. There have been sound advances, such as the introduction of the programming language Ada and its various Programming Support Environments. Yet some in the industrial real-time computing community still use languages such as "C" and employ limited dynamic tasting as the sole means of verifying the functionality of the product.

Considering the utility and application of the real-time software produced, it has been estimated by the General Audit Office of the United States that 40% of all real-time software developed for US government agencies is never used operationally, due to lack of functionality, speed, presence of errors, late delivery and budget crises. The primary causes of failure in real-time projects can be listed as:

1. Failure to produce an adequate engineering specification for the total product or system and to keep this in step with changing requirements.
2. Lack of sound software specifications.
3. Starting on the development of executable programs far too early in the life cycle, with too large a team of programmers.
4. Failure to acknowledge the verification (testing) requirements in the early specifications.
5. Too much reliance on dynamic testing as a means of checking conformance between the specification and the implementation.

This serious situation has resulted, in part, from the unwillingness of many academic teams to work collaboratively with industry on real-world products. Valuable advances in real-time computing techniques are not being passed on and hence developed in the harsh financial regime of the commercial world.

It is hoped and believed that this ASI will help in some way to fill this void between academics, industrial design teams and the policy makers at the head of the major computer and control companies.

The State-of-the-Art in Real-Time Computing

Lonnie R. Welch

New Jersey Institute of Technology
Newark, NJ 07102
U.S.A.

The emerging generation of complex software systems presents significant challenges that must be addressed with new development technologies. Such systems are highly distributed and employ many heterogeneous processors, some of which may be parallel processors. Additionally, there are many non-functional requirements (related to timing, reliability, security and fault tolerance).

Development of a complex system proceeds from a requirements specification to a design of a software system that satisfies the requirements. Following the design and specification of the system modules, libraries of previously implemented modules are searched for components matching the specifications of design modules. Since multiple implementations of a component may exist, one must select an implementation for use in a particular application. To select the appropriate implementation, its effects on the non-functional requirements of the system under development are analyzed. An implementation of a module is chosen and it is assigned to a processing element (PE) of the computer system, and the system is analyzed. If all constraints can be met, the process of retrieval is repeated with the next module. Otherwise, the implementation is modified. There are two degrees of freedom for such modifications. Either an alternate implementation of a component may be chosen, or a component may be reassigned to a different PE. The process of modification is repeated until the criteria are satisfied, or until some fixed number of attempts has been made, at which time the system design "fails" to meet the requirements. When a design failure is detected, the system design is modified and the synthesis process repeated. Only a fixed number of designs is tried before the system requirements are deemed to be "unreasonable" and are therefore modified.

The development of software for complex systems can be very costly, partially due to the absence of automated techniques for software development and analysis. The status quo is in such a state that techniques are needed for

1. complex requirements specification so that analyzability and expressivity are both satisfied,
2. analysis of design tradeoffs,
3. automatic retrieval of components based on functional specifications,
4. assignment of modules to processors and
5. efficient and accurate prediction of complex system behavior.

The Role of Academia, Industry and Government in Real-Time Computing

Leo Budin

University of Zagreb
Faculty of Electrical Engineering
Avenija Vukovar 39
4100 Zagreb
Croatia

There is an agreement between various authors and authorities that today's most pervasive generic technology is information technology. It penetrates into all branches of economy, without exemption, and has an impact on all phases of every enterprise. No other known technology has diffused so deeply in so dissimilar sectors such as: industry and offices, traffic and banks, science and health care, education and publishing. Needless to say, the significant part of this diffusion process is related to real-time computing.

Therefore, beside the basic research and education in the field of real-time computing, the academia should promote interdisciplinary activities in order to foster the transfer of knowledge and technology to diverse application areas. The transfer is possible only if the absorption capacity exists from the human resources side. It is the people who have new ideas, create solutions, devise processes, operate and maintain the systems.

Therefore, the education of not only computer scientists and engineers but also of specialists in the application areas is an essential factor for the future of the field. Computing professionals have to communicate with engineers in other fields, and, therefore, need to understand the fundamentals of engineering systems. On the other side, professionals in the application fields have to be enough familiarized with the computing component of their systems in order to communicate, mainly through specification and validation processes, with real-time experts.

The question how to shape the curricula to meet the above requirements is not easy to answer. It would be desirable if this NATO ASI could provide some recommendations and encourage further discussion of this issue. It seems to me that different kinds of continuing education programs (courses, seminars, workshops, etc.) can help to disseminate the important developments and knowledge generated in the last couple of years to the above mentioned parties. One of the main problems is that considerable amount of technical knowledge is created in companies where it is considered relevant to competition between them. The role of academia is to overcome this problem by fostering the basic research and systematizing the public knowledge that is continuously produced, independently of secrecy between companies.

The Role of Academia, Industry and Government in Real-Time Computing

Günter Hommel

Technische Universität Berlin
Institut für Technische Informatik
Franklinstraße 28/29
10587 Berlin
Germany

As I am coming from a university, I will concentrate on the role of academia in real-time computing. Universities fulfil a double function: research and education. Another panel is going to discuss future research in real-time computing so that I will address education issues. Prerequisite for real-time computing is a thorough knowledge of sequential programming techniques as normally taught in undergraduate courses. As real-time systems are complex program systems, modularization is an important aspect but there are no special issues compared to large sequential systems.

As real-time systems often control technical processes, the natural mapping of the concurrency in the environment is a concurrent program system. This is very often but not necessarily the case. In safety-critical applications where interrupts and non-deterministic behavior cannot be tolerated the controlling program is sequential and strictly polling the I/O devices. Nevertheless, for most applications knowledge of concurrent programming is essential. This includes, of course, problems of synchronization and communication.

In our university those concepts are addressed in an undergraduate course in systems programming where computer science students design and implement a small operating system kernel. The problem of real-time computing is postponed to essentially two graduate courses with laboratory exercises and a one term project. In the first course we concentrate on problems of controlling the sensors and the motors of a robot with one computer. The second course introduces problems of distribution and fault-tolerance. Failures and communication are modelled using deterministic and stochastic Petri nets. At the end of the term the students have implemented a fault-tolerant, fail-safe distributed real-time system that controls trains of a toy railroad.

Last years term project was to recognize arbitrarily oriented objects on a conveyor belt using a vision system. A robot had to grasp the objects and move them to a pallet where they were stored in the desired position and orientation. Real-time computing is the heart of systems engineering but real-time computing is not sufficient to realize a whole technical system. Since several years we had realized that neither computer scientists nor electrical engineers are educated in a way to solve the difficult task to analyze a technical system and to design and implement a hardware/software system that controls this system.

It is not sufficient to learn programming after having studied electronics. In the curriculum of electrical engineering fundamentals of discrete mathematics and fundamentals of discrete structures and the algorithms on those structures are not contained. Students do not gain experience in structuring and designing complex software systems.

On the other hand side it is not sufficient to have a course on digital electronics after having studied computer science. In the curriculum of computer science fundamentals of analysis, as e.g. differential equations or integral transformations, are missing which are essential for systems or control theory.

Basic physical knowledge to understand technical processes is missing as well. It is common for both disciplines that it is very hard to familiarize in the corresponding other discipline as essential fundamentals are missing. Normally it is impossible to gain this knowledge already working in an industrial environment. This was the reason that we started a new curriculum one year ago that combines fundamentals from computer science and electrical engineering. We have already very positive reactions from industry (e.g. Siemens). They are very interested in scientists with this kind of education.

Towards Process-Oriented Technology Transfer between Academia and Industry

Petri J. Pulli

Technical Reserch Centre of Finland (VTT)
Computer Technology Laboratory
P.O. Box 201
90571 Oulu
Finland

1 Viewpoint

A *process view* on technology transfer is proposed, instead of picking up a single-shot programme for promoting contemporary hot topics.

2 Samples of Existing Attitudes

- **Industry**
  - Opportunity-oriented R&D (Yogi Bear style: "if you come across an apple on the road, pick it up"),
  - Watch-competition R&D,
  - Trouble-shooting R&D (John Wayne style).
- **Academia**
  - Lonely riders: "I don't know what the needs of the industry are right now, but my approach sure is something worth publishing, and maybe somebody could try it for the industry, but I am not the one to get hands dirty",
  - Bounty hunters: "Sure I can become an expert in this field in two weeks, I've done that several times before",
  - Piggybackers: "Yeah, I could participate in this joint project just to get funding for what I'll be doing anyway",
- **Government**
  - Lack of vision: "I have to be careful that nobody can come and blame me for spending this piece of R&D money on the wrong things. Here's what I'll do: I'll split the money up for such small projects that nobody can figure out the whole, and some of the projects are bound to succeed".

3 Suggestions

Technology transfer should become a continuous process involving joint R&D projects and circulation of people between industry and academia. All this should be supported by government institutions with the respective charter.

- **Industry**
  - Encourage bright young people to participate in joint R&D projects, and to visit prominent university groups,
  - Support long-term relationships with academia in forming advanced groups (pooling of resources),
  - Continuous improvement of processes, not just trouble-shooting or looking for new opportunities.
- **Academia**
  - Allow research groups of size 3 ... 9 to be formed,
  - Adjust promotion criteria to encourage long-term research and team-work,
  - Encourage co-operation with industry.
- **Government**
  - Read Parkinson and Deming,
  - Minimum bureaucracy,
  - Develop long-term visions,
  - Form strategic projects with.
    * Number of partners 3 ... 7,
    * Involve both universities and companies,
    * Encourage innovative small companies to participate,
    * Minimum participation per partner 3 persons for 3 years,
    * Encourage demonstration of results in real industrial processes,
    * Accept and take risks.

What Role Should Be Played by Slovenia in Real-Time Computing Research, Development and Technology

Matjaž Colnarič

University of Maribor
Faculty of Technical Science
62000 Maribor
Slovenia

In Slovenia, computer science and control systems research have a non-neglectable tradition. In the last time also the domain of real-time computing is significantly gaining interest. The research is mainly done in the two universities, several scientific institutes and industrial R&D laboratories.

Research and development potential in Slovenia can be characterised by the following facts:

- Due to the economic situation we are experiencing in our country in the last years, the funds for basic research in most research areas are limited.
- Because of the obvious reasons we can not count on massive industry production of, e.g., control systems, thus the R&D represents a considerable share in the final cost of a product. This and the overall economic situation in industry are negative motivations for their own development.
- Because of the above reasons there exists available qualified research and development potential. It would be possible to organise teams which would in short time be able to participate in R&D projects.
- The mentality of Slovene people is more or less homebound, although we also experience the run-away of experts caused by lack of working positions (and/or inappropriate conditions). It is my belief that shorter stays abroad (few months) and most of the work done at home would be the most productive arrangement.
- We already possess the infrastructure in terms of computer networks of mainframe and local computers. Unlike many other countries we have well organised computer communications and our scientists are in every moment accessible via e-mail. We also have enough personal computers but generally lack modern workstations and certain special hard- and software equipment.

From the above it can be concluded that the main problem of our research and development teams is financing of the projects. There is research and development potential available and we believe we have relevant knowledge and experience that could be useful for the cooperation in international projects. Opening of Slovenia towards Europe and the rest of the word and its inclusion in international organisations also formally enables that.

The Next Generation of Real-Time Operating Systems and Languages

Phillip A. Laplante

Fairleigh Dickinson University
Madison, NJ 07940
U.S.A.

The next generation of real-time operating systems and languages must focus on solving chronic problems facing real-time designers such as:

- specifying temporal behavior
- providing schedulability analysis
- supporting object-oriented paradigms
- providing tools

In addition, these problems must be addressed so as to support a wide variety of architectures, from standard von Neumann, to non-von Neumann such as

- systolic
- wavefront
- transputer
- dataflow
- optical

It is clear that no currently available operating system/language combination satisfies these needs.

While unambiguous specification of timing behavior is naturally required in real-time systems, it is unclear whether it should originate at the operating system or language level. Most real-time languages facilitate the specification of temporal behavior and schedulability analysis by either restricting the language to remove indeterminate constructs or extending the language to provide temporal control. In some cases the language can be constructed in conjunction with the operating system to provide temporal control. While any of these approaches seems reasonable, a real-time language/operating system combination must pick one paradigm and adhere to it.

Much has been written about both the support of object-oriented programming languages in real-time and the object-oriented approach to real-time operating systems. Recent research seems to indicate that both these directions are promising. For the former, the major problems to be overcome appear to be; garbage collection algorithms that are suitable for real-time, the performance penalties of

Phillip A. Laplante

late binding due to function polymorphism, and priority inversion problems due to operator inheritance. Object-oriented design seems to have many supporters, however the greatest hurdle to be overcome is the lack of tools. Practical tools for the specification, generation, testing, and maintainence of real-time systems is a persistent problem that must be solved quickly.

Finally, little has been written about the behavior of real-time systems in heterogeneous, distributed architectures such as systolic, wavefront, and dataflow machines. These hardware solutions are finding there way rapidly into industry and one of the challenges facing researchers is to find tools and techniques that allow for real-time system design without the need for considering the underlying architecture.

In summary, the basic challenge facing researchers and practitioners designing real-time operating systems and languages, is to provide environment that allows for the seamless design, code generation, and testing in a way that guarantees system performance, but allows the designer to ignore the underlying hardware.

Next Generation of Real-Time Operating Systems: Industrial Prospective

Borko Furht

Department of Computer Science and Engineering
Florida Atlantic University
Boca Raton, Florida 33431
U.S.A.

The presentation begins with discussing major driving forces which will impact the next generation of real-time operating systems. These are:

1. Approval of the IEEE POSIX standards 1003.4 (Real-time standard), and 1003.4*a* (Threads).
   Once these standards will be approved (expected time frame is end of 1992 to middle of 1993), every real-time operating system in order to be successful, must comply with the standard. In other words, the domination of proprietary real-time operating systems will be over!
2. Big players, such as IBM, DEC, Hewlett-Packard, and Sun, have entered the real-time computer battle by introducing their real-time UNIX operating systems. Their RT UNIX systems contain a fully preemptive kernel, fixed priority schedulers, and run on powerful RISC-based systems. These are IBM, AIX, DEC OSF/1, SUN Solaris 2.0, and HP/RT.

The discussion continues with the presentation of three current methodologies in designing real-time OS: real-time executives (such as VRTX, PSOS+, VxWorks, OS 9000), full-blown real-time UNIX OS, and distributed systems (such as Chorus, Mach, and Alpha), and a debate about which way to go.

In expanding the application range of real-time UNIX systems, we forecast the trend in providing a scalable UNIX architecture. This scalabale architecture begins with the full-blown RT UNIX, consisting of development, networking, file system, and RT kernel elements, and ends to a small RT UNIX kernel for embedded applications. The other two RT UNIX architectures include diskless system with RT kernel and networking, and the system with RT kernel, networking, and file system. This approach can be referred to as top-down.

We also foresee the trend in expanding real-time executives by providing scalable architectures. They will use a bottom-up approach, beginning with nano kernels to micro and regular RT kernels, and expansions with networking and file systems, as well as with the POSIX interfaces. The nano kernel approach will offer minimal primitives, such as multiple threads management, and a basis for the development of custom RT kernels needed for specific applications.

The discussion concludes with a summary that the major trends will be in developing scalable RT operating systems which comply with POSIX standards. Complying with standards will mean that all systems will have more or less the same functionality, however there will be still differences in the implementation of various functions. This means that real-time performance will vary from one to another implementation. The winner(s) will be those systems who provide scalability along with the best real-time performance.

Finally, in spite of the requirements to comply with standards, there will be still space for research in real-time OS. Suggested topics include: improving real-time performance, distributed real-time OS, which are still in their initial phase, real-time development tools, performance measurement and improvement tools, and so on.

The United States Navy's Next Generation Computer Resources Program and the Testing Issues of Standardized Real-Time Operating Systems

Timothy Jodoin

United States Navy
Naval Air Warfare Center
Aircraft Division
Patuxent River, MD 20670
U.S.A.

The Next Generation Computer Resources (NGCR) Program will provide the basis for standardized embedded computer hardware and software products for all U.S. Naval weapons systems in the mid-1990's and beyond. As such, through a set of commercially-based interface and protocol standards, it will assure that mission critical computer hardware and software systems, produced to perform the same types of functions as the current computer systems, will be compatible within and between systems regardless of manufacturer or technology used (technology independence). NGCR standards will be applicable to all mission critical computer resources (MCCR) encompassing shipboard, airborne and shore-based platforms, and will provide various performance levels to meet the diverse computer processing needs of future Naval systems. Areas of interface and protocol standardization include operating systems, local area networks, graphics, backplanes and database management.

With the rising complexity of todays Navy MCCR, it is becoming necessary to provide the capability for heterogeneous computers to interoperate in a reliable manner. Thus, the Navy is adopting Open System Architectures and desires to utilize standardized Operating System Interfaces along with industry. The Navy is concerned in these areas with ensuring the specification, analysis and verification of these standards, as well as analyzing and verifying their implementation in a real-time operating system. Hence, the Navy is interested in being able to test both conformance and performance of operating systems built to meet the requirements of the standards.

Two issues facing the Navy in terms of conformance testing the interfaces of a real-time operating system are (1) how to demonstrate interface services which, in effect, are transparent to the operation of an application, in this case, a test suite, and perform a pass/fail analysis, and (2) how to generate a generic test suite capable of testing both full service real-time operating systems and small service restricted real-time operating systems (for example, an aircraft flight control computer).

In terms of performance testing Operating System Interfaces, the Navy's goal is to ascertain the ability of the defined interfaces to meet the requirements of Navy applications. In this effort the Navy is working with industry, specifically

in the Institute for Electrical and Electronic Engineers (IEEE) 1003.4 Real-Time
Working Group, in developing real-time extensions to the IEEE 1003.1 base standard. The preeminent test issue facing the Navy is the need to develop objective
performance metrics intended for real-time computer systems.

These represent some of the issues the Navy is addressing in its work with real-
time operating systems in the NGCR Program.

Building Systems the Old Fashioned Way

Andrew Bernat

Computer Science
The University of Texas at El Paso
El Paso, TX 79968
U.S.A.

Most real real-time systems are hybrid systems with certain deadlines which must be met, others which are slippable and other computations which may run as resources permit. In astronomy, computers are used to drive the telescope, rotate the dome, control the instrument and record, display and even reduce (analyse) the data. Some of these tasks have no real deadlines: data reduction can always be done later, off-line, but with a reduction in the ability of the scientist to modify his/her experiment as the evening progresses. Some of these tasks have soft deadlines: rotating the dome may be delayed as long as the slit still clears the telescope field of view; displaying the data need not be 100% up-to-date. Still other tasks must meet hard deadlines: the telescope must be driven consistently across the sky to keep the object centered; the instrument must be controlled as required to record data at precise intervals, etc. But even some of these hard tasks have widely varying time scales. The result is a very complicated system.

Past systems have been built via cyclic runtime executives in C code with hand tweaking. Why are more modern techniques not used? Not because programmers are static, but because:

- the old techniques work,
- the problems which are of interest to academics are not necessarily those problems of interest to engineers or industry,
- the field of real time programming by necessity deals with many low level aspects of programming thus losing the power of abstraction,
- the best way to transfer new ideas is through the sending forth of well trained students, not papers.

This work is supported by the National Science Foundation through grant CDA 9015006.

Hard, Soft, and Hybrid Computer Systems

Raymond K. Clark

Concurrent Computer Corporation
Westford, MA 01886
U.S.A.

In many cases, the distinction between hard and soft real-time systems may reveal more about the design and implementation of computer systems than it does about the inherent properties of the physical system being controlled or simulated. While a strict definition of a hard real-time system states that even a single missed deadline can result in a disaster, we should strive to ensure that situations jeopardizing system integrity primarily reflect the nature of the physical system being controlled, rather than the design of the application.

For low-level real-time systems — e.g., those that perform sampled-data control system calculations — the computations performed are typically very predictable, reside on a single machine, and must satisfy strict time constraints. In this domain, hard real-time systems with rigidly structured applications are often employed when possible.

For higher-level systems — e.g., supervisory control systems — behavior and environment may be much more dynamic and involve the coordination of a number of separate machines. Although designers may attempt to structure applications in this domain in the same manner as those of the low-level systems, the complexity is much greater and more flexible techniques are often appealing.

Low-level and higher-level systems, however, are not entirely different. While some time constraints in higher-level systems may be soft in nature — that is, they can be missed without serious consequences — others may have hard time constraints that must be satisfied to provide acceptable system behavior. Conversely, some low-level systems can be structured such that the failure to satisfy certain time constraints need not result in disaster.

In fact, many systems actually contain a mixture of computations with both hard and soft time constraints. Moreover, the consequences resulting from the failure to satisfy a time constraint are application-specific. Real-time systems must be able to execute critical computations in a timely way; in a system featuring both hard and soft time constraints, the application must be able to specify both time constraints and the relative functional importance (or potential cost) for any given computation in order for the system to determine which computations to perform. Particularly in complex systems, dependencies among computations should be analyzed carefully, either statically or dynamically.

Hard, Soft, Hybrid Real-Time Systems and Their Uses

Werner Kriechbaum

IBM AIX-FSC
Poccistraße 11
80336 Munich
Germany

Whereas — at least from a theoretical point of view — hard real-time systems are quite well-defined [1], [2],soft real-time is a rather elusive term, at least as soon as one attempts a "hard" definition. Therefore a discussion of different kinds of real-time is probably better started by looking at the different user needs instead of attempting a definition pleasing to the theoretician. Users — and seen with the eyes of a system designer, users doesn't only mean end-users struggling with some application, but developers using operating system kernel routines as well — are not extremely interested in whether the operating system they use is hard, soft, or hybrid, they simply want to get their job done.[1]

As illustrated in Fig. 1 real-time applications in industrial control will become even more multi-leveled as they are today. Whereas the base layers of such an architecture like axes and machine control have to deal with rather clear cut "traditional" real-time problems, deterministic timing becomes less important in the top layers like within-plant or inter-plant communication. But whenever such top layers are used for "mission control" tasks like the optimization of machine or assembly-line usage, two novel design problems arise:

1. The classical real-time layers have to deal with an, at least partially, unpredictable environment. They are not isolated anymore from rather not time-critical requests coming from e.g. the accounting department.
2. On the other hand, applications dealing with interplant communication or accounting, totally separated from the real-time world today, have to have at least as much real-time features as are needed to enable them to talk with a low-level application in a non-disastrous way.

Besides these requirements caused by the integration of real-time and non real-time applications, any operating-system nowadays has to meet some additional constraints arising mainly from the need to minimize costs during all phases of its life-cycle; it has to use

---

[1] Despite the fact that the real-time community will easily agree that DOS is not a real-time operating system at all, there is a considerable amount of DOS-based software used for real-time applications like the control of NC machine tools.

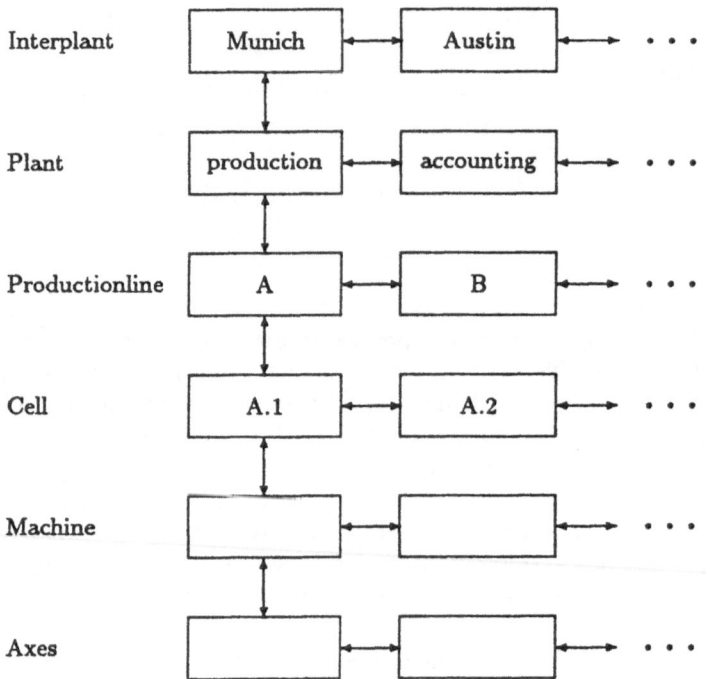

Fig. 1. CIM Scenario 2000: This network gives an example of the level of integration aimed at in the next generation of industrial control systems. The main feature of all such designs is the integration of office and control applications to provide mission control capabilities like optimizing machine usage and dynamic scheduling of production lines.

- *open system standards.*

  Adherence to open system standards — which to most people means Posix 1003.∗ conformance — implies that the operating system has to have a considerable amount of UNIX-affinity, in the design of the system call interface as well as in the set of tools and utilities provided for developers and end-users.
- *open GUIs.*

  Since MIT's X11 is the de facto standard for the design and implementation of graphical user interfaces, it will be used even in the real-time layers of such an architecture, nonwithstanding the fact that X is non-deterministic by design [3].
- *open hardware.*

  As reflected for example by Esprit's OMI project [4] there are increasing efforts to use standard off-the-shelf RISC microprocessor designs not developed specifically for real-time applications in industrial control.

As a consequence of such a system architecture, characterized mainly by a gradual change of hard real-time requirements from layer to layer, it does not seem appropriate to separate hard and soft real-time. It seems more natural to view the hard real-time part as limiting case of soft real-time. The Benefit Accrual model of real-time scheduling [5] allows the specification of "hard" and "soft" timing constraints in a homogeneous manner. Therewith it offers not only a very promising base for the implementation of such large-scale integrated real-time systems, but a theoretical framework for a metric for real-time hardness as well.

References

1. H. Rzehak, *Real-time Operating Systems: Can Theoretical Solutions Match with Practical Needs*, this volume.
2. J.A. Stankovic, *Real-time operating systems*, this volume.
3. A. Nye, *The X Window System Series*, Volume 1: Xlib Programming Manual O'Reilly & Associates, Inc, Sebastopol 1990, 229–264.
4. *Commission of the European Communities*, Esprit — Open Microprocessor systems Initiative, The Synopsis, Luxembourg 1992.
5. E.D. Jensen, *Asynchronous Decentralized Realtime Computer Systems*, this volume.

Hard, Soft, Real-Time Systems and Their Use

Helmut Rzehak

University of the Federal Armed Forces Munich
Werner-Heisenberg-Weg 39
85579 Neubiberg
Germany

The Term "Predictability"

A slightly modified definition of Lawson, which I would like to call "strong predictability" is:

In a time interval from ti to tj the exact behaviour can be reproduced from the externally observable state existing at ti.

With respect to this definition most (may be almost all) existing real-time systems are not strong predictable. This is not a contradiction to deterministic laws, but the observable state is a projection of the whole system state, and therefore we do not know the whole system state exactly. Examples are the position of the read/write heads of the disk or the working progress of the running tasks. It is similar to weather forecast: Despite of deterministic physical laws we cannot give an exact prediction because we do not now exactly the initial state.

Instead of giving a definition of some kind of weak predictability I strongly claim for considering predictability not as a binary or triary quantity but as a continous measure let us say in the Interval [0,1]. This corresponds to the fact, that a set of possible internal and external states at ti is mapped to a set of states at tj, and the power of it depends on a low or high predictability. Giving a picture: a high predictability maps through a small funnel, low predictability through a wide one. This leads to the thesis that systems have many sources of nondeterminism. For real-time systems we have to reduce the influence of this nondeterminism for establishing an acceptable level of predictability.

Hard versus Soft Real-Time Systems

The paradigm of hard deadlines has the advantage to be clear, but mostly it does not describe exactly real world problems. For leaving this paradigm and reasoning about missing time constraints we have to ask for at least two dimensions:

- how far is the deadline missed, and
- how often may this happen.

The term "Soft Real-Time" lacks in precision. We urgently need metrics for more precise soft real-time constraints.

A New Specification/Design/Implementation Paradigm for Real-Time Avionics Architecture and Systems

Alfred Anderman

Rockwell Space Systems Division, MS/FB96
12214 Lakewood Blvd
Downey, CA 90241
U.S.A.

1 Summary

The Software Productivity Consortium's new "Ada-based Design Approach for Real-Time Systems (ADARTS)" bridges the gap between systems requirements, software requirements, software design and Ada implementation by a series of well defined steps. ADARTS extends real-time structured analysis principles, such as the Ward/Mellor and Hatley/Pirbhai methods to generate specifications, applying object-oriented design methods and Clements/Heninger cost reduction perspectives to Ada implementation.

ADARTS formalizes system decomposition into manageable partitions, and allocates partitions for distributed processing, with concurrent tasks packaged into "information hiding modules" to make them resilient to change. ADARTS is used by many Consortium members, including Rockwell. It should also be used at the Systems Engineering level for avionics design, before architecture and hardware are selected, besides its main application for Software Engineering.

2 Discussion

ADARTS addresses the need for both task and information hiding structuring criteria by integrating four separate methodologies:

1. *"Real-Time Structured Analysis and Design (RTSAD)"* using finite state machines;
2. *"Design Approach for Real-Time Systems (DART)"*, originally applied to an industrial robot controller design, emphasising system decomposition into concurrent tasks and defining interfaces between them;
3. Naval Research Lab's *"Software Cost Reduction (SCR)"*, first used for the Onboard Flight Program of the A-7E aircraft; identifying three types of orthogonal structures, each derived from different sets of criteria: (a) *Modules* based on information hiding; (b) *Uses* determining executable s/w subsets;

and (c) *Tasks*, the decompositions of runtime system activities; also iden-titifying system modes (superstates), and transitions, with each transition table encapsulated in a mode determination module;

4. *"Object Oriented Design (OOD)"*, using Booch concepts of abstractions and objects as information hiding modules classified as (a) *Servers* providing operations for other objects, (b) *Actors* using operations from other objects, or (c) *Agents*, both providing and using operations.

The key systems engineering aids are: 1) Structuring the system as a hier-archical set of data flow/control flow diagrams that can be checked for comple-teness and consistency; 2) RTSA spec including system context diagram, exter-nal events list, data dictionary, and physical timing constraints; 3) Concepts of transforming data flow diagrams into state transition diagrams; and 4) Control transformations executing state transition diagrams and coordinate data trans-formations by means of event flows, using either Warc/Mellor or Hatley/Pirbhai approaches.

Acknowledgement

Ideas and comments received from Dr. R.B. Setzer, Software Metrics Specialist, Software Engineering Department, are hereby acknowledged.

What is the Right Specification/Design/Implementation Paradigm for Real-Time Applications?

Constance Heitmeyer

Center for High-Assurance Computer Systems
Naval Research Laboratory
Washington, D.C. 20375
U.S.A.

In recent years, a large collection of formal methods has been developed for specifying, analyzing, and verifying real-time computer systems. A major problem is how to apply these methods to the development of real-world computer systems. There are two important issues:

- When in the software life-cycle of real-time systems should formal methods be applied and how?
- What should be the relationship between formal specification and analysis of timing properties and formal specification and analysis of nontiming properties?

When and How to Apply Formal Methods

Studies have shown that correcting errors late in the software life-cycle (e.g., during initial system operation) can cost up to one hundred times more than detecting and correcting errors earlier. In our view, substantial reductions in software development costs will accrue if formal methods are used to detect and weed out errors during the requirements and early design stages of software development. During this period, two formal specifications should be developed: a formal statement of the system's critical timing properties and a system model that specifies the required system behavior, including its timing behavior. The next step is a formal analysis that tests the consistency of the model with the critical timing properties. In addition to being useful during early software development, formal methods are also useful later on when better estimates of the system's timing parameters are available. The formal specifications developed earlier (and probably updated to reflect new or changed requirements) provide a framework for performing additional analyses of a system's timing properties.

A More Unified Approach to Formal Specification and Analysis

In real-time, safety-critical systems, it is rarely the case that one is concerned with timing properties alone. Most often, an analysis is needed of timing and other critical system properties, such as security, reachability, deadlock avoidance, fault-tolerance, and safety. To prevent duplicative effort and to achieve high confidence that a set of specifications satisfies more than one class of properties, a more unified approach is needed to specifying a system and analyzing a system's consistency with different classes of properties. With such an approach, formal specification and analysis of timing properties would proceed as follows:

- A single system model is defined. This model captures all of the system requirements - functional, timing, accuracy, reliability, etc.
- Formal methods are applied to improve the model's correctness.
- The subset of the model that deals with timing is extracted. In this subset, details about functional behavior, data types, and other nontiming behavior is abstracted away.
- A formal analysis is performed using a proof system that allows the specifier to reason about the model at the appropriate semantic level and that provides user-friendly feedback.

What is the Right Specification/Design/Implementation Paradigm for Real-Time Applications?

Harold W. Lawson

Lawson Publishing and Consulting Incorporated
Torshammarsvägen 11
18133 Lidingö
Sweden

Based upon my experience, there is only one reasonable answer to the "right" paradigm given the fact that real-time applications and systems must be dealt with abstractly and concretely by a variety of vested interest parties. These parties most often have varying backgrounds and abilties to understand real-time system solutions. Consequently, the "right" paradigm must be "designed for understandability", that is, it is understandable to all vested interest parties in terms that each party can comprehend.

Given application requirements, the paradigm must provide a natural solution to the real-time application. The selection of a paradigm is somewhat analogous to that of food preparation by master cooks on the one hand and as an industrial process on the other. The best results are achieved when the best ("right") ingredients and a good ("right") recipe are employed. Master cooks use creativity in deviating from the known ingredients and recipes, perhaps establishing a new and better paradigm. However, once selected for an industrial process, the paradigm must be understandable, rational, economical and reliable.

It is my view that we must emphasize TIME in the paradigms for real-time applications; especially in the paradigms for time and safety critical systems. However, this time orientation should also be considered for non-safety (even service oriented) paradigms, particularly as the cost/performance ratios of hardware resources change. Straightforward time based approaches reduce software complexity thus improving upon many critical real-time abilities such as testability, verifiability, reliability, diagnosability, and so on.

To be successful, the paradigm must be a consistent part of a holistic view of the treatment of the real-time application(s) implemented in a system. Thus, it must be tone setting for all "ingredients"; namely, the means of specification of application functions, the behavioral description, the resource structures and the mappings between behavior and resources. To be rational, economic and reliable, it must be supported by tools for managing design, development, integration, maintenance, and change.

We will not achieve the right paradigms for real-time systems by concentrating upon traditional software engineering aspects, for example, the software technical convenience of event driven approaches. We do not build real-time systems for the convenience of software engineers. The paradigm must focus upon the essential properties of the application, the appropriateness and quality of the ingredients used in implementation and the industrial processes surrounding real-time system products.

What is the Right Specification/Design/Implementation Paradigm for Real-Time Applications?

John A. McDermid

Dependable Computing Systems Centre
University of York
York YO1 5DD
U.K.

1 Introduction

The aim of this short paper is to set out the author's views on the issues which must be addressed by a real-time systems specification, design and implementation method. This is a very broad topic, so the main focus is on timing issues, and on the overall specification process. More specifically the paper sets out views on how specifications are, or should be, derived progressively from high level requirements, and considers the nature of systems architectures, which defines both the needs for high level design specification, and the constraints on implementation.

The ideas are presented in a direct manner, with the minimum of rationale. However there is an implicit rationale. The ideas have been developed over some years, based on observations of the way real systems are developed, and the constraints on real systems' development. They represent a view of how to provide a "rational development process" recognising the constraints of real systems development projects. Clearly, in the space available, all we can do is to present broad ideas, rather than to define a precise structure for a development process and method.

2 Structure of the Development Process

The ideas presented are based on the (non-standard) idea that development is concerned with six "information domains", i.e. collections of information which need to be modelled at some stage in the development process. These domains bear some relationship to the stages of a waterfall model, but there is no assumption that the information is derived in "waterfall order". The domains are:

- *fundamental requirements* — the definition of key objectives for a system; these will typically be in terms of the goals of the organisation which the system is serving, or strategic (technical or marketing) goals for the system, e.g. for a flying control system to maintain an aircraft in its flight envelope, if necessary limiting pilot actions;

- *derived requirements* — refinements of the fundamental requirements, taking into account the constraints of the real world, e.g. control loop iteration rate based on the rate of divergence of the controlled system;
- *logical architecture* — definition of the network of system components needed to satisfy the requirements, based on an assumption of infinite and perfect resources, e.g. definition of a set of objects and their communication structure;
- *physical architecture* — definition of the network of system components needed to satisfy the requirements, based on knowledge of the available resources, failure rates, etc. in the underlying hardware, e.g. a set of replicated processes, voters, etc., reflecting, but not identical to, the logical architecture;
- *detailed design* — internal design of the system components, e.g. abstract definition of data structures and algorithms;
- *implementation* — program code.

It is important to realise that the above information may arise in any order, or concurrently, e.g. it is common for the logical and physical architectures to evolve together. There is similarity in the drivers for the progression from fundamental to derived requirements and for that from logical to physical requirements. In both cases the change is from an "ideal world" model of the requirements or design, to one which takes into account the constraints of physical reality. The distinction is that in the requirements the concern is with the reality of the system environment; in the case of architectures, the constraint is the limitations of the implementation hardware (and the way in which it is, or can be, affected by the environment).

Like all models of the development process the above is a (considerable) simplification and an abstraction; it is hoped, however, that it reflects accurately the key shifts in perspective that occur through the development process.

3 Specification of Real-Time Properties

We can consider the specification of real-time properties in terms of the above domains. In general the above timing issues are relevant in each of the domains:

- *fundamental requirements* — few, if any timing requirements; the only examples might be mission times, e.g. the typical flight time for an aircraft, but these tend to be constraints or influences, rather than "hard" requirements on the system;
- *derived requirements* — properties reflecting the physics of the controlled system, typically:
  - end to end response times for sporadic events;
  - period and response times for periodic events, plus jitter constraints, i.e. allowed variation on the response times;
  - precedence and offset relations between units of computation;

- possibly benefit/utility functions representing more subtle timing constraints than the more classical deadlines;

- *logical architecture* — this mainly acts as a "link" between the derived requirements and physical architecture, but worst case execution times (WCETs) may be specified;

- *physical architecture* — definition of the properties of the system components and communication structure:

  - WCETs for schedulable program fragments;
  - network delays;
  - deadlines, etc. inherited from the derived requirements and allocated according to the design decomposition;

- *detailed design* — the main requirements are WCETs for code fragments;

- *implementation* — here the concern is with actual WCETs derived from program analysis, not specifications.

The aim at each stage is to be able to show that specification at the previous stage has been satisfied. Thus at logical architecture the aim is to show that the specified properties of the logical architecture, if realised, will meet the requirements. This is, inevitably, a fairly weak verification. Physical architecture can be verified much more precisely against the derived requirements, using the relevant scheduling theory to show that the deadlines, etc. will be met. In a well-defined method it should be possible to predict timing behaviour accurately from the physical architecture, subject only to the programs being implemented to satisfy their WCETs.

4 Producing Suitable Methods

No single method is capable of representing all the above properties. What is required is a careful integration of a number of techniques. The aim is not to produce a "monolithic" specification method, but to provide a set of related methods, or techniques, all of which can be related back to the same underlying model of the system. Using an analogy with databases, the methods represent a set of views on the overall model of the systems (projections from the schema and data).

There are some examples of pairwise integration of methods, e.g. Statecharts and RTL, but the real challenge is to integrate enough different techniques to describe systems in a "sufficiently complete" manner that it is possible to have confidence in the timing properties (the accuracy of predictions of timing properties) early in the development process. This remains a major challenge to the developers of real-time specification methods.

In order to get the necessary analytical power, mathematically based, or formal, methods are required. Many candidate methods are available, but it is beyond the scope of this paper to survey and analyse these methods.

5 Commentary

The above description of requirements for real-time specification methods is necessarily abstract and brief. It is hoped that the benefit is that it sets out, albeit succinctly, requirements for development methods for real-time systems, and gives an indication of the process framework in which such methods must fit. This information is necessary to guide the process of developing and evaluating concrete development methods.

Object-Oriented Real-Time Computing

Michael L. Nelson

Naval Postgraduate School
Dept. of Computer Science
Monterey, CA 93943
U.S.A.

Object-oriented programming (OOP) shows great potential in several areas, including real-time (RT) systems. The primary benefits of OOP (encapsulation and reusability) are extremely useful in the RT arena. This position paper briefly describes the benefits of object-oriented (OO) real-time (OORT) computing. For a more thorough introduction, refer to (Nelson 1992) [1].

Unfortunately, most OOP languages (OOPLs) were not designed for RT applications. That is, they do not contain constructs for enforcing timing constraints. However, all OOPLs do provide the benefits of increased encapsulation (the internal values of an object are accessible only through its established interface) and reusability (a new class, called the subclass, inherits all of the variables and methods defined for an existing class, called the superclass).

We have developed a series of equations that are useful in determining which objects/classes to load on which processors in a distributed system. These equations determine computation and communication costs for objects, classes, and class hierarchies. Calculations such as these should also be quite helpful in meeting RT scheduling deadlines.

OO operating systems (OS) is another area from which OORT systems can benefit. An OO OS consists of several objects working together to accomplish the tasks normally expected of an OS. These objects, such as a scheduler, can easily be replaced by another object which is better suited for a particular application. OORT systems can also benefit from OO simulation. This can be either an OO simulation of a RT system (i.e., the simulation is not done in RT), or an OORT simulation (i.e., the simulation is done in RT). OOP is particularly well-suited for simulation systems in that real-world objects and their activities can readily be simulated as objects with a set of methods to manipulate them.

In summary, OOP is not a 'cure-all' for all of our problems. It is simply a better approach to many (if not all) programming projects. Inheritance allows for increased system reusability, which is helpful in any application. Encapsulation allows for increased system reliability, which is crucial in RT systems.

References

1. Nelson, M.L., *Object-oriented real-time computing.* NPS Technical Report NPSCS–92–010, Monterey, CA, August 1992.

What is the Right Specification/Design/Implementation Paradigm for Real-Time Applications?

L. Simoncini

Department of Information Engineering
University of Pisa
Via Diotisalvi 2
Pisa
Italy

The use of a *functional paradigm*-based [3] coarse-grained dataflow computational model and notation for design description languages [2], [1], may help in satisfying many of the challenging requirements for the design of predictably dependable real-time systems. The advantages of such an approach reside in the potential for parallelism it admits, in having the property of referential transparency which allows for a degree of inherent fault tolerance and in the property of composability which puts in direct relation the general behaviour of a system with that of its constituent parts.

The principle of *referential transparency* states that the value of an expression depends on its subexpressions only through their value — anything else, like internal structure or order of evaluation is irrelevant. Therefore *equational reasoning* can be made on functional programs, as a basis for proofs and transformations. The same principle is a basis for dealing with *spatial redundancy*, by which multiple simultaneous evaluation of the same expression always yield the same value, and *temporal redundancy*, by which multiple evaluations of the same expression at different times always yield the same value. Moreover the *absence of side-effects* and *no sharing* enforces both *atomicity* property and the easy structuring in *recoverable actions*. The principle of *minimal privilege* is enforced, since only the values which are necessary for evaluation are passed from one subexpression to another.

Finally *structural models for software reliability assessment* can be used since the data which are required for those models are more easily gathered. Both *failure rate* and *mean sojourn time* of individual modules are more simply determined since modules are simple, not nested and atomic; the *frequency of transitions* across the interface between every pair of modules depends only on the application and not on the interaction with the support and the *probability of failure on transition* across the interface between every pair of modules is more easily evaluated since the independency among modules implies that each module generates failures at its own rate.

References

1. A. Bondavalli, L. Simoncini, *Functional Paradigm for Designing Dependable Large-Scale Parallel Computing Systems*, International Symposium on Autonomous Decentralized Systems, ISADS'93, Kawasaki, Japan, 1993 (to appear).
2. L. Simoncini, *Design Description Languages for the Design of Predictably Dependable Real-Time Systems*, IFIP 12th World Computer Congress, Madrid, Spain, 1992, 598–598.
3. D.A. Turner, *Functional Programming and Miranda*, IFIP 12th World Computer Congress, Madrid, Spain, 1992, 32–41.

Formal Methods for Real-Time Systems

Leonor Barroca and John McDermid

Dept. of Computer Science
University of York
York Y01 5DD
U.K.

We believe that formal methods are both under-used and over-sold and consider here when and to what extent it is appropriate to use formal methods in the development of safety critical systems.

We advocate the presence of formal methods throughout the several phases of the software life cycle. There is no unified methodology that can be proposed for the whole development; we would use formal methods to produce top-level specifications for systems, but carry out development by a systematic application of stepwise refinement supplemented by formal refinement where there are adequate techniques. In the phase of Requirements Analysis both the environment and the system are described, first building a model of the real world and then specifying the model of the computer system. The capture of the requirements is a vital stage and it is advisable that at least a set of well established guidelines be followed.

The representation of cause-effect relationships and non-functional requirements such as time, resources, ..., should be done in a formal framework from which the subsequent development can be achieved mainly by enrichment.

Safety should be explicitly treated here dealing with the presence of failure. We would advise that when it comes to the definition of the model of the computing system, still as part of the requirements, it should be stated formally; namely, relations between inputs and outputs, preferably in some notation that could be easily animated.

It is against this model that the correctness of the final program is verified. In the Design phases we would use an eclectic approach to specification. For example we would use a notation such as Timed Statecharts to represent concurrent and communication structure but specify the effects of the individual actions in another formalism such as Z; here, we would also advise the use of modularity, taking probably a more object oriented approach such as Object Z.

We would define a set of transformation rules that would allow the verification of the preservation of behaviour, as structure and detailed functionality are added. Refinement, as design becomes more detailed, should be carried out in a semi-formal way.

We would also derive a number of theorems, e.g. stating that the system will not deadlock, or giving a top-level statement of safety policy, but would probably reason about these theorems informally.

We would use animation and simulation techniques, and methods such as Real Time Logic [3] to analyse timing properties. We would also link the formal techniques, so far as possible, to standard safety techniques, e.g. fault tree analysis. It would seem quite possible to apply such techniques in a manner analogous to the use of fault trees on programs [4].

When implementation is considered, we would link the specifications to techniques for schedulability analysis [1]; [2]; [5] and program timing analysis [6].

We would use code verification techniques, e.g. SPARK, for the most critical code.

In summary we would supplement existing good practices with the use of formal specifications in order to gain clarity in top level specifications, to aid consistency checking specifications and to assist in validation through derivation of key properties from the specifications.

Formal methods can be used effectively in industry. The techniques are sometimes over-sold and it would appear to be very easy to over-state their value. The theoretical benefits are very great and fairly clear, but the limitations are far more subtle and so it is rather more difficult to articulate them clearly and accurately.

Also there is a temptation in trying to stimulate the use of formal methods to stress their value and to 'skate over' the limitations. This may not be deliberate over-selling but it has a similar effect. Thus we stand by the assertion that *formal methods are both over-sold and under-used*, but recognise that this is a simplification of a complex situation.

Since their use has been limited to date, our assertion about the benefits of wider use seems to be clearly true!

References

1. Audsley, N. C. & Burns, A., *Scheduling Real-Time Systems*, YCS 134, Dept. of Computer Science, University of York, 1990.
2. Audsley, N. C., Richardson, A. B. M. F. & Wellings, A. J., *Hard Real-Time Scheduling: The Deadline Monotonic Approach*, Proceedings 8th IEEE Workshop on Real-Time Operating Systems and Software, Atlanta, GA, USA, 1991.
3. Jahanian, F. & Mok, A. K., *Safety Analysis of Timing Properties in Real-Time Systems*, IEEE Transactions on Software Engineering SE–12(9), 1986, 890–903.
4. Leveson, N. G. & Harvey, P. R., *Analyzing Software Safety*, Transactions on Software Engineering SE–9(9), 1983, 569–579.
5. Tindell, K., Burns, A. & Wellings, A., *Allocating Real-Time Tasks (An NP-Hard Problem made Easy)*, Real Time Systems, 1992. to appear.
6. Zhang, N., Burns, A. & Nicholson, M., *Analysing Assembler Code for Program Execution Time Estimation*, Spirits Workshop, 1992.

The Role of Formal Methods and Algorithms in Real-Time Computing

Fabio A. Schreiber

Dip. di Elettronica
Politecnico di Milano
Piazza Leonardo da Vinci
20133 Milano
Italy

I firmly trust in the need for formal methods in specification and in verification/validation of real-time systems to get 100 % confidence in their performance and dependability, especially when safety is a main concern. However, I still see a very long way to go before they are widely accepted and used by the practitioners community. There are several reasons for that:

1. **cultural** — our believes notwithstanding, most of real-time programmers are still assembler programmers the same way as most of commercial application programmers are Cobol programmers, and scientific application programmers are Fortran programmers (if you don't believe it, just scrap the surface and see!), so they are not ready to accept and understand the often awful mathematical notation and machinery required for formal techniques;
2. **practical** — at the state-of-art, only small and well understood pieces of the whole system can be treated formally, so let us concentrate on the most critical parts and leave the rest to the traditional methods. Moreover, formal techniques are applied to source code; they should be applied also to prove the correctness of the compiler and of other tools (e.g. mathematical libraries), not only to the real-time application software;
3. **structural** — starting from low level program verification, formal methods have been pushed up to the specification level. However, we cannot leave statistical dependability assessment techniques totally off the game since formal specification again needs validation against the designer original thought; therefore there will always be a passage point from informal to formal and the risk of making formally undetectable errors is there![1]

A second point I want to mention as worthy of further research is that in many control algorithms, the effect of *load conditions* should be *formally* considered in the validation process, since they can cause *instability* situations, such as thrashing, cascaded shutdowns, etc., which cannot be detected by a static verification technique.

References

1. J.C. Laprie, B. Littlewood, *Viewpoint*, CACM Vol. 35, No. 2, 1992.

Formal Methods: Yes but How ?

Janusz Zalewski

Dept. of Computer Science
Southwest Texas State University
San Marcos, TX 78666-4616
U.S.A.

There is certainly no doubt that formal methods should be used, as far as possible, in the specification and design of real-time systems [2]. The number and quality of articles published on formal methods grow significantly from year to year. Their use, however, is still not very effective. In this note, I am trying to give a brief summary of such applications, followed by some suggestions which may contribute to a more widespread use of formal methods in practice.

By a formal method I mean a specification or design technique, which uses proofs (proof systems) for verification purposes (to check that the implementation is correct). This definition eliminates some methods which are systematic and rigorous but lack mathematical proof techniques. In addition, I am looking only at those methods which have been recognized more widely, that is, are presented in at least one book or in a significant number of articles.

An important point, to obtain a clear picture of formal methods, is to collect statistics on their use in real-time systems, on three different levels (as demonstrated in documented examples):

Level 1 — toy (classroom) examples, presented by paper and pencil (such as the elevator or railroad crossing specs used in several books and articles [1, 4]).
Level 2 — lab examples, experimental systems, supported by a real implementation which has been verified (such as an elevator control system running in the lab, on a real hardware, or simulated on a computer).
Level 3 — real life examples, such as a product (to be) released or deployed, or operational systems built at least in single quantities (such example would be the clinical cyclotron control system [3], if it actually ran).

Such statistics clearly show about 99% of applications to be on Level 1, some one percent on Level 2, and a number close to ε on Level 3.
This is certainly not, what an advocate of formal methods would like to see. But why is this so? To give a diagnosis, it is helpful to look at those aspects of real-time systems technology, which already reached a certain level of maturity. By taking a closer look at the implementation phase of real-time systems development, one can see, for example, that in one of the major real-time projects,

the use of **standards** is emphasized on each of the following implementation layers: Ada as a programming language, POSIX.4 compliant real-time kernel on the operating system layer, and Multibus II architecture on the hardware layer. The military mandates similar standards in their applications. Relating those observations to the use of formal methods, one can derive a conclusion that serious applications of formal methods will probably start no sooner than some of these methods are fully standardized. Moreover, methods which are not standardized have a very little chance to be applied on level 3 of this classification. At this point of time, however, there are only 2 serious activities to standardize formal methods: VDM and Z, none of them being real time specific.

One other important factor, contributing to a broader use of formal methods in real-time systems, is **education**. It is necessary to encourage and consequently promote including of formal methods in the academic curricula. Such promotion may take place by funding educational and training programs, distributing courseware materials, elaborating case studies, etc. These activities would generate more familiarity with formal methods among college graduates.

Another factor which could significantly help to establish the use of formal methods, would be the availability of (public domain) **tools**. Looking at the applicability of other techniques based on pure mathematics, one can think of FFT (Fast Fourier Transform) and various other transforms: they were mathematically well developed long ago, but only the emergence of software packages made them useful in practice. Current, commercially available, software engineering tools, even though sometimes based in principle on formal methodologies, are not easily accessible in academic environments due to pricing policies. Tools support is something what this community badly needs now.

The last important factor, which may have a positive impact on future, is generating more **diversity** in promoting the use of formal methods in real-time systems. This requires more agressive policies, such as giving this subject better publicity, organizing meetings and symposia, broadening interest among potential users, attracting different research centers, technology transfer to industry, enhancing information flow, increasing public awareness, improving management. One example of such activities is the creation of VDM-Europe working group — sponsored by the European Communities; no similar group or organization exists in the real-time systems community yet.

The four components mentioned above are, in my opinion, the key important factors on the way to the maturity of this technology.

References

1. H. Barringer, *Up and Down The Temporal Way*, The Computer Journal, Vol. 30, 1987, 134–148.

2. D. Craigen, K. Summerskill (Eds.), *Formal Methods for Trustworthy Computer Systems (FM89)*, Springer-Verlag, Berlin, 1989.
3. J. Jacky, *Formal Specification for a Clinical Cyclotron Control System*, Software Engineering News, Vol. 15, No. 4, 1990, 45–54.
4. J. Ostroff *Temporal Logic for Real-Time Systems*, Wiley, New York, 1989.

Formal Methods for Fault-Tolerant, Real-Time System Design

Jack Goldberg

Computer Science Laboratory
SRI International
Menlo Park, California 94025
U.S.A.

Fault-tolerant design for real-time systems may be necessary when the cost of failure and doubts about the perfection of a system's components are sufficiently high. Unfortunately, experience has shown that fault-tolerance functionality is itself a significant source of design error. This is not surprising considering the subtle, time-sensitive impact of faults on component functions and interactions. The complexity of fault effects and the need for very high confidence in designs of critical systems place fault-tolerant, real-time designs beyond the power of informal design verification techniques.

SRI's research on formal verification of fault-tolerant, real-time designs started in the late 1970s, in connection with the SIFT flight-control computer prototype. Early proofs of design correctness for voting and clock synchronization were tedious and limited in scope and thoroughness, but they established the feasibility of formal proof methods for fault-tolerant designs.

Recent work at SRI and elsewhere has resulted in advances in the power of verification tools and increased understanding of fault-tolerance design issues. A major objective of current work is to produce formal, computer-aided verifications for some major building blocks and to develop real-time, fault-tolerant architectures that simplify the job of formal verification.

We will describe an application of SRI's PVS verification system to algorithms whose correctness depends on the relative magnitudes of time intervals.

Next-Generation Real-Time Database Management and Databases

Paul J. Fortier

Naval Undersea Warfare Center Div.
NUWC, Newport, RI 02841-5047
U.S.A.

The conventional database execution model views transactions as an atomic sequence of reads and writes executed on a monolithic database. Transactions in the conventional model act as units of execution and recovery. To provide these features database items written by a transaction remain inaccessible to other transactions until commit. This model of transaction's execution has well served conventional database processing applications where safety was of the utmost importance, and performance secondary. Unfortunately this model is not applicable to engineering, real-time, and control oriented applications. These applications require database services which allow more concurrency with shorter contention durations, support long transactions, and user controlled consistency and recovery.

Conventional database management solutions for next-generation engineering, real-time, and control oriented application's port present technology to the new domain. The problem with conventional database representation and execution management based on a monolithic database and global serializability is that they aren't conducive to next-generation applications database requirements. Motivations for next-generation databases include integration of an organization's operational databases, unconventional information usage patterns, increased processing capacity and turnaround requirements, greater availability of database items and improved reliability. New applications include, air traffic management, computer controlled manufacturing, military command, control and communications (C^3), spacecraft, avionic control applications, computer aided design teams, and software engineering environments. These applications contain processes and tasks with varying transaction duration, real-time deadlines, frequent interaction with the environment under control and operate on diverse data types. Transactions within these applications are unconventional and do not necessarily require transaction-level serializability. Correctness of the database system is measured by its ability to acquire information in a timely manner and maintain applications requirements for consistency and correctness.

Next-generation systems required high throughput, fast response, loosened consistency and forward recovery from a transaction processing and database environment. Conventional algorithms and mechanisms support neither timely, nor selective application of consistency and recovery in the processing of transactions.

Correcteness criteria based on transaction level serializability cause increased delays, and are too restrictive for next-generation systems. Recovery based on transaction undo and redo result in the inability to meet next-generation applications requirements. Conventional database management systems force all transactions to incur the same overhead and delays.

Currently researchers are investigating the use of embedded semantic information from transactions and database structures to increase concurrency, by allowing nonserializable scheduling of interleaved transaction steps over separately maintained database partitions. Further research focuses on forward recovery protocols to maintain real-time services, for failure safety and loose coupling of transaction execution.

Real-Time Databases

John A. Stankovic

University of Massachusetts
Amherst, MA 01003
U.S.A.

The questions posed by the panel moderator include: what are the correct transaction and data models, the correct database architecture, which applications require real-time databases, and what are the open research questions. I'd like to address these questions in an integrated fashion, twice: once for soft real-time databases (SRTDB) and once for hard real-time databases (HRTDB).

In the SRTDB area applications include program trading in the stock market and airline reservations, as well as parts of HRTDBs. To date, most research work has focussed on SRTDBs. Here we see that the transaction model has been to simply add timing constraints (such as deadlines) and value information to the transaction, but retaining the full ACID properties of transactions. The architecture in these studies has been a centralized database system. The research has developed cpu scheduling algorithms, concurrency control, conflict resolution, disk scheduling, real-time buffering, deadlock resolution, and transaction restart policies in an integrated manner, where each of these policies explicitly addresses time. Results have sometimes been contradictory and have only been attained for testbeds (such as RT-CARAT at the Univ. of Massachusetts) and simulations (such as those done at the Univ. of Wisconsin, Virginia, and Princeton). Real application characteristics and workloads are needed. New systems must be developed to extend the work from centralized to distributed architectures, from the standard transaction model (with time and value added) to various forms of nested transactions with varying degrees of ACID properties, from the simple relational model to object oriented models, and from soft to hard real-time.

Applications for HRTDBs include industrial process control, automated navigation, telecommunications, and command, control and communication systems.

HRTDBs will initially be of two types:

1. a fairly typical hard real-time subsystem dealing with the sensors and actuators and the corresponding low level control loops interfaced to a SRTDB (as described above) for dealing with the plant data that requires more permanency; and
2. an integrated model (schema) that can describe data along a spectrum from

the data of sensors and actuators to permanent plant data, data can have a lifetime associated with it, and transactions span from simple tasks that literally have no properties typically associated with transactions all the way to the full ACID properties.

I will not discuss the first model except to say that such a model can be more easily implemented in existing plants. In the second model, the architecture requires sensors and actuators, one or more main cpus, main memory with both a stable and non-stable part, various disks, including solid state disks for better predictability, and a bounded network connecting distributed nodes. The stable main memory will be used for supporting the ACID properties of hard real-time transactions. The overall system will be modeled as an active, object oriented database with all that this entails. Other research issues include recovery in real-time (e.g., when and how to abort a transaction so that more important transactions can execute as soon as possible is a difficult problem), how to control the interaction between different transaction semantics, how to deal with knowing only approximate resource requirements of certain queries, how to exploit RAID I/O architectures for predictability, reliability and improved performance, and how to build the system to facilitate analyzability.

VOTRICS: A Highly Predictable Fault Tolerant System Architecture

Bernhard Appel

Alcatel Austria – ELIN
Research Centre
Ruthnergasse 1-7
1210 Vienna
Austria

Abstract

VOTRICS is a fault-tolerant system architecture intended to provide a variety of control systems with high availability and reliability. VOTRICS provides message passing services between actively replicated components. Event triggered applications in loosely as well as tightly coupled computer systems are supported.

Introduction

The VOTRICS modules running in each replicated component communicate via network links. Due to hard real-time requirements VOTRICS is implemented in a strictly periodic way. The cyclic nature decreases the complexity of the algorithms used and allows to prove that time requirements are met subject to any assumptions made concerning failures and workloads.

VOTRICS consists of following components: the communication layer, which provides a global and consistent view of all messages and a global time base, the voter, which determines the correct messages to be forwarded to the applications, the error monitor process, which supervises the functionality of the system, and the router, which serves incoming and outgoing messages.

The communication layer, the key component concerning predictability, provides the exchange of synchronization messages between the replicas. The scheduling is time-driven, so the time behavior of the communication layer protocol is not affected by any single fault occurred. As the arriving time of the synchronization messages is known, it can be reacted immediately on a missed message. The time-driven protocol requires that all replicas start their protocol machine at a synchronized point of time, which is achieved by a well synchronized time base and the agreement on the next activation of the protocol.
VOTRICS uses a time-budget based scheduling strategy for the voter and the error monitor activities. In each period a time-budget of logical execution time is foreseen for these activities. Each class of activity has certain logical time-costs.

Activities are performed as long as a budget is left. This mechanism ensures that voter and error monitor activities finish in a consistent state before the next VOTRICS period starts. Replica determinism is therefore reached by local schemas and identical actions in the replicas.

The remaining time till the next VOTRICS period starts is consumed by the handler running in the background.

Future work will focus on a better adaptability of VOTRICS to varying load conditions. In the current implementation a fixed period between communication layer instances is used. By introducing adjustment of the period length and the length of the synchronization messages the performance behavior can be tuned dynamically to the observed load condition. A longer period increases the throughput of VOTRICS and decreases the average message transfer latency.

Predictability Versus Adaptability

Steven L. Howell

Naval Surface Warfare Center, Code U33
10901 New Hampshire Avenue
Silver Spring, Maryland 20903
U.S.A.

The issue is particularly interesting when considering the class of large, complex, real-time, time-critical, highly reliable systems. In this case, large means systems with several million lines of high level software code built on distributed and parallel architectures. While the architectures of these systems may be exceedingly complex, these systems still require highly predictable and reliable behavior. Systems of this class are found in military, telecommunications, commercial avionics, nuclear, and business applications. Many of these systems operate in a highly adaptive, unpredictable and changing environment; therefore, the systems are required to be highly reactive. Also, the complexity of these systems' architectures increases the probability that a portion of the system will fail. If the system is designed to be highly adaptive, its ability to overcome the complex environments and potential faulty behavior may be greatly enhanced.

Many systems' workloads are non-uniform. These systems enter periods of time when they are under stress, then enter times when they are not fully loaded. It is usually not important for the system to be optimized for non-stress situations (resources available are typically more than enough). However, it is critical that the system reacts appropriately during the overload periods. A highly adaptive system must be careful not to over-optimize itself to non-critical situations, making the system difficult to be reconfigured in a timely manner for the critical situations.

Historically, adaptability has been designed into the system in a very structured manner.
Modes are often used to describe the various behaviors the system must provide for given environmental conditions (scenarios) and/or system states. An example are avionics systems, whose expected behavior depends on the current weather. Definition of reduce functionality *failure modes* given hardware/software faults is another example of the use of modes. A system designed with modes can be viewed as providing a coarse level of adaptability. If particular events occur, the system will transition to a new mode of operation. The system is designed such that the number of system modes and the expected delay to transition from one mode to another is well understood.

One reason why this approach has been used in the past arises from the fact that many large complex systems are life-critical or safety related. Therefore, not only does the system need to be highly dependable, this dependability must be validated before the system is fielded. If the adaptiveness is built-in in a non-deterministic or highly complex manner, then the validation of such systems becomes extremely difficult, if not impossible. The complexity of the large systems has increased partially due to the reduction of cost/size over the past two decades in hardware; therefore, the ability to validate even non-adaptive systems has become increasingly difficult. An additional increase burden on system validation may result to systems that are undependable when executed on cases not previously tested.

Mathematical proofs used to show the ability of complex reconfiguration schemes to maintain behavior are many times not adequate. This is because the proofs need to make simplifying assumptions that may or may not be valid under all operational conditions.

Adaptive behavior is a necessary attribute for systems that need to operate in complex and changing environments. However, the approaches explored should meet the following criteria:

(1) provide analysis during the system engineering phase;
(2) amenable to validation after system implementation, and
(3) maintain the ability to predict the system's behavior under new system/environmental scenarios.

Revolutionary approaches which don't meet these three criteria, while interesting, will not be applicable to this wide class of large, complex, real-time systems.

Predictability Versus Adaptability in Real-Time Computing

Thomas F. Lawrence

Rome Laboratory
C3AB, Griffiss AFB
525 Brooks Road
Rome, NY 13441-4505
U.S.A.

The dichotomy of "adaptivity vs predictability" is as ill founded as the old "communism vs capitalism". Just as capital is fundamental to any economy whether socialist or not, so predictability is essential to real-time systems whether adaptive or not. Two connotations of predictability that are relevant include: (1) the ability to anticipate the environment external to the information processing system, and (2) the ability to understand and determine the degrees of behavior of the internal real-time system state. Both of these issues are of importance to real-time systems since in these systems the internal system state is highly synchronized with the external environment. Stated another way, correctness in real-time systems is contingent not only on the ordering of internal events but on the ordering of both internal and external events. This synchronization in part defines real-time systems. Adaptivity is the ability of the system to adjust its internal state to be consistent with both the current internal system resources and external environmental condition. Adaptivity might be better opposed with the word "rigidity". Consequently adaptivity and predictability are two aspects of a real-time system and are not mutually exclusive. A system can be both highly predictable and highly adaptable. However, in gerneral low predictability and high adaptivity is assumed.

For any scheduling to be useful predictability must exist, that is, the model being used to schedule tasks must be valid. The question is how far into the future one can predict. The real issue then is the degree of predictability. Only the simplest of systems are predictable (e.g. phases of the moon can be predicted years in advance). Command and Control systems and their environment, due to their complexity, have limited degrees of predictability perhaps in the order of minutes or seconds. However, it is important to realize that even though there is limited ability to predict the behavior of a complex world, the behavior of adaptive systems can be understood.

Though the behavior of an adaptive system under a given set of conditions can be understood, it may be difficult to test or model all permutations of conditions which may be relevant to the application. Highly predictable systems of today deal with simple situations either in terms of the application (e.g. periodic tasks) or in terms of the limited number of states the information processing system can assure.

The Role of Standards in Real-Time Computing

C. Douglas Locke

IBM Federal Systems Company
6600 Rockledge Drive
Bethesda, MD 20817
U.S.A.

1 Introduction

Having participated in the IEEE POSIX 1003.4 "Realtime" extensions [1],[2],[3], including process and thread-level functions as well as profiles, it has become apparent that there are a number of important attributes of standards in the real-time systems arena. These can be characterized along two dimensions; a set of attributes that illustrate the importance of real-time standards, and a set of attributes that seem to lead to the conclusion that real-time standards could be inappropriate. This discussion will cover each of these sets of attributes in turn, followed by some brief conclusions.

2 Why Use Standards for Real-Time Systems?

The ability to move applications from one computing hardware architecture to another, i.e., application portability, has been an elusive goal in the field of real-time systems. When real-time systems were small, with relatively low complexity, portability was seldom a concern, since maintaining the operating environment, including languages and operating systems, was not a major part of the overall life-cycle cost. For example, 20 years ago, this author designed and developed a real-time executive program, including I/O and interrupt handling, priority scheduling, dispatching, error management, and initialization. This implementation was done in assembly language, and required about 400 source lines of code; it supported an avionics mission application with about 35,000 source lines of code.

Modern applications, about 2 orders of magnitude larger, require infrastructures that are 2-3 orders of magnitude larger to handle the far greater demands for real-time resource management. For example, the application described above used about 12 tasks. Modern applications will require about an order of magnitude more tasks.

With such growth, it is increasingly financially imperative that the interface between the application and the operating system be standardized to permit applications to be designed and implemented independently from potentially obsolete hardware architectures. As new hardware, such as processors, communications media, and I/O devices, are developed, existing systems will be able to take advantage of them if they no longer require a complete redesign to migrate. Such migration could be done during normal maintenance cycles. Implementation personnel would not require major retraining when moving from one project to the next as they usually do now.

Real-time systems would be constructed on a base of Commercial Off-The-Shelf (COTS) hardware and software. Such software, with a dramatically larger user-base, would have the benefit of greatly increased maturity, resulting in greatly enhanced reliability and reduced long-term maintenance.

3 Why Not Use Standards for Real-Time Systems?

First, standards represent the lowest common denominator of technology. Standards can be created only for technology that has been widely and consistently implemented in the domain in which the technology is to be used. In the case of POSIX real-time extensions, for example, each part of the application interface is based on existing implementations in various real-time operating systems, although there are probably no existing implementations that support all functions. Attempts to prematurely standardize interfaces that, however promising, have not been widely implemented and used in existing systems invite unusable standards. An example of a standard not based on existing implementations was the rendezvous in Ada. Subsequent implementation and use uncovered significant problems that are now a principal focus of the Ada update called Ada 9X.

Second, it is widely feared that standardization will stifle research in technologies competing with the standard. It has been observed, for example, that funding sources for operating system research have been reduced following the success of the UNIX operating system (resulting in the POSIX standardization effort.) It is feared that premature real-time standards would thus present a significant problem for real-time research, particularly in view of the fact that a large proportion of the real-time research topics are concerned with operating system issues, such as scheduling, communications, and synchronization.

A related problem is that because of the relative immaturity of real-time research, accompanied by the likely reluctance of developers already in a relatively high-risk position to deviate from standards-conforming infrastructure products, it is possible that the existence of standards might slow the development and acceptance of advanced real-time technology. In addition, educators may exhibit a similar tendency as has been observed in language research to limit undergraduate real-time concepts to those supported by standard products.

4 Conclusions

In spite of these concerns, the major cost savings possible for real-time systems developers mean that there is really no question of whether real-time standards will be created and used, there is merely the question of what they will be. It is quite true that they will not be technologically exciting, but it is very likely that they will be quite effective in a fairly wide domain of applications, particularly those with significant periodic components, or aperiodic components whose response times can be adequately met using periodic techniques, such as sporadic servers [4] or cyclic executives.

Thus, the cost savings are too great to permit delay in real-time standards development. The concerns about the possible reduction in funding of real-time research must be addressed by the community by pointing out the great potentials of further advance through research over the mature, but overly simplistic approaches currently possible through standards. This will be increasingly important as the exponential advances in hardware performance make it possible to produce dramatically more complex applications.

References

1. *Portable Operating System Interface (POSIX) Real-time Extensions*, P1003.4a Draft 13, IEEE Technical Committee on Operating Systems, October, 1992.
2. *Threads Extensions for Portable Operating Systems*, P1003.4a, Draft 6, IEEE Technical Committee on Operating Systems, February 26, 1992.
3. *Standardized Application Environment Profile (AEP) — POSIX Realtime Application Support*, P1003.13 Draft 5, IEEE Technical Committee on Operating Systems, February, 1992.
4. Sha, L., Goodenough, J. B., *Real-Time Scheduling Theory and Ada*, IEEE Computer, Vol. 23, No. 4, April 1990, 53-62.
5. Locke, C. D., *Software Architecture for Hard Real-Time Applications: Cyclic Executives vs. Fixed Priority Executives*, Journal of Real-Time Systems, Vol. 4, No. 1, 1992, 37–53.

The Role of Standards in Real-Time Computing

Ulrich Schmid

Technical University of Vienna
Department of Automation
Treitlstraße 3
1040 Vienna
Austria

Standards have been defined in almost every traditional engineering discipline for a long time. Computer industries became aware of the importance of widely accepted standards particularly with the development of computer networks. Today, they are sometimes viewed as a panacea: there are standards for networking (e.g. IEEE 802.x), operating systems (e.g. POSIX), hardware (e.g. VME bus), etc. This is also true for real-time systems. In Europe, for example, there are numerous firms offering the development of customary real-time applications ranging from small embedded systems to geographically distributed factory automation and industrial process control systems. They usually combine a considerable experts' knowledge within some field of application with the use of industrial standard components. Actually, these industries would not be able to survive economically if such hardware (e.g. VME-bus CPU- and I/O-modules) and software standards (e.g. kernels like VRTX) were not available.

The major deficit of the industrial standards mentioned above, however, lies in the fact that many of them are built upon an insufficient conceptual basis: Does it actually make sense to worry about a RTEID (Real-Time Executive Interface Definition) or ORKID (Open Real-Time Kernel Interface Definition) standard while taking it as granted that static priority scheduling in conjunction with traditional interprocess communication facilities are to be used? Similar arguments apply to any real-time UNIX implementation, including the "celebrated" POSIX.4 (real time extensions) standard/draft, of course. Admittedly, the situation is particularly complicated for real-time systems due to the necessity of an integrated approach: Scientific research has pointed out that usual modularization concepts are worthless for real-time systems, unless both hardware and software components are integrated within a global scheduling concept.

Anyway, the actual problem with ill founded standards does not lie in applications built upon it. Instead, it is the "inertia" of already established standards against being replaced by novel ones (primarily resulting from the obvious desire to preserve existing hardware, software, and know-how), which causes serious problems. A typical example is the well-known Ethernet standard IEEE 802.3, which is based on a definitely unstable MAC collision resolution algorithm. In the meantime, much better ones have been developed (e.g. INRIA's Deterministic Ethernet), but nobody seems to be really interested in using them.

Therefore, it does not make sense to define standards for real-time systems at the moment — only because they are needed. Scientific research has to provide a sufficient conceptual basis first, before standards should be allowed to evolve.

Tradeoffs in Real Time Protocol Standardization

*Carlos Sêrro**

INESC–Instituto de Engenharia de Sistemas e Computadores
and Instituto Superior Técnico
Technical University of Lisbon
Rua Alves Redol, 9
1000 Lisboa
Portugal

1. Over the past few years, research in the area of real time (RT) protocols for distributed systems has progressed to the point where a fairly large number of multiple access Local Area Network (LAN) protocols have been proposed.

2. Furthermore, fault tolerance aspects of some RT protocols have been developed or are being developed that will shift towards the Medium Access Control (MAC) layer some of the functionality that was previously regarded as being implementable only in higher protocol layers. The flexibility in usage that comes with this approach will eventually lead to wider application scenarios.

3. It seems reasonable, then, to state that the progress in the area of general purpose, multiple access LAN RT protocols is steadily growing and a point will be reached soon where standardization becomes necessary.

4. The ISO OSI model is generally regarded as unsuitable for that purpose due to the complexity of the layers placed between the RT application and the MAC layer. Although generality of implementation is clearly a strong point of the OSI model (specially in internetworking environments), the complexity that comes associated with it becomes a disadvantage when tight RT constraints have to be met.

5. A tradeoff between complexity and generality, on one side, and RT constraints, on the other, should then be reached for best effort systems and for systems that must have a guaranteed timing behavior. This is, in the author's opinion, the fundamental issue in RT protocol standardization.

6. Other important tradeoffs should also be addressed:

   a) generality versus specialization of operation in a wide variety of implementation scenarios: automated manufacturing systems, process control, traffic control, automotive control, to name but a few;

   b) tight versus loose RT constraints: certain RT applications require fast response times while others can cope with slower time constraints;

* This work was made while the author was on sabbatical leave at the Electrical and Computer Engineering Department, University of California, Irvine, with grants from INESC and FLAD – Fundação Luso–Americana para o Desenvolvimento

c) RT LANs using high bandwidth channels versus RT Wide Area Networks (WANs) and Metropolitan Area Networks (MANs) using medium or high bandwidth channels: the cost of communication is basically dependent on the complexity of the network topology and on the cost of actually distributing the cable between the nodes; the RT requirements and constraints should take into account those restrictions.

Meeting all these different and sometimes constrasting requirements is a difficult issue that standardization at the RT protocol level may help to alleviate by providing some form of common operational framework for academia, industry and government to use.

Statement on a Concept for Dynamic Testing in Four Sequential Steps During Software Development

Rudolf Lauber

Institut für Regelungstechnik und Prozeßautomatisierung
Universität Stuttgart
Postfach 80 11 40
70511 Stuttgart
Germany

Concerning the life cycle I see at least two major activities which are needed in developing a real-time system (and which are not needed in developing an information system), (see Fig. 1):

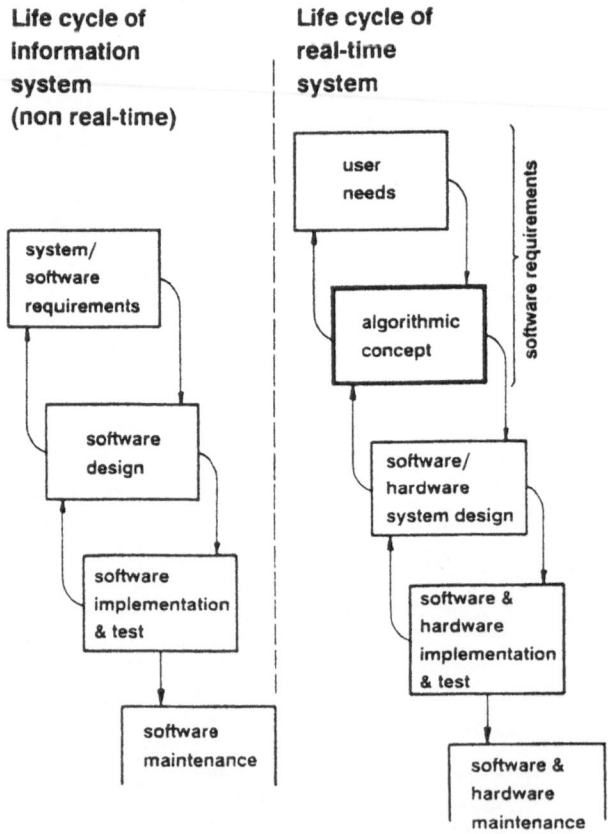

Fig. 1. Difference between the life-cycle of an information system (non-real-time) and of a real-time system.

1. An algorithmic concept (how to monitor and control the technical process) is needed before we can start to design real-time software.
2. A dynamic test of the coupled system (consisting of the computer system and the technical process) is necessary.

We propose to do dynamic testing on each level, e.g. (see Fig. 2):

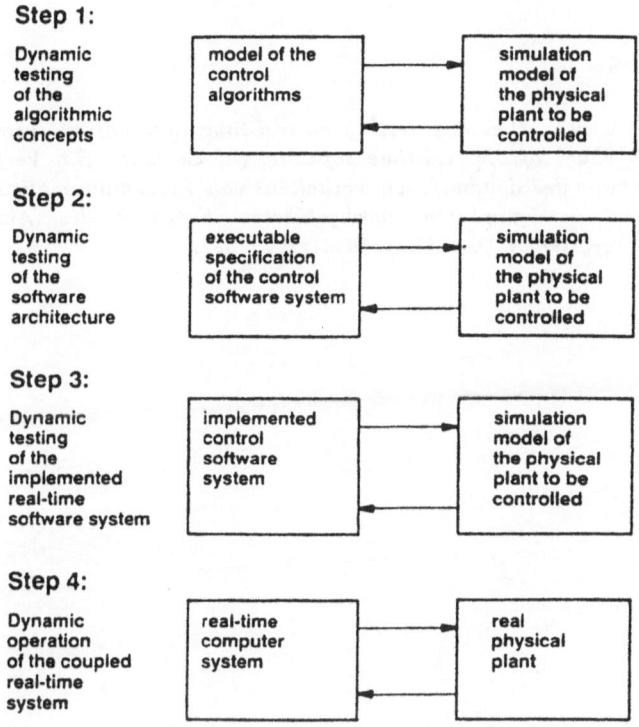

Step 1:

| Dynamic testing of the algorithmic concepts | model of the control algorithms | → | simulation model of the physical plant to be controlled |

Step 2:

| Dynamic testing of the software architecture | executable specification of the control software system | → | simulation model of the physical plant to be controlled |

Step 3:

| Dynamic testing of the implemented real-time software system | implemented control software system | → | simulation model of the physical plant to be controlled |

Step 4:

| Dynamic operation of the coupled real-time system | real-time computer system | → | real physical plant |

Fig. 2. Dynamic testing sequence consisting of 4 test steps.

– on the level of the algorithmic concept (step 1)
– on the level of software design (or software and hardware design) (step 2)
– on the level of implementation (step 3)
– on the level of the real physical plant (step 4).

The following errors or deficiencies can be detected:

– Step 1: Errors or deficiencies of the basic concept, of control algorithms etc.
– Step 2: Errors or deficiencies of the interaction of software modules and tasks, including the influences of the real-time operating system (based on estimates of runtime conditions).

- Step 3: Errors of the real-time software system implemented in a certain programming language.
- Step 4: Remaining errors which were not detected in steps 1 to 3 (possibly because the simulation model of the plant was not sufficient).

A dynamic testing system for step 2 has been realized. It is described in detail in [1].

References

1. Geier, Ulrich, *Dynamic testing of real-time automation systems during the design phase of the real-time software*, (in German: *Ein Verfahren zur Untersuchung des dynamischen Verhaltens von Prozeßautomatisierungssystemen während des graphisch durchgeführten Entwurfs des Automatisierungs-Softwaresystems*), Diss. Univ. Stuttgart, 1992.

Dependability of Telecommunication Software

Lambert J.M. Nieuwenhuis

Royal PTT Nederland NV
PTT Research
2260 AK Leidschendam
The Netherlands

During the last years, the use of real-time computing systems in vital applications has increased enormously and, probably, this development will continue in future. Due to these developments, possible failures of computing systems may cause fatal accidents or unacceptable social and environmental damage. Therefore, the dependability, i.e., the reliability and availability, of these computing systems is of great importance from both a social and economical point of view. Hence, scientists and engineers are confronted with the problem of designing and constructing highly dependable real-time computing systems. The scope of designing and constructing dependable systems is not limited to the physical components of such systems but includes the entire software life-cycle, i.e., the specification, design, construction, validation and verification of the system.

The developments in the field of real-time systems are of great importance for public telecommunication network operators like PTT Telecom in the Netherlands. The current state-of-the-art on *Reliability Engineering* is hardly sufficient to meet the reliability and availability requirements of today's telecommunication systems. In future telecommunication systems, the dependability is even of more importance because of a significant increase of complexity and much more vulnerable architecture of the network and the services. The dependability of future telecommunication systems will be based on fault tolerance in the various layers of the infrastructure. Unfortunately, the strength of fault tolerance is also its weakness. The subsystems that control the interventions to prevent failures are designed to affect operation of the entire network. Consequently, design or implementation faults in such subsystems may cause failures of the entire network and services. The nine-hours, nationwide blockade of AT&T switching systems on January 15, 1990 was caused by a software fault in such a fault handling subsystem.

The telecommunication market in Europe is divided amongst a large number of independent (national) Public Network Operators. PTT Telecom is such an operator, mainly providing public telecommunication services in the Netherlands. The services are provided by means of a multi-vendor network, e.g., the switching systems of the network are manufactured by different suppliers. The networks of the various countries in Europe are different. Therefore, PTT Telecom is confronted with the problem of specification, validation and verification of large scale, complex, real-time, distributed software systems.

The ultimate solution for this problem will probably be based on the use of formal methods. Formal specification can provide the basis for automatic verification and validation of the system. However, the development in the field of formal methods proceeds very slowly and formal specification of the entire telecommunication network and services will not be feasible in near future.

Because of our limited ability to control the *product*, attention is also paid to the *process* with which the product is developed. Complex, real-time software for future telecommunication systems must be produced through a standardized development process. Not only Quality Assurance systems like ISO 9000 or the SEI Software Maturity Model will be required but Public Network Operators also demand for measurements based on standardized metrics (like Bellcore's RQMS). Such data is used to determine the parameters of reliability models like for example Reliability Growth Models, which are used to estimate the dependability of telecommunication systems during the operational phase.

Using Integration Architectures for Systems Development

Wilhelm Rossak

Systems Integration and Real-Time Computing Laboratory
Department of Computer and Information Science
New Jersey Institute of Technology
Newark, NJ 07102
U.S.A.

So called Mega-systems [2], [3], especially in the form of "systems of systems" [1], can be seen as a network of independently developed, but interoperating systems. The combined functionality of the systems constitutes and represents the satisfaction of an overall coherent mission. As mega-systems have to cover the functional requirements of a comprehensive application domain, it is very likely that time constraints will apply to parts of the system network and further complicate the development and maintenance process [3].

To be able to take care of this aspect and other problems on the level of fully flagged, interdependently developed systems, the development process relies heavily on an additional element of coordination. This control level utilizes the concept of an integration architecture [1] to provide a flexible but coordinated development approach in multiple parallel projects.

An integration architectures is an engineering standard [2], [3]. It applies to every project in the application domain and guarantees that the systems can finally be integrated into a mega-system (a system of systems). It acts as a kind of reference model for system design and specifies the external "appearance" of each developed system (as component of a system of systems) by providing standards and guidelines for system decomposition, interface handling, communication, data storage, etc.

This type of architecture/design is a standard that does not focus on the internals of single systems and projects. It supports the engineer to structure and guide the development process of an application domain rather than that of a single system and constitutes a framework for other, more system/project oriented standards (as we know them).

Even though integration architectures are domain specific rather than general purpose guidelines, we believe that there will be a set of predefined and standardized general purpose architectures. These architectures will have to be generic enough to be adapted and instantiated for the needs of a specific domain, e.g., to take care of stringent real-time constraints. This also means that there must be a kind of "standard/architecture adaptation step" in the related integrated process model [2], [3].

References

1. H. Eisner, J. Marciniak and R. McMillan, *Computer-Aided System of Systems (S2) Engineering*, Proceedings of the 1991 IEEE/SMC International Conference on Systems, Man, and Cybernetics, Charlottesville, VA, IEEE Computer Society Press, October 1991, 531–537.
2. W. Rossak and P.A. Ng, *Some Thoughts on Systems Integration — A Conceptual Framework*, Journal of Systems Integration, Kluwer, Vol. 1, No. 1, 1991, 97–114.
3. W. Rossak, T. Zemel, A.T. Stoyenko and P.A. Ng, *On Real-Time Aspects in Systems Integration*, Research Report, Computer and Information Science, New Jersey Institute of Technology, CIS-92-12, 1992.

Software Life Cycle of Real-Time Systems

Theodor Tempelmeier

Fachhochschule, FB Informatik
Marienbergerstraße 26
83024 Rosenheim
Germany

The following theses on the software life cycle of real-time systems have been derived from the author's practical experience in various aerospace and manufacturing automation projects.

Thesis 1:

Design is most important in the life cycle

One can learn from operational systems that the early and latter phases of the software life cycle must have been successful (to a certain degree): Without an implementation the systems would not work at all and without an analysis of the requirements the systems would not fulfill the user's needs. However, the designs in these systems are often horrible, i.e. impossible to understand and hard to maintain. Frequently, a redesign of existing systems has to be undertaken to cope with the problems of bad designs.

A second reason for the importance of the design phase is related to predictability. In [2] two approaches for achieving predictability, the top layer approach and the layer-by-layer approach, are described. In both approaches it is mandatory to have a clear and understandable design. In the top layer approach (this is the one preferred by the author), full comprehension of the design may be even more crucial than in the layer-by-layer approach.

Generally, a design has to comprise *all task and module specifications* in the system, enhanced with timing constraints and other information. Clearly, elements for fail-safe or fail-soft error handling are also part of the design. The design has to be described *very precisely and unambiguously* on one hand and must be *easily comprehensible* on the other hand. Tool supported graphical design notations with underlying textual representations are currently the appropriate choice.

Thesis 2:

Embedded systems are most difficult with respect to the software life cycle

Software, computer hardware, and other surrounding hardware equipment are usually *developed concurrently* for embedded systems. In practice, there is no easy solution to this concurrent development scheme because of the usually tight time schedules. Life cycle models which at least address this problem are of great help. They provide clear terminology, describe deliverables, and show all interrelationships. The life cycle model of the German military [1] must be mentioned here as a positive example. It is even adapted outside the military community voluntarily and is currently being put to international standardization.

Thesis 3:

Bringing all state-of-the-art knowledge fully into practice is the most efficient short-term solution to many problems

Research may be necessary to investigate better life cycle models or to find new software development paradigms eventually. However, highest short-term benefits could be obtained by bringing the state-of-the-art knowledge on software development to the practical projects and by exploiting the existing framework of software life cycles whole-heartedly.

References

1. *General Directive 250*, Software Development Standard for the German Federal Armed Forces, V-Model (Software Life Cycle Process Model), August 1992. Obtainable at: IABG, Dept. ITE, Einsteinstrasse 20, D-8012 Ottobrunn.
2. J.A. Stankovic, K. Ramamritham, *What is Predictability for Real-Time Systems?*, Real-Time Systems, 2, 1990, 247–254.

What Should We Focus on in the Next Five Years?

Toward Future Software Products Based on Time and Functions

*Giovanni Cantone**

University of Rome at "Tor Vergata"
Department of Electronic Engineering
Laboratory for Computer Science
Via della Ricerca Scientifica
00133 Roma
Italy

Let us try to answer the panel question by looking at real-time computing and engineering from the following points of view.

Internal point of view

Questions: Which theoretical, methodological and/or technical real-time problem are we faced with that we should solve in the next five years?

Goals: In the next five years, the activities of the RT community should include investigations on

   i. concurrent computation models for timeliness; virtual and real machines (organizations and languages) for time-predictable and time-dependable control systems;

   ii. deterministic worst-time versus stochastic response-time bounds: feasibility, costs, trade-off, application-area;

   iii. abstraction, inheritance, instantiation, packaging, reuse of time properties of objects.

External point of view

Questions: Are our channels to/from neighbouring fields of engineering, for instance electronic, control, dependable, software (say data processing) and performance (say mean time) engineering — well-defined, dimensioned and "installed" for the next five years? What should we import (resp. export) from (resp. to) them? Which loosely coupled relationships should be enforced, why and how?

Main goals: While such relationships with Control and Electronic engineering are to be maintained and exchanges with Dependable engineering should be

* This paper was partially supported by the "Progetto Sistemi Informatici e Calcolo Parallelo" of CNR under Grant No. 90.00705.PF69

enforced, tight partnerships should be established with Software engineering in order to get reciprocal advantages.

The present context

Questions: Which are the expected trends of the hardware/software industries? Do they affect the real-time research and production trends; how?

Status: The present general context of any computer related engineering is the "software crisis".

Goals: To address hard/software technology to produce massive products, i.e. to apply computer based artifacts to almost any aspect of both the social, the family and the individual human life. This includes formal and informal knowledge, and detection and handling of signals and events; it is strongly determined by the necessity of continuously interacting with the world; timeliness, time-flexibility, synchronization and time-dependability are some of the most important aspects of contemporary life. Computer-based future products call thus for combining the knowledge from diverse areas of the computer science, real-time, dependability, parallel, and software engineering specially included. For the sake of brevity, let us emphasize relationships between real-time engineering and software engineering only. A topic of the software engineering experimental research at the present time is the Software Factory Engineering. This can be divided into two related sub-topics: the engineering of the Software Process and the Reuse of Software Experiences. Some questions follow which are expected to be answered from by "Real-Time Software Engineering" in the next years: Which techniques should be employed to design, implement and control timed software (production) processes? Does timeliness affect the quality of products and processes? Should time related experiences be arranged, packaged, generalized, and reused? How?

What Shall We Focus on in the Next Five Years?

Lars-Berno Fredriksson

Kvaser AB
Box 4076
511 04 Kinnahult
Sweden

Focus on Controller Area Networks!

The experience of designing plants as well as machines with Controller Area Networks is very encouraging. Controller Area Networks have lots of advantages:

1. Simple management of the development work:
   One module corresponds to one activity in the project plan.
2. Simple specification:
   For each module the messages to be received and transmitted and the timing of them as well as the mechanical response of them must be specified.
3. Short development time:
   Modules can be developed simultaniuosly by different working groups. System integration facilitated.
4. Simple verification and testing:
   Each module can be tested against a computer simulation of the rest of the system. The whole system can be verified step-wise.
5. Simple further development:
   The system can be further developed module by module. New modules can be added and old ones deleted.
6. Inexpensive standard modules can be provided by multiple suppliers.

With all the above advantages there ought to be some drawbacks, otherwise most machines would already show a Controller Area Network design. Yes, there are a few drawbacks and one or two of them are inconspicuous:

- The need for multi-disciplinary engineers and/or a new organization of the development departments.
- The linguistic problem.

More obvious problems are:

- Proper treatment of timing.
- Lack of computing methods for electronic shafts, gears etc. ...

The development of a module in Controller Area Network requires a close co-operation between engineers of different specialties. Just a matrix organization is not enough as the engineers need a rather deep knowledge about the specialty of their colleagues in the working group. The mechanical engineer has to know quite a lot about electronics, micro controllers and data transfer in order to understand how this affects the mechanical design and vice versa. A module is always a compromise between mechanics and electronics. Just the use of some words can be confusing: What is a message? Is it a set of data transferred between nodes, the position of cogwheel "A" just now, or, maybe, the parameter "temperature" in a controller program? To my experience everybody in a working group has a firm and clear opinion about what a word means. The problem is that the interpretation of one and the same word can be very different for each one of the working group depending on their education and earlier experience.

In the development of "CAN Kingdom" we tried very hard to find words and a model that were neutral to any line of engineering. E.g. we used the word post instead of mail as a "mail box" gave system engineers the wrong picture. We use the model of a "postal system", so everybody can see that the problem is not just to transfer data. It takes time to write a letter, transfer it and to read it. Some time is also needed to collect something to write about and when a letter is read it takes some time to act upon it. This highlights the problem of proper treatment of timing. Finding models better than "CAN Kingdom" may make the work easier but will not solve the problem of understanding and timing. To make the education of engineers broader will not solve the problem either as we need specialists to make advanced designs. The lines in a matrix organization are still lines of specialty and in the projects there is no time for education. We have to find models that can be used as a common base for the education of different kinds of engineers and new ways to organize development departments in order to make efficient use of Controller Area Networks.

In a mechanical design power and information can be transmitted very fast. The dynamic behavior of a gearbox, a shaft and a load can be fairly well predicted by computing. The importance of the stiffness of the gearbox and the shaft is obvious to the mechanical engineer. These components can be exchanged for electronic counterparts in a network but immediately we face problems: What is the stiffness of an electronic shaft? How do I compute it? What are the natural frequencies and how do I find them? The damping factor? These problems are not only related to the nodes but also to the data exchange between the nodes.

Controller Area Networks is a tiny part of the field of Real-Time Computing but a very important field. It does not only contain real-time problems but also parallel processing. With the introduction of the CAN protocol supporting chips on the market the development of Controller Area Networks gained speed. The main target for the chip manufacturers is the car industry but there is a great interest also in other industries. In Europe there are many ongoing projects within the fields of textile machinery, hydraulics, robotics, farming equipment, dairies and packaging machines. Only a tiny fraction of the potential of Controller Area Networks is used. Education, development organization and computing methods suitable for Controller Area Networks are indeed areas to focus on in the next five years.

Next Step: Responsive Multicomputer Systems

Miroslaw Malek

The University of Texas at Austin
Dept. of Electrical and Computer Engineering
Austin, TX 78712
U.S.A.

After parallel and distributed computer systems are now well established, the next step should be focused on ensuring their dependability, especially in real-time applications. I call such dependable real-time systems responsive and am convinced that the need for such systems will grow rapidly. Robotics, avionics, communication, multimedia and even point-of-sale terminals are just a few examples of an ever-expanding number of applications in which responsiveness is vital.

The challenge for the nineties is to form a marriage between fault tolerance and real time [1]. How to effectively integrate system attributes, such as dependability parameters, with service attributes, such as timeliness, remains an open question. Optimization of responsiveness requires a good understanding of fault models, system models and their characteristics. This is difficult in any case, but especially in a multicomputer environment. The challenges here are across the board, from responsive processors and memory design to responsive operating systems and applications.

To succeed in maximizing responsiveness, we must create formal methods and languages for specification, design and verification of responsive systems, formulate algorithms for responsive scheduling and responsive protocols, and develop testing methods and evaluation tools. Finally, prototypes incorporated into real-life environments must be built, tested and measured in order to establish the levels of responsiveness which can be attained. Our approach is founded on two basic paradigms — the omnipresence of consensus and the inevitability of probability.

Consensus plays a fundamental role in dependable multicomputing. It is vital in synchronization, reliable communication, diagnosis, reconfiguration and scheduling. Probability cannot be avoided, as systems are becoming too complex for deterministic analysis and as faults themselves are probabilistic. In most real systems, then, we must accept that only probabilistic guarantees can be given. Maximizing the probability of a timely execution of tasks, even in the presence of faults, is one of the major challenges of the near future as dependence on computers grows at an accelerated pace.

References

1. M. Malek, *Responsive Systems: A Marriage Between Real Time and Fault Tolerance*, Keynote Address, Proceedings of the Fifth International Conference on Fault-Tolerant Computing Systems, Nürnberg, Germany, Springer-Verlag, Informatik-Fachberichte 283, September 25, 1991, 1–17.

What Should Be Focussed on in the Next Five Years?

M.G. Rodd

Dept. of Electrical & Electronic Engineering
University College of Swansea
Singleton Park
Swansea SA2 8PP
U.K.

In my opinion, there are four vital issues to be tackled over the next five years.

- Safety/reliability,
- useable real-time design tools,
- genuine distributed real-time data bases, and
- real-time artificial intelligence techniques.

We have seen over the last five to ten years too many disasters. Our plants are becoming increasingly complex and as a result are increasingly failing. There is a significant anti-technology swing throughout the whole of the developed world and a total mis-trust by the undeveloped world. We are to blame. We have allowed systems to be used which are simply far too complicated to be serviceable. We have put software into use which we cannot validate or verify. We still have to admit to producing 1 line in 300 lines of coding in error. Now we are developing AI systems which we are pronouncing as suitable for industrial control and yet their very nature allows them to reason and draw conclusions which cannot be anticipated. We simply cannot go on developing systems which we cannot truly validate.

As good as most of the current software engineering environments are, in practice the bulk are of little or no use when handed over to real, genuine, industrial control engineers. Abstract computer science terminologies and concepts which are totally foreign to practicing engineers, yield tools that are totally unacceptable — and this is reflected in their level of use by the real industry. The bulk of our software engineering tools, too, are incapable of supporting complex real-time interactions, and this is a further cause for concern.

The question of developing genuinely distributed real-time data bases is of fundamental importance in all future control systems. It is now acknowledged that to move towards reliability in control, total autonomous action by local controllers is essential. This has two consequences. In the first place the data is genuinely distributed and must be maintained where it is most urgently required, i.e. the point of use. This typically requires us to retain data throughout the plant, but at the same time, though, such data must be replicated. A distributed database is not one which is only distributed in the sense of accessing data, but in which the data is genuinely distributed. However, the data is real-time information and is useless unless it is time-stamped! The consequence, from the point-of-view of redundancy, is that we must be capable of ensuring data consistency — despite data being distributed throughout the plant!

Despite what so many computer scientists are saying, I believe very strongly that we ignore the challenge of AI techniques to our peril. The sheer number of industries who have already adopted even naive, 1st generation AI products, such as Real-time Expert Systems and fuzzy logic, must be telling us something! The number of site licences sold by leading vendors of AI systems is very impressive, and, given their high costs, must mean that they are being taken very seriously. Thus we must really begin to understand the real-time problems which have to be faced by AI systems. Many of these, such as time-conscious and predictable behaviour are parallel to so many problems faced in the real-time computer field already. However there are some very fundamental problems which must be addressed as we move AI systems from the non real-time arena to the hard real-time world. The issues here include:

- The need to handle multiple problems simultaneously.
- That these simultaneous problems interact with each other.
- That the goals of a system often will change dynamically.
- That most reasoning processes will be strictly time-limited.
- That only genuinely logically- and temporally-predictable systems will ever be acceptable in critical situations.

Ignoring the current adoption of AI techniques by industry will render much of our research in real-time computing totally irrelevant.

What Should We Focus on in the Next Five Years?

Jacques J. Skubich

Charge des relations Internationales
Departement d'Informatique
I.N.S.A Bat. 502
69621 Villeurbanne Cedex

Personally, I think it seems to be tricky to give only one answer, so I'd rather ask some questions:

- Which answers do we have to give to whom?
- Do we know what the needs are?
- Who needs something?

Of course, we have to carry on with research in most of the domains we have been speaking about since the beginning of the NATO Advanced Studies Institute: Distributed Real Time Computing, Fault Tolerance Computing, Real Time Software Quality, Standardization, ...

But when I say "Real Time", I immediately think of Real Time industrial applications and the real Time industrial developers' job. What are the needs? I think that if usually one assimilates Real Time application coding to assembly language coding, it is due mainly to the fact that there does not exist any Real Time Development Environment. Real Time developers need user-friendly Real Time Development Environments in order to be freed from a lot of tedious things and to be able to implement all Real Time related mechanisms in an easy way: Fault Tolerance, Distribution, ...

Sometimes ago it was said that Real Time Computing was not mature. To my mind that is right, and a part of the solution is to make efforts to provide people with convenient and user-friendly tools.

On the other hand, if we consider the educational point of view, one has to notice that Real Time techniques Education is not a monolithic education and that usually there does not exist only one Real Time Computing course but several ones according to the fact that they are taught by people who have various scientific origins and who teach Real Time from their own point of view. We will have to make some pedagogical efforts in order to try to determine how a Real Time Computing course will have to be like. What will our students have to know and to learn in order to be able to perform within the frame of their future job considering the expectations of Industry?

Somebody said that Real Time teaching nowadays is limited to standard-based solutions, what partly still is true. So I think that Real Time development Environments could also be a major solution to this problem. Their use will help us to focus on the essential part of teaching, and that means *design and creativity*.

What Should We Focus on in the Next Five Years?

Alexander D. Stoyenko

Real-Time Computing Laboratory
Department of Computer & Information Science
New Jersey Institute of Technology
Newark, New Jersey 07102
U.S.A.

As far as the requirements of modern applications are concerned, real-time systems have definitely come of age. Unfortunately, this is not true of our ability to engineer such systems. We strongly believe that the following four crucial points need to be addressed — in the next five years and probably beyond — if the gap between what is required and what can be done is to be narrowed or, at least, kept constant.

First, modern and future systems are (or will be) — in addition to being real-time — fault-tolerant, secure, reliable, maintainable, traceable, and of course functional. Existing system engineering techniques — from requirements specification through implementation and operation — seldom or never address more than a small number of these (conflicting) characteristics. Typically in fact, most techniques address a single one. Clearly then, we need to develop techniques that work on as many as possible of these characteristics in an integrated fashion and properly. The recent trend towards responsive systems as well as the treatment of integrated system design factors are steps into the right direction but, clearly, much more work needs to be done.

Second, modern and future systems often are very large and dynamic, and are expected to adapt in a timely, rapid and correct (predictable) fashion to frequently changing environment variables and conditions. These systems are expected to run on modern computer architectures, which often are (highly) parallel and utilize many heterogeneous resources. Again, however, existing engineering techniques — developed mostly within the cyclic executive model and typically treating real-time applications as consisting of a relatively small number of heavy, largely independent and coarse processes, executed on a small number of processors and making use of a small number of mostly homogeneous resources — fail to address these systems. Consequently we badly need new techniques that will consider — at the very least — complexity, predictability, adaptibility and performance.

Third, academia, government and industry need to work much closer together. One severe problem is lack of professional success metrics that encourage cooperation. Somehow, academics should think more in terms of building systems, or at the very least, prototyping their ideas — the "publish-or-perish" syndrome is obsolete, dangerous and quite simply has to give way to accommodating system builders. Industrial practitioners need to share their technology engineering and marketing expertise more openly (with each other as well as government and academia). While legitimate proprietory concerns should certainly continue being addressed, a company's Patent and Intellectual Property Office should not be used to police and ultimately destroy professional dissemination of ideas and expertise. The government should encourage collaborative efforts through funding, favorable patent and legal laws, and other mechanisms. While much of the spending is currently decided upon through either political ("pork-barrel") or random (or worse) academic reviews ("dice-roll"), we feel that evaluation of all proposals by expert well-mixed panels of practitioners and researchers would be better.

Fourth, there simply is not enough cooperation across the Atlantic (and other fundamental barriers). While NATO is clearly the undisputed leader in facilitating such cooperation, national and regional organizations and agencies also need to address this concern.

Instrumentation for Real-Time Programs in Parallel Environments

Aldo Esposito

Direzione Studi, Italian Air Force Academy
Via Domitiana
80078 Pozzuoli (NA)
Italy

Distributed and parallel computer systems are being incorporated into real-time environments at an increasing rate. Distributed computer systems with interconnecting networks give the potential of high reliability with dynamic adaptation to modifications from the environment or internal faults. Parallel processors are ideal for the task of simulating large production plants where numerous actions and interactions simultaneously are taking place: the various real-life processes can be programmed onto different processors thus allowing a more dynamic model to be created. The multi-processor machines are ideally suited for plant monitoring, inspection or remote surveillance systems, that require *virtual reality* techniques, 3D graphics or complex signal processing. To guarantee that deadlines within these applications are meet, high performance obtained by the multiplicity of processors is necessary.

Generally speaking, the execution time T of a program depends on the inputs (tasks, data, commands), on the environment (architecture and attributes of its resources) and on the algorithms for controlling and scheduling the system activity. Parallel computers increase the complexity of evaluating T. Additional features that affect overall system performance within a parallel environment include: distribution and management of memory, network topology, management of task queues and process synchronization, multiuser features (cluster of processors per user), parallelism in programming languages, I/O mechanism.

In order to evaluate performance indices, the complex interaction of the many architectural, hardware and software features of parallel systems requires the use of different tools specifically designed. To develop good instrumentation techniques, it is necessary to study monitoring tools during the system design phase. In this way, the additional performance measurement hardware and software are directly inserted into the system, thus obtaining a performance instrumented computer. The additional hardware allows easy access and storage of performance- critical informations in the computer system. The additional software allows the user to specify which measurements to make, according to the specific evaluation goals. Moreover, by using an integrated design, the conflicts between computational processes and performance data measurements can be reduced to a minimum, to achieve a flexible noninvasive monitoring.

For parallel applications performance analysis, modelling supports based on dynamic models are necessary to identify tuning actions between workload and resources in order to meet system requirements. Models can be validated by using measurements tools under real operating conditions and are usually classified into simulation and analytical models. Petri Nets (PN) are well-suitable for modeling the concurrency (the activities can be *graphically* viewed by following the path of the tokens in the places). The generation of PN and their reachability tree has been automated and adopted within some CASE tools. Unfortunately, massive parallel systems are difficult to be modelled by PN because of the explosion of the state space.

In Generalized Stochastic Petri Nets (GSPN) the transitions belong to two different classes: timed and immediate. The reachability tree of a GSPN is a subset of the reachability tree of the associated standard PN, because precedence rules introduced with immediate transitions do not allow some states can be reached. Moreover, by dividing states in tangible and vanishing, according to time spent for enabling timed and immediate transitions respectively, it is possible to define an embedded Markov chain over tangible states only, so reducing complexity for the system solution.

In conclusion, in order to be able to predict the program's temporal behaviour within parallel computers, specific architectures must be defined, including also performance measurement hardware. Moreover, due to the many parameters involved, numerous monitors and powerful software packages are needed to evaluate the system and numerically solve the problem automatically generated from the model description.

References

1. Ajmone Marsan M., Balbo G. and Conte G., *Performance Models of Multiprocessor Systems*, MIT Press, 1986.
2. Cantone G. and Esposito A, *An Initial Approach to Response Time Verification of Critical Programs*, CSCI-CNR Wshop. on Massively Parallel Systems, Napoli, Oct. 1987.
3. Cantone G., Esposito A. and Gragnani F. S., *Predicting Temporal Behavior of Highly Distributed Processes*, Proc. Computer Architecture Conf., Lecce (I), Oct. 1991.
4. Chu W. W., Sit C. M.. and Leung K. K., *Task Response Time for Real-Time Distributed Systems with Resource Contention* IEEE Trans. Soft. Eng., Vol. 17, No. 10, October 1991, 1076–1092.
5. Colnaric M. and Halang W. A., *Architectural Support for Predictability in Hard Real Time Systems*, Proc. Int. Wshop on Real-Time Programming, Bruges, June 1992.
6. Croll P. R., *Safe and Deterministic Real-Time Programming in a Nondeterministic Parallel Processing System*, Proc. Int. Wshop on Real-Time Programming, Bruges, June 1992.
7. Esposito A. and De Pietro G., *Estimating the Execution Time of Parallel Programs*, IEEE Microarch. Magazine (to appear).

8. Esposito A. and Vaccaro R., *Performance Measurements and Instrumentation for Distributed Memory Parallel Machines*, EC Newsletters (to appear).

9. Halang W. A., *A priori execution time analysis for parallel processes*, Proc. of the Euromicro Wshop on Real-Time Systems, Como (I), June 1989.

10. Halang W. A. and Stoyenko A. D., *Constructing Predictable Real Time Systems*, Kluwer Academic Publ., 1991.

11. Jeffrey J. P., Fang K. Y. and Chen H. Y., *A Noninvasive Architecture to Monitor Real-Time Distributed Systems* IEEE Computer, Vol. 23, No. 3, March 1990, 11–23.

12. Malony A. D., *Multiprocessor Instrumentation: Approaches for Cedar*, in Instrumentation for Future Parallel Computing Systems (M. Simmons et al. eds.), ACM Press, 1989, 1–33.

13. Park C. Y. and Shaw A. C., *Experiments with a Program Timing Tool Based on Source Level Timing Schema*, IEEE Computer, Vol. 24, No. 5, May 1991, 48–57.

14. Shin K. G., HARTS: *A Distributed Real-Time Architecture*, IEEE Computer, Vol. 24, No. 5, May 1991, 25–35.

15. Stoyenko A. D., *A Schedulability Analyzer for Real-Time Euclid*, Proc. IEEE Real-Time Systems Symp., San Jose (CA), December 1987.

16. Szczerbicka H., *A Combined queueing network and stochastic Petri-net approach for evaluating the performability of fault-tolerant computer systems*, Performance Evaluation, Vol. 14, No. 3/4, 1992, 217–226.

17. Vaccaro R. and Vanneschi M., *Design Methodologies for General-Purpose Highly-Parallel Computers: Physical Machine and Architectural Supports*, IEEE Microarch. Magazine, Vol. 6, No. 1, 1991, 21–26.

CORTO: High Availability in a Real-Time System

Carlos Almeida and Keith Marzullo

INESC
R. Alves Redol 9
1000 Lisboa
Portugal

The area of building *embedded real-time systems* is one in which the applications being designed are more advanced than the available underlying system support. Examples of such applications can be found in several fields, including robot control, avionics, and plant control systems. These systems all have hard real-time requirements: if a deadline is missed, then the result is catastrophic. Furthermore, such deadlines must often be met even in the face of bounded processor or network failures. Yet, the principles for building such systems are still being developed and the availability of systems supporting these principles is very limited.

One of the most important characteristics required by a real-time system is *predictability*, and predictability can be met in part by ensuring that all timing constraints are met. In order to meet timing constraints, the worst case execution must be computable. Hence, all actions need to be time bounded in order to compute the cost of a given thread, and a scheduling policy must be used that guarantees resource contention does not cause deadlines to be missed.

Even ignoring predictability, the development of fault-tolerant applications can be a complex task when the programmer does not have supporting software tools. At Cornell, we have developed the ISIS toolkit that supplies a group programming paradigm for building fault-tolerant programs. However, the current version of this system is not suitable for building real-time programs. ISIS runs on top of UNIX and contains no scheduling support for writing predictable real-time applications.

Our goal is to create an environment that supports the development of hard real-time systems even in the face of resource loss. *Corto*, the system we are building, will support the basic programming abstractions of ISIS; namely, ordered delivery of messages to groups of processes and agreement on membership. Corto will also support the predictable scheduling of processes and communication that systems like ARTS and RT-Mach provide.

Multicast Protocols:
Combining Real-Time and Reliability

Dick Alstein

Eindhoven University of Technology
Dept. of Mathematics and Computer Science
P.O. Box 513
5600 MB Eindhoven
The Netherlands

We address the problem of developing protocols for reliable multicast in a shared-memory multiprocessor. The protocols must have bounded completion time, so that they are suitable for use in a Real-Time system.

A multicast service, found in many parallel and distributed systems, enables a sender to transmit a message to a predefined set of destinations, a *multicast group*. The multicast service is called reliable if it satisfies the requirements of

1. *Unanimity:* a message must be either accepted or rejected by all correctly functioning receivers,
2. *Non-triviality:* if a message is sent by a correct sender, it must be accepted by all correct receivers, and
3. *Ordering:* correct receivers receive the messages in the same order.

Additionally, the protocols are intended to function in a real-time sytem. Because a process using the multicast service must complete its task before a certain deadline, we also require the multicast to satisfy timing requirements. Specifically, send and receive operations must be completed in bounded time.

Several protocols for reliable multicast exist. However, these protocols all use communication channels to transmit data. In contrast, our protocols use the common memory of a shared-memory system for communication.

Senders deposit their messages in a mailbox (a block of common memory), from which receivers then read.

To prevent loss of data in case of a mailbox failure, the mailbox is replicated. If the replicates are located in different memory modules, with independent failure probabilities, the probability of failure of the whole mailbox can be made negligibly small. Messages are written in every mailbox replicate, so that at least one copy of the message will remain available.

Two protocols for reliable multicast in a multiprocessor system have been developed. The basic protocol tolerates only crash failures of processes, while the second protocol can also handle timing failures. Both protocols satisfy the requirements, and are tolerant of memory crashes.

As an example of an application of the protocols, consider a set of replicated data items, replicated for higher availability. The set of processes that hold a copy of the data should form a multicast group, and updates should be sent to that group. The properties of the multicast service guarantee that the copies of the data receive all updates, and in the same order, thus maintaining a consistent view of the data.

Towards Heterogeneous Real-Time Knowledge-Based Systems

Vladimir Bacvanski

Aachen University of Technology
Lehrstuhl für Informatik III
Ahornstr. 55
52056 Aachen
Germany

Knowledge-based (KB) technology failed to provide a number of features significant for applications in real-time environments. Real-time KB systems have to provide support for making tradeoffs between processing power, response time, data space, inattention and degradation. There is also a problem of time semantics which have to be included in the knowledge representation.

Current expert system development tools provide only one unchangeable inference engine, and it is often the case that this inference engine is not appropriate for the use under real-time conditions. Moreover, current KB systems have serious problems regarding integration with conventional components. All these problems force developers of real-time applications to implement their systems in a fully conventional way, without benefits of high-level abstractions of knowledge representation languages.

A compilation of KB systems into a highly efficient object-oriented strongly typed language, enriched with constructs for real-time programming could be the way to overcome current deficiencies of KB systems in a real-time context. This approach offers the possibility to develop systems in sophisticated environments on a much higher abstraction level than it would be possible using conventional technologies. The utilization of rigorous software engineering techniques enables building reusable libraries of abstractions for KB representation, which could be refined to meet demands of particular applications.

Another result of the proposed approach is a unified but secure data model which diminishes the mismatch between KB and conventional systems, facilitating the interfacing among various components of complex software. These implementation decisions provide a ground for extending the application scope of KB systems to the real-time area. Advances in object-oriented languages for programming real-time applications, especially the introduction of real-time (active) objects, explicit timing constraints on operations and periodic tasks with rigid timing constraints offer the possibility to adequately implement real-time KB components and to enrich the KB component library with components designed for real-time processing and knowledge representation. The commonality of implementations will further facilitate integration between different components in heterogeneous real-time applications and ease managerial and training issues, thus reducing development costs.

Propagating Quantitative Temporal Constraints into the Software Design: A Formal Approach for Practitioners

Reinhold Bareiß

Institute for Control Engineering and Industrial Automation
University of Stuttgart
Pfaffenwaldring 47
70569 Stuttgart
Germany

When designing safety critical hard real-time systems, there is an urgent need for powerful and practically usable methods to assure the correctness and to support the evaluation and validation of the temporal behavior of real-time systems already on the level of the software design. To provide help for both aspects, we propose a formal method based on constraint propagation. The underlying idea is to derive all temporal relationships inside the software design from the environmentally motivated temporal constraints and the user-defined temporal system requirements.

By this strategy, we consequently exploit the fact that the computer for process control is totally subordinate to the temporal behavior of the plant. The following aims are reached:

- We are able to calculate formally the lower and upper time bounds within which the elementary, pure sequential functionalities (for instance procedures, functions, etc.) have to deliver their output parameters in order to satisfy the given time constraints and to keep the entire system running regularly.
- We can calculate quantitatively the whole framework of temporal relationships within which the real-time system acts in worst-case at maximum work load. This information forms the basis for visualizing the temporal behavior in a time diagram and is useful for evaluating the temporal behavior of the entire real-time system. Furthermore, with the complete knowledge of the actual concurrency an experienced engineer will be enabled to recognize possible bottlenecks.
- Because the propagation technique is a formal one, the propagated time constraints in the software design are correct against the given temporal constraints and requirements.

To make this formal method accessible for practitioners, we took the following measures:

- The specification method is a pure graphical one. It is based on easy understandable communicating state machines. Further, the method is based on interval semantics in time. Thus, the temporal behavior of, for instance, a plant can be specified error-free by using lower and upper time bounds.

– The propagation technique can be automated completely. That means, the "end-user" does not see what happens inside. He just gets the results.

Scheduling Tasks and Traffic in Fieldbus Based Real-Time Systems

Carlos B. Cardeira[1], Z. Mammeri[2], F. Simonot[2], J.-P. Thomesse[2]

[1] Sistemas - DEM - Instituto Superior Técnico
  Avenida Rovisco Pais, 1096 Lisboa Codex, Portugal
[2] CRIN, (Centre de Recherche en Informatique de Nancy)
  Ensem, 2 av de la Forê de Haye, 54516 Vandœuvre Cedex, France

In this communication we present fieldbuses as real-time systems networks, and how they are suited to a pre-run-time schedulability analysis of hard real-time systems.

Fieldbuses are networks of interconnected sensors, actuators, instruments and control machines, at the lowest hierarchical level of a CIM architecture, replacing traditional 4–20mA centralized connections. We compare the characteristics of a fieldbus generated traffic with other industrial networks protocols like MAP, MiNiMAP or FEIS.

We discuss the motivations for fieldbus like wiring cost reductions, smart instrumentation, reliability as well as some of the disadvantages like availability.

We present the fieldbus as an entity providing the services of a real-time distributed data base, and we find scheduling of both tasks and network traffic as the essential tool to maintain the consistency of the real-time distributed data base. To do this global (tasks and networks) schedulability analysis, we began our study by a bibliographic research for current practices for pre-run-time scheduling and how existing algorithms are or are not adapted to our needs. We'll present the results of this research, based on current practices for handling time, precedence, resources and allocation constraints.

There is the need for mixed solutions for tasks representation and we'll present our conclusion that real-time logic is a good tool to represent most tasks constraints.

At last, we'll discuss how Smart Instruments may influence existing scheduling algorithms. Smart instruments may take decisions that were before taken by centralized machines, leading to the dispersion of the system intelligence. As a consequence, these systems ask for distributed parallel scheduling algorithms, in order that each node maintains the consistency of the real-time data base, and takes consistent decisions.

Real-Time: The Uncertainty Between Sensor and Process Requirements in Computer Vision

Matthias F. Carlsohn

Am Heiddamm 36g
28355 Bremen
Germany

The real-time capability of computer vision equipment is still one of the key features which defines the level of complexity those systems can deal with. In every case, it affects directly the overall performance and costs of a system, respectively. Therefore it has to be defined carefully according to the real-time demands of the particular application.

In computer vision, one usually has to deal with two real time definitions which does not fit into the raw classification of the RT-community, i.e. into hard- and soft-real-time. Additionally, from the application point of view, the customers are mostly not aware about the difference between sensor real-time and process real-time, although this difference is sometimes in the range of some orders. The uncertainty about time constraints of the task and the accordingly derived requirements the solution really needs is due to the fact that computer vision systems often use standard sensor components, as e.g. TV-cameras, delivering images at a rate of 40ms cycle time, i.e., depending on resolution and colour, a permanent data stream of around some 100 Mbits/s is generated. Consequently, all components within the image processing chain have to keep in line at least with this cycle time, in order to produce outputs on image input speed. Of course, the use of those standard components is beneficial with respect to the decrease of costs for the sensor periphery, but the number and complexity of operations per time slot is rather restricted. This bottle-neck can only be dilated by introduction of parallelity in the processing either in space or in time, making use of special architectures and multi-processing (in pipe-lines or spatial parallel structures) and of course any reasonable mixtures of both.

The increasing variety of camera sensor elements like CCDs as line or array configurations allow to adapt processing speed of all components of the vision system to the time requirements of the processes under inspection or control via the automatic visual analysis or feedback.

As a matter of fact, most off-the-shelf frame grabbers and special purpose boards for high speed signal processing have been designed for standard video camera input and are expensive, respectively. Nevertheless the complexity of algorithms which can be performed by these boards within a TV-standard time cycle are often poor compared to sophisticated solutions which are described in literature. For that reason processing is often still applied to binary images only instead of exploiting the gray value information. Additionally, only few functions like binary correlation with simple masks and coarse edge detectors are already "hard-wired" in silicon. Consequently, vision algorithms applied under time constraints close to video speed, seldom achieve a higher complexity than simply counting pixels in some intelligent way.

It should be remarked that beside those vision systems which are conventionally labeled by "real-time", there exist also "real-fast" implementations which are mostly unique, for special purpose, rare and expensive.

In future, standardization has to decrease the costs for the engineering of operating systems for parallel and multi-processing hardware, image processing user-interfaces, function libraries, i/o-drivers for dedicated imaging periphery, debugging tools and test beds. If finally, those components will be standard modules of a vision tool box, there will still remain a lot of individual adaptation, as e.g. for uniquely designed sensor-illumination arrangements and integration into the production environment. But as long as computer vision has the image of some kind of art which only inventors can deal with, the whole branch of this technology will suffer from a non-continuous business success.

Near Real-Time Pattern Recognition in a Special Purpose Computer with Parallel Architecture

Matthias F. Carlsohn

Am Heiddamm 36g
28355 Bremen
Germany

In computer vision the term real-time possesses some uncertainty, because of the demands defined by standard camera sensors and the requirements of the processes under inspection sometimes differ by orders. An example shows the necessary system complexity. In image pattern recognition, the segmentation of interesting image objects from their image background and the characterization of the object properties by their describing features are the pre-requisites for an object classification. Both process steps are usually of great computational complexity and time consumption, respectively. Consequently, a processing in video real-time is only possible by a supporting computer architecture.

The presented system is a hybrid hard- and software implementation of a region-based and scan line-oriented segmentation method including an inherent feature extraction [1].

A set of concurrent single processes are mapped onto an appropriate parallel processor architecture. An associated communication structure assures the proper synchronization of the processes and supports the inherent data exchange within the loosly coupled parallel structure of processes and processors.

The basis of the segmentation algorithm is the binarization of a gray value image using a set of related gray value thresholds, spanning a nested set of binarization intervals. This is equivalent to decompose the gray value image into a set of mutual related binary images, which are in fact a stack of binary slices of the gray value information, projected onto subsequent planes of a certain level within the gray value range of the image. Here, the principle of graceful degradation of (gray value) information is realized. The segmented objects are described symbolically by a heterogeneous set of features.

An iterative assignment procedure uses programmable object signatures for application-dependent selection of the interesting objects and of course, also for combining similar object candidates, i.e. those, consistent with respect to their feature attributes of adjacent binary slices of the threshold hierarchy, to one representative item.

The assignment can be adapted to the data of the particular application [2] and is controlled by a set of rules. These can be formulated in a simple meta-language, which uses the features as variables and numerical thresholds of tolerance ranges as constants for the related entities as some kind of alphabet. Basic logic and arithmetic operations and a simple grammar determine the related expressions.

The symbolic representations of the objects have to be inversely transformed into an iconic data structure again, so that false-coloured object masks can be generated and overlayed to the appropriately delayed real-time video sequence. This visual feedback of the segmentation results enables an optimal adjustment of the control paramenters for the process.

References

1. C. Anderer, U. Thönnessen, M.F. Carlsohn, A. Klonz, *Ein Bildsegmentierer für die echtzeitnahe Verarbeitung,* 11. DAGM Symposium Mustererkennung, 2.–4. Oktober 1989, Hamburg, Informatik-Fachbericht 219, K. Burkhardt, K.H. Höhne, B. Neumann (Eds.), Springer-Verlag, Berlin, Heidelberg 1989, 380–384.

2. U. Thönnessen, D. Ernst, H. Gro, *Entwicklung einer segmentbasierten Beschreibung von Ereignissen in Bildfolgen,* 13. DAGM Symposium Mustererkennung, 9.–11. Oktober 1991, München, Informatik-Fachbericht 290, B. Radig (Ed.), Springer-Verlag, Berlin, Heidelberg 1991, 499–506.

Verification and Validation in the Life-Cycle of Real-Time Software Development

Özer Ciftcioglu

Istanbul Technical University
Electrical Engineering Faculty
P.O. Box 17
Teknik Universite 80191
Istanbul
Turkey

Abstract

Rapid advances in computer technology as hardware and software have provided the capability to develop complex real-time systems. While these advances have enabled significant increases in system efficiency and has allowed the development and operation of systems that were earlier impossible, it has also introduced the inherent drawback of system induced failures. In the real-time computing environment, for a complex system, the software components are highly interdependent and therefore identification and resolving software problems early in the life-cycle is necessary to prevent the probable catastrophic failures in actual utilization. In general, the software development cycle is divided into phases of requirements, implementation and testing. The basic objectives in verification and validation (V&V) of software requirements and design specifications are to identify and resolve problems and high-risk issues during the life-cycle of real-time software development. In this respect the real-time software requirements have to be carefully determined and they should comprise the following features.

a) Statement of the functions which software is expected to perform and the description of the required level of performance.
b) Overall architecture of the software product and its components.
c) Design specifications.

The V&V process involves the interrelations of the activities associated with the above features. In particular, verification is the process of determining if the products of a given phase of the software development cycle fulfill the requirements established during the previous phase. Validation in the process of evaluating software at the end of the software development process to ensure compliance with software requirements [1].
With respect to real-time computing, there are several important V&V issues in the design of real-time software system. One of the important features of real-time systems is the critical nature of the software execution speed with reference to external events. If the time is not available to complete a task, the execution fails unless appropriate measures are taken. A second critical feature

of the real-time system is limited memory capacity. Real-time software typically can execute in an environment where the size of the program or the I/0 data can exhibit problems. Having these critical features in mind, the consideration of the following V&V issues on the life cycle of real-time software development take an important place:

a) Consistency
b) Completeness
c) Reliability
d) Maintainability
e) Testability
f) Portability

Above, some concepts differ in hardware designs relative to their software counterparts. Reliability is one example as software reliability differs from hardware reliability. Another example is the verification and validation concept which takes different forms in hardware systems applications where it is rather difficult to establish a unique definition of V&V which applies to all engineering systems [2]. In this respect V&V is a concept which is not to be built in the hardware system as, however, the case is reverse for the concept of reliability. On the other hand, an independent V&V effort can be implemented on a software so that quality can be built into the software by means of provisons that the features, with respect to the above-stated items, of V&V issues are favorably implemented in the life-cycle of real-time software development.

References

1. *IEEE Standard Glossary of Software Engineering Terminology*, Los Alamitos, Calif., IEEE Std. 29-1983, IEEE-CS order No. 729, 1983.
2. J. A. Wise, V. D. Hopkin, P. Stager (eds.), *Verification and Validation of Complex Systems: Human Factors Issues*, NATO ASI Series F, Vol. 110, Berlin, Springer-Verlag 1993.

Real-Time Rule Based Control of Robot Motion

M. Kemal Cılız

Electrical Engineering Department
Boğaziçi University
Bebek, Istanbul 80815
Turkey

This short talk will focus on the real-time control of mobile robot motion using rule based techniques. Motion control rules are generated in the form a fuzzy rule base based on the experimental data obtained through experiments. Actual implementation is carried out on an industrial mobile robot for locomotion experiments.

Intelligent control of mobile systems allows for hierarchical structures that utilize sensory data with various levels of accuracy. This talk discusses real time control of robot motion. At the lowest level of hierarchical control, a control strategy should be established to derive appropriate control actions in real time. Uncertainties in the world description are represented by fuzzy memberships and then used in the generation of a fuzzy rule base for motion control. These rules are executed in real time by the use of an inference mechanism (decision making) and then the outcome (the decision) in the form of control signals is applied to the robot's actuators for motion control. Actual implementation is achieved in real time for an industrial robot.

Resource Management and Security in Supervisory Control Systems

Raymond K. Clark

Concurrent Computer Corporation
Westford, MA 01886
U.S.A.

Increasingly, supervisory control real-time systems flexibly manage physical processes in a dynamic environment. Several steps can be taken to effectively manage the target applications for a significant class of these systems.

First, an operating system (OS) can be used to provide services that applications typically need, reducing the expense required to produce the system and promoting a common framework for applications.

Second, the operating system can support a programming model that permits the application to communicate sufficient information to the OS to allow it to effectively manage the resources that are shared by the computations comprising the application. This should be contrasted with alternative approaches that attempt to constrain the application to eliminate dynamic resource sharing.

Third, for a robust application, the OS must be able to determine which application computations should be performed during temporary or permanent overloads. Associating computations with meaningful physical-world activities allows application designers to assert parameters that enable the scheduler to handle overloads gracefully. Furthermore, relatively complex scheduling algorithms may be appropriate in systems requiring graceful degradation under overload.

Fourth, resource management, in both the OS and the application, should be integrated. For instance, queues used to pass work through a system influence execution order, just as the system scheduling algorithm does. Eliminating such queues, or adopting a queuing discipline that complements the scheduler, integrates management decisions.

The Alpha Operating System kernel has adopted these steps, providing an object-based programming model featuring distributed threads that freely extend across nodes in a distributed system, that serve to associate computations with real-world tasks, and that accommodate concurrency and synchronization. (Many, notably J. D. Northcutt and E. D. Jensen, have worked on Alpha.)

Recent work has focused on the design of a secure version of Alpha, investigating methods to provide high assurance in a secure, real-time computer system. This is particularly interesting since secure computer systems typically restrict resource sharing and the ability to control resources precisely, while real-time systems demand effective use and precise control of resources. Alpha's threads and scheduling policies lend themselves to the resolution of this apparent conflict.

The Need for a New Generation of Integrated Systems Software for Real-Time Applications

Sadegh Davari and Charles McKay

Dept. of Computer Science and Engineering
University of Houston - Clear Lake
2700 Bay Area Boulevard
Houston, TX 77058-1098
U.S.A.

There is an increasing need for mission and safety critical (MASK) computing applications. Some of the future MASK applications will be large, long lived, complex, non-stop, remotely distributed, real-time, fault tolerant and expensive. Examples include the FAA's advanced automation system, NASA's proposed manned missions to Mars, and DOD's needs for improved automated support for command, communications, control and intelligence. Such applications cannot be safely and affordably mapped to concepts and components of systems software that were not designed to support the life cycle of MASK applications. Operating systems, database management systems, data communications systems, user interface systems and applications cannot be constructed with different paradigms and technology and then somehow be *certified* for collective use in hard real-time, safety critical environments. Issues such as distribution, fault tolerance and survivability, and non-stop operation further complicate these challenges.

The authors are part of the MISSION research team. MISSION is a NASA funded research project focused on improvements in the life cycle support of MASC applications such as those described above. The team has proposed a generic solution architecture for a new generation of integrated systems software designed especially for this target environment. The generic solution architecture is composed with an object based paradigm and includes support for firewalled partitions, software monitors for systems level fault tolerance and survivability and a MASC kernel with twelve features not found as an integrated set in today's systems software. The features of the architecture have been selected to facilitate/enable rigorous reasoning about the structure and behavior of MASC applications and systems. The features have also been selected to facilitate predictable, real-time performance.

Testing by Executing Logic Specifications

Miguel Felder and Pierluigi San Pietro

Politecnico di Milano
Dipartimento di Elettronica e Informazione
Piazza Leonardo da Vinci 32
20133 Milano
Italy

The importance of executing formal specifications to validate requirements has been widely advocated. By executing requirements, we perform testing in the early phase of the development process.

TRIO is a first-order logic language developed at the Politecnico di Milano for specifying real-time systems. TRIO is one of several extensions of classical temporal logic that introduce a quantitative view of time, so that time distances can be measured. Special care was paid to constructively verify the satisfiability of a formula. Two main algorithms based on the Tableaux method were proposed and implemented:

Satisfiability of a TRIO formula:
Dealing with finite domains, the satisfiability of a TRIO formula is decidable. Hence, in order to validate requirements expressed as a TRIO formula, one may try to prove the satisfiability of the formula by constructing a model for it.

Checking a history against a TRIO formula:
The tableaux algorithm can be adapted to verify that one given temporal evolution of the system (called history) is compatible with the specification.

We are currently investigating the definition of suitable methodologies to perform testing and analysis activities based on TRIO specifications of real-time systems.

The above mentioned algorithms are more suitable to support white-box testing. Moreover, testing methods referring to the structure of the specification formula can be found and used to define suitable coverage criteria, in a way similar to what has been done in structural testing. To this purpose, we point out the duality among the algorithms for stating the satisfiability and history-checking TRIO formulas. While the history-checking algorithm can decide whether a *given* history or evolution trace of the system satisfies the specification formula, the satisfiability algorithm can be converted into a test case generator, since it *generates* models of the formula which can then be used as test cases for the (prototype) implementations of the specified system.

Another research direction is the study of testing in-the-large. TRIO was extended to allow the construction of specifications of complex systems in a systematic and modular way. This extension, called TRIO+, is an object oriented language.

It is possible to perform test case generation directly on TRIO+ specifications. This activity comprises:

- partial testing, i.e., testing only some parts of the specified system even when some other components have been specified informally or are left unspecified;
- composition of test cases, allowing the specifier to obtain test cases for a complex system starting from those of its components, and vice versa;
- test case classification and reuse, which can be done by exploiting the information available in the inheritance relation among TRIO+ classes.

Finite Time Semantics for Executable Logic Specifications

Miguel Felder and Pierluigi San Pietro

Politecnico di Milano
Dipartimento di Elettronica e Informazione
20133 Milano
Italy

By executing formal specifications it is possible to observe the behaviour of a specified system and check whether specifications capture the intended functional requirements. A specification formalism very suitable to real-time systems is Temporal Logic with a metric of time [5, 6]. It allows to express complex temporal conditions and properties in a precise, quantitative way. In general, however, temporal logic specifications are not executable, since the classical undecidability results for a first-order calculus apply to them as well.

To solve the problem, various proposals have appeared in literature.

1. The recent work [1] defines a real-time logic, TPTL, where quantification over time is not allowed, thus yielding a decidable — but less expressive — language.
2. Other solutions allow temporal quantifications, achieving decidability by using only finite domains. The result is a language as expressive as a first-order logic, although as powerful as a propositional logic. Execution algorithms have been successfully designed [3] following a finite time semantics.

A specifier usually does the natural assumption of an infinite time domain. The more finite models approximate infinite models the more such methods are useful. The definition of semantics and algorithms for the finite domain case must allow the best possible approximation.

(a) One of these solutions is [4]. A conventional false (or true) value is given to every formula (or part of a formula) whose evaluation time does not belong to the time domain. This results in a very counterintuitive semantics.
(b) Another finite solution disregarding the approximation issue is presented in [2]. The language has a couple of dual temporal distance operators: a strong operator Δ and a weak one ∇. $\Delta_t F$ is true iff there exists a time instant x which is at a distance t from the current one, and F holds at x. $\nabla_t F$ is true iff F holds at x and x is at a distance t from the current instant, or x does not exist. The solution does not support any approximation: a specifier must use Δ and ∇ to explicitly deal with a finite time domain.

(c) Another semantics is proposed in [7], leading to a valuable approximation. Let F be a formula, D the set of values for time variables occurring
in F. The truth value of F is evaluated restricting the time variables
domain D to $D'=\{t \in D$ s.t. the evaluation of F uses only time instants
belonging to the time domain$\}$. If D' is empty, then a conventional value
is assigned to F. According to this semantics, many cases that, following
definiton 2(a), lose their intuitive meaning, are correctly interpretated.
However, trivial cases of poor approximation still arise. For instance,
consider the intuitevely equivalent statements "Tomorrow will be the
case that it was raining the day before" and "Today it is raining". According to semantics 2(c), they are not equivalent, because if the time
domain is finite and "tomorrow" does not exist, the first statement is
not evaluable, while the second is true or false.

We propose a new solution to the finiteness problem. Our proposal consists of:

1. a three-valued semantics: appropriate truth tables ensure that the meaning
   of the third value is "unknown";
2. a conventional value for every predicate, to be used in the future of the time
   domain, and another conventional value to be used in the past;
3. an evaluation that does not "stop" whenever the current time instant does
   not belong to the time domain.

We claim that our solution allows a better approximation of infinite domains
with finite ones. For instance, all the known approximation problems are solved.
Current work is being devoted to prove approximation theorems, and to define
and implement execution algorithms for the proposed semantics.

References

1. R. Alur and T. Henzinger, *A Really Temporal Logic*, Proceedings of the 30th
   Annual Symposium on Foundations of Computer Science, IEEE Computer Science Press, 1989, 164–169.
2. E. Ciapessoni, E. Corsetti, A. Montanari and P. San Pietro, *Embedding Time
   Granularity in A logical Specification Language for Synchronous Real-Time Systems*, to appear in Science of Computer Programming.
3. M. Felder and A. Morzenti, *Specification Testing for Real-Time Systems by
   History Checking in TRIO*, Proceedings ICSE 14, Melbourne, Australia, May
   1992.
4. C. Ghezzi, D, Mandrioli and A. Morzenti, *TRIO: A Logic Language for Executable Specifications of Real-Time Systems*, Journal of Systems and Software,
   June 1990.
5. R. Koymans, *Specifying Message Passing and Time-Critical Systems with Temporal Logic*, PhD Thesis, Eindhoven University of Technology, 1989.
6. A. Morzenti, *The Specification of Real-Time Systems: Proposal of a Logic Formalism*, PhD Thesis, Dipartimento di Elettronica, Politecnico di Milano, 1989.
7. A. Morzenti, D. Mandrioli and C. Ghezzi, *A Model Parametric Real-Time Logic*,
   Politecnico di Milano, Dipartimento di Elettronica, Report 90.010, 1990, to
   appear in ACM Transactions on Programming Languages and Systems.

Formal Specifications for Real-Time Fault-Tolerant Systems

E. B. Fernandez

Dept. of Computer Science & Engineering
Florida Atlantic University
Boca Raton, FL 33431
U.S.A.

The objective of our current work is to develop formal methods to specify real-time, concurrent, fault-tolerant systems in a multilevel fashion. This is a continuation of the work described in [1] where we developed a layered architecture and a CSP-like language to formalize and describe fault-tolerant mechanisms.

An application can be described by a set of classes that describe its static structure [2]. A design model such as the ones in [2] or [3] can describe the process structure that represents its behavior.

The functional requirements can be described using a formal language such as a combination of an object methodology and Z [4], to generate what we call Formal Functional Specifications (FFS). Adding criticality information, timing constraints, and safety constraints we can obtain a set of formal specifications incorporating these constraints, we call these Fault-Tolerant Formal Specifications (FTFS). We add now rules that summarize design constraints at the configuration level, e.g., *two copies of a critical process should go in different processors*, to obtain the Fault-Tolerant Configuration Formal Specifications (FTCFS). Finally we add constraints that describe architectural features such as rings of privilege, memory segmentation, etc. to obtain the Fault-Tolerant System Formal Specifications (FTSFS). These represent assignment of objects and processes to the architectural features intended to optimize the fault tolerance ability of the complete system.

This is not a decomposition hierarchy, i.e., the lower levels are not more detailed; it is rather a process-view hierarchy, showing the effect of constraints and the computational environment on the placement of the process/object.

References

1. Ancona, M., G. Dodero, V. Gianuzzi, A. Clematis, and E. B. Fernandez, *A system architecture for fault tolerance in concurrent software*, Computer, Vol. 23, No. 10, October 1990, 23–32.
2. Rumbaugh, J., M. Blaha, W. Premerlani, F. Eddy, and W. Lorensen, *Object-oriented modeling and design*, Prentice-Hall, Englewood Cliffs, N. J., 1991.

3. Järvinen, H. -M., R. Kurki-Suonio, M. Sakkinen, and K. Systä, *Object-oriented specification of reactive systems*, Proc. IEEE 12th Int. Conf. on Softw. Eng., 1990, 63–71.

4. Spivey, J. M., *The Z notation*, Prentice-Hall, Englewood Cliffs, N. J., 1989.

Real-Time Systems Theory and Practice
Can We Bridge the Gap?

Borko Furht

Department of Computer Science and Engineering
Florida Atlantic University
Boca Raton, Florida 33431
U.S.A.

This discussion begins with the question: what is the impact of the universities and the real-time research community on the real-time systems industry, whose total market has been estimated to be approximatelly $45 billions. Their impact and influence are very low.

The RT industry is going through a transition period: from expensive proprietary real-time systems to relatively inexpensive open real-time systems, based on industry standards. Niche RT computer companies, such as Harris, Concurrent, Encore, and Modcomp, have all introduced RT systems based on off-the-shelf RISC technology, and traditional UNIX operating system, modified for real-time. They face very tough competition from the large computer manufacturers DEC, IBM and HP, who were some time ago in RT computer business, then abonded it, and recently re-entered the battle. They also offer similar open RT systems. Newcomers, such as Sun and Silicon Graphics, who have never been in RT business, suddenly began offering RT systems.

In summary, the competition in the real-time open systems arena is very tough, and these companies are hungry for innovations in order to add values to their *open systems* and beat the competition. There are many practical research areas where the RT reserach community can assist and develop new RT technology. The topics, discussed in this presentation, include:

(a) **Software tools for Real Time:**
CASE tools for real-time, object-oriented design, tools for evaluating and measuring performance of RT systems, tools for RT system analysis and improving their performance, and integration of modern graphics tools and multimedia into RT development tools.

(b) **Real-Time architectures:**
RISC processors for real-time operation, which will provide support for RT OS, RT scheduling, and fault-tolerance. They will have built-in sempahores, and provide fast context switch. Multiprocessor and parallel architectures for real-time with improved I/O capabilities, better cache solutions for RT, improved throughput. Innovative distributed architectures.

(c) **Real-Time Operating Systems:**

Improve RT performance of RT UNIX, incorporation of RT scheduling algorithms, multi-threaded kernel and its RT performance, RT UNIX for embedded applications, distributed RT UNIX.

(d) **Real-Time Languages:**

Implement RT language on RISC systems, adding real-time features (such as scheduling) to C, C++, ADA.

Real-Time Communication Networks

Damas P. Gruska

Institute of Informatics
Comenius University
Mlynska dolina
842 15 Bratislava
Slovakia

A common feature of different types of parallel machines and distributed systems is the presence of many processing elements and interconnections among them. It does not matter whether the systems are of one chip size or of a worldwide telecommunication network size.

Process Algebras belong to basic tools for specification and verification of these systems viewing them as "communicating systems". In general, standard Process Algebras as Hoare's *Communicating Sequential Processes*, Bergstra and Klop's *Algebra of Communicating Processes*, Milner's *Calculus of Communicating Systems* abstract many real properties of actual systems as duration and structure of actions, location of processes, properties of an interconnection network and so on.

Since for many applications these properties are crucial there is a research going on extending the existing abstract calculi, defining more sophisticated semantics for them and so on. For modelling real-time behaviour of concurrent systems several timed process algebras have been suggested. But, while abstract calculi express system properties which are more or less independent on level of system description, the less abstract calculi depend much more on those levels. For example, on one level we can incorporate reasoning on durations of actions (expressed in some time units) into a calculus and we can still abstract real properties of an interconnection network. For another level, speaking about durations of actions (using finer time units) we cannot neglect time needed for start of communications since (re)configuration of a network might take some time units.
For these reasons specially low level timed calculi have to take into account also reasoning about interconnection network properties as a capacity, a communication speed and so on.
The resulting calculi are tailored for some existing type of a network and in this sense they are less general then abstract ones. It seems that since the calculi lack an elegancy of abstract ones they are still simple enough to be used for specification and verification of concurrent real-time systems.

Usability of ATM Connections for Sensitive Real-Time Systems

Karl Jonas

Technische Universität Berlin
Prozeßrechnerverbund-Zentrale
10623 Berlin
Germany

Introduction

Expected real-time applications like video telephony, video conferences and document retrieval can either take advantage of human's ability to cope with missing pictures or bad audio quality, or of — time consuming, therefore inconvenient — retransmission.
Things are different when we look at delay- and loss-sensitive real-time systems. They require guaranteed delivery with a given (maximum) transmission delay. Since one design aspect of Asynchronous Transfer Mode (ATM) is, that delay and cell losses caused by congestion are shared amongst all existing connections (and therefore should be small enough to be ignored by most of them), sensitive real-time traffic needs a traffic specific transmission scheme.

Achieving Faster Transmission in ATM

Transmission delays derive from

- long connection-set-up delays;
- slow transmission;
- cell buffering;
- retransmission due to errors/lost cells;
- long connection-release delays.

No Set-Up Delays: Connectionless Transmission in ATM

ATM offers a pseudo-connectionless transmission, using predefined (or pre-set-up) virtual connections for the routing through the network. This speeds up transmission significantly for short-term connections.

Speeding Up the Standard: Doing it in Parallel

CCITT has recommended a speed of 155 Mb/s and 600 Mb/s for the access to B-ISDN. The use of parallel physical connections increases the transmittable bandwidth between peers to infinity.

No Buffers — No Delay

Buffers in the ATM switching fabric are needed as soon as more than one input port of a switch is allowed to access a certain output port at a certain time. The drawback of a buffer is obvious: transmission delay. Two approaches eliminate the need of buffers in the switch. Although very specific, they might still fulfill the needs of certain applications:

1. A certain output port can only be accessed by one dedicated input port.
2. A certain output port can only be accessed by a certain input port at a certain time.

Pre-transmission instead of Re-transmission

If cell loss is still assumed to happen a preventive multiple transmission of cells is sensible if bandwidth is available and time counts.

Congestion Control

Congestion control schemes are currently subject of a lot of investigations and will not be tackled here.

Guaranteed Service Parameters

Two approaches make it possible to avoid congestion and guarantee Quality of Service (QoS) parameters like transmission delay and cell loss rate even with an underlying ATM network:

1. dedicated physical connections and
2. priorities.

Conclusions

ATM is usable for (delay- and loss-)sensitive real-time traffic. Some restrictions appear to the network, like the use of dedicated physical paths or of a strict priority scheme like HoL.

The use of connectionless services can speed up transmission significantly, as well as the introduction of parallel physical connections.

Use of unbuffered switches is only necessary for very special applications, and probably an expensive solution.

Pre-transmission is sensible on bad communication links, especially for bursty traffic. A considerable reduction of retransmission due to cell loss can be expected.

Dedicated links and strict priority schemes are the means to achieve guaranteed performance, to prevent network congestion and to allow reliable statements concerning quality of service parameters like delay, cell loss and delay jitter.

Real Time Computing Requirements of the "Fieldbus"

Cemil Keles, Erdogan Narli

Dokuz Eylul University
Department of Electrical and Electronics Engineering
Bornova
35100 Izmir
Turkey

Abstract

Attempts have been made to standardize Fieldbus which is especially used for factory automation. Real time communication, data base and control are important topics in this type of automation system. Therefore, the requirements related to these topics must be defined exactly and it should also cover future requirements. In this paper, these requirements are discussed and some suggestions are given following a short information about fieldbus.

1 Introduction

The increasing complexity of automation tasks and the related trend towards increasingly decentralized intelligent units has led to an extreme rise in the demand for an exchange of information between all levels and components of an automation facility. A global network can not be used forever in a factory.

If we consider CIM (Computer Integrated Manufacturing — Fig.1) model, it is necessary to use a diversity of networks adapted optimally to the respective requirements of each level in the hierarchy. The reason is that devices from different information levels place extremely diverse demands on a communication system. For example, the response time aspects of the Sensor/Actuator level differ from the other levels of the CIM model. If we use OSI (Open System Interconnection) reference model for communication, integration of these networks into an overall system and thus uninterrupted communication can be achieved by using identical or similar structures in the application layers of the individual networks used in the hierarchical structure.

2 What is the Fieldbus?

The main task of the Fieldbus is to link sensors, actuators, controllers and process computers with the system intelligence in the production and manufacturing area. Together with its hardware, the Fieldbus (Sensor/Actuator bus) meets

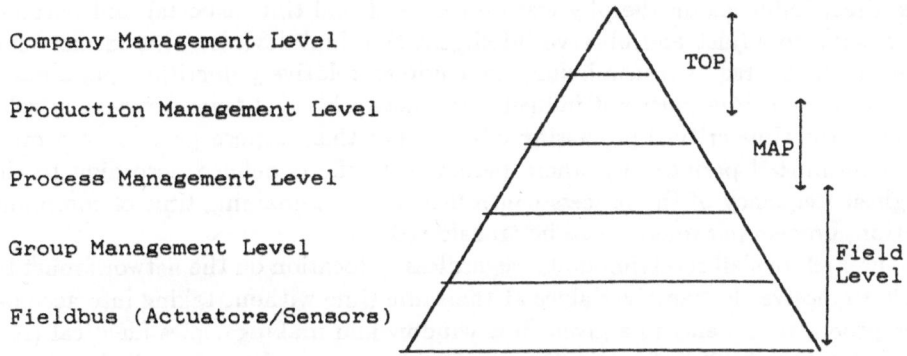

Company Management Level

Production Management Level

Process Management Level

Group Management Level

Fieldbus (Actuators/Sensors)

TOP

MAP

Field
Level

Fig. 1. Computer Integrated Manufacturing Model.

communication requirements between these devices. At the same time the information they supply can flow into the factory information system.

About 25 years ago, the 4–20 mA analogue interface established itself as the defacto standard in instrumentation at the field level. With the advent of digital technology, the situation has changed to benefit from the advantages of digital technology, such as economy, more information, reliability and safety.

3 Real Time Requirements of new Fieldbus

Fieldbus is different from general communication networks. Since the network in the field level will be used to control manufacturing processes, it has to meet certain specific constraints and requirements. Some constraints are technological. Other constraints are the result of objective of such a network. For example, the bus must provide communication facilities with various time constraints (periodic sampling, life time of data, and time response). Moreover, some requirements, such as full distributed computing (distributed algorithms, distributed data, and distributed control), reliability, application modularity and scalability must be fulfilled.

These lead us to define the concept of REAL TIME. A real time network is a network able to exchange variables(process data) while respecting time constraints. In addition, the application must be executed and organized in such a manner that the data is taken from process in a homogeneous way and the calculations and commands are executed respecting control theories. Time constraints can take on several forms. Response time which is the delay necessary for an entity to react to another entity's request must be as small as possible. However when truly automated applications are involved the response time aspect is not enough. The transmission system must also provide data at proper instant.

A universal Fieldbus must be capable of transmitting both process data and parameters without any noteworthy mutual influencing. Here process data (such as switch status or control signals for contactors and valves) is characterized by its direct influence on the physical process and real time aspects) and parameters serve to adjust and observe intelligent terminal devices. This means that, during the course of transmission, the complex relatively uncritical parameters in relation to time must not influence the network's real time response in relation to the time-critical processing of data. For this purpose process data must be transmitted periodically where period of traffic is defined according to the highest frequency of the process controlled. In the remaining time of communication, process parameters can be transferred.

In the Fieldbus all receiving units, regardless of location on the network must be able to receive the same variables at the same time without taking into account the propagation delay in a given time window and making copies identical (real time data base). Therefore the timing of exchanges must be controlled and guaranteed. A knowledge of the timing of producer variables and their delivery time informations are also given to user. It is more important for a data consumer to be sure that the data were correct, rather than for a producer to be sure that data had been correctly received after a certain time. A data variable can be produced by one producer (application process) but can be read and used by any number of receivers (broadcasting). This means that it is not necessary to give each device a unique address. We can then see that a Fieldbus should not only be a communication system but must also offer genuine real-time distributed database services. Therefore client/server model which is based on peer to peer communication and can only be used for communication needs of coordinating two application processes. So, client/server model is unsuitable for field communication.

In addition to these, the transmission technique used must be simple and cost-effective, giving preference to existing industrial standards. Therefore only physical, data link and application layers of ISO/OSI model is used for open communication on the field level. All other layers are superfluous to a working Fieldbus model.

4 Conclusion

Using new digital technology, real time requirements of the Fieldbus can be fulfilled. Especially, using digital computers, intelligent sensors and actuators etc., consortia of the process can be eliminated. Some consotiums such as FIP, Profibus, Bitbus etc., have started to provide some solutions in their national standards.

References

1. J.Warrior and J.Cobb, *Structure and Flexibility for Fieldbus Messaging*, Control Engineering, October 1988, 18–20.
2. T.Phinney, *Fieldbus- The Bottom-up Approach to an Open DCS*, Control Engineering, March 1991, 52–55.
3. J.P.Thomesse et al., *Factory Instrumentation Protocol: Model, Products and Tools*, Control Engineering, September 1991, 65–67.

4. R. Mackiewics, *Looking at Manufacturing Message Specifications*, Control Engineering, March 1991, 49–50.
5. G.G.Wood, *International Standards Emerging for Fieldbus*, Control Engineering, October 1988, 22–25.

Robust Sampling for Process Control

Marten D. van der Laan

University of Groningen
Dept. of Computing Science
P.O. Box 800
9700 AV Groningen
The Netherlands

Keywords

Analog-digital conversion, Data Acquisition, Digital Signal Processing, Approximation theory.

1 Introduction

In most process control applications analogue inputs have to be processed by digital controllers. In such systems, *sampling* is a very important operation in the control loop. Traditionally, point measurements of a signal are taken at equidistant times. According to the *Nyquist criterion*, the sampling frequency should be at least twice as high as the highest frequency occurring in the time-continuous signal. The reconstruction quality is assured by Shannon's sampling theorem, which says that a frequency band-limited signal, sampled in time from minus infinity to plus infinity at a frequency exceeding the Nyquist frequency, can be perfectly reconstructed from its samples.

However, *the requirements for this theorem cannot be met in practice*, because signals are not perfectly band-limited and sampling can only be carried out during finite time. Moreover, a practical device is not able to take true point measurements. In general, analogue-to-digital converters are used, which perform an integration within a narrow interval. It can be concluded that the value of the sampling theorem for real sampling applications is limited.

2 The local integral sampling operator

In order to study alternative sampling concepts, a theoretical framework has to be developed. Assume a time-continuous signal $x(t)$ is observed during a finite time interval $[0, T]$. The signal can be interpreted as a vector in an infinite-dimensional signal space. Sampling is an operation which represents the signal by a finite sequence of numbers, the samples. Reconstruction is the inverse operation, which restores a time-continuous signal $\hat{x}(t)$ from the samples. If N independant samples are taken in the interval $[0, T]$, the reconstructed signal is a vector in a N-dimensional subspace of the original signal space. In this light, the combined operation, sampling plus reconstruction, can be studied as an approximation problem: Given a N-dimensional subspace, extract the samples in such a way that the error between the original signal and the reconstructed signal assures a minimum.

Theoretically, many operators exist which solve the approximation problem. For practical applications, however, the combined sampling/reconstruction operator must fulfill the following requirements in order to minimise the processing expense:

- The operator should be linear (in the mathematical sense).
- Every sample should be obtained using the same procedure, i.e., the operator should be invariant to time shifts.
- The parameters should be calculated at equidistant points.
- The operator should be causal, i.e., future values are not to be used. If a small time delay is allowed, a finite part of the future signal may be used.

An operator which meets these requirements is the *local integral sampling* operator. The interval [0,T] is divided into N subintervals. In each subinterval the observed signal is integrated, thus yielding N samples. The ith sample is

$$x[i] = \int_{iT/N}^{(i+1)T/N} x(t)dt.$$

The integration is carried out in the analogue domain. The reconstruction may be achieved by a straightforward spline interpolation. The subspace thus becomes a spline space. The combined local integral sampling operator and spline interpolation provide good approximation with respect to the supremum norm. Contrary to the commonly used mean square norm, this norm gives an upper bound to the absolute error, which is important for Real-Time control systems. It should be noted, however, that a reconstruction is not required in process control applications: controllers generate their control signals based on the samples.

3 Evaluation and Application

It can be shown that the local integral sampling has the following advantageous properties compared to traditional sampling:

- Inherent noise suppression by the integration process, without extra processor load for digital post-filtering.
- No redundant data required for digital noise filtering, yielding a lower sampling frequency.
- Decreased sensibility to power-frequency disturbance by carefully selecting the integration period as a multiple of the power frequency.

- Decreased sensibility to spikes due to integration.

The local integration can easily be implemented in hardware, providing a low cost, robust sampling module. For further numerical analysis of the signal, the representation in a spline space yields high numerical stability. The method is therefore a serious alternative to traditional sampling methods.

A Real-Time Image Processing Language?

Phillip A. Laplante

Fairleigh Dickinson University
Madison, NJ 07940
U.S.A.

1 What is the Need for a Real-Time Image Processing Language?

Real-time image processing is widely used in multi-media systems, virtual reality and simulation, and remote command and control. Unfortunately, there is no standard language to support image processing in a real-time framework. Moreover, it is unwise to assume that other real-time programming languages can support the specialized needs of image processing.

2 What are the Goals of a Real-Time Image Processing Language?

A real-time image processing language must provide those constructs needed for real-time as well as those for image processing. These include:

- Methods for enunciation of concurrent processing, synchronization, and timing constraints, while in some way, guaranteeing response times at compile time.
- A framework for efficient image description, storage and manipulation.
- Support for various digital electronic, sequential and parallel architectures and possibly bulk optical architectures.

Other desirable features include

- Support for object-oriented paradigms.
- Built-in exception handling.
- Storage and execution time optimization strategies.

At this juncture, there is apparently no language with these features. It is therefore, imperative that more research be focused on the development of said language.

Static Analysis:
Hard Real Time is Hard, "Big Time!"

Stephen P. Masticola[1] *and Thomas J. Marlowe*[2]

[1] Department of Computer Science
Rutgers University
New Brunswick, NJ 08903
U.S.A.
[2] Department of Mathematics
Seton Hall University
South Orange NJ 07079
U.S.A.[***]

Hard real time (HRT) programs are correct only if they produce a correct output within a specified time. Failure to meet timing constraints can be disastrous, and can be caused by subtle bugs that are difficult to find by testing [3]. While formal methods are often proposed to deal with this problem [11], these cannot presently handle large systems in full generality. We believe that the real-time community should adopt programming language methodology, e.g., static anomaly detection, to certify that programs meet termination [9] and timing [5] constraints.

HRT applications may have complex requirements, making assembly language programming unreasonably complicated. It is also hard to ensure safe translation from such intricate specifications into intermediate code without auxiliary analysis or testing. Moreover, we cannot afford (literally) to neglect issues of efficiency, i.e., optimization and parallelization. HRT optimization requires harder static analysis than conventional programs, since semantically "safe" optimizations can cause missed deadlines, and since previously uncoupled phases of compilation must interact for best results [8].

Several languages [5], such as Real-Time Euclid [6], have been proposed for HRT systems. Most are akin to more common languages, modified to eliminate constructs problematic for HRT (e.g., run-time loop bounds), and to add features desirable for HRT (e.g., timing exceptions). HRT programming is harder in languages lacking the problem features, but the programming language technique of partial evaluation [10] can help to prove hard time bounds on at least some programs that include them.

While some of the added HRT features are clearly needed, there are penalties for adding them: increased complexity of both the semantics of the language and the safety verification of programs. Ada [1], perhaps the most egregious example

---

[***] In affiliation with the Real-Time Systems Laboratory of the New Jersey Institute of Technology.

of this sort of "creeping featurism," is consequently difficult to learn, tedious to compile, and nightmarish to analyze.

We propose, instead, that HRT languages should not only be predictable and schedulable, but also simple. Simplicity benefits all parties: the language designer, the compiler writer, and the programmer. The language should have few primitives, and these should interact only in predictable, well-defined ways. Design of the language and the analysis techniques should proceed together, to assure efficient program analysis. The language specification should include a formal semantics, including time, to facilitate correctness proofs of anomaly detection and optimization algorithms (as well as potential proofs of user program correctness). We suggest that, although current specification languages appear simple, they may cause problems in translation or efficiency.

Static analysis of hard real time languages is hard — and necessary. Formally defined "reduced instruction set languages," in the spirit of CSP [4], Occam [7], and Scheme [2], help to keep the complexity of HRT analysis reasonable, and are easier to understand and utilize.

References

1. American National Standards Institute, *ANSI/mil-std 1815A (1983) Reference Manual for the Ada Programming Language*, U.S. Gov't. Printing Office, 1983.
2. W. Clinger and J. Rees, ed., *Revised Report on the Algorithmic Language Scheme*, LISP Pointers, Vol. 4, No. 3, July 1, 1991.
3. U.S. Government Accounting Office, *Patriot Missile Defense: Software Problem Led to System Failure at Dhahran, Saudi Arabia*, GAO/IMTEC-92-26, February 1992.
4. C.A.R. Hoare, *Communicating Sequential Processes*, Prentice/Hall, 1985. ISBN 0-1315-3271-5.
5. W.A. Halang and A.D. Stoyenko, *Comparative Evaluation of High-Level Real-Time Programming Languages*, Real-Time Systems, Vol. 2, No. 4, November 1990, 365-382.
6. W.A. Halang and A.D. Stoyenko, *Constructing Predictable Real-Time Systems*, Kluwer, 1991. ISBN 0-7923-9202-7.
7. Inmos, Ltd., *Occam Programming Manual*, Prentice/Hall, 1984. ISBN 0-1362-9296-8.
8. T.J. Marlowe and S.P. Masticola, *Safe Optimization for Hard Real-Time Programming*, 2nd IEEE Int'l. Conf. on Syst. Integration, Morristown, NJ, June 15-18, 1992.
9. S.P. Masticola and B.G. Ryder, *A Model of Ada Programs for Static Deadlock Detection in Polynomial Time*, SIGPLAN Notices Vol. 26, No. 12, December 1991, 97-107.
10. V. Nirkhe and W. Pugh, *Partial Evaluation of High-level Imperative Languages, with Applications in Hard Real-Time Systems*, ACM 19th POPL, 1992, 269-280.
11. J.S. Ostroff, *Survey of Formal Methods for the Specification and Design of Real-Time Systems*, in: Tutorial on Specifications of Time — Abstractions, Design Methods, Languages, K. M. Kavi ed., IEEE Press, 1991.

GranAda: A Distributed Real-Time Language

Peter M. Müller

Technische Universität Berlin
ITI PDV
Franklinstraße 28/29
10587 Berlin
Germany

Distributed real-time systems consist of an arbitrary number of autonomous processing nodes. In the absence of shared memory, cooperation between these processing nodes is achieved by message exchange on some communication media. In common, distributed real-time applications are designed as tasks or processes interacting with communication and synchronization primitives.

Distributed real-time systems are implemented with "High Level Languages" (HLL). We believe that an appropriate HLL should possess suitable language constructs to express parallelism, communication, synchronization, time control, and error recovery within a distributed environment. Further, it is necessary to specify the software units of distribution and to express their mapping onto the processing nodes. If an HLL does not possess such constructs, the implemented software relies on operating and communication system facilities (Hardware- and Architecture- dependent), restricting its portability.

Moreover, some other aspects are important: Are there some language features that facilitate the incorporation of redundancy schemes, increasing system availability in spite of faults or failures? Second, is it possible to anticipate subsystems' failures (and subsequent repairs) and to implement certain modes of degradation (i.e., mode changes) and fail-safe behavior in a straightforward manner? Third, is there a possibility to maintain a long-lived application easily, i.e., carry out evolutionary changes, e.g., rearranging hardware or exchanging software components, without halting the entire system?

Currently, we develop the programming environment Granular Ada (GranAda) at the Technical University of Berlin. GranAda is an integrated language approach, based on the programming language Ada [2] that tries to give solutions to the aspects and questions encountered above. See [1] for a more detailed discussion.

References

1. P. Müller and G. Hommel, *GranAda: A Programming Environment for Implementing Distributed Real-Time Applications*, 1992 Proc. Int. Symp. on Artificial Intelligence in Real-Time Control (to appear), June 1992.
2. U.S. Departement of Defense, *Reference Manual for the Ada Programming Language*, ANSI/MIL-STD-1815A, 1983.

Real-Time Database System Design

Hidenori Nakazato

Department of Computer Science
University of Illinois at Urbana-Champaign
Urbana, IL 61801
U.S.A.

1 Motivation

Due to the rapid development in the integrated circuit technology, a microprocessor can handle more computation. We can cram more computation into a small package than before. With this development, computers are increasingly used as embedded systems. Because embedded systems need to interact with the physical world, they usually have timing constraints. In other words, they are real-time systems. Increasing computational power makes the processing of more data in an embedded system possible. In addition, data storages are getting smaller and less expensive. This development in the data storage technology also helps to attract real-time applications that require to handle large amounts of data. Real-time database systems have a potential to be used frequently. An air traffic control system needs a database of planes and airports. An automobile navigation system needs a map database. There are many possibilities of real-time applications using databases.

2 Issues to be Studied

A model that is suitable for a real-time database needs to be identified. The commonly used relational model is appropriate for business applications such as a banking system. A different model may be necessary for a real-time database where the behavior of tasks, such as data usage of the tasks, should be well known before the system becomes operational.

We need to satisfy timing constraints in real-time database systems in addition to other requirements. Therefore, scheduling is an important issue. In a database system, tasks require exclusive data access. We need to control this exclusive access carefully because the exclusive access blocks other tasks from executing and the blocking may cause timing constraints violations of other tasks. In particular, we should avoid deadlock and starvation. This is one requirement for a scheduling algorithm for real-time database systems.

In traditional database systems, the objective of scheduling (or concurrency control) algorithms is to maintain a serializable execution and to avoid interference

among tasks. In other words, maintaining the consistency of database states
before and after task executions is the only objective. In addition to the serializability, there are more consistency issues which need to be addressed in
real-time database systems. Namely, they are external consistency and temporal
consistency.

The external consistency is up-to-dateness of data in a database. Since a real-
time system has to respond to the state of the physical world, the data used
to produce results must be up-to-date. In many real-time systems, tasks are
executed periodically in order to respond to the change in the physical world.
The external consistency requirement defines how frequently the tasks need to
be executed.

In order to produce correct results from the contents of a real-time database,
the data used to produce the results must accurately reflect the state in the
physical world. If the used data are taken at different times, they may not reflect
the correct state. In other words, those data must exist simultaneously in the
physical world at a certain time. This is the temporal consistency. If values of
two data can exist simultaneously in the physical world, we say that the data
are temporally consistent. We need a mechanism to guarantee the temporal
consistency.

From the above mentioned requirements: the timing constraints, the serializability, the external consistency, and the temporal consistency, we should be able
to find scheduling and concurrency control algorithms for real-time database
systems. The algorithms must have schedulability conditions. By satisfying the
schedulability conditions, the algorithms must guarantee that all requirements
are satisfied.

Distributed Transport Systems and Aspects of Real Time

Klaus Rebensburg

Technische Universität Berlin
Prozeßrechnerverbund-Zentrale
10623 Berlin
Germany

Abstract

Integrated Broadband Technologies use the expression **real time** for their advanced service definitions for distributed systems. Real-time techniques on protocol level include the prediction of resource parameters and handling of quality of service parameters as well as best effort strategies to handle them within well defined borders. QoS guarantees are given for real-time data occurrences like voice and video streams as well as for combined events like synchronized voice and video streams, joint viewing and conferencing. Besides well defined advanced service profiles which have to be negotiable between service provider and service user a cross layer approach for QoS handling and resource reservation is required to fulfill these demands. The author presents results from project BER-KOM which uses an innovative Transport System Platform for various Reference Broadband Applications and expresses his position and questions for the panel discussion on the future of real-time systems.

1 Introduction

The word **real time** is used in sometimes completely different contexts and with different meanings. My dictionary says: *real time - the actual time during which something takes place (the computer may analyze the data in real time (as it comes in), real-time adj.*

My *pre*-professional life taught me that **real time** means time-sharing. It was 1969 when we used the first industrial time-sharing approaches on Hewlett Packard HP 2100 computers in the field of electronics. As students we were happy to develop application software in a concurrent manner.

My *first* professional life had to do very much with some computer's real-time features mostly found in so called embedded systems. Input/output and processes had to be in time, sometimes they were related to absolute (or relative) time references. We used so called "real-time operating systems" and real-time languages and believed in them.

During my *second* professional life I migrated to distributed systems and networking (connecting real-time process control systems on campuses). Some people felt networking to be a contradiction to their real-time world because of the increase in complexity, unpredictable behavior and possible loss of performance. Open Systems Interconnection (OSI) came up and there was a time when MAP (Manufacturing Automation Protocol) was heavily discussed. People also told me that Ethernet can never support real time because there is no *guarantee* that transport happens in time because of possible collisions. But some things of my former real-time world still remained valid. Various experiments with advanced transport systems with guaranteed QoS have been done within BERKOM and especially within TUBKOM which is TUB's highspeed networks testbed.

2 Distributed Transport Systems and Real Time

With the discussion about private (local) and public networks which have to support end-to-end video and voice, multimedia channels and even synchronized multiple streams of video, voice and data the word real time appeared again but now in a different context: *"the ability to complete protocol processing functions within the transmission time of a packet so that protocol processing never falls behind network traffic"* is a definition we find in the XTP (eXpress Transfer Protocol) transport system documents.

Real time plays a role in the discussion about *transport services* (TS) and their corresponding *quality of services* (QoS). Different transport services are being discussed in the framework of *real-time distributed system applications*: acknowledged and unacknowledged datagram, multicast, isochronous stream, and highspeed bulk data transfer. TS and QoS definition depend on the nature of the real-time application.

The nature of on-line voice and video streams and joint editing apparently is demanding QoS like end-to-end delay, delay-jitter and throughput and some synchronization which have to be guaranteed to have fun at both the senders as well as the receiver's side. Some applications' demands can be derived from a sentence like this: *better deliver 10 pictures per second with guaranteed quality in time than 25 pictures which cannot be reconstructed in real time as a video event.*

2.1 Real Time Transport Services for Distributed Systems

The initial meaning of Real Time varies *in different context of digital technologies.* We find it as actual time or duration where something takes place, within real-time distributed applications, with transport systems of digital video and audio, in interactive systems, or with remote control systems.

Real-Time Transport Services are services which provide guaranteed levels on delay, delay jitter, throughput and other QoS parameters. Some aspects of Real Time Transport Service are:

- Transport service definitions containing connection-mode, fastconnect, acknowledged and unacknowledged connectionless, transaction mode, multipeer stream mode service,
- QoS parameter definitions with selectable QoS parameter (error, control, flow control), threshold and best effort QoS parameters,
- Protocol mechanisms for provision of the transport service (flow and error control, selective retransmission, acknowledgment strategies, fast connection establishment and closing technique).
- Virtual circuits and resource reservation.

2.2 Quality of Service Parameters for Real-Time Communication

Within the relationship of transport service and QoS defintions differences in transport service are to be considered dependent on connection mode, connectionless mode and transaction mode.

Real-Time QoS Requirements are fulfilled within guaranteed levels of transit delay, delay jitter, send interval, priority, user data size, throughput, selectable error detection and correction, selectable flow control and active group integrity.

- QoS Parameters are classified in respect to their different processing:
- best effort QoS: where the TS provider will do its best to reach the QoS required by the TS users. Nothing will be done in case the TS provider is unable to maintain the required QoS parameter.
- compulsory QoS: If a compulsory QoS is not satisfied after its negotiation, then the TS provider must reject the connection.
- threshold QoS: After its negotiation the TS provider will have to monitor the transport connection and to issue a special indication primitive to the TS users whenever it notices its inability to maintain the requested threshold values.

Whenever the word **guarantee** is used for a transport system there are different options:

1. check the quality of service sometime in advance before the communication takes place by collecting static resource parameters. Notify or cancel the connection when the QoS can not be reached. The result can be frustrating when you collect guarantees e.g. for the internet coming to a transmission delay of e.g. 20 minutes.
2. check the QoS sometime in advance and while communicating. Notify or cancel the connection when the QoS can not be reached.
3. check as you do in 2). Derive a best effort strategy dependent on dynamic resource utilization parameters.

Consensus seems to use the word *QoS-guarantee* in conjunction with a certain context only and mentioning some prerequisite conditions, but intentionally ignoring some unavoidable exceptions. If a well defined policy of communication is derived then these kinds of guarantees lead to a transport system for real-time data as we described them before (on-line voice, video,...). Of course there still can happen many exceptions as we find them within embedded systems (there is still some accepted probability of a lost connection, some lost packets which may be recovered by different kinds of retransmission, or exceptions as they happen in station management of FDDI). But people in the field of networking don't care too much about it as long as it is possible to define a *name* for it, the *restrictions* and *upper and lower limits* of QoS parameters.

Entering the concrete implementations of high-speed protocols we get a little impression how advanced real-time mechanisms are handled:

Example: XTP resource reservation protocol mechanisms

- The bandwidth at the intermediate and endsystems can be reserved during the fastconnect based on the requirements in the FIRST packet.The origin indicates, respectively in the rate_req and burst_req fields of the address subsegment included in the FIRST packet, its initial desired data rate in bytes/sec and its expected output burst size in bytes. Only the burst and rate parameters can be required in XTP 3.6.
- If the XTP entity or the intermediate system receiving the FIRST packet cannot support the required rate and burst, it sends a DIAG XTP packet in response.
- The receiving XTP entity or the intermediate system can require the change of the rate and burst of the peer by way of sending CNTL or RCNTL packets.
- As the CNTL and RCNTL packets flow back to the sending XTP entity, updated values for rate and burst will arrive and affect the output rate and the resource reservation.

TDP 3.6. resource allocation combined with the fastconnect setup is shown in Fig. 1.

Example: XTP Concept for extended QoS provision for real time systems

- Establishment of channels providing different QoS requirements of the multimedia applications (delay, delayjitter, throughput).
- Introducing the threshold values of QoS parameters which are used at the intermediate and end systems as reference values for allocation and adjustment of resources.
- Specification of the QoS requirements of the target (needed for the bidirectional transmission mode).
- Negotiation of the QoS parameters during the channel setup phase (allows the source and the target to obtain the actual negotiated QoS values of the virtual circuit based on which they can refuse or accept the connection).
- Use of a flow specification structure (similar to FlowSpec of ST-II) which can have different versions of specifications. This flow specification structure must contain also the flow specification requirements of the reverse direction.

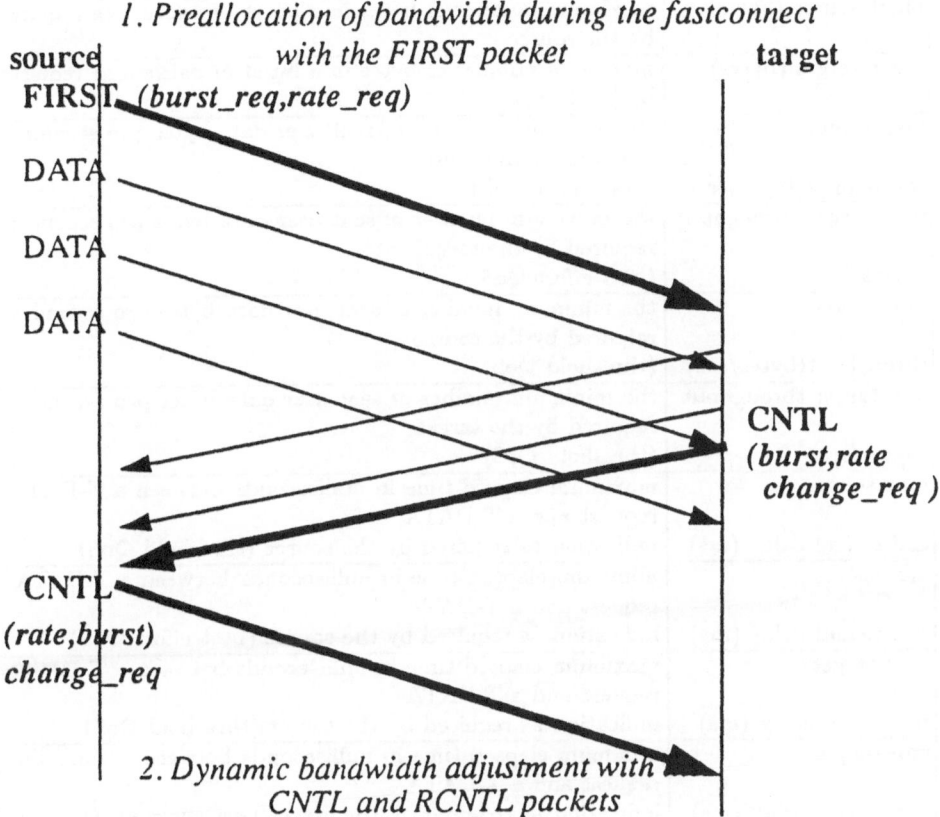

*1. Preallocation of bandwidth during the fastconnect
with the FIRST packet*

source   target

FIRST (*burst_req,rate_req*)

DATA

DATA

DATA

CNTL
*(burst,rate
change_req)*

CNTL
*(rate,burst)
change_req*

*2. Dynamic bandwidth adjustment with
CNTL and RCNTL packets*

Fig. 1.

**Example: Negotiation of QoS parameters and resource reservation for
a virtual circuit in an extended XTP version**

– Preallocation of resources during the channel setup with the FIRST packet.
– Adjustment of resources at the intermediate system and source based on the
  actual flow specification values in the PATH response packet (with ACCEPT
  flag set).
– Accepting or releasing the connection based on the actual received flow specification values at the source.

There is done some research on resource administration (and reservation) leading to network layer and transport layer protocols which are able to include
related data into negotiation of QoS. An example is ST-II where we find as a
basis for the calculations of node/link/network resources depending on services
parameters like expected % use of bandwidth, bit error rate, precedence, priority
of reservation of resources, reliability, probability of packet loss, trade-offs, flags
to specify demands, recovery time-out, time to indicate error on a path, limit on

burst source (bytes)	maximum number of bytes in a burst of packets as required by the source
burst target (bytes)	maximum number of bytes in a burst of packets as required by the target
max source throughput (bytes/sec)	the maximum number of sent user data bytes pro second as required by the source (best effort QoS)
max target throughput (bytes/sec)	the maximum number of sent user data bytes pro second as required by the target (best effort QoS)
min source throughput(bytes/sec)	the minimum number of sent user data bytes pro second as required by the source (threshold QoS)
min target throughput (bytes/sec)	the minimum number of sent user data bytes pro second as required by the target (threshold QoS)
max source end-to-end delay (ms)	maximum elapsed time in milliseconds between a T-DATA request and a T-DATA indication as required by the source (threshold QoS)
min source end-to-end delay (ms)	minimum elapsed time in milliseconds between a T-DATA request and a T-DATA indication as required by the source (best effort QoS)
max target end-to-enddelay (ms)	maximum elapsed time in milliseconds between a T-DATA request and a T-DATA indication as required by the target (threshold QoS)
min target end-to-end delay (ms)	minimum elapsed time in milliseconds between a T-DATA request and a T-DATA indication as required by the target(best effort QoS)

Table 1. Example: Flow Specification Structure for real time applications

cost, maximum cost the sender can afford, limit on delay, maximum end-to-end delay, limit on PDU bytes, smallest allowable message size, limit on PDU rate, smallest allowable packet transmission rate, min. Bytes X rate, smallest allowable bandwidth, accepted mean delay, computable expected delay, accepted delay-jitter, max. acceptable delayjitter.

Looking towards the initialization process we see data being handled like this: Number of buffers, buffers configured and allocated, % CPU time available, allocated CPU-time per byte, various pointers to resource fields for CPU usage and buffers usage, selected available network services, bandwidth, bandwidth to send one byte, to send one packet, cost for a client, cost per byte, cost per ms, cost per packet, cost per received byte, cost per byte sent, drop-rate, delay to receive a byte, delay variance, seconds to send a packet and its variance.

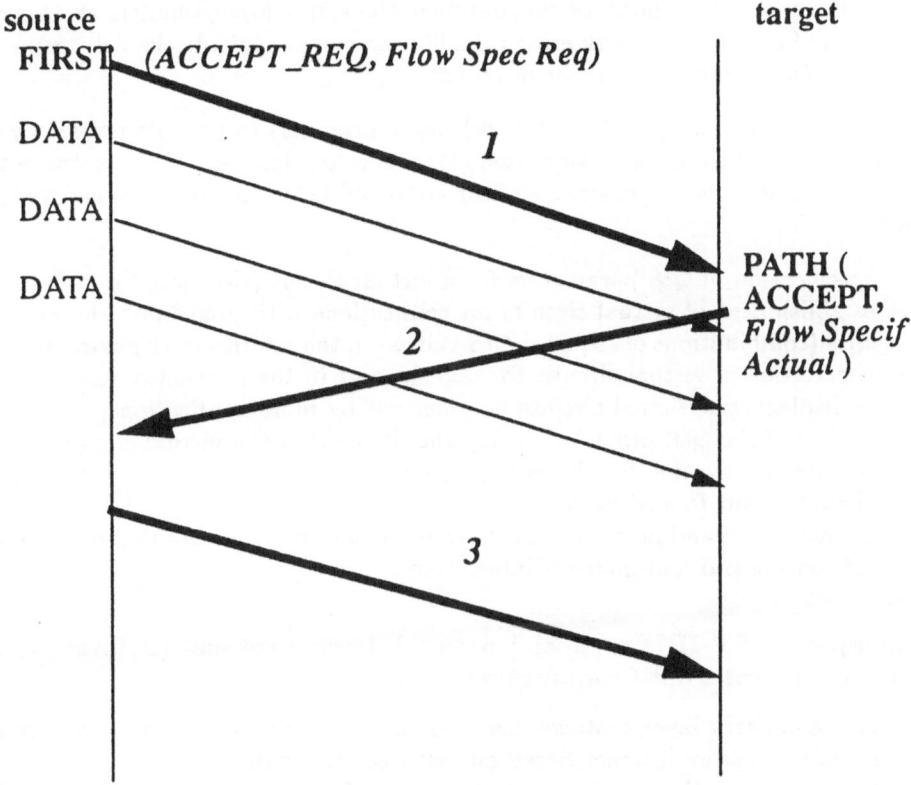

Fig. 2.

2.3 Communication Resource Reservation — Aims and state of the art

Behind the idea of binding resources we find the use of techniques to map TS and QoS parameters (selected flow control, error control, throughput, delay) onto communication resources like buffers, bandwidth, and processing time.

State of the art:

- Communication systems with asynchronous character do not provide guaranteed bandwidth and delay bounds.
- Some networks, such as FDDI with its synchronous service mode and DQDB with its isochronous service, can guarantee the bandwidth requirements of the applications.
- Further problems appear with the operating system design - workstation operating systems, which are scheduled based on fairness rather than urgency can not guarantee a bounded delay. More promising guarantees we find in new versions of the POSIX standard and Realime-UNIX of some workstation manufacturers.

- Mathematical methods for calculation of the actual needed buffers and bandwidth for a given network error rate, flow and error control acknowledgement protocol mechanisms can be obtained.

Facilities of the transport and network layer protocols to provide the QoS parameters of real-time connection-mode transport services (for applications with predictable flow control characteristics) are listed below as virtual circuit facilities:

- specification of QoS parameters for a virtual circuit (channel),
- establishment of virtual circuits for connections with predefined characteristics (combinations of required QoS values) in the internetwork environment,
- negotiation of virtual circuits for QoS support in the internetwork,
- multiplexing of virtual circuits for their use by more applications,
- control of the QoS provision during the life time of the virtual circuit,
- resource reservation for the virtual circuit,
- virtual circuit failure recovery,
- maintainance and accessing the state information describing the virtual circuit on the end and intermediate systems.

Example — ST-II is a special network layer protocol (defined by a RFC of the Internet Community).

- It is a network layer protocol designed to provide an end-to-end guaranteed service across an internet based on resource reservation.
- ST-II supports the management of streams of packets with controlled bandwidth, delay and other flow characteristics to either single or multiple targets.

Example — XTP is a network and transport layer protocol designed for high speed communications and flexible transport services

- supports applications with different flow, error control, and throughput requirements on end-to-end virtual circuits from one source to either single or multiple targets in the internetwork.

Example — The Tenet real-time protocol suite designed especially for real-time communication is a

- protocol suite designed to provide guarantees by reserving resources for channels, but making the resources available to non-real-time traffic if they are not actually being used at the time. It consists of
- the Real-time Channel Administration Protocol (RCAP) provides control services for the Tenet real-time protocol, the
- Real Time Internet Protocol (RTIP) — a connection-oriented network layer protocol which provides delivery of fixed size packets over a simplex channel, with client-specific bounds on packet delay, jitter, and loss rate at a guaranteed bandwidth chosen by the client, the

- Real-time Message Transport Protocol (RMTP) — a simple transport protocol which uses a RTIP as an underlying network layer protocol to provide delivery of arbitrarily-sized messages with guarantees on delay, jitter, loss rate, and bandwidth, and the
- Continuous Media Transport Protocol (CMTP) — which provides a stream like interface for continuous media clients that generate data at regular intervals.

Some other approaches for real time systems and distributed systems on the scientific market:

- Dash Resource Model (Berkeley) with workload, delay defining sessions, a deadline-workahead policy, regulated packet transmission, network access time model (estimation), and the
- Session Reservation Protocol (SRP) as an instantiation of the TCP /IP protocol hierarchy (CPU for protocol processing, network for data transmission).

Remember that when we discuss QoS our attention can not only be directed towards layer 4 (transport). This layer uses underlying services from layer 3 (network) which uses services of layer 2 (data link) etc. Every layer utilizing computer resources has its own contributions to successful services, QoS, and real-time behavior. There are still some more aspects of real time in lower layers to be considered when reserving resources (e.g. FDDI synchronous mode). Even the physical media is a resource itself; a fact becoming more and more important when migrating to gigabit communication systems (some megabytes of data can always be on their way between hosts).

2.4 The means of handling real time in protocol stacks

First choices of today's mechanisms for resource administration are e.g. TCP urgent mechanism, message priority, priority of channels, threads, lightweight threads, and multi process mechanisms. Advanced choices are:

- Have end-to-end sessions, have a view at all resources, have a collective components' establishment procedure, negotiate.
- Scheduling of CPU protocol processing per message, software interrupts, kernel processes, some automatic identification of virtual circuit receivers (close to hardware), user process model, describe and administrate firmware, hardware resources for best effort processing.

As usual we are faced with problems of complexity, lack of knowledge about intermediate systems, surprises about advanced users' demands.

3 Panel Theses about present Real-Time Systems within today's Networks

In General: The world of "Real Time" meets the world of the "communication community" now!
The main issue of communication transport systems today is

- to fight against lack of their own resources,
- to optimize their performance under the given constraints of physical laws.

Transport systems meet operating systems when they use the real world of

- Application Programming Interfaces (API) like sockets, TLI, XTI, XOPEN system calls,
- and protocol stacks included in the kernel (TCP, XTP, IP, UDP, ...),
- and interface drivers (Ethernet, FDDI, ATM, ...).

Future transport systems and their features being seen now are based on the trust on growing real-time capabilities and facilities of modern operating systems.
The user's view: Real-Time Properties are declared and handled as Quality of Services (QoS) (kinds of delay, transit delay jitter, throughput, ...).
More than ever the demands on transport systems are driven by user's requirements!

Example: Multimedia, Voice, Conferencing — the collapse of present OSI model.

More than ever a certain kind of customers' satisfaction is orign for the design of communication stacks!:

- Pictures, Voice, even continous streams of them (not just bytes!),
- Synchronized events directly driven and evaluated by human beings.

There is a gap between the offer of software-models, algorithms on one side, and user demands on the other side:

- throughput is still declared by bytes/sec not TSDUs per second,
- transit delay jitter is being discussed with users of ATM networks,
- at the same time it is made invisible by smoothing of adaptation layers,
- QoS are introduced but cannot yet be verified,
- people talk about the QoS peer-to-multipeer,
- and have never elaborated suitable handshake strategies for this.

Absolute guarantees concerning real time for distributed systems are impossible. Some relativated guarantees (directed towards the network provider's and user's needs) are sometimes considered useful.

4 Panel Questions about the future of real-time and distributed systems

Is it not yet the time to define real time by a kind of subjective cost/benefit driven best effort of a system (including a dynamic escape strategy and a well defined cost driven behavior when violations occur)?
Is it not yet the right time to include all views of costs accompanying every QoS

parameter on its way through 4–7 OSI layers?

Is there not another way of handling real time and distributed systems in the near future than a mixture of:

- non negligible operating system services (and constraints), like sockets, ...,
- some predictable parameters only for protocol handling (delay of media per km),
- some mathematically based algorithms to support predictability here and there,
- some vague assumptions about resources like buffers, processes, media, following a sufficiently predictable approach,
- some resource reservation strategies based on well defined static resource assumptions (CPU speed, cycles per packet),
- some resource reservation strategies mostly based on worst case assumptions,
- few resource reservation strategies based on dynamic behavior of the network,
- some resource management including obscure hardware components disturbing a clean software structure (OSI layers),
- on-line selectable sophisticated negotiation strategies (in-band as well as outband) adapted to the actual users demands?

Don't we ask for too much flexibility when we approach the dynamic choice of scheduling strategies due to static and dynamic demands?

Being aware of this complex mixture within protocol stacks, is there any hope of solid ground in the near future in terms of

- applying an overall queuing theory,
- applying an intelligent general purpose distributed scheduler,
- applying an overall resource reservation strategy, (it is an internetworking problem also!) (including upcoming resources of gigabit networks — data on the media)
- having a unique distributed real time operating system model in the network?

Or isn't it easier to redefine the words "guarantee" and "real time" in a very flexible way and open them for multiple views?

References

1. Protocol Engines Inc., Ed.: *XTP Protocol Definition*, Revision 3.6, 11.2.1992.
2. Parris, Collin J., Ferrari, Domenico, *A Resource Based Pricing Policy for Real-Time Channels in a Packet-Switching Network*, March, 1992. /pub/techreports/tr-92-018.ps.Z from icsi-ftp.Berkeley.EDU.
3. Ferrari, Domenico, Verma, Dinesh C., *A Scheme for Real-Time Channel Establishment in Wide-Area-Networks*, 1990, /pub/techreports/tr-92-018.ps.Z from icsi-ftp.Berkeley.EDU.

4. R. Jain, K.Ramakrishnan, *Congestion Avoidance in Computer Networks with a Connectionless Network*, Layer: Concepts, Goals and Methodology. Proceedings IEEE Computer Networking Symposium, 1988.

5. K. Rebensburg et al., *Milestone Reports Project IsBn*, BERKOM, Technical University Berlin, 1991, 1992.

6. M. Chen, *A Services Features Oriented Congestion Control Scheme for a Broadband Network*, IEEE ICC Proceedings, 1991.

7. K. Bala, I. Sidon, K. Sohraby, *Congestion Control for High Speed Packet Switched Networks*, IEEE INFOCOM Proceedings, 1990.

8. M. Moran, B. Wolfinger, *Design of a Continuous Media Transport Service and Protocol*, Computer Science Division, University of California, Berkeley, 1992.

9. C. Lowery, *Protocols for providing Performance Guarantees in a Packet Switching Internet*, International Computer Science Institute, Berkeley, California.

10. Banerjea, Anindo, Mah, A. Bruce, *The Real-Time Channel Administration Protocol*, The Tenet Group, Computer Science Divisio, University of California, Berkeley and International Computer Science Institute, Berkeley, California.

11. Huitema, Christian, Dabbous, Walid, *Minimal Complexity for the Simplest protocol*, IEEE Infocom '91.

12. C. Topolcic, *Experimental Internet Stream Protocol*, RFC 1190, October 1990.

System Level Real Time Distributed Diagnosis

*Carlos Sêrro**

INESC–Instituto de Engenharia de Sistemas e Computadores
and Instituto Superior Técnico
Technical University of Lisbon
Rua Alves Redol 9
1000 Lisboa
Portugal

Recently, a number of system level distributed diagnosis algorithms have been presented in the literature. None of them, however, explicitly addresses the issue of time constraints in meeting their diagnostic goals. Also, bounds on diagnostic latency prove to be difficult to establish.

Most of the work in this area has been directed towards asynchronous systems. Although important, this work can not meet the stringent deadline requirements of real time (RT) systems due to the absence of a global clock synchronization paradigm. As a consequence, no exact agreement regarding diagnostic system status can be achieved in bounded time, and only partial diagnostic information can be obtained.

System level distributed diagnostic has, however, been obtained for RT systems in special situations:

(i) when a TDMA broadcast medium is used, and even then only to detect link faults and, sometimes, also node faults; or

(ii) for point to point communications, with node faults being detected.

In both cases, group membership protocols have been designed where overall agreement is implicit in bounded time regarding the presence or absence of nodes and/or links in one particular group. Hence, the problem of performing general system level RT distributed diagnosis concurrently with normal processing throughput is largely an open and important research problem.

Contributions from the work in asynchronous as well as synchronous diagnosis can be beneficial to help solving this problem if time constrained messages and task deadlines are included, providing diagnostic latency can be significantly reduced by reducing the number of test and diagnostic messages.

---

* This work was made while the author was on sabbatical leave at the Electrical and Computer Engineering Department, University of California, Irvine, with grants from INESC and FLAD – Fundação Luso–Americana para o Desenvolvimento

Simulation-Based Analysis for Real-Time Systems Development*

Frederick T. Sheldon[1], *Seung-Min Yang*[1] *and Trina L. Bornejko*[2]

[1] Computer Science Engineering Dept.
University of Texas
P.O. Box 19015
Arlington, TX 76019
U.S.A.
[2] Avionic Systems Division/SMEE
Wright-Patterson AFB
U.S.A.

Abstract

This research approach is focused on the investigation of a) Real-Time Distributed (RTD) Systems Development, and b) Simulation.

The approach addresses the application of computer simulation and modeling of real-time control systems within a distributed context. Our premise is to apply a simulation-based technique to analyze the reliability and timeliness of such systems. In addition, this research will investigate how to model and describe failure conditions, as well as determine their containment and recovery strategies.

1 Motivation

Some examples of RTD systems include: manufacturing process control, life or flight critical applications, and autonomous land vehicles. The critical nature of large RTD control systems requires rigorous design and verification of timeliness and reliability [1]. Such analyses can be done using mathematical, simulation and/or testbed based methods [2]. As the environments in which real-time systems are embedded become more stringent and complex, the difficulty in specifying such systems precisely, describing the interactions among tasks and their environment, and in designing and verifying their correctness will become even more formidable. Many mathematical models are not applicable for analyzing complex real-time systems due to the approximation or simplification of many parameters. In addition, a formal method for dynamically verifying the system is either unsuitable for the application or is ignored. Consequently, this work advocates the development of a practical formalized approach to simulation-based analysis for systems of this nature.

---
* This work is being supported by NASA Langley Research Center and the Integrated Diagnostics program office at Wright Patterson, AFB.

2 Objectives

The primary objective of this work is to develop a simulation method for system models which:

- Considers the reliability and timeliness of system performance.
- Realizes and/or executes program dependencies (i.e., relationships holding between program statements) for both a) control dependencies, and b) data dependencies.
- Realizes execution behavior of distributed computation based on synchronization models for:
  a) message-passing based systems [3], and
  b) shared variables based systems.

This research effort is developing a formalized simulation method for performance modeling of discrete event systems (i.e., ascertaining correctness and efficiency), as well as problems of a nature related to the mapping of the simulation itself onto a distributed (or parallel) architecture.

The approach will provide a dynamic execution environment that will enable the designer to run a given system model against various environmental scenarios to rigorously measure and verify the desired behavior. This approach will emphasize reliability and timeliness of the correctness criterion (i.e., defined by the system models).

3 Research Focus

Systems are primarily stochastic and ergotic in nature. A simulation-based analysis avoids the difficulties of obtaining closed-form solutions (based on static analytic approaches) to intricate multi-activity concurrent process problems [4]. The analysis will thus focus on the precise stochastic nature (including failure states and steady state behavior) of the processes which characterize performance.

In more specific terms, a system model is defined as an abstraction of the RTD system, which consists of both a conceptual and physical model. The conceptual model controls activities which sense and control the dynamics of the functional description, while the physical model defines the structural architecture. The behavioral model is the visible part of the system which displays how the reactive and dynamic activities of the system are affected by different simulated environmental stresses [5].

In a real-time system, the specification of system correctness contains constraints related to time in the real world. These constraints may be expressed as explicit functions of time, or they may be implicit in the other constraints (e.g., in the allowable relative positions and velocities of two aircraft). Thus, in a real-time system, all constraints on resources and correct behavior are compounded by the addition of strict timing constraints. This significant problem for real-time systems will be investigated.

The different timing requirements of real-time systems may place different constraints on the processing such as

a) response time deadline,
b) validity of the data,
c) periodic execution, and
d) coordinating inputs and outputs.

The judicious use of test models, simulations, tracing at runtime, and analysis of runtime results can prevent the costly and inefficient building of prototypes as a way to test requirements and perform cost/benefit studies on individual features and candidate architectures. For distributed and/or parallel machines, performance is especially critical and must be measured and fed back to the designer as part of the simulation development environment. Our simulation framework will address the following:

Characterization and formalization of the simulation-based analysis approach and real-time target domain, Simulation of concurrent distributed (parallel [6]) models/computations that are used to confirm analytical estimates for system verification and validation, Performance as it is affected by

a) the system topology (or architecture),
b) the mapping tasks to processors [6],
c) synchronous (time-driven) and asynchronous (event-driven) contexts, and
d) the scheduling of tasks and messages.

Integration and experimentation of an example of the simulation framework, including analysis and validation of the outputs.

References

1. K.M. Kavi and S.M. Yang, *Real Time Systems Design Methodologies — An introduction and survey*, The Journal of Systems and Software, Vol. 18, 1992, 85–99.
2. S.M. Yang, K.M. Kavi and F.T. Sheldon, *A Development Model for Large, Complex, Real-Time Embedded Systems*, Submitted to Special Issues of IEEE Software, 1992.
3. V. Madisetti, J. Walrand and D. Messerschmitt, *Synchronization in Message Passing Computers: Models, Algorithms and Analysis*, Proc. of SCS Conf. on Modeling Simulation, San Diego, January 17–19, 1990, 35–48.
4. R.C. Tausworthe, *A General Software Reliability Process Simulation Technique*, Jet Propulsion Laboratory (Cal. Inst. of Technology, 4800 Oak Grove Dr., Pasadena, CA 91109) Publication 91–7, April 1, 1991, 1–53.
5. D. Harel, *Biting the Silver Bullet: Toward a Brighter Future for System Development*, IEEE Computer, January 1992, 8–20.
6. R.M. Fujimoto, *Parallel Discrete Event Simulation*, Comm. of the ACM, October 1991, 30–53.

Functional Versus Non-Functional Requirements Analysis

Marco Spuri

Scuola Superiore di Studi Universitari
e di Perfezionamento S'Anna
via Carducci 40
56100 Pisa
Italy

Specification languages are usually intended to serve as the foundation for a streamlined software development process in which only one complete *formal* description of the system is written [13]. Other representations (*e.g.* implementation code) consistent and correct with respect to the requirements specifications should be generated automatically from the original description. Due to the differences in the characteristics of systems developed for different applications domains, each specification language must occupy a niche. This justifies the great efforts for the development of languages particularly suitable for hard real-time systems. Several motivations for the need of design methods specifically thought for such systems can be found in the literature (see for example [2], [10], [4]).

In particular, what makes the traditional formalisms unsuitable for real-time applications are the so called non-functional requirements (*e.g.* time stringent constraints). Time domain is not explicitly treated in many of them and the solutions proposed by several researchers are not considered satisfactory since in order to prove real-time properties of time-critical systems it is often necessary to know many details about the execution environment (*e.g.* the tasks scheduling policy) [6].

This has led to two kinds of approaches: formalisms for both functional and non-functional requirements analysis [10], [6], [1], [9] and design methods in which the two aspects are treated in some way separately [2], [8], [7], [4]. The former approach is generally based on abstract models of the system (*e.g.* Timed Transition Models or Time Petri Nets) and/or some kind of temporal logic. The goal is to mechanically prove real-time temporal logic properties, given the specifications of the system and some safety assertions. In the latter case, instead, the design process is usually neither fully formal nor fully informal [7]. The specifications of the system are given by some language which generally has its own graphical editor. Timing properties (*i.e.* schedulability analysis) are stated during the development process and in particular before and after the coding activity. The main aim is to discover timing problems as soon as possible during the process. Of course, software engineering principles (*e.g.* abstraction, information hiding, hierarchical decomposition) and real-time devoted facilities are provided.

At present only the latter approach seems to be practical. A complete formal analysis generally abstracts away from elements that could be crucial [3]. It seems very difficult to take all the execution environment constraints into account in an abstract model, while it appears to be more manageable in a schedulability analysis. In fact, this is a simplification of a formal analysis, in which the semantics of the tasks is partially considered in estimating the worst case execution time [11], and a timing analysis is done under certain assumptions on the tasks structure, relations and schedulability policy.

The complexity of formal proofs is also a hard obstacle to overcome. For several researchers [5], [6], [10] automated analysis of large finished design is not likely to be practical, at least in the next years (consider that much debate goes even on the practical usefulness of formal verification techniques proposed over 20 years ago [3]). This approach may indeed be considered for the verification of smaller subsystems.

All this suggests that the role of formalisms in real-time design is increasing. This should lead to a greater integration of functional and non-functional requirements analysis in the future hard real-time design tools, giving a more accurate prediction of the system behaviour. However, this accuracy may be achieved only utilizing knowledge of implementation- and hardware-dependent information [12]. How this can be effectively accomplished in a complete formal analysis is an open question.

References

1. Berthomieu B., Diaz M., *Modeling and Verification of Time Dependent Systems Using Time Petri Nets*, IEEE Trans. SE-17, No. 3, 1991, 259–273.
2. Burns A., Wellings A.J., *HRT-HOOD: A Structured Design Method for Hard Real-Time Systems*, Submitted to the J. of Real-Time Systems, 1991.
3. Ghezzi C., Jazayeri M., Mandrioli D., *Fundamentals of Software Engineering*, Prentice-Hall Editions, 1991.
4. Gomaa H., *A software design method for Real-Time systems*. Comm. ACM, Vol. 27, No. 9, 1984, 938–949.
5. Jaffe M.S., Leveson N.G., Heimdahl M.P.E., Melhart B.E., *Software Requirements Analysis for Real-Time Process-Control Systems*, IEEE Trans. SE–17, Vol. 3, 1991, 241–257.
6. Jahanian F., Mok A.K., *Safety Analysis of Timing Properties in Real-Time Systems*, IEEE Trans. SE–12, No. 9, 1986, 890–904.
7. Kopetz H., Zainlinger R., Fohler G., Kantz H., Puschner P., Schütz W., *The design of Real-Time Systems: from specification to implementation and verification*, Software engineering J., Vol. 4, 1991, 72–82.
8. Lark J.S., Erman L.D., Forest S., Gostelow K.P., Hayes–Roth F., Smith D.M., *Concepts, Methods and Languages for Building Timely Intelligent Systems*, J. of Real-Time Systems, Vol. 2, 1990, 127–148.
9. Liu L.Y., Shyamasundar R.K., *Static Analysis of Real-Time Distributed Systems*, IEEE Trans. SE–16, No. 4, 1990, 373–388.

10. Ostroff J.S., *A Verifier for Real-Time Properties*, J. of Real-Time Systems, Vol. 4, 1992, 5–35.
11. Puschner P., Koza C., *Calculating the Maximum Execution Time of Real-Time Programs*, J. of Real-Time Systems, Vol. 1, 1989, 159–176.
12. Stoyenko A.D., Hamacher V.C., Holt R.C., *Analysing Hard Real-Time Programs for Guaranteed Schedulability*, IEEE Trans. SE-17, No. 8, 1991, 737–749.
13. Zave P., *An Insider's Evaluation of PAISLey*, IEEE Trans. SE-17, No. 3, 1991, 212–225.

An Overview of the HOOD Software Design Method

Theodor Tempelmeier

Fachhochschule, FB Informatik
Marienbergerstraße 26
83024 Rosenheim
Germany

Abstract

HOOD or Hierarchical Object Oriented Design has been developed as the standard software design method of the European Space Agency (ESA) for Ada projects. It is used in all major space programs and in the European Fighter Aircraft program. The *concepts* and the *method* in HOOD are described in detail. Aspects of the application of HOOD are also discussed.

1 Introduction

Hierarchical Object Oriented Design (HOOD) has come into existence under a contract of the European Space Agency (ESA). HOOD is the mandatory design method for ESA's major space programs and is also used in other real-time projects. To date, HOOD is prevailing in a variety of versions:

HOOD 2.2	April 1988
HOOD 3.0	September 1989
HOOD 3.1	Juli 1991
HOOD 3.1.1	currently in preparation
HRT-HOOD	September 1991 ("Hard Real-Time"- HOOD)

Deviations from these versions are common among users of configurable HOOD tools. The following overview is based on the most up-to-date and available version 3.1 [7], [5].

Developed by a French-Danish consortium (CISI, Matra, CRI), HOOD is now governed by the HOOD Technical Group and the HOOD User Group which everybody can join for a (significant) fee.

HOOD claims to be especially suited for software architectural design, but also to be appropriate for the detailed design and coding phases.

Originally, HOOD was oriented towards software systems to be implemented in Ada. In the latest version [7], HOOD is said to be "fully compliant with Ada program development", and at the same time it is emphasized that "all HOOD definitions are now independent of the target language. HOOD is not another representation of an Ada program". Despite of this claim, the basic concepts of HOOD are most easily understood by showing their similarity with the corresponding Ada constructs. The following chapter will be organized accordingly. It is assumed that the reader is familiar with the Ada package construct or with a module concept of any other language.

2 Concepts in HOOD

2.1 Basic Concepts and Graphical Representation

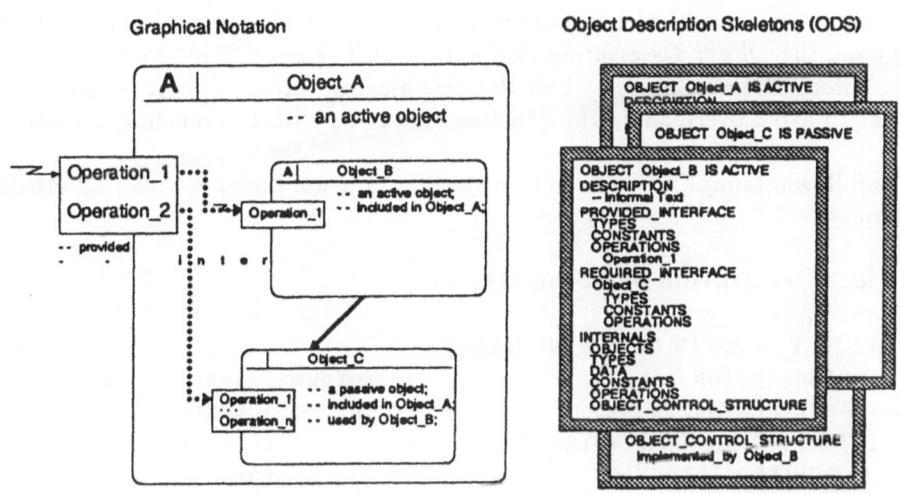

Fig. 1. Basic concepts.

An *object* in HOOD is similar to the definition in object-oriented design [1] and largely corresponds to an Ada package. In its graphical representation (cf. figure 1) a round-cornered rectangle is used, where a protruding rectangle shows the exported operations of the object, i.e. its services *provided* to other objects or its "specification" in terms of Ada. Internal elements of an object are not visible to the outside world, of course. If an object is *included* within another object (this conceptually corresponds to nesting in Ada), HOOD calls the objects child object or parent object respectively. HOOD defines the *use*-relation between two objects in terms of one object requiring the provided operations of the second object; this is equivalent to importing resources from another object or referring to another package by a with-clause in Ada. The use-relation does not refer to specific operations, only to the used object as a whole.

HOOD distinguishes between *active* and *passive* objects. Active objects are marked with the letter "A" in the upper left corner. An object is said to be active, when it has *constrained operations* in its provided interface. An operation is constrained when it might block or delay a potential caller. With this in mind, active objects are vaguely similar to Ada tasks and passive objects may be seen as Ada packages without tasks. However, this simplification does not hold in some unreasonable cases (as shown in [11]) due to the HOOD rule stating that "passive objects may include active children ...".

As in Ada, there is no inheritance or dynamic binding in HOOD.

2.2 Object Description Skeletons

Behind every graphical representation in HOOD lies a textual representation scheme, the *Object Description Skeleton (ODS)*. The ODS allows for more precise information on objects than the graphical notation. This is meaningful in order to avoid overloading the graphical notation with too much information.

The following simplified view of an object description skeleton shows all essential elements:

Object Description Skeleton (ODS)

```
OBJECT  name IS ACTIVE_OR_PASSIVE
  DESCRIPTION                      -- informal text
  IMPLEMENTATION_OR_              -- informal text
SYNCHRONISATION_CONSTRAINTS
  PROVIDED INTERFACE               -- Ada syntax;
    TYPES & CONSTANTS              -- exported resources
      OPERATIONS
      EXCEPTIONS
  REQUIRED INTERFACE               -- Ada syntax;
    list of (                      -- imported resources
    Object_name
    TYPES & CONSTANTS
    OPERATIONS
    EXCEPTIONS
    )
  DATAFLOWS                        -- semiformal
  EXCEPTION_FLOWS                  -- semiformal
```

```
OBJECT CONTROL STRUCTURE
  DESCRIPTION
  list of (constrained_operation_name)

  -- end of visible part --

  INTERNALS                              -- Ada syntax;
    OBJECTS                              -- included objects;
    DECLARATIONS                         -- provided and/or
                                            included;
    OPERATIONS                           -- included operations;
OBJECT_CONTROL_STRUCTURE (ObCS)
    --   ...                             -- see text below
OPERATION_CONTROL_STRUCTURES (OpCS)
    list of (subprogram_body)            -- for all provided/
                                            included
                                         -- operations

  END OBJECT name;
```

Most fields in the ODS are obvious and easy to understand. Only the *Object Control Structure (ObCS)* needs some explanation.

As known from above, active objects are characterized by the presence of constrained operations. It is the purpose of the ObCS to describe the details of interaction when calling constrained operations. Hence, only active objects do have the ObCS field in their ODS.

Informally, the ObCS specifies the tasking, synchronisation, and communication structure of the software unit. The ObCS's are thus of fundamental importance, especially for real-time systems.

In [7] it is suggested that Ada rendezvous syntax and semantics or another formal notation may be used for describing the ObCS. Also, any implementation language with corresponding calls to operating system primitives is allowed. This freedom in specifying one of the most important aspects of real-time systems seems questionable with respect to the overall system structure, language independence, and portability.

The Object Description Skeleton also serves as a standard interchange format for different HOOD tools.

2.3 Further Concepts

This subchapter briefly surveys some further interesting concepts in HOOD (cf. fig. 2). For more details the reader is referred to [7].

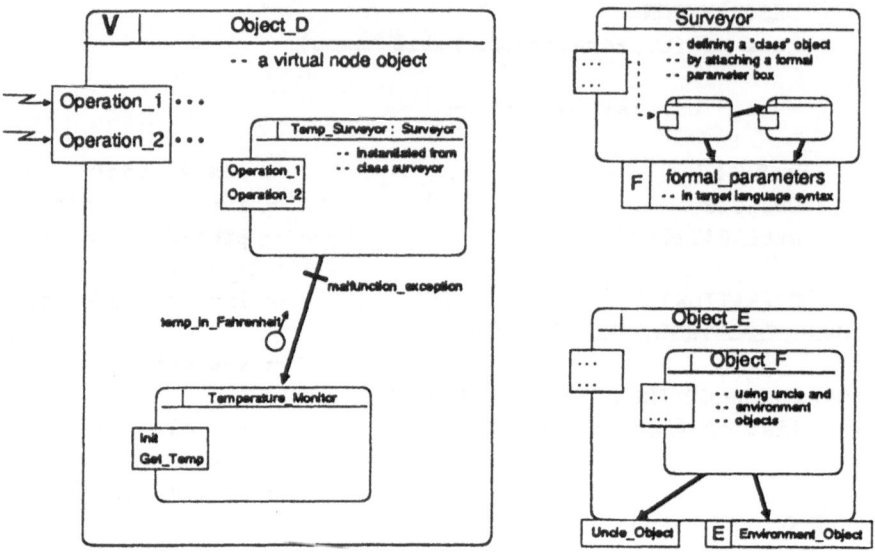

Fig. 2. Further concepts.

"Class" objects in HOOD largely correspond to Ada generic units. They should not be confused with the class concept of object-oriented programming languages such as C++.

Exceptions are defined analogous to Ada.

Dataflows are denoted by arrows with a circle.
Because dataflows are only informal names, consistency between the dataflows in the graphical diagrams and parameters of subprograms in the ODS cannot be enforced — in contrast to [2], [4] for instance.

Environment objects (marked with the letter "E") stand for objects which are outside the current design. This may be an external piece of software which is supplied by another team or company. However, this may also denote another of the parallel HOOD design trees (see chapter 3), which together form the system to design.

Finally, *virtual_node* objects (marked with the letter "V") are used to form distribution units to be allocated to different physical processors. Certain restrictions exist for virtual nodes to make them suitable as distribution units.

HOOD provides a set of approximately 125 rules which summarize major aspects of the concepts (and parts of the method).

3 The Method in HOOD

"method: ... a planned way of doing something" [8].

As the term "hierarchical" indicates, HOOD employs a top-down decomposition scheme. The internal parts of an object are designed by devising some included child objects (cf. fig. 3). These are refined in turn, and so on.

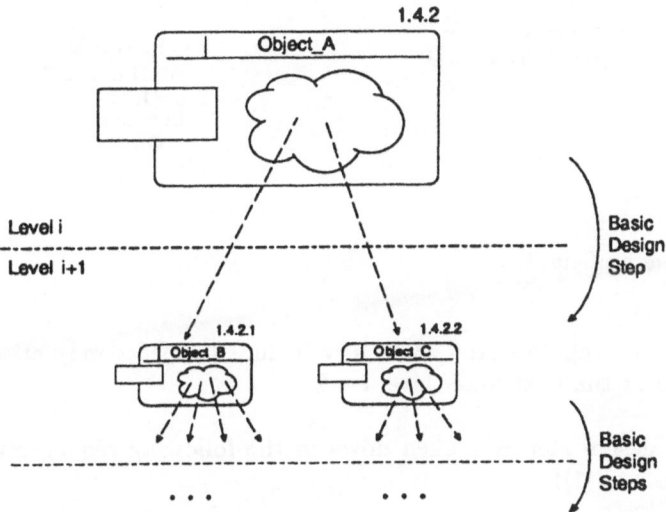

Fig. 3. Hierarchical decomposition.

The decomposition of an object is termed a *Basic Design Step (BDS)* in HOOD. Applying basic design steps successively results in a *Design Process Tree*, which is equivalent to the overall include structure. The design process tree thus comprises one top level element and all its hierarchical refinements. One design process tree or *a set of* design process trees may represent the "system to design" since version 3.1, thus weakening the strictly hierarchical scheme of earlier HOOD versions (see figure 4). "Classes" must not be declared within a design process tree; they are only allowed as root objects, thus forming the so-called class space.

During hierarchical decomposition each object is seen from two different points of view (cf. figure 3). At level i the internal elements of an object are *specified*, i.e. a preliminary ODS with the appropriate provided interface is defined. At the next lower level $i+1$ all preliminary ODS's are completed, i.e. their internal parts

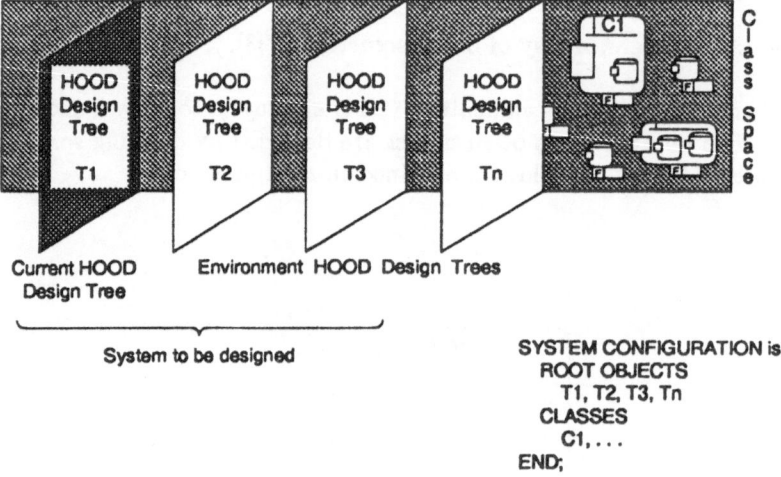

SYSTEM CONFIGURATION is
ROOT OBJECTS
T1, T2, T3, Tn
CLASSES
C1, ...
END;

Fig. 4. System configuration.

are specified; during this step some new included objects may arise which are again refined at the next lower level $i + 2$.

Every basic design step is broken down in the following sequence of activities (which is close to [1]):

1. Problem definition
   1.1 Statement of the problem
   1.2 Analysis and structuring of the requirement data
2. Elaboration of an informal solution strategy
3. Formalisation of the strategy
   3.1 Identification of Objects
   3.2 Identification of operations
   3.3 Grouping operations and objects
   3.4 Graphical description
   3.5 Justification of the design decisions
4. Formalisation of the solution
   — define parent object description skeleton
   — define (incomplete) child object description skeletons

Details on this sequence of activities and other design guidelines are separated from the HOOD reference manual and included in a user manual [6].

For every object a chapter which follows the above sequence of activities is included in the HOOD design documentation. Numbering the objects according to the design process tree and combining this numbering scheme with the scheme from above yields the *HOOD Chapter Skeleton (HCS)*. For instance, 1.4.2.2 H 3.1 denotes chapter 3.1 ("Identification of Objects") of the second child of object 1.4.2.

It should be pointed out that other methods exist which seem to be of superior or at least equal usefulness as compared to HOOD, most notably the method of Nielsen/Shumate [9], [10].

4 Application of HOOD

Application of HOOD is supported by a number of tools from Cadre, Intecs, IPSYS, Sema, Systematika, TNI, and others. These tools currently support version 3.0 or version 3.1 with deviations and intermediate forms.

All tools can generate Ada target code. (Ada code generation is partly specified in the HOOD reference manual and can be influenced by *pragmas* in the ODS).

Positive aspects of using HOOD are its object orientation and especially its sequence of work steps which guides unexperienced developers through design.

On the negative side, the concepts in HOOD are very vague and open to (mis-)interpretation. Detailed criticism on HOOD may be found in [11]. Obviously, using the concepts of Ada directly, e.g. [2], [4], would provide for much more preciseness; the possibility to apply the HOOD method or some other set of guidelines would still exist.

There is little practical experience on large scale application of HOOD which is based on the new HOOD versions and open to the public. Almost all applications which are published or known to the author exploit HOOD's vagueness to cope with problems such as reported in [11]. Three examples shall be given:

- *Project 1:*
  The tool/method has been changed in a way that an active object of HOOD is seen as an equivalent to an Ada task, which is *not* true in HOOD.
- *Project 2:*
  The application of HOOD is reported as having been successful. However, the presentation of parts of the design shows violations of important HOOD rules. The design is thus *illegal* in HOOD.
- *Project 3:*
  The tool/method is changed to allow "classes" within design process trees and to include task types. Task types are *not available* in legal HOOD, and "classes" outside the class space are *illegal* in HOOD.

All these projects use Ada as target language. Obviously, using other target languages and calls to the operating system, as it is claimed to be possible in HOOD, would result in even more tailoring.

5 Conclusion

HOOD does not introduce excitingly new aspects. The concepts in HOOD are sometimes strange and vague, while the method may be acceptable. There have been positive ideas in the first versions of HOOD. It still has to show up whether the development of HOOD from version 2.2 to version 3.1 has been going into the right direction.

References

1. G. Booch, *Object-Oriented Development*, IEEE Transactions on Software Engineering, SE–12, February 1986.
2. R.J.A. Buhr, *System Design with Ada*, Prentice Hall, Englewood Cliffs 1984.
3. A. Burns, A. Wellings, Development of a Design Methodology — Volume 2: HRT-HOOD — *A Structured Design Method for Hard Real-Time Systems*, Task 3 Deliverable on ESA-ESTEC Contract 9198/90/NL/SF, York, UK, September 1991.
4. Teamwork/Ada User's Guide. Release 4.0. Cadre Technologies Inc., Providence December 1990.
5. B. Delatte, M. Heitz, J.F. Muller, HOOD *3.1, the adult age*, in: F. Hass (ed.): Proceedings of the Second Symposium "Ada in Aerospace", 11–15 November 1991, Palazzo Barberini, Rome. EUROSPACE, Paris, France 1992, 363–376.
6. HOOD Working Group, HOOD *User Manual. Issue 3.0*, European Space Agency, Noordwijk, The Netherlands, Dec. 1989, (Version 3.1, by: HOOD Technical/User Group, to appear 1992).
7. HOOD Technical Group, HOOD *Reference Manual. Issue 3.1.* HOOD User Group, HRM/91–07/V3.1, July 1991. Note: This is the up-to-date defining document for HOOD.
8. Longman Dictionary of Contemporary English, Longman, London 1987.
9. K. Nielsen, K. Shumate, *Designing Large Real-Time Systems with Ada.* McGraw-Hill, New York 1988.
10. K. Shumate, M. Keller, *Software Specification and Design. A Disciplined Approach for Real-Time Systems*, Wiley & Sons, New York 1992.
11. T. Tempelmeier, *Some Critical Comments on HOOD*, in: F. Hass (ed.): Proceedings of the Second Symposium "Ada in Aerospace", 11–15 November 1991, Palazzo Barberini, Rome, EUROSPACE, Paris, France 1992, 343–353.

Configuring Hard Real-Time Distributed Systems

Ken Tindell

Department of Computer Science
University of York
Heslington
York YO1 5DD
U.K.

My work is concerned with configuring automatically distributed hard real-time systems. A large facet of this work is the development of analysis which can take a given configuration of a distributed hard real-time system and determining whether the timing constraints are met. To do this I have developed extensive scheduling theory, assuming a static priority pre-emptive scheduling algorithm. I have been largely successful in developing this theory, and can now determine worst-case response times (i.e. the time between a task being released and the task terminating after executing for a bounded of computation time) for a number of different task types. One of the most powerful and expressive pieces of theory allows a set of task transactions to be described: each transaction consists of a set of tasks which are released at fixed offsets in time relative to each other. The transactions can be used to implement distributed hard real time systems, and allow complex timing patterns to be described.

Another component of my work is developing analysis to bound the delays when sending messages between processors in a distributed system. The analysis has been applied to two different bus arbitration protocols. More importantly, however, the analysis has been applied to two different delivery protocols. For the first time the overheads of communications (such as DMA cycle stealing and packet assembly) can be properly accounted for.

The analysis work is integrated into a complete system model for use by the configuration approach (configuring, say, task placement, communications parameters, and so on). The configuration algorithm is a multi-parameter global optimisation algorithm, and uses the analysis developed to obtain a measure of how good a particular configuration is. This measure is then used to guide the algorithm to finding good configurations (i.e. ones where all the timing constraints, and other simple constraints, are met).

My work tries to put on a firm engineering foundation the approaches that have been used for years to build hard real-time systems. Previously systems were analysed and configured by hand: using rules-of-thumb to obtain static schedules, and using knowledge of the problem to configure the system. It is now possible to entirely automate this process.

Towards Provable Correct Real-Time Systems

Ronald M. Tol

University of Groningen
Dept. of Computing Science
P.O. Box 800
9700 AV Groningen
The Netherlands

Abstract

Systems in hard real-time environments must be highly dependable. We state that this can be achieved by developing real-time systems using formal methods.

To prove this statement we construct an important part of a real-time system, viz., an operating system kernel, using formal methods. The operating system kernel is specified and verified using Hoare-style logic and the Boyer-Moore theorem prover.

At the moment, part of the verification process has been completed, i.e., a number of kernel routines has been manually verified using Hoare-triples, and a stripped-down version of the kernel has been mechanically proven correct using the Boyer-Moore theorem prover. We expect to have the kernel completely mechanically verified within the next two years.

1 Real-time Systems

Real-time systems are used to control external devices in a timely manner. Since we are considering hard real-time systems, we have strict timing conditions, that must not be violated under any circumstances.

For these systems there is a need for dependable software and hardware. A step in this direction is the use of software engineering techniques, methods and tools.

Especially, computer support can be of great help in:

— automation of routine tasks,
— avoidance and early detection of specification and design errors,
— control of complexity,
— systematic development, and
— relative ease of change.

But for safety-critical applications, i.e., applications in which the violation of timing constraints endangers the process and human life, this is not sufficient. Here the correctness, both functional correctness and correctness of the time behaviour, of the software (and hardware) needs to be assured.

Formal methods, like Hoare-triples [5], wp-calculus [6], RTL [8], or temporal logic [9], are to be used to specify and verify programs.

Since humans make errors, the verification process should be mechanized, using so-called theorem provers. An example of such a prover is the Boyer-Moore theorem prover [4].

2 A Provable Correct Real-Time System

2.1 The Approach

Our approach is to build a general-purpose provable correct real-time system, using the above mentioned methods and tools, in an essentially bottom-up manner.

On top of reliable hardware, a small but powerful real-time operating system is built. This basic architecture is mechanically proven correct. This is a non-trivial, tedious task, but, fortunately, has to be performed only once. On top of the basic architecture, the application programs can be run. For every application, only the specific application program has to be proven correct, since the basic architecture is correct. Using a language in which it is easy to express real-time, this should be a relatively easy task.

A similar approach is taken at Computational Logic in Austin, TX, [2, 3]. However, their research does not involve real-time.

2.2 The Project

Currently, we are developing a new computer architecture for hard real-time environments [7]. The architecture consists of special-purpose hardware (realized by Programmable Gate Arrays in the prototype version), a processor for the real-time operating system kernel, and Transputers for the application programs and the operating system's shell functions.

The kernel supports the real-time features of an extended version of the real-time programming language PEARL [7].

As mentioned above, formal specification and verification of the system is necessary to use the system in safety-critical applications. This means, that, for the software part, a formal verification of the correctness and the time behaviour of the kernel and the modules of the operating system shell has to be carried through. Since the kernel is quite small, viz., some 30 simple procedures with altogether less than 1000 lines of PEARL-code, this should be feasible.

At the moment, part of the verification process has been completed, i.e., a number of kernel routines has been manually verified using Hoare-triples, and a stripped-down version of the kernel has been mechanically proven correct using the Boyer-Moore theorem prover. We expect to have the kernel completely mechanically verified within the next two years.

The Boyer-Moore theorem prover is of special interest, because an operating system kernel has been verified with it [1]. This kernel, however, was not developed for real-time purposes.

3 Conclusion

To come to a predictable, dependable and timely operation of real-time computing systems in hard real-time environments, formal specification methods and (mechanical) verification need to be used.

In our approach we construct such a system by proving the real-time system correct. The correctness proof of the complete system is divided into two independent proofs: the correctness proof of the basic architecture and the correctness proof of the application programs.

Since they are independent, the basic architecture has to be proven correct only once, and for every application a correctness proof of the application programs has to be performed.

References

1. W. Bevier, *A Verified Operating System Kernel*, PhD thesis, University of Texas at Austin, 1987.
2. W.R. Bevier, *KIT and the short stack*, Journal of Automated Reasoning, Vol. 5, No. 4, December 1989, 519–530.
3. W.R. Bevier, W.A. Hunt, Jr., J. Strother Moore, and W.D. Young, *An approach to system verification*, Journal of Automated Reasoning, Vol. 5, No. 4, December 1989, 411–428.
4. R.S. Boyer and J. Strother Moore, *A Computational Logic Handbook*, Academic Press, 1988.
5. E.W. Dijkstra and W.H.J. Feijen, *Een methode van programmeren*, Academic Service, 1984.
6. D. Gries, *The Science of Programming*, Springer-Verlag, New York-Heidelberg-Berlin, 1981.
7. W.A. Halang and A.D. Stoyenko, *Constructing Predictable Real Time Systems*, Kluwer Academic Publishers, Boston-Dordrecht-London, 1991.
8. A.K. Mok, *Towards mechanization of real-time design*, In André M. van Tilborg and Gary M. Koob, editors, Foundations of Real-Time Computing: Formal Specifications and Methods. Kluwer Academic Publishers, 1991.
9. A. Pnueli and E. Haral, *Applications of temporal logic to the specification of real time systems*, in M. Joseph, editor, Formal Techniques in Real-Time and Fault-Tolerant Systems, LNCS 331, 1988, 84–98.

Real-Time Systems in the Field of Mechatronics

Martin Törngren and Jan Wikander

DAMEK Research Group
Dept. of Machine Elements
The Royal Institute of Technology
100 44 Stockholm
Sweden

Mechatronics can be defined as an integration of mechanics, electronics and computer engineering sciences by combining knowledge from these fields in research and product design and implementation. The main goal of the "DAMEK mechatronics research group" is to improve the functionality of mechanical components and systems by use of a mechatronic approach. DAMEK research is therefore focused on the two following areas: Control theory applied to control of mechanical systems and real-time systems. In the research there is a specific emphasis on motion control applications such as vehicle dynamics control systems and industrial robot control systems.

Real-time systems as an important subtopic of mechatronics is well illustrated by a mix of ongoing and planned research activities at DAMEK. Most of these activities are associated with the design of real-time machinery. *Real-time machinery* refers to machines consisting of modular mechanical components which incorporate processing elements which are close to actuators and sensors and are interconnected and communicate through some communication medium. Distributed control is achieved by allocation of control functions to the processing elements which constitute nodes in a distributed computer system. There is a two-dimensional interaction between the nodes within a real-time machine. The nodes interact in two ways; on one hand through the communication system and on the other hand and most importantly through the dynamic mechanical system (machine) or its environment. The dynamic mechanical system puts certain demands on processing capacity, information interchange and timing which has to be fulfilled by the distributed computer system.

An initial study of issues in the design of real-time machinery has been performed by Törngren [1]. Requirements of ordinary discrete-time control theory applications considering distributed control implementation are investigated and suitable base architectures of distributed real-time computer systems (DRTCS) for such applications are proposed. Time and synchronization, allocation, scheduling, communication architectures and fault detection/tolerance are identified to be important design parameters of DRTCS. Control approaches based on complete dynamic models of industrial robots for state feedback control and parallelisation of the control algorithms in order to achieve acceptable performance is being investigated by Lind [2]. Another project deals with modelling/design of real-time systems by use of the object oriented approach and adapting such approaches to handle temporal behaviour [3].

An objective of future planned projects is to perform a comprehensive study of theories and models for distributed control implementation in real-time machinery. A cross technological approach is necessary in order to obtain realistic and accurate requirements of modern control approaches and in order to find optimal solutions.

References

1. M. Törngren, *Distributed Control of Mechanical Systems*, Licentiate thesis, 1992:6, Dept. of Machine Elements, The Royal Institute of Technology.
2. H. Lind, M. Kuroki and J. Wikander, *Dynamic Control of Direct-drive Robot*, Using Transputers, Proceedings Robotikdagar, Linköping, May 1991.
3. E. Brorson, C. Eriksson and J. Gustavsson, *Real-Time Talk, an Object Oriented Language for Hard Real-Time Systems*, Presented at the 18th IFAC/IFIC workshop on Real-Time Programming, Bruges, June 1992.

Off-Line Scheduling of Hard Real-Time Distributed Systems Using Windows

Jack Verhoosel

Department of Mathematics and Computing Science
Eindhoven University of Technology
P.O. Box 513
5600 MB Eindhoven
The Netherlands

The last decade dependability of computer systems has become a more and more important topic in computing science. Dependability of a computer system includes besides correct functionality also *timeliness*, i.e., hard real-time constraints imposed on the tasks of the system must be satisfied. In our opinion, timeliness can only be guaranteed when the event rate of the environment is bound and all hard real-time tasks are scheduled *off-line* incorporating all resources. An approach for off-line scheduling of tasks in hard real-time distributed systems is presented.

The hardware resources consist of a set of homogeneous processors, a set of communication media, such as busses and point-to-point links, and a set of physical devices, such as sensors and actuators. An application is comprised of a set of processes, each one privately managing a set of devices. The processes implicitly define a set of hard real-time executions. Each execution is represented by a directed acyclic graph of non-preemptable beads, each bead being part of the execution in a process or part of a communication between processes. Each bead is executed on a processor which takes a particular execution time and during the bead several physical devices or a communication medium can be accessed. In addition, between two successive beads a device can be accessed.

Beads have to be executed according to four kinds of constraints:

1. *Absolute timing constraints*, that restrict a bead to be executed between an earliest start time and a deadline (to enforce periodic behaviour of executions),
2. *Generic relative timing constraints*, that enable synchronization of and precedence relations between beads,
3. *Data-dependency constraints*, that allow overlap in time of beads on the same processor and
4. *Consistency constraints*, that guarantee consistent use of physical devices and communication media.

The off-line scheduling approach for distributed systems consists of four steps. First, each process and the devices managed by it are assigned to a processor

using heuristics that help to find the best assignment according to schedulability, load-balancing, device-balancing, minimum communication and maximum
parallelism criteria. In addition, beads that represent communication are inserted between any two adjacent beads of different processes. Second, in order to
reduce the amount of context switching, successive beads in the same process
are grouped into *blocks*, used in subsequent steps as non-preemptable off-line
scheduling objects. Constraints on beads are translated into similar constraints
on blocks. Third, a *window*, i.e. a time interval, is assigned to each block such
that if, each block is scheduled in its window, *all* constraints are satisfied and
thus scheduling of blocks at a processor can be done independently of schedules
at other processors. For instance, satisfying absolute timing constraints requires
the window of a block to lie between the earliest start time and the deadline of
the block. In order to strive for blocks to remain schedulable, window assignment
is subject to certain schedulability conditions. Fourth, for each processor a schedule is constructed such that no block is preempted, no two blocks overlap unless
they are related by a data-dependency constraint and each block is scheduled
in its window. If one of the steps cannot be finished successfully, backtracking
is incorporated by adjusting the outcome of the previous step using feedback
information that expresses the cause of failure.

Formal Methods and Algorithms for Parallel Real-Time Computing

Lonnie R. Welch

New Jersey Institute of Technology
Newark, NJ 07102
U.S.A.

Parallel computers are becoming increasingly popular as vehicles for speeding up the execution of programs, enabling more real-time processes to execute and to meet deadlines than would be possible otherwise. Formal methods are useful for exploiting parallelism in real-time systems and some techniques used to develop parallel algorithms are useful for developing predictable real-time systems.

The use of formal methods is helpful for the extraction of parallelism from real-time programs and for the prediction of program execution times. We have developed parallelism extraction techniques that work for real-time systems composed of processes that use modules encapsulating objects or ADTs. A directed acyclic graph is used to show the call relationships among the processes and objects of a program and to represent inter-object parallelism. The amounts of parallelism and communication costs between objects are used to assign objects to processors in a way that optimizes performance. Process execution times are approximated using functions that incorporate knowledge of object method execution times, the numbers of invocations between objects, and the hardware characteristics of the parallel computer. Once an assignment of processes and modules to processors is made, the fact that all processes meet deadlines can be verified by applying proof rules like those defined by Alan Shaw.

Algorithms developed with paradigms such as PRAMs and meshes often include constraints useful for predicting program execution times. For example, all processors may exchange data with their "eastern" neighbors simultaneously. Assuming a direct connection between each processor and its neighbor to the east, no contention for communication links occurs. Thus, no variable length delays occur due to contention management techniques. Prediction of process execution times as a function of the number of PEs is also useful. Typically, parallel algorithms are developed assuming an infinite number of processors and time/space performance analysis is performed on the algorithms. These techniques should be extended to consider the behavior of the programs when the number of processors is finite. Such techniques would allow one to answer questions such as, "How many processors are required for deadlines to be met?".

Techniques for Complex Systems Development

Lonnie R. Welch

New Jersey Institute of Technology
Newark, NJ 07102
U.S.A.

In the Real-Time Computing Laboratory at NJIT, we are studying the techniques of vertical integration and automatic synthesis in the context of complex systems[1].

Vertical integration refers to the treatment of hardware, operating system, programming language and application as a harmonious unit. We have designed a RISC-based processor that employs instruction pipelining and on-chip memory to increase performance. To further improve performance and to achieve dependability, the processor is used as a node in a distributed memory computer that supports asynchronous remote procedure calls (ARPCs). The nodes may be interconnected by a time-sliced token-ring to maintain predictability. Our operating system kernel provides minimal functionality, enabling variable process scheduling policies, distributed execution, and adaptability. Our programming model allows real-time processes that use abstract data objects (ADOs) and abstract data types (ADTs). The language run-time system performs automatic synchronization of data accesses and allows separate compilation of generic ADTs. Predictability of application programs is achieved by requiring that loops and recursion be bounded, that module instantiation be static, and that pointers be avoided. By integrating all layers of a complex system, predictability becomes feasible.

Construction of an application for execution in a vertically integrated environment can be performed by applying automatic synthesis techniques. We are developing a requirements specification language that allows multiple system views, each allowing one characteristic of the system requirements to be examined and modified. For example, there are views relating to parallelism, performance, fault tolerance, functionality, security, and timing. From the requirements specification, module design specifications are derived, and implementations of the modules are produced. For analysis and maintenance purposes, it is important to be able to trace requirements to implementation details. When a system is automatically synthesized, traceability is simplified, since the synthesizer is

---

[1] Complex systems have non-functional requirements related to timing, dependability and security, and employ distributed parallel processors.

less likely to overlook details that a human could inadvertently overlook.

The automatic synthesis proceeds from the module designs to the implementation, replication and distribution of the modules. Implementation may be performed by reuse, or by (automatic or manual) code generation. Replication of modules may be performed to meet performance or dependability requirements. Assignment of modules to processing elements (PEs) is done in a way that allows all requirements to be satisfied.

Formal Methods —
How to Make Them Understandable
and Usable for Engineers?

Reinhold Bareiß

Institute for Control Engineering and Industrial Automation
University of Stuttgart
Pfaffenwaldring 47
70569 Stuttgart
Germany

Report of a *'birds-of-a-feather'* discussion

List of participants:

B. Appel	R. Bareiß
L. Budin	J. Cullyer
C. Ghezzi	J. Goldberg
R. Lauber	R. Lichtenecker
S. Masticola	H. Steusloff

Motivation and Introduction

The discussion was motivated by a long term observation, that each time when theoretically oriented computer scientists deeply involved in formal methods talk with "engineers from practice", they don't really understand each other. However, on the background of increasing importance of formal methods in many technically oriented application domains with high safety and reliability requirements, a cooperation between both parties becomes more and more important. This requires a common understanding.

To reach this, the discussion was a chance for everybody to get various sights of the very complex topic.

To start the discussion, the question of "what are the benefits for using formal methods in industry today?" was asked provocatively by comparing the most referred benefits of formal methods in literature, as for instance the verifiability and the claim of being a common basis for communication with the degree of maturity and availability of tool support being a precondition for use in industry.

Looking at formal verification we must recognize, that this can be used in ordinary industrial applications only (not belonging to the category of very small but highly safety critical applications) if powerful and easy to use proving systems are available. But systems with that features are not available yet. So, formal verification is not possible in practice yet!

Looking at the notations of formal methods we have to say that these are often cryptic and the specification of even rather small systems becomes quickly complex. As a consequence, the understandability is suffering and the specification's meaning for being a common basis for communication tends to be diminished.

Considering this state of the art, it is not amazing that formal methods are hardly used in industry. Besides of tiny but highly critical applications (proofs can be done manually), the main benefits of formal methods are simply not exploitable in practice yet.

On the other side, if we observe the way how software-systems are actually developed in practice, we can also state, that this has little to do with professional engineering but very much with 'modern art' and sometimes simply vocational work. It's often ad-hoc, chaotic and without long term strategies.

Thus (even with engineers) it is becoming common sense that the development of software-systems needs a sound basis as other engineering disciplines do have it too. But how will it look like? Is it somewhat combining the pragmatism of current CASE-technology with the sound and formal basis of formal methods?

Discussions and their results

The discussion was lively and in the end it had to be broken off rigorously. For me, the main remarkable results have been:

- During the discussion it became implicitly obvious, that one of the main reasons for misunderstandings between engineers and computer scientists are the different sizes of systems implicitly referred to as small, medium and large systems. If an engineer talks about a complex specification, he may mean the specification of a control system for a complete chemical plant. If a theoretically oriented computer scientist talks about a complex specification, he may mean the specification of a safety critical interlocking function. In terms of the complexity of both systems there are orders of magnitude between them. The difficulties both "parties" have to face are completely different. This becomes obvious in the fact, that when engineers are talking about computer aid they stress the aspect of supporting the structuring and designing process. People deeply involved with formal methods hardly feel the need for such kind of support.

- The argument that introducing formal methods into practice requires much training first was discussed very controversely. Experience shows, so one of the arguments, that costs for training people, for instance in HOL (higher order logic), are about 150 000 US$. It was mentioned, that one of the reasons for these high costs are the missing curriculums. On the other side there was the counter-argument, that learning a formal method is as difficult or as easy as learning a programming language, because roughly spoken, a programming language is also just like a formal method based on some kind of formalism. In both cases their use requires a full understanding of the underlying formalism.

- In the discussion today's development process using formal methods was outlined by an experienced expert as follows: The specification is developed by a team of highly qualified experts. The discussion deals with how the features of the system can be specified within the underlying mathematical model of the formal method. Without formal verification, the generally promised increase of quality of the specification using formal methods is in fact mainly caused by the high degree of redundancy by developing a formal specification in a team. The formal method is just needed indirectly as a "vehicle" for communication purposes. Required formal proofs have to be executed to a far extent manually. To increase the confidence in the generally complex proofs, it is checked afterwards by a second group of experts. It was also pointed out, that the application of formal methods today is still a very exhausting job. Experience shows, that experts will do this job only for 2–3 years.

- The visions for easily applicable and industrially usable systems in the future have been different. There was one position, that the question of usability is mainly a question of a good human communication interface (HCI). Until the year 2010 it would be possible to hide the formal method behind an excellent full-graphical HCI. Essential changes in the formal models haven't been considered as really necessary. In a second vision, a "2. generation" of CASE-tools was requested, which combines the pragmatic aspects of current CASE tools — based on a collection of ad-hoc formalisms and methods — with a sound formal basis. The formal model should integrate methods for supporting the structuring and designing process as well as methods suitable for formal specification. To reach this, a formal framework consisting of a coherent set of formal sub-models is needed. This would be an ideal basis for completely mechanisable analysis techniques, based on sub-models and combinations of them. It became clear, that this kind of so called "approximate reasoning methods" will be very useful in industrial applications because of their easy use. Surely, they won't deliver that deep results as formal verification, but generally they deliver results being exact enough for nearly all practically relevant cases.

- One way to make formal methods easily understandable and usable for practitioners has been considered to apply them in the field of domain specific application machines. Although there was common understanding about their need, their importance and their advantages — to my surprise — this field hasn't been really discovered by researchers yet.

Minutes of the Birds-of-a-Feather Session on "Real-Time Systems Education"

L. Budin[1], *M. Colnaric*[2], *J. Skubich*[3], *J. Zalewski (Convenor)*[4]

[1] University of Zagreb, Croatia
[2] University of Maribor, Slovenia
[3] Jacques Skubich, I.N.S.A. de Lyon, France
[4] Janusz Zalewski[‡] (Convenor), SW Texas State University, U.S.A.

Those who expressed interest:

Andrew Bernat, University of Texas at El Paso, USA.
Carlo Ghezzi, Politecnico di Milano, Italy.
Wolfgang Halang, FernUniversität Hagen, Germany.
Michael Rodd, University of Swansea, UK.
Carlos A.J. Serro, Inst. de Eng. de Sistemas e Computadores, Portugal.
Hartwig Steusloff, Fraunhofer-Institut, Germany.
Alex Stoyenko, New Jersey Institute of Technology, USA.

1 Introducing Participants

Participants introduced themselves briefly, describing their major activities and interest regarding teaching "Real-Time Systems" courses, as well as their expectations regarding the work of this group. Remarkably, attending participants formed a mixture of faculty from Computer Engineering, Computer Science, and Electrical Engineering departments.

2 Identifying Objectives of the Group

J. Zalewski presented the initial list of Objectives, to focus the work of this group.

Immediate Objectives

I1 Exchange information and share experience.
I2 Discuss software and hardware tools used, or to be used, in classes.
I3 Develop and exchange examples, case studies, sample problems, assignments, test questions, exams, and other courseware.

[‡] Minutes approved on: October 13, 1992. Written and distributed by: J. Zalewski.

Long-Term Objectives

L1 Consider the best paradigm for teaching Real-Time Systems.

L2 Develop modular curriculum (or, at least, syllabus).

L3 Set up a permanent Interest Group (under IEEE/CS Real-Time Systems Committee or IFIP WG 5.4 Computerized Process Control).

Other Issues

− prerequisites
− textbooks
− special topics lying on boundaries with other disciplines (such as Real-Time Expert Systems, Reliability and Safety, etc.)

3 Discussion of the Objectives

In discussion, the following points were made regarding modification of, or additions to, the current list of objectives of this group.

L. Budin, supported by J. Skubich (who called it a pragmatic point of view), proposed the following:

L0. Formulate educational objectives, in terms of *"what every student needs to know to meet market's demands."*

J. Skubich suggested to contact also respective IFAC TC and extend the objective L3 by adding the phrase:

"... or IFAC TC on Computers, WG on Real-Time Programming"

L. Budin, supported by all present, suggested to modify the objective L2 to have the following wording:

New L2. Define the course contents in terms of Knowledge Units, perhaps in a form of a partially ordered graph, to allow tuning various implementations of the course according to actual circumstances, such as departmental needs, available faculty, etc.

A brief discussion revealed the need to define suggested duration of each Knowledge Unit, in lecture/lab hours. Total course duration may vary widely, as reported by participants in a table below:

	Lecture hours	Lab hours
Budin	24 mandatory/24 electives	Vary widely
Colnaric	30	30
Skubich	20 mandatory/20 electives	80
Zalewski	42	Approx. 20 hrs in open lab

The discussion of objective L2 raised a new question, formulated by L. Budin and J. Zalewski as the following objective:

L4. Describe a desired course sequence of which Real-Time Systems is a component. This sequence should include not only prerequisite courses but also suggested follow-up or extensions to a Real-Time Systems course.

J. Zalewski presented one possible sequence from SWTSU, on which Real-Time Systems could be based:

- Hardware leg, including "Introduction to Computer Architecture" and "Small Scale Computer Systems"
- Software leg, including "Operating Systems" and "Software Engineering."

Addressing objective L1, J. Zalewski presented briefly his paradigm as an example of a hierarchical approach to teaching Real-Time Systems course:

(a) RT Specification and Design Methods
(b) RT Language Constructs
(c) RT Kernels and Scheduling
(d) RT Architectures.

Although the suggested distribution of topics is even, 25% of time spent on each of the above levels, this can be easily adjusted, say, by putting more emphasis on the highest level (Spec and Design) and teaching in a top-down manner, as in Computer Science departments, or more emphasis on the lowest level (Architectures) and teaching in a bottom-up manner, as in Electrical Engineering schools.

In the discussion which followed, all four levels were briefly reviewed and amended.

(a) L. Budin and J. Zalewski suggested that specific Formal Methods should be included in the RT Specification and Design level. None of the attendees use them in their current courses. J. Zalewski mentioned using DARTS approach (originated from H. Gomaa's works) in his classes, supported by a new Shumate's book (Software Specification and Design: A Disciplined Approach to Real-Time Systems, Wiley, 1992). J. Skubich reported on the use of graphics in the Specification and Design phase, in his courses (as also presented in his ASI lecture).

(b) M. Colnaric suggested to allow and keep as much diversity in this paradigm as possible, by concentrating on teaching concepts rather than just teaching how to use tools. For example, on the Real-Time Language level, rather than using one particular language to teach real-time programming constructs, concepts should be taught using a programming language (or languages) as a vehicle. A brief review revealed the following languages used in respective Real-Time Systems courses:

Instructor	Language
Budin	C
Colnaric	PEARL
Skubich	PL/M
Zalewski	Ada

Furthermore, regarding teaching RT language constructs, J. Skubich proposed as one of the paradigms: "Teach parallelism and concurrency as early as possible in a course sequence."

All participants agreed with this, with J. Zalewski suggesting to use the SEI (Software Engineering Institute) Curriculum Modules on Concurrent Programming as a basis. Respective reports, which can be obtained via ftp from ftp.sei.cmu.edu, are as follows:

- D.W. Bustard, Concepts of Concurrent Programming, SEI-CM-24
- M.B. Feldman, Language and System Support for Concurrent Programming, SEI-CM-25

(c) On a kernel level, one of the issues is whether to teach designing and writing RT kernels in this course, or move it to a prerequisite operating systems class, and use commercial kernels instead. In this view, J. Skubich reported on the use of VRTX and J. Zalewski on LynxOS, in respective universities.

(d) On a hardware/architecture level, two issues were mentioned briefly:

- use of advanced multiprocessor buses, such as VMEbus, Multibus I and II, and Futurebus (Colnaric and Zalewski)
- writing device drivers (Skubich).

4 Conclusion

The group solicitates proposals of paradigms, other than those mentioned, for teaching Real-Time Systems courses. They will be discussed by the group, proposed for use, and distributed to all interested parties.

The group will seek affiliation with one or more organizations, such as IEEE, IFIP and IFAC, and try to form a Joint Interest Group.

One issue which has been left open is whether the proposed work should focus on undergraduate or graduate Real-Time Systems course.

Actions

The following actions were assigned:

1. Distribute the list of books suitable for use in Real-Time Systems courses (J. Zalewski)
2. Contact IFIP WG 5.4 and IEEE/CS RTS Committee with respect to setting a Joint Interest Group (J. Zalewski)

3. Contact IFAC TC on Computers for setting a Joint Study Group (J. Skubich)
4. Prepare a brief outline of the lab exercises at INSA (J. Skubich)
5. Report by the end of November on the progress of work (J. Zalewski)

"Birds-of-a-Feather-Group" on Safety Critical Systems

W. J. Cullyer[1] and J. A. McDermid[2]

[1] Dept. of Engineering
University of Warwick
Coventry CV4 7AL U.K.

[2] Dept. of Computer Science
University of York
York YO1 5DD
U.K.

This special interest group consisted of 16 delegates at the ASI and met on four occasions to debate the specific issues raised by safety critical real time control systems. In order to protect both human life and the environment of the Earth, certain classes of automated control systems in industries such as nuclear power, aviation and railway signalling are subject to independent analysis and certification, before operational use is permitted. There is universal agreement that such independent checks are essential when human life is at stake. The papers by Cullyer and McDermid in these Proceedings give more details.

The group agreed that the subject is deeply rooted in the technology of so-called "embedded computer systems". By embedded systems we mean those applications of computer hardware and software in which the equipment is hidden from public view, within the electronics bays of aircraft, deep inside the protection mechanisms of nuclear reactors, inside the engine compartments of cars and in hundreds of similar real-time control systems. If such equipment malfunctions, there may be accidents leading to loss of human life.

The techniques which have been developed for the specification, design and verification of such systems are intended to provide a practical route for the development of such highly critical systems, at a cost which is acceptable to the operator of the potentially hazardous plant or vehicle. The best available techniques are based on:

1. Hazard Analysis, to determine the risks to human life and to the Environment.
2. Derivation of unambiguous specifications for the required real time control system.
3. Decomposition into hardware and software, with the critical functions clearly delineated.
4. Implementation of software using subsets of internationally defined high order programming languages.
5. Verification of the software against higher level specifications, using a combination of static analysis and dynamic testing.

6. Corresponding development of the safety critical hardware, using languages such as VHDL.
7. Integration of the software and hardware.
8. Validation of the integrated system against the original customer requirements.
9. Certification for operational use by an independent agency.

The knowledge of these techniques is not widespread and only a handful of vendors worldwide are competent to carry out equipment development in the mannner listed above.

The technological base for safety-critical systems is improving, but only slowly. It was agreed that safety-critical electronic hardware is ceasing to be a major problem. Microprocessors and memory are now so cheap that everyone in the avionics, nuclear power and railway industries uses triplicated or quadruplicated processing elements to guard against random failures during operational use. For example, the Boeing 777 flight control system employs quad-ruplicated control channels, each fitted with three different types of microprocessors.

The high costs and development problems arise from the computer software, which ideally should be of the same excellent integrity as the underlying electronic components. This is far from being achieved. Despite the use of formal mathematical methods in a few application areas, notably military systems, the group concluded that these techniques are not widely accessible to industrial design teams, because the mathematical basis is not understood by many engineers and the associated automated tools have a number of limitations including poor user interfaces.

On the topic of training, there appears to be little tuition available on an international basis to help scientists and engineers improve their skills in the safety-critical marketplace. Attempts in the UK to introduce a modular training scheme has been thwarted, largely by the onset of economic recession.

The safety critical systems group at this ASI concluded that the techniques for the specification, design and verification of safety critical real time control systems are immature. Although much of the mathematical base is well understood, there is a major need to apply the existing knowledge to practical control systems and hence improve the maturity of the techniques. Our ability to make such progress internationally is dependent in part on the availability of Training courses and matching funding, since this topic cannot be absorbed solely in the design centres, but requires additional professional qualifications, gained partly in the class room.

What Will We Get from Real-Time Research Within the Next 50 Years (1992-2042)

A Surprising Review as Seen from the Year 2042

Klaus Rebensburg

Technische Universität Berlin
Prozeßrechnerverband-Zentrale
10623 Berlin
Germany

- **1992:**

  It was in St. Maarten where a group of more than 100 computer scientists surprized the rest of the world by stating that they have been doing real-time research for years in order to generate automated solutions for problems and in spite of their efforts and in spite of tricky schedulers, excellent methods, fast CPUs and networks, not all problems concerning real-time have yet been solved.

- **1999:**

  A sophisticated prediction method for schedulers arises using witches (the witch processor 'wp').
  Concept: 'wp's usually know things before they happen!
  New real-time-concepts derived: Look ahead 1 step and do now, look ahead 2 steps and do later, have visions and think.

- **2010:**

  Introducing 'reverse time' processors, first success to overcome Einstein's Relativity Theory, 'shortest deadline last', 'longest deadline first' now very easy! This was considered as the victory of 40 years discussion about scheduling strategies.

- **2020:**

  A new concept, supported by tools — 'do it right':
  New concept: 'do it right the first time' (no fault tolerance needed),
  Advanced concept: 'do the right thing at the right (any) time'! this was considered as the victory of Real-Time Artificial Intelligence.

- **2021:**

  Breakthrough on universal broadcasts:
  'Telepathic Networks': Every information available at any place at any time.
  New concept: Solve problems of other people at any time you desire.
  Very new concept: Do control before you measure.

- **2030**:
  Invention of a new dimension for real-time with mechanical problems: First industrial use of anti gravity, real-time compression of movements and masses possible now.

- **2041**:
  Breakthrough with formal methods and language constructs: Introduction of a new class of general 'solve_the_problem' constructs.
  New command: 'solve_the_problem_now at any cost'.
  Advanced command: 'solve_the_problem_now with cost constraints'.
  Very advanced command: 'solve_the_problem_now without any costs'.

- **2042**:
  A shock! The whole development of the last 50 years is considered to have been a failure.
  More direct approach now: Invention of the 'money generating machine' for the use by everybody.
  Consequence: A 'general problem generator' will have to be invented.
  More shocking consequence: All problems will have to be regenerated again to have fun like mankind had 50 years ago in 1992.

Switching back in real-time:

Above we stated the solutions for every problem we have been able to foresee until now (1992). New problems will arise when scientists meet again at the next ASI on Real-Time Computing.

List of Participants

Mehmet Akşit	Universiteit Twente, Enschede, The Netherlands
Carlos M. R. Almeida	INESC, Lisboa, Portugal
Dick Alstein	Technische Universiteit Eindhoven, The Netherlands
Alfred Anderman	Rockwell International Corporation, Downey, CA, U.S.A.
Cesare Antonelli	Universita di Roma "Tor Vergata", Italy
Bernhard Appel	ALCATEL Austria-ELIN Forschungszentrum GmbH, Wien, Austria
Vladimir Bacvanski	Rheinisch-Westfälische Technische Hochschule, Aachen, Germany
R. Bareiß	Universität Stuttgart, Germany
Leonor Barroca	University of York, U.K.
Jay S. Bayne	Bailey Controls Company, Wickliffe, Ohio, U.S.A.
Kim Bengtsson	Defence Material Administration, Stockholm, Sweden
Andrew P. Bernat	The University of Texas at El Paso, U.S.A.
Gottfried Bonn	Fraunhofer-Gesellschaft, Karlsruhe, Germany
Uwe W. Brandenburg	Berlin, Germany
Ron Bruckman	Digital Equipment Corp., Merrimack, NH, U.S.A.
Giorgio Bruno	Politecnico di Torino, Italy
Leo Budin	University of Zagreb, Croatia
Carl Burmeister	Digital Equipment Corp., Englewood, CO, U.S.A.
Giovanni Cantone	Universita di Roma "Tor Vergata", Italy
Carlos Batista Cardeira	Instituto Superior Tecnico, Lisboa, Portugal
Matthias Carlsohn	Bremen, Germany
Andrea Castella	Politecnico di Torino, Italy
Jean Chabert	Digital Equipment France, Mont Saint Aignan, France
Michael Chang	Naval Surface Warfare Center, Dahlgren, VA, U.S.A.
Roderick Chapman	University of York, U.K.

Bo-Chao Cheng	Kearny, NJ, U.S.A.
Özer Ciftcioglu	Istanbul Technical University, Turkey
M. Kemal Cılız	Bogazici University, Istanbul, Turkey
Raymond K. Clark	Concurrent Computer Corporation, Westford, MA, U.S.A.
Matjaz Colnarič	University of Maribor, Slovenia
W. John Cullyer	University of Warwick, Coventry, U.K.
Sadegh Davari	University of Houston - Clear Lake, TX, U.S.A.
Klaus Ecker	Technische Universität Clausthal, Germany
Aldo Esposito	Accademia Aeronautica, Pozzuoli, Italy
Heidemarie Fahn	Universität der Bundeswehr München, Neubiberg, Germany
Sergio M. M. de Faria	Universidade de Coimbra, Portugal
Miguel Felder	Politecnico di Milano, Italy
Eduardo B. Fernandez	Florida Atlantic University, Boca Raton, FL, U.S.A.
Paul Fortier	Naval Undersea Warfare Center Division, Newport, RI, U.S.A.
Lars-Berno Fredriksson	Kvaser AB, Kinnahult, Sweden
Borko Furht	Florida Atlantic University, Boca Raton, FL, U.S.A.
Hector Garcia-Molina	Stanford University, CA, U.S.A.
Remy Gaudy	Digital Equipment France, Mont Saint Aignan, France
Carlo Ghezzi	Politecnico di Milano, Italy
Jack Goldberg	SRI International, Menlo Park, CA, U.S.A.
Damas P. Gruska	Comenius University, Bratislava, Czechoslovakia
Petter Haave	SINTEF, Trondheim, Norway
Wolfgang A. Halang	University of Groningen, The Netherlands
Dieter K. Hammer	Technische Universiteit Eindhoven, The Netherlands
Robert Harrison	Naval Surface Warfare Center, Dahlgren, VA, U.S.A.
Constance L. Heitmeyer	Naval Research Laboratory, Washington, DC, U.S.A.
Jon Holt	University College of Swansea, U.K.
Günter Hommel	Technische Universität Berlin, Germany
Steve Howell	Naval Surface Warfare Center, Silver Spring, Maryland, U.S.A.
E. Douglas Jensen	Digital Equipment Corporation, Maynard, MA, U.S.A.
Timothy Jodoin	Naval Air Warfare Center Aircraft Division, Maryland, U.S.A.
Karl Jonas	Technische Universität Berlin, Germany
Daniel Juttelstad	Naval Undersea Warfare Center Division, Newport, RI, U.S.A.

Nedim Karaca	Hacettepe University, Beytepe-Ankara, Turkey
C. Keles	Dokuz Eylul University, Bornova-Izmir, Turkey
Christian Kelling	Technische Universität Berlin, Germany
Kane H. Kim	University of California, Irvine, CA, U.S.A.
Werner Kriechbaum	IBM AIX-FSC, München, Germany
Rakesh Kushwaha	Linden, NJ, U.S.A.
Marten D. van der Laan	Rijksuniversiteit Groningen, The Netherlands
Philip Laplante	Fairleigh Dickinson University, Madison, NJ, U.S.A.
Rudolf Lauber	Universität Stuttgart, Germany
Thomas Lawrence	Rome Laboratory, C3AB, Griffiss AFB, Rome, NY, U.S.A.
H. W. Lawson	Lawson Publishing and Consulting Inc., Lidingö, Sweden
Reiner Lichtenecker	FernUniversität Hagen, Germany
C. L. Liu	University of Illinois at Urbana-Champaign, U.S.A.
Jane W. S. Liu	University of Illinois at Urbana-Champaign, U.S.A.
C. Douglas Locke	IBM Federal Sector Company, Bethesda, Maryland, U.S.A.
Fernando J.P. Lopes	Universidade de Coimbra, Portugal
Imad Mahgoub	Florida Atlantic University, Boca Raton, FL, U.S.A.
Miroslaw Malek	The University of Texas, Austin, TX, U.S.A.
Stephen P. Masticola	Rutgers University, New Brunswick, NJ, U.S.A.
David P. Maynard	Austin, TX, U.S.A.
John A. McDermid	University of York, U.K.
Gee-Gwo Mei	IBM Thomas T. J. Watson Research Center, Yorktown Heights, NY, U.S.A.
Frank Merkel	Fraunhofer-Gesellschaft, Karlsruhe, Germany
Aloysius K. Mok	The University of Texas, Austin, TX, U.S.A.
Peter Müller	Technische Universität Berlin, Germany
Hidenori Nakazato	University of Illinois at Urbana-Champaign, U.S.A.
Michael L. Nelson	Naval Postgraduate School, Monterey, CA, U.S.A.
Lambert Nieuwenhuis	PTT Research, Leidschendam, The Netherlands
Christos Nikolaou	University of Crete, Heraklion, Greece
Ulf Olsson	NobelTech, Järfälla, Sweden
A. Pedar	NASA Ames Research Center, Moffet Field, CA, U.S.A.
Carlos M. Puchol	Austin, TX, U.S.A.
Petri Pulli	Technical Research Centre of Finland (VTT), Oulu, Finland
Klaus Rebensburg	Technische Universität Berlin, Germany
Michael G. Rodd	University College of Swansea, U.K.
C. Gary Rommel	Eastern Connecticut State University, Willimantic, CT, U.S.A.

Wilhelm Rossak	New Jersey Institute of Technology, Newark, NJ, U.S.A.
Dario Russo	IRSIP–CNR, Napoli, Italy
Helmut Rzehak	Universität der Bundeswehr München, Neubiberg, Germany
Pierluigi San Pietro	Politecnico di Milano, Italy
Ralph Sasse	Berlin, Germany
Ulrich Schmid	Technische Universität Wien, Austria
Fabio Schreiber	Politecnico di Milano, Italy
Carlos Serro	INESC, Lisboa, Portugal
Frederick Sheldon	University of Texas at Arlington, U.S.A.
Kang G. Shin	The University of Michigan, Ann Arbor, MI, U.S.A.
Luca Simoncini	Universitari e di Perfezionamento S'Anna, Pisa, Italy
Jacques J. Skubich	I.N.S.A., Villeurbanne, France
Marco Spuri	Universitari e di Perfezionamento S'Anna, Pisa, Italy
John A. Stankovic	University of Massachusetts at Amherst, U.S.A.
Hartwig Steusloff	Fraunhofer-Gesellschaft, Karlsruhe, Germany
Matthew Storch	University of Illinois at Urbana-Champaign, U.S.A.
Alexander D. Stoyenko	New Jersey Institute of Technology, Newark, NJ, U.S.A.
Moiez A. Tapia	University of Miami, Coral Gables, FL, U.S.A.
Theodor Tempelmeier	Fachhochschule Rosenheim, Germany
Ken Tindell	University of York, U.K.
Ronald M. Tol	Rijksuniversiteit Groningen, The Netherlands
Martin Törngren	Kungl. Tekniska Högskolan, Stockholm, Sweden
Valentijn Vande Keere	Universiteit Gent, Belgium
Jack Verhoosel	Technische Universiteit Eindhoven, The Netherlands
Lonnie R. Welch	New Jersey Institute of Technology, Newark, NJ, U.S.A.
Karin Wendland	FernUniversität Hagen, Germany
Janusz Zalewski	Southwest Texas State University, San Marcos, TX, U.S.A.

NATO ASI Series F

Including Special Programmes on Sensory Systems for Robotic Control (ROB) and on Advanced Educational Technology (AET)

NATO ASI Series F

NATO ASI Series F

Including Special Programmes on Sensory Systems for Robotic Control (ROB) and on Advanced Educational Technology (AET)

NATO ASI Series F